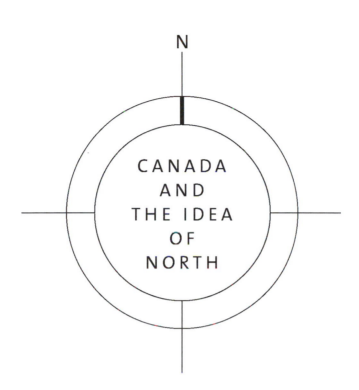

N

CANADA
AND
THE IDEA
OF
NORTH

CANADA AND THE IDEA OF NORTH

SHERRILL E. GRACE

McGILL-QUEEN'S UNIVERSITY PRESS

Montreal & Kingston · London · Ithaca

For Elizabeth and Malcolm,
and for John,
who has been there too

© McGill-Queen's University Press 2001
ISBN 0-7735-2247-6
Legal deposit 1st quarter 2002
Bibliothèque nationale du Québec

Printed in Canada on acid-free paper

This book has been published with the help of a
grant from the Humanities and Social Sciences Federation
of Canada, using funds provided by the Social Sciences
and Humanities Research Council of Canada.

McGill-Queen's University Press acknowledges
the financial support of the Government of Canada through
the Book Publishing Industry Development Program (BPIDP)
for its activities. It also acknowledges the support
of the Canada Council for the Arts for its
publishing program.

National Library of Canada Cataloguing in Publication Data

Grace, Sherrill E., 1944–
Canada and the idea of north
Includes bibliographical references and index.
ISBN 0-7735-2247-6
1. Canada, Northern. 2. Canada, Northern, in literature.
3. Canada, Northern, in art. 4. National characteristics,
Canadian. I. Title.
FC95.G72 2002   971   C2001-902121-6   F1021.G72 2002

This book was typeset by Dynagram Inc. in 10.5/13 Cartier Book and TheSans.
Book design by Glenn Goluska

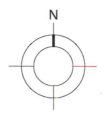

CONTENTS

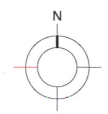

COLOUR PLATES, ILLUSTRATIONS, AND FIGURES

COLOUR PLATES

ILLUSTRATIONS

FIGURES

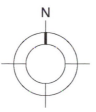

ACKNOWLEDGMENTS

The research and writing for this book could not have been undertaken without the prior work and shared experiences of many others. The scholars whose work I have read and greatly appreciated are mentioned in my Bibliography and in my notes, and it is always important to stress how much any scholarly undertaking like this one relies on, and is profoundly informed by, the published work that has gone before. As a student of literature, however, I am especially indebted to the creative writers in this country, many of whom have written about the North so wisely and so powerfully. It is from their words, as from the visual art, music, drama, and film that depict the North, that I have drawn my inspiration.

In addition, it is a personal pleasure to thank many individuals, groups, and institutions for the contributions they have made to this book and, indeed, to the joy I have had in preparing it. Over the years I have debated the meanings of North with several generations of graduate students, and for those always stimulating discussions and insights, thanks is never enough. I have also been able to present papers on northern topics at many conferences, and the responses and encouragements I have received, not to mention the many things I have learned from the work of fellow participants, constitute some of the chief privileges of academic life. My thanks and sincere appreciation for kindnesses and help to David Archer, Joan Backus, Gwen Boyle, Kathy Chung, Ann Cowan, Marlene Creates, John Flood, Judith Currelly, Peter Dickinson, Sandra Djwa, Patti Flather and Leonard Linklater, Louise Forsyth, Carole Gerson, Bryan Gooch, Stefan Haag, Gabriele Helms, Casimir Lindsey, Mary Lu MacDonald, Ross Mackay, John Moss, Richard Prince, Aron and Elaine Senkpiel, Antoine Sirois, Mary Shiel, William Straw, Phil Thomas, John Twomey, Doug Udell, Jack Warwick, Angela Wheelock, and Graeme Wynn; to members of Green College, UBC, who listened to my unformed ideas; to my colleagues Laurie Ricou, Ray Hall, Cole Harris, Allan Smith, Julie Cruikshank, and John O'Brian, each of whom read drafts of chapters and gave me helpful advice. Although a formal credit is provided with each illustration, I want to offer special thanks here to all the individuals who gave me permission to reproduce their works in this book; thanks also to Margaret Thompson for her poetry, to Mary Carpenter for her stories, and to many archives, galleries, and

ACKNOWLEDGMENTS

libraries across the country for their kind assistance – the University of Saskatchewan Archives, the Yukon Archives in Whitehorse, the National Archives of Canada, the National Library of Canada, the British Columbia Archives, the RCMP Library, the Fondation René Richard, UBC Special Collections, the Art Gallery of Hamilton, the McMichael, the National Gallery of Canada, the Vancouver Art Gallery, the Art Gallery of Ontario; to Geoff Kavanagh and Ink and Stink Productions, the CEAD for their prompt help with Quebec playscripts, to Dianne Kennedy and the Vancouver Canadian Music Centre, and to the Lawren Harris Estate; to my colleagues in the 1994 SSHRC research group on race and gender for sharing so much interdisciplinary knowledge – Veronica Strong-Boag, Avigail Eisenberg, Joan Anderson, Gabriele Helms, Matt James, and Paddy Rodney; to Robert Lecker for asking me to guest-edit the volume that developed into *Representing North*; to Margaret Tom-Wing for her help with the index; to Jill MacLachlan for her patient help with permissions; to Joan McGilvray and Susanne McAdam for transforming a typescript into an elegant book, and to Aurèle Parisien, my editor at McGill-Queen's University Press, for his encouragement and interest. It is customary on these occasions to thank the Social Sciences and Humanities Research Council of Canada, but I do so here with profound gratitude because so much of the kind of research this book has required could simply not have been done without the Council's support. Very little of what appears in the following chapters has been previously published, but it is a pleasure to acknowledge the following journals for publishing articles, parts of which I reproduce in the book: *Mosaic*, the journal of the Japanese Association of Canadian Studies, *The Northern Review*, and *Theatre Studies in Canada*.

As always, there are a few people to whom I owe very special thanks. First among them is Lisa Chalykoff for her invaluable help with the research, her patience with my questions, and her sense of fun and discovery, though Lisa has still to go north. My special thanks also to Eve D'Aeth of Whitehorse, who, with Lisa and me, prepared the collection of plays called *Staging the North*; that shared enterprise introduced us all to a wealth of dramatic work based on ideas of North and to the joys of collaboration. To Susan Kent Davidson, who has once more guided me and my manuscript through the northwest passage of preparation with her accustomed wisdom, navigational skill, and good cheer, I can only say: sailing with Susan almost makes the ordeal fun. Finally, I want again to thank John, this time for his enthusiastic company on our northern travels, for his help with details, his photography, his lively discussion of plays and films, and for his deep understanding of why the North matters. I hope that this book will show readers how important the ideas of North are and how an informed understanding of them can prepare the way for political action and scientific change.

S.E.G.
Vancouver, 2001

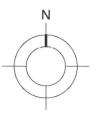

INTRODUCING NORTH

Follow me: I seek the everlasting ices of the north,
where you will feel the misery of cold and frost, to which I am impassive.
The Creature to Dr Frankenstein

This book is about Canada. A moment's reflection will remind anyone that other countries besides Canada have large northern regions and think of themselves as northern nations. Lawren Harris and J.E.H. MacDonald were inspired by the Scandinavian paintings in the 1913 Buffalo exhibition in large part because they depicted the North, what MacDonald called "the mystic north." Russia has a vast North, at once colder and more urbanized than Canada's. Iceland, Finland, and Greenland are geographically northern, and both Greenland and Norway have indigenous populations that have much in common with Canadian Inuit. Now that Nunavut is a political reality, comparisons with and lessons learned from Greenland's experience with home rule are inevitable.

If I were to allow my attention to wander, any number of northern images from outside Canada would catch my eye, such as Peter Hoeg's *Smilla's Sense of Snow*, the powerful Danish film set in Greenland called *Zero° Kelvin* (to my mind the most terrifyingly northern film yet made), Jón Gunnar Árnason's stunning sculpture *The Sun Craft*, based on northern myth, which guards Reykjavik's harbour, or several examples of American representations of Alaska and the Canadian Arctic in film, memoir, and fiction, with novels like Audrey Schulman's *The Cage* or Andrea Barrett's *The Voyage of the Narwhal* as representative examples. The sheer scope and variety of the North is perhaps nowhere more evident than in the Northern Encounters '99 multidisciplinary festival for the performing arts from the eight circumpolar countries, hosted in its first two years by Canada. An event like this is an unequivocal reminder that the circumpolar world is a geographical reality and, more and more, a geopolitical force to be reckoned with.

But this book is about Canada. Why? Because I am Canadian and my love for and desire to understand this stubborn, complex, infuriating place that I call home drives me to ask, not "where is here?" – Frye's old question – but what and who is here, and how the *here* called Canada has been constructed, represented, and articulated. One of the greatest challenges of a book like the one I have tried to write is that the subject will not stay still. Canada is not over. Indeed, at the beginning of the twenty-first century, the country is facing some splendid new beginnings as well as some persistent challenges. But it seems to me that now, more than ever before, it is important for Canadians to look north and in looking north to celebrate the creation of Nunavut, to appreciate the dependence of the South on Canada's northern resources, to recognize the crucial role we must play in safeguarding an Arctic environment and in articulating policies for a circumpolar world.

In order to look north now, at the beginning of a new century, with informed vision and understanding, it is essential to come to terms with how we got here from there, when there in 1867 (and before) was also defined as North. What Canadians mean by such enigmatic phrases as "the North" or the "true north strong and free" is constantly changing, and we have located North almost everywhere within our national borders; even Vancouver, where I sit writing and facing north, is now as often called Hollywood North as it is Lotus Land. For anyone living in Montreal in the 1860s or 1870s, North was the *pays d'en haut*; by the turn of the century, the discovery of gold in the Klondike had extended our northern reach and led to a reshaping and renaming of a part of the country. And it has always been this way: North is an idea as much as any physical region that can be mapped and measured for nordicity.

The discussion and analyses that comprise *Canada and the Idea of North* are organized in four main parts. The Prologue provides a quick tour of the terrain to be covered in the four central parts of the book. It is a kind of map or a set of aerial snapshots intended to introduce a number of ideas of North which form the main topics to be addressed in detail. I call this opening section a prologue not only because it comes before other matters or because it prepares the way for the explorations of later chapters but because it is here that I introduce the voices of others who have talked about, written about, and spent time in some version of North. It is a prologue of many voices that introduces what I conceive of as the dialogues in parts 1 to 4; thus, I take a quick look at paintings, drop in on two politicians, eavesdrop on explorers as they argue about the Arctic, sample popular culture, and, above all, listen to Glenn Gould, whose *Idea of North* has inspired my own thinking. I return to personal reflections – my own voice and position – in the Epilogue, which I call "Magnetic North" and which I see reflected in the mask/sculpture I have chosen for Plate 1: Don Proch's *Magnetic North*. I did not discover this work until the fall of 2000, when it was exhibited at Vancouver's Douglas Udell Gallery, many months after I had written my Epilogue. But it is precisely this kind of congruence of ideas, this uncanny, if no longer surprising, coincidence of North in my life and in the lives of other Canadians that demonstrates the fundamental premise of this study: no matter who, when, or where we are, we are shaped by, haunted by ideas of North, and we are constantly imagining and constructing Canada-as-North, as much so when we resist our nordicity as when we embrace it.

Part 1, "Writing the North," is divided into two chapters. Chapter 1, "Representing North," is devoted to two essential topics: my theoretical approach and a discussion, an overview really, of certain theorizations of Canadian identity and landscape that must be recognized as part of any discussion of North, or of any cultural analysis of a Canadian imagined community. Because I insist upon a plurality of ideas of North that are in constant flux yet are persistent over time, across a very wide field of endeavour, and are capable of being isolated for analysis, I call this phenomenon the *discursive formation* of North. This term, and the methodology it invokes, were developed by Michel Foucault; therefore, I devote some space to explaining why and how I work with the method. However, Foucault's method does not serve all my purposes, so in chapter 1 I introduce other theoretical concepts and analytical tools upon which I also draw in the subsequent discussions. The remainder of chapter 1 is devoted to others' analyses of Canadian culture as these pertain to northern landscape and identity. In this context, no one can escape Northrop Frye or Margaret Atwood, but there are other cultural analysts whose work has influenced my thinking and who have contributed significantly to discussion and debate. Like myself – and unlike Foucault – these writers are applied theorists, but what we all share with Foucault is the understanding that texts of all kinds, discourse of all kinds, are representations and that representations have great power. In a sense it is this power of representation (of Canada-as-North) that is my subject.

Chapter 2 moves from theory and theorization to aspects of historiography and geography. Here I must stress the word *aspects*. I am not attempting to write a history of Canada-as-North or even to assess every historiographic contribution to my subject. In keeping with my Foucaultian approach and my understanding of *all* discourse as representation, I have selected for consideration what I see as some key formative discussions of Canadian history and geography. My choices have been determined by the impact of the writing about history and place – the historio*graphy* and geo*graphy* – as these pertain to the discursive formation of North. Thus, a historian like W.L. Morton and a physical geographer like Louis-Edmond Hamelin are grist for my mill because, to the extent that the *writings* of these men have reached other scholars, general readers, and students of Canadian history and geography, these writings, these ideas of North and of Canadian identity, have helped to construct who we think we are. They have helped to represent us to ourselves and to the world and have proved strategically useful in times of national crisis.

Parts 2 ("Articulating North") and 3 ("Narrating a Northern Nation") continue the analysis of texts and representation as I pursue the discursive formation of North across other disciplines, such as forms of mapping, viewing (notably through photographs), and painting, and through varieties of performance, such as music, theatre, and film. Chapter 3, "Visualizing the North," looks at practices of cartography, in the literal sense of map-making and in the metaphoric sense of mapping, at the objectification of people and events, and at painting. I make no attempt at exhaustive summary of materials in any of these disciplinary categories because I am primarily interested in tracing how the discursive formation of North operates across disciplines in a complex interdiscursive and interdisciplinary manner; therefore, I turn from actual maps to a maplike painting by Lawren Harris or Paterson Ewen, from images of the Klondike Gold Rush, one of the major events of Canadian history in the North, to a specific instance of Klondike discourse and imagery (particularly as this is located in photographs). In the section on painting I talk about only one painting and one poem, not about painting in general. In other words, I am not concerned with disciplinary boundaries, and I disrupt these whenever I can on the assumption that such boundaries limit understanding of culture, hinder insight into the connections that sediment ideology, and occlude rather than reveal power relations. Throughout chapter 3, I pay special attention to the ways in which ideas of North have inscribed complex, interrelated, and mutually reinforcing attitudes of racism, sexism, and class prejudice in Canada. The Great White North, I argue, is anything but an innocent notion or a lighthearted Mackenzie-Brothers joke, and the "true north strong and free" may only be true, strong, and free for some of Canada's citizens.

Chapter 4, "Performing North," is devoted to analyses of music, drama, and film, and to some of the ways in which these different media, or art forms, draw upon and deploy the ideas of North circulating in the larger culture. For example, it certainly came as a surprise to me to discover how many Canadian classical composers respond to the North, whether they choose to set poems to music and let the words carry the northern discourse or whether they stretch the limits of non-programmatic forms to evoke cold, ice, and snow. Glenn Gould, of course, is in a class by himself, and his *Idea of North* epitomizes the interdisciplinary attractions of North that I find so appealing and so necessary. But the North is not only celebrated in classical compositions, as Stan Rogers and Susan Aglukark always remind us, and films, feature-length and documentary, provide a wealth of popular material for anyone investigating images of northern identity. The theatre must face its own special challenges when it wants to perform the North, so playwrights, from the late 1920s to the present, keep inventing new ways to stage the northern stories that connect them with the history, geography, and politics of North.

Chapter 5, "Fictions of North," is the only chapter that might appear at first glance to have a disciplinary bias. It is here that I examine a wide variety of narratives about North, from children's stories and autobiographies to popular novels. My chief focus, however, is upon serious fiction, by which I mean novels by some of Canada's recognized, major novelists, who are also essayists, poets, and literary critics. I have called all these works *fictions* to foreground their fictionality, their imaginative made-up-ness, but it would be a mistake to suppose that novels and history are discrete phenomena, or that stories, even those written for children, do not utilize and recreate the documentary record. In fact, some of these texts flaunt their own fictionality while undermining the truth claims and exposing the ideological investments of historians and geographers. Rudy Wiebe's *A Discovery of*

Strangers, for example, takes what we have been taught to believe were the facts of Sir John Franklin's first Arctic expedition and turns the facts inside out to show the reader other fictions and other truths. When all is said and done, it is probably the novelist who has the greatest impact on the Canadian imagination (however that is defined) and on the discursive formation of North because, throughout the twentieth century, the novel has remained a widely accepted and disseminated form; novels and novelists are popular in a way that poets and poetry, playwrights and plays are not. Novels, especially popular novels, stay in print or are turned into movies, and novels, especially by major writers, are translated, put on school and university syllabi, and studied at home and abroad.

Part 4, "The North Writes Back," consists of a single chapter, and it is the chapter I knew I was working towards from my earliest conception of this book. It is called "Writing, Re-Writing, and Writing Back" because here I attempt to discover, to listen to, to pay attention to some of the voices of Inuit and northern First Nations speakers, writers, activists, artists, and historians who have written about their northern homes, have re-written the stories and histories concocted in the South to exclude them, and written back in protest, anger, and pride to the dominant discourse, which has constructed the North as a homogeneous, empty space, outside of history, a place of romance, danger, challenge, mineral resources, and so forth for white, southern men. More by accident than design (it appeared late in 1998, just as I began to work in earnest on chapter 6), my main example of writing back is a novel, a novel everyone should read – Thomson Highway's tour de force, *Kiss of the Fur Queen*. As with earlier chapters, I have not separated the disciplines in chapter 6 but deliberately marshalled evidence across disciplines, juxtaposed texts, mixed genres and media – in short, done all I can to confound the assumptions analysed in preceding chapters, to disrupt disciplined boundaries, and to identify – to listen for – an alternate discursive formation of North(s). Moreover, I have tried as much as possible to disappear so that others' voices may be heard. In the last analysis, of course, I know I cannot disappear. As I confess in my Epilogue, this narrative is my invention, my fiction, my responsibility.

Although this is already a long book, with many different parts, much remains to be done, and there are a great many examples of the discursive formation of North that I mention only in passing or do not deal with at all. Poetry is one, and while I frequently quote poems and even examine one in great detail, I have not dealt at length, in a concentrated way, with this literary genre. My reasons are, first, that Ian MacLaren has already written extensively on poetry about the North, and second, that poetry seems to fall naturally across the entire book; if it is in no single place, that is because it is everywhere. Cartography, especially if expanded to include surveying, air photography, and satellite imaging, is a very large subject and a powerful instrument of imperial control, but I have only considered a few of its modalities. Health care, another important subject, is an area I have largely avoided because I do not have the expertise to assess what has been written about medical practices in the Canadian North. And much more still needs to be said about the impact of Christian missionaries across the North. Between them, health care and religion represent the extremes of southern neglect of and interference in the North, and these extremes also contribute to the dominant representation of North as empty, inhospitable, out of sight and mind, and irrelevant, except as a source of the natural resources consumed in the South.

Just as I have not been able to address all aspects of North, so I have not considered all paintings of the North, all songs about the North, or all popular images of North, and I am certain that I have not found all the books written about the North. I have tried to gather together as many images and illustrations as possible while keeping in mind the logistical difficulties of reproduction and the need to choose images that illuminate my arguments. The Bibliography is not selective; I have included everything relevant I have read to date, in the hope that this extensive listing will be of use to others. In keeping with the book as a whole and with my methodology, it is an interdisciplinary bibliography, the kind of bibliography our library classifications make so difficult to develop.

In *Canada and the Idea of North* I have harvested my thoughts, reading, and travel experiences over twenty years in an effort to understand what Canadians have meant by and continue to understand as North. This has been a personal journey – a search for my own answers. I hope that the discussion and the journey it inscribes will hold answers for others as well. What is more, I dare to hope that my passion for North will be infectious, that it will tempt others to go north, to read about North, to discover their own North, to realize how much southern Canadians, indeed, all peoples living south of sixty, depend upon a healthy, viable northern environment, and to value the lifestyles and lives of those – human beings and animals – who live north of sixty. Canada is entering the twenty-first century with renewed talk of a Mackenzie Valley pipeline on the one hand and news of polar bears dying and open, ice-free waters at the North Pole on the other. How will we navigate our way through these perilous, competing needs and demands? I do not know, and this book is not an attempt to answer such momentous questions. However, the more we know about the ideas of North that have shaped Canadian culture, policy, and history, the better able we will be to think through the issues. So this is my invitation: "Follow me: I seek the everlasting ices of the north, where you will feel the misery of cold and frost, to which I am impassive." Except that the words of Dr Frankenstein's Creature must be revised. The ices of the North may not be everlasting, and none of us can afford to be impassive. Follow me while there is still time.

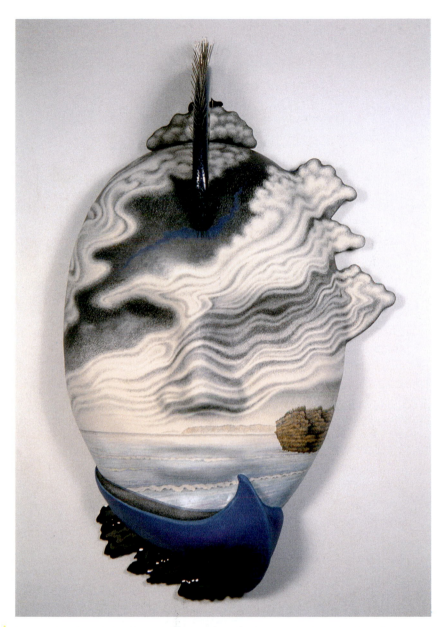

Plate 1   Don Proch's *Magnetic North Mask* (2000), 20 × 15 × 6 in., is a mixed media *tour de force* that embodies and recapitulates a complex iconology of North. Proch uses silverpoint, graphite pencil, and coloured pencil on a fibreglass-backed white ceramic surface. The top arc is black and blue fibreglass, inlaid with crosscut animal bone and studded with chrome-plated brass pins; the area below the canoe is nickle-plated and chrome-plated copper with a sandblasted surface pattern. © Don Proch. Collection of John and Sherrill Grace. Reproduced with permission of the artist and courtesy of the Douglas Udell Gallery.

    In this mask Proch has captured the face of Canada's nothern landscape through the visual metaphors of canoe, water, rock, and magnetic attraction. The human contours of the mask, however, remind a viewer that this landscape is above all an idea of North, a human construction of an imagined landscape.

Plate 2　William Blair Bruce, *The Phantom Hunter* (1888), recently renamed *The Phantom of the Snow*, oil on canvas, 59.5 × 79.25 cm. Collection of the Hamilton Art Gallery, Bruce Memorial, 1914, and reproduced with permission of the gallery.

Plate 3   Lawren S. Harris, *Winter Comes from the Arctic to the Temperate Zone* (c 1935), oil on canvas, 74.1 × 91.2 cm. Collection of the McMichael Canadian Art Collection, 1994.13, and reproduced with permission of the Lawren Harris Estate.

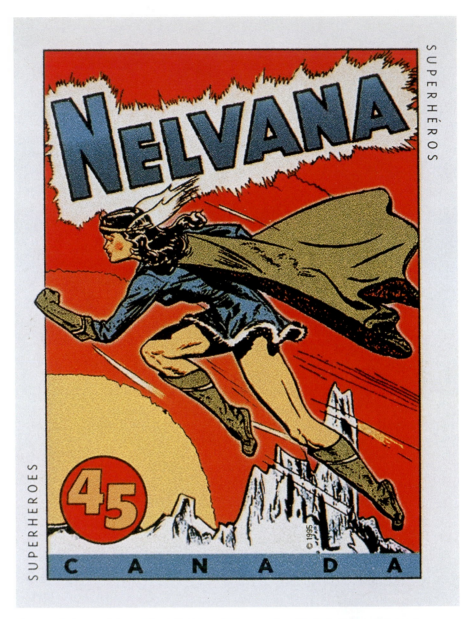

Plate 4   Nelvana of the Northern Lights as she appeared on the forty-five-cent stamp from the October 1995 series commemorating Canadian comic-book heroes. © Nelvana Limited. Reproduced with permission.

Plate 5 Jack Shadbolt, *Bush Pilot in the Northern Sky* (1962), acrylic and ink, 27 × 40 in., concept sketch for the Edmonton International Airport mural. Photograph by Robert Keziere. Reproduced with permission of Doris Shadbolt and courtesy of the University of British Columbia Special Collections Library (44:UBC 1935/174).

Plate 8   René Richard, *Trappeurs au repos* (1969), oil on canvas, 33 × 34 in. Collection of M. and
Mme N. Dion. 2001 ©, all rights reserved, Fondation René Richard. Reproduced courtesy of Normand
Dion and with the permission of the Fondation René Richard.

In this painting Richard captures the chill, bleak beauty of his *grand Nord*. His human figures and
dogs appear to be hunched together against the cold, while at the same time being incorporated into,
made one with, an abstracted landscape.

Opposite page
Plate 6   Lawren S. Harris, *Lake and Mountains* (1928), oil on canvas, 130.8 × 160.7 cm. Collection of the
Art Gallery of Ontario, Toronto: Gift from the Fund of the T. Eaton Co. Ltd., for Canadian Works of Art,
1948. Reproduced with permission of the Lawren S. Harris Estate. Photo: Carlo Catenazzi.

Plate 7   Gwen Boyle, *Tuning* (1993), glass, whalebone, and metal installation with sound tape of
magnetic resonance, a naturally recurring phenomenon captured by the artist near the Magnetic
North Pole. Collection of the artist and reproduced with her permission.

Plate 9   Jin-Me Yoon, *A Group of Sixty-Seven* (1996), a selection from the installation project of 135 cibachrome photographs on paper, Vancouver Art Gallery Acquisition Fund VAG 97.2 a-999999. Photograph by Trevor Mills. Collection of the Vancouver Art Gallery. Reproduced with permission of the artist.

Through these images, Korean-Canadian artist Jin-Me Yoon installs a new group of Canadians within a familiar Group of Seven landscape, thereby claiming that national landscape, with its northern identity, as theirs. The images function as a mode of "writing back" to a dominant, Euro- and central-Canadian politics of identity.

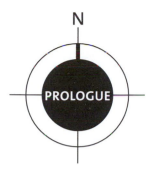

N

PROLOGUE

IDEAS OF NORTH

I've been intrigued for quite a long time ... by that incredible tapestry of tundra and taiga country ... I've read about it, written about it occasionally, and even pulled up my parka once and gone there. But like all but a very few Canadians, I guess, I've had no direct confrontation with the northern third of our country. I've remained of necessity an outsider, and the north has remained for me a convenient place to dream about, spin tall tales about sometimes, and, in the end, avoid.
Glenn Gould, *The Idea of North*

The idea of North is a Canadian myth.
Without a myth a nation dies.
This piece is dedicated to the splendid and
indestructible idea of North.
R. Murray Schafer, *North/White*

To all of us here, the vast unknown country of the North, reaching away to the polar seas, supplies a peculiar mental background.
Stephen Leacock, "I'll Stay in Canada"

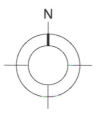

IDEAS OF NORTH

If you were to visit the Hamilton Art Gallery tomorrow, chances are you would be able to see a famous Canadian painting prominently displayed on its walls. Chances are you would have seen the image before in histories of Canadian art because the painting played an important role in establishing a reputation for Canadian art in France in the last century. Whether you had seen the image before in a book or were seeing it in the gallery for the first time, you would almost certainly be fascinated by its quality of chill, ominous mystery.

The canvas is not especially large (151.1 cm x 191.4 cm), but its power is not a function of size. In the foreground, just to the left of centre, a hooded figure with snowshoes strapped to his back kneels in the snow. All around him, and receding into distant drifts, lies moonlit snow. The sky is dark, but if you look closely there are a few stars; however, it is not the stars, the night sky, the pale snow, or even the fallen trapper that holds your attention. To the left of this man, just beyond his outstretched arm and clearly discernible against the snow, is a figure walking away from the man, into the picture plane and out of the painting. Who or what is this? Another trapper? A ghost? Or, given the precise resemblance of the fallen trapper to this ghostly presence, is this figure the trapper's *Doppelgänger,* his very soul, and thus the image of his death?

The painting I have just described is Blair Bruce's *The Phantom Hunter* (1888; see Plate 2), and it was "an immense success" at the 1888 Paris Salon (Murray, 21).[1] Today it is Bruce's most famous painting, and it enjoys a privileged place in the iconography of Canada's northern imagination. In chapter 3 I will return to this image of Canada-as-North to examine the semiotics of its representation in detail, but something more about the genesis of this painting is worth a mention here. Bruce's inspiration for *The Phantom Hunter* came from a poem by Charles Shanly called "The Walker of the Snow" (1867). Charles Dawson Shanly, who emigrated to Upper Canada from Ireland in 1826 at the age of twenty-five, fancied himself an artist and a poet, but if he is remembered at all today it is for this one poem and the impact it had on Bruce.[2]

"The Walker of the Snow" is a simple narrative poem based on legends or folktales about the "Shadow Hunter," a figure who bears some resemblance to the

Windigo of northern Ojibwa and Cree mythology. The speaker in the poem, a servant or guide, tells his "Master" about an encounter he has had – and survived? – with the Shadow Hunter "Who walks the midnight snow" (26) and kills men who pass through the valley alone on cold winter nights. The hunter wears a grey hood and appears suddenly beside you just as you are about to enter the valley; more importantly, he leaves "no foot-marks on the snow" (28). The climax of the guide's portentous tale comes just as he and his Master are about to enter "the valley / Of the Walker of the Snow":

> Then the fear-chill gathered o'er me
>   Like a shroud around me cast,
> As I sank upon the snow-drift
>   Where the Shadow Hunter passed.
>
> And the otter-trappers found me,
>   Before the break of day,
> With my dark hair blanched and whitened
>   As the snow in which I lay.
>
> But they spoke not as they raised me;
>   For they knew that in the night
> I had seen the Shadow Hunter,
>   And had withered in his blight.

Even today in a postmodern Canada, where we can build towns like Inuvik on the permafrost, take oil from the Beaufort Sea, escape from wind chill and temperatures of −30° into the West Edmonton Mall (with its southern simulacrum of igloos and North), and transport the great Canadian Shield to downtown Toronto, it is difficult to shrug off this poem. It is difficult because the poem reminds us, just as it did Blair Bruce at the end of the nineteenth century, that our northern world is a dangerous one. The poem, like the famous painting it inspired, reminds us forcibly of things we might like to forget.

But perhaps you cannot make a visit to the Hamilton Art Gallery or lay your hands on Shanly's obscure poem. What ideas about the North might you get by watching Robert Flaherty's *Nanook of the North* or reading Herman Voaden's plays? *Nanook of the North,* which is readily available on video, was first released by Pathé Films in New York in 1922, but it was largely filmed at the Revillon Frères fur-trading post at Port Harrison (now Inukjuak), Ungava, in 1920. The film made Flaherty famous and popularized the image of the "Eskimos" as childlike, fur-clad, smiling primitives around the world.[3] In the opening sequence of the film Canada is equated with the North of Hudson Bay and Ungava, which are described as "the hunting ground of Nanook and his followers ... a little kingdom ... occupied by

Illus. 1. This still from the beginning of Robert Flaherty's famous film *Nanook of the North* (1922) erases provincial boundaries to map Canada as the northern areas of Ungava and Hudson Bay. Viewers can orient themselves in this strange world of the "Eskimos" by referring to American co-ordinates. Reproduced from *Nanook of the North*, edited by Robert Kraus, with permission of International Film Seminars Inc. and the Robert and Frances Film Study Centre.

less than three hundred souls" (see Illus. 1). The Eskimo subjects of the film are constructed as representative of all Inuit, and the actors are never identified by their real names *as actors*. Instead, we come to know them as "Nanook," the "great hunter," and his family as we watch Nanook hunt walrus, spear fish, harpoon seal, and build an igloo against a background of snow and rafted ice. The film closes with a shot of Nanook's peaceful sleeping face before cutting to a final shot of the family's igloo and the caption: "Tia Mak (The End)." Compared with the Norths of Shanly and Bruce, Flaherty's North is liveable, and the cheerful, if bizarre-seeming, inhabitants are quite at home.

Eight years after *Nanook* the southern Ontario playwright Herman Voaden published *Six Canadian Plays* (1930), the volume in which he announced his new northern vision for a Canadian theatre. Voaden, who was deeply influenced by the Group of Seven, believed that a truly Canadian drama must use Canadian subjects and largely northern settings. The six plays he edited for the volume used these subjects and settings, and Voaden illustrated the book with production photographs, drawings of northern scenes by Lowrie Warrener, three black and white plates of paintings by members of the Group – Arthur Lismer's *A September Gale – Georgian Bay* (1921), Lawren Harris's *Above Lake Superior* (1924),

J.E.H. MacDonald's *Solemn Land* (1921) – and with Tom Thomson's *The West Wind* (1917). Voaden's introduction was, in fact, a manifesto linking Canadian nationalism, nordicity, and the arts.[4]

At the same time as he was encouraging others to write northern plays, Voaden was creating his own dramatic method for putting the North on stage: symphonic expressionism (see Illus. 2). For his own plays, plays like *Northern Storm, Northern Song, Symphony,* and, most importantly, *Rocks* (1932), Voaden used silver-grey-blue lighting on the simplest, abstract sets to evoke a northern atmosphere that would make the "North," as he put it, "a participant in the action, an unseen actor" (quoted in Grace, 1989, 128). By all accounts these lyrical and stylized sets were powerful evocations of a mystical North that Voaden (like Harris) believed essential to Canadian art and identity. However, the human drama in these plays, or even in the later *Murder Pattern* (1936), is secondary to that of nature itself, and Voaden's North, modelled upon the Haliburton area and the Laurentian Shield, is an overwhelming and uncompromising, albeit majestic, force.

If attention to Canada's North (or to Canada-as-North) were restricted to a handful of poets, painters, filmmakers, and playwrights, it might be easy to dismiss *the North* as a romantic myth, an idealized but dramatic setting of limited, if none the less genuine, interest. But such attention has not been so narrow, and before I stop to ponder further the four ideas of North presented thus far, I want to consider four more. According to Rudy Wiebe, Vilhjalmur Stefansson (1879–1962), arguably Canada's greatest Arctic explorer, "is so fascinating a character that he must be avoided" (*Playing Dead*, 105). But he cannot, of course, be avoided. Stefansson organized three expeditions to the Arctic and wrote several important and very popular books about his explorations, about the Inuit, and about Arctic history and legend. He was an explorer, "an anthropologist by profession" (Stefansson, 1921, v), an ardent advocate of the North, and an extremely interesting writer. It is as a writer that Stefansson is important here because it was he, above all others, who argued for the *friendliness* of the Arctic and who attempted – in the most eloquent, yet strategically deployed prose – to dispel a series of what he believed were ill-founded prejudices, errors of fact, and negative assumptions about the North.

Stefansson's most famous book is *The Friendly Arctic* (1921), written after his Canadian Arctic expedition of 1913–19. In it he sets out to convince his readers (who are assumed to be Arctic sceptics, in Canada and the world over) of the significance of what he has just accomplished: survival in the Arctic for almost five years, with his research team, by living off the land instead of attempting (like Franklin and so many other non-natives before and after him) to carry everything with him. Putting aside the grim facts of tragic deaths, near-fatal illnesses and accidents, and terrifying (for this reader, at least) weather and physical conditions, Stefansson's message is that the North is, after all, a friendly place, rich in resources and high in potential for development and settlement. All we must do to realize this potential is to set aside the negative twaddle proliferating in the South

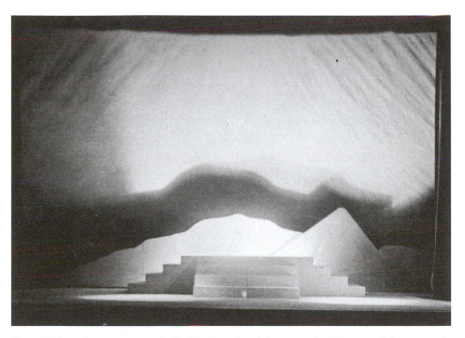

Illus. 2. This set for Herman Voaden's play *Rocks* (1932) illustrates the influence of the Group of Seven, in particular of Lawren Harris, on Voaden's ideas for set design and lighting. Reproduced with permission of the Voaden Estate and courtesy of York University Archives and Special Collections (Y.U. 1319).

about the North and learn from the Inuit. "It is the mental attitude of the southerner," Stefansson insists, "that makes the North hostile. It is chiefly our unwillingness *to change our minds* which prevents the North from changing into a country to be used and lived in just like the rest of the world" (687, emphasis added). By the time the reader has reached the final chapters of this 800-page tome, she must be persuaded by Stefansson's rhetoric and sheer narrative skill, if not by his facts, tables, photographs, and the header "The Friendly Arctic" at the top of every page, that "the polar regions are ... friendly and fruitful" (6).

Unlike most other explorers, who begin by describing exhaustively their equipment, Stefansson begins with two chapters devoted to discrediting received ideas based on errors and misunderstandings accumulated in reports by early British explorers, who would not learn from the Inuit, and repeated until they were accepted as truth. In his biting critique of Flaherty's *Nanook of the North* Stefansson called this type of negative stereotyping and expedient, self-serving rhetoric the *Standardization of Error,* but in *The Friendly Arctic* he is content to call the phenomenon "The North That Never Was."[5] One by one he tackles the seven cardinal sins committed by non-northerners against the North, and he demolishes each in turn, often by using what today we might well call deconstructionist methods. First to dissolve is the idea of "eternal ice," which will not hold up before the facts of precipitation and glacier formation. Next he makes short work of the notions that the North is always covered in snow and that it suffers an "everlasting winter of intense cold" (13). Montreal, as Stefansson points out, receives more snow than many parts of the Arctic, and summer temperatures in the western sub-Arctic and Arctic often reach 90° F. "People," he exclaims, "are willing to believe any horror of the North if it centers around cold and ice" (15). Then he inveighs against the term "Barren Ground" or Barrens, calling it "libelous" (16). Associated with this commonly accepted, albeit misleading name are the adjectives "lifeless," "silent," and "dark." And it is easy for him to list the exquisite flowers and abundant wild-life that actually do exist across this not-so-lifeless tundra, filling it with colour and sound, as Ernest Thompson Seton had joyfully confirmed in his *Arctic Prairies* (1912). Even the "depressing effect of darkness" during the long northern winter is exaggerated, according to Stefansson, because for explorers and missionaries to describe the North as lifeless, silent, and dark is to enhance their own reputations as "intrepid adventurers" (16).

The Friendly Arctic is legitimated in several ways, from the usual maps and photo-graphs to a substantial appendix and strategic foreword and introduction. The foreword includes letters and tributes from the president of the (American) National Geographic Society, the prime minister of Canada, Robert L. Borden, Admiral Robert Peary (the putative American discoverer, in 1909, of the North Pole), and Major General Greely (another American Arctic hero).[6] The most important of these appearances is that made by the "Rt. Hon. Sir Robert Laird Borden, P.C., G.C.M.G., Prime Minister of Canada, Under Whom The Expedition Was Carried Out" (xxi), who writes the formal introduction. With Borden's support, the Canadian government assumed "entire responsibility for the Expedition, as any lands as yet undiscovered in these northern regions should be added to Canadian territory" (xxi). In short, Canada financed the expedition, although only five members of the fifteen-member team (eight of whom would die) were Canadians, the most famous being Diamond Jenness.

The story of the Canadian government's interest in the Arctic is a long one, and I will return to it in chapter 2. At the moment it is enough to say that Borden and his government were keenly interested. Borden had read Stefansson's *My Life with the Eskimos* (1913), and he had listened carefully to the anthropologist's ideas about northern settlement and development. Whether to sell the expense to Parliament and the Canadian taxpayer or because he sincerely believed in Stefansson and shared his vision, Borden cautiously, yet warmly, praised the expedition for adding "many thousands of square miles" to the country, for increasing scientific knowledge, and for dispelling "many illusions with respect to Arctic conditions" (xxiv), illusions that would impede development.

This was not the first time that a Canadian government or Canadian businessmen had cast entrepreneurial eyes at the North, and it would not be the last. In July 1946 Lester B. Pearson, at the time Canadian ambassador to the United States (but soon to be recalled by Mackenzie King to take up new duties as deputy minister of External Affairs), announced that " 'Go North' has replaced 'Go West' as the call to adventure." He made this announcement in an article called "Canada Looks 'Down North,' " published in *Foreign Affairs: An American Quarterly Review,* and he went on to outline the seriousness with which Canada viewed "the responsibilities and the opportunities that attach to our ownership of this vast area" (639). The year 1946 was a strategic moment in which to publish what I am tempted to call this *mission statement.*[7] It was an occasion to remind the world of Canada's Arctic sovereignty (something the Americans might question in the wake of their Second World War activities in Canada's North) and an opportunity to stress the potential for and significance of northern development. "A whole new region," Pearson explained, "has been brought out of the blurred and shadowy realm of northern folklore and shown to be an important and accessible part of our modern world" (642). Pearson went on to itemize the "great wealth in the Land of the Midnight Sun" in gold, in the "precious pitchblende" that yields radium, silver, and copper, and in uranium. He hinted that the "snowy wastes of the Canadian North have many more mineral secrets of that kind to yield" (646), and, while he acknowledged the recently formed Canada/United States *private* research body, the Arctic Institute of North America, he stressed the importance of independent Canadian government research initiatives like "Exercise Musk Ox."

In words and phrases that echo other voices stretching back into the 1860s, Pearson concluded his remarks by reminding his readers that the "Canadian Arctic is ... *no country for weaklings* and its economic development will test the finest qualities of *the men of the North*" (emphasis added, 647).[8] If Pearson had not quite fully accepted Stefansson's rosy vision of a friendly Arctic just waiting for human settlement and development, he had none the less, and for a variety of reasons (from sovereignty to symbolism), moved the idea of North further up the Canadian political agenda. Not surprisingly, perhaps, it would be the Conservatives under John Diefenbaker who would transform a "Northern Vision" into a successful election platform. On 12 February 1958 in Winnipeg, during his now famous campaign-opening speech, Diefenbaker proclaimed, in what Peter Newman has described as "a frenzy of rarely equalled oratory" (218): "We are fulfilling the vision and the dream of Canada's first prime minister – Sir John A. Macdonald. But Macdonald saw Canada from East to West. I see a new Canada. A CANADA OF THE NORTH!"[9] Whatever else can be said about Diefenbaker's "Northern Vision," which I revisit in chapter 2, the Canadian public responded by returning the Conservatives to power with 208 seats, the largest single party majority ever won to date in a Canadian federal election.

By 1935–37, when Lawren Harris painted *Winter Comes from the Arctic to the Temperate Zone,* it was no longer necessary for him or for other members of the Group of Seven to fight for their northern vision of Canada. The critical attacks had largely ceased; the original Group had disbanded, to give way, in 1933, to the Canadian Group of Painters, and Harris himself had moved on from the country north of

Lake Superior to the Rockies and from houses, northern Ontario landscapes, and Rocky Mountain glaciers to abstraction. Despite these changes, he could look back and say that his "work was founded on a long and growing love and understanding of the North, of being permeated with its spirit" (*Lawren Harris, 7*). Exactly what Harris meant by "the North" and "its spirit," however, cannot be neatly formulated and put aside as settled. Along with A.Y. Jackson and Frank Johnston, Harris's North expanded to include areas far north and west of Algoma and Lake Superior.[10] More than any other member of the Group, Harris wrote about the North in comments that have been published, printed, quoted, and reprinted until it has become a critical commonplace to associate him centrally with the "mystic North," the "replenishing" North, the "spiritual clarity" and "flow" of the North, and a national ideal of northernness.[11]

Of all the Harris paintings I might have chosen to contemplate here – among them images that are much more familiar, or images with a direct influence on other artists – *Winter Comes from the Arctic to the Temperate Zone* (see Plate 3) captures succinctly many of the ideas of North that are circulating in my examples thus far. The first striking aspect of the canvas is the limited palette: the pure shimmering blue mountain- or glacier-like shape rising in the background is balanced, but not displaced, by the creamy white, snow-clad shapes of tree and shoreline in the foreground. These two massive vertical forms mirror each other across the smaller horizontal, deeper blue form of an island, which is in its turn surrounded by a greyish-white-to-blue skirt of ice. On the dominant vertical axis of the painting, the eye moves from the distinct cold blue tips of mountain or glacier down to the tree top and down again to the frozen but barely identifiable shapes in the foreground, until, at the very bottom of the picture plane, the eye rests on spots of yellow, the only warm touches in the entire composition. From there the gaze travels back up the painting and off the top of the canvas towards an imagined Pole.

If we shift from the vertical to the horizontal axis, further interesting possibilities arise. The line of apparent horizon bisects the canvas as if to suggest that the majestic blue mountain is resting just at that point. How extraordinarily large it must be, therefore, to rise so high above everything else, as if it could tilt our perspective on the world and force us to *look up* north. On second thought, it is perhaps *not* resting on or at the horizon after all, because moving up both sides of the mountain are sets of lines, first grey on darker grey, then thin blue, then bands of grey or green or brown moving out on either side to the edge of the image that seem to reach above the mountain and to escape the picture frame altogether. These lines and forms, extending up both sides of the upper half of the painting, closely resemble the kind of shoreline that can be found across the Canadian Arctic, and their presence turns the painting – *almost* – into a simple topographical map. Or, if not a map, then, together with the treed landforms lying across the lower half of the canvas, an inner frame containing, controlling, and connecting three ideas of North: temperate zone of boreal forest, barren (Stefansson notwithstanding) ice-surrounded island of the Arctic, and high Arctic mountain or glacier pointing further upwards towards – what? The Pole? The Ultima Thule of the northern imagination? Godhead?

What Harris has done in *Winter Comes from the Arctic to the Temperate Zone* is to join the more southerly Canadian North of Shanly and Bruce with the far North of Stefansson. By joining them visually, by imaging their symmetry and mirroring duplication, he is constructing an allegory of Canada-as-North, moreover of a multiple Canada as unified in and by North.[12] Where Blair Bruce represents North in an overtly narrative genre, Harris abstracts it to enhance its symbolic value. Where Bruce felt he had to (or wanted to) create his Canada North in a studio in France, Harris insists dramatically that Canada is *here*, and that it is filled with snow, water, and ice, mapped by landforms and shorelines. For both painters North is deeply spiritual, an awesome *home*, a romantic place of death, but also of transfiguration.

For Canadians like Voaden and Harris, the North was indeed God's country, and they understood that epithet in the most idealistic, spiritual sense (Harris, remember, was a Theosophist). However, the idea of "God's country" had much more popular roots, which have spread deeply in the fertile commercial ground of popular culture over the last hundred years. Putting aside for the moment the movies explicitly using the term (beginning with Nell Shipman's *Back to God's Country*, 1919, to which I return in chapter 4), let us look briefly at a popular image that is inextricably bound up with ideas of North that many of us will remember from childhood: the *Men in Scarlet* and *Sergeant Preston of the Yukon*.[13] Images of the Mounties, with the North-West Mounted Police often casually conflated by the Americans with the Royal Canadian Mounted Police, proliferated in radio serials or movies about Canada, whether they were made in Canada or were the much more common American radio and Hollywood ones. Pierre Berton claims that of the 575 Hollywood films made about Canada between 1907 and 1956, the overwhelming majority represent the country as vaguely northern or Arctic, and 256 feature the Mounties (*Hollywood's Canada*, 111). Of these, *Rose-Marie* was the most popular, receiving three separate treatments (in 1928, 1935, and 1954), and the 1935 sound version, starring Jeanette MacDonald and Nelson Eddie, is famous.

While Sergeant Preston owes much to the earlier Canadian Mountie radio serial *Men in Scarlet* and to movies, including *Rose-Marie*, this northern hero probably reached more Canadians than any of his predecessors because he was aired serially on CBC radio during the late forties and early fifties, and he starred in seventy-eight episodes on CBC television between 1955 and 1958. Although the radio tapes of *Sergeant Preston of the Yukon* are difficult to locate today (a few reels are available in the National Archives in Ottawa), videos of the hugely popular television series are more easily accessible. The stories are fairly predictable: they are set in the Yukon, of course, usually in or around Dawson City at the height of the Klondike Gold Rush (1896–98); wicked machinations occur in such immoral spots as the

Gold Nugget Saloon; and the evil geniuses are often French Canadian seduc-
tresses, lying, greedy thugs with names like "Pierre Renau," and duplicitous half-
breeds. The incorruptible Preston, however, always gets his man, despite fierce
blizzards, numbing cold, and howling winds, with the help of his wonder-dog
King. The radio serial (like *Men in Scarlet* before it) provided dramatic sound-effects
of blowing wind, barking dogs, and cries of "Mush!" The television series (with
some episodes from 1955 now available on video) exploits scenes of glorious
chases, dramatic shoot-outs, and rustic log cabins, with the good sergeant *always*
in dress uniform and groups of "Eskimos" or "Chilkat" Indians (played by whites)
looking surprisingly alike and all speaking a pidgin English. Clearly, authenticity
was not important; heroic masculine adventure with a strong, clear moral message about law and order in Canada's North was. That this North so closely resembles the American west is perhaps obvious only in hindsight.

The forties and fifties were in fact very rich in popular images of the Canadian
North. One might say that the younger generation of voters who would bring
Diefenbaker his stunning majority in 1958 were brought up on *Men in Scarlet*, Sergeant Preston, and such explicitly northern comic-book heroes as *Dixon of the
Mounted*, *Nelvana of the Northern Lights* (otherwise known as Alana North, secret
agent), and, in Quebec, *Fleur de Lys*. The Nelvana comics, which appeared from
1941 to 1947, were the brain-child of Adrian Dingle and Franz Johnston, who had
left the Group of Seven, changed his first name from Frank to Franz, and spent
five months in the sub-Arctic and Arctic at Great Bear Lake and Coronation Gulf in
1939. Nelvana was a white Goddess figure, daughter of the Inuk Koliak, King of
the Northern Lights, and a mortal woman, very loosely based on Inuit mythology
but made more "attractive" and "up to date," "with long hair and mini skirts"
(Dingle, quoted in Bell, 5; see Plate 4). In addition to her extraordinary powers –
she could travel at the speed of light on the Aurora Borealis, make herself invisible, transform others, control communications – Nelvana was, like her father, im-
mortal. Together with Sergeant Preston she was Canada's most complex, even
"indigenous" guardian of the North, a North that *she*, unlike Preston, embodied
and represented.[14]

It is tempting to imagine Glenn Gould, who was born in 1932, listening to *Men in
Scarlet* and Sergeant Preston on the radio or reading *Dixon of the Mounted* and *Nelvana of the Northern Lights*; he was, after all, an inveterate radio listener and quite
comfortable with popular culture. It is tempting, but I have no evidence for it.
What apparently inspired Gould to create *The Idea of North* in 1967 lies elsewhere:
with school maps of the Northwest Territories, reproductions of Group of Seven
paintings on schoolroom walls, aerial photographs, and geological surveys.[15] *The
Idea of North*, which has inspired much of my own thinking about the North, was
commissioned as a centennial project for CBC *Ideas* and first broadcast on 28 December 1967. Three months later, on 26 March 1968, it aired on CBC's Northern
Service *Tuesday Night*. Gould's introductions for the two broadcasts differ in inter-

esting ways and clearly demonstrate his awareness of the differences between southern and northern Canadian audiences.[16] But by 1968 Gould was not finished with his "sound documentary," as he called it. In 1970 he adapted it, adding visuals and actors to the score and music, to create the CBC television version of the work. Since then *The Idea of North* has been recorded on vinyl (in 1971) and on compact disk (1992), where it is one of three sound documentaries in Gould's *Solitude Trilogy*; moreover, it has come to be seen as the governing metaphor for the man himself in François Girard's 1993 feature film *Thirty-two Short Films about Glenn Gould*.[17]

But just as Gould's *Idea of North* has had several incarnations that, by the nineties, had recuperated Gould himself, making him over as (or into) North, so the original composition as broadcast and recorded does not inscribe a stable or a unitary *idea* of North. Gould's North is, in fact, contrapuntal and multiple, just as are the voices that we hear. These refuse absolutely to be reduced or distilled to a single vision, a unifying idea, or a master narrative, despite the apparently privileged voice of one of the speakers. *The Idea of North* develops out of the "interaction of [the voices of] five characters" carefully chosen by Gould to represent five different responses to the North and a broad knowledge of most areas of the sub-Arctic and Arctic, from Southampton Island in Hudson Bay to Tuktoyaktuk on the eastern side of the Mackenzie delta, where it joins the Beaufort Sea. The five characters are an "enthusiast," represented by nurse Marianne Schroeder, a "cynic," represented by sociologist Frank Vallee, a "government budget-watcher," represented by civil servant R.A.J. Phillips, and someone who could "represent that limitless expectation and limitless capacity for disillusionment," a position filled by James Lotz, anthropologist and geographer (*Glenn Gould Reader*, 392). All three of these men have published extensively on the North, but the fifth voice, that of Wally Maclean, who acts as narrator, is there to encompass all the characters' positions, to serve as "pragmatic idealist" or "disillusioned enthusiast" (392) – in short, to philosophize about the North.

The piece opens with Schroeder's enthusiastic voice remembering her first flight over Hudson Bay to Coal Harbour. After a few seconds Vallee's cynical comments overlay hers, only to be drowned out, as it were, by Phillips' (see Illus. 3). Then suddenly, and for the only time, Gould speaks to introduce his composition with the words I have quoted to introduce this Prologue: "I've been intrigued for quite a long time ... by that incredible tapestry of tundra and taiga."[18] He continues long enough to introduce W.J. Maclean, a surveyor-turned-philosopher whom Gould met on his own trip north on the Muskeg Express from Winnipeg to Churchill in June 1965. Wally then takes over briefly to establish a certain ironic, contemplative context for the piece before passing the polylogue to the British-trained geographer James Lotz. At that point *The Idea of North* moves from voice to voice, introducing a wide range of accumulating, shifting, sometimes contradictory, sometimes bitter or angry, always keenly felt *ideas* of North. One man complains about our obliviousness of the people and the place; another man speaks of

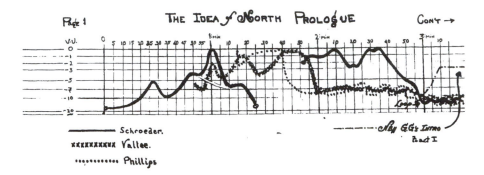

Illus. 3. Glenn Gould's chart for the first three minutes of the Prologue to his *The Idea of North* shows the "scoring" of three voices. Glenn Gould Papers, National Library, MUS 109–5–40. Reproduced with the permission of the Glenn Gould Estate.

his "love affair with the North"; yet another insists that it "takes a strong person" to live in the North because when problems arise, you "can't get away" from that "desert island" of the North. Marianne Schroeder, immediately standing out as the only female voice, reflects upon the fact that the isolation forces one to recognize "a sense of sharing this life" with the few people nearby, and this idea is emphatically endorsed by Lotz. From time to time Wally returns to comment upon the others and to remind us that he is "indeed, a northern listener."

Inevitably, each "character" turns to the question of the relationship of the North to the rest of Canada, to the idea of nation, and to the way the North shapes the southern individual who goes there. These reflections flow smoothly into observations about some of the harsh realities of the North – poverty, alcoholism, starvation, racism, and sexism. And so the polylogue continues, swaying back and forth, like the train, from one voice to another, from romance and myth to harsh facts, from dreams of Eldorado or Utopia to the terrifying realities of the present. Then, late in the composition, an extremely important theme is introduced: the future of the North. One man sees this future positively, as being just like that of the rest of Canada; another sees it practically, as a future of dramatic developments like drilling for oil in the Beaufort Sea; and another (Lotz, the geographer) imagines the North emerging as the place to go for creation, recreation, re-creation, the place to go for universals and knowledge "on a global scale."

Underneath these voices but occasionally rising over them is what Gould has called the "basso continuo" of the train carrying us all further and further north. According to Lotz, it is not only the going or being there but the process of seeking North that has enriched him immensely. As the composition draws to its close – as we are about to arrive *there* – Wally takes over against the rising progression of the final movement of Jean Sibelius's Fifth Symphony, not so much as "a northern listener" now but as a synthesizer and a philosopher of the North. Our inner gyro-compass, according to Wally, guides us into the challenge of the unknown, which is summed up by the North, and it leads Wally (via William James) to the conclusion that the North will unite us all because it represents the "common enemy ... Human Nature" and, thus, "the war that you can afford to be against." "The moral equivalent of war," says Wally, "the moral equivalent for us is going North."

So just what is this "peculiar mental background" that, as Leacock would have it, "the vast unknown country of the North, reaching away to the polar seas, supplies"? Whatever it is, it is powerful enough to form the cornerstone in Leacock's popular essay "I'll Stay in Canada"; it is what defines Canada and being Canadian for Leacock; it is, Leacock assures the British editor who had asked him if he would not retire "home to England," why he will stay in Canada. However, Leacock is, typically, honest and astute about this "appeal" of Canada's "great spaces," "isolation," and "climate," for, as he goes on to say in the sentence following the one I use to introduce this prologue, he has never gone north and never shall (291). In fact, he is perfectly content just thinking about the North stretching away outside his Montreal window. But Leacock has put his finger on what is, for me, one of the most important aspects of North: North is a "*mental background*"; it is, as Gould reminds us more than thirty years after Leacock, *idea*. Now this is not to say for a moment that there is no actual geographical North, although, as we shall see in chapter 2, even our best geographers have struggled to define it.

Throughout this book I consider the *creation* – sometimes very deliberate and self-conscious, sometimes more emotional and intuitive – of North as idea, or, put another way, the creation in words, sounds, images, signs, and symbols of a northern *mentality. My* capitalization of the word North (although it is also capitalized by many of those whose work I will be examining) is intended as a small reminder *passim* of this fundamentally *created* status. North is not *natural*, *real*, a geological or meterological matter of treelines, eskers, permafrost, snow, and temperatures that can dip as low as −81° C (the all-time Canadian low recorded at Mayo, Yukon – see Illus. 4). North, while it has certainly been naturalized as essential to Canada, is a human construct, like Canada itself. It has become part of what Bourdieu calls the "habitus," and we have learned to accept it as a given. North is a discursive formation (a term, along with habitus and others, which I examine in chapter 1), and as such it has done and continues to do a great deal of ideological and practical work. Moreover, it has accumulated a wide range of fascinating, contradictory associations, a set of familiar, compelling stories, a particular rhetoric and an aesthetic that resemble at points those of the desert (and with good reason, because large stretches of the high Arctic are northern desert), a constellation of stubborn stereotypes and seemingly intransigent exclusions. North is gendered, raced, and classed; it permeates all aspects of our culture, from painting to comic strips, from politics to classical music, and it encompasses the entire country from the St Lawrence to the Cariboo, from Labrador to the St Elias Mountains, from Winnipeg to Coppermine, Baffin to Dawson City, Ellesmere to Herschel.

Illus. 4. This photograph, taken on 3 February 1947, shows the record low registered, to date, on an alcohol thermometer at Mayo, Yukon. Reproduced courtesy of the photographer Gordon McIntyre. © Gordon McIntyre.

North is multiple, shifting and elastic; it is a *process*, not an eternal fixed goal or condition. It is, above all, Other, and as such emphatically a construction of southerners (or in earlier stages Europeans, Romans, Greeks), paradoxically invoked to distinguish *us* from those who are more southern. The *we, my, us,* or *our* that is tacitly assumed as authoritative speaker or attentive listener *rarely* lives north of sixty and cannot possibly inhabit North. One result of the southernness of North, of course, is that ideas of North tend to serve southern Canadian interests, be they psychological, spiritual, physical, material, or political. Thus, the familiar descriptions of North as deadly, cold, empty, barren, isolated, mysterious, and so on create a dramatic atmosphere for challenge and adventure. One of the most "likely stories" (as Kroetsch calls them) about North is the narrative of courageous men battling a dangerous, hostile, female *terra incognita* to prove their masculinity and the superior force of their technology, or to die nobly in the struggle, or to map, claim, name, and control unstructured space, even if only on paper. But of course this construction of North necessarily contains its opposite, a friendly North of sublime beauty, abundance, natural resources waiting to be exploited, and of great spiritual power; this North is "God's country." I say *necessarily* because, as is true of any discursive practice or formation, it exists by negating or subsuming what it is not, or does not articulate. What North negates on the human level is not human presence altogether – the well-known *emptiness* of Group of Seven canvases notwithstanding – but the full multiplicity of humanity. Thus, North represents "Eskimos," Indians, the RCMP, white male romantics, adventurers, explorers, etc., and colourful "characters" like Wally Maclean, in prescribed, homogeneous, stereotypic forms, which strike us today as ridiculous, ignorant, sexist, ethnocentric, and, at times, racist. It is only very recently that northern voices have begun to be heard in their own speech, arts, and politics.

In my last chapter, "The North Writes Back," I will consider some of these voices and reflect upon what northerners are telling southerners about *their* home and native land. But before I reach that point I must establish the theoretical basis for my examination of North and its representational strategies, and explore in detail some of the many formulations of North found in the geography, historiography, political discourse, and the arts of Canada. If we are to understand how North has shaped and, I believe, continues to shape Canada (individuals, groups, regions, and the nation-state), then we must trace the discourse of North in as many of its manifestations and formulations as possible; we must be alert to its shifts, modulations, and nuances, the degree to which, like the polar ice or Magnetic North, it moves. Canada *cannot* abandon the idea of North, but Canadians can understand the idea and learn to accept, perhaps even to moderate or change, the ongoing story. If Frobisher Bay can become Iqaluit, Pelly Bay return to Arviligjuaq or Kurvigjuak, and Nunavut emerge from the NWT (itself once Rupert's Land), then anything can happen on a voyage north.

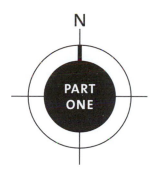

WRITING THE NORTH

To write is, in some metaphoric sense, to go North. To go North is, in some metaphoric sense, to write.
Robert Kroetsch, *A Likely Story*

There is a saying that after five years in the north every man is an expert; after ten years, a novice. No man can hope or expect to absorb it all in a lifetime, and fifteen generations of explorers, whalers, fur traders, missionaries, scientists, policemen, trappers, prospectors, adventurers, and tourists have failed to solve its riddles. To me, as to most northerners, the country is still an unknown quantity, as elusive as the wolf, howling just beyond the rim of the hills. Perhaps that is why it holds its fascination.
Pierre Berton, *The Mysterious North*

À partir du moment où le Nord fera vraiment partie des préoccupations du pays, les affaires pan-canadiennes ne pourront plus être décidées seulement par les seuls citoyens du Canada de base. On en serait alors arrivé à vivre un "national" (le tout de la nation) qui aurait cessé d'être équivalent du seul "principal" (le Sud où la majorité électorale est centralisée).
Louis-Edmond Hamelin, *Le Nord Canadien et ses référents conceptuels*

I conclude, therefore, with a paradox. The ultimate and the comprehensive meaning of Canadian history is to be found where there has been no Canadian history, in the North.
W.L. Morton, "'The North' in Canadian Historiography"

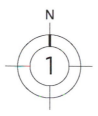

REPRESENTING NORTH

I can think of few more obviously interdisciplinary subjects than the North. Everyone is interested in it, and it has attracted just about every type of non-northerner, from scientist, explorer, whaler – all those Pierre Berton mentions – to poet, painter, sculptor, musician, photographer, filmmaker, social worker, missionary, nurse, doctor, geographer, historian, and literary critic. The North has inspired all these people – to one degree or another, in one form or another – to write, read, and talk about it, to represent it, to imagine it, to, in some sense, *go there*. Above all the North has been and continues to be written about and represented in verbal images and tropes, and in a range of sign systems besides language. Indeed, what we know as North is the product of this writing, these representations. The real north (or norths) is not, for the moment at least, the issue. It is not, in all its particularity, complexity, and diversity, what I am writing about.

In *Canada and the Idea of North* I am writing about and analysing the activity of representing North within and across a range of signifying practices over the last 150 years. In the chapters that follow I explore a selection of representations of North from a wide range of fields, or disciplines, such as history, geography, politics, popular culture, and the arts, from literature to drama, classical music, film, and painting, in order to analyse how they create their representations of North; how they signify, and what they mean; and how they construct meaning, specifically how they construct what we (southerners? some northerners? Canadians-at-large? non-Canadians?) understand as North, both the North in Canada and Canada-as-North.

These chapters, as indeed the entire book, have been set up in accordance with a few basic guidelines or principles that are informed by my methodology and conceptual framework. For example, to a degree my selected representations are organized historically: my overall structure begins in the past and moves into the present. This chronology and general historicity are important for many reasons, but for the moment suffice it to say that North is an idea or a phenomenon that Canadians live with; it exists in and evolves over time. However, no sooner have I mentioned history in connection with North than I must acknowledge the equally important domain of geography. We cannot talk about, write about, imagine, or depict North without placing it somewhere. North is both historically lived and changing *and* spatially configured, even if (for all but specialists) *very* vaguely and imprecisely. Thus, the co-ordinates of my conceptual framework are representation, time, and space, or, put another way, spatio-temporal representations. Just as the very terms historio*graphy* and geo*graphy* suggest writing, writing is what, to a significant degree, if never exclusively, connects my co-ordinates.

Because what I am examining is a body of writing *about* and representations *of* North over time and within numerous spaces, I have attempted to handle my materials with sensitivity to the multiplicity of ideas, styles, voices, and concerns involved. Fairly early in my research I became aware of two things: one, that the representations I was examining (indeed, had access to) were very largely by southern Canadians (and others – Americans, British, French), and two, that northerners, who comprise many different native and non-native groups, seem to have had, until fairly recently, few opportunities for self-representation in the South. The very existence of this latter realization, of course, opens up an enormous range of complex questions and considerations: Why do southerners so overwhelmingly dominate the field of representation? What mechanisms (economic, social) work to silence or exclude northerners? Were they really silenced or, just as seriously, not heard, and what do they have to say? Was and is North *North* for them, and if not, how do they write or tell and represent their place? Who were and are these many northerners anyway? With these observations and questions in mind, I have organized my writing of North in order to maximize voices. Thus, I open with a multi-voiced Prologue and conclude with an Epilogue, and the four parts in between I see as dialogue. I have consciously attempted a dialogic organization of what, in the last analysis, is often re-presented, re-accentuated speech. The wealth of illustration in these pages is another deliberate dialogic strategy, for not all representation of North is verbal. In choosing this dialogic approach I am mindful of Tzvetan Todorov's reflections at the end of *The Conquest of America: The Question of the Other*. Todorov outlines two dangers that he faced in writing about such a politically and morally charged series of events as the conquest – to try, on the one hand, to reproduce voices (of the Conquistadors and the Amerindians) "as they really are" (250) and thus to appear to do away with himself, or, on the other hand, to repress the Other (Spanish and Aztecs) in favour of himself and make them puppets: "Between the two," Todorov tells us, "I have sought not a terrain of compromise but the path of dialogue. I question, I transpose, I interpret these texts; but I also let them speak" (250).

To invoke the Todorov of *The Conquest of America* is to invoke more than the dialogical method of Mikhail Bakhtin that informs that study. I will turn to Bakhtin and his broader influence on my thinking in a moment. But first a *caveat lector* (as it has been for me a *caveat scriptor*): for reasons that I hope will become clear and shall repeat in various ways, I do not see "the North" as an exclusively pernicious master narrative that has, in a postmodernist, poststructuralist, postcolo-nialist world outlived its purpose and can be/*must* be discarded. Neither do I see "the North" as a myth, if by that term is meant a fanciful narrative with no useful relationship to fact. There are many aspects of the representations of North that are destructive and repugnant. They are often racist and sexist and almost always imperialist, even when that imperialism is within the Canadian nation-state; they are by no means always positive adventures, uplifting encounters with mystic grandeur, and so forth. The representations of North are as beautiful, powerful, inviting, disturbing, exclusionary, and exploitative as the individuals creating and using them *according to accepted standards and ideas of the day.* My task is not to judge and lay blame but to try to understand a set of practices that has told us in the past and continues in the present and foreseeable future to tell us – as a people, as a nation – who we think we are. That certain aspects of these representations are, by today's standards, factually wrong or morally problematic does not mean that we should reject the idea (or ideas) of North, even if we could. Not only are our "nordicity" (as Hamelin calls it) and our sub-Arctic and Arctic geography inescap-able physical realities, but the North is deeply embedded in all that we do, even, I would suggest, when we flee south. North, I will argue, is fundamental to who we are, to that "imagined community" (as Benedict Anderson so aptly puts it) of Can-ada, with all its contradictions, failures, compromises, and successes. We will not change Canada by jettisoning the idea of North but by interpolating new voices into the dialogue, by actively participating in the unfinalizable process of what I call the discursive formation of North.

THEORIZING REPRESENTATION

For a cultural study as broadly interdisciplinary as *Canada and the Idea of North* tries to be, I have found it necessary to draw upon a wide range of theories and cultural analyses. For example, Benedict Anderson has helped me to understand the evolu-tion of Canadian nationalism; Edward Said has been a formative influence upon my thinking about the construction of North as a fundamentally orientalizing project; Anne McClintock, Judith Butler, Diana Fuss, Elizabeth Grosz, and Teresa de Lauretis have guided my attempts to articulate the role of race, gender, and class in representations of North, not just as isolated sites of discrimination or exclusion but as complex interconnected regimes of power.[1] Julie Cruikshank and James Clifford and George Marcus have provided me with illuminating evidence of the *degree* to which culture is written and some of the ways in which that writing can be opened up to include the narrativized knowledge of the Other. And the social semiotics of Robert Hodge and Gunther Kress has, for some time now, enabled me to move back and forth more comfortably and confidently between sign systems (including language) and to understand them as socially constituted practices.[2]

What all these theorists share, regardless of their many differences and special interests, is a central focus on the role of language and narrative as constitutive of identity, a recognition of language as one among many sign systems, an interest in the dynamic nature of social formation, culture, discourse, a privileging of diachrony without disregarding synchrony that permits the possibility of change and transformation, a recuperation of some form of the subject and with it – importantly – a concept of agency, and an attention to social processes and interaction. Of paramount importance for me is the fact that all these theorists address the world; they are all turned towards the world in which we must live, and they explore the ways in which language, texts, semiotic systems, and discourse are strategies or forms of representation that work in, are put to use in, the world.

To speak of the world, in this case that part of it called Canada, is to be immediately reminded of the need for a clear understanding of the modalities and the power of representation. The problem is an old one: do our human representations (in whatever sign system) *refer* to an accessible, stable, material or social reality exterior to the self that can be mimetically captured or recuperated? If so, how do they operate? And what is this self that does the representing? I begin on the assumption that we can and do represent a world both exterior to us and of which we are inextricably a part. Our "will to representation" (a term I adapt from Nietzsche and Foucault via Ann Jefferson)[3] may arise from our need to understand, to make meaning in and of the world, but the practice of representation is enormously complex because our representations of the social world are constitutive of it, shape it, construct what we accept as that world. Moreover, we are not, neither as individuals nor as members of groups, such as modern nation-states, free to represent ourselves or anything or anyone else just as we wish. To practise representation at any level is to participate in a complex, already-in-process activity; it is to employ and deploy tools, codes, signs already in use and heavily invested with constructed meaning. However, I do not accept Barthes's view (or that of other thinkers who argue similarly) that representation is only "a carpet of codes" unrolling in nothing more than an endless "circularity" (*S/Z*, 55). At the same time, however, extreme caution is necessary with representation because it is at best a necessary practice that mediates socially constructed images of the self and the world, while at its worst it can block the real by replacing it and directing our attention or desire away from complex lived experience of a heterogeneous reality towards a simulacrum. Postmodernity is, to a large extent, experienced as a virtual global space for the commodification of knowledge and for electronic communication.[4]

My approach to the practice of representation is through a social semiotics that allows me to analyse the details of a particular system (a specific text, painting, cartoon) while remaining acutely aware of the larger social activity or work of representation that contributes to what Diana Fuss calls in her important study of Fanon "colonial regimes of representation."[5] In order to do this I have developed a conceptual framework that draws on Foucault and Bakhtin because, for all their apparent differences, their theorizings have enough in common to make this conjunction viable and enough difference to make them complementary. Between them I place Pierre Bourdieu's notion of the habitus, which helps me to understand where and to what degree the practice of representation informs our consciously acknowledged *and* unconsciously accepted and performed beliefs. By means of this Foucaultian/Bakhtinian conjunction grounded on the notion of habitus, I am able to organize representations of North, to identify and situate the links, continuities and discontinuities, iterations, and so forth of the practice of representing North, and to account for the changes, contestations, interpolations of marginalized voices, the complexities of what Adrienne Rich has called the "politics of location" (in race, gender, ethnicity, and class).[6] What I am mapping is, I believe, nothing less than a major component of the articulation, through representation, of Canada itself, its nationalism and its nationhood.

I have already described the organization of this study as dialogic (in the Bakhtinian meaning of the term) and as informed at every level by my understanding – and appreciation, I must say – of Bakhtin and his circle.[7] My discovery of Bakhtin in the late seventies was critically liberating and enabling. However, Bakhtin has not helped me to understand and map North at its most abstract, generalizable, macrolevel. For that I have turned to Foucault, and to what I have come to call the discursive formation of North. But before I describe what I mean by this term, it might be wise to consider briefly where I see the theories of Foucault and Bakhtin converging.[8] For a start – and a crucial one – both recognize the centrality of language to social relations, forms of power, and ideology. Both see language as *constitutive* of social relations instead of as instrumental (that is, as a tool used to express or communicate a pre-existent truth). Both delight in the resisting or contestatory capacity of discourse, which they posit as a *field* of inescapable and valuable social and cultural struggle that is always lived, in process, ongoing. They are both attempting (if at very different discursive levels) to map conceptual histories of the *process* of cultural discourse, and in doing so both (somewhat paradoxically perhaps) invoke spatial configurations in metaphors, tropes, and turns of phrase, such as Bakhtin's "chronotope," that remind us constantly of the spatio-temporal domain of all discourse (and all representations).[9]

Although they focus on different manifestations of constraint, both Foucault and Bakhtin give us incisive analyses of those social forces that contain, order, and control – discipline in both senses of the word – discourse: Foucault focuses on institutions and disciplined knowledge; Bakhtin focuses on monologic regimes of discourse and elite groups (be they social groups or literary genres). The differences between, yet compatibility – indeed, complementarity – of their approaches to the social constraints on discourse are especially clear if one compares Foucault's "Discourse on Language" with Bakhtin's essays "Discourse in the Novel" and "The Problem of Speech Genres." While Foucault locates the "rules of exclusion" ("Discourse," 216) *outside* of discourse and describes them as activated by society's "profound logophobia" (229), Bakhtin identifies centripetal and centrifugal forces ("Discourse," 271–2) *inside* the word itself, the inner dynamics, as it were, of the heteroglossia within which we must live and which we embody in flexible, diverse speech genres ("Problem," 79). Moreover, both are profoundly interdisciplinary in so far as their theories and concepts are migratory, *not* discipline-based or -bound: both resist narrow disciplinary categorization and application.[10]

But there is one final congruency of Foucault and Bakhtin that, while in itself debated and problematic, is of importance to my aligning of the two, and that is their theories of the subject. Neither Foucault nor Bakhtin accepts the Cartesian subject. For both the human subject is non-Cartesian (though they differ in how they define/characterize this subject), and for both the subject retains some form and degree of agency. Now this business of the subject has been much discussed and hotly debated by feminists and cultural theorists, who wish to negotiate some space in the powerful discourse of poststructuralism for those newly present (visible, audible, self-representing, desiring) subjects who have been hitherto ignored, erased, repressed. As Nancy Harstock put it in her critique of Foucault: "Why is it that just at the moment when so many of us who have been silenced begin to demand the right to name ourselves, to act as subjects rather than as objects of history [that is, of Western history], that just then the [Western] concept of subjecthood becomes problematic?" (163)

With Bakhtin the subject is less problematic. Indeed, Bakhtin insists that dialogic relations "must be embodied ... they must become discourse" by receiving "an *author*" (*Problems*, 184); dialogics posits an absolutely central concept of intersubjectivity whereby subjects are mutually constructed in the dialogics of their utterances, which are themselves, by virtue of heteroglossia, already thoroughly dialogical; Bakhtin's subject is a present, speaking one that "cannot manage without another ... cannot become [him or herself] without another" (*Problems*, 287). Foucault, of course, goes by no means so far, and in *The Archeology of Knowledge* (his key text for my purposes) he is careful not to invoke such a subject. And yet, even in the *Archeology* some notion of a subject as a "speaking subjectivity" (122) keeps returning – in the margins, between the lines.[11] Lois McNay argues, convincingly I think, that in his later work Foucault struggled to articulate a notion of the subject through what he called "techniques of self." As McNay explains it, the Foucaultian "individual comes to understand him/herself as a subject" by means of "techniques or practices of the self" (49).

Thus, while I do not claim that Foucault and Bakhtin agree absolutely – they would be of less use to me if they did – their agreement on key concepts is enabling. Where Bakhtin tells me *how* to deal with representation in discourse at the level of the multi-voiced word and *why* it is necessary to do so, Foucault tells me how to map the field, the terrain of representations of North. And I have not forgotten the habitus, which, as Bourdieu reminds us, is that "embodied history, internalized as a second nature and so forgotten as history" (56): the habitus "is what makes it possible [for 'agents,' for *us*] to inhabit institutions, to appropriate them practically, and so to keep them in activity, continuously pulling them from the state of dead letters, reviving the sense deposited in them, but at the same time imposing the revisions and transformations that reactivation entails" (*Social*

Practice, 57). Bourdieu tells me where to look for the social practice of a discursive formation of North and how deeply installed it is in our "imagined community" of Canada, how thoroughly imbricated it is in Canadian nationalism.[12]

To think of North as a Foucaultian discursive formation is useful in many ways. However, to say more precisely what it means to speak of the discursive formation of North requires a return to *The Archeology of Knowledge*. To begin, then, archeology is a method; it "only ever means a certain mode of approach" (66). Archeology does not take everything into account, as Foucault makes very clear in "Questions on Geography" (65). Discursive formation is a sufficiently clear, orderly concept; it can be grasped, located, analysed. In the concept of discursive formation we can see the crucial constitutive activity of discourse at work, and thus the power it has to construct identities of nation, class, gender, race, etc. (although these are not Foucault's own concerns). An archeological approach to the discursive formation of North allows me to take the following conditions into account: the living, processual nature of all discourse and the dynamics of knowledge, which is not static but shifting (hence the usefulness of such terms as paradigm shift or cognitive shift), the transdisciplinarity of discourse, which is always crossing boundaries, intersecting, overlapping, duplicating, and reinforcing (or resisting) domains of knowledge and of power, and the analogies, at times homologies, between and among disciplines and institutions that facilitate corrections and comparisons. While privileging words, language, and textuality, neither the archeological method nor the concept of discursive formation forecloses on the material or social world or on our experiences of it. To the contrary, as Foucault always reminds us when speaking of his methods and concepts, his theorizing was firmly rooted in his own explicit experiences with psychiatry and penal institutions. Thus, *an* archeology of the discursive formation of North isolates for study those sites where the relations of power and knowledge work to construct identities over time and in a certain real and imagined space: North.

But let me move still closer to his method and concept. In *The Archeology of Knowledge* Foucault is at pains to explain (to legitimate) his method. Archeology is *not* a lot of things: it is *not* interpretive (139); it is *not* about a search for origins or ends; it is *not* directed at content; it is *not* trying to capture essences or Truth; it does *not* personalize discourse by identifying it with *oeuvres* or great men; it does *not* totalize a theme or construct a master narrative (although powerful themes, tropes, and representations inevitably come up for consideration). Most important for Foucault, archeology is *not* a history of ideas (138), which he sees as unmethodical, lacking in objectivity and rigour. No, Foucault's archeology is a descriptive methodology for identifying discursive formations (or what he also calls a "discourse-object") and their constitutive statements, and for examining their rules of operation.

Archeology is the method I have used at the *macrolevel* of my investigation in order to identify (to gather in an archive) the discursive and representing practices, statements, positivities (discursive rules), and interdiscursive configurations that comprise a discursive formation – here, of North. Archeology highlights the historicity of discourse (while embedding spatialization in its very terms and metaphors), the *processes* (changes, transformations, shifts, continuities *and* discontinuities) of discourse, and the cross-disciplinary "fields" of discourse and its sites of analogy and difference (160). It facilitates the mapping of discursive formations and the discovery of active relations between discursive and non-discursive forms. As Foucault puts it, a discursive formation is "the general enunciative system that governs a group of verbal performances" (116) – which I must qualify by adding, verbal and *other representing* performances.[13] A discursive formation can be said to constitute a field of relations according to "the law" of a series of "statements" (107). It is "essentially incomplete," because living in time and space, and it is an enunciative process (which I expand beyond the verbal) that cannot be identified with speaking, representing, authorizing subjects. It is "the group of statements that belong to a single system of formation" (107), or, as Foucault says in his clearest description of the concept: "Whenever one can describe, between a number of statements, such a system of dispersion, wherever, between objects, types of statement, concepts, or thematic choices, one can define a regularity (an order, correlations, positions and functionings, transformations), ... we are dealing with a *discursive formation*" (38).

Statements are the key constitutive *units* of a discursive formation (Foucault's preferred term is "enunciative functions" [106], not units), and yet statements can be simple sentences (a familiar enough notion) or "a series of signs" (98). Statements are always part of a "network of statements" (99); therefore, for my purposes, I will find the discursive formation of North by locating a single statement and then looking for the network to which it belongs and within which it operates. Above all, a statement must be capable of being used and repeated. "Thus the statement circulates," Foucault tells us, "is used, disappears, allows or presents the realization of a desire, serves or resists various interests, participates in challenge and struggle, and becomes a theme of appropriation or rivalry" (105). The statements and their discursive formation, which archeology enables us to locate, are, if you will, the *what*, the object of study. They are the constitutive parts in a system of relations for producing (creating, organizing, disseminating) knowledge. A discursive formation and its statements, *when approached archeologically*, will not yield analysis or interpretation. Nevertheless, as Foucault knows full well and as his description of statements ("realization of desire," "resists various interests," "challenge and struggle," "theme of appropriation or rivalry") implies, describing the system is never enough. Being human we want to know what ideological investments have been and are being made and legitimated in discursive formations. We want to know who or what controls them, uses them, and to what end. For me this necessitates asking: *who* is served by a discursive formation of North, and *how* and *why*? Which is also to ask, of course, who is *not*.[14] It is at this mesolevel of my study that I turn, not to Foucault and his theory of genealogy but to Bakhtin, Bourdieu, Said, Fuss, McClintock, and the others mentioned above, because it is only by paying attention to the ways in which statements are used to serve or resist, to participate in struggle, to enter into operations of appropriation and rivalry that I can assess the meaning and impact of a discursive formation of North in social and artistic discourses and in life, in this "imagined community" of Canada. To move from Foucault through Bakhtin and Bourdieu to recent theories of race, gender, class, nationalism, and so forth is to move from the what to the how and the why, from a system to its consequences.

Before I turn to what I am doing differently from those others who have already discussed and theorized the North, let me pause to situate the discursive formation of North and to summarize the three levels of my study – macrolevel, mesolevel, and microlevel. Archeologically, for example, Stefansson's *The Friendly Arctic* contains a very large number of statements that are constitutive of the discursive formation of North. They circulate and contribute to, are part of, a very large network of relations that are, collectively, part of the process. These statements vary in type; there are sentences, verbal arguments, photographs, maps, tables, charts, lists, and appendices. To describe this text in this rather blunt way is to treat it quantitatively and to make it quantifiable within the larger formation of which it is a constitutive part. To treat it qualitatively requires a significant shift in focus from the what of quantitative description to the how and why of qualitative analysis and interpretation. It is also to shift from the macrolevel to the mesolevel of analysis. At this intermediate level we can appreciate how passionately, overtly, deliberately, and skilfully Stefansson marshals his materials – his language and his other modes of representation – to argue the case for a *friendly* Arctic that will serve precise political, social, economic, and national ends. Moreover, he does this by entering the already powerful and widely circulating system of the discursive formation of North with fists flying. He breaks his way into the system, forcing a rupture, creating a discontinuity, resisting and challenging, while at the same time necessarily relying on the very discursive formation within which he must operate, by which he is himself ruled and appropriated. At this level Stefansson has entered into a dialogue with many others who have written about, studied, explored, and represented the Canadian Arctic. Even in this text, which at times might sound like a monologic rant, Stefansson is *extremely* sensitive to other voices, some of which are quoted directly, some of which are re-presented intertextually and re-accentuated. The final effect of *The Friendly Arctic* is not unlike that of a debate in which the reader is left to listen and decide for herself.

But I cannot stop there. To move to the microlevel is first to grasp a single discrete statement constituting *The Friendly Arctic*, then to identify its network of relations within the discursive formation of North, and finally to interpret, evaluate it in comparison with other analogous or homologous statements. I could take Stefansson's title – the friendly Arctic is a descriptive statement: the Arctic is [capable of being] friendly – but I will choose instead a simpler-seeming, more categorical grammatical statement: "The North is cold." Now this statement is not a truth or a fact or a definition, as Stefansson sets about so brilliantly, in "The North That Never Was," to demonstrate. Stefansson does not stop to consider its origin or its end. However, he knows that this statement is repeatable, that it can be used, manipulated, transformed (which is what he hopes to do with it), even discarded. He knows that it travels across related discursive fields and disciplines, and that it is part of a network of statements (for example, the North is barren, silent, always snow-covered, always dark).

The network of statements that concerns Stefansson is delimited by the purposes and available space of his book. However, the statement "The North is cold" has a much greater circulation than Stefansson has time or space to consider. If we move outside *The Friendly Arctic*, we can easily find other statements of "The North is cold." Take John Moss's question – "what does cold mean, where survival depends on the solidity of winter?" (13) – or consider for a moment the photographic proof (see Illus. 4) of Canada's record-breaking lowest temperature, registered at Mayo, in the Yukon, at 8:00 a.m. on 3 February 1947, when the alcohol thermometer fell below −80° F.[15] The thermometer demonstrates that "The North is cold" is not restricted to verbal statements but is fully representable in other sign systems. The very same can be said of Blair Bruce's *The Phantom Hunter* (see Plate 2), which tells us that the North is so cold it kills you. All these statements are representations of the North that construct it while, at the same time, in each case, always referring to a real Arctic or northern place or experience (Mayo is not in the Arctic, although it is certainly farther north than Bruce's Hamilton home). In order to compare such specific statements in different sign systems, to consider how they work and why, in whose interests, it is necessary to work at the microlevel, to make semiotic comparisons, to ask *who* is using the statement and from what position they are speaking, writing, representing. What was cold in Mayo on 3 February 1947 might not have felt cold near Fort Nelson, B.C., on 7 January 1982, when the thermometer dipped to −96° F, and neither Stefansson in his study nor Bruce in his studio was as cold as the North he represented. Both the semiotics of representation and the agency and subject position of the speaker/writer (here add painter and photographer) are relevant and necessary to understanding the discursive formation of North. Finally, this example of analysis at the microlevel is a reminder that the physical North is always there, a sharply visible or blurred image, lying beyond the North. But the object I am examining is not pre-discursive – the actual ice storm that hit Montreal in 1998 notwithstanding. North is not the physical facts of meteorology, permafrost, or building the DEW Line. North is a discursive formation, with articulations, representations (including photographs of "the Ice Storm" – see Illus. 5), processes, transformations, and a "schema of correspondences [among] ... temporal sites" (*Archeology*, 74), of which *Canada and the Idea of North* is a part.

CRITICAL DISCOURSES OF REPRESENTATION

Inevitably some of the other parts of this discursive formation of North are criticism and/or theory by other critics and theorists. With them my comments are always in dialogue because, on the one hand, they have made their constitutive

Illus. 5. "Collapsed Powerline, Boucherville, Québec" is one of the images from "Lethal Beauty" (1998), a photoessay by Montreal photographer Benoit Aquin. Aquin's images function as powerful *aides mémoires* of Canadian nordicity, which reaches down to our southern borders, and of our vulnerability, despite sophisticated technology. Reproduced courtesy of the artist. © Benoit Aquin.

contributions to the on-going formation of North and, on the other, I have learned from them even when, as is sometimes the case, I cannot agree with their descriptions or cannot share their approach to the North. Many, if not all these attempts to describe, articulate, or theorize the North are post-1950; indeed, at first glance it seems that, perhaps since Meech Lake (1987), there has been a rush of voices struggling to create and enter a debate about Canada and the North. However, a closer look reveals that Canadians have been attempting to define themselves and Canada by invoking the North or their nordicity for a very long time. Many of these voices are literary, and range from the scholarly Northrop Frye to the essays of Margaret Atwood or Robert Kroetsch (although there is no line drawn in the snow that divides the scholar from the artist on this subject). But there are other contributors to the critical discourse, writing from well beyond the disciplines of literary studies and literature; I am thinking of Lawren Harris's essays as well as the considerable discussion of the North in the history of fine art, preceding and provoked by the Group, and of R. Murray Schafer, whose *Music in the cold* (1977) is nothing less than a manifesto on the condition of Canadian creativity and identity *as nordicity*: "All the energy of the world," he proclaims, "radiates from the Magnetic North Pole. CANADIAN PROVERB (ought to be)" (64).[16] And then there is Herman Voaden in the Canadian theatre of the thirties, Stephen Leacock, whose 1922 *Adventures of the Far North* foreshadows Pierre Berton's *Arctic Grail* (1988) and Farley Mowat's *Top of the World Trilogy* (1960 to 1973), and always Stefansson, who, in 1922, was the first (to my knowledge) even to speak of *theorizing* the North.

What chiefly characterizes these critical, descriptive, and theoretical writings is their secondary nature; these are not primary texts but self-consciously secondary ones that are trying to make sense of what has already been said and written about the North, or about its representations, and about Canada as a northern nation. I cannot examine them all in detail, but I would argue that they fall, more or less, into three categories and a few of them warrant closer attention.[17] In the first category I include those studies that focus on a generalized northern landscape of Canada (on Canada *as* northern landscape) and see in it either the image of our worst fears or the nexus of complex ambivalent desires of attraction and repulsion, escape and freedom, failure and death. The second category includes a number of much more carefully situated studies that focus on problems of ethnography, aesthetics, and the representation of specific Arctic or sub-Arctic experiences and locales. The third category includes a number of studies that are overtly theoretical and analytical; often these works construct North in order to deconstruct it or to reconstruct and reimagine it; sometimes they are extremely personal and philosophical. The first has contributed to the myth, a largely literary and pictorial one, of North as a negative, overwhelming presence; the second provides a wide spectrum of analysis with greater concern for the social realities of time and place and the practices of representation; the third returns us to a dreaming, contemplative subject for whom the meaning of North is a paradoxical reality conjured from the abstractions of philosophy and its near cousin, theory.

Frye is in many ways responsible for the literary/cultural critical construction of Canadian nature as a "sinister and menacing" monster (*Bush Garden*, 142) that inspires "stark terror" (138) in all who contemplate it. Frye's Canada, and thus Frye's North, of course, is circumscribed by the Laurentian Shield. To enter this country, Frye tells us, is to be "silently swallowed by an alien continent" (217) in which the imagination quickly takes refuge within a garrison mentality (226). In his tendency to take an eastern, largely southern Ontarian, part of Canada for the whole, Frye is not much different from such contemporaries as Harold Innis, Donald Creighton, and, to a lesser degree, W.L. Morton (to whom I turn in the next chapter). His "bush garden" trope (borrowed from Atwood: *Bush Garden*, x) has given rise to descriptions of our literary landscape as a *Haunted Wilderness* (Northey) and of our winters as having a *Northern Imagination* (Mitcham).[18] According to these critics, despite the splendour of *our* Northland (as it is so often styled), the quest-like journey north of characters in plays, poems, novels, and films usually leads to isolation, madness, violent death, to what Margaret Atwood, quoting Robert Service, calls *Strange Things.* In *The Wacousta Syndrome*, for example, Gaile McGregor pushes the deadly bush-garden trope still further by insisting that both the literature and the painting of Canada (by which she means predominantly the Group of Seven) construct an image of the North as inimical to human habitation and deeply threatening to the human imagination, which, as a result, is obsessed with isolation and death.[19] The Canada that McGregor constructs from these limited tropes is one largely derived from artistic representations of a narrow strip of mid-northern Ontario, which in her theorizing becomes an imperialist metonymy that stakes its claim to Canada as a whole. This metonymic construction of Canada-as-North, where North is northern (just north of *southern*) Ontario, is by no means confined to Frye and McGregor.

In many ways the mystical northern vision of Voaden and Harris fuels the notion of North as pure but overwhelmingly white, silent, and spiritual, as *opposed* to material, or bodily, presence. People are seen either as absent from or quickly rejected by – or, if they stay, absorbed into – this critical construction of the Great White North. This focus on spirituality and human absence is stressed by Ann Davis in her close comparison of Harris's Arctic work with that of his American contemporary Rockwell Kent: where Kent's canvases represent a human, personal (and self-aggrandizing) view of the North, "Harris gives no hint of man's presence" because "the sublimity of the north appealed to his scepticism, while its beauty and ruggedness gratified his patriotic desire for a suitable inspirational means of national identification" (*A Distant Harmony*, 131).[20] Thus, from Harris and Voaden in the twenties to Frye in the late sixties, Margot Northey in the seventies, Allison Mitcham, Gaile McGregor, and Ann Davis in the eighties, and Atwood in *Strange Things* (1995), we can trace a critical construction of a deadly, inhuman North characterized by mystery, danger, and adventure and typified by the 1917 disappearance of Tom Thomson, which has circulated from geographical, historical fact to critical trope and poetic myth –

Tom Thomson I love you ...

I love your bent trees   and I love your ice
in spring   candled into its green rot
and I love the way you drowned   all alone

with your canoe   and our not even knowing
the time of day   and the grave mystery
of your genius   interrupted   is *our* story   (Kroetsch, *The Stone Hammer Poems*, 50)

– and back again: "There was no indication of how he had come to drown. But everyone knew, or thought they did: the Spirit of the North had claimed him as her own ... Tom Thomson's death was found significant because it fitted in with preconceived notions of what a death in the North ought to be" (Atwood, *Strange Things*, 19).

Yet North and death are not merely synonyms, as even Atwood allows. In his study of French Canadian writing (including Quebec authors and those from other provinces), *The Long Journey* (1968), Jack Warwick provides a detailed historical study of the *pays d'en haut* tradition, from the seventeenth century to the 1960s, in which he takes great pains to trace a multi-faceted "literary tradition of the North" (4) that has produced such heroic figures as the *coureur de bois* and the *voyageur*. Where Frye and his followers find a hostile bush garden represented in the works of anglophone and francophone writers and artists, Warwick finds the trope of a long journey that carries the male hero into the *pays d'en haut* on personal, artistic, and national quests (where *national* is understood as French *rayonnement*), or that locates imaginative possibilities for regeneration (even salvation) and revolt against social constraint in *le Nord*. The North that Warwick maps is both more precisely delineated in time and space than Frye's or McGregor's and more complex (see Illus. 6).[21] Despite the at times deadly and negative aspects of the *pays d'en haut*, Warwick insists that the "persistent dream of freedom in the forest" (128) is the current legacy of this literary tradition; in the works he considers, the *pays d'en haut* remains an imagined place of truth, peace, vitality and escape.

Despite her many witty representations of the North as deadly – "a frigid but sparkling fin de siècle femme fatale, who entices and hypnotizes male protagonists and leads them to their doom" (*Strange Things*, 3) – Margaret Atwood knows full well that the North is much more complex than that. She has often written about North (in *Surfacing*, most notably, but also in stories like "Death by Landscape" and "The Age of Lead" from *Wilderness Tips* and in many poems), but her most sustained non-fiction consideration is *Strange Things: The Malevolent North in Canadian Literature* (1995). Her subtitle is, I suspect, a humorous salute to the dominant academic critical tradition stemming from Frye, but her main title is of course from Robert Service's macabre Yukon poem "The Cremation of Sam McGee":

> There are strange things done in the midnight sun
>   By the men who moil for gold;
> The Arctic trails have their secret tales
>   That would make your blood run cold;
> The Northern Lights have seen queer sights,
>   But the queerest they ever did see
> Was that night on the marge of Lake Labarge
>   I cremated Sam McGee.   (*Songs of the Sourdough*, 57)

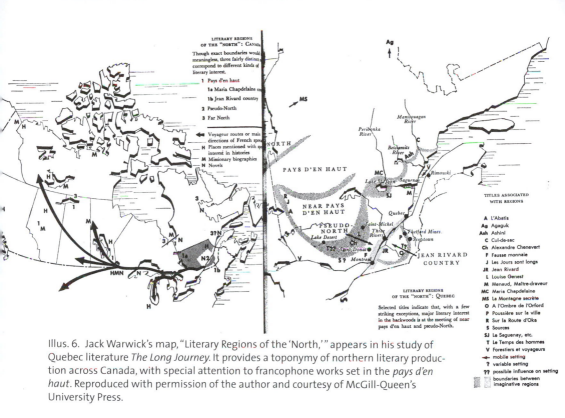

Illus. 6. Jack Warwick's map, "Literary Regions of the 'North,'" appears in his study of Quebec literature *The Long Journey*. It provides a toponymy of northern literary production across Canada, with special attention to francophone works set in the *pays d'en haut*. Reproduced with permission of the author and courtesy of McGill-Queen's University Press.

In the four lectures that make up *Strange Things* Atwood takes us on a dazzling tour of some of the more grisly episodes in Canadian history and literature, from Sir John Franklin's demise t«o other deaths-by-mystic-North in Robert Service's Yukon and E.J. Pratt's Atlantic to Gwendolyn MacEwen's chilling verse-drama *Terror and Erebus*, and Mordecai Richler's "outrageous burlesque of the Franklin story," *Solomon Gursky Was Here*. From these she moves to the somewhat more up-lifting "Grey Owl Syndrome," named for Archie Belaney and including a wide range of non-native literary characters who go native, usually in the North, where they hope to find "salvation and new life" (35). But this positive note is quickly exchanged, in the next lecture, for an exploration of those who are "driven crazy by the North" (62) and become Windigos. Her fourth and final lecture brings her back to gender, to the *femme fatale* image of the North and to the fate of women who go North to become either "the victim of the North – or ... more likely, its incarnation" (114). Whatever else I might say about *Strange Things*, this much is clear: Atwood's North is much more than malevolent; it is parodic, tricky, alluring, hungry, inescapably part of who we are as Canadians, and fun.

If this first category of critical studies and theorizings produces a dominant narrative of a generalized North as malevolent female or hostile bush garden, with a muted subtext of North as place of freedom, purity, and regeneration, my second category celebrates specific Norths and the people who live there or dared to pass through. These works range from collections of literary/cultural studies (Carlsen, *Literary Responses to Arctic Canada*; Grace, *Representing North*; Moss, *Echoing Silence*) to the meticulously researched and argued analyses of northern aesthetics by Ian MacLaren. Most of the work in this category is cross- or interdisciplinary, and reaches back to Stefansson in *The Friendly Arctic* (1922) and Stephen Leacock in *Adventures of the Far North: A Chronicle of the Arctic Seas* (1922) and forward to Farley Mowat and Pierre Berton. Indeed, I would stretch this category to include the dialogic ethnography of Julie Cruikshank in *Life Lived Like a Story* (1990), Hugh Brody's *Maps and Dreams* (1981), the passionate debate of "The True North Strong and Free Inquiry Society" published in *The Arctic: Choices for Peace & Security* (1989), and the complex installation art of Marlene Creates' *The Distance between Two Points Is Measured in Memories, Labrador 1988.* Unlike my first category of texts, this one cannot be easily summarized because it does not boil down to a few stereotypic or mythic formulations about how North has been constructed. If these studies have anything in common it is the closeness with which they examine the evidence, the critical pressure they bring to bear on specific aspects of the discursive formation of North, and their careful scrutiny of myth.

Leacock's *Adventures of the Far North* is a good example of what I mean for two reasons: first, it is a celebratory retelling of the explorations of northern and Arctic Canada by the Elizabethan Frobisher and by Samuel Hearne, Alexander Mackenzie, and Franklin (his two overland expeditions and his fatal naval search for the Northwest Passage); and second, it stands as a precursor to a long list of such retellings, the best known being Mowat's *Top of the World Trilogy* (*Ordeal by Ice, The Polar Passion,* and *Tundra*) and Berton's *Arctic Grail* (though Berton's further retellings for children in the Adventures in Canadian History Series are yet other examples of the phenomenon), which begin by assuming that the North *they* are representing is *constitutive* of Canada and *the stories are Canadian* (not British). What Leacock, Mowat, and Berton construct is a naturalized version of exploration as Canadian history in which the men whose narratives they recycle are viewed for the most part as noble, intrepid Canadian heroes, even when they fail.[22]

Ian MacLaren's work on northern aesthetics makes a major critical contribution to contemporary appreciation not only of *how* the Canadian North and Arctic were represented by the artists who illustrated the explorers' narratives and the explorers themselves (as in the case of Samuel Hearne, Robert Hood, and George Back) but also of *what* was at stake in these representations. Aesthetics, as MacLaren demonstrates, dictates the semiotics of visual imagery and style that, in turn, conveys the moral and ideological investments of individual artists or explorers, and of the British Empire. Thus the predominance of a picturesque aesthetic (as distinct from the sublime) in the work of artists like W.W. May amounts to "an aesthetic strategy for survival in high latitudes" ("The Aesthetic Map," 94) because "the chief ideological thrust of the picturesque" was to control nature and bring it into harmonious subservient co-existence with man ("Commentary," 288). This kind of informative close study of North can be found, of course, in numerous articles on specific authors, artists, or explorers, but one other example of such scrutiny worth noting here is the trio of studies of Glenn Gould's *The Idea of North* in *Representing North* (see Hjartarson, McNeilly, and Dickinson), which treat that work by comparing, juxtaposing, and contextualizing it with the Group of Seven, geographical concepts of nordicity, and poetic versions of documentary. The result of such interdisciplinary exploration is not only a better understanding of Gould but, equally important, sharper insight into the critical work of re-presenting and, thus, of constructing North.

By including Cruikshank's and Brody's texts in this second category, I am necessarily pushing the boundaries towards those more philosophical and theoretically self-conscious works I have reserved for category three. But what is especially notable about *Life Lived Like a Story* and *Maps and Dreams* is the way their authors acknowledge their own constitutive role in the representation of others' stories. This is both a methodological strategy and an urgent reminder to the reader of how materially *we* (southerners, non-natives) have affected both the people of the North and North itself. As Brody notes, sadly I think, "Canada could achieve something in the North that no country has ever done" (280): the operative word here is "could." Something can only be achieved, however, if we learn to listen to another narrative logic – the logic of Dene elders, for example, or the logic of memory as Marlene Creates represents it in her installation art, where assemblages of personal maps, portrait photographs, and brief personal narratives by northern Labrador Inuit, Naskapi Innu, and white settlers sit side by side with each other and with actual pieces (sod, rock, wood, etc.) of the Labrador land (see Illus. 7). What Creates' critically engaged act tells us is that, like the cultures of the Inuit, Innu, and settlers of northern Labrador, our identity is shaped by the land of which we are an inextricable part and that we deny our place in nature at our peril (Creates, 15).

"I was a Kabloona" (155) says Gontran de Poncins about halfway through his famous ethnographic travel memoir, *Kabloona* (1941).[23] And Kabloona he will remain. *Kabloona*, in fact, is not so much about the Inuit of the Kitikmeot area of Gjoa Haven and Pelly Bay, regardless of what the book's promoters and editors might say; it is about Jean-Pierre Gontran de Montaigne de Poncins (1900–62) and, as he tells us himself, the "substitution of the Eskimo mentality for the European mentality within myself" (xxvii). For a few months during 1938–39, and only after phases of acute resistance, resentment, and revulsion, de Poncins's journey into the exotic terrain of the Other takes him into the heart of his own identity, much of which he would like to reject. For those few months he masquerades as an Inuk, all the while knowing that he is not and never could be an Inuk. During his long journey into the *pays d'en haut*, this French aristocrat does tell us a great deal about the Arctic and the Inuit, who look after him and with whom he lives. In both the intense personal focalization and the detailed representations of what he learned, heard, and experienced while he was sojourning there, *Kabloona* points forward to several of the works that I am including in this third category of

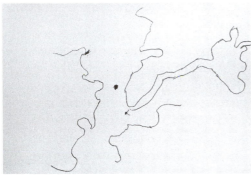

I was born in Utshimasits. That's the one, you know, the old place. Island over here. And then over here right in there, that's the old place, Old Davis Inlet. That's where I was born, 1931, something like that. Naskapi Indians is what they call us. Mushuau Innu is what we call ourselves. In the winter we went in the country. Inside you know. About August everybody went in the country. Pulled it you know, had to use the canoe. Got to stay in there all winter. Hunt caribou, fox, anything. Mink, otter. And then come out all people in June. Summer got to work at the fish and wood. Get wood. Got to use an axe. And a bucksaw. And some use a chain saw. All place, lots of wood. Two days now didn't make a fire. Nobody to give me wood.

Illus. 7. Marlene Creates' "Gilbert Rich, Labrador 1988" is an assemblage of two black and white photographs, a memory map drawn by Rich, his story panel, and a piece of wood from Davis Inlet, cut with an axe. © 1988, CARCC.

Marlene Creates' eighteen assemblages, called *The Distance between Two Points Is Measured in Memories, Labrador 1988*, celebrate the identity of individual Labradorians in autobiographical stories and maps about the times and places that define them. For Rich, a Mushuau Innu from Utshimasits, identity is remembered through the wood he chops, his story, and in his drawing of Old Davis Inlet, where he was born.

overtly philosophical, self-reflexive, or theoretical texts. R. Murray Schafer's *Music in the cold*, while passionately personal like *Kabloona*, is also a nationalist representation of North and northern values, and Schafer reverses de Poncins's formulation: "I am a Northerner," he asserts:

I say prayers for the souls of the animals I eat.
My heart is pure.
My mind is as cool as an ice-box.
"And the cold of the forest will be in me until my extinction." (66)

In *Music in the cold* Schafer sees no hope for *Canadian* art, which is "an art of the North," unless Canadians stop going, stop *being* South and become, once more, "the unpainted observer in a Group of Seven painting," who, like Harris and Thomson, can "hack it in the bush" (66).

Schafer's message here, in the aggressive images of *Music in the cold* and in his more measured preface to *On Canadian Music*, is the same as Rudy Wiebe's in *Playing Dead*. Where Schafer insists "We are all Northerners, sharing a million acres of wildness in the imagination. That is our only uncounterfeit resource, and we should seek to draw more directly from it" (x), Wiebe protests: "I need wisdom. Wisdom to understand why Canadians have so little comprehension of our own *nordicity*, that we are a northern nation and that, until we grasp imaginatively and realize imaginatively in word, song, image and consciousness that North is both the true nature of our world and also our graspable destiny we will always go whoring after the mocking palm trees and beaches of the Caribbean and Florida and Hawaii; we will always be wishing ourselves something we aren't, always stand staring south" (*Playing Dead*, 111). Like de Poncins, Wiebe has gone North to discover himself, "to walk into the true north of my own head between the stones and the ocean" (119). Like Leacock, Mowat, and Berton, he retells some of the stories of other kabloonak who have gone North and re-presents their discoveries (Robert Hood's and George Back's of Greenstockings, Albert Johnson's of an Aklavik grave, Franklin's, Frobisher's, Stefansson's). Unlike most kabloonak, however, he also *listens*, and re-presents some of the stories of those who have always been there (Joe Nasugaluaq, Mable Stefansson, Felix Nuyviak, Nellie Cournoyea, William Nerysoo, and others), and he concludes with a song/poem called "My Breath" by Orpingalik of the Netsilik Inuit (recorded by Knud Rasmussen). As with Marlene Creates' work, Wiebe's *Playing Dead* has a lot to tell us, not just about the North or about others who have tried to represent it but about ourselves and our representating of North, and, like Creates, Wiebe learns to value *here*, "true NORTH, not PASSAGE to anywhere" (114), and the wisdom of native northerners: "Songs are thoughts sung out with breath when people are moved by great forces and ordinary speech is no longer enough" (Orpingalik, recorded by Rasmussen, quoted by Wiebe, 119).

I will come back to the songs, representations, and wisdom of native northerners in chapter 6. For the moment, however, it is but a short step from de Poncins's ethno/autobiography to the personal theorizings of North by Robert Kroetsch, Aritha Van Herk, and John Moss. Kroetsch was one of the first Canadian writers to theorize North, as distinct from writing it in novels like *But We Are Exiles* (1965) and *Gone Indian* (1973) and in poems about Tom Thomson or Albert Johnson. In his essay "The Canadian Writer and the American Literary Tradition" (1971) Kroetsch distinguishes Canadian from American writing by characterizing it as northern. Canadian writers, he explains, have "a peculiar will towards silence," and "this silence – this impulse towards the natural, the *uncreated* ... – is summed up by the north" (11). This North, Kroetsch romantically insists, is not a frontier to be pushed back and conquered but "a true wilderness, a continuing presence" (11), which we can draw on without physically going north at all because it is a psychological space and an imaginative trope. Although his readers did not necessarily know it in 1971, when Kroetsch was south in Binghampton, New York, this Canadian writer had in fact gone north, in 1948 at age twenty, to Great Slave Lake, the Mackenzie River, Inuvik, and Tuktoyaktuk to be precise, and he went north to write a novel. "Why I Went Up North and What I Found When He Got There," first published in 1989 and reprinted as the introductory essay in *A Likely Story: The Writing Life* (1995), is one of the most ironic and illuminating commentaries we have on the North, on how and why we are driven to represent and construct it, and on how, as both imagined and real place, it escapes our shaping and shapes us. When Kroetsch went north to write his novel, he took with him his southern baggage, his preconceptions, his knowledge of Albert Johnson, Franklin, and Samuel Hearne, and Joseph Conrad (32). When he got there, he discovered beyond all the silence, all the stories, not those stories he would write *about* the Other but stories *by* the Other, by Vital Bonnet Rouge, the Dogrib river pilot, and by that great river Deh Cho (Mackenzie). By going north and listening, he learned to read the landscape and the "shifting narrative" of the river. It was, Kroetsch explains, Vital who "had shown me how to move through the slant and recurring passages that are the quest of northward journeys" (40). North, Kroetsch is telling us, is nothing less than the stories we learn how to tell by going north, by reading the rivers, by *listening*.

Even Aritha van Herk must write about and write North, despite her assurances that, for her, to be in the Arctic is to be "finally free of words" (*In Visible Ink*, 2). The paradox that van Herk articulates is the one experienced by so many male scholars, critics, and theorists before her – that "ultimately this page of Arctic is not written or read by insignificant me. No, it (agent) reads and writes me. I am its text, impressionable, inscribable, desirous of contamination, a page open to its tattoo, marking" (5). How far she has come from Frye, or even Atwood, and their constructions of a terrifying malevolent North! How very far from de Poncins, with his horror of contamination and his fear of being read. How far from all the mappings of representations by Warwick, Leacock, MacLaren, Mowat, and Berton – or has she? Van Herk hears the silence, feels the cold, recognizes the mystery and power of North to erase, efface, invisible her, but like Schafer, Wiebe, and Kroetsch she accepts the difference between South and North and she struggles to do the only thing she can – to write it down in words. North for van Herk, even more than for Kroetsch, is a theory about presence and writing, even a somewhat Foucaultian theory. She writes: "Even more extreme is the illusion of absence that is truly presence, tremendous presence, with no need to articulate itself narcissistically, being so much a *hereness*. This space, this landscape, this temperature, question all *document* and instead document me, without reference to an other; decipherable as glass I am, and fragile as any silenced voice, a tracement of arctic essence ... I am effaced, become an enunciative field, a page untouched by pen, no archive and no history. Happily" (8).

Enduring Dreams: An Exploration of Arctic Landscape (1994) is, in a sense, a reply to and a replication of the critical tradition I have charted thus far. Speaking in the first person, in what often amounts to a deeply personal, lyric, even romantic "I," John Moss meditates on the Arctic landscapes of Baffin Island, of the Mackenzie River and delta, and on how these land and river spaces feel as he moves through, across, and over them. His journeys north, whether physical, psychological, or writerly, have become his passion and obsession, have become part of him. He is always taking notes, field-notes; he is always testing his physical endurance (enduring dreams are nightmares of endurance) – "an honouring of the body as landscape" (65); he is always searching, like de Poncins, for himself. In a hybrid style that mixes aphorism with poetry, brief passages of prose description and reflection, and much citation/re-presentation of others' words, Moss makes a kind of gentle narcissistic love to himself as Arctic landscape.

Enduring Dreams is also the record of Moss's love affair with almost everything that has ever been written about the Arctic. At one point in his narrative, just after he has tantalized himself with the possible choices for reading (will it be Hearne? or Frobisher? or Hornby? or Stefansson and Rasmussen? or "the greatest challenge – to read Robert Peary"?), he pauses to reflect: "Here will be the chance to measure narrative in terms of the landscape it subsumes and to explore the landscape for what has been distorted or concealed" (44). And Moss quotes from and alludes to a great many northern texts, reinscribing geography and history, celebrating many of those who have gone north and written about it before him. He is also, to his credit, acutely aware – like Wiebe, Creates, and van Herk – of the sexist and racist constructions of North that he has inherited and of the southern colonialist power of that narrating, representing tradition. He knows the Arctic is an invention and Canada a fiction (33). He knows this, and yet he dares to hope that, by moving "through the landscape literally with books in hand" (43), he can "escape the world as text" and "perceive meaning in landscape, instead of imposing it" (43). And yet, if this legacy of writing North that Moss invokes, celebrates, and reinscribes in *Enduring Dreams* tells us anything at all about the North and ourselves, it is just this: we cannot escape text; we do not perceive an *original* landscape (the very word implying its own human construction) freely, neutrally, directly; our perceptions, like our knowledge, are culturally mediated. But Moss has uncovered something far more enduring and more central to our constructions of North than its malevolence (or friendliness), or Canadians' apparent obsessions with isolation, silence, and death. "We are caught," Moss tells us, "between geography and history in Canada, between naming and story. Exploration has taken the place of significant event and we yearn to venerate surveyors and cartographers, Hearne and Mackenzie, Franklin, Thompson, Fraser, writers all, and foreigners. We name the landscape for them, as they, for us. We are a nation in writing, perennially rewriting ourselves" (94).

My last example of critical contribution to the discursive formation of North is also an example of theorizing, but a more scholarly, abstract, less personal, and more theoretically focused example than those of Kroetsch, van Herk, or Moss. In chapter 4 of *Places on the Margin*, "The True North Strong and Free," geographer Rob Shields applies an approach he has developed largely from Foucault, Henri Lefebvre, and Bourdieu to selected places "on the periphery of cultural systems of space" (3), such as Brighton beach and the Canadian North. He argues that these places are examples of *social spatialization*, which (after Lefebvre) means spaces socially constructed by discursive and non-discursive practices (7). Thus, he argues, the "Canadian North ... forms the mythic 'heartland' of Canada but remains a zone of Otherness in the spatial system of Canadian culture" (4). Shields recognizes the fundamental dualism underlying what he insists (misleadingly, as we shall see) is the "masculine-gendered, liminal zone" (163) of North, on the one hand, and a socially spatialized economic hinterland on the other.[24] What he does theoretically with this dualism, however, is to underrate its power to inform cultural constructions of reality, and to overrate its negative impact. By conceptualizing "True North" as the social spatialization of a dominant, southern Ontario elite and then identifying the myth as fundamental to Canadian nationalism (195), he participates in the dualism (right/wrong, good/bad) he seems to want to interrogate and escape. As the continuous tradition he identifies (in quotations, references, allusions to works from the nineteenth and twentieth centuries) demonstrates, North, whatever evil uses it has been put to (Shields stresses racism and internal colonialism of the North), cannot be easily jettisoned or transcended by re-territorializing the North.

Where Shields agrees, importantly, with Cruikshank, Wiebe, van Herk, Creates, and Moss is in his recognition of the separate realities of the norths of Canada and of northerners, in his acknowledgment of difference between South and North. It is this awareness that leads him to suggest that the "literal re-territorialization of the North, the re-drawing of maps, would make the North suddenly *someone's*, a place where people dwelt and appropriated the land as their own" (198). What he misses, crucially I think, is that this re-territorializing has been in process for some time, in the Yukon, in the Northwest Territories, and in Nunavut to be sure, but also in the re-textualizations and reconfigurations of a host of literary writers, dramatists, visual artists, and musicians who exist outside the social spatializations of Shields's discourse and beyond the margins of his text.[25] Moreover, these representations do not erase North or render it irrelevant so much as reinvent new ideas of North that breathe new life, northern life, and introduce new voices, into an ongoing dialogue. This shift that both displaces while it includes is strikingly evident in one small example. Between 1945 and 1956 the name *Northern Review* (subtitled first *New Writing in Canada* and later expanded to *Northern Review of Writing and the Arts in Canada*) signalled an important literary journal formed by the merger of two competing groups of poets based in Montreal and Toronto.[26] In the 1990s *The Northern Review* (subtitled *A Multidisciplinary Journal of the Arts and Social Sciences of the North*) began to be published by Yukon College in Whitehorse, and to privilege northern voices *without excluding others*.

"How do we plot the narrative of the nation that must mediate between the teleology of progress tipping over into the 'timeless' discourse of irrationality?" The question is put by Homi K. Bhabha in his essay "Dissemination: Time, Narrative and the Margins of the Modern Nation" (142), and I would rephrase it here by asking how we can represent (and thereby construct) the northern narrative of Canada so that it resists the colonizing totalizations of the "True North" myth while recuperating and installing in its plot, images, and discourse the multiple representations and voices of Canadian nordicity. The critical work that I have surveyed thus far offers a number of clues because it throws into sharp relief (a relief that allows us to see both figure and ground, North and South) the following characteristics of the discursive formation of North. First, there is a consistent and relatively stable, coherent, twentieth-century tradition of Canadian theorizings of the North, from the modernist Frye, looking for and creating a grand narrative of a malevolent North, through many detailed descriptions of topoi and sites, and the romantic quests of Wiebe, Kroetsch, and Moss, to the postmodernist deconstructions of van Herk or Shields. Each of these writers, most of them aware of those who preceded them, attempts to describe, chart, map, and interpret what, to paraphrase F.R. Scott, we have written in the full culture of our occupation ("Laurentian Shield," *Collected Poems*, 58). Within this lively tradition there is a strong element of the romantic and personal southern response to a variously located northern landscape of cold, snow, ice, mystic beauty, and alluring danger, a response that persists in constructing North as a grail, a test (notably for men), and as a place to find not the Other but the self. No single figure so completely represents this tradition as does Tom Thomson, as I discovered while writing *Inventing Tom Thomson*. This continuing, accumulating attention to North by southern critics, scholars, and writers attests more forcibly than any one formulation could to the importance of the representations of North in Canadian culture and to the constitutive role played by those critics who participate in the discourse.

Not surprisingly, a number of new statements have entered the discursive formation as the boundaries of the enunciative field shift: North is no longer seen only as cold, barren, silent, and so forth; the old stereotypes are often challenged by new tropes. Native northerners play an increasing part in the representation of North, even when that part is limited to an acknowledgment of their prior exclusion; thus, a writer like Wiebe will not only include their voices within his dialogic text but will turn to them for wisdom. Perhaps most importantly, North has come to be understood as a problematic southern construction that is heavy with the ideological baggage of the past and a legacy of political exploitation or neglect of the norths. What these critics also show us is the degree to which North is a geographical proteus; without necessarily loosening its imaginative grip on southerly or easterly parts of the country, North has moved ever more west and north until, with Wiebe, Kroetsch, van Herk, and Moss, it lies – without explanation or apology – well north of sixty in the Yukon, Northwest Territories, Nunavut, and the high Arctic. There has been as well a gradual naturalization (indigenization, if you will) of those "foreigners" (as Moss calls them) who explored, mapped, painted, wrote about, and sometimes died here. Franklin has become a *Canadian* story (see Grace, "Re-inventing Franklin"), and searches for him (or for new episodes in the story) continue right into the twenty-first century, as James Delgado's summer 2000 voyage with the *St Roch* has shown (see Howell).

This critical, theorizing tradition also highlights, however, the unfortunate balkanization of our attempts to understand how North has come to signify, what it means and why. Most of these secondary forays north are strictly disciplinary, with, at best, a limited tapping into history or comparison of fiction with painting (Warwick, Frye, McGregor, MacLaren), at worst a suspicious dismissal of what a novelist has to say (Shields). What I want to do is to charge headlong across as many disciplining boundaries as possible because, like Stefansson (who, yes, I will invoke), I can think of no more interdisciplinary subject than North. What I want to do is to explore (discover, chart, name, map) and read the discursive formation of North by opening it out to include what other writers – geographers, historians, and politicians – and artists have contributed to the ongoing process of constructing a northern nation.

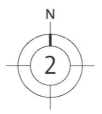

N

2

CONSTRUCTING A
NORTHERN NATION

As one of Canada's greatest geographers tells us, "The North is more than an area, it is a passion" (Hamelin, *Canadian Nordicity*, 9). Because Louis-Edmond Hamelin recognizes the North as a passion – an idea, an emotion, to some degree a subjective construction – he also recognizes the mutability and variability that constitute its power and longevity. One of the most exciting aspects of Hamelin's North is its changing face, and in tracing those lineaments the contemporary geographer joins hands with a historian like W.L. Morton, writers like Rudy Wiebe or Elizabeth Hay, and artists like Judith Currelly and Marlene Creates. A lot has happened to the representation of North over the past 140 years, but nothing is more striking than this capacity for change. From a concept thoroughly imbued with a raced, gendered, and classed imperialist ideology, North has shifted to include critiques of this ideology and resistance to its hegemonic power; it has expanded to include the voices, perceptions, and representations of those hitherto excluded. Inevitably, of course, what we think of as our nordicity (to use Hamelin's term) has also shifted further and further north. But if North has shifted, expanded, changed, what has happened – is happening – to Canada?

The discourse of primary concern in this chapter is that produced by geographers, historians, prophets and proselytizers, political scientists and politicians, many of whom refer to and cite certain poets, novelists, and painters. From the set of discursive characteristics that emerge in and with the discourse – characteristics that I want to consider in detail – one must be stressed above all others: the blurring and overlapping of boundaries that creates a complex, duplicating interdiscursivity of North. At several points geography intersects with historiography, which is always merging with popular pseudo-historical narrative, which in its turn fades into political rhetoric. This interdiscursivity is at once extraordinarily powerful, self-reinforcing and -legitimating, and difficult to tease into separate strands for analysis. A case in point is the cartography of North because, regardless of *who* is writing *when* with *whatever* notion of North, maps will be used to explain, illustrate, prove, debate, problematize, legitimate – in short, *to create* – the North, and these maps range from the highly technical (and exquisitely beautiful) productions of skilled cartographers in the *Historical Atlas of Canada* to impassioned pleas to preserve our sovereignty by setting aside our "Mercator mind-set" (Honderich, 212) to the embodied map cover of Aritha van Herk's "geografictione" *Places far from Ellesmere* (see Illus. 8), to major works of art like Jack Shadbolt's mural *Bush Pilot in the Northern Sky* (1963; see Plate 5) or Paterson Ewen's 1973 *Northern Lights*, to a satiric piece like Greg Curnoe's 1972 image of North America as Canada and Mexico, without the United States, or Judith Currelly's new works called "Northern Maps, Legends, and Legacies" (2000).[1] This book is itself never far away from maps and mapping, and I will, perforce, return to the cartography of the northern imaginary in the next chapter. But it is first of all necessary to chart the salient features of the interdiscursive construction of this northern nation.

Of the dozen or so topographical features that I see in this discursive landscape, none is more intriguing than the emotion with which the most scientific of scientists and social scientists speak of the North. One is constantly aware of the difficulties they face in their efforts to define and locate North and, as a consequence, the extraordinary investment (in nothing less than personal, professional, and national identity) represented by these efforts. If Hamelin's language is not enough to convince his readers of how deeply he feels (this man of graphs, tabulations, and indices), then listen to another of our great geographers, Ross Mackay, describing the surface appearance of ground over permafrost as "stones arranged in circles or garlands a few feet across, like stone necklaces" (92). But intrigue gives way to bafflement as one hears again and again the chorus of lament over how the North is ignored, neglected, forgotten, and absent from the minds of Canadians. Thus, Morris Zaslow, the author of two major volumes on the history of the North, begins by stating: "Canadians fail to recognize or often forget, that they are essentially a northern people" (*Opening*, xi) – a failure that his meticulous study should address by virtue of the facts he marshals and by the sheer weight of his own volumes. On 8 December 1953 Prime Minister St Laurent described Canada as having "administered these vast territories of the north in an almost continuing state of absence of mind" (quoted in Hodgins "The Canadian North," and in many other articles and books), just as he was about to create the Department of Northern Affairs and National Resources, and Hamelin, who lists examples of our indifference, explains this "limited interest" in the North as an "apathy" resulting from negative and distorted images of the North (*Canadian Nordicity*, 8).

If St Laurent, Zaslow, and Hamelin sound like R. Murray Schafer in *Music in the cold* or Rudy Wiebe in *Playing Dead*, it is because they are all saying the same thing. Amazingly, and despite thousands of volumes – explorers' narratives, novels, poems, geographical studies, historiography, popular fiction – written about the North, despite the maps, the art, the films, the flights of impassioned rhetoric and the imaginative tropes, we persist in believing, we repeat it until we believe it, that we fail to understand ourselves as a northern nation. Perhaps, *pace* Queen Gertrude, I might say: methinks the gentlemen do protest too much – perhaps. And yet there is something real in this lament, something deeply felt and

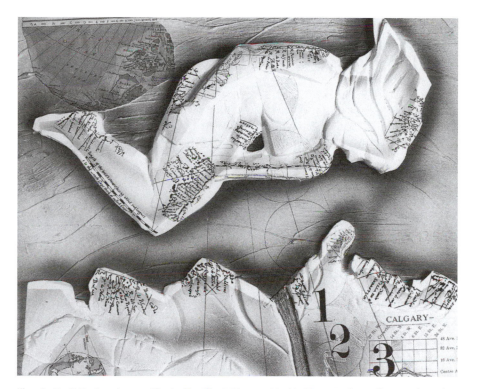

Illus. 8. Scott Barham's cover illustration for Aritha van Herk's *Places Far from Ellesmere* (1990) represents Ellesmere Island as a woman floating north of the Canadian mainland on a personal map of van Herk's home and native land. Reproduced with the permission of Red Deer Press.

believed to be true about our identity generally as Canadians and, more specifically, as northerners living in the provincial norths and the territories. Perhaps it is not so much an absence of mind – although absences should never be confused with neutrality or conflated with indifference – as a profound ambivalence. On the one hand, *we* love *our* North (however carelessly or romantically we define it) and see nordicity as our uniquely defining quality; on the other, we fear and loathe it and reject everything that might remind us (in the land and in our minds) of our inescapable northern latitude, climate, and topography. As John Merritt (in 1989 the executive director of the Canadian Arctic Resources Committee and legal counsel for the Inuit Tapirisat of Canada) puts it, after itemizing, as did Stefansson before him, all the pejorative generalizations about the Arctic, Canadians deal with their nordicity "in a profoundly schizophrenic way": "On the one hand, Canada's nordicity … and things associated with nordicity, like hockey, Group of Seven paintings, and Bob and Doug Mackenzie, are badges of national identity. At the same time, travel agents do a lively business in February sending people south, and Canadian cities look like they were designed for a southern California climate" (*The Arctic*, 22). What is more, ambivalence has its usefulness. How better to have your North and leave it too? – leave it, that is, until it is deemed to have some particular (strategic? monetary?) value. This is the burden of Ken Coates's charge in *Canada's Colonies*, where he claims, first, that "neglect ... has characterized southern response to the Canadian North" (12) – by which he means the Yukon and the NWT – and, second, that "Canadians exhibit a curious lack of faith in the land that supposedly informed their character" (13). Catch-22.

But it is not just the emotion, the ambivalence, or double-think, and the seemingly endless difficulty in locating North that characterize the interdiscursivity of geography, historiography, and political rhetoric. As with the novelists, poets, and artists, there is a powerful, complex subtext here, a subtext and *politics* of identity that is personal, regional, and national, raced, gendered, and classed. To ask where North *is* and what North means is to open a veritable Pandora's Box on identity, so it should scarcely be surprising to find the stakes claimed to this real and imagined territory passionately articulated and intensely debated and defended. The discourse of this subtext is heavily masculinist, even today; it assumes an objectifiable feminine Other in the physical terrain that can be (indeed, must be) penetrated, revealed, put to use, tamed, and controlled. It also assumes and reiterates the male author's first-hand physical and intellectual *knowing*, experience, and expertise, a knowledge that circles back to confirm his masculinity; as historian Arthur Lower has phrased it, "I am sure I am a better scholar because I know the bush ... can split wood, make a bough bed, snare a rabbit, run a rapids" (*Unconventional Voyages* [1953], quoted in Hodgins, "The Canadian North," 10). Moreover, the language – images, key tropes, strategies of naming, and citation – used to represent North quickly becomes familiar. The best places to look for this language are the introductions, conclusions, and occasional asides in essays and books where, in a displaced first-person voice and focalization masquerading as the objective, scientific third person, a reader hears the personal voice of the writer and sees with *his* eyes. There is as well a fundamental narrative pattern, what I would call a diegetic morphology, to much of this discourse. This is especially apparent in a persistent search for origins, an obligatory genealogy, and a quixotic desire for closure or stability, even amongst those who recognize the fundamental instability and necessary processual character of North (I am thinking here of West, Coates, Wreford Watson, and Hamelin, among others). The genealogical component of this discourse is interesting for several reasons, not least for its very persistence and the degree to which it exceeds what one might think of as a scholarly acknowledgment of sources. There is a surplus here that indicates a psychological need to follow in the footsteps of, to retrace, all those who have gone before and, by so doing, to place oneself in a tradition before finalizing it.

I am reminded by this genealogical compulsion of Harold Bloom's theory of precursor and ephebe (a theory applied to poets). One of the most extraordinary, because so flamboyant, examples of what I mean is the painter Toni Onley's book *Onley's Arctic*, which includes colour plates of paintings, first-person narrative exposition, maps, charts, and diary excerpts, the very construction of his book mimicking explorers' narratives and recalling a work like Hamelin's *Canadian Nordicity.* Thus, Onley on Beechey Island – "SEPTEMBER 11 Lat.74° 20'N Long. 90° 00'W" – names A.Y. Jackson in 1927, Sir Edward Belcher in 1854, Franklin in 1845–46, and "the messages from people who have braved it to this spot in the intervening years," and tells us, "I leave my own message in an Edgeworth tobacco tin and place it with the bottle beneath the cairn" (35). History, Onley asserts, is *frozen* here: but the paradoxical genealogical compulsion belies him because, like the others, he longs to add himself to that history and *then* to seal it shut, to finalize and close the northern story with himself inside it.

Similarly, when Louis-Edmond Hamelin introduces and explains his "northern index" (see Illus. 9) and VAPO (*valeurs polaires*) measure, he observes: "Mental structures may constitute the most powerful determinants of a region. By this, images may be created whose weight may come to surpass that of the most easily identifiable physical realities such as freezing. Thus 'reality' is, in part, the product of the interpretation put on things. The Canadian North is not exempt from this mental evolution" (*Canadian Nordicity,* 17). Thus, in the scientist's language of measurement, Hamelin explains "freezing" by referring to a "mental evolution" that includes all those ideas of nordicity he has inherited, as a geographer, from other geographers, scientists, and social scientists, plus his own attempts to measure the ecumen (in criteria 7, 8, 9, and 10) before calculating and thereby stabilizing nordicity. Using his index, the "mental evolution" and production of "reality" can be contained, controlled, and finalized in VAPO measures, and the problem of nordicity resolved.[2] Unfortunately, however, what is often missing from these genealogies, and from the subtext of identity more generally, is awareness of the enormously varied and rich northern discourse of creative writers and artists. When writers or painters are cited, they will predictably be the same few – Robert Service, Jack London, Stephen Leacock (more rarely), and members of the Group, especially Harris and Jackson, or Tom Thomson. The result is a narrowing of vision that leads a political scientist like D.A. West, for example, to conclude that the "North ... becomes a fact that is produced by northern specialists who operate under the general title of Northern and Native Studies" ("Researching the North in Canada," 116–17).[3]

And yet – the desire to know, name, identify, represent North persists, and the picture remains tantalizingly incomplete. North, as it were, seems to recede ever northward like Frankenstein's monster, only to catch us unawares from behind (from the South)! Far from being a drawback, or a sign of failure on the part of geographers, historians, political scientists, or artists, however, this intransigent mutability, this resistance to measure and closure, is the beauty and strength of North. The constant shifting of *all* the parameters – physical and metaphysical – of North is what constitutes its greatest VAPO/value as an index to, a sign for, a representation of our identity. In the exciting ongoing debate not only over *where* North is but also over *what* its history is and *who* can tell it lies the creation of Canada itself, and North is *neither* synonymous with Canada *nor* different from it (from

Illus. 9. Louis-Edmond Hamelin's "Summary table for the calculation of the northern index" is reproduced from *Canadian Nordicity: It's Your North Too* (1978), translated by William Barr, with the author's permission. Hamelin's indices, which include meteorological and socio-cultural factors, have become a familiar means for measuring degrees of Canadian nordicity.

Criteria	Classes	Polar Units or VAPO
1. *Latitude*	Up to 90°	100
	80°	77
	70°	55
	60°	33
	45°	0
2. *Summer heat*	0 days above 5.6°C (42° F)	100
	40 days above 5.6°C	80
	60 days above 5.6°C	70
	80 days above 5.6°C	60
	100 days above 5.6°C	45
	120 days above 5.6°C	30
	135 days above 5.6°C	20
	>150 days above 5.6°C	0
3. *Annual cold*	6650 degree days below 0 °C (32°F)	100
	5550 degree days below 0 °C	85
	4700 degree days below 0 °C	75
	3900 degree days below 0 °C	65
	2900 degree days below 0 °C	45
	1950 degree days below 0 °C	30
	1250 degree days below 0 °C	15
	550 degree days below 0 °C	0
4a.Types of ice Frozen ground	Continuous permafrost 457 m(1,500 feet) thick	100
	Continuous permafrost less than 457 m	80
	Discontinuous permafrost	60
	Ground frozen for 9 months	50
	Ground frozen for 4 months	20
	Ground frozen for less than 1 month	0
4b. Floating ice	Permanent pack ice (Arctic Ocean)	100
	Pack ice on peri-Arctic seas (e.g., Baffin Bay)	90
	Pack ice for 9 months	64
	Pack ice for 6 months	36
	Pack ice for 4 months	20
	Pack ice for less than 1 month	0
4c. Glaciers and snow cover	Ice sheet 1,524 m (5,000 feet) thick or more	100
	Ice sheet 700 m (2,300 feet) thick	96
	Icecap about 304 m (1,000 feet) thick	60
	Névé	20
	Snow cover of less than 2.5 cm (1 inch)	0
5. Total precipitation	100 mm (<4")	100
	200 mm (<8")	80
	300 mm (<12")	60
	400 mm (<16")	30
	500 mm (>20")	0
6. Natural vegetation cover	Rocky desert	100
	Tundra clumps; 50% cover	90
	Sparse tundra; almost continuous	80
	Dense tundra and shrubs; humid steppe	60
	Open woodland (subarctic; parkland; bushes)	40
	Dense forest (coniferous or broad-leaved)	0

southern Canada); it is not either/or but both/and: it is a part of the imagined community called Canada and a defining characteristic, a crucial metonymy, for the whole. It is North and north(s) co-existing in interdiscursive interdependency.

Of the many toponymic features of this discursive landscape that I have briefly sketched there are three key sets of statements that warrant detailed scrutiny. These are: the shifting parameters of North in time, space, in the language of definition and belonging, and in the constancy of "double-think"; the highly contested questions surrounding national identity and unity, of regions versus a centre, of North versus South, and the politics of North (including issues of sovereignty, internal colonialism, and resource development, which emerge in peaks of activity during the Klondike, then the 1920s, the Second World War and after, and the 1990s); and finally, the rhetoric of race, gender, and class that underlies each of the first two and is imbricated, at every level, in the wider discursive formation. All three are, of course, interrelated and overlapping categories, and each constitutes a multifaceted, complex statement within the discursive formation of North. They cannot be grasped for analysis by approaching them from one side or another, through geography alone or through history alone, for example. As Foucault warns us, we must look for statements in their dispersion across a wide discursive field. What is more, we must be alert to the dialogics of these statements

7.	Accessibility other than by air (heavy transport, including water transport, pipe line, and winter road)	No service Seasonal service: Year-round:	once per year for two months forth three months for six months or two seasons by one means (with difficulty) by two means by more than two means	100 80 60 55 40 20 15 0
8.	Air services (either private or government)	Charter flights, 1,600 km (1,000 miles) Charter flights, 480 km (300 miles) Charter flights, 160 km (100 miles) Charter flights, 48 km (30 miles) Regular service, twice per month Regular service, weekly Regular service, twice weekly Regular service, daily or better		100 80 65 60 40 25 15 0
9.	Resident or wintering population			
9a.	Inhabitants in settlement	None About 25 About 100 About 500 About 1,000 About 2,000 About 3,000 >5,000		100 90 85 75 60 40 20 0
9b.	Population density of the area 250,000 km² (or 100,000 miles²)	Uninhabited 0.004 per km² (0.01 persons per mile²) 0.4 per km² (1 person per mile²) 1 per km² (2.5 persons per mile²) 2 per km² (5 persons per mile²) 4 per km² (10 persons per mile²)		100 90 70 50 25 0

10.	Degree of economic activity	No production, none foreseen
		Exploration but no exploitation
		  Reserves known
		  20 persons living off the land; airstrip
		Low level of commercial sea fisheries
		Gathering, extraction, or handicrafts
		  Radar site; small factory, light
		  investment
		Mineral concentration, storage, terminal
		  Small scale agriculture
		Major "secondary" enterprises; well
		  developed agriculture
		Interregional centre with multiple services;
		  heavy investment
				100
				
				80
				75
				60
				
				50
				
				30
				
				15
				
				0

and to their paradoxical stability within change. To explore these three sets of statements is to participate in and contribute to an increasingly self-critical and theorized debate about Canada and the idea of North.

When Schafer proclaimed his Canadian proverb – "all the energy of the world radiates from the Magnetic North Pole" (*On Canadian Music*, 64) – he hit upon the perfect image for North. It is important that he chose the Magnetic, not the geographic North Pole, because the Magnetic Pole *moves*. Like the Arctic ice pack, it shifts; it will not be pinned down. What is worse, the closer you approach it, the more will the Magnetic North Pole send your conventional compass needle veering wildly off any fixed course.[4] Magnetic North, then, encapsulates a North whose parameters seem always to be shifting, a North, I would go so far as to say, that cannot be understood apart from this protean capacity. Canadian geographers and historians are well aware of this capacity of North to defy their maps, statistics, measurements, and analyses, and Bruce Hodgins summarizes the changing boundaries of North very aptly when he tells us that he sees "the Canadian North as a territorially shifting concept" ("The Canadian North," 4). In the nineteenth century North was seen as defining what today we might think of as the southeastern area of the country around the Great Lakes and the St Lawrence, with the *pays d'en haut* stretching west and further north with the voyageurs and explorers, and this concept is still with us to a not inconsiderable degree because of the iconographic power of the Group of Seven. But just a glance at a cartographic attempt to locate North (see Illus. 10) helps to explain why Quebec and Ontario should feel they have some special claim on nordicity: all the lines for delineating the North – be it the Shield, the treeline, or the permafrost – dip furthest south in those provinces. And the speed with which "the Ice Storm" of 1998 has been incorporated into northern discourse is a further reminder of this claim (see Aquin, and Illus. 5).

Others, geographers, political scientists, and especially historians, have increasingly insisted on a more northerly location of North. Even in the nineteenth century, as narratives like Charles Tuttle's *Our North Land* (1885) demonstrate, North was not confined to the Laurentians and Algonquin Park or even Temagami and Témiscamingue. Tuttle was a vociferous champion of the Hudson Bay route for grain and other goods through Manitoba to ports on Hudson Bay (like Fort Churchill), where ships would complete transportation through the Bay and Hudson Strait to the Atlantic Ocean and across to European markets. To sell this vision and to legitimate his arguments, Tuttle undertook an expedition, in July–August 1884, up the east coast of Labrador to Baffin Island, then west through Hudson Strait, and across the north end of the Bay to Marble Island (site of Captain James Knight's last stand).[5] The Geological Survey of Canada began its illustrious and important work in 1842 and gradually reached into the most northern parts of what is today the Yukon, the Northwest Territories, and the Arctic archipelago. The survey was followed north by the RCMP (known until 1919 as the North-West Mounted Police) when gold was discovered in August 1896 on Rabbit Creek (later called Bonanza) in the Klondike River watershed in the Yukon, and from there the RCMP established posts across the North from Herschel Island to Ellesmere.[6] And as all studies of the fur trade make clear, the North and Northwest were integral to the economic and territorial parameters of Canada-as-North from the seventeenth century, when the great company of adventurers was formed (on 2 May 1670), to the early twentieth, when the last Revillon posts were sold and the HBC fur trade fell into decline (see Ray, 168–9). In his simple but elegant theory of the creation of Canada, Harold Innis told us as early as 1930 that "Canada emerged as a political entity with boundaries largely determined by the fur trade. These boundaries included a vast northern temperate land area extending from the Atlantic to the Pacific and dominated by the Canadian Shield. The present Dominion emerged not in spite of geography but because of it" (*The Fur Trade in Canada*, 393). And while Innis has been challenged and critiqued, notably by historians like Creighton, who sees Canada as an artificial product of British and American imperialism, his formulation of Canada-as-North has sunk deeply into the Canadian consciousness.

But as the idea of what Douglas West calls "the nordification of the North" ("Researching the North in Canada," 109) has caught on, giving increased credibility and authority to "a northern political voice" for northerners living in the terri-

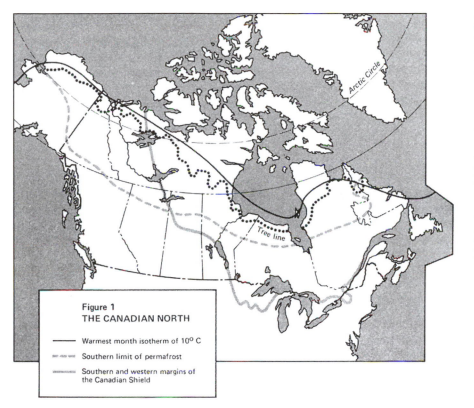

Figure 1
THE CANADIAN NORTH

——— Warmest month isotherm of 10° C

▬ ▬ ▬ Southern limit of permafrost

▬▬▬▬▬ Southern and western margins of
the Canadian Shield

Illus. 10. "Where Is the North?" from *The Canadian North* (1977), edited by Bruce Hodgins, Jamie
Benidickson, Richard Bowles, and George Rawlyk, illustrates some of Hamelin's nordicity indices
in cartographic terms. Reproduced with the permission of Bruce Hodgins.

tories, so too has our need to acknowledge North as (in Bruce Hodgin's words) "a
territorially shifting concept."[7] And to my mind no geographer has done this
better than J. Wreford Watson, whose 1969 study, "The Role of Illusion in North
American Geography," constitutes a poststructuralist theorizing *avant la lettre* of
geography and North. He begins with what looks like, in hindsight, a most
Foucaultian assertion: especially when we try to account for "new environments,"
he points out, "it is not what people actually see there so much as what they want
to see, or think they see, which affects their reaction" (10). This is precisely the
point that Todorov is making in *The Conquest of America*, where he shows how what
Europeans wanted to see destroyed millions of people. But Wreford Watson continues to drive home his point by reminding us that "a mental image of a place is
built up [from] what men hope to find, what they look to find, how they set about
finding, how findings are fitted into their existing framework of thought, and
how those findings are then expressed ... The power of illusion is a major factor
in the making of geography, particularly where it affects decision-making" (10).
And Stefansson would agree with this statement – as would Stefansson's many

detractors, who accused him of manipulating language to further his dubious cause (see Waiser).

On analysing what he neatly calls the *"geography of the double illusion"* (23), Wreford Watson traces two competing discourses of North: one is the four-hundred-year-old rhetoric of North as barren wilderness blocking the way (or hiding a secret passage) to the Orient; the other, more recent rhetoric is closely associated with men like Stefansson and his admirers (for example, Richard Finnie in *Canada Moves North*, 1948), who insist that the Arctic is friendly, resource-rich, and capable of extensive development, even settlement. Underlying these illusions and their competing rhetorics, according to Wreford Watson, is a truth or, at the very least, "a more realistic view" (24) of the North that lies between the extremes of barren wasteland and fruitful, friendly Eldorado, and between the Great Lakes and the Beaufort Sea. But is there a more realistic rhetoric of North? Is there a northern reality – or set of realities – that can be faithfully represented in language or maps, by VAPO measures or any quantifiable set of statistics? On the one hand, Wreford Watson seems to imply that there is, and there is certainly an important cadre of writers (geographers, historians, and other social scientists) who have in recent years developed an influential third rhetoric (as neither frozen waste nor resource-rich oasis) of North; on the other hand, he leaves us with a crucial injunction to pay more attention to the geography of the mind: "the subject we call geography should pay at least as much attention to the climate of the mind as to the climate, to the morphology of thought as to geomorphology ... The place of perception is critical to the perception of place. Increasingly we must write the geography of countries in terms of the country of the mind" (26). This Borgesian advice may sound strange coming from a geographer in the late sixties, but it identifies tendencies that emerged in theories of spatialization, cartography, and in the writing of geography in the latter half of the twentieth century, what in many ways Hamelin has addressed. The geo*graphy/grafictione* of North is a fascinating site for competing, shifting, ideologically invested rhetorics and cartographies; it opens up enchanting vistas on the process of discursive formation, on the politics of location – or, more precisely still, the chronotopes of North! – and the degrees to which these rhetorics become part of the Canadian habitus.

Between the rhetoric of northern negation and the rhetoric of northern affirmation lies an emerging rhetoric of northern realism that locates the real North north of sixty. Three of the earliest proponents of a "real" North are R.A.J. Phillips, James Lotz (two of those northern voices in Glenn Gould's *Idea of North*), and William C. Wonders. Wonders, a geographer with special interest in the Northwest, has examined the changes that have occurred there, more particularly in the Yukon and in the Mackenzie District of the NWT, with a view to balancing the "attractive" notion that the Northwest is "a land still essentially untouched" (146) with the facts of impact from two major historical developments: missions and the Klondike Gold Rush. His study, "The Canadian Northwest: Some Geographical Perspectives," traces the results of these developments through education, the introduction of agriculture, concentration of population and settlement, major changes to transportation, environmental degradation (such as removal of trees and diversion of streams to facilitate mining), and the introduction of wage labour and of tourism, and his points are conveyed throughout in a dispassionate language reinforced by many excellent documentary-style photographs, which alternate, in a striking visual dialectic, between spectacular aerial panoramas to close-ups of mission gardens, school children, townsites, aircraft, and mining equipment. Even more than the objective prose, with its careful mapping, naming, and marshalling of statistics, these photographs convince the reader of the truth of Wonders's argument: the Northwest has changed. The vast expanse of uninhabited, unmarred natural beauty stretching "south-east up the Pelly Valley in the Cordillera region of the Yukon" (from the caption to the first photograph, 148) has given way, we are shown, to vast mining operations and well-planned townsites.

Integral to both verbal and visual semiotics in this article is a more important and far-seeing message, the message Wonders concludes with. Despite the remarkable developments and human achievements in the Northwest, there are problems and warning signs. "Cultural stratification," Wonders tells us, "is reflected all too often in native 'ghetto' areas in northern communities and contributes to the serious social problems" (164). The "utildor maze at Inuvik," while a remarkable engineering feat, "can scarcely be regarded as a work of art" (104). The genuine work of art, or so Wonders suggests, with an over-the-shoulder glance, back, as it were, to his first photograph of the majestic Pelly Valley, is the pristine North of wilderness and adventure: "Landscape remains a fresh unspoiled asset of the Northwest over much of its area and it is to be hoped that it will so continue" (165). The North, in short, must not be changed so radically that this "wilderness heritage" (105) is lost. Wonders's *real* North must have room for both wilderness and development.

Unlike Wonders, geographer and anthropologist Jim Lotz adopts a more engagé, impassioned voice, even though his ultimate message is much the same. He begins his classic study *Northern Realities: The Future of Northern Development in Canada* (1970) as an outspoken and idealistic Canadian nationalist, with remarks about northern policies that are laced with anger and reflections on the North (his focus is the Yukon) that convey his love and respect. Like so many before and after him, he laments Canadian indifference and chastizes our ignorance. "It is northern-ness that binds Canadians together," he insists: "Canada is a northern nation, lying along and beyond the edge of the settled temperate world ... The 'north' is not just 'up there,' held behind the line of the sixtieth parallel. It covers most of the country" (27). Quoting W.L. Morton (31) and Wally Maclean from Gould's *The Idea of North* (32), he reminds us that "the north runs in our bones, whether we know it or not, pacing us, warning us, guiding us, helping us to tell the reality from the image" (29).

The reality *from* the image? Interesting. For, as Lotz nevertheless goes on to show, the image *is* the reality: without an image of North we cannot see the North at all, let alone the fine distinctions that Lotz himself is one of the first to draw between the "Northerner's North" and the southerner's ideas of North, between "outside" and "inside" the North (20). If Lotz's anger is directed at outsiders, southerners, a paternalistic central government, and American imperialism (during the Klondike and again during the Second World War), it is also aimed at those insiders, "the old Northern Whites," who are Eurocentric and racist. The future he recommends for the Yukon is one run by and for native northerners, and it includes social development from within (as distinct from economic exploitation from outside), respect and empowerment for natives, a northern university, planned development, and environmental protection that will facilitate recreation and tourism. Much of what Lotz called for in 1970 has in fact come to pass, but not simply because of facts or a rhetoric of realism, telling "the reality from the image." In a language that recalls Stefansson and Finnie (though *crucially* without their Social Darwinism), Lawren Harris and Herman Voaden, and points forward to Kroetsch, Wiebe, and Moss, Lotz concludes by appealing, past reason, directly to our imaginations, to the idea of mystic North, to our nationalism: "If, in our scientific era, we can combine science and human concern in that spirit that can only be called religious, we may yet be able to better the human condition. In the north, the force of a greater presence comes to one with great clarity; and this force implies an integration, a oneness, a wholeness that man never ceases to seek" (249).

In *Canada's North* (1967) Richard Phillips concentrates on Canada north of sixty and expends considerable space and energy in marshalling socio-historical and geographical facts about the North, while acknowledging that there are "many norths" (7). Beginning with the Vikings, he goes on to describe Arctic exploration, the creation of the Hudson's Bay Company, the competitive development of the fur trade, and the Klondike Gold Rush. He recounts in some detail twentieth-century challenges to Canada's Arctic sovereignty (adding to the already familiar lament about government indifference) before and during the Second World War, what he sees as the pernicious effects of missionary activity among the Inuit, the critical role of the RCMP, the development of air transportation in the North (notably with famous bush pilots like "Wop" May), and the creation (in December 1953) of the new Department of Northern Affairs and Natural Resources (DNANR). Chapter 11 he devotes to what he calls the "Modern North"; here he takes an inventory of what the future promises through the formation of research groups like the Polar Continental Shelf Project (in 1959), the development of major northern studies centres at universities across Canada, and the increase in writing (albeit largely by southerners) about the North – for example, he mentions Farley Mowat, Edmonton journalist Bob Hill, Yves Thériault, James Houston, NFB films, and the first northern journal, *The Eskimo Way*, begun in 1959 and edited by Mary Panegoosho. In these ways, Phillips concludes, "the wide open spaces of the

North where men could go to escape the world are rapidly narrowing. The North is becoming a part of Canada" (196).

As this comment implies, however, there is a complex subtext to *Canada's North*, a discernible romantic nostalgia for the appeal of the mystic North. At the same time as he can see and praise economic development of mineral resources and tourism – "Canada can live handsomely on its northern inheritance" (200) – and calls for a greater involvement of, indeed control by, northerners in future "nation-building" (298), Phillips is drawn to the romantic image of North as a place of escape, adventure, and dream – for white men, government officials, and civil servants like himself. His rhetoric of realism is shot through with a rhetoric of loss; the concrete facts of a modern North jostle uneasily with a poetics of North. Thus, Phillips frames his argument for Canada's North with lines from T.S. Eliot's *Burnt Norton* and begins by echoing Eliot:

> At the end of the earth, it is cold.
> At that point where the earth stands still, and time stands still, it is
> dark for half the year ...
> This is the permanently frozen sea ...   (3)

It is not so easy, after all, to distinguish time past from time present or to redeem the future; in any case, "human kind / cannot bear very much reality" (Eliot, 190). And my point is this: it is impossible to stabilize the rhetoric or the boundaries of North. Just as the negation invites affirmation and affirmation requires negation, so this rhetoric of realism is thoroughly dialogized, and in it I can hear all the other voices.

A DISCOURSE OF HISTORY

Historiographic representations of North are extremely illuminating, and I would argue that W.L. Morton occupies the pivotal position here. Like Wreford Watson with geo*graphy*, Morton understood that history is historio*graphy*, a story, a writing into existence; he would have agreed with Robert Kroetsch that we do not have an identity until someone tells our story, that the fiction (the *storying*) makes us real (Kroetsch, *Creation*, 63). Morton's representations of North are pivotal for other reasons as well because, from the vantage point of the twenty-first century, we can look back and see him as the only major historian of his generation to enunciate clearly the need for a northern historiography, a history of the North that would disclose "the ultimate and the comprehensive meaning of Canadian history" ("The 'North' in Canadian Historiography," 239). Prior to Morton's major book *The Canadian Identity* (first published in 1961) and his 1970 address to the Royal Society of Canada, "The 'North' in Canadian Historiography," the *historical* problem of defining and representing North had not been directly addressed. Proponents of the Laurentian thesis, like Creighton, saw no historiographic value in the North, while Innis, who most certainly did understand the historical significance of the North, moved increasingly to the analysis of communications after 1930. It was not until after *The Canadian Identity* that our historians began to focus more critically on the question of the North by stepping back far enough, as Carl Berger did in 1966, to see how the North was historied in the nineteenth century. Since 1970 the historiography of the North has flourished, evolved, and become infinitely more nuanced, complex, and challenging.

In "the true north strong and free" Carl Berger takes us back to the 1860s, to Confederation, and to the Canada First Movement. According to "the rhetoric of the day," he reminds us, "Canada was 'the Britain of the North,'" and her "unique character [was believed to derive] from her northern location, her severe winters and her heritage of 'northern races'" (4). I will return to Berger's important essay in the discussion of my third set of statements; for the moment, I want to follow Berger's lead back to the 1860s and the nationalist northern vision of men like R.G. Haliburton and W.A. Foster (both founding members of Canada First).

The Men of the North and Their Place in History, a lecture delivered to the Montreal Literary Club in March 1869 by lawyer and Canada Firster Robert Grant Haliburton, quickly caught the public's attention; it was carried in the newspapers and published as a pamphlet by John Lowell that year. Haliburton's message was a passionate one, and his purpose nothing less than to articulate the future and destiny of the young Canadian nation. He began with a flourish of assertions and rhetorical questions (he was, after all, delivering a speech): "A glance at the map of this continent, as well as at the history of the past, will satisfy us that the peculiar characteristic of the New Dominion must ever be that it is a Northern country inhabited by the descendants of Northern races ... From the past we may draw some augury as to the future. Is the northern land which we have chosen, a congenial home for the growth of a free and dominant race? What is the stock from which we have sprung? Who are the men of the north and what is their place in history? Can the generous flame of national spirit be kindled and blaze in the icy bosom of the frozen north?" (2) Haliburton's answer was a resounding yea because, in the Social Darwinian rhetoric of the day (a rhetoric that persisted well into the twentieth century), the North produces conquerors, leaders, and visionaries. If the United States was busy formulating its manifest destiny, Haliburton was not far behind, and providence was on Canada's side: "to the end of time the North is destined to be 'the Scourge of God' upon the overrated and overrating South" (6).

But what does Haliburton understand as North? Well, for a starter, North is *not* the degenerate, effeminate South. Haliburton's North equals winter, frost, snow, "pine woods," the "cold north wind" (10); it is the "stern ... home of the brave and true" (11). It is the young Dominion, with, to be sure, the ambition to stretch to the Pacific and the North Pole, but above all defined by the borders of 1867, with its central Ontario and Quebec heartland. There, in Hamelin's near North around the St Lawrence and the Great Lakes, Haliburton placed the "apostles of a new, of a Northern, of a Christian civilization" (8).

Of course, Haliburton was not alone in these views, nor was he the only one to link the North inextricably with Canadian nationality. National identity was *the* key concern of the day, and politicians like George Brown and Macdonald himself were aware of the importance of the North: in the mid-1850s Brown viewed Rupert's Land, the possession of the HBC, as a "vast and fertile territory which is our birthright," and in 1869 Macdonald explicitly addressed Canada's need to control the entire northern territories with a clear view to posterity (Hodgins, "The Canadian North," 7–8). What distinguishes Haliburton and the Canada Firsters from more general ambitions for northward expansion is the nationalistic fervour and the sexist-racist rhetoric of their speeches and publications. In *Canada First; or, Our New Nationality; An Address* (1871) W.A. Foster insisted that Canada must assert its difference from the United States and free itself from dependence on Britain. "Unless we intend to be mere hewers of wood and drawers of water," he inveighed (in these now so familiar words), "we should in right earnest set about strengthening the foundations of our identity" (30). As Foster saw it, Canadians needed only to recognize their nordicity to be masters of their imperial/national identity, "for we are a Northern people, – as the true out-crop of human nature, more manly, more real, than the weak marrow-bones superstition of an effeminate South" (16). As Carl Berger reminds us, these views were further disseminated by other Canada Firsters like the poet Charles Mair, and they continued to be promulgated by fiction and non-fiction writers alike (Berger, 17–19). But perhaps the most striking of these xenophobic literary nationalists is William Taylor, whose *Canadian Seasons* (1913) fairly rings with pronouncements on the superiority of a Canada that is defined by its northernness. In poems celebrating each of the four seasons, such as "Grasses and Hay," "Summary," "Invocation" (which Berger quotes at length, 3–4), and "The Blizzard," Canada's northern climate and nordic races are singled out for special praise. This point is emphasized in "The Northern Flora":

It needs the ozone of our northern clime,
The storm and cold, to soar to the Sublime!
Free Northmen broke the chains of ignorance
And shook dark nations from their bestial trance;
Let southern satyrs dance to Piper Pan,
The rugged North alone, can grow A MAN!   (Taylor, 17)

Simultaneous with this boosterism, which conflated Canada (and a Canada of limited geographical scope at that) with North, there was a much more careful focus on specific aspects of the North by federal and provincial politicians and self-appointed apostles. Canada purchased Rupert's Land from Britain in 1870 (with Britain transferring all its remaining territories to Canada in 1880), thus giving concrete existence to a Canadian Northwest beyond Lake Superior and north of 60° latitude, and the provinces of Quebec, Ontario, and later, Manitoba and Saskatchewan jostled to expand and consolidate their northern boundaries right up to the early years of the twentieth century. From Confederation to the outbreak of the Second World War both Quebec and Ontario politicians and businessmen were pushing hard to colonize and develop (through mining, farming, railway expansion) their northern areas. It is worth remembering that, through the nineteenth century, many francophones identified the salvation of Catholic francophone identity with the North, and that for Quebec, at century's end, in the words of Father F.X.A. Labelle, "le nord ... sera un jour la force, le boulevard de notre nationalité" (see Morissonneau, 28–30, and Zaslow, *Opening*, 167).

Charles Tuttle's *Our North Land* (1885), bristling with the self-legitimating gestures of maps, photographs, and statistical charts, argued loudly for a northern transportation route across the prairies from the Pacific to ports on Hudson Bay. An influential Senate committee report on the Mackenzie River basin, released in 1888, predicted – and made recommendations for – extensive development of the entire middle North, from Hudson Bay and the Arctic west to the Athabasca, Mackenzie, and Peace rivers (see Zaslow, 78–9). The Geological Survey played a new and vital role in this vast area from the mid-1870s through to the 1890s, as important books like J.B. Tyrrell's *Across the Sub-Arctic of Canada* (1897) remind us, and the discovery of gold in the Klondike brought issues of far northern (far, that is, from the central Canada of Canada First) resources and sovereignty to national attention with new urgency. The parameters of North were shifting. For various reasons, however, this "irregular and spasmodic" (as Zaslow calls it, 281) northward movement of our provincial and national frontiers was not to take on major historiographic significance for several more decades. In the meantime, the idea of Canada-as-North articulated by writers like Haliburton and Foster, and captured so powerfully in the 1920s by the Group of Seven, would assume a hegemonic position within the popular imagining of the nation.

It should hardly be surprising to find professional historians commonly constructing the North, when they considered it at all, as a colonial hinterland, very much like the West, there to serve the interests of the central Canadian heartland of southern Ontario and Quebec. This idea of North is implicit in the title of Donald Creighton's *Dominion of the North: A History of Canada*, first published in 1944. Creighton's history is political history, a historiography of great men and parties in power; he is interested in the discovery and founding of a new nation. There are few natives, women, or workers in Creighton's *Dominion*, and very little North beyond the "northern colonies" of late eighteenth-century British North America – in other words, "the old empire of the St Laurence" (272). The endpapers of the 1957 hardback edition of the book cut off the top of Ellesmere Island and do not name Baffin Island or the Beaufort Sea (while continuing as far south as New York and San Francisco). To all intents and purposes, Creighton's Canada is the political result of American manifest destiny and British indifference (320). Even when Creighton speaks directly about the North – for example, to describe the transfer of Rupert's Land – that area holds little importance for him except in so far as it serves the needs of the Laurentian heartland (as the fur trade had done and prairie wheat would do). Creighton describes the North after 1920 as "the great new impulse of Canadian life" (473), but it would appear that what he means by North is the Canadian Shield. What he designates as "the new north" (473–4) seems to comprise everything from the forty-ninth parallel to the Pole, including the Yukon and the NWT. This "new north" he characterizes as a "vast empire ... thinly populated by a curiously mixed assortment of races and classes" (474).

It is in the context of this historiography of Canada that we must place W.L. Morton and the historians of North who follow him – Morris Zaslow, Kenneth Coates, William Morrison, R. Quinn Duffy, Arthur J. Ray, and others. There can be no doubt that Morton was speaking, in 1961 with the publication of *The Canadian Identity*, as a politically conservative, federalist, and devout anti-continentalist; like John Diefenbaker, Morton was from the West and understood, from the inside, as it were, the value of margins and marginalized (even othered) voices and perspectives in the narrative of evolving Canadian identity. Perhaps his greatest insight was this privileging of margins in an evolving historiography; for Morton the parameters of Canadian identity, like the parameters of North, were not stable or finalized. I can imagine him, were he alive today, applauding the ongoing evolution – the unfinalizability – of Canadian history and national identity at the beginning of a new century.

Morton's creative quarrel with Canadian history began in 1946 with "Clio in Canada: The Interpretation of Canadian History," in which he denounced the imperialistic ideology inherent in the Laurentian thesis of Creighton and others (106). At this point in his career Morton's chief concern was the treatment of the West by central Canada and the economic/political hegemony of the metropolitan centre, which, he argued passionately, misleads and deceives, "cruelly, children of the outlying sections" of the country, thus fostering "a nationalism cut athwart by a sense of sectional injustice" (108). But Morton makes one other especially important point in this early essay about the nature of internal Canadian imperialism by the so-called centre, a point of crucial significance for the historiography of the North: he warns us against "a political imperialism of the metropolitan area" that will force the "uniformity of the metropolitan culture throughout the hinterlands" (108). This is a point to which he will return in his 1970 paper for the Royal Society, but between these two papers, in 1946 and 1970, comes his influential study *The Canadian Identity*.

This book is, to date, one of the most frequently quoted (it is pre-eminently quotable) of Canadian histories. Moreover, it contains Morton's elegant comments about Canada and the North that have become so familiar through citation, repetition, and resituation in others' texts. Tracing our European history from the Vikings and Norman fishermen (a northern-races manoeuvre reminiscent of Canada First, albeit without the strident racism), Morton insists that Canada has "had a distinct, a unique, a northern destiny" (4). From this foundational theory he elaborates a complex and subtle narrative of Canada-as-North and the Canadian northern frontier, in sharp distinction from the American western frontier, as "perpetual" (72). He argues that our "national life ... rests on a Northern economy" (83), and his description of the country as "largely arctic or sub-arctic in climate" (83) amounts to a decisive claim that Canada *is* the North. Thus, our history must be determined by our "northern character" (89), from which it will articulate the history of "a distinct and even a unique human endeavour, the civilization of the northern and arctic lands" (93). From this conclusion it is but a short step, and a logical extrapolation, to Morton's observations about the "northern quality" (echoing, whether consciously or not, Herman Voaden and Lawren Harris), "the wilderness venture," the "seasonal rhythms" of our lives, and that perpetual northern frontier line that "runs through every Canadian psyche" (93).

But what that line marks – and the mark is crucial, I think – is Morton's implicit acknowledgment of a "northern *and* arctic" (emphasis added) country. In chapter 4 of *The Canadian Identity*, "The Relevance of Canadian History" (first presented as a paper in 1960), he makes several observations about the Arctic, from paternalistic comments about the "Eskimos" to the historical importance of the Northwest Passage, which still challenges us "to fathom the deep secrets of the north and to measure the hair-breadth's difference between disaster and success in northern development" (108). He goes so far as to lament Canadian neglect of Arctic sovereignty and, something quite rare among our historians, discusses "the northern outlook of Canadian arts and letters" (109) with reference to a range of poets and painters, and suggests that satire will be an important component in our culture because "northern life is moral or puritanical" (109). It is no wild exaggeration to suggest that these ideas both in part derive from and, in turn, contribute to the discursive formation of North that connects Morton with the nineteenth century, the Group of Seven, Stephen Leacock, E.J. Pratt, Northrop Frye, Margaret Atwood, Rudy Wiebe, and Robert Kroetsch.[8] Morton calls this art – in a formulation I want to stress – "the art of the hinterland" (109), and he allows that there is a different art specific to the baseland.

In short, Morton begins to see and articulate two crucial aspects of Canada in *The Canadian Identity:* the first is a culture of difference that characterizes North (as well as West) – *difference from* eastern Canada, the southern baseland, the hegemonic and imperialistic metropolitan centre; the second is a distinct and important Arctic presence, with real challenges for the sovereignty, development, identity and history of Canada. "The 'North' in Canadian Historiography" carries these insights several steps further. After a critical aside on Stefansson's overly optimistic prophecies about Arctic settlement, Morton predicts a pattern of "outpost" settlements in a North that he clearly places in the provincial norths and north of sixty. "The development of the North," he insists, has its own characteristics, different in quality, scale, and sociology from the historical development, agricultural and industrial, of southern regions (230). In effect Morton has here expanded his formulation of Canada-as-North in *The Canadian Identity* into the norths-in/of-Canada. He is simultaneously retaining his idea of Canadians as uniquely northern and refining that idea, through the strategic recognition of difference, to acknowledge ideas of norths as part of and crucial to a larger Canadian whole. Thus he allows that "every man and every scientist has his own 'North'" (229), while arguing that by "North" he means "all that territory beyond the line of minimal growth of the known cereal grains" (230). Morton's own parameters of North shift as he speaks/writes.

In the remainder of the essay Morton goes on to call for a distinctly northern historiography and a specific history *of* the North. This is a radically new call for a new historiography that simply ignores the traditional concept of history existing only where the farmer has first storied the land (232). Although he does not go as far as, in hindsight, we might today like, in his recognition of the existence and validity of First Nations oral history he prepares the way for a strategic resistance to the agricultural claim on culture, and he directly acknowledges the influence of the North on Canadian history as stemming, in large part, from the contacts between and among different cultures (236).

It is at this point that Morton describes the North in the terms that have irritated critics like political scientist Douglas West: "We ignore the North," Morton says, because "its coldness, its emptiness, its menace, and its promise [are] too terrible" (237).[9] Then, in an astonishingly post-structuralist, Lacanian move (both *avant la lettre*, to be sure), he theorizes the difference of North as lack, void, vacuum, and puts the rhetorical question: "How ... can ... freezing emptiness ... arctic void ... silent space ... mean anything at all?" (237) His answer follows swiftly: "even a vacuum has meaning," and if we do not develop the North and its Canadian story, someone else will. In short, Morton is calling for the creation of northern historiography as an essential but distinct and different part of Canadian history, and he concludes "with a paradox," that Canadian history can only find its full meaning where there has been (up until 1970) a *lack* of official Canadian historiography – "in the North" (239). Lack, silence, void, and "freezing emptiness" are not mere nothingness; they are the necessary opposites of South, the very palpable signs of northern difference waiting to be invoked, storied, told, heard, and *listened to* by all Canadians. As with Lawren Harris before him, in a canvas like *Winter Comes from the Arctic to the Temperate Zone* (see Plate 3), or Cole Harris after him (see my discussion below of "Maps as a Morality Play"), Morton reads the signs of a Canadian ethos in a North that stretches southward in an unbroken continuity; he situates the morality play of Canadian history on the different stage of the North: "The North makes necessary an absolute dependence on one's fellows, on cooperative skills, on communal capital. So, in ever-lessening degrees southward, does southern Canada" (239).

In the preface to Morris Zaslow's *The Opening of the Canadian North, 1870–1914* (1971) Morton explains the vision of the Canadian Centenary Series called *A History of Canada*, of which Zaslow's two volumes are a part. As executive editor of the series Morton stresses the importance of this major "co-operative" endeavour, the "general theme" of which "is the development of those regional communities which have for the past century made up the Canadian nation" (ix). The North is the only region to be the subject of two volumes, and Zaslow's monumental history (continued in *The Northward Expansion of Canada, 1914–1967*) is now widely acknowledged by specialists of northern history as ground-breaking. Emerging from Zaslow's vast array of statistics and detailed analyses is an intricate and shifting picture of North that includes the largest image of a complete Canadian nation-state and, within those sea-to-sea-to-sea boundaries, a series of provincial, sub-Arctic, Arctic, and high Arctic norths that gradually emerge into sharper focus and prominence.

In volume 1 Zaslow provides convincing proof that the North, albeit variously defined and situated vis-à-vis the growing metropolitan South, was always important to individual Canadians and to governments. Volume 2 shifts the focus from a larger sweep of the territory to a series of close-ups of individual people who have lived, worked, and died in specific parts of the North and to crucial developments of northern resources on which, Zaslow reminds us, the South depends (mining, hydro-electric power, pulp and paper, etc.). The norths that emerge in this volume are individualized, diversified, and personalized by the historian who creates their story. Zaslow is also among the first (possibly *the* first major Canadian historian) to consider the lives of northern native people in precise detail and to describe the negative impact on them of imported diseases, southern technology, the depletion of northern wildlife, and the degradation of the environment, government relocation policies, and missionary competition for souls. Clearly, for Zaslow, the emptiness of the North is a relative condition, and the people who have lived and continue to live there have intrinsic value and historical significance.

That said, however, Zaslow's North is a part of Canada, and northern history, in all its rich complexity, is Canadian history. He writes positively of Diefenbaker's "Northern Vision" as helping to move the "concept of developing the North as a national duty [to] political centre-stage" (*Northward Expansion,* 332), and hints that the next phase of northern history, from 1967 to the end of the century, will be told by northerners *for* northerners, including northerner First Nations.

The Northward Expansion of Canada, 1914–1967 did not appear until 1988 (seventeen years after *The Opening of the Canadian North*), and already between 1967 and the late 1980s at least two quite distinct northern academic historiographies had emerged. One is the line stemming directly from Morton and Zaslow that treats the North as Canada, as do Shelagh Grant, Bruce Hodgins, and John Honderick, for example, or historians of the fur trade such as Jennifer Brown, Sylvia Van Kirk, and Arthur Ray. The other is a much more aggressively northern history that constructs Canada as South in contrast to a North struggling to assert itself in the face of southern colonizing expediency and indifference. This second northern history has been developed by popular writer-historians such as Pierre Berton, Hugh Brody, and

Farley Mowat, southerners with special expertise like Thomas Berger, geographer R. Quinn Duffy, and sociologist Frank Tester, and professional historians like Kenneth Coates and William Morrison, whose credentials include living and working in the North. Alongside this second category of northern historiography is another kind of social scientific writing about the North that increasingly validates or, indeed, centres on northern First Nations' histories – I am thinking here of the important work being done by Valerie Alia, Julie Cruikshank, Penny Petrone, and David Woodman, to mention only a few. It is these writers, together with Coates and Morrison, and a journal like *The Northern Review*, who are creating, even as I write, the "New Northern Vision" (233) that Coates asked for in his 1985 history of the Yukon and Northwest Territories called *Canada's Colonies*.

Once again, my concern is not to compare and weigh these histories/stories of North, to claim that one is better than the other, but to identify the shifting parameters of the historiography itself and to stress the degree to which this writing contributes to and participates in the discursive formation of North. Let me take one final Foucaultian "statement" of North as an example of what I mean. As I have already noted, Canada has had two journals called *Northern Review*. The literary journal was formed in late 1946 by the merger of two competing small magazines devoted to modernist Canadian poetry, *Preview* and *First Statement*.[10] This *Northern Review*, edited by the crusty Canadian nationalist John Sutherland, was based (with Sutherland) in Montreal and Toronto, and, although it began with a pan-Canadian editorial board of poets (several of whom resigned in 1947), it was dominated by Sutherland, his nationalistic concerns, and his preferences for a group of eastern and southern Canadian anglophone poets like Irving Layton, Raymond Souster, and Louis Dudek. By the time it died with Sutherland in 1956, it was an increasingly regional, conservative voice. "Northern," clearly, signified little more than the near North of the Group of Seven – the Laurentians, Algonquin Park, and Lake Superior; it was an adjective with a vague, generalized Canadian significance. The second *Northern Review* – *The Northern Review: A Multidisciplinary Journal of the Arts and Social Sciences of the North* – begun in 1988, the year in which Zaslow's second volume appeared, is published by Yukon College.[11] Its editors are northerners, and its mandate is to publish works (scholarly, literary, and artistic) "that pertain to human experience in and thought about the North" (editorial note to 1.2). Here "northern" signifies those parts of Canada, like the Yukon and the NWT, that are north of sixty. And so the North shifts ever northward; *The Northern Review*, while not denying that Canada is North, chooses a focus that Sutherland would not have dreamed of or approved.

A DISCOURSE OF ORIGINS AND IDENTITY POLITICS

When Harold Innis tells us (as he did in 1930) that "Canada emerged as a political entity with boundaries largely determined by the fur trade" (393), he is articulating a theory of national origins. There are, of course, other theories of our national origin – some that would modify Innis or reject him or, indeed, dispute the very concept of origins as a eurocentric chimera. Creighton, for example, in *Dominion of the North*, traces our national origins to the expedient political manoeuvring of larger military-political and imperialist forces, those of the British Empire and of the emerging continental imperialism, in the nineteenth century, of the United States. Innis sees our national boundaries as a political response to a naturally (climate, topography, natural resources) determined economic imperative; Creighton sees them as the arbitrary result of power politics. Both ascribe our national origins to the arrival of white men in North America. Between and outside these extremes are other theories. Morton asserts that "Canadian history began when the Vikings carried their maritime frontier" (*Canadian Identity*, 4) to the so-called New World, but from that point he shifts immediately (and like Innis) from time to space – the Canadian Shield is central to Canadian history – and from a glimpse of an originary moment to a much more complex, regionally differentiated, spatialization of our national history. More recently, and in one of the most significant texts published in this century – volume 1 of the *Historical Atlas of Canada: From the Beginning to 1800* – Cole Harris invokes Innis and locates the origins, not of *Canada*, to be sure, but of what we would come to know as Canada, in the late Wisconsinan glacial period (18,000–10,000 BC), with the first evidence of human civilization; in other words, he makes of these earliest indigenous peoples the first, *original* Canadians, a point he acknowledges in "Maps as a Morality Play" (167). And for each First Nation there is another version of origins, one that focuses on the creation of the world and of a people rather than of a nation-state.

Whether or not we can agree about origins, or even why origins matter, it is clear from the *Historical Atlas*, from Innis, Creighton, and Morton (among many others), that where we locate our beginnings in time and how we account for our national/international boundaries affect *absolutely* how we define our nationality, our national identity, and, informing both of these, our national unity. The counter-argument, or contra-position, to all attempts to explain and defend our characteristics, identity, and society as a nation – to answer Frye's "where is here?" by saying, *here* is Canada – is the regional. *Here* is the Maritimes, Vancouver Island, Toronto, the Ottawa Valley. Literary critic Frank Davey has gone so far as to say, in *Post-National Arguments*, that at the end of the twentieth century there is no need for a Canadian national identity because each of us is at once regional and global.[12] But whether we support the argument for a national identity or for a regional/global one, North and the discursive formation of North constitute centrally formative factors determining the construction of that identity. This is not to say that North is *the* decisive or *only* factor determining the construction of identity; it is to say, however, that Canadian identity, be it national or regional, has always been thought, articulated, and represented as northern, even when (perhaps especially when) we are, as John Merritt ironically noted, flying south in February. The familiar Canadian debate over region versus nation has a particular force and urgency in the context of North.

In his important, and still very relevant, 1980 analysis of Canadian studies, "On the Concept of Region in Canadian History and Literature," William Westfall describes some of the ways in which the national versus regional debate has been framed in this century. Until the 1970s, when, he suggests, new and more positive scholarly attention began to be focused on regions, claims for a strong national identity were couched in anti-regional terms, and "the metaphor of a northern land" was used "to proclaim national values at the expense of regional ones": "The north itself might be a region, but the central thrust of this northern mythology emphasized the way a single environmental experience affected the whole of Canada. The adverse climate of the north would temper the Canadian character, dissolve regional and ethnic divisions, and fashion a united and racially purified country" (5). The North, in short, and as so much of the primary material I have already considered shows, emerged in the nineteenth century as a unifying symbol of national identity. Nordicity, after all, is one of the few things most Canadians (including today's Québécois) have in common. To celebrate the North as a symbol of national unity and Canadian identity is to make a virtue of geographical reality and socio-economic necessity, to differentiate us from the United States (becoming thereby a key component in an anti-continentalist rhetoric and political agenda), and to focus attention on larger, greater, more important and more abstract things than divisive regional concerns. Inevitably, this nationalizing aspect of the discursive formation of North has contributed to the erasure of differences among regional norths and to the neglect of provincial norths, of the territories, and of the high Arctic, except as reservoirs of natural resources for exploitation and political co-option by southern interests.

But Westfall is correct, I think, in pointing to the 1970s as marking an important watershed, and not only in scholarly theorizing and studies about Canada and the North. Perhaps in response to the nationalist fervour of 1967, which gave us, with so much else, Gould's *The Idea of North*, perhaps in response to a growing weariness with nationalist efforts to hold the country together, and perhaps in response to an overdue and increasingly urgent need on the part of the country as a whole to acknowledge and address the social, economic, and political needs of northerners, the 1970s and 1980s witnessed a proliferation of studies about the regional norths. One hundred years after the discovery of gold in the Klondike put the Yukon on the world map, this Canadian territory has developed an extraordinarily rich, multi-voiced and layered story through the scholarly work of academic historians like Coates and Morrison, journals like *The Northern Review*, hundreds of popular studies of all aspects of the Gold Rush (including a sophisticated CD-ROM called *Klondike Gold*, released in 1996 to mark the official anniversary of the discovery), ground-breaking work by ethnographers like Julie Cruikshank, and a flourishing literary and artistic industry centred in Whitehorse.[13] Although there has not been a single factor of such magnitude as the Klondike to centre attention in the NWT, a strong sense of regions and regional identities has emerged there as well. Hamelin's "conceptual referents" and "nordicity index" (*About Canada*, 21) have played an incalculably important role in, as it were, representing these norths as distinct regions of great particularity and interest, worthy of our most serious study. The development of Inuit arts (sculpture, print-making, and weaving), while certainly serving a Canadian national identity, has also strengthened regional and community identity through the creation of arts co-ops and centres on Baffin Island, Inuit art journals, and events like the Inuvik Northern Arts Festival.[14] *Up Here: Exploring the True North*, a magazine aimed at the southern tourist trade, is published in Yellowknife, supported in part by businesses from across the NWT, and it has become an important vehicle for regional news, popular history, and local advertising. And personal narratives by white settlers in the NWT like Ernie Lyall and Georgia, together with a popular television series like *North of Sixty* (see Warley), have helped to create the insider perspective that contradicts and undercuts the nationalist rhetoric. Emerging into clear and undeniable focus is what I would describe as a strong regional aspect to the discursive formation of North that exists alongside, sometimes in competition with, the still dominant national discourse. This emerging discourse is the main topic of my penultimate chapter, "The North Writes Back."

It would be a mistake, however, to pretend that the North is predominantly imagined or imaged as regional or *from the inside*. Moreover, national and regional, outsider and insider perspectives, are not mutually exclusive either/or sites. Indeed, the very opposite, I would argue, is true. The discursive formation of North includes *both* in an ongoing unfinalizable process of identity- and nation-formation. North coexists with the norths, and *together* they construct the complex, always changing, imagined community of Canada. The very creation of Nunavut within the Canadian nation-state signals and situates that process. I have suggested elsewhere that the North has been evoked at critical moments of *national* interest and nationalist concern (see *Representing North*, 1, and "Canada Post"). This interest and concern inform debates on national (as opposed to colonial) identity, sovereignty, and development, all three of which are intertwined and have coalesced to create peaks of intense focus on general notions of nordicity or activity in the North. These peaks occurred in the late 1860s and early 1870s (largely due to Canada First), in the late 1890s in response to the Klondike, in the 1920s with the Group of Seven on the one (much more southerly) hand and the Arctic activities of men like Stefansson, Jenness, Camsell, and Richard Finnie on the other, during and immediately after the Second World War because of the overwhelming presence of Americans in the Yukon and the NWT, with Diefenbaker and his "Road to Resources" northern vision at the end of the fifties, and then from 1967 to the present in a steadily mounting chorus of voices calling for attention to the North as our circumpolar destiny and responsibility at the end of the twentieth century. And just as *The Northern Review* and *Up Here* have provided fora for regional northern voices, so important magazines like the *Canadian Forum*, *The Beaver*, and *Canadian Geographic*, the first two of which began in 1920, have consistently privileged and celebrated Canada-as-North.[15]

John Diefenbaker's sweep to power, in March 1958, was fought, and arguably won, on his northern vision: "I see a new Canada," he proclaimed in his opening campaign speech from Winnipeg's Civic Auditorium on February 12: "I see a new Canada – a Canada of the North" (Diefenbaker ts, 6). To be sure, Diefenbaker was not the only prime minister to draw attention to the North or to capitalize on Canadian fascination with ideas of North; Macdonald, Borden, and St Laurent were not oblivious of its importance or magnetism. But no prime minister before or since capitalized on the idea of North so effectively or accomplished more in the North than did Diefenbaker in the five years following this 1958 election.[16] In his opening campaign speech he set forth the party's "new principles" and "new objectives" with regard to the North in ringing tones:

We ask from you a Mandate: a new and stronger Mandate, to pursue the planning and to carry to fruition our new *National Development Programme for Canada.*

This national Development Policy will create a new sense of National Purpose and National Destiny. One Canada! One Canada, wherein Canadians will have preserved to them the control of their own economic and political destiny. Sir John A. Macdonald gave his life to this Party. He opened the West. He saw Canada from East to West. I see a new Canada – a Canada of the North.   (6)

Having touched all the right buttons of unity, destiny, and new development, Diefenbaker goes on to elaborate what he sees in this northern future: "the development of the national resources for the opening of Canada's northland" (transportation, communications, hydro-electric power), the maintenance of "Canadian sovereignty in the Arctic," "a vast programme on Frobisher Bay," and a "Roads programme for the Yukon and Northwest Territories" to advance exploration for oil and minerals (7). Then, with repetitions of phrases like "One Canada" and "Canada First" (this surely no casual allusion), and rhetorical flourishes on "faith," Diefenbaker rises to eloquent, prophetic heights: "There is a new imagination now. The Arctic. We intend to carry out the Legislative Programme of Arctic research, to develop Arctic routes, to develop those vast hidden resources the last few years have revealed. Plans to improve the St. Laurence and the Hudson Bay Route. Plans to increase Self-Government in the Yukon and Northwest Territories. We can see one or two provinces there ... Completion of Confederation by developing a self-governing North" (8–9).

Easy though it may be to scoff or to pick holes in Diefenbaker's rhetoric and logic from the practical perspectives of policy and implementation, as a statement in the discursive formation of North this speech is a classic. The dominant message is national – Canada *is* North, and the resources of the North exist to serve the whole country – but running through the speech, like a motif in a regional subtext, is the importance of distinct separate norths deserving of full provincial status within a greater Confederation. This is a promise that Diefenbaker could not keep, a vision he could not possibly realize. As Kirk Cameron and Graham

White succinctly put the matter in their 1995 study *Northern Governments in Transition*, "problems with government are endemic in the North ... and the widespread social ills of the North may prove impervious to any set of constitutional arrangements" (140). Decades after Diefenbaker's speech, the challenge of northern development and autonomy is still before us, as Nunavut illustrates.

The other challenge that resists easy resolution and still contributes to the discursive formation of North is sovereignty, the sovereignty, in an international forum, of the Canadian nation-state. This concern constitutes a major site of discursive attention from at least the middle of the nineteenth century, and it has been repeated and reformulated in political speeches, scientific and scholarly research, films, narratives both fictional and non-fictional, plays, and the visual arts. From the Canada First rhetoric of Haliburton and Foster to Charles Tuttle, the federal government's concern (albeit belated) over the American presence in the Klondike, which led directly to the expansion of the NWMP and Geological Survey activity across the sub-Arctic and Arctic, the political context for Stefansson's 1913 Canadian Arctic expedition, to the films made by Richard Finnie for the Canadian Government Motion Picture Bureau – *In the Shadow of the Pole* (1928) and *The Arctic Patrol* (1929) – sovereignty has been asserted, debated, and questioned, but never set aside. The building of the Alaska Highway by the Americans during the Second World War, the DEW Line after the war, missile testing over northern Canada, and the intrusion into Canadian Arctic waters by the American ships ss *Manhattan* (in 1969) and the *Polar Sea* (in 1985) have all fuelled continuing analysis of sovereignty over the past fifty years. In November 1969 the *Canadian Forum* devoted a special issue to the North, including Michael Galway's articulation of two strategic principles for assuring Canada's Arctic sovereignty, and since then several major scholarly studies of our sovereignty have appeared, the most important being John Honderich's *Arctic Imperative: Is Canada Losing the North?* and Shelagh Grant's *Sovereignty or Security? Government Policy in the Canadian North, 1936–1950*.[17] It is interesting, though hardly surprising, that the 1989 public inquiry of "The True North Strong & Free Inquiry Society," published as *The Arctic: Choices for Peace and Security*, has much more to say about Canadian sovereignty in the Arctic than it does about either peace or security.

If one were looking for a particular set of statements to represent all aspects of the national/regional interdiscursivity of North, one could hardly find a better place to look than the story of the Klondike. The claims staked along that river and its tributaries were to more than gold. From its very beginning – a moment debated in most of the many books about the Gold Rush – Canadians were pushed aside by the thousands of Americans flocking to this Eldorado.[18] The American George Carmack is usually credited with the discovery, instead of the veteran Canadian prospector Bob Henderson or any of the First Nations men and women of the area (a subject I return to in chapter 3), and of the millions of dollars mined from those Yukon creeks, most went south, out of the country. Mounting federal government concern over sovereignty, law and order, and customs duties led to the creation of a virtual police state, albeit a benign, paternalistic one, in the closing years of the nineteenth century, and with the formal creation of the Yukon Territory in 1898 began the tensions between region and nation that characterize thinking and inflame passions in the Yukon to this day. The variations in the story of the Klondike, the shifting perspectives and claims, the growing awareness on the part of historians, ethnographers, and others that many voices, notably those of women and native peoples, still need to be incorporated into the story, all these characteristics mark the Klondike as an exceptionally rich site for the archeology and genealogy of the discursive formation of North. Most of all, the story is not over. When Ken Coates called for a "New Northern Vision" (233) in *Canada's Colonies*, he may not have foreseen the precise form that new vision would take or just how central and symbolic the Klondike would be. A decade after his 1985 book appeared, and just in time for the centenary of the Klondike, magazine, television, flyer, and urban billboard advertisements proclaimed that Molson beer, like Inukshuks, stand on guard for us (see Illus. 11), that out future security and prosperity lie in the Eldorado of the North, with the advice of the Toronto-Dominion Bank, and that the best mutual funds are in the "True North."[19]

Writing in the mid-sixties, on the eve of Canada's centenary, for a collection of essays called *Nationalism in Canada*, historian Carl Berger was one of the first Canadian intellectuals to draw our attention to aspects of Canadian identity that are questionable, and he did so in a balanced yet unflinching and unequivocal manner. The historical moment was right and the warning timely. At the end of "the true north strong and free," and after a quantity of explicit quotation that proves his point, Berger tells us: "If Canadian nationalism is to be understood, its meaning must be sought and apprehended not simply in the sphere of political decisions, but also in myths, legends and symbols like these [about the North]. For while some might think that Canadians have happily been immune to the wilder manifestations of the nationalist impulse and rhetoric, it seems that they too have had their utopian dreamers, and that they are not totally innocent of a tradition of racism and a falsified but glorious past" (24). Berger is referring, of course, to the rhetoric of Canada Firsters like R.G. Haliburton, William Henry Taylor, the poet Charles Mair, and erstwhile Firster George T. Denison, to the romantic, rugged views of Charles Tuttle, and to the imperialistic Social Darwinism of George Parkin, and he traces the influence of their branch of northern supremacy into the twentieth century – to Gilbert Parker, Ralph Connor, Robert Service, and Vilhjalmur Stefansson (20–1), among others.

Bruce Hodgins is by no means so gentle with these men. Dismissing the views of Haliburton as "racist rantings" ("The Canadian North," 4), a description to which I would add "and sexist," he notes that the "theme of Canada as North," which necessitates a homogenization of distinct regions and peoples, continues on through this century in the thought of Parkin, George Grant, Charles Paradis, Vincent Massey, and "the novels of Margaret Atwood and the sophisticated musings of

Illus. 11. Molson Canada, which sponsored the August 1995 rock concert in Inuvik, advertised Molson Dry by evoking a sense of shared nordicity through the symbols of the Inukshuk and the Molson label. This image appeared as a full-page colour advertisement in newspapers and on television during the summer of 1995 and represented a clever appeal to national identity and patriotic spirit through the semiotics of cold, purity, and pride. Reproduced with permission. © 1995, Molson Canada.

W.L. Morton" ("The Canadian North," 5). I do not wish to imply for a moment that Hodgins is labelling all these writers racist, because he is not. He is making another, much more subtle and important point: to the degree that historians, writers, artists, and others overlook the particularities of the norths (regional or territorial), they must also overlook the diverse complexity of the North, and to the degree that they idealize North as the source of a unique Canadian identity, they ignore the actual, often third-world living conditions of northerners.

In addition to the overt racism of Haliburton and his fellows, a racism that, our history tells us, if it tells us nothing less, is still with us (see Kitigawa, Ward, and Bannerji), much of the past *and present* discourse of North is sexist, and assumptions about class are also deeply imbricated in the discursive formation of North.

The racism has been recognized and condemned by Berger, Hodgins, and others. What has not been addressed is the degree to which a form of white nordic supremacy underpins much of the praise of North as a land of spiritual purity (for Lawren Harris, Herman Voaden, and R. Murray Schafer, for example) that is perceived as free of the incipient degeneracy of some generalized South. That this degeneracy goes hand in hand with effeminacy underscores one of ways in which sexism combines with racism to construct South in negative terms against a Great White North of and for real men. Two general groups of human beings are either excluded from or at best marginalized by this discourse – First Nations peoples, who have been living in the North (and norths) for thousands of years, and the women who have been here all this time, who frequently helped white explorers, or who came with Euro-Canadian men to prospect, farm, settle, and so on. It is these groups whose voices are largely excluded in, say, Robert Ballantyne's popular novels for boys (see R.S. Phillips), Ralph Connor's Glengarry and prairie novels, Hugh MacLennan's *Two Solitudes*, which begins with a paean to the Laurentian Shield, Robert Kroetsch's *But We Are Exiles* and *Gone Indian*, or even Gabrielle Roy's *Le Montagne secrète*, with the result that North has been constructed and represented as a feminized space in which to test white male identity, virility, and competence. Native peoples and women are also largely excluded from our histories; to read Creighton, Morton, and Lower, for example, or most of the historiography of the Yukon – right up to the 1980s – is to imagine a nation where these groups play at best a minor, dispensable role.

To be sure, this combined sexist/racist representation of North is changing, along with a more general sensitivity to what is and is not socially acceptable and a growing awareness of the social injustice that results from these views. To some degree this shifting boundary of identity politics explains – if it does not justify – how, in 1885, Tuttle could describe the "Eskimos" as "poor creatures" (74), filthy (87), ugly, utterly without religion (87), and as speaking "gibberish" (79), the poet D.C. Scott could write of Indians as a "weird and vanishing race" ("The Onondaga Madonna"), or how Charles Camsell (himself of Métis background) could exclaim, as late as 1946, that the "same racial stock [British] which has carried the flag around the world will also carry it to the farthest north" (277). Many more contemporary writers, including Carl Berger, R.A.J. Phillips, Hamelin, Lotz, Harris, Thomas Berger, Rudy Wiebe, Ken Coates, John Moss, and Charlene Porsild, have begun to set the record straight. What is not fully recognized, even by these writers, I think, is the degree to which ideas about race are complicated by gendered social relations and stereotypes, and by class prejudices, which take the form of southern elitism and disregard for the natives and for non-native wage-workers in mining or other isolated towns and settlements. The three categories of identity (and there are others like ethnicity, sexual orientation, and language) are interconnected and, together, inextricably constitutive of the habitus.

We have had to date some excellent studies that tackle the *interconnections* of race and gender, with some attention to class, in the fur trade (see Sylvia Van Kirk and Jennifer Brown). However, too little attention has been paid to the complex ways in which the discursive formation of North has been rigidly raced, classed, and gendered, and to the encouraging ways in which some of our political scientists, historians, geographers, novelists, playwrights, and visual artists have begun to dismantle the discourse. They work to undermine the discourse first by introducing new perspectives and voices, but second, and even more importantly, by demonstrating the degree to which racist assumptions are bound up with sexist ones and the images (positive and negative) of both race and gender are classed: they cannot be understood in isolation from each other or approached as mere by-products of or add-ons to our representations of North.[20]

At several points in the chapters that follow I return to the question of race/gender/class in the discursive formation of North, explicitly in the case of Kate Carmack, in the representations and counter-representations of North by writers and artists, and in my sixth chapter, "The North Writes Back." However, if it is continuing change, openness, plurality, freedom from discrimination, and social equality in a *new* true North strong and free that we seek, we could do worse than hold before us as a *practical* ideal the story and example of Nunavut, with its reality of an aboriginal northern homeland and a consensus form of government. Nunavut, as Kirk Cameron and Graham White have put it, constitutes "a powerful and visionary step forward for Canada's Aboriginal people and for Canada itself" (111).

Despite the continual lament that the North is not valued or understood as important, indeed, essential to the Canadian identity, to what makes us a distinct imagined community, and to the geopolitical reality of Canada as a circumpolar national state, a very great deal of Canadian attention has in fact been paid to the North. The archive is vast and still growing. North constitutes an enormously complex discursive formation whose transferability (across disciplinary boundaries and historical periods), signifying power, and flexibility make it one of the most long-lived of Canadian national(ist) markers. Not surprisingly, the North, like the north*s*, has changed profoundly over time; in this sense North is a classic Bakhtinian chronotope, what Arthur Ray has called "a geography of change" (xvii). Inscribed and reinscribed in/as the discursive formation of North are the signs of its shifting parameters, its national and/or regional characteristics, and its representations of identity as raced, gendered, and classed. Equally unsurprising, Canadian fascination with the North gives no indication of waning. To the contrary, advertisements relying on the iconography of North, massive state-supported and -identified exhibitions such as *The Group of Seven: Art for a Nation*, postage stamps celebrating northern comic-book heroes of the 1940s like Nelvana of the Northern Lights, or scenes of Inuit and Arctic life, or the Klondike, the creation of Nunavut in 1999, ongoing searches for Franklin, and the consequences of global warming all serve to keep the North at the forefront of regional *and* national imagination and consciousness. This obsession with North should not, however, blind us to the reality of economic neglect and colonialist exploitation by southern Canada or to the severe social problems experienced by many northerners living in the provincial norths, the Yukon, the NWT, Labrador, and Nunavut. The territories are grappling *today* with a highly complex mix of social problems that has characterized native and non-native encounters in Canada for at least the last 250 years.[21]

The North has served competing claims to identity – regional/national, colonial/imperial (with Canada as both the object and the subject of imperialist acts), national/continental, and national/international-circumpolar. There is every indication that it will continue to do so, because the mapping of Canada-as-North, like the map of our internal borders, is constantly changing. The cartography of the northern imaginary, as I try to show in the next chapter, is a system of representation open to the endless re-mappings and subversions of our postmodern age. The questions of what and where North is, along with how and why it matters, have been constantly argued, and the dialogue continues. Is it hostile or friendly, barren or fruitful, an Eldorado or a deadly trap? Is it *here*, all around us, or north of sixty, north of the treeline and the permafrost? Is it the Yukon, Nunavut, and the NWT, or is it Lac St-Jean, Sudbury, Edmonton, and Prince George? Is it the quintessential place of unspoiled wilderness adventure, or is it home? Well, it depends. North is both/and, not either/or. North is the paradox of Canadian history with a VAPO for "le tout de la nation." The truth about North, as Morton, Hamelin, and MacEwen tell us, depends on our position:

> If you consult the polestar for the truth
> of your present position, you will learn that you have no
> position, position is illusion   (MacEwen, "Polaris," 21)

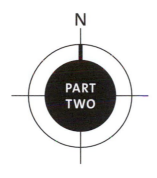

N

ARTICULATING NORTH

The arctic circle
is a threshold
in the mind,
not its circumference.

North is
where all parallels
converge
to open out
Henry Beissel, *Cantos North*, Seventh Canto

One could not live in the north country very long without seeing plainly what
white civilization had done to the Natives. White men had brought such "refining"
influences as whisky, thievery, adultery, syphilis and tuberculosis to the tribes,
and they had systematically robbed the Natives at the same time ... Native people
of North America were once great people, and they will be again, not because
of white "civilization" but in spite of it.
Eva MacLean, *The Far Land*

They were tracking an indomitable ghost that moved as if weather did not exist
and laid tracks in whatever deadly spot it pleased, up cliffs and over ice-skimmed
running water that could catch you with one snap of its innocent deadly surface.
Rudy Wiebe, *The Mad Trapper*

The north focusses our anxieties. Turning to face north, face the north, we enter our
own unconscious. Always, in retrospect, the journey north has the quality of dream.
Margaret Atwood, "True North"

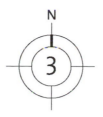

VISUALIZING NORTH

SEEING CARTOGRAPHICALLY

In his 1988 study "Maps, Knowledge, and Power" Brian Harley began an investigation of cartography that has caused something of a stir among geographers and in recent issues of *Cartographica*. Noting that maps have always been, like guns and warships, "the weapons of imperialism," serving to maintain "the territorial *status quo*" (283), Harley goes on to argue that maps have usually served the powerful in society by silencing or excluding others, and that they will probably continue to do so: "The social history of maps, unlike that of literature, art, or music, appears to have few genuinely popular, alternative, or subversive modes of expression. Maps are preeminently a language of power, not of protest" (301). By treating maps as language and situating them firmly in the context of political, religious, and social power, Harley reminds us of just how profoundly maps constitute and participate in our "cultural mythology."[1] However, while he is no doubt correct in claiming that cartography does not easily permit subversion or "genuinely popular, alternative" representations of the physical world that we can recognize *as maps*, the cartographic system is not quite as impenetrable and resistant as he suggests. There are numerous examples, from a metaphorics of mapping to actual maps, that challenge the supposed hegemonic, stable authority of the map, and it is to some of these mappings that I now turn.

If I call these mappings visualizations of North rather than representations, it is because the jury is still out on this question. On the one hand, maps can refer to a real world – road maps help me get around – but, on the other, they can also be artistic, imaginative constructions of a world we want to be there. However, I am interested less in defending either side in the debate than in exploring some of the many ways in which maps contribute to the discursive formation of North and constitute some of the specific cartographic statements in the archive. This archive must, of course, include the national sphere of the historical atlas, which, in Canada, has passed through three stages of development: Lawrence Burpee's pioneer effort of 1927, D.G. Kerr's *A Historical Atlas of Canada* of 1960, and most recently the three-volume *Historical Atlas of Canada*. These major efforts at mapping the nation, or at staging what Cole Harris so aptly calls the "morality play"

("Maps," 163) of Canada, are complemented (perhaps even challenged) by a host of specific maps with other, often regional, purposes. And no subject or territory seems to invite and rely upon maps more obsessively than the North. Pick up almost any book, from children's fiction to social science, on the subject and you will find maps. Films, paintings, videos, and CD-ROM all exploit the cartographic potential of the northern map. As often as not these texts will also rely on a range of cartographic metaphors: thus Ian MacLaren can construct an "Aesthetic Map of the North" between 1845 and 1859 using a map (of course) and several illustrations of paintings to explain the language and ideology of Sublime and Picturesque depictions of the Arctic, and John Honderick, using numerous maps, can attack the "Mercator mind-set" that undermines our ability to take our sovereignty and military presence in the North seriously and blocks our capacity to recognize "ourselves as a circumpolar country" (212).

Maps in particular serve a number of purposes in books, articles, films, artwork, and so on. They inform by assisting a reader or viewer, who will be unlikely to have detailed knowledge, to follow an argument or an adventure. They delight by illustrating a text or contributing to a painting, supplementing in design, colour, and composition the larger narrative of the work. They legitimate and authorize the writer, speaker, artist in numerous ways, most obviously by asserting (whether truthfully or not) that the author has been *there*, seen *that*, and knows what he/she is talking about. By informing, illustrating, and legitimating, maps exhibit an enormous discursive and, thus, cultural power; they claim knowledge of and thereby mastery over a part of the world – here, the North, or a part of the North.

Maps often provide the reader, like the writer, with a surplus power through knowledge. A splendid case in point is the effect of maps in books about Sir John Franklin's third and fatal 1845 expedition in search of the Northwest Passage. Today's writer and reader are able to see from the start what Franklin could not see, what *his* maps did not show, and we are thereby subtly placed in a superior position of knowledge and power over Franklin. This power, however, is ironically undercut for us because now the search is not for the Northwest Passage but for Franklin himself and for the ships *Terror* and *Erebus*, which we still cannot locate, despite our superior maps. The fascination with Franklin and his men that continues, either to send us to the Arctic with research teams or to inspire us to dream, imagine, paint, and write about their death and disappearance in the North, is always played out in maps, and none of these is more apposite, I think, than the map at the beginning of Zoom's adventure in *Zoom Away* (see Illus. 12). This is the perfect example of mapping the northern imaginary: it certainly looks like a traditional map, with lines of latitude and longitude clearly marked, but this flattened section of the globe defies any rational effort at representation or location; it matches no known map of the high Arctic, despite its emphatic claim to mark the North Pole. As such, of course, it is an ideal invitation to the children's narrative

Illus. 12. In this illustration by Eric Beddows for the children's book *Zoom Away* (1991), by Tim Wynne-Jones, Maria, Zoom's guardian and good angel, shows the adventurous little cat where his Uncle Roy's ship was heading when it was last heard of. Zoom is about to set off for the far North in search of his Franklin-like uncle, but unlike those who searched in vain for Franklin, Zoom's story will have a happy ending. Reproduced with the permission of the artist. Illustration © 1985, Eric Beddows.

fantasy that follows when Zoom, the little cat, takes the magic door to the Northwest Passage in search of his missing uncle, Captain Roy (see Grace, "Gendering Northern Narrative," 163–4).

But is this subversive mapping? Does it protest anything? Probably not. And yet, when placed, as one statement, beside so many other maps of the North, particularly those associated with Franklin and the Northwest Passage, it does ruffle gently our assumptions about the scientific objectivity of maps. It disturbs, if only a little, our belief that maps definitely tell us what is *really* there and not just (as Wreford Watson reminds us) what we want to think is there. It problematizes our knowledge and our power through parody – a playful, ironic imitation-with-difference that catches us unawares to remind us of our Cartesian and Mercator mind-set. A similar effect is achieved by the map at the beginning of *Nanook of the North* (see Illus. 1), although in this case the imaginary North is less benign than in *Zoom Away*. In *Nanook* the whole of Canada (at least the part that is shown) is North, and *that* North is a bleak, empty space somewhere to the north

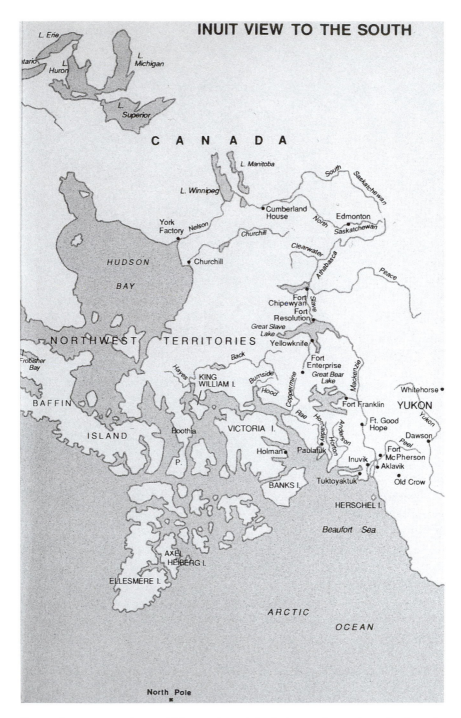

Illus. 13. "Inuit View to the South" from Rudy Wiebe's *Playing Dead* reminds readers from the start of the book that a south-centric vision is not the only possible way of imagining the country. Reproduced with the author's permission.

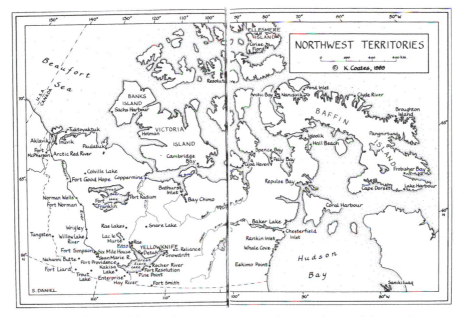

Illus. 14. This 1989 map of the Northwest Territories provides a good sense of the area, its scope, component parts, and sheer size, prior to the formation of Nunavut in 1999. Map by Stuart Daniel, Starshell maps; reproduced with permission from *The Modern North* by Ken Coates and Judith Powell. © Ken Coates.

of Chicago and New York (see Grace, "Exploration as Construction," 132–3). The extreme simplicity of the map constructs the image of a primitive *terra incognita* transformed into the desired object of our bemused, curious, voyeurs' gaze thanks to Robert Flaherty, Revillon Frères, and twentieth-century science and technology.

In order to examine northern cartography more fully, with Brian Harley's important challenges in mind, I would like to take a wider view of the matter and suggest a mapping of the maps. At the centre (and dominating Western, Euro-Canadian cartographic practice and discourse, as Harley tells us) are those scientific, objective maps in gazetteers and atlases that promise us precise representations of reality. Around the cartographic periphery, and at its extreme margins, are those Borgesian, Swiftean maps of playful fantasy, like the one Zoom will imagine for the Arctic. In between the determinedly Cartesian and the wildly non-Cartesian are a range of maps that represent something, to be sure, but first and foremost refer to and rely on our familiarity with *other maps*. The in-between maps I want to consider are Warwick's *Pays d'en haut* (Illus. 6), Rudy Wiebe's "Inuit View to the South" (Illus. 13), Aritha van Herk's Ellesmere, island-as-woman-as-island (Illus. 8), Kenneth Coates and Judith Powell's "Northwest Territories" (Illus. 14), Inuit and Nunavut maps (Illus. 15 and 16), and one of the memory maps from Marlene Creates' *The Distance between Two Points is Measured in Memories* (Illus. 7).

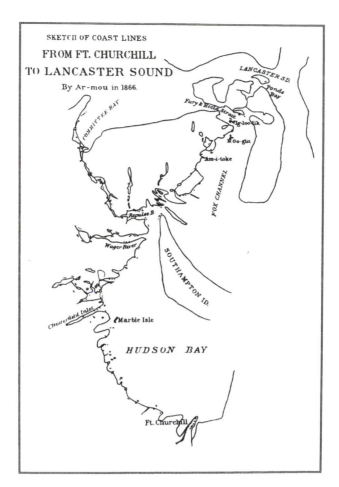

Illus. 15. As this map demonstrates, the nineteenth-century Inuit had a detailed cartographic understanding of their world. In 1866 the Inuk Ar-mou drew an accurate sketch of the western coastline of Hudson Bay from Fort Churchill north to Lancaster Sound. Reproduced from David Woodman's *Strangers among Us*.

For comparison – to measure deviance, if you will – I suggest we keep in mind the "Where Is the North?" map (Illus. 10) from *The Canadian North*, but a few caveats are also in order: first, there is little use in maintaining the Cartesian/non-Cartesian distinction evoked by Rundstrom, because to map means to objectify within Western culture; second, even the most assertively scientific maps demand an ability to read them, to decode their sign system, that must be learned through the study of cartography and other maps: and third, all maps, even the most fantastic or speculative, must obey the rules of reference and representation, which makes them inescapably available to an archaeology of geography, and here part of the discursive formation of North. Finally, my examples of maps that exist between the extremes

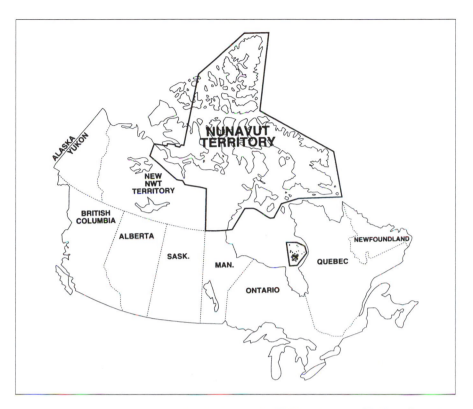

Illus. 16. On 1 April 1999 the map of Canada changed. In his "New Canadian North as of 1999" John David Hamilton shows the boundaries of Canada's newest territory – Nunavut. As he explains, the population of Nunavut (meaning "Our Land") is largely Inuit, while the **NWT** contains Dene, Métis, Inuvialuit, and whites. Reproduced with permission from *Arctic Revolution*.

of the "Where Is the North?" map (Illus. 10) and Zoom's North mark different degrees of separation, lie at varying degrees of marginality from the centre of gazetteer or atlas. The Warwick, Wiebe, and van Herk maps visualize the subversion that Harley ponders, while the Coates and Powell, Inuit and Nunavut maps, and Creates' memory maps are radical re-mappings of what we thought we already knew. The move here, as I see it, is from traditional, utilitarian, scientific/instrumentalist cartography through artistic subversion to a variety of reinscriptions that, however quietly, inobtrusively, reconstruct by reimagining the reality we expect to find referenced by maps. By snatching these maps from their original contexts and replacing, re-presenting them here, I too want to subvert and reinscribe cartographic practice. By facilitating the dialogue that Robert Rundstrom calls for (6–7), I want to dialogize, in precisely Bakhtin's terms, these visualizings of North.

Warwick's two-part *Pays d'en haut* map visualizes several points about Canada and the North that are argued in his critical text. First and most obviously it traces the location of French Canadian novels in terms of the geographic spaces contained in the diegesis (the basic story elements of the plot). From this tracing we can quickly see *where* the heroes of these novels go and where their stories take place (or are set). Second, this map compares the fictional geography and diegesis of space with the historiography of the voyageurs and missionaries, whose routes took them from Montreal across the Great Lakes to southern Manitoba, and from there northwest beyond Great Slave Lake right up to the mouth of the Mackenzie, or due north into what would become northern Manitoba, as well as west and south. Third, Warwick's map marks off degrees of nordicity; working from a chronotopic base transferred from narrative (novel, history, biography) to cartography, it classifies literary areas of Far North, Pays d'en Haut, Near Pays, and Pseudo-North as degrees of *textual* nordicity. The map is circular, enclosed within the textually devised and constructed world of narrative. To read this map – to make *sense* of it – requires that we accept Western cartographic conventions and easily transfer them to an undeniably textual and imaginary world that in turn legitimates the map. It also helps if we know the novels, in which case the map grounds, authorizes, establishes as *real* (so to speak) the narrative territory claimed by the text. Finally (at least, for my purpose here, because more could be said about this map), some interesting political and more generally ideological points are asserted by this map, such as, for example, that the French mapped *all* of Canada (of what would *become* a nation-state), that they mapped it as North, and that Quebec, as a northern region, is the key defining metonymy of national Canadian space and identity.

Paterson Ewen's massive painting *Northern Lights* (1973, 167.5 cm × 244.0 cm, acrylic, oil, dry pigment on galvanized steel and gouged plywood, in the Art Gallery of Ontario but not available for reproduction) makes a similarly nationalist statement, if in somewhat different and more humorous terms. Ewen's globe, resting against the black ground of outer space, puts the Aurora Borealis and Canada, especially Arctic Canada, at the centre of pictorial space. Indeed, an enlarged map of Canada fills most of this space, at one and the same time to exaggerate the importance and centrality of Canada in the global perspective and to stress the idea of Canada-as-North, of Canada as dominated by our nordicity and lit up, from within the space of the nation, by the Northern Lights.

Ewen's map of Canada barely reaches south to the Gulf of St Lawrence, while our northern coast, the Beaufort Sea, the Arctic archipelago, Hudson Bay, and Baffin Island lie across the middle of the image where Earth's curve meets an outer space filled with stars and planets (created by gouges in the plywood). The Aurora Borealis sits on the curve like a crown, right at the centre of the image; it is constructed of "strips of galvanized iron with the colours of the spectrum on it" (Ewen, quoted in Teitelbaum, 128). From this dominant position the Aurora lights up the darkness of space, with five brightly coloured slashes of colour dancing on the left of the image and Canada itself glowing beneath its crown of lights in warm hues of orange, yellow, green, and blue. Speaking of his inspiration for *Northern Lights*, Ewen has said: "I was in Algonquin Park on a snow-shoe trip and there was a very exciting aurora borealis and when I got back from the trip I said that's going to be my next painting" (quoted in Teitelbaum, 128). This is not Rudy Wiebe's mapping of a northern perspective on the South so much as a southerner's recognition of how deeply South the North comes into Canada, or, to put it another way, how northern the whole country is and can be visualized as being. *Northern Lights*, albeit in a very different visual language, reminds me of Lawren Harris's message in *Winter Comes from the Arctic to the Temperate Zone* (see Plate 3).

The first thing you see on opening Rudy Wiebe's *Playing Dead: A Contemplation Concerning the Arctic* is the map "Inuit View to the South." It faces you, as part of an endpaper in a hardback book might, before the half-title, title, and copyright pages. This, it insists, is how the world really looks (see Illus. 13). More important perhaps than this optical reversal, with Canada disappearing off the top of the page, is the toponymy. Not all the place names in the Arctic are there, and they are not always given in their primary, native languages (why, indeed, is Deh Cho not shown instead of, or at least alongside, Mackenzie? Why Frobisher Bay and not Iqaluit?), but many of them are given, and different languages jostle each other for attention, reminding us of the heteroglossia of our world. *This* North is named: Tuktoyaktuk, Old Crow, Aklavik, Holman, Boothia, and Yellowknife, and there is history, cultural encounter, linguistic diversity, ethnic multiplicity, and difference of naming strategy represented here, instead of order and homogeneity. The map hints at the polyphony of the North by dialogizing its text. Its great rivers, old forest, and some of its lakes appear to fill up and occupy what usually appears as unnamed, empty space. To the south – where we are – nothing! The centre of the world is the North, the Arctic archipelago, Hudson Bay, and the Mackenzie basin. These are the places we need to think about and locate in the meditations that follow. This is the North-as-Canada, and the rest of the country scarcely matters. Wiebe, of course, not only wants to help us see the geographical locations and the routes of explorers, lost patrols, and mad trappers who story the Arctic; he wants us to know what it feels like to be written out of history, like so many of the Dene and Inuit who people his meditations and occupy the places and the pages of his text. "Inuit View to the South" reorients the southern viewer by turning our familiar versions of the world upside down and thus estranging us, reminding us (to paraphrase the title of Wiebe's later novel) that we are the strangers discovered on the land. Wiebe's map pushes beyond the overt manipulation of the *pays d'en haut* and the exaggeration of *Northern Lights* into parody by literally turning the world on its head (what Bakhtin would describe as carnivalizing). It is a gesture that my next map takes even further.

The cover of Aritha van Herk's *Places Far from Ellesmere*, created by Scott Barham, is a work of art (see Illus. 8). It is also a map, constructed by collage, mapping maps on maps over maps, which matches the verbal collage of van Herk's text, her "geografictione." It plays with Canadian geography and cartography to defy, while exploiting, *real* maps. It is, in short, a cartographer's nightmare, the North-as-woman (which all those male explorers already knew in their dread), embodying our desires and our selves. *Elles mere*. What this map/cover represents is what the text implements – a series of interpenetrating, overlapping (and thus layered) "EXPLORATIONS ON SITE," where the site is several places at once but first and last the text, the map, the imagined self. This map is the most subversive of the ones I am gathering here because, like the text it so aptly presents to us, it invokes and parodies our received notions and unacknowledged assumptions about Canada-as-North and about mapping Canada. We will not *get it* if we cannot read maps. By using this knowledge and fragments of the *real* maps of this country, the image forces us to begin rethinking what is elided by or contained in the map, not under it or beyond it but *with/in* it. This image, like van Herk's text, dialogizes Canada and North and turns each (as much as any two-dimensional document can) into a process. Working within the conventions of that Cartesian Mercator mind-set of which Rundstrom speaks, the image jump-starts a dialogue with those conventions, forcing us to react, to disagree, dismiss, inquire further, to open the book (is this a historical atlas of Canada? an explorer's map of the Arctic?). The image radically decentres Canadian geography by insisting that Ellesmere is not up there but right here (with Calgary in the lower right corner), that North *is* what we imagine, what we desire it to be, a place that we fashion in our image.

My next four examples are not so much subversive maps as re-mappings; they do not destabilize or parody so much as inscribe new information and, in the process, *replace* and supplement received cartographic information. They return us directly to the real world of socio-economic and political lived experience. Coates and Powell's "Northwest Territories" (Illus. 14), which appears at the beginning of *The Modern North: People, Politics and the Rejection of Colonialism*, appears to be quite straightforward. It has familiar co-ordinates, scale, and toponyms. But there are some subtle differences here from what we have come to expect from maps in social scientific books like this one as it describes itself. To begin with, the NWT fills the frame. Canada is not named, except in small print, to mark the Canada/USA border, which, according to the authors, runs through the Beaufort Sea along the 141st meridian to the Pole (a point not accepted by the United States in 1989). Alaska, the Yukon, and the southern provinces, all of which we are accustomed to seeing on maps of the country, simply do not appear. Moreover the print, or typeface, for names, while following rules of scale, seems informal – like a hand-painted script – and suggests an intimate, personal knowledge that qualifies, if only slightly, the abstract objectivity of many toponymic maps in scholarly texts. Finally, it is a *busy* map; its area is full of places, topographical markers, rivers, and dizzying shorelines. This North is *home* to a whole complex of signs that carry every bit as much positional importance as Vancouver, Edmonton, Toronto, Montreal, or Ottawa. What the map visualizes for us is a decolonized North, one that is self-determined, seen in terms of itself instead of as a decentred hinterland extension of Canada.

Maps incorporated into advertisements in *Up Here: Exploring the North* for the hotel chain Inns North execute a similar centralizing, self-determining performance, except that the commercial intention demands that such maps show how the NWT relates to a larger scene. In these cartographic ads much of the rest of Canada (Yukon and parts of six provinces) is shown. However, the places named are nicely selected invitations to the tourist, and as text sidebar tells us, there are nineteen Inns North to serve us when we travel the North. The map, in fact, is only one element in a complex marketing semiotics that includes text, numbers, and colour (in one example we see red triangles and black letters on a white ground shading to deep turquoise, with the trademark name in turquoise and dark blue). This occupied North, we are told, is dedicated to excellence and is easy to reach. *Up Here* is a glossy, beautifully illustrated, and very informative magazine published in Yellowknife. Advertisements, like those for Inns North, contribute not only to the financing of the magazine and the economy of the region but also to the celebration of the physical beauty, cultural diversity and richness, and to the entrepreneurial independence of the North.

My next map (Illus. 15) opens on to an/other world. Drawn in 1866 by Ar-mou, an Inuk from the area near Southampton Island to the northwest of Hudson Bay, it shows, as David Woodman tells us, "Inuit familiarity with the coast from Churchill to Ponds Bay" (*Strangers among Us*, 100). As a map it shows the relative area and importance of the mid-nineteenth-century Iguligmiut world, as well as Ar-mou's cartographical knowledge and skill. As Rundstrom reminds us (see also Sparke), a map such as this is part of a particular culture, an Inuit culture that knew its world exceptionally well. The dialogue and dynamic (Rundstrom, 6), or what I prefer to call the dialogics of this map, arise from and are made accessible first by the imposition on it of English toponyms, but second and more importantly by its reaccentuation and replication within Woodman's 1995 text, where it is an example of the kind of indigenous information so often spurned by Europeans and southerners who came North to find some trace of the missing Franklin.[2]

My last map is a "memory map," and it forms one segment in one of eighteen five-part assemblages in the Land Art installation/exhibition *The Distance between Two Points Is Measured in Memories, Labrador 1988* by Marlene Creates.[3] Each assemblage (see Illus. 7) consists of a black and white photograph of a Labrador inhabitant (Inuk, Naskapi Inu, or Euro-Canadian settler), hung beside his/her memory map, a brief typed text describing the significance of the remembered place, and a black and white photograph of the place and surrounding landscape. On the gallery floor in front of the assemblage lies a piece of the land (sod, wood, rock) from that place. Very clearly, Creates has intervened in these landscapes and places; just reproducing them for gallery display indicates a range of arbitrary choices and an overall control over image exercised by the artist and, finally, by the exhibition space. What is at once extremely personal, intimate, embodied, and situated is presented for public view in an urban, environmentally controlled, artificial setting; pieces, literally, of the North have been brought south.

The risk is great. Are these displayed images appropriations? Are they mechanistic reifications? Are they voyeuristic? Are these subjects, people and places, displaced, made into mere objects of a curious southern gaze? I think not. The biggest risk is the one faced by the southern viewer, because these assemblages use several instances of familiar technology from photographic reproduction, typewriter print, and hand-drawn map to remind us of human agency and the human construction of memory and place. Creates calls the entire series a memory map, referring not only to the map segment itself but to the total assemblage as a series of assemblages. What she reminds us of thereby is the profound degree to which mapping is not a scientific, objectifiably accurate abstraction separate from the person (and the technology) who makes it. Maps chart the experiential interrelation of the self with its cultural context and its physical world. These memory maps remind us that we are all map-makers and that we map what matters most to us. They are, I would argue, precisely the kind of "process cartography" and "autobiographical ethnography" (3) for which Rundstrom calls. They do not subvert or parody or, perhaps, even re-map. They remind us of where maps come from and that they are made. Such maps can be made anywhere, but that these are maps of the North is just one more eloquent reminder that the North is a part of those who live there.

RE-VIEWING THE KLONDIKE

When Robert Service announced that "there are strange things done in the midnight sun / By the men who moil for gold" (*Songs of a Sourdough*, 57), he could not have imagined what he was starting. A later Robert, Robert Kroetsch, blames (or praises?) Service for sending him north: "I have a suspicion," Kroetsch tells us, that "it was that one verb, *moil*, that tricked me into wanting to write and into beginning to write by going North. I should have checked a dictionary instead of applying for a job; to moil: to work hard, to toil, to slave" (*A Likely Story*, 14). But it was not just Kroetsch who was influenced, *lured*, one is tempted to say, by Service's mystique of the Yukon and the Gold Rush of 1896–98. Service has been and continues to be one of the most widely read and translated of writers; his *Songs of the Sourdough*, first published in 1907, has never been out of print. It exists today in a fine edition illustrated by Yukon artist Ted Harrison, and open-air readings of Service's poems are a major tourist attraction in Dawson City. He is celebrated in Scotland, where he was born, and quoted by generations of Canadians, including Margaret Atwood.[4]

When we imagine the Yukon today or read almost any of the dozens of books about the Gold Rush, we are seeing images and reading a story profoundly influenced by Service, and this is the image of the Yukon that many Yukoners continue to celebrate to the exclusion of all others, and thus to the exclusion of a more complex, conflicted construction of Yukon history. To be sure, Service is not single-handedly responsible for this discursive formation of the Yukon, but his version fitted a need in 1907 and it has become gospel. For Service the North *is* the Yukon of the Gold Rush years, an imagined territory for determined and desperate men who pit themselves against a demonic, female landscape whose law is to drive mad, drown, or otherwise destroy all but the strongest and fittest men:

> This is the Law of the Yukon, that only the
>> Strong shall thrive;
> That surely the Weak shall perish, and only the
>> Fit survive.
> Dissolute, damned and despairful, crippled and
>> palsied and slain,
> This is the Will of the Yukon, – Lo! how she
>> makes it plain!   ("The Law of the Yukon," 18)

Her preferred sons were, not surprisingly, "Sired of a bulldog parent," "with the hearts of Vikings," and the power to fight, win, and dominate her by "Ripping the guts of my mountains, looting the beds of my creeks" (16). Service's monstrous female Yukon waits to be ravaged by R.G. Haliburton's "Men of the North."

Service's Yukon is also an almost exclusively male world, a female landscape of dangerous allure, staggering beauty, and maddening deceit made for miners like Sam McGee, sourdoughs, and "the Arctic brotherhood" ("The Parson's Son," 19), a place where men go to be alone, to seek adventure, to answer "The Call of the Wild" (27), and to fall under "The spell of the Yukon" (23). Service's Yukon does not include Indians at all, and the women who inhabit it bear small relation to the actual women of the Klondike like Kate Carmack, Emilie Tremblay, or Martha Black, let alone the larger Yukon (see Den Ouden).

Until very recently, however, the only women to figure on the discursive stages of the Klondike were prostitutes, can-can dancers, and seductive, unscrupulous females like "the lady that's known as Lou," who will betray a man to his death and pinch his poke into the bargain ("The Shooting of Dan McGrew," 56). These are the entertainers and "camp-followers" who are there "to mine the miners," as the common locution still has it. We now know, of course, that non-native women made up only 12 per cent of the population at the height of the Gold Rush, that prostitutes were a minority, and that can-can dancers were never part of Dawson City life.[5] Moreover, Dawson City quickly attracted women from all walks of life, from intrepid miners and businesswomen to loyal wives, dedicated teachers, and nurses (see Backhouse). And yet the myth of a violent, licentious Gold Rush frontier represented by Diamond Tooth Gertie and a miner panning for gold continue to dominate the popular image, not only of the Klondike but of the entire Yukon. This is precisely the point of Jacques Languirand's play-cum-musical *Klondyke* (1971), where the space of the Klondike and the events of the Gold Rush are staged as male dionysiac disruption of established, female social order. The Klondike, says Languirand, was a collective adventure in which "le Clan des males domine" (228).[6]

The other dominant narrative construction of the Yukon, however, cannot be attributed to Robert Service and is much more narrowly confined to the discursive formation of the Klondike. This is the story of discovery – the discovery of gold – and it is a story, among other things, of an American invasion of the Canadian North that stripped the creeks of much of their gold, that carried the wealth out of the country, and, in at least one major competing narrative – that of Canadian prospector Robert Henderson – brushed aside the history-making discovery claim of Canada. It is a story, not unlike that of American filmmaker Robert Flaherty and *Nanook of the North*, where Canada is conflated with the United States, which then exploits and controls, whether in actual or discursive mining, both the wealth and the narrative of the North: in the case of Flaherty it is Ungava; in the case of George Carmack, the Klondike.

However, in what follows I want to offer an alternative reading of the discovery of gold in the Klondike and of women's and native participation in the story of the Yukon. It is a reading, a retelling, that tries to displace some of the most familiar statements in the discursive formation of North by re-placing the story in a Canadian context as one of the most significant events in our history. I offer it as an addition to the ongoing retellings of the Gold Rush already begun by Ann Brennan, among others, in her recuperative history of the Canadian Katherine Ryan in *The Real Klondike Kate*.[7] In focusing upon Kate Carmack, who is like Katherine Ryan in so far as she has largely been erased from Yukon history and the story of the Klondike, I am reintroducing her into the discourse, and thereby disrupting the formation itself by modifying the familiar statements about discovery, gold, and white masculine adventure in Service's land of the midnight sun.

Patricia Yaeger begins her afterword to *Feminism, Bakhtin, and the Dialogic* with the startling claim that "it's sexy these days to talk about silence" (239). What she has in mind, and is both critical and sceptical of, are poststructuralism's "lacunae, the rupture, the *mise en abyme* ... the *aporia*, the *differand*, the unknowable," which she characterizes as the "phantasms," "negativities," and "slim deliriums [that] have become our textual goddesses, our political deities" (239). Although Yaeger is suspicious of this poststructuralist obsession with silence, she none the less goes on to make a strong case for the critical and theoretical need to understand silence and silencing, and her method of choice is Bakhtinian dialogics because dialogics permits a move from theory to practice, from method to socio-political goal. "The business of the dialogic imagination," she insists, "is to elicit these forbidden [or silenced, negated] vocalities and show them at work" (240).

Now I could not agree more with Patricia Yaeger, both in her suspicion of sexy silences and in her call for a dialogic elicitation of hitherto repressed/silenced voices. However, the case of "Kate Carmack" is a difficult one. Not only does her voice *appear* to have vanished, but she has been almost entirely excluded from the written, published record of the Yukon Gold Rush and the *discovery* of gold on the Klondike. Even in the accessible oral accounts by native elders, accounts in which she has an important place, *her* voice is missing. There are many reasons for this silencing, of course, and if I stress *appear* and *missing*, it is because I believe it is possible to locate traces of her voice: for example, I have been told that there are some written documents in her hand but that these are not yet available to researchers; and there are a few newspaper quotations. However, it now seems certain that all references to Kate in George Carmack's diaries and papers were excised by his second wife Marguerite, and when Kate died in 1920, in poverty and obscurity, she had had neither the opportunity nor the means to record her story.[8]

Nevertheless, no one doubts that she had a voice, a presence, a position. Moreover, I think it important that the effort to recover and listen be made. What we have to work from, to *listen to*, are the stories of others with whom she spoke, like family members in Carcross and the occasional reporter who purports to quote her. We have photographs that tell an eloquent story, and we have many accounts of the Klondike Gold Rush that can be sifted for clues. In other words, Kate has not vanished without a trace, and if she is missing, lost, then surely she can be found, or more can be found out about her if we look for her in her historical and discursive context. So I must begin with questions in a kind of archeology and genealogy of the discursive formation of "the Klondike," which itself is part of the discursive formation of North. Who was Kate Carmack? What is her story? Why is it so hard to find her and her story? What other stories block access to hers? Where must I go to "elicit" her "forbidden" vocality? "Where," as Rudy Wiebe once asked, "is the voice coming from?" The answers, when they come, will be inextricable parts of a dialogue and must be listened to dialogically.

These questions, like the dialogue in which they are embedded, involve a complex network of assumptions about identity, which means, of course, that these questions are as much about race, gender, class, culture, and discursive and social power as they are about a real woman who came to be called Kate Carmack. So where to begin? Here are the available facts.[9] Kate Carmack was born Shaaw Tláa, one of eight children (six of them girls) in a Tagish/Tlingit family living near contemporary Carcross in southern Yukon sometime during the late 1850s or early 1860s (Cruikshank, *Reading Voices*, 129–30). After several deaths from influenza had struck her family, including her Tlingit husband and first child, she returned to her mother and married a white man (the widower of her sister), George Washington Carmack (1860–1922). Carmack, an American prospector (although there is some debate about how serious or skilled a prospector he was), was a friend of her brother Keish, known as Skookum Jim, and it was George who named her Kate, and thus Kate Carmack. By the mid-nineties, Kate and George had left Carcross to try their luck prospecting downriver in the vicinity of the Klondike, where Kate gave birth to her daughter Ahgay (renamed Graphie Grace by George) on 11 January 1893 (Shiell, 61). During these years, it is agreed, George lived an Indian lifestyle and was frequently called a "squaw man" – a term of racist opprobium, with negative overtones for gender and class.

At this point Kate's story becomes tangled in stories about the discovery of gold on Bonanza Creek, which led to one of the greatest gold rushes of all time and was certainly, as William Wonders makes clear, one of the two most important nineteenth-century events in the development of the Canadian Northwest. The facts that are agreed on, in both the written and oral record, are that in August 1896 an experienced Nova Scotian prospector, Robert Henderson, met Carmack, who was fishing with his Indian family (Jim and Dawson Charlie), and advised him to try his luck in the area of Rabbit Creek, but also insulted the Indians who were with Carmack. Thus, when Carmack's party found gold, they did not tell Henderson, but the assault on the Klondike had begun. Carmack always claimed that he himself had found the first gold on Rabbit Creek on 17 August 1896, but the actual discovery was disputed by Skookum Jim, who insisted that he had found the first nuggets. Whatever happened, Carmack staked the discoverers' double claim, with single claims for Jim and Charlie, and renamed the creek Bonanza. Kate is not mentioned as a discoverer, or even as being present, by either Carmack or her Tagish menfolk. Indeed, she is rarely mentioned at all in written accounts, and then only in passing, until 1989, when the role of women in the Klondike began to receive more attention.

By 1900, after the Carmacks and their co-discoverers (Jim and Charlie) had made small fortunes and gone south to Seattle to spend and, on George's part at least, to invest, the marriages and lives of all were in trouble. The Seattle newspapers published sensational stories of alleged wild, drunken brawls involving Kate and her relatives, and George was preparing to abandon Kate and marry a white American woman, Marguerite Laimee. In 1901 Kate returned, with Graphie, to Carcross to live, with no financial support from Carmack, until her death from influenza in 1920. Moreover, she lost Graphie, who joined her father in Seattle in 1909 and never saw her mother again. This removal of their daughter from her Indian mother and native roots was something Carmack had wanted from the first breakdown of his marriage with Kate – a marriage he denied had ever existed – and it has been called a kidnapping (Cruikshank, *Reading Voices*, 133). For any mother this separation and loss would be a terrible blow, but the race, class, and matrilineal cultural context for this loss made Kate's experience extreme.[10] No longer a "squaw man," George Carmack had returned to his American family with *his* child, and resumed his American roots and identity. In short, during the years immediately before and after the 1904 La Scala première of Puccini's great opera *Madama Butterfly*, the story of Cio Cio San and Benjamin Franklin Pinkerton was re-enacted in the life on a Yukon stage, with Shaaw Tláa and George Washington Carmack in the leading roles.[11]

Some of the silences, or gaps in the narrative, to which I have alluded can now begin to be named. First, there is the racism itself. Surprisingly few accounts of the Klondike recognize the racist assumptions underlying this story. For example, Henderson's remarks about Jim and Charlie are often glossed over as unfortunate, or are simply ignored (see Adney, 282–3, Gates, 136, Hamilton, 67), and

Pierre Berton indianizes George Carmack in his comparison of Carmack with Henderson, claiming that Carmack "wanted to be an Indian" (*Klondike*, 41), while at the same time orientalizing Jim as a handsome, good Indian who wished to be a white man (428).[12] Berton goes on to note that Carmack, for whom he has a clear distaste, quickly dropped his Indian identity when he struck it rich and no longer needed his native family: "In that instant of discovery something fundamental had happened to Siwash George: suddenly he had ceased to be an Indian. And he never thought of himself as an Indian again" (47). Berton only mentions Kate as Carmack's "silent, plump" black-haired wife (43).

Which raises the problem of gender and the profound sexism of almost all accounts of the Klondike. There are two interrelated problems here. One is the more general issue of gender. The story of the Klondike has always been a male adventure story of epic proportions, and the heroes of such a story must be men – *real* men. They are Parsifals seeking the Holy Grail, or Odysseuses seeking adventure, overcoming terrible obstacles, and returning – the return is essential! – to tell their tale, or Don Quixotes tilting at windmills in their blind fever for gold (in which case their tale has a somewhat different moral, as in Service's "The Cremation of Sam McGee"). Or they are adventurers in search of King Solomon's mines, clutching their maps of Sheba's breasts and obsessed with the desire to ravish the land for its hidden treasure. That the land is constructed as a female hoarding her treasure by male writers from Service to Carmack himself should come as no surprise; as Anne McClintock reminds us, speaking of Ryder Haggard's immensely popular novel *King Solomon's Mines* (1885), narratives of exploration and adventure inscribe "a long tradition of [white, European] male travel as an erotics of ravishment" (22).[13] Relatively few women went to the Klondike, and those who did, with the exception of Martha Black, have been systematically ignored, until very recently that is (see Backhouse, Brennan, Cruikshank, Kelcey, Mayer, Shiell, and Wheelock). According to the conventions of adventure or quest narratives, women figure only as the space to pass through or the place to which a man returns, as to Penelope, with his real or narrative gold.

More than one hundred years after the Klondike, women are still denied membership in the Yukon Order of Pioneers, and this fact points to the related issue of sexism within a patriarchal society. By moving from gender to explicit sexism, I wish to shift ground considerably, from the culturally legitimated constructions of gender identity as feminine and masculine that are elaborated in narratives such as those of adventure in the wilds, prospecting in difficult circumstances, which entails great physical strength and endurance, and even the writing of autobiographies, to actual living conditions, laws regarding citizenship, ownership of property (including children), and marriage, to freedom of movement and the availability and recognition of productive labour. Although I cannot go into any of these categories in detail, I can extrapolate from the many written accounts, narratives, and histories to suggest that the Klondike was anything but a congenial place for women. They have been written out of the histories not because they were not there at all but because they were largely discounted as citizens (Canadian women could not vote in the Yukon until 1918, and were not legally "persons" until 1929) and workers, even by those men who benefited from their practical skills and constant labour. The real work and glory of the Klondike were preserved for white men, and women, native or white, played no acknowledged part; it was enough if they did the laundry, cooked in tents, sewed mittens, hunted and trapped, and so on, to keep the miners well supplied or to bring in cash. They were expected to remain silent in the background, if they were there at all.

The women who were always already there, of course, were native women like Kate, and marriage "à la façon du pays" was common. As both Sylvia Van Kirk and Jennifer Brown make clear in their discussions of the fur trade, the "manner of the country" included serious personal, social, and economic relationships and commitments for both the white husbands and their Indian wives; native peoples did not consider these marriages to be casual liaisons. Initially, at least, fur trade marriages were honoured by the men and by the courts, but both Van Kirk and Brown agree that, by the mid-nineteenth century, attitudes were changing: overt racism combined with the sexist attitudes of a Victorian patriarchal society led to increased abandonment of native or mixed-blood wives, to an anxiety that daughters especially be removed from Indian influence, and to the treatment of Indian women as playthings and prostitutes whose racial origins were given as the basis of *their* sexual licentiousness.[14]

In his recent discussion of the Gold Rush, *Gold at Fortymile Creek*, Michael Gates confirms that, because white women were scarce, "miners married Native women or, more frequently, entered into less formal, short-lived liaisons with them" (86). What he does not consider is the impact on these women, their cultural traditions, their agency, and their work – except to note that these women were "of considerable advantage to the early miners because of their familiarity with the country and their ability to look after themselves" (86). Gates goes on to claim that, when white women did appear on the scene, "*social pressures* ... created a distance between white women and Native women, placing the latter much lower on the social ladder" (87, emphasis added). The question left unasked here is: what social pressures? The answer is that, where an intensely sexist patriarchal social order exists under acute stress (financial, psychological, and moral for the white miners, legal and political for official elites), fears about success, authority, and degeneration, what Anne McClintock describes as "racial contamination [that threatens] white male control of progeny, property and power" (47), are bound to determine attitudes and behaviour. White men and women were no more free of these attitudes in the Yukon than elsewhere (perhaps less so), and a woman like Kate was swept up and aside by this foreign culture.

It is well to remember that the late nineteenth century was not only the period of Victorianism and British imperialism; it was also characterized by Social Darwinist theories of survival of the fittest and, in Canada, deeply engrained ideas about the North as a place of purification and white supremacy. Racism cannot be separated from sexism in our consideration of the Klondike, because they operate together to reinforce prejudice and oppression. Although issues of class are rarely considered directly in accounts of the Gold Rush, class is also an integral part, with race and gender, of the "social pressures" Gates refers to. Thus, to be a "squaw man" is to be seen as lowering oneself, as behaving in an uncivilized manner, because to the Victorian mind, as Kipling's familiar formulation has it, non-whites are "lesser breeds without the Law" (219). The lowering and "racial contamination" come from consorting with Indians, more importantly from marrying one, who can never hope for acceptance into civilized, white, middle-class society.

The silences surrounding and erasing Kate Carmack's and Shaaw Tláa's voice are, then, silences about race, gender, and class, and the complex ways in which they work systemically within the historical and discursive context of the Klondike to obliterate most Indians and certainly any female ones. George Carmack was a product of his time; he used his Indian family when he needed them and discarded them when they got in his way. There is no evidence in the record that he understood the social pressures experienced by Kate (or Jim and Charlie) when she was abruptly transplanted to Seattle or California. And his concern for Graphie, whatever understandable parental feelings we allow him, was predictable. He wanted her to be *his* daughter, a white girl who, as he instructed his sister Rose, must always "look nice and clean" and "never ... go out with soiled clothes" (quoted in Johnson, 121).[15] As McClintock reminds us, for late Victorian patriarchal culture "métissage ... generally and concubinage in particular, represented the paramount danger to racial purity and cultural identity *in all its forms*" (48, emphasis added).

But what about Kate? Between Tappan Adney's 1900 *Klondike Stampede* (reprinted in 1994) or Marguerite Carmack's 1933 publication of her husband's *Experiences in the Klondike* and Mary Shiell's 1996 article "Rediscovering Kate Carmack, True Queen of the Klondike" lie sixty-three years of legend, excision, contradiction, and exaggeration. And yet the discursive formation of the Klondike contains statements repeated and duplicated across genres, media, languages, and cultures that allow other voices to be introduced into the narrative, that open a gap for the emergence of other perspectives and expose the monologism of the dominant version of events.

If the dominant story gives us a faint image of Kate as a "silent, plump" temperamental woman (and James Johnson's construction of her in his 1990 *Carmack of the Klondike* is certainly negative), the muted story is quite different.[16] Native elders tell us about a woman who was a dutiful daughter, living in the traditional way of her people, when she met Carmack. She was also a great asset to any husband because she was skilled. In the words of Mrs Kitty Smith:

He's got wife.
He's all right!
She does everything, that Indian woman, you know –

hunts, just like nothing,
sets snares for rabbits.
That's what they eat.
I know her: that's my auntie Kate Carmack.
(quoted in Cruikshank, *Reading Voices*, 133)

Some newspaper articles and oral accounts suggest that it was Kate, not George or Jim, who actually found the first gold nuggets in Rabbit Creek on 17 August 1896 (see Little and Shiell). And a few, supposedly accurate quotations of Kate's remarks appear in newspapers. For example, in the *Klondike Nugget* for 10 November 1900 she is quoted as saying: "Yellow hair she come to town. Tagish Kate she no good after that" (quoted in Wheelock, 12). However, as Angela Wheelock rightly points out, the *Klondike Nugget* presented biased and inaccurate accounts of the Carmack "divorce" that should not be taken at face value. Certainly the pictures painted of Kate by the Seattle newspapers are sensational and appallingly racist and sexist, so it is difficult to believe that she could get an objective hearing from journalists.[17] If her fragment of reported speech is accurate, it speaks eloquently of Kate's awareness that she had been cast aside as inferior, not just by comparison with another woman but with a *white* woman.

Photographs of Kate Carmack tell yet another story, a silent speaking story to which I would now like to turn. According to Johnson, the family portrait photograph (see Illus. 17) was taken in the spring of 1898 during their first visit to California. It is a conventional studio image of a late-nineteenth-century middle-class family. Everyone is serious, especially the shy little girl. George looks every inch the confident Victorian paterfamilias, his gold-tipped cane the sign of his authority and prosperity (as is the professional photograph itself, of course). Kate is, for me, the most interesting and expressive presence. Hers is a handsome, strong, intelligent face, the slight smile complimenting the direct, intense eyes. Both her central, elevated position, standing behind George and Graphie, and her apparent tension – is she not leaning forward towards the camera? – impart a certain force or energy to her person, a keenness to her gaze. Around her neck hangs the famous gold nugget necklace given to her by George as the sign of his wealth and her decorative function. But the gold is ironic: it is the central sign of what brings this group together in the photography studio, and as such it points beyond the group to the economic basis of the family and the state. It also operates as a key symbol, a metaphor, if you will, for the decorative value of a necklace and a wife, in this case a necklace made of nuggets found in Canada's North and worn by the woman who, as Indian and female, represents the fruitful territory that Service describes, in "The Law of the Yukon," as waiting "for the men who will win [her]" (17). Another aspect of its symbolic value, however, lies in its metonymic status as a part of Carmack's treasure. Where the semiotics of the necklace as sign point beyond the image to the economic power relations (of race, gender, class, *and nation*) informing and sustaining the image, the semiotics of its symbolism return us to

Illus. 17. These studio photographs of George and Kate Carmack with their daughter Graphie Grace and of Kate alone were probably taken c 1898. Clearly visible in both pictures are Kate's famous gold nugget necklace and rings (including a wedding band). Reproduced with permission of the Yukon Archives, from the A.C. Johnson Collection (82/341 #22 and 82/341 f.2 #21).

George Washington Carmack, so-called Discoverer of the Klondike, owner of the gold, the woman, and the child.

In the companion photograph (see Illus. 17), Kate appears alone, seated in a more relaxed pose, but unsmiling. This photograph must have been taken on the same day as the family portrait: her dress is identical and so are the props – the flowers and the bench on which Graphie sits and Kate leans in the group portrait. The dress itself appears to be made of black silk or taffeta, with the raised puff sleeves, pleated bodice, and standing collar typical of ladies' quality formal day dresses in the 1890s.[18] This, together with the necklace and what looks like a gold buckle, bracelets, and rings, confirms Kate's position as the wife of a very well-to-do man. The dress, jewellery, and hair-do further proclaim this woman to be a middle-class American wife. And yet this woman is not what, at first glance, she appears to be: her non-Caucasian racial identity is clear in her face, and her prominent hands are not those of a lady unaccustomed to work. Shaaw Tláa is visible in this photograph of Kate. What is equally visible, I would argue, is an Indian woman trying to pass for a white woman, cross-dressing as an American wife, transvesting as Mrs George Washington Carmack. Why would she do this? Why should she want to, and what choice did she have? What are her chances of success?

To make a start at answering these questions – since I cannot ask them of Shaaw Tláa or Kate but only of her cross-dressed simulacrum – I need to make a distinction between current theoretical categories of mimicry and masquerade.[19] Diana Fuss is helpful here because, like Anne McClintock (64–9), she sees mimcry as a social practice that is potentially subversive but also subjugative and thus difficult to use in a progressive politics (24–5). Mimicry, in short, is an unstable, uncontrollable practice; it can backfire on the mimic to betray him or her. Both Fuss and McClintock agree with Bhabha in identifying mimicry as fundamental to the "cultural hybridity" (McClintock, 69) experienced by colonizers and colonized in the power politics of imperialism. Clothes, gold, and formal photographs, like maps, mining claims, and court documents, are instruments of social power; they contribute to and participate in the construction and legitimation of identity – for individuals, families, and nation-states. If you were not white, male, and American in the Klondike, you would have had difficulty asserting your identity or your claims. If you were Indian, female, and "Canadian" (a problematic designation for a Yukon First Nations person), you simply did not exist. In order to find or occupy a place in this imperialist American narrative, you would have to practise the mimicry of "racial transvestism" (McClintock, 69, 202), which is what Kate tried to do. Through her hairstyle, clothes, jewellery, and "marriage," she tried to go white. However, no one in Seattle, California, or in Dawson City, I suspect, would go along with her act. No one, least of all George, who must have expected this mimicry from her – why else take her south in the first place? – would accept or validate her assumed identity. They knew she was *almost the same but not white*

(Bhabha, "Mimicry," 89). Certainly, they could not tolerate or even understand her Tagish self. The case of Kate Carmack was that of the "colonial other" trapped "between difference and similitude, at the vanishing point of subjectivity" (Fuss, 23). She was, moreover, quadruply colonized and othered – as woman, as Indian, as lower class (or beyond class, a lesser breed "without the Law"), and as living in the Canadian North.

The case was never the same, or even parallel, for George. As we have seen, he was called a "squaw man" during his life and after. He had twice married Tagish women, had lived like an Indian with his Tagish family and, for a time at least, shared their home and cultural values, and learned something of their language. Although he never went as far as Archie Belaney by becoming a Yukon Grey Owl, for a time he masqueraded as an Indian. And this is where the necessary distinction with mimicry must be made. There was no serious risk involved in George's racial masquerade; he could and did use his disguise only to discard it, if not, as Berton claims, in that moment of discovery, at least by 1898, when he went home to the States, returning easily, and as a celebrated success, to a white, male, American, middle-class identity that was now reinforced by his wealth, luck, and individual prowess (at least as he told it) in the hard game of prospecting. It was to his benefit to play the role of an Indian in the full knowledge that, when the time came, he could return to being white; he could, in short, perform the role, take off his mask, abrogate the social and familial codes of Tagish culture – even deny any knowledge of them – and continue his *chosen* life as a wealthy, famous American. He could even succeed in claiming the child as *only* his and, thus, as white.

Kate Carmack/Shaaw Tláa had none of this power or choice. Either she must become what she was not allowed to be by mimicking it to the life, or she must be discarded and denied. Where George could transcend his former obscure class, Kate could not do so because her race and gender bound her, within a racist, sexist structure, to what Euro-Americans defined as her class, which was in turn inextricable from her race and gender. She had no choice but to return, penniless, to Carcross, to lose her daughter, and to die, finally, of a white man's disease. Despite this lack of choice, she continued to call herself and to be called Kate Carmack.

In another well-known photograph taken a year before her death, she appears as a very poor, old, heavy woman (see Illus. 18). Her face is in shadow, but she is smiling for the camera with a quiet dignity. To compare this photograph with the 1898 one of the Carmack family or of Kate herself (see Illus. 17) is to be reminded not only of the passage of time but of the categories of race, gender, and class that defined Kate Carmack, silenced her, and kept her in her place. There is small doubt here about the image, and no sign of mimcry: this is Shaaw Tláa, an aging Indian woman, who is poor and alone. This photograph, when reproduced by Johnson (132), is accompanied by a photograph of her dilapidated cabin (135) and by Johnson's commentary; he tells us that she lived "a lonely and embittered

Illus. 18. In this 1920 photograph Shaaw Tláa (formerly Kate Carmack) stands outside her home in Carcross, Yukon. The caption written across the bottom of the image reads: "Kate Cormack. The Discoverer of [the Klondike]." Kate frequently claimed that she, not George, was the real discoverer of gold in Rabbit Creek. Reproduced with permission of the Yukon Archives, from the Bill Becht Jr. Collection (88/140 #2).

life ... in a cluttered cabin," told tourists that she, not George, discovered Bonanza, and that drink ruined her looks (135). This picture, however, juxtaposed with the 1898 ones and seen in context with the mores and events of the day, tells another story, one, I believe, that captures something of Kate's own voice.

Like Madama Butterfly, that other exotic, eroticized female who fascinated the late-nineteenth-century masculine imagination, Kate Carmack was *married for convenience* and discarded for a real American wife. To George Washington Carmack belong Benjamin Franklin Pinkerton's words:

> E al giorno in cui mi sposerò
> con vere nozze a *una vera sposa*
>   *americana!*[20]

Like Butterfly, Kate tried to go white and American through a mimicry of dress, class, customs, and naming that could not, in the last analysis, transform her. Like Butterfly, she was robbed of her only child in a move that signified the ultimate power-play in a politics of gender, race, class, and cultural identity. When she died, not by her own hand, it is true, but from complications arising from influenza, as Shaaw Tláa, she could have said, with Cio Cio San: "Si voglion prendermi tutto!" ("They want to take everything from me!") By *translating* Kate *through* Butterfly, Shaaw Tláa through Cio Cio San, and the unknown story through the well-known one, by contextualizing her story in its time and place through categories of race, gender, and, to a degree, class, and by listening to the evidence of the loud dominant discourse side by side with the muted discourse that cannot speak, I have tried to give Shaaw Tláa /Kate Carmack, not a voice, perhaps, but a position from which to speak in a dialogue that *includes* her, that reintroduces her as an individual woman and as a representative of a group, as well as a Foucaultian statement in the discursive formation of North.

On one level, that of the interplay of socio-historical forces of imperialism and colonialism, which are imbricated with oppressive practices of race, gender, and class, her story is anything but singular. It is in fact emblematic of the othering that Todorov describes in *The Conquest of America*. Like the story of the Mayan woman to whom he dedicated his book, Kate's "story, reduced to a few lines, concentrates one of the extreme versions of the relation to the other" (246). Rather than retell it as tragedy, however, by making Kate into a Butterfly, I have chosen a contextualizing, dialogic repositioning of her and her story. This dialogue could be greatly expanded to include Stefansson's Fanny, Flaherty's Alice, Hood's Green Stockings, and many more.[21] In her poem "Susanne's Lament" from *Squaring the Round*, Margaret Thompson approaches the dialogue from a different angle. She goes so far as to create a voice for the discarded Cree wife of HBC Chief Factor William Connolly and to interpolate that voice into the story of Fort St James and the history of the Hudson's Bay Company. Thus, it is

"Susanne's" voice that confronts the reader – the white twentieth-century reader – with profound questions:

> What am I?
> Wife, but no wife,
> Singled out from my Cree sisters –
> Such a favour –
> To be what?
> A familiar talisman
> To hold the crowding spruce at bay,
> To fill the empty air with sound,
> To blot out the grim water
> And endless iron hills;
> A coverlet,
> To comfort and swaddle,
> To blunt the cruel edge of winter air
> Through parchment windows;
> A coarse earthen vessel
> For borrowed passion;
> Nursemaid,
> Skivvy,
> Easy to kick aside as a cold hot water bottle.
> Did I not merit constancy?
> But he waved his hand
> And flew like a wintering bird
> [...]
> And what do I feel?
> Who enquires about the feelings
> Of a discarded boot?
> It has served its purpose,
> And so have I.   (18–19)[22]

IN THE MIND'S EYE

At the beginning of this exploration of Canada and the idea of North we visited the Art Gallery of Hamilton to see Blair Bruce's famous painting *The Phantom Hunter* (Plate 2), and it is time to revisit the painting. It is also time to revisit Charles Shanly's "The Walker of the Snow," the poem that inspired Bruce and that would have a continuing effect on the Canadian imagination through Bruce's painting, and in its own right. The northern world of Shanly's poem and Bruce's painting is the world of legend, myth, and imagination, a world of spine-tingling mystery, of the uncanny, and of ghosts. It is a world seen in the mind's eye, and it proves Earle Birney quite wrong when he proclaimed that Canada is haunted by its "lack of ghosts" (*Ghost in the Wheels*, 49).[23]

Of course, the mind's eye that the poet and painter use is akin to the eye of the cartographer, photographer, and historian. The very metaphor inscribes that Cartesian split of mind and object, self and other, that is, as Timothy Mitchell reminds us, inseparable from a representation of reality that turns the world into an exhibition and the objects of that world into exhibits (295–7). Such an objectification of people and place constitutes an act of appropriation that seeks to control, order, and exploit the people and places thus objectified in the best interests of the dominant subject group or, to return to my metaphor, the dominant eye. According to Said (upon whom Mitchell draws) and Todorov, this process of objectification and appropriation is at the root of imperialist aggression and its manifestation in what Said calls "orientalism." It is perhaps easy to argue that maps abstract, objectify, and order reality, and not much more difficult to see the construction of the Klondike as a story of white, male, American discovery and adventure that erases other presences/stories, but in the exploration of poetry and painting that follows I will suggest that these aesthetic texts display the same hegemonic power, something literature and art specialists have not always been willing to allow. Shanly's "Walker" and Bruce's "Phantom" represent the North by visualizing it *in certain ways* and not in others. What those ways are and how they function are the questions I want to address through an examination of the comparative semiotics of each text, a semiotics that will finally return us to representation and social reality.

First a brief comment on the semiotic approach I will take and why I find such an approach useful. As the material considered thus far amply demonstrates, North is a complex construction. It comprises many ideas of North and many norths. North is, in short, a discursive formation existing in and changing over time. In many ways North resembles Said's Orient in that it inscribes and embodies an exhibition of a world (and here I mean a national and geographic area, although there have been historical instances of northern peoples, especially Inuit, brought south for display in so-called natural habitats)[24] for purposes of control, development and commodification, and exploitation, be it political, military, economic, social, or even spiritual. Our understanding, both as attributing meaning to and as interpreting the meaning of, the North derives from and is constructed by cognitive manoeuvres that entail an ordering or staging of reality through representations such as mapping, historiography, photography, poetry, and painting. When we *read* these representations, we are ascribing meaning to them, granting or denying them the status of reality or truth. Every time we do this we are working with signs, manipulating codes, engaging in a semiotic activity or, more importantly, in the process of social semiotics.

From its beginnings in the theorizing of Ferdinand de Saussure and C.S. Peirce, semiotics was viewed as a structuralist pursuit that was limited to the synchronic and abstract study of signs and sign systems. As a result, semiotics was thought of as disconnected from history, social processes, and culture. As Hodge and Kress remind us, however, sign systems cannot be separated from context, time, and history – in short, from social process. Using the theories of Bakhtin and Voloshinov, notably the concepts of dialogics and the utterance (18–19), they open up semiotics to history, to diachrony, and to social practice. Through what they call "social semiotics" they show how semiotics functions in other than verbal sign systems in a dynamic, interactive semiosis that is constantly experiencing constraint and resistance over time. The social semiotics developed by Hodge and Kress, on which I will rely in the following discussion, recognizes the profoundly diachronic and interdisciplinary nature of a semiotics that must be contextualized, studied in as many contexts as possible, and recognized as ideologically inflected at all times.

After a fascinating extension of a conventional structuralist analysis of the red, amber, and green signals of a traffic light to include a range of social contexts and ideological meanings, Hodge and Kress warn us that "semiosis is never simple, clear and rational, even when it is operated by electricity" (39). Bearing that warning in mind, I have summarized in Figure 1 the salient features of their social semiotics with a view to the poem and painting that I want to examine.[25] From the outset Hodge and Kress stress the importance of contexts for any semiotic act; thus, I have given examples of three contexts (genre, canon, tradition/convention) specific to the disciplines of literature and fine art (poem and painting), and three examples of social contexts (laws, institutions, metanarratives), but other contexts internal to a particular system could be shown as oriented to the semiosic plane, just as other contexts external to a particular system could be shown as oriented to the mimetic plane. Hodge and Kress also stress the dynamic, interactive, diachronic nature of the semiotic system itself, and this I indicate with arrows and connecting lines; social semiotics does not concern itself with origins or originary moments but with how and what signs mean in complex contexts. This crucial aspect of meaning as a process occurring in time and space cannot be captured at all satisfactorily in a schematic, two-dimensional drawing.

The three central terms in Figure 1 demand some explanation. In brief, the semiotic act puts signs to work in order to represent something on the mimetic plane. The most basic unit for semiotic analysis is therefore the text created by these signs; thus, the text sits at the central point of my illustration, and for my purposes the texts are "The Walker of the Snow" and *The Phantom Hunter*. However, no text comes into existence *sui generis* or by magic. It is the product of a complex interaction of forces in many different contexts. Above all, a text is determined by what Hodge and Kress call a "logonomic system," which is a normative system or set of rules that serves the dominant power in social relations by constraining the possible meanings of any semiotic act (4–7). According to Hodge and Kress, logonomic systems must be highly visible and understood by all members of a community (here, poets, painters, readers, art lovers, literary and art historians, many Canadians) or the rules will not work, but logonomic systems are also the key sites for contestation and resistance.

Figure 1
Social Semiotic Contexts

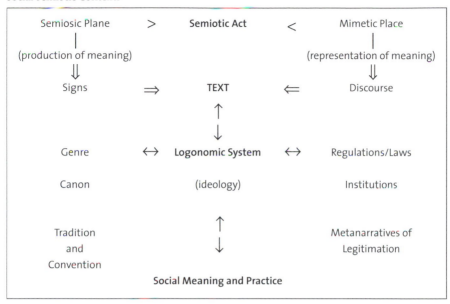

In considering my texts I will be placing them at the centre of a number of contexts and exploring their production of meaning both synchronically and diachronically; it is diachrony that will return the discussion to consideration of wider social issues and thus to the contribution of my two texts to the discursive formation of North and the Canadian habitus. I shall also be borrowing a few other terms and concepts from Hodge and Kress, but these will be explained as I go. So, now, the poem and the painting.

Shanly, who had worked for the Montreal-based *Punch in Canada* as an editor during the 1840s, retired from that work in 1850; by 1857 he was working full-time in New York for the *Atlantic Monthly*, where his poem was first published anonymously in May 1859 (see Chalykoff). This publication brought the poem to the attention of contemporary readers: Blair Bruce was captivated by it after coming across it in John Burrrough's *Locusts and Wild Honey* (1879), and William Lighthall included it in his anthology *Songs of the Great Dominion* (1889). It was still deemed worthy of note by 1910, when C.M. Whyte-Edgar included it in *A Wreath of Canadian Verse*. In other words, this poem, which might seem uninteresting or very minor today, enjoyed some popularity in Canada both before and after Bruce discovered it. Reading it today, one can, I think, see why.

THE WALKER OF THE SNOW
Speed on, speed on, good Master!
    The camp lies far away;

We must cross the haunted valley
　Before the close of day.

How the snow-blight came upon me
　I will tell you as we go,
The blight of the Shadow Hunter
　Who walks the midnight snow.

To the cold December heaven
　Came the pale moon and the stars,
As the yellow sun was sinking
　Behind the purple bars.

The snow was deeply drifted
　Upon the ridges drear
That lay for miles between me
　And the camp for which we steer.

'Twas silent on the hill-side
　And by the sombre wood,
No sound of life or motion
　To break the solitude.

Save the wailing of the moose-bird
　With a plaintive note and low,
And the skating of the red leaf
　Upon the frozen snow.

And I said, "Though dark is falling,
　And far the camp must be,
Yet my heart it would be lightsome
　If I had but company."

And then I sang and shouted,
　Keeping measure as I sped,
To the harp-twang of the snowshoe,
　As it sprang beneath my tread.

Nor far into the valley
　Had I dipped upon my way
When a dusky figure joined me,
　In a capuchon of gray,

Bending upon the snowshoes
  With a long and limber stride;
And I hailed the dusky stranger
  As we travelled side by side.

But no token of communion
  Gave he by word or look,
And the fear-chill fell upon me
  At the crossing of the brook.

For I saw by the sickly moonlight,
  As I followed, bending low,
That the walking of the stranger
  Left no foot-marks on the snow.

Then the fear-chill gathered o'er me
  Like a shroud around me cast,
As I sank upon the snow-drift
  Where the Shadow Hunter passed.

And the otter-trappers found me,
  Before the break of day,
With my dark hair blanched and whitened
  As the snow in which I lay.

But they spoke not as they raised me;
  For they knew that in the night
I had seen the Shadow Hunter,
  And had withered in his blight.

Sancta Maria, speed us!
  The sun is falling low, –
Before us lies the valley
  Of the Walker of the Snow!

This is a narrative poem in the form of a dramatic monologue, spoken by an unidentified man who is accompanying another man identified only as "good Master" in the opening line. Aside from the obvious and intense addressivity of the narrative – an "I" telling a "you" or an "us" his tale – there is no further direct mention of the listener *within* the poem until the first line of the last verse. The "good Master" is positioned, as are the readers of the poem, as listener(s), and we are held, like Coleridge's Wedding Guest, by the suspense of the tale and the obsession of the teller. The story starts on a most ominous note: "We must cross the haunted valley," the exact valley where the story we are about to hear took place some time ago; exactly when is not clear, and that uncertainty is significant because it removes the story from the limits of one special moment in time and makes it timeless – that is, possible at any time. The valley in question is inhabited by something called "the Shadow Hunter," who wears a "capuchon of gray," and on that fateful night about which we are hearing, he appeared suddenly beside the speaker. However, this presence neither spoke nor left any footmarks on the snow. Instead, the speaker became terrified, sank to the snow, and was not found until daybreak.

At this point in the narrative (the penultimate verse) the story becomes confusing and the sense of mystery, even dread, doubles because the speaker tells us that the men who found him did not say anything to him, "For they knew that ... [he] had seen the Shadow Hunter, / And had withered in his blight." What, precisely, we must wonder, happened to the poor man whose tale we have been hearing? Was he injured? Did he recover? Is he – and this is *the* question – dead? What, in short, does "withered in his blight" mean? If he died on that terrible trek through the Shadow Hunter's valley, he could not now be speaking to a "good Master" or to us. Or could he? The closing verse suggests that he survived his ordeal and has lived to tell his tale and, dread prospect, pass once more through this valley of the shadow of death. But another possibility hovers over the poem and is unresolved at the end: either the *two* men in the poem (master and companion, guide, or servant) face the valley together, and this tale simply adds excitement and a *frisson* of the supernatural to their otherwise tedious, lonely night, or the speaker of the poem is not what he seems. He might be a ghost himself, an avatar of the Shadow Hunter (though he seems much more garrulous than that ghostly presence is described as being – "no token of communion / Gave he by word or look"), or he might be addressing us all from the depth of our inner fears about being alone and tired on a cold, moonlit night, surrounded by nothing but snow-filled space in the middle of the northern wilderness, in which case he is a hallucination and we are in greater trouble than we thought.

The story itself will not resolve these questions for us because the diegesis seems quite straightforward: a man is entertaining his companion during a long snowshoe trek through the wilderness, and, as we all know, a good story requires some mystery to raise the adrenalin, especially on a cold winter night. Usually we tell these kinds of stories around a campfire, or in the relative safety of a cabin or tent, and all the fun is in the telling, in scaring our listeners. However, the relative safety factor is distant here: "The camp lies far away," and between here and there "lies the valley / Of the Walker of the Snow." In short, the ordeal of crossing the valley lies ahead of as well as behind us. It must be repeated. If we turn away from the simple story to the semiotics of the poem, many other complications and options come into view, and what first appeared to be a simple story with a gothic twist becomes much more. A synchronic examination of the semiotic codes of the poem will not tell us everything (the poem must be returned to diachronic and mimetic contexts), but it will tell us a lot, and moreover facilitate comparison with the painting by Bruce.

Hodge and Kress suggest that among the most important signs in a text are those dealing with space (proxemics), modality, and syntactic structures (parataxis and hypotaxis), because these signs carry certain meanings about human relationships of solidarity and power and about ideology, and when we read these signs *in a specific context* we understand them as having value, as signifying truths or realities. Also important are what Hodge and Kress call metasigns or "sets of markers of social allegiance (solidarity, group identity and ideology) which permeate the majority of texts" (82). Examples of metasigns are frames (as in frames around paintings), accents in speech that also indicate class, education, ethnicity, etc., size, colour, and gender, and these categories of signs are often most effective when they are most transparent or most taken for granted, in which case they work unconsciously (88–91).

I have already commented in passing upon the spatial codes of the poem, so this is a useful starting point. The first thing to stress is that this poem is spatially and temporally framed; it is a type of story within a story that contains an embedded narrative. The overall structure, then, is hypotactic, and the frame comprises the first two and last verses, which situate the speaker and his "Master" in a present time on this (the near) side of the valley, far from the safety of camp over there. Inside this frame we have the story of a past event that took place in the space-between of the outer frame story, that dangerous space not yet, but about to be, entered again. The hypotactic structure reinforced by the frame story contains and controls, places boundaries around, the events and experiences of the inner story. The person controlling and manipulating the frame and its contents is the teller of the tale, even though he addresses his companion as "good Master," which suggests that he is of lower rank or class than his addressee. Moreover, the speaker has special knowedge and thus the power to urge his companion to "Speed on, speed on" so they can get through the valley before nightfall and spare themselves the danger of the Shadow Hunter. The ambivalence of the ending is repeated in the choice of these spatial codes because the person who at first appears to be powerless (he is only a guide or servant, and his tale is about his own helplessness) turns out to hold all the cards: he knows about the valley; he knows about the Shadow Hunter (he's been there and done that), and he knows how the story ends. It is we, his "Master," his listeners and his readers, who are helpless before the tale, the teller, the valley and the Shadow Hunter, and our own worst fears about the northern wilderness. Once we are into the inner story we are trapped until the teller frees us, and we may even feel trapped before that story begins because we are already out there, with the only way to reach some civilized safety lying before us in the valley.

Once we are into the inner story, other things happen too. What exists on one level as a strictly controlled proxemics – here and there are sharply demarcated, as are here and the camp, just as now and then are perfectly distinct, and I and you seem clearly separate – dissolves on another level and loses its clear boundaries and distinctions. Once we enter the valley, it becomes difficult to distinguish self from other, reality from fantasy, absence from presence – even, perhaps, life from death. The inner story and the valley represent a liminal space, and it is this liminality that is so difficult to understand or negotiate. However, the speaker (and the poet, of course) provides several markers to assist us in the form of meta-signs of colour and gender. We enter the valley of the Snow Walker on a "cold December" night, just as the "pale moon and the stars" come out. This pale, whitish light, reflected by the "deeply drifted" snow, creates an eerie, uncanny world in which it is hard for the human eye to see well and where shadowy shapes and presences can startle us. The associations of the moon with madness and magic are deeply familiar in Western culture, and both the moon and the valley carry gender inflections that do not need to be spelt out by the poet or the teller: this man has entered a female space under the sign of the female moon. He is alone in this "sombre," "frozen" place, where there is nothing to be heard but the "wailing of the moose-bird." The only touch of colour is in a "red leaf," which is oddly incongruous in this white, December snowscape. Its very incongruity and singularity invite speculation about its meaning and why it should be worthy of mention at all: it must be a dead leaf, but why then is it still red, and why is it "skating" as if it had a life of its own? Both its colour and its movement suggest, among other possibilities, that it is a sign of blood, and thus of the life's blood that will abandon the story-teller. Whatever it signifies in that place at that time, it is not human and provides no community for or connection with the man; to the contrary, it underscores the isolation and non-humanness of his situation.

Colour continues to be stressed in the poem after the appearance of "a dusky figure ... / In a capuchon of gray," but it is negative, an absence of colour. Now the moonlight is "sickly," and where one would expect to see the darker colour of footprints in the snow, there is nothing but snow. Indeed, the story-teller himself becomes white: his "dark hair [is] blanched and whitened / As the snow" in which he is found lying by the "otter-trappers." The boundary between man and nature, life and death, self and other has been blurred and rendered uncertain, indistinguishable. However, the gender of the "dusky figure" is given; "he" does not speak or communicate with the story-teller, but anyone familiar with Western iconography will recognize this masculine presence in his "gray" hood as death. Death in the form of this ghostly male "Shadow Hunter" travels, as does the story-teller, who, we should remember, is himself a hunter, as the story-teller's only companion. In at least one reading of the situation, he *is* the story-teller or his *Doppelgänger* (and thus his soul), which passes from him and leaves him behind as part of the feminine, natural world he has dared to penetrate.

But this conflation of the "Shadow Hunter," whose very name is a sign of his status, and the hunter/story-teller of the inner tale, can be more fully grasped by considering the modality of the participants in the poem as they operate both inside and outside the frame. Modality, in the social-semiotic sense that Hodge and Kress employ it, describes the relation between speakers or agents that is gauged by lesser or greater degrees of affinity: the higher the affinity between two speakers or between speaker and hearer, for example, the greater their solidarity with each other and their agreement about the "truth" or "reality" of the semiotic system that produces meaning on the mimetic plane, whereas the lower the affinity, then the greater power one agent exerts over the other and the greater the probability of contestation over what is understood on the mimetic plane (*Social Semiotics*, 12–24). Modality is therefore a crucial site for the "working out, whether by negotiation or imposition, of ideological systems" (124) because modality registers participants' responses to affinity by gender, class, race, and so forth (127). However, as Hodge and Kress insist: "The modality of a message … is not a single or simple truth value. It is nearly always a complex, even contradictory package of claims and counter-claims" (127).

Let's return now to the poem and pick it up where we left it – with the conflation of the Shadow Hunter and the story-teller. By entering the "valley / Of the Walker of the Snow," our story-teller has trespassed or transgressed. He has entered a deadly female space (valley), watched over by the moon on a frozen December night, and he will not be allowed to emerge on the far side, where the camp and safety (presumably with many other men) are to be found. However, on the semiosic plane, what begins as very low affinity between the man and the valley, with its "ridges drear," "sombre wood," "wailing" bird, and a single "red leaf," seems to be alleviated when someone appears to accompany him – seems, that is, until the level of affinity drops even further. This figure is a "dusky stranger" who refuses to communicate, even to the point of leaving no human marks on the snow. But oddly, and as if in contradiction to this low affinity, which should indicate resistance and refusal of the situation by the story-teller, the man sinks to the snow and dies, or at the least becomes one with the snow, merged with the non-human natural world to the extent that the otter-trappers will not speak (from fear? horror?) when they find him. Contradictory as this sudden affinity with the frozen North might seem, this is precisely what the listener/ reader should expect, because the story-teller has succumbed to a greater force, the force of nature, the North, death, call it what you will, and he has been forced to acknowledge her "truth" and "reality."

Once again the problem of the ending that I outlined above begins to arise, except that this time I am approaching it not as an element of diegesis but as the expression of modality between the players in the scene. The story-teller thinks there really was a ghostly presence stalking him, and he wants his "Master" to believe him so that they can "speed on." Whether or not the "Master" believes him is never clear, because when we move out of the inner story and return to the frame story in the final verse, we receive no indication of the "Master's" response. What we do learn is that the "us" of the poem (presumably speaker and "Master") are about to enter the valley at the same time of day as the story-teller did before – then "the yellow sun was sinking," and now "the sun is falling low." *If* there is a strong affinity between the story-teller and his "Master," then surely they will hurry and safeguard each other, but *if* they cannot agree about what has happened, then a struggle will occur and they may both succumb to the reality of the valley. Or, what is also possible here, the story-teller may himself be the Shadow Hunter or the hallucinatory projection of the Master's fear. It may already be too late.

But there is another relationship in this poem that demands attention – that between the poem as told by the hunter/story-teller persona and us, the poem's readers, who exist outside the narrative frame. Blair Bruce was one of those readers, and I will turn to his modality in a moment. What affinity do we recognize here, or more precisely, what is my modal orientation to the speaker? My relationship is highly conflicted and contradictory. I have no affinity with the faceless "Master" or with "the Walker of the Snow"; to the first I am indifferent, except in so far as I suspect that he is a stand-in for me, and about the second I am sceptical. I am, however, attracted by that valley in all its moonlit otherness, and I resist the suggestion that it is fundamentally deadly. Why should I be alarmed, after all? This is only a poem, in a fusty old book, and I am safe at home, or camp, or in some civilized place. Nevertheless, I cannot resist the power of the speaker, who has captured my interest as he did Blair Bruce's and left me with the clear message that the North is fatally dangerous and alien, that it/she will kill me if I am not careful. Despite all the possible readings of the codes of the poem, which create at least three interpretations of the ghost and the ending, one thing seems irrefutable: it is madness and certain death to venture out alone at night into the frozen valleys of the North; neither the necessity of work (hunting, trapping) nor the possession of knowledge about the wilderness nor the company of a guide will save you. There is no room to negotiate with the power of the North, and this voice has come back from the dead, from the frozen wastes, to tell me so.

And yet I am safe because I am outside the frame, except that in that space I am susceptible to being haunted by the powerfully represented images of the North produced by the semiotics of the poem. My position, therefore, is not absolutely secure, because I have been manipulated into accepting a construction of North that may or may not be true but is conveyed with the force of truth by the poem. In Figure 2 I have summarized the key metasigns and modalities of the poem to illustrate how relationships are structured. Within this structure of narrative and relationships the key tension is spatial: at one side is safety (the camp, the book containing the poem), but between here and there lies the valley, the space of danger, of the *imagined North* and of the North as constructed by our haunted imaginations. The ambiguity and uncertainty that arise from this tension shape our response to the story itself (the diegesis) and to the characters (story-teller, Shadow Hunter, and "Master"), but more importantly, this tension controls our reading of the signs and thus our interpretation of the poem on the mimetic plane. All that readers will agree on, I suspect, is that we have just read a scary

Figure 2
"The Walker of the Snow"

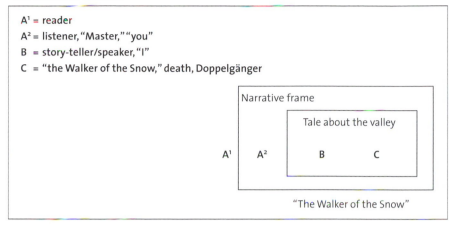

A¹ = reader
A² = listener, "Master," "you"
B = story-teller/speaker, "I"
C = "the Walker of the Snow," death, Doppelgänger

Narrative frame

Tale about the valley

A¹   A²   B   C

"The Walker of the Snow"

story, that something unpleasant can happen to you if you stay out in the Canadian North at night in winter, that the North is frozen, silent, alien, and deadly, and that we, happily, are safe at home. We will never know (or never agree about) what happened on that December night in that valley. Of course it is this tension, this undecidability, that makes the poem interesting, even today, when it might well seem trite and aesthetically dated. And it is this tension that Bruce captures so effectively in his painting.

The Phantom Hunter was painted in France during 1887–88, after Bruce returned there to paint at Giverny, but the subject was intended to represent Canada, and Bruce took great pains to get the northern and Canadian details just right. According to Joan Murray, he had come back to Canada from Europe in 1885 to recover from a nervous breakdown.[26] While here he sketched a snowbank scene in the lane behind the family's Hamilton home, and this scene became the basis for his canvas. However, the subject of the fallen trapper was, as we now know, inspired by Shanly's poem, which Bruce read during his year at home. In a 13 November 1888 letter to his father he describes this Salon painting (which was a great success) and explains that it is based on a "legend ... from the old story lore of Early Canada": "I first read it in [the] form of verse in the works of John Burrows, the American naturalist and writer, which is I believe a very well known book in America. The poem is entitled the 'Walker of the Snow.' The 'Walker' is simply 'old Jack Frost' personified – and his victims are killed by his frosty breath. But the hunters in their love of the Supernatural have put their story in such a form that this walking ghost has been the result" (*Letters Home*, 167).

Joan Murray, the leading scholar of Bruce's work, believes that "the fallen figure of the trapper" represents Bruce's own collapse and disorientation of 1885–86, and she says that the "face, so far as it can be seen, is his face" (21). Judging from photographs of Bruce, we could read the painting as a self-portrait; if we assume that it is, then the feelings of isolation and helplessness that pervade the painting carry added force. There can be no doubt that Shanly's poem moved Bruce deeply and that he identified with it in some fairly profound ways: not only was it about Canada and the North (really Canada-as-North), which mattered greatly to Bruce, but he found a depth of serious meaning in it that is belied by his casual tone in the November letter to his father.[27] The image suggests that Blair Bruce at least identified with the story-teller in the poem, like him collapsed before the greater force of the North, and like him needs to share his tale with us.

The Phantom Hunter (see Plate 2) is a narrative, mimetic painting, with representational figures in a recognizable northern snowscape; it is executed in a loosely impressionist style and is much less cold and sombre in reality than it appears in reproductions.[28] The shapeless, vague white of the snow is in fact both warmer and more mysterious than one might think because flecks of peach tones appear beneath the white pigment to give the snow an inner warmth and glow. The sky, though mostly dark greys and blues, especially dark on the left, has surprising areas of pale turquoise, and there are stars in the sky, one of which, the North or Pole Star, is very bright. The total effect is of an ethereal serenity rather than a stark or harsh frigidity; there is both mystery and delicacy in the scene. As well, landscape is indeterminate; the drifted snow and lack of trees could indicate a place anywhere from northern Ontario to the Yukon or even the high Arctic.

The hunter's dress, however, pulls us further south than the polar extreme, and his position in the foreground, just right of centre, dominates the scene. But the title of the piece reminds us that this painting is not so much about the hunter as the phantom, and by telling us that this semi-transparent figure striding away from the fallen man is a phantom, Bruce is dematerializing his presence and placing greater stress upon psychology than the supernatural, which remained a possibility in the poem. Bruce goes one crucial step further than Shanly in identifying this figure, because close comparison of the two figures reveals that they are virtually identical in details of dress and face. But before I return to these two and the relation between them, there are several other apects of the composition and elements in the scene that should be noted. The most important of these is the footmarks in the snow. These enter the picture plane from beyond the frame at the bottom left corner of the picture and they move into and across the foreground to circle around behind the kneeling figure; they are not connected with the phantom who, like Shanly's Shadow Hunter, leaves no footmarks on the snow. Moreover, these are not snowshoe marks but footprints, because the man has taken off his snowshoes. Behind him on the snow lies his rifle.

The deep space of the painting is almost entirely filled with snow, and this snow is empty of any objects (no red leaf, no wailing bird) and devoid of any angles or planes that would provide some sense of volume or perspective – until, that is, the eye reaches the upper third of the image. At this level the snow is mounded, and two curved banks and hollows appear, but apart from dark shadows at their centres, they are empty. There are no markers or indicators of direction, nothing from which a lost person could take his bearings, and on the far right of the image this seemingly empty, trackless, unmarked snowscape recedes over the horizon. Unless one knew the poem, one might suppose nothing existed beyond the horizon, but with the poem in mind it is reasonable to imagine that the hunter's camp lies that way, far over there on the other side of the valley that has been entered from the left.

But it is the two figures that hold the eye and make such an indelible impression on the imagination, and in this configuration it is the outstretched left arm of the hunter, especially his hand, that focuses the image. The tension along the line of that outstretched arm is palpable, and yet it is not a gesture of much force: the hand almost seems relaxed (no fist, no clutching fingers), and the arm is not so much tensed as wearily extended out from the sinking torso. The line of the arm is reinforced, propped up in a sense, by the shadow-filled footprint. The contrast between the hunter and the phantom is strong. Where the first is collapsing on to the snow (the posture is not a crouch), on to the horizontal, the latter is erect and moving purposefully away; his back is turned to the hunter, of whose presence he seems oblivious, and the phantom is the only vertical thing in this emphatically horizontal world, while he is also and decidedly *not of this world*. What I am describing here is the proxemics of the figures, the way they are oriented in space, but the single most compelling feature of this spatial relationship is the gap between the two figures, just beyond the slightly curved, gloved fingers. We can read that gap as an implied connection between the two figures or we can read it as empty space, mere air, like the phantom. But on the flat surface of the painting we can actually see what fills that gap because it is what surrounds and is engulfing the hunter: the snow. The only substance that is really present with the hunter is this snow, which we can even see through the body of the phantom, and it seems to fill up almost all the available space of the composition.

Then there is the frame, a metasign that is taken for granted around a painting (at least it is in conventional paintings). On this painting the frame serves to cut out or select a slice of reality from its larger context and to hold it together, to concentrate and control it so that it can be viewed and understood. Given the size of the piece (close to 4 feet by 5 feet) and the size of the figures (half to three-quarter life-size), the scene needs framing, holding in place, and control. After all, it would not do for that phantom to come gliding into *our* presence. And yet, is that not precisely what appears about to happen? If the moment unfroze, would not that ghostly presence leave the space of the painting and enter ours? As with Shanly's poem, the narrative conveyed by the relationship of and contrasts between the hunter and the phantom takes place in time as well as space. There is an implied before and after, an anticipated next scene in the drama. Just what it will be we can guess but never know. But let me linger a moment longer over this matter of the frame because it is important; as long as it stays in place, the forces in the painting stay put. In addition to the directionality of the phantom, who seems about to leave the picture plane at roughly the point where the footprints enter it, there are two points at which we are forcibly reminded that the frame is an arbitrary imposition upon a larger scene and space: these are the footprints themselves, notably the partial one at the bottom left of the image, and the hunter's shadow, which extends off the right side of the picture (a similar implied extension could be seen in the horizontal lines of the snowbanks and the horizon). These slight details add considerably to the tension and power of the scene because they indicate that what lies outside the frame is more of what lies inside it, and that the story continues beyond the frame that contains what, in Shanly, is the inner story. In other words, the metasign of frame in the two works is homologous. In both texts it orders, hypotactically, the events and meaning of the narrative; it discriminates exactly between in there and out here; it marks the boundary between the familiar and the strange, the safe and the threatening, the ordered world and a world without apparent order. The visual frame is a narrative frame.

The world inside the frame is full of ambiguity, blurred; indeed, there is a lack of boundaries. Even the phantom has blurred edges, and the hunter, whose shape stands out sharply for the moment, is fast becoming one with his surroundings. Colour and gender signs, while seemingly obvious or transparent (to use Hodge and Kress's term), enhance the liminality, the vague unmarked quality of the scene. White predominates, with blues and greys used to relate the night winter scene with the phantom and the hunter's shadow. Affinity, however, is low. The strong blue/grey areas are not contiguous, and there is no solidarity in the relationship of the participants. As with the poem, the hunter is overwhelmed, forced to submit to the greater force of nature. Here the only red appears on the hunter himself, in his sash and in the trim on his gloves. He is for the moment the only sign of life within this frozen, dead place. There is no red visible on the phantom's clothing, and this absence suggests that, with the phantom, life itself departs the scene. Gender also seems clear: the human protagonists of this drama are male, just as they were in the poem, and the female presence lies in the curved, hollowed, mysterious, and deadly landscape. This presence is, in fact, present through absence – the absence of anything vertical or phallic, except the phantom, in an otherwise empty and horizontal space. When the phantom leaves and the hunter dies, he will become, like the story-teller in the poem (and as the phantom already is), one with the snow, indistinguishable from the North that surrounds him.

If the spatial relation of the two principal figures within the frame indicates low affinity as a result of their contrasts and the paratactic disposition of the images, there is none the less and paradoxically a very strong identity asserted by the obvious similarity of the two shapes: with a few rather important exceptions, they are identical. What are we to make of this? On the one hand they are separate, disconnected, isolated from each other by the snow; on the other, they are the same, as if someone could be in two places at the same time. This, of course, is what makes the painting so memorable. The modality of the participants is ambiguous and unresolvable by the third participant in the scene: the viewer.

This is the point at which I think we find the sharpest difference with the poem, and it is a difference that is unavoidable. Bruce has provided no surrogate for the viewer *inside* the frame; there is no equivalent to Shanly's "Master." However, a painter knows that the viewer is there, must be there, and must be built into the scene somehow. How do we locate the viewer, and thus account for her/his modality? As viewers we are understood to be standing in front of the painting, in the space, as it were, of the outer frame and outside the physical frame around the image (unless, as is most probable today, we are sitting looking at a book, but then I would argue our position as viewer is parallel, if not quite identical, with that of the gallery visitor). If the painting works, we are held there, fascinated, chilled, horrified perhaps; it is the painting as a whole that addresses itself to us. Because the painting is realistic (highly representational), we understand that we share this northern reality that lies beyond the horizon and outside the safely containing frame, that there, but for the grace of the frame, is me. Thus, the affinity we acknowledge as we stand there – or again, my modal orientation towards this speaking picture – is dramatically clear: my affinity is with the hunter. If I were caught alone in the frozen wastes of the North, I would end up just like him – the only fully human presence in the scene. I am not as drawn to the winter scene as I was with the poem, and thus my affinity with the natural world is quite low, but I am certainly in solidarity with the fallen man. Trapped within the world of the painting, I become, like him, subject to the greater power of that world.

The metasigns and modalities of the painting can be summarized in the same configuration as the poem (see Figure 3). But I exist outside that pictorial world, in the safe space of the gallery (or my study), so I have the privilege of feeling secure. Except that, as was the case with the poem, in my mind's eye I will retain the image of the hunter and the phantom. I will be haunted by this vision of a North that is cold, alien, female, and absolutely deadly. Art, the very force that can tame this North, has represented it in such powerful signs and images that it controls and dominates my orientation to the painting on the semiosic plane, and to the North on the mimetic plane. Once again, North has been constructed as everywhere out there and as cold, alien, inhuman, and overwhelming. There is, I think, less undecidability about Bruce's painting than there is about Shanly's poem, because once a subject is rendered in pigment, especially when the rendering is representational, certain realities appear fixed once and for all. The *frisson* of uncertainty is strong, however, and it arises from the phantom and from the snow-filled world (our world outside the frame) into which he seems about to step.

A synchronic semiotic analysis of these texts helps us to understand the range of meanings produced by them, and it also alerts us to their ideological content. Each text creates and exploits considerable tension and anxiety about the status of being a human being in this world, but the gender of the humans involved and the nature of the world are carefully proscribed: the people are male; the world is the Canadian North viewed, in their mind's eye, with complex feelings of desire

Figure 3
The Phantom Hunter

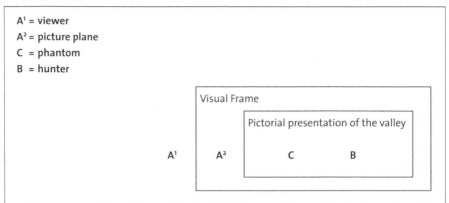

A¹ = viewer
A² = picture plane
C = phantom
B = hunter

Visual Frame

Pictorial presentation of the valley

A¹   A²   C   B

and revulsion. Both texts inscribe a need to enter the frozen valley, despite the warnings or, in the case of the painting, a general atmosphere of the uncanny inspiring dread. In both the valley is mysterious and beautiful, and in both texts the male victim (for surely, in the poem's inner story, he is represented as victim) succumbs to the force of the North with little or no struggle or protest. Paradoxically, however, and most importantly, the artist controls the semiotic system and the story because he is able to tell us about what he has seen in that valley; he has, in a sense like Dante, returned from that frozen hell to create a work of art, to objectify the experience and put it to work – for himself and for the wider culture.

In their day these texts were popular; they spoke to their consumers in a language that was understood and appreciated. The poem was quoted by contemporaries and anthologized. Moreover, it influenced a painting that enjoyed great success in late nineteenth-century Paris and has been frequently reproduced as a canonic Canadian work in the twentieth century and as one of two major canvases that established Bruce's reputation.[29] Shanly's poem also impressed Howard O'Hagan, and the effect of the story is apparent in O'Hagan's novel *Tay John* (1960). This is not the place to open a discussion of that novel, but it is worth noting what O'Hagan said about the poem in his 1979 interview with Keith Maillard.[30] When Maillard asked O'Hagan about his experiences of strange presences in the mountains, O'Hagan replied:

Well, it's very hard to talk about that. I fully notice it when I've been alone in the wintertime. And it would seem that there was someone keeping time with my snowshoes, just off a distance. I couldn't see him. But this has been better portrayed than I could ever do it by a French-Canadian writer whose name I've forgotten in a poem called ... "The Walker of the Snow." It's set in a canyon north of Montreal or Quebec, I forget. When men went through that canyon, they felt this presence, or they heard this man snowshoeing in unison with them. The faster they went, the faster he kept up with them ... It was a very moving poem.   (quoted in Fee, 34)

Now, the poem was not written by a French-Canadian, but O'Hagan is probably correct in thinking that the source of the story is an oral tale or legend from *le Nord*. More than seventy-five years before O'Hagan, Blair Bruce described the story as from "old story lore of Early Canada" (*Letters Home*, 167), and thus from Quebec. It may also have associations with northern Ontario and Quebec Ojibwa stories about the Windigo, who is known for stalking lone trappers, among others, and eating them.[31]

I will return to the Windigo in chapter 6, but at this point a few general observations about it are useful. Windigos always appear at night in the winter; they are quintessentially northern monsters who prey upon hunters travelling alone. Moreover, they are genderless, humanlike monsters that can take on the shape of a man. They are usually associated with overwhelming hunger, even starvation, and thus with cannibalism, although they are also capable of driving men mad. The Windigo is a projection of some of our deepest fears of the wilderness (of extreme cold, starvation, and isolation), and it inscribes one of the most basic taboos of human cultures: the prohibition against cannibalism. Although I would not go so far as to argue that Shanly's poem and Bruce's painting are about Windigos, I would suggest that the residual power of horror that is not resolved or staged in either text has to do with cannibalism, not in the sense that another starving person is going to eat the story-teller, the hunter, or ourselves (in so far as we identify with these central protagonists in the two texts) but in the sense that there is something (Shadow Hunter/Walker or Phantom) out there that is going to get us. That something is the North, a deadly female space filled with ice and snow and dangerous valleys that will absorb us, destroy us by swallowing us up and transforming us – blanching and whitening – until we are one with her. This horror is too awful to depict. It must be implied, carried in a complex, seemingly contradictory set of codes that mark the Walker and the Phantom as male because they represent the soul or spirit of the victim, whose agency can only be tolerated and allowed meaning when it is gendered masculine.

Cannibalism, especially associated with frozen northern wastes, was not far from public attention in the mid-nineteenth century. By 1848 news of the fate of Franklin's 1845 expedition in search of the Northwest Passage was making headlines in newspapers around the world. It would continue to do so for the next decade as the searches for survivors, or at least for signs of what had happened, continued, and public interest in the fate of Franklin and his crew has been periodically revived right up to the present. But no one created a greater stir than did Dr John Rae in October 1854, when he reported news about members of Franklin's party who had left "accounts of their sufferings in the mutilated corpses of some who had evidently furnished food to their unfortunate companions."[32] Rae was vociferously criticized for his claims and for daring to publicize them, and his reputation has suffered ever since. He openly mentioned the forbidden and unmentionable; he broke the taboo of silence. In 1879 the subject of cannibalism again surfaced to shock Canadians when the Cree hunter "Swift Runner" (Katistchen) was executed for murdering, then eating, his family (see M.A. Macpherson). Can it be too much to suppose that the connection between a frightful death involving cannibalism and the North was very much before the mind's eye in the last decades of the nineteenth century, and that the very possibility of such a thing was too horrible to contemplate? I think not. There is a tangible and very powerful social context here within which it is important to place "The Walker of the Snow" and *The Phantom Hunter.* They were telling the right story at the right time, and they were telling it well. What they wisely refrained from telling, their contemporaries would understand.

The diachronic dimensions of the social semiotics of these two texts can be extended to include many other historical, scientific, artistic, and political elements, of course. Both texts are drawing upon Darwinian concepts of survival of the fittest, which were already inscribed in the Canadian habitus, as Haliburton's *Men of the North* shows and as the 1896 Gold Rush would continue to demonstrate, nowhere more emphatically than in Robert Service's poems. Both texts exhibit a wide knowledge of literary and artistic traditions of the Gothic and Sublime, and quite possibly of Coleridge's "Rime of the Ancient Mariner." Moreover, both texts demonstrate their creators' awareness that an exotic Canada-as-North would, so to speak, sell. They recognized the appeal of their subject and, by using it, contributed not only to their own reputations but to a much broader conception of Canada that is still with us. If Shanly's poem is forgotten, it none the less lives on subterraneously in others's works, and Bruce's painting affects us directly in the gallery or in art history books.

The basic narrative in the poem and the painting (of a man pursuing or being pursued at night by death) is familiar enough in Western culture; think only of Mary Shelley's monster or of Goethe's "Erl King." *Doppelgängers* are also familiar occurrences in nineteenth- and early twentieth-century literature, painting, drama, and eventually film, and ghosts have a long and illustrious history. Because they draw upon such a deep well of mythic, symbolic, psychological, and social meaning, these texts constitute interesting and important statements in the discursive formation of North; they construct a Canada that *is* North and a North that is cold, snow-filled, silent, deadly, and female. It will drive you mad and destroy/devour you. Its very emptiness and otherness are to be feared and conquered. The vulnerability and passivity of the male victims function as a warning, not against entering the North but against giving in to it, becoming one with it. The image of defeat in the mind's eye, haunting the imagination, serves as a powerful reminder of our need to prevail, to possess and dominate, to "speed on" in the assertion of our superiority over this meaningless, shapeless force, this place without order *until we supply it*, in art, story, civilization.

But I do not want to conclude this chapter on such a chillingly imperialistic and orientalizing note. North would not be a discursive formation if it did not include opposing or complementary stories and multiple ideas of North. One of the most haunting and extraordinary of these is Gabrielle Roy's *La Montagne secrète* (1962).

Roy's novel has two protagonists, a painter, Pierre Cadorai, and the North. The North in this novel stretches from the mouth of the Mackenzie River south and east through the Northwest Territories and around Hudson Bay to Ungava. While the entire North is beautiful to Pierre, he finds the goal he has been searching for in the hallucinatory realm of Ungava, and it is a mountain, more beautiful than any other, that reveals itself to the artist in all its glory and then tells him that through the artist alone it shall exist. Roy's artist is utterly possessed by this vision, and, as we might suspect, it nearly kills him; he is caught by a sudden blizzard and without food he nearly dies.

La Montagne secrète is remarkable for many reasons, and I examine it closely, with Roy's other northern fiction, in chapter 5. The story functions as an allegory of Canada-as-North (and the entire sub-Arctic and much of the Arctic is included in Roy's North), for which the mountain stands as both symbol and goal. This Canada, however, can only reach full existence if its artists will love and paint it, devote themselves to it utterly. To return to the old world, assuming anything of value could be learned there, is tantamount to a betrayal; it separates the artist from his very life's blood and soul. In effect, Roy has turned the story of *The Phantom Hunter* and "The Walker of the Snow" inside out. For the northerner, it is the South, civilization, Europe that destroys the soul and kills.

PERFORMING NORTH

THE SOUND OF THE NORTH

In an attempt to explain the recent popularity in Canada of Czech composer Leoš Janácek, Canadian Opera Company artistic director and principal conductor Richard Bradshaw has remarked that "there's a 'starkness of the North' aspect to Janácek's plot [in *Jenufa*] that appeals to Canadians" (Charles, 57). The remark is intriguing. On the one hand, it is so familiar as to be taken for granted: the North is stark; Canada is northern; therefore, starkness of plots (and music?) will touch Canadians. On the other hand, it ignores several questions: how is Janácek's popularity explained in other, less northern countries? What is "stark" about the North? What or where *is* North anyway? But Janácek is not my problem here, and if I raise him and Bradshaw's observation at all, it is because of the fascinating range of issues, questions, and assumptions buried in this casual remark.

As W.L. Morton has told us, Canada has been constructed as North from the time of its European discovery, and the positive evaluation of this northernness, according to Harold Innis, was measured in the quality of fur: the farther north the animal, the better the pelt. The negative evaluation, as centuries of searches for the Northwest Passage demonstrate, was the depiction of Canada as a frozen waste, and not even Stefansson could dispel that myth. Whether as a "friendly" place of potential resource wealth and a space for dangerous adventure or as a barren land empty of little but snow, ice, wolves, and the threat of starvation and death, Canada has come to be equated with the North. What the explorers, traders, geographers, historians, and politicians constructed in economic, cartographic, historiographic, and political terms, our artists have trained us to see, feel, and recognize as a Canadian identity. We have been – and continue to be – constructed and represented as "the men [sic] of the North," whose "place in history" (Haliburton, 1) is to guard "the true North strong and free," with a "Northern Magus" (Trudeau) for a prime minister and a wine labelled "49 North."[1]

But what about music, "what will this [cold and ice] do for music?" (Schafer, *Music in the cold,* 64) Do composers and singers construct or re-present "the North" or Canada-as-North? Is it possible to *hear* as well as see, feel, and recognize a northern identity? The short answer to these questions is yes. And it is yes not only for

Canada but for the other Nordic or circumpolar countries as well. Moreover, this music, in all its forms, is often enlisted in the search for and articulation of national identity, whether or not the popular singer or classical composer *intends* his or her music to represent the nation or to perform a northern identity. The extensive June 1997 Northern Encounters Festival for the Arts, hosted by Canada, with contributions from eight northern nations, is only one case in point; bringing together almost two thousand artists, the festival was a "celebration of 'northernness' through music, art and culture of the eight circumpolar countries."[2]

Examples of Canadian northern popular and folk music come quickly to mind: Stan Rogers' haunting and justly famous "Northwest Passage," the folksongs of the Yellowknife-based group The Gumboots, the Innu group Kashtin, the 1996 Juno award–winning Dene group from the Yukon called Jerry Alfred and the Medicine Beat, collections of ballads like *The Beauty of the North* (1994) or the more light-classical pieces of *North Country: The Music of Canada* (1976). At one extreme of this popular discourse is the kind of legendary song that everyone has heard about but few can sing like "When the Ice Worms Nest Again." Complete with a questionable construction of race and gender, a dubious courtship, and a very shaky metre, the famous ditty entertains us with visions of love in an igloo. The first verse sets the scene:

> There's a husky dusky maiden in the Arctic;
> In her igloo she is waiting there in vain,
> But some day I'll put my mukkluks on and ask her
> If she'll wed me when the ice-worms nest again.[3]

And in his country/jazz ballad "Canadian Man" Paul Brandt updates the courtship:

> Canadian Man
> At your service from the land of the chill
> If I can't warm you baby nobody will
> A genuine Canadian Man

At the other, more serious extreme is Susan Aglukark, whose recent success, south as well as north of sixty, extends and complicates the northern repertoire in important ways.[4]

However, sung lyrics relying on verbal text and the human voice can represent northern experience far more directly than can instrumental music, especially if it is non-programmatic, and the distinction here cannot be simply drawn between popular and classical forms. Several classical composers have set explicitly northern texts to music, and others have been directly inspired by specific northern paintings to capture, in musical language alone, the qualities of snow, ice, extremes of cold, isolation, space, silence, austere beauty, and dread – all qualities we experience as northern and uniquely Canadian. In the discussion that follows

I will explore some classical orchestral or instrumental pieces by such composers as Harry Freedman, Diana McIntosh, Harry Somers, Barbara Pentland, John Weinzweig, Alexina Louie, R. Murray Schafer, and François Houle, and comment in passing on songs and programmatic compositions as different as Violet Archer's "The Lonely Land," Murray Adaskin's Inuit songs, and Glenn Gould's *The Idea of North*. While I can make no claim to be exhaustive or technically analytical, I do want to identify some of the strategies used by Canadian composers to express (even to represent) the North in musical idioms that contribute to and participate in the discursive formation of North. There is a wealth of musical discourse out there, often recorded and broadcast by CBC FM (now Radio 2), much of it powerful and highly accomplished, and this music, like the historiography, art, and geography, is part of the complex, interrelated (often interdisciplinary) field of cultural and national discourse about the North. The sound of the North is an inescapable part of our imagined community.

The theoretical problems that must be faced in any consideration of musical texts as part of a discursive formation are many and perhaps more intransigent than those that arise in a comparative treatment of the semiotics of poetry and painting. These problems occur on all three levels of my analysis – the macrolevel, the mesolevel, and the microlevel – but are particularly challenging on the latter two. It is not, I think, especially difficult to identify those classical compositions that, in one way or another deal with North (with popular songs, ballads, and so forth, it is easy); their verbal texts (when a text is set), dedications, titles, or special contexts (such as festival premières) self-identify them, often with additional certainty provided by the composer's imprimatur in commentaries, introductions, and interviews. Usually these musical statements (compositions) are consciously connected by the composer with other statements in the discursive formation of North with which she or he is already familiar: thus Glenn Gould, fascinated from childhood with the North, creates *The Idea of North* for the 1967 centenary; R. Murray Schafer, building on considerable rural if not far northern wilderness experience, wide knowledge of the arts in Canada (notably the Group of Seven), and a carefully developed philosophy, calls for an explicitly Canadian/northern music in *Music in the cold* and proceeds to write such music in *North/White*; and François Houle, reacting to media coverage of the 1998 Ice Storm, recycles electronically, in *Au coeur du litige*, the sounds of freezing rain, brittle ice, and media sound-bites (in French and English), in the effort "to get to the heart" of what unifies Canada: ice, cold – in short, winter. Moreover, these musical statements are sometimes, as in the case of Schafer, explicitly nationalist.

To move to the mesolevel of analysis is to push the argument for meaning through interpretation a step further; it is to assume that a musical composition can be treated as a textual statement like any other, to say that it *represents*, that it is not a closed, abstract, self-referential system but a system that *means* on the mimetic plane and can therefore be interpreted, that notation has more than musical significance. Now musical purists will immediately reject such an argument for meaning as perverse or frivolous, if not worse, but I am none the less making it – cautiously, self-ironically at times, and only to a degree and only with certain compositions. I make no global claims for my theoretical assumptions or practice. I am encouraged, however, to venture boldly here by such recent musicologists as Susan McClary, who acknowledges that it is "an intimidating task" to try to release music from the hegemony of formalist critque (20), and Catherine Clément.[5] Music, it seems to me, can and does create, replicate, communicate, and participate in social meaning. Why else would those of us who are not composers or professional musicians choose to listen to it? Why else incorporate music into a play or provide a score for a film, where music performs an important role in the semiotic system. The shift to the microlevel, which takes analysis to the very medium itself, to its language, details of convention, genre, structure, and canonic (or canon-resisting) traditions, is the most difficult for all but the expert, and most music experts reject the enterprise (McClary is a path-breaking exception). I am not an expert in this sense but an amateur (a lover – informed but casual, promiscuous) of music; therefore, my attempts to track the musical statements in the discursive formation of North through the meso- to the microlevel are few and carefully circumscribed. What I can affirm is that the tracking can be done with interesting results, and that the macrolevel alone provides, in astonishing quantity and quality, an undeniable northern sound.

I have arranged my examples of northern music in three categories: compositions inspired by Canadian painting, compositions for voice and text, and non-programmatic music.[6] Without doubt the place to begin a review of music inspired by expressly *northern* Canadian painting is Harry Freedman's *Tableau* (1952) and *Images* (1957–58). *Tableau for String Orchestra*, usually considered Freedman's first mature piece, is a twelve-tone composition of about eight minutes' duration that develops a lyric quality at its close. According to Freedman, it was inspired "by a brooding Arctic landscape of ice and snow" (Elliott) that hung in the Winnipeg School of Art when Freedman was a student there in the late 1930s. Although the painting has not been identified, some assume that the canvas was a Lawren Harris; however, in a review of *Tableau* John Kraglund refers to a painting of a flat landscape with "a tiny Eskimo village in the distance" (quoted in Parsons, 15).[7]

The piece is hauntingly beautiful: adjectives like lonely, spacious, and brooding – with a sonorous, eerie, possibly threatening undercurrent – come to mind to describe it. A sense of isolation and great space is created through the wandering melody, carried, echoed, and sustained by the first violins, and this atonal melody conjures up the image of a lonely human or animal figure moving across the uneven tundra. A darker, brooding, even threatening mood pervades the scene at those points when the violas, cellos, and basses enter to bring the piece to full orchestration, punctuated by a series of strong staccato chords, as if to overwhelm and subdue the animate form of the violins.[8] The sharp contrasts and shifts in the basically "two-part counterpoint" (Parsons, 16) create tension that is both spare and direct. But the violins return to bring the piece to an almost serene close on a softly fading chord (*sul ponticello* and without vibrato).

Images is a more complex work in three movements, each inspired by a Canadian painting: the first movement, "Blue Mountain," is based on Lawren Harris's *Lake and Mountains* (1927), the second, "Structure at Dusk," on a non-objective work of the same name by Kazuo Nakamura, and the third, "Landscape," on a Jean-Paul Riopelle canvas. But it is only the first movement that I want to consider here. Harris's canvas (Plate 6) depicts a massive, jagged mountain, with low, dark hills at its feet and talon-shaped clouds above, in his familiar cool tones of blues, greens, dark grey-brown, and white. The lake and shoreline, occupying the immediate foreground, impart dramatic tension and mystery to the piece. Where the sharp points of stump and rock appear to warn the viewer/adventurer of danger, the lake seems to lead us on into the landscape and the white light streaming forth from an invisible, distant source. This initial ambivalence is intensified by the contrasting horizontal and vertical lines.

Freedman interprets the canvas by stressing its mystery, spaciousness, and intensely spiritual remoteness. After a stunning opening six-bar crescendo broken by his distinctive "snap-motive" (Proctor, 68), Freedman leads our ears into the soundscape (as Harris leads our eyes into his scene) by means of a melody announced in the first violins: horizontal and diagonal lines, which work to control our visual entry into a mysterious middle-distance in the painting, are matched in the music by the gently emerging melody. Parsons stresses the importance of semitones, leaps of a fourth, countermelody (with dissonance), and " 'blue' notes [Freedman has had a lifetime interest in jazz] like the minor second and major/minor third" (39) as key elements in the composition for capturing the cold, stark northern scene. As in *Tableau*, Freedman develops striking contrasts and, thereby, tension by shifting from the violins to the low strings, which in "Blue Mountain" are further intensified by bass clarinet, bassoons, and trombones. The final effect is above all one of majesty and power, and of a cold, mysterious realm that can evoke in the listener an imagined North.

But Freedman is not the only Canadian composer to be drawn to visual images of the North for musical inspiration. Diana McIntosh has developed a performance and lecture philosophy around her belief that composing and painting are profoundly interrelated activities. In the seventies she toured Canada introducing audiences to contemporary Canadian music and art; she has said that "such techniques usually get the listener's imagination going ... and through the paintings I'm able to break down this mental barrier ... to contemporary music" (quoted in MacMillan, 4). She has also composed from paintings: *Paraphrase #1*, for example, is a solo piano piece inspired by Harris's *Maligne Lake* (1924). Derek Healey's *Arctic Images* (1971), a sixteen-minute composition for orchestra, is based on Cape Dorset prints and uses a number of performance techniques and Inuit drumming to create a sense of icy solitude, stillness, and mystery (see Parsons, 56–8). Michel Longtin's *Au Nord du Lac Superieur* (1972) is a purely electronic composition with every sound synthesized and no concrete elements. This thirteen-minute work (only one of several Longtin pieces with northern themes) was inspired by Harris's Lake Superior canvases, notably *North Shore, Lake Superior* (1926).[9]

In setting words to music, several composers have used Inuit songs. For example, Harry Freedman and Serge Garant have both created works based on *Anerca*, Edmund Carpenter's edited collection of Inuit poems, using voice with musical accompaniment that ranges from the discordant, expressionistic score of Garant to the simpler piano dialogue of Freedman.[10] Diana McIntosh's *Kiviuq, an Inuit Legend* (1985) is a more ambitious work for chamber orchestra and narrator. Divided into five movements and lasting for approximately twenty-five minutes, the composition weaves the narrator's voice, as he tells the story of Kiviuq and his wife (an important story in Inuit myth), with the music that expresses and dramatizes Kiviuq's actions in a "Kiviuq rhythm" and a "Kiviuq theme" (4–5); the narrator's voice coexists dialogically *with* the music, rather than dominating it or reducing it to background accompaniment.

In her 1978 suite of three songs called *Northern Landscape* Violet Archer set three poems by Canadian modernist poet A.J.M. Smith for piano and mezzo-soprano or baritone. Archer's choice of poetry is significant because Smith's spare, modernist verse is well suited to her equally modernist, atonal idiom. The poems she chose to set to music are "Swift Current," "Sea Cliff," and "The Lonely Land." All three capture aspects of the Canadian landscape, notably its northern qualities, and all three are highly visual minimalist and imagist pieces: these are not poems *about* Canada so much as poems that re-present or express something believed to be essential to Canada – its water, rocks, and "jagged fir."

"The Lonely Land" is the most important of Archer's choices and one of the most frequently anthologized of Smith's poems.[11] It comprises four carefully balanced, stripped-down sentences arranged in a tall vertical column on the page. Each sentence is spaced as a separate paragraph of free verse, with no end rhyme or formal capitalization but with a tightly controlled system of assonance, alliteration, and repetition. Key words, like "snap," stand alone for stress and visual/aural effect:

Cedar and jagged fir
uplift sharp barbs
against the gray
and cloud-piled sky;
and in the bay
blown spume and windrift
and thin, bitter spray
snap

at the whirling sky;
and the pine trees
lean one way.

The final four lines ("This is the beauty / of strength / broken by strength / and still strong") are the closest Smith comes to nationalist sentiment or overt message in a poem that is primarily meant to convey the sights, sounds, and feel of the "the lonely land."

In her "Lonely Land" Violet Archer has done much more than merely set the poem to music.[12] She has created a powerfully mimetic composition in which the piano and voice are fully integrated to reflect the rhythm, emotion, and sense of the verbal text. The music is spare, with an angular melodic line, a dramatic use of dissonance, and strong harmonic progressions, which capture precisely and effectively the rhythmic qualities of alliteration and onomatopoeia in the poem. This imitative approach works particularly well at several points, such as the "stagger and fall" repetition evoked with repeated triplets, or in the descending line that pauses on a single note to mimic the long vowel (see Figure 4) of "and the pine trees lean one *way.*"

Glenn Gould's *The Idea of North* is, of course, in a class by itself, but no exploration of the soundscape of North can afford not to consider it. The entire composition was constructed by Gould in the studio from the interviews he taped with his "characters," who never met each other and whose texts were elicited in response to Gould's questions about the North and their experiences there. To round out his imagined North, Gould travelled on the Muskeg Express to the end of the line in Churchill, on the west coast of Hudson Bay, and he chose characters who would represent four contrasting perspectives on the northern experience: "an enthusiast, a cynic, a government-budget-watcher [and] someone who could represent that limitless expectation and limitless capacity for disillusionment which inevitably affects the questing spirit of those who go north seeking their future." The fifth character, a sort of narrator-cum-philosopher, reflects on the comments of the others, at times adding his own observations but always keeping the larger issues of human fate and civilization in mind. For Wally Maclean the North is, finally, the moral equivalent of war because it is the battleground for the ultimate test of human nature, which will only survive if it can accept the challenge to coexist without contaminating and destroying one of the purest places on earth.

The Idea of North has been discussed before and in some detail (see Dickinson and McNeilly). Here it is important to remember what motivated Gould to create his contrapuntal sound documentary in the first place. In his introduction to the piece he explains that the North had fascinated him since boyhood and that he dreamt of going there. He recalls poring over maps, aerial photographs, and geological surveys, and of suspecting that the Group of Seven had not captured all there was to say about the grandeur, mystery, and challenge of the North. In other

Figure 4
Bars 17 and 18 of Archer's "The Lonely Land"

words, Gould was influenced by the evolving construction of Canada-as-North and was aware of the myths of the North circulating in the culture. More precisely, he was fully self-conscious about the role of the Group of Seven in contributing to this image of the country and prepared to carry on where they left off, to push their imagining of country further. With *The Idea of North* Gould was, in short, invoking, adding to, interpolating his voice and the voices of his five speakers into the discursive formation of North.

He was also aware of the romantic fallacy he was toying with – especially for a man who loathed the cold and would never use planes to explore a landscape that could only really be reached by plane (unless one took to canoes, ice-breakers, and dog teams). But Gould was serious about this passion for the North. Although he questioned his own "quasi-allegorical attitude toward the north," he insisted that "something really does happen to most people who go into the north – they become at least aware of the creative opportunity which the physical fact of the country represents, and, quite often I think, come to measure their own work and life against that rather staggering creative possibility" (liner notes). It is interesting that, in measuring his own creativity against the North, Gould chose to counterpoint the human voice with the sound of a train. The only music in *The Idea of North* is the symphonic language of Sibelius; Gould himself must be listened for in the interstices of sound, in the silences and spaces that separate while they integrate the elements of the work. When Timothy Wynne-Jones recreated Gould in his children's novel *The Maestro* (1995), he was careful to have his hero's great composition destroyed by fire; it is not for his musical compositions that we revere and mythologize Gould.

Several other Canadian composers, however, have attempted either to express their own responses to the North or to capture aspects and qualities of a northern or Arctic landscape in absolute (non-programmatic) music.[13] The source, or object, of their inspiration is signalled by descriptive titles (*North Country, Edge of the World, Suite Borealis*, for example), but the sound of the North can also be located in the textures, tempi, and tonalities of the work. Taking his cue from Brian Cherney, David Parsons argues that a set of distinct characteristics recurs when Canadian composers wish to represent the North: "These include long, high string lines, wide register spacing, delicate orchestration, and thin textures" (Parsons, 13). Just what the composer wishes to convey in his or her northern language is less easily determined, or, perhaps more to the point, how the listener responds to and hears the music is open to interpretation.

North Country: Four Movements for String Orchestra (1948) by Harry Somers is a fascinating example of non-programmatic northern music that exploits the distinct musical language described by Parsons while remaining richly evocative and ambiguous.[14] The composition is relatively short (ranging in performance from just under thirteen to almost fifteen minutes), and the contrasts between and among its four movements emphasize the tight, contrapuntal aspects of its structure. The first movement opens with high, thin violins above deeper, widely spaced chords on the violas and cellos. The sense of dramatic tension and expectation increases with the ostinato in the violins and a refusal of tonal resolution (in McClary's terms, a rejection of the masculine ending). The long pauses between chords bring the movement to a dramatic close that prepares the ear for something about to happen. This expectation is answered in the light, playful, rapid pizzicati and slow glissandi of the second movement, which in turn give way to the quiet, sinuous phrasing, the shimmering of strings, and very quiet close of the third. The fourth movement is brief, energetic, and abrupt; according to Cherney, its brevity creates a lack of balance (38).

Interpretations of *North Country* are bound to vary, but few listeners can fail to recognize some qualities of northernness and thus of Canada in Somers' music. Although we know that Somers added the title after the piece was written, and that he had spent considerable time canoeing in northern Ontario during the period of composition in the forties (Parsons, 12–13), it is unnecessary to tie the music precisely to geographical location; it is important, however, to acknowledge his success in setting the North (or his idea of North) to music. To Cherney this music suggests the "bleakness, ruggedness, and loneliness" of northern Ontario (35). Parsons carries this reading further by insisting on the sense of an overwhelming and threatening landscape conveyed by the music (14); *North Country*, he concludes, evokes "an autumn scene ... full of sorrow (evident in the yearning melodies and generally minor tone) at the loss of summer and the apprehension of the harsh winter to come" (15).[15] And in his introduction to the CBC broadcast of the 15 October 1991 Edmonton Symphony Orchestra's performance, with Uri Myer conducting, Ken Winters exclaims that to him *North Country* "sounds like Canada" with its own "limitless north," not like the music of Grieg and Sibelius. "When I hear this music," he tells his listeners, "I feel the huge Canadian spaces, the keen Canadian winds, and I shiver" (quoted from the New DAT tape).

While I would agree with Parsons that *North Country* ends on an autumnal note, I do not hear *North Country* as threatening or negative. If the four movements correspond to the four seasons, then in my reading the longest, first movement is winter, and the sense of waiting and expectation created by the tempi, absence of resolution, and dramatic contrasts between the violins and deeper cello chords is an appropriate preparation for the burst of energy in the second movement. Here there is nothing ominous; the North in spring is animate, full of life, sunshine, and activity conveyed by the whimsical pizzicati and glissandi of the violins. The third movement stretches out in clear expansive phrasing to create the serene, contemplative mood of summer. To be sure, this mood includes staccato interruptions, the minor, yearning melody that Parsons stresses, but the overall feeling of the music is one of tranquillity. As a representation of autumn, the fourth movement is fittingly brief. It is energetic and stops abruptly, as if in mid-phrase, instead of resolving the startling contrasts repeated here from the first movement. The refusal of closure holds open the cycle (in the music and in nature) of renewal. Rather than hearing *North Country* as a negative representation of a hostile landscape, I would argue that Somers has captured the variety, drama, energy, beauty, and expectation of the North; his North, if not Arctic, is much friendlier than Parsons allows.

John Weinzweig's *Edge of the World* (1946) is another matter. His North is the high Arctic world of tundra and ice above the treeline, and the music for this eight-minute symphonic poem differs in significant respects from *North Country*. Weinzweig uses a full orchestra with timpani and gong and incorporates characteristics of Inuit music and dance songs. The dramatic opening crash hovers over the entire piece, to be echoed at intervals in the sounding of the gong, while the melodic theme is established by the violins in their upper register and echoed by the woodwinds (most effectively by the clarinet), which capture a lonely, haunted quality that southerners have *learned* to associate with the Arctic.[16]

According to the composer, "the edge of the world is a dark northern wilderness – the scene of man's conflict with the hard unyielding grimness of ice and rock. The shadows of adventurers stalk the ancient trails through the sharp crackling stillness of an Arctic night" (quoted in Parsons, 56). It is this human element that we neglect when we focus exclusively on the ice, cold, and emptiness of the North and the fear it inspires. *Edge of the World* is more complex than this because it evokes sensations of epic drama and human effort (be it in the evocative Inuit melodies and rhythms or in the contrasting registers that suggest generalized human struggle). The North that Weinzweig creates is alluring, even exotic (what the southerner hears as representation of the Inuit recurs throughout), and therein lies its danger and its challenge. As Weinzweig reminds us, the Arctic has for centuries been a challenge to native and non-native alike, and it is filled with the presence of the Inuit and the ghosts of non-native "adventurers," some of whom, like Franklin and his men, never returned south. Like Gould and Schafer after him, Weinzweig sees the North as a stage for dramatizing the human struggle to survive. Though not "the moral equivalent of war" (Gould) or the core of Canadian identity (Schafer), it is none the less inhabited, historied, and ours.

The fundamental differences, as well as similarities, suggested by this brief consideration of two contemporaneous non-programmatic works like *North Country* and *Edge of the World* also apply in some recent compositions. Perhaps most importantly, however, the norths represented in these works differ; just as we (in the South) must learn not to reduce the North to a single, homogeneous abstraction, so we must also learn to hear the differences in the sound of the North, and these differences are a function of musical modality and structure as well as the result of a composer's skill and intention (or ideology). Barbara Pentland's *Suite Borealis* (1966) for piano and François Morel's *Nuvattuq* (1967) for solo flute necessarily create less textured and more abstracted musical images of North. In the former the North is symbolic and well south of sixty; in the latter the title evokes the Arctic or sub-Arctic regions of northern Quebec, Ungava, or even Baffin Island, although the music was not intended to represent or express the North. François Houle's *Au cœur du litige* (2000), like the Pentland composition, gives expression to an event that reminds southern, urban Canadians of their northern situation – the 1998 Ice Storm – by counterpointing media news coverage with solo clarinet and violin to create a "palimpsest of voices" (CD liner notes).

Suite Borealis is an austere, loosely serial composition in five parts: "Unknown Shores," "Settlements," "Rapids," "Wide Horizons," and "Mountains." In her own description of the work Pentland calls it "a sort of 'Pioneers' Progress' [that] expresses various feelings, colours, sensations which the changing regions symbolize" (quoted from RCI Anthology, 10). Although there is little sense of northern coldness or the emotions of terror and dread that Parsons finds in most landscape compositions, the suite does capture an unmistakable sense of vast space and open terrain. Morel's *Nuvattuq* (an Inuktitut word for breath) is more about the making of the music itself than it is about the sound of the North. The key connection to the North is the title, which is well chosen to suit both the solo instrument and the creative force of breath in both Inuit and European mythology.[17] A secondary link is in the choice of the flute which, together with the clarinet, has come to be so closely associated in the southern mind with northern solitude and ice. The sound of the North, while still abstract and intellectualized, is much more obvious in Morel's *Iikkii* (1972), a composition for eighteen solo instruments that was inspired, according to Morel, by the feeling of extreme isolation described by Québécois poet Saint-Denys Garneau (Morel, quoted in program notes). Although Morel insists that he did not set out to write northern music, he none the less called it, upon completion, *Iikkii* (an Inuktitut word for coldness) and prefaced the work with the following lines from Maurice Beaulieu's *Il fait clair de glaise*: "Verdure glaciaire, et toi, toundra / Vous m'êtes fraternelles" ("Glacial greenery and you, tundra, are my brothers").[18] Houle's radiophonic composition is if anything even more abstract than Pentland's or Morel's work, and it is overtly political. He uses digitally improvised, recycled news items, in French and English, to comment on nationalist declarations by the media, but he stages the Ice Storm by pushing both clarinet and violins to their limits. The result is a high-tech, anti-romantic encounter between a deliberately constructed *nature* and contemporary human response. (For a more romantic, albeit ironic, representation of the storm, see Benoit Aquin's *Lethal Beauty*, Illus. 5.)

Like these pieces by Pentland and Morel, the last three compositions I want to consider are attempts to capture the spirit or separate identity of a northern environment. They are not narrative (even *Suite Borealis*, despite Pentland's comments, is not human-centred) or even descriptive so much as expressive. What they attempt to express, albeit to different degrees, is the abstract essence or otherness of the North. Malcolm Forsyth's *Atayoskiwin, Suite for Orchestra* (1984) evokes a personified North with a spiritual life and visionary energy independent of human presence. To be sure, there is tremendous and subtle power here, a power perhaps more accessible to the northern Cree, from whom Forsyth takes his title, than the southern non-native, but it is not a destructive or hostile power so much as an uplifting, potentially empowering force characterized, as Forsyth has pointed out, by "majesty" and "quiet."[19] Alexina Louie's *Winter Music* (1989) is a startling and exquisitely evocative composition that almost conjures up winter before our eyes and ears. Originally written for the Vancouver New Music Society, it is scored for solo violin, viola, cello, and bass, flute, oboe, clarinet, bassoon, harp, and percussion, with the woodwinds creating the sensation of eerie space familiar from Somers, Weinzweig, and Morel. In *Winter Music* high, thin, sustained notes on the violin, followed by gentle glissandi, create a magical quality of icy, delicate beauty. Rapid bowing on the cello suggests falling snow, and a series of ascending chords in the strings suggests the accumulation of snowdrifts. Percussion (the chimes in particular) is used to introduce not a threatening note but a tinkling, brittle sound, and the harp introduces qualities of lightness or softness. In short, Louie's winter world, which could be as far south as Toronto (where she lives), is full of life, delicacy, and beauty; it is only the strong minor progression, which concludes the piece, that introduces a heavier, more sombre stillness. *Winter Music* reminds me of what Lawren Harris said in *Winter Comes from the Arctic to the Temperate Zone* (Plate 3) and of what R. Quinn Duffy tells us in *The Road to Nunavut*: "Winter unites all Canadians in what is frequently referred to nowadays as their 'nordicity'" (xiv).

Gwen Boyle has pushed her search for the sound of the North right to the pole. *Tuning* is not a musical composition but an installation sculpture. The work was created after Boyle had suspended a magnetized steel rod from a tripod very near the magnetic North Pole in June 1989. She was expecting the rod to move but she was not expecting to hear it sing: "out of that clear Arctic atmosphere," she explains, "harmonics began to resonate from the sculpture, as if it were 'tuning' the shimmering sea ice" (Boyle, "Artist's Statement"). Fortunately, she was able to record the sound and then to build it into the installation piece shown at the Richmond Art Gallery in the fall of 1993. *Tuning* is an extraordinary experience.

The viewer/listener enters a large white space in a round, high-ceilinged room. Glass plates hang from a bar across the centre of the room over four huge whale bones set amidst shards of green glass – and this space is filled with a high-pitched humming sound, soft, delicate, unearthly, and persistent (Plate 7). What Boyle has done is to take Murray Schafer's lessons in *The Tuning of the World* and transform them into a work of art.

Of all the composers I have considered thus far, with the possible exception of Gould, Schafer has said the most about being a Canadian and about composing "music in the cold," which is an explicitly northern music. His key text in this regard is not in fact a musical composition but a poetic manifesto: *Music in the cold* (1977). Before I look at that text, however, it is important to consider where Schafer is coming from, geographically and philosophically, and how and why he argues for a Canadian music shaped by climate and geography.[20] Schafer's music springs from what he calls the soundscape, and he demands that his audiences abandon their overdetermined reliance on the visual and on urban civilization to become attuned to the sounds in/of the natural world around them. For Schafer that natural Canadian world is northern; in the preface to *On Canadian Music* he stresses "the importance of the Canadian climate and geography," and reminds us that, "as various as this is, it is our best unifier, transcending ethnic extraction or allegiance of any other kind. We are all Northerners, sharing a million acres of wildness in the imagination. That is our only uncounterfeit resource, and we should seek to draw more directly from it" (x). His message is at once nationalist and, in a sense, ecological; like Hamelin and Wiebe, he sees nordicity as what unites Canadians from all parts of the country regardless of race or ethnicity, and he wants us to recognize our nordicity as inherent in our natural environment, which it is incumbent upon us to preserve and protect against "rape ... by the nation's government in conspiracy with business and industry" (*On Canadian Music*, 62).

Schafer's national, ecological, and musicological position is interesting in the context of an investigation of the wider parameters of Canadian identity, but in the context of the discursive formation of North his position is especially illuminating because he overtly connects culture with ideology, the arts with politics, history, and the hegemony of an industrialized, corporatist elite, and the physical place in which we live with the habitus. It is evident from his essays (and from a work like *North/White*) that he is highly self-conscious about his Canadian context and his participation in and contribution to the discourse of North. For example, in "A short history of music in Canada" from *On Canadian Music*, he claims that the "rugged austerity of the Canadian North has prompted a response from many composers" (7), including Freedman, Somers, and Claude Champagne, and in his "Program Note" for *North/White* he invokes Gould by citing and reaccentuating "the idea of North": "Canadians," he warns, "are about to be deprived of the 'idea of the North,' which is at the core of the Canadian identity. The North is a place of austerity, of spaciousness and loneliness, the North is pure, the North is temptationless. These qualities are forged into the mind of the Northerner; his temperament is synonymous with them" (63). Whatever one thinks of Schafer's rhetoric and rather simplistic geographical determinism (not to mention his romantic idealism, which rivals Harris's), there is little doubt that Schafer believes passionately that a great deal is invested in the construction of North.

As is clear from "The Canadian Soundscape," Schafer's larger point is that we are as constructed by our geography and soundscape as is any imagined community or national identity that we might construct from the physical and social elements of our experience of place (see Stephen Adams, 57–9). In this essay Schafer maps the soundscape of the Canada he has known from childhood, beginning with the call of the common loon. Why the loon? Because the loon (common, red-throated, Arctic, and yellow-billed) makes its home in Canada, can easily be heard by most Canadians, and its call is unforgettable (83).[21] And he continues with the aural navigation recorded by Frederick Philip Grove in *Over Prairie Trails* (84), the surprising quiet of a blizzard (85–6), the silence and isolation of our natural environment in winter (87), and the railway that once "constituted a genuine Canadian soundmark" (89). Reaching into his personal notes from the years he lived in the Monteagle Valley in Ontario, Schafer finds a potential score for the soundscape that captures all the seasons but stresses the sounds of winter – "tree branches snapping," the "thwoom, thwoom" or "thwak, thwak" of snowshoes, the cry of migrating geese or just the sound of their wings, the howling of wolves, snow sliding from the roof "like a man clearing his throat," falling icicles that sound like a "glass xylophone," and the "erratic explosions like gunfire" of the forest at –35° (89–94). In other words, what Schafer is constructing here (he would say he and we are constructed by it) is the soundscape of Canada as a set of statements in the discursive formation of North. That his desired Canada *is* North (Canada-as-North) is equally certain – certain, that is, once we get away from the cities, the corrupting, despised South against which he inveighs in *Music in the cold*.

On its own, *Music in the cold* is a bizarre, idiosyncratic text.[22] However, in the context of the discursive formation of North it constitutes an important statement, at once intensely personal and public. It is, at moments, a lyrical lament for a lost northern ideal and an aggressive political challenge to the status quo of "slack-jawed indifference" and creeping Americanization. The diegetic core around which Schafer builds his allegory of Canada-as-North is a story of a northern nation run amok by becoming its opposite: the South. As the following passage demonstrates, Schafer draws upon a wide range of other statements from the discursive formation of North to create a bitterly ironic imagined community:

We became one of the richest nations in the world.
We were invincible.
We were gearing up to become Number One.
We stood straight like the North West Mounted Police.
We gritted our teeth and grimaced for the photographers.

Those "few acres of snow" (Voltaire) had been beaten by our cement
industry. We were dropping geodesic domes in the arctic and
building slick, fabulous cities over the woodchips of grizzled forests.
We wrote paradise into our constitution.
The world applauded and flooded in to see how we had done it.
We became the most powerful nation in the world.
We lived in glass houses hundreds of feet in the air.
We no longer went South.
We were South.
[...]
No one had seen snow for fifty years, except for a few outdoor freaks who
flew up to the Yukon for weekends to chase polar bears on snowmobiles.
We lived on avocados and flamingo-meat
We all grew double chins.

This may not be the friendly Arctic Stefansson envisaged, and it is certainly not
the dominant discourse that I have explored thus far, but it relies on and assumes
knowledge of that discourse to make its point: this is what awaits us if, as Rudy
Wiebe protested in *Playing Dead*, we continue to neglect our nordicity and persist
in "whoring after the mocking palm trees and beaches" of the South (111). It is the
fate courted by the characters in Mansel Robinson's play *Colonial Tongues*, to which
I shall return.

Like R.G. Haliburton and so many others, the only hope Schafer holds out in
Music in the cold is a return to the North. But where the evolving discursive formation (from Haliburton and the Canada Firsters to F.R. Scott, A.J.M. Smith, and the
Group, to St Laurent and Diefenbaker) represented Canada as growing northward,
as becoming more and more northern, Schafer, living in the later half of the twentieth century, locates the fundamental paradox of that northern discourse in the
collapse of the narrative itself, in its tectonic slide southwards:

Millions fled south.
The rest could no longer carry on.
They took down the signs reading Canada.
We surrendered.
Glaciers descended into the basements of cities and toppled
Skyscrapers like dry weeds.
Wolves howled derisively at night – 0000 0000 0000
Zero
Zero
Zero
Zero.

Only then, at ground zero, when North has reclaimed its territory and "All is still,"
will a small group of "Rough men ... themselves half wolf," sitting around a camp-

fire, begin again to construct a new northern nation and, once more, as "men of the North," reclaim their "place in history." The "music in the cold" that Schafer calls for will be a music rooted in the northern soundscape, beginning with the howl of the wolf; it will be restrained, quiet, "composed of tiny events," and it will be created, apparently, by real men, like Schafer.[23]

North/White is Schafer's closest musical formulation of the ideas in *Music in the cold*. It is a short composition (eight minutes in my recording) for orchestra and snowmobile, intended, as Schafer explains, to dramatize our technological abuse and destruction of the North by "pipelines and airstrips, highways and snowmobiles" ("Program Note" for *North/White*, *On Canadian Music*, 62). The piece opens with a single protracted note followed by shimmering notes in the strings that are suddenly blasted by heavy percussion and screaming synthesized sounds. One of the most unpleasant of these latter sounds is a low, repeated *glubbing* that conceivably mimics the sound of oil moving through a pipeline. After this, the high strings are interrupted at increasingly short intervals by jarring bell sounds, heavy horn blasts, and percussion. Whistling and the flapping of two masonite boards evoke Arctic wind (Stephen Adams, 128). Finally, a hammering, percussive barrage of noise drowns out the rest of the orchestra, and over this we hear the droning of a machine (the snowmobile) that represents all the heavy machinery, from planes to trucks and mining equipment, that we use to open up, develop, and exploit the North. The last sound we hear is the ugly *glubbing* that fades into silence. As Stephen Adams suggests, Schafer's emphasis on "quasi-technological sounds" may work to drown out the purity of the North (suggested by the strings) rather than lament its loss (128).

North/White is not pleasant to listen to. It is not meant to be. Using musical signs in a semiotics that represents the northern soundscape as it exists in Canada today – a jarring mix of delicate, natural sounds and abrasive mechanical ones – Schafer asks us to cherish both the northern environment and our identity. Consistent with his philosophy throughout his work, physical geography and the indigenous soundscape shape us, make us what we are, as much by their real, acoustic presence as by their contribution to and participation in the discourse of our nordicity. To "chop into the North," Schafer warns, is "to chop up the integrity of [our] own minds." In Schafer's formulation, we cannot imagine ourselves if we can no longer imagine North (*his* idea of North): "The idea of North is a Canadian myth," and "without a myth a nation dies." Therefore, *North/White* "is dedicated to the splendid and indestructible idea of North" ("Program Note," 63).

Although Schafer's musical statements are strident and politically confrontational, he is not alone, even among musicians and composers, in his nationalist evocation of North. The sound of the North created by his fellow composers and, behind them, the poems or outdoors experiences or paintings that have attracted and inspired the music *all* contribute to the discourse. Central to this discourse, of course, is that lodestone of northern representation and ideology, the Group of Seven, whose images link Herman Voaden, Harry Freedman, Diana McIntosh, Glenn Gould, Michel Longtin, Violet Archer (via A.J.M. Smith), and Schafer with each other and with the present. In the closing years of the twentieth century, as Canadians reassessed their identity, it was no accident that 1996 was marked by the massive retrospective exhibition called "The Group of Seven – Art for a Nation," and that June 1997 was devoted to the Northern Encounters circumpolar music festival. These important events, like the music of Somers and the others, articulate and perform aspects of who we are.

Just how powerful the discursive formation of North will be to the socio-political reality or cultural symbolism of Canada in the twenty-first century and what it will contribute to the habitus as a unifying force for a renewed Canadian "imagined community" remains to be seen. The Northern Encounters Festival suggests a re-location, in contrast to the vision of the Group of Seven, of the discursive formation to a wider, circumpolar sphere. Such a relocation and displacing is another reminder that the "we" implied by the Group exhibition and assumed by terms like Canada and Canadians is problematic, always open to reformulation and revision. Whether we can imagine going all the way north to Schafer's exclusive and primitive community (no further north, after all, than an Ontario wilderness lake or the Rockies) or up to the high Arctic with Boyle, or whether we prefer to turn back south sooner, geographically and imaginatively, with Longtin or Archer or Forsyth, we can hear the sound of the North all around us. As François Morel puts it: "I am a Northerner, of course. The attraction of the North is not peculiar to me; it is also found among poets, artists and other musicians ... It is the poetry you get from a northern environment" (Morel, quoted in Parsons, 60).

PUTTING THE NORTH ON STAGE

To shift from the sound of the North to the creation of a northern play is not as great as it might at first appear. Songs tell stories, whether they are the popular songs of Aglukark and Rogers, the folksongs of Wade Hemsworth, or the classical song cycles inspired by poetry, and films require sound-tracks. There are even a few Canadian musical plays about such northern events as the Cariboo Gold Rush and the Yukon Quest dog-sled race and about northern icons like Tom Thomson.[24] As I survey the stage at the turn of the twenty-first century, the only form I cannot find much sign of is opera: Gwendolyn MacEwen's *Terror and Erebus*, which began as a verse-play for radio in 1974, has been set to music for solo baritone voice and ensemble by composer Henry Kucharzyk, and the oratorio received its world première in the Glenn Gould Studio on 17 June 1997 as part of the Northern Encounters festival. Henry Beissel's mythic masterpiece *Inuk and the Sun* has been recast as an opera, with music by Wolfgang Bottenberg, but it has yet to be performed in Canada.

As one might expect, the stage is no stranger to northern discourse. Indeed, the theatre has proved to be one of the most contentious places for articulating and presenting ideas of North (see Grace, *Staging the North*, xii–xx). From the 1920s on, debates have swirled around the technical problems of trying to put the

North on stage, and playwrights and critics have argued over the suitability of northern themes for dramatic treatment. Nevertheless, there is a vital tradition of Canadian plays about the North, and, like every other aspect of the discursive formation of North, the dramatic statements are complex, varied, and often contradictory. In the discussion that follows I situate these statements in their historical context by tracing briefly a southern genealogy of plays about the North. More importantly, however, I explore the categories of northern play that have emerged over the past seventy-five years because it is in the differences between plays that dramatize historical events and figures or celebrate a mystique of northern adventure, freedom, and death, and plays that analyse and critique that dominant version of a beautiful, if deadly, heroic North, that I locate the tensions and the vitality in the theatre's contribution to and replication of a discursive formation of North.

In his 1977 essay "Is There a Canadian Drama?" Brian Parker argued that Canadian theatre had been slow to develop in large part because Canadians lacked an appropriate myth. Parker recognized the centrality of the North for Canadian identity and praised the capacity of poets, novelists, and painters to represent the North, but he believed that the myth of the North was "antidramatic" (155). He could not imagine a dramatic art that could put such a non-human landscape on stage, and he dismissed the early efforts of Herman Voaden, Merrill Denison, and Gwen Pharis Ringwood to stage the North. Nevertheless, playwrights have kept trying to do just that, usually by focusing on human experience and psychology and by resisting the temptation to reproduce a detailed replica of a northern landscape.

When Herman Voaden published his edited collection *Six Canadian Plays* in 1930 and "dedicated" it "to the north" (xviii), his purpose was to encourage the writing of Canadian plays about Canadian subjects and places. He wanted to foster a *Canadian* theatre, and he believed passionately that such a theatre would spring from a desire to dramatize "the north." He did not ask what "the north" meant or where it might be located. Voaden's North was the country stretching north of Lake Superior, the country painted by the Group of Seven; it was up and out there; it was ultimately, for Voaden, synonymous with Canada. In Voaden's mind a Canadian theatre would *naturally* be northern, whether it took a realist form to explore human relations and social issues, a romantic form to explore historical subjects or heroic struggles, or a variety of more experimental forms that might, as in his own plays, exploit the connections between drama, music, and the visual arts (see Grace, "Re-introducing Canadian 'Art of the Theatre' "). As Voaden knew, plays about the North are not limited by a northern landscape but embedded in it.

The strongest tradition of northern plays is still based in southern Canada, and its genealogy, which begins with Denison and Voaden, peaks with Mansel Robinson's *Colonial Tongues* (1995) and Judith Thompson's *Sled* (1997), and shows every sign of continuing in the twenty-first century. Because these plays are presented to southern, urban audiences, often on main stages of major theatres, they represent a North that mirrors southern ideas of North, that dramatizes social, psychological, and ethical problems that concern southerners, and that sees the North in terms of the South. Given the population base, the economics, and the existence of theatres and publishers in the South, it is hardly surprising that southern playwrights would get more exposure in print, at fringe festivals, and in main-stage productions. There are alternatives to this southern tradition, of course, and these come from theatre companies based in Whitehorse, Yellowknife, Igloolik, and Pond Inlet. Yet to date very few of the plays written and produced in the North have been published or produced south of sixty. During the 1980s and 1990s the Playwrights' Union of Canada published scripts of some of these plays, and in 1992 two publications appeared with work by northern playwrights: *Canadian Theatre Review*'s special issue on the Arctic called *Beast of the Land*, and *Writing North: An Anthology of Contemporary Yukon Writers*. *Staging the North* (1998) is the first collection of plays to place southern and northern plays side by side, and these juxtapositions demonstrate the discursive shifts and the proliferation in *ideas* of North that have occurred since the era of Dension and Voaden.

The context for dramatizing the North is complex, multifaceted, and by no means confined to the theatre. The earliest films (a subject I will examine shortly) used the North as their subject and setting – Nell Shipman's *Back to God's Country* (1919), Robert Flaherty's *Nanook of the North* (1922), and the oft-reprinted *Rose-Marie* (1936) come immediately to mind – but, as Pierre Berton has told us, this was but the tip of the celluloid iceberg (see Berton, 1975). And, as we have seen, radio drama was not far behind film. From the mid-thirties to the late forties Canadian children listened to shows like *Renfrew of the Mounted*, the all-Canadian *Men in Scarlet*, and the immensely popular *Sergeant Preston of the Yukon*. To the sounds of howling blizzards and cries of "Mush," the valiant Sergeant would pursue his man over the frozen air waves. By the fifties Preston had moved to television, and in 1959, weary of American bowdlerization of the national symbol, the CBC introduced *RCMP*, a popular series starring Gilles Pelletier. During the 1990s *North of Sixty* enjoyed a highly successful run on CBC television (see Warley).

None of this material influenced Denison or Voaden, of course, although it may well have had an impact on later artists such as Gould, Schafer, and Judith Thompson. In putting his North on stage, with plays like *Northern Song* (1930), *Wilderness* (1931), and in the set-designs for *Six Canadian Plays*, Voaden took direct inspiration from the paintings of the Group of Seven, especially those by Lawren Harris, and Tom Thomson; his sets were stylized rocks, hills, and trees flooded with silver-grey or blue light (see Illus. 2). The result was an abstract and idealized North of cold, austere beauty that lured but overwhelmed the men who answered her call to adventure. Denison's North was neither as romantic nor as complex, and Voaden's image of the North was in no small part a challenge to Denison's volume of plays called *The Unheroic North* (1923). Denison's characters are crude country yokels or defeated northern Ontario farmers. In *Brothers in Arms*, for example, any remnant of romantic charm associated with a "hunting camp in the backwoods" (9), where the action takes place, is stripped away to expose it as a "God-forsaken hole" (10).[25] Ringwood also wrote plays with northern settings: *Still Stands the House* (1939) is a psychological drama that is inseparable from the blizzard that dominates and destroys her isolated prairie family, and *The Road Runs North* (1967), with music by Art Rosoman, is a celebration of Billy Barker and the 1860s Gold Rush in British Columbia (see Grace, "Staging the North in B.C.").

During the late 1950s and early 1960s the Inuit and their Arctic landscape were put on stage in some striking ways that, by today's standards, seem inept and appropriative (see Grace, "Representations of the Inuit"). The most problematic attempt was David Gardner's 1961–62 production of *King Lear*, starring William Hutt (see Illus. 19). Gardner wanted a *Canadian* setting for the play, which meant a *northern* setting, and he decided to mount an Arctic *Lear* complete with harpoons, mukluks, and snow goggles to create a suitably primitive impression. The Fool was recast as "part seal, part penguin [sic], and part wise, old owl" (Garebian, 152).[26] *The Great Hunger* (1958), by Leonard Peterson, is a white southern Canadian's well-meaning attempt to examine the plight of an Inuit family caught between a traditional lifestyle of hunting and shamanism and Christian values, which make little sense in their Arctic world. Peterson adapted this material from actual accounts of Inuit lives as recounted by white anthropologists and missionaries like Gontran de Poncins, Diamond Jenness, and Raymond de Coccola, but the play itself fails to do justice to the cultural complexities of encounter because it is cast in the form of a conventional Western tragedy with a deeply embedded Christian plot-line turning on sin, guilt, and punishment.

Representation of the Arctic and the Inuit Other is much less problematic when the southern playwright moves away from such culturally embedded and hegemonic modes as tragedy to comic forms, satire, and myth. Henry Beissel's *Inuk and the Sun* (1974) is the best example I know of of a play by a southern Canadian about the Inuit.[27] Beissel was fascinated by Inuit mythology; to present his dramatization of a boy's passage to manhood, he combined myths of Sedna, the goddess of the sea, who must be placated if the seals and other animals are to be available for the Inuit to hunt, with Bunraku-style puppets to enact the human and spirit roles (see Illus. 20). Beissel's Inuk is a northern Everyman, and his story is a dramatization of the cycle of death and life that privileges the survival of a group over an individual's story. In *Question Time* (1975) Robertson Davies constructs a satiric allegory of Canadian political life that stars an Inuk shaman who convinces a Canadian prime minister that life is worth living and Canada worth serving, as long as he remembers the importance of the North. This comic yet biting play is aimed straight at southern audiences and parliamentary procedures; there is no attempt to represent Inuit realities here. Not until 1989, and Mordecai Richler's *Solomon Gursky Was Here*, would there again be such an approach to the far North.

During the 1970s, 1980s, and 1990s the dominant discourse for staging the North, first articulated by Voaden, as heroic, alluring, and mystical, continued to

Illus. 19. William Hutt as the "Eskimo" (or Arctic) King Lear in the 1961–62 Canadian Players production, directed by David Gardner. Photograph by Lutz Dille, who is represented by the Stephen Bulger Gallery, Toronto. Reproduced by the Special Collections Centre, the Toronto Public Library, with the permission of William Hutt and Lutz Dille and courtesy of David Gardner.

provide the stimulus for some of the most powerful plays written by southern Canadians about the North. A new discourse begins to emerge as early as 1969 with Herschel Hardin's *Esker Mike & his Wife, Agiluk*, but I want to consider what the dominant discourse looks like on the boards before turning to a few powerful attempts to unsettle it.

Some of the most important dramatic statements in the dominant discourse are those that recreate historical figures and events. In his introductory manifesto to *Six Canadian Plays* Voaden had identified historical romance as a key contributor to a northern mythology and identity; he knew likely subjects could be found in Arctic exploration and northern adventure, although he could not have foreseen the exact subjects or their treatment. Both Gwendolyn MacEwen's *Terror and Erebus*

Illus. 20. Henry Beissel's classic play *Inuk and the Sun* received its Stratford premiere in 1973 with staging concept and puppets by Felix Mirbt. The play was directed by Jean Herbiet and Felix Mirbt with Silvia Maynard as Sedna, Goddess of the Sea, and puppeteers Ian Osgood, Jill Courtney, Maxim Mazumdar, and Felix Mirbt. The production photograph was taken by Henry Beissel and is reproduced courtesy of Henry Beissel and Felix Mirbt.

and Geoff Kavanagh's *Ditch* explore the deaths of Sir John Franklin and his crew in the mid-1840s on their ill-fated search for the Northwest Passage. In *Who Look In Stove* Lawrence Jeffery dramatizes the final weeks in the lives of John Hornby and his companions, all of whom starved to death on the Barrens in 1927, and in his unpublished play "Canoe Lake" Kavanagh re-creates one of the most mysterious of Canadian heroes – Tom Thomson, "the prophet of the North" (44). Even with the story of a madman and killer there is room for a sense of awe and fascination, especially when that man was Michael Oros, who kept diaries and had romantic illusions about life as a northern bushman. Oros is brought to life with some of that aura still in place in Philip Adams' expressionist nightmare *Free's Point*.

Despite their considerable differences, each of these plays constructs an image of North as a place of extremity and masculine adventure. Women have no place in this world, in part because the relationships are deeply homosocial, or openly homosexual (as is the case in *Ditch*), and in part because the North is a place to which men go to escape what they believe women represent: the comfort of home, civilization, safety, and boredom – in short, the feminine. There is a dreadful irony in the suspicion that lies just below the surface of the dialogue and the narrative in these plays and that constructs the North, be it bush, tundra, ice, a lake in Algonquin Park, or the Barrens, as female. Paradoxically it is MacEwen (the only female playwright in this group) who dares to say it aloud, to voice the horror of that suspicion through the voice of Rasmussen, who, reflecting on Franklin's disaster, knows he has to "drive and press on down / Into the giant virginal strait of / Victoria," even though "she might not yield":

> She might not let you enter,
>   but might grip
> And hold you crushed forever in her stubborn
>   loins,
>   her horrible house,
> Her white asylum in an ugly marriage.[28]

Franklin and his men, at least as MacEwen imagines Rasmussen remembering them, came all that way from England to find, not a Victorian angel in the house but their overwhelming Other. The North, or Canada-as-North, in *Terror and Erebus* is a deadly female trap.

This trap is by no means so graphically described in *Who Look In Stove* and *Ditch*, but it is a trap for its male adventurers all the same. *Ditch* also examines the Franklin disaster; however, Kavanagh does not privilege the high heroic perspective of the officers. The two characters in this one-act tragedy are merely sailors, ordinary seamen, who are left behind when Crozier and the surviving men abandon their ships in a futile trek south across King William Island to the mainland, and who come to accept their love for each other as they die. Their deaths are, in a sense, transfiguring, but they have had to come here, to this frozen, desolate place to find the truth about betrayal, hatred, and love. When the play was staged at Tarragon's Extra Space theatre in 1994, the program included a reprint of the famous Victoria Point Record (the only written document to have survived the disaster and a key point of reference in the play), and Stan Rogers' song "Northwest Passage" was played at the end as the lights went down. The effect of this play with such staging and presentation is, at one and the same time, to decentre the Franklin story by focusing on two of the sailors and constructing those men as gay, and to reinvest the story with all the pathos and human interest of failed human struggle against overwhelming odds; in Kavanagh's hands, Whitbread and Hennesey, not Franklin and Crozier, are the true heroes of the event.

In *Who Look In Stove* Jeffery tells the story of the last few months in the lives of John Hornby and his two companions, Harold Adelard and Edgar Christian, who was a cousin of Hornby's and a boy in his teens when Hornby set out for the Barrens in 1926. However, instead of presenting the story – it could hardly be called the *action* – of the play from Hornby's perspective, Jeffery chooses Edgar as his central character, and we experience the futility, endurance, anger, and loyalty that surround the three men in their final, desperate isolation through Edgar's registering of these emotions.[29] As we move through this minimalist one-act play, tension mounts, not through what the men do – trapped in their cabin and growing progressively weaker, there is little they can do – but through what they say and refuse to say. Silence steadily overtakes the play, as activity, interaction, even the conversation of the men shrink to nothing. Like the men, we watch life being stripped down to its barest minimum until, in the final moments, Edgar is left to repeat, with long pauses between them, the words that he actually wrote, in life, on the top of the cold stove, where he had placed his diaries, and that Jeffery has immortalized: "Who ... Look ... In ... Stove" (93–4). The play ends with a slow fade from brilliant white to blackout as the audience listens to the final verse of the fifth song from Mahler's *Kindertotenlieder*.

Who Look In Stove is a quintessentially northern play for several reasons. It is a story, based on actual events and on the written record (Edgar's diary and final letters to his parents), of adventure, adversity, and death in the sub-Arctic; the characters are driven by their lust for adventure but forced into isolation, near madness, and starvation; and it is an all-male story, in which Jeffery emphasizes the homosocial bond that is especially strong between Hornby and Edgar. In re-creating these men, of course, Jeffery has constructed a psychodrama of extremity and represented a dramatic truth, and the fictionality of his creation is a central theme in the play. There is no attempt to put the landscape on stage because such realist detail would detract from the main interest of the play: the *impact* of the landscape on the minds and bodies of the characters and on their embodied words.

Throughout the drama Edgar insists on using words, on finding the right words to communicate with his companions and with his diary. And Jeffery has stayed fairly close to the diary for his description of failing health, small fragments of conversation and observation, and timing. In the Exile Editions publication he includes Edgar's diary and final letters at the end, but in the play itself documentary is offset and balanced with art. Jeffery, like Edgar, never lets us forget that the greatest adventure, the most difficult and yet the most necessary, is the adventure of words and representation, never more so than when one is faced with the overwhelming languagelessness of the North and the silencing of death. Edgar's death matters *in the play* because he speaks and writes; his final gesture is a semiotics of writing and a plea to be heard. Indeed, this passion to write and be read, to tell and be heard, seems inextricable from the discursive formation of North (see Grace, "Re-inventing Franklin"). Either we must write about it, if we go there, or we must read about it if we do not, and if there is no instantly available written record, we will search forever, in disbelief, until we find something in words to anchor our experience. Thus we have Kavanagh replicating and rearticulating the Victoria Point Record, Jeffery replicating and rearticulating Edgar's diary, and MacEwen reminding us that the flesh of Franklin's men is "a mildewed chart" (*Afterworlds*, 44), that in the North, finally, it is our bodies that leave a "graph in the snow, a horrible cipher, / a desperate code" (53).

Even Philip Adams' play about Michael Oros, *Free's Point*, is based on a written record, the diaries kept by Oros, confiscated by the RCMP and available to the playwright.[30] But one does not need to know about the written record (unlike Jeffery, Adams does not highlight that connection) to appreciate the degree to which words are the centre of the character Tahltana Free Mick's existence. He is nothing without them, and the play emphasizes that reality by presenting the story as a frantic monologue that frames Mick's remembered/replayed dialogue with his hallucinated double, and murder victim, Heinz. Like the other plays about actual northern events and heroes or anti-heroes, *Free's Point* ends in death, and Mick's final words are significant. In his delusion he thinks he has become one with the North and that this means transcendence: "When the land takes its sweet victory and we are made one with the wind ... there are no other blessings we can receive that take us to where we are perfect ... cleansed" (278). It is this desire for purity and transcendence *through* death that characterizes so much northern discourse, as the next group of plays I want to consider makes very clear.

The representation of North as an idealized space of beauty, freedom, and adventure or escape underlies, to varying degrees, each of the plays I have just considered. In those plays, however, the complications presented by an actual historical record, however modifed and reaccentuated it may be, tie the play to document and a documentary mode.[31] Plays such as Voaden's *Wilderness*, Beissel's *Inuk and the Sun*, and Thompson's *Sled* are free to celebrate this idealized North and to privilege its spiritual and mythic aspects in the themes, dramaturgy, and set designs of the plays. Odd as it may seem, in their vision of North these plays actually have a lot in common with stories and novels, from nineteenth-century fiction for boys (see Phillips in *Representing North*) to mythic narratives like *Tay John*, or a postmodern "geografictione" like Aritha van Herk's *Places Far from Ellesmere*. In making this sweeping comparison, I am not suggesting that these plays are heavily narrative or non-dramatic but that they can claim a degree of licence from fact and are thereby freer to envisage a symbolic, mythic North in a landscape of the imagination.

Thus Voaden calls for a lyrical expressionist style in *Rocks* (a recasting of *Wilderness* in his "symphonic expressionist" mode), and he uses lighting and music as much as the characters' speeches to carry the play's message of transfiguration.[32] In a sense it does not matter *where* the play is set; the hero, whom we never see, dies in the North, and his mother and lover are left to reject or accept that loss in lament or transfiguring vision. *Inuk and the Sun* has the very simple plot of myth. It is a quest play, in the form of a hunt, that takes its hero on a cyclical journey into manhood and a search for the sun, which will restore the animals to the land and save the Inuit from starvation. But if the plot is simple, the presentation of it is not. Henry Beissel is a poet, and the textures, phrases, shifting registers of language from prose to poetry make this a verbally rich play. He has also drawn on Inuit and Greek myth to create a subject that, while located somewhere in the Arctic, will resonate with more southern cultures. Add to this the aural effect of a chorus (of seals) and the stylized visual beauty of masks and puppets, and the final effect is one of dramatic ritual. Like Voaden, Beissel has been deeply influenced by Irish theatre, especially that of Yeats, and by Japanese theatre. Although *Inuk* can be performed by actors, Beissel prefers Bunraku puppets, which frees the theatre from naturalism (see Illus. 20). "All art," he insists, "has its place in the imagination and nothing is more persuasive than a puppet, because you would never take it for anything but a creation of the imagination" (Glaap interview, 55).[33]

In *Sled* Judith Thompson gives us a play that recapitulates the discursive formation of North in startling and familiar ways (see Grace, "Going North"). It is a hybrid work, mixing symbolism and realism to create a mythic journey from South to North and from life (or a kind of urban life-in-death) to death, and it identifies its female characters with a natural world of snow, cold, and the Northern Lights. The plot is a complex doubling of interconnected story-lines: a middle-aged Toronto couple, Annie the singer and Jack the cop, go to a northern Ontario lodge for a weekend's respite from the city and a troubled marriage. When Annie goes for a midnight walk along the snowmobile trails, she is shot by a drunken local who has stolen a snowmobile to poach moose. Meanwhile, back in Toronto, on Clinton Street, a young woman called Evangeline waits for the return of her lost brother and shares memories with her Italian-Canadian neighbour. After Annie's violent death in the snow, Kevin, the man who shot her, makes his way to Toronto hoping to find his mother and sister, while Jack, the bereaved husband, returns to his house, which is almost next door to Evangeline's.

Kevin turns out to be Evangeline's lost brother, who was kidnapped when a baby and taken to North Bay, where he grew up. This disastrous upbringing has not made a pleasant human being of him; he wants to dominate (sexually and economically) his sister, and he is almost killed by Jack, who falls in love with Evangeline because she reminds him of Annie and, like Annie, is closely associated with nature and the North. However, Evangeline shoots Jack before he can strangle Kevin, and, on the advice of Annie's ghost, the two siblings flee north following the North Star. The play ends with Evangeline about to give birth on the very spot where Annie died. The Northern Lights, which have played an increasingly important role throughout the play and are associated with the dead in the mythology of most northern First Nations cultures and in Inuit culture, fill the night, while the ghost of Annie appears singing her song from the beginning of the play.

The fundamental binary opposition on which this play rests is that of North/South, where North is situated no further north in Ontario than Algonquin Park, and South is a central Toronto neighbourhood. Thompson's description of her experience on a ski trail in Algonquin Park provides crucial insight into her construction of North in *Sled*, and thus of this binary in which North is so firmly inscribed: "I was alone with this exquisite stand of birch and the light going down and I felt a rush of a kind of St Francis of Assisi ecstasy, in communion with nature, and I thought 'only in Canada.' At the same time I felt this note of a deeper kind of danger. I felt fear with a kind of ecstasy."[34] By now, this formulation of a northern experience should sound very familiar: the combination of aloneness, ecstasy, communion with nature, and holy terror have come to be read as synonymous with North. Moreover, this equation is central to the construction of a Canadian identity and of Canada-as-North, and in *Sled* Thompson is attempting to create nothing less than an allegory of Canadian life.

Sled repeats, participates in, and contributes to, the identity constructed in the opening and closing sequences of *Thirty-two Short Films about Glenn Gould* (1993), in Malcolm Forsyth's *Atayoskiwin* (1984), in Robert Kroetsch's *Gone Indian* (1973), by R. Murray Schafer in *Music in the cold* (1977) and *North/White* (1973, where a snowmobile is brought on stage as part of the performance), in the closing scenes of Howard O'Hagan's *Tay John* (1960), in Harry Somer's *North Country* (1948), in Voaden's plays, and by Blair Bruce in *The Phantom Hunter* (see Plate 2). Drawing upon her own, clearly profound experience and on this wider context, which she can assume her audiences will know, Thompson mystifies North as the Other – our *uncanny* "Home and Native Land." Her North, like Voaden's, like Lawren Harris's, is spiritual, beyond precise articulation or realist representation; it is an aesthetic object removed from the welter of social realities and problems that she associates, in the play, with South. And so her characters, especially her female characters, go North to find themselves – in death and in a promise of rebirth that lies beyond the end of the play, in symbol and myth.

But there are *real* norths, with real people living there with real problems, and there is another group of plays, still written by southern playwrights, that probe and question and expose these problems. In these plays it is southerners, who only see the North as a source of raw materials to be exploited, or as a place where they can live out their fantasies, who become the focus of the playwright's critical gaze. Herschel Hardin's *Esker Mike & his Wife, Agiluk* was the first play to examine the catastrophic effects of southern, white interference in the Arctic, but in *The Occupation of Heather Rose* Wendy Lill provides an equally damning and more moving confrontation with such interference. In *Colonial Tongues* Mansel Robinson shifts our attention away from interracial and intercultural conflict in the Arctic or remote northern communities to focus on the results of our ignorance and neglect of the near North, of small-town northern Ontario. Robinson includes in *Colonial Tongues* all that Thompson left out of *Sled*, and for my purposes his play provides important ballast to hers. Despite their differences and unique qualities, each of these three plays shares a desire to unsettle and decentre the dominant northern discourse that I have been considering thus far. They all stand North on its head and show it for the southern construction it is. At the same time, and this is what makes all three plays to my mind so powerful, they all celebrate the lives of northerners, and they all confirm the importance of a more inclusive, less destructive concept of Canada-as-North.

Set in the tiny Inuit community of Aklavik in the mid-1960s during the development of Inuvik on the eastern side of the Mackenzie delta, *Esker Mike* is a savage exposé of the fundamentally racist, and deeply sexist, behaviour of the representatives of white culture in all their dealings with the Inuit and Dene of the area. Esker Mike is a white trapper, a selfish, lazy, stupid brute, always on the lookout for welfare and always complaining that Agiluk will no longer sleep with him. Agiluk, who has borne too many children already, only to see them farmed out to the Catholic or Anglican church schools in Inuvik, has decided that she has had enough: "When Esker Mike can feed us, then that hole will open up again. Why should my children go to Inuvik? I want them to eat out of their own hands" (22). This face-off forces Esker Mike to marry Agiluk, in the hope that marriage will oblige her to do her duty by him. However, the wedding turns into a Brechtian farce, with the Anglican minister and the Catholic priest competing for souls. By the play's end, however, the useless whites are unable to stop the inevitable tragedy; Agiluk kills her remaining two children and is arrested. In the view of the arresting constable she is almost as crazy as Esker Mike, and the dead babies are "two heaps of dead Eskimo. Or is it whale meat?" (84) Agiluk will be sent south to face white justice, leaving Esker Mike to move in with another Inuit woman, and the steady rape and exploitation of the North will continue. What the church does not interfere with, the government officials will, and the police are there to see that law and order prevail.

It is not a pretty picture, but then the story of interracial relations and southern development in Canada's North has not been a happy one, as so many actual events and subsequent studies have made clear.[35] If *The Occupation of Heather Rose* is less harsh than *Esker Mike & his Wife, Agiluk*, it is only because of the mode of the play. Heather Rose is a young white nurse who has been sent to a remote northern community to provide health care for the local Indian band, but the entire play – a one-act monodrama – takes place after she has returned south to confront Miss Jackson, her boss and the woman from Northern Medical Services who trained her and sent her to this community. But Miss Jackson never shows up. While she waits, Heather tells us what she saw, experienced, and learned; she has, in short, come back from the brink of madness, from a "heart of darkness" for which she is partly responsible, and, like Conrad's Marlowe (whom Lill invokes in a prefacing quote to the published text), to make us feel, to make us hear, above all to make us listen.

The *us* in this play is a white southern audience, comprising those Canadians who, like Miss Jackson, have no understanding of real northern conditions but think they have a right – a duty even – to bring southern, Euro-Canadian values, food, ideas about health care, land claims, and education to a people whom they cannot imagine as having any values or culture of their own. The results of this ignorant interference are terrible, and the play ends with Heather Rose reliving the death from solvents of a beautiful teenaged Indian girl. Heather, of course, can do nothing to save Naomi; her Western medicine is useless. She leaves the North having understood the arrogance of her Florence Nightingale assumptions, and the social problems of the native community remain unsolved: the white storekeeper continues to peddle illegal booze; the local river is still full of chemical pollutants; a southern-style education remains irrelevant to the native's lives; and Nurse Rose's medical supplies never arrive. *The Occupation of Heather Rose* is a moving plea for understanding, sensitivity, realism, and the rejection of arrogant, colonizing, racist attitudes that insist on seeing the North as a playground for white adventure or as a source of southern wealth. It is a portrayal of defeat, not by northern realities alone but by the illusions about North that are absorbed from the dominant discourse. It is finally a portrayal of humility: "There was no connection," Heather realizes, "between the Romance of the North and my tired lonely existence as a Northern Nurse" (316).[36]

Colonial Tongues brings its social and cultural message closer to southern Canadians' home, and it explicitly expands the idea of North into the idea of Canada. This play takes the world of Thompson's *Sled*, and of so many romantic, idealized norths, and turns it inside out. Like *Esker Mike* and *Heather Rose*, it demystifies the romance of the North to show its audiences and readers how close the North is and how important it is to national life. The play has two temporal settings, but both parts of the story take place in the same physical place – a working-class family home in a small northern Ontario single-resource town. The play opens on 30 June 1967, the day before Canada Day in our centenary year. The Barnett family of mother, two sons, and a daughter are facing eviction and break-up: the father, who had worked for the railway, is already gone, killed in the Korean war; the elder son is about to decamp to join the American army in Vietnam; the daughter wants away from the dying town and dissolving family as fast as possible, and the younger brother is busy in the back yard building a model steam engine for the Canada Day parade. In 1967 the mother, Edna, is trying single-handedly to hold the family together and to keep her place in her house and town. The *present* action of the play takes place on 30 June 1995, only by this time the town is a ghost town; the older brother is presumed missing in action; the daughter has become a ruthless developer married to an American tycoon, Edna has died; and the younger brother, Butch, is desperately trying to rebuild the family home and the entire town.

Butch, however, is staging more than a renovation project. He has brought his sister home to force an acknowledgment from her that she and their older brother (who is actually alive in Florida), and Canadians like them, are the ones responsible for the destruction of the North and, thus, of Canada. The action from 1967 is in a sense his memory play, his remembering of what he witnessed as a boy on that day, and so urgent is his need, so powerful his creative memory, that he brings Edna back to life. The dramatic energy of the play resides with this mother and son because they are the creative forces in the world, as Mansel Robinson imagines it. They are alike in other ways as well – feisty, mouthy, passionate, loyal, tenacious, proud of who and what they are, and possibly, just possibly, victorious in the end. Neither Edna, who in 1967 holds on to her home, ironically, by renting it out, nor Butch, who in 1995 is unable to wring a single sensitive or unselfish feeling from his sister or bring his absconding brother back, is able to stave off the consequences of greed, exploitation, globalization, branch-plant closures, corporate and government cost-cutting, all of which lead directly to the collapse of the local economy and the shutdown of the railway. Neither is able to undo the past. However, both are able to remember the past, to retell it, to make others listen, and it is this capacity that makes them victorious in the end.

The beauty of *Colonial Tongues* is not just that it is so emphatically about real life; any Canadian who travels into the provincial norths will find the kind of towns Robinson describes and the kind of working-class people who are his characters. The beauty of this play lies in its language. The Barnett family characters use an immediate, direct vernacular that we can associate with credible small-town, working-class Canadians, but Edna and Butch are the most verbal, the most eloquent in this family. They are the bearers of local history, the story-tellers who remind us that without a history and a shared family story we are nothing. There is a scene in which Butch waxes almost rhapsodic about the terms for building, and this scene crystallizes, for me at least, one of the key ideas of the play. Madison, the American-tycoon husband of Butch's sister, is goading Butch about his rebuilding. According to Madison, "businessmen are the craftsmen of the 21st Century" (399), but Butch knows his craft well: "furring, kerfs and nosing," he replies, "… all carpentry is poetry" (399). Madison is not listening: he shoots back: "The aesthetics of this century are the aesthetics of warfare," but Butch insists: "half-lap and blind dowels," "… bull nose boards" (399). Poetry indeed, a working-man's poetry.

But the war of words continues:

MADISON: Time and distance have been liquidated by the new alchemy.
BUTCH: They fill the boxcars with southern PCBs and shitfilled Pampers and they ship the garbage north to us.
MADISON: We're all nomads now.
BUTCH: "You want jobs?" they say. "Become a garbage dump for Toronto, Montreal, for Vancouver and you'll have all the jobs you can handle." They starve us out and then they give us shitty diapers to suck on.
MADISON: Even the rules are fluid.
BUTCH: They're taking apart this country family by family, town by town.
MADISON: Think of it as national euthanasia. Home towns? Provinces? Nation states? Phantoms from the past.   (401)

At this point Madison picks up the Canadian flag and prepares to set fire to it, but Butch seizes his builder's drill, places it against Madison's cheekbone, and proposes a little demolition of his own. The point is made. Madison drops the flag. There is a line this northerner will cross to protect his home.

In performance this scene is funny, witty, bitterly ironic, a *tour de force* of duologue and timing, but on the evening I was in the theatre there was an audible gasp when the nasty American made to burn the Canadian flag and a sigh of relief when the local yokel, this guy straight out of a Mackenzie brothers' beer ad, stopped him with his drill. But this scene is more than a stunt or a pitting of the poetry of carpentry against the crass babble of postmodern cliché, because it goes to the heart of the play and celebrates the creative power, verbal and manual, of an ordinary Canadian to see the truth of northern exploitation by the South and to describe exactly what he sees. *Colonial Tongues* is finally about northern voices having their say, telling it like it is; it is a play about discourse by a playwright who is a master wordsmith. Robinson's wider message is that we must listen to these authentic northern voices before it is too late. The story of the North is not about adventure, romance, heroics, terrifying and dramatic deaths of famous men struggling to endure unthinkable hardships or to accomplish amazing feats. It is a story of small towns, railroads, families, of traditions, history, and the building of a nation. The last word should go to Butch Barnett, whose very name says a lot:

> BUTCH: But we gave it away. This place. The north. We had everything we needed. We could have built a home. But we volunteered to build our own coffins instead. We don't run a thing anymore. It's all run by somebody from somewhere else. We turned this place into a colony of a colony. (385)

As these Canadian plays about the North demonstrate, the discursive formation of North takes its place easily on the stage. Staging the North (as I have called this process elsewhere) is not a matter of putting elaborate realist sets of rocks, snow, pine trees, and igloos on the boards but of exploring the multifaceted capacity of North to fascinate, haunt, repel, lure, and trouble the southern Canadian imagination. Among the many things that these statements in the discursive formation of North have in common is, in fact, this quality of haunting. These plays are full of ghosts – from the ghosts of Franklin and his men, of Hornby and young Edgar, of Tom Thomson, and of Mick and Heinz (who comes back from the dead to make his point) to the more idealized ghosts of romance and myth such as Voaden's lost lover, Beissel's spirits, and Thompson's Annie. Even the plays that seek to displace the dominant discourse by interpolating their alternative statements into this haunting produce their own ghosts – dead babies, dead teenaged Indian girls, a nurse who comes back from the dead (almost) to speak to us, and in *Colonial Tongues* the most pervasive ghost of them all: the ghost of Canada itself. And while these ghosts take many forms, some of which are forceful reminders of that phantom hunter in Bruce's painting, they are usually accompanied or presaged by the Northern Lights, whose very existence signifies the mysterious vitality and otherness of North.

In the mythology of northern native peoples, including the Inuit, the Northern Lights are signs of great power and are usually associated with death, whether as a violent death involving loss of blood or a joyful state of spiritual travel and transformation.[37] Certainly, death is a central theme and a common ending for all the plays I have examined. Either the key players are already dead and must be remembered by those who survive, or the characters move, inescapably, towards death, which may come as a transforming release or as a terrible annihilation. Very few of these plays hold out any hope for a death that leads to rebirth: *Inuk and the Sun* is the most positive in this regard, although even here one knows that the cycle will repeat itself. *Heather Rose* may hold out a slim promise of better things to come, but that possibility is left with the audience or reader to realize, and *Colonial Tongues* may be read as ending in a desperate gesture of faith in the creative, restorative power of art (and of rebuilding), or as a deranged man's hallucination of a dead mother/country and a vanished past. What all these plays insist on, and in this they share much with fiction, visual art, historiography, and narrative poetry, is the felt need to name those who have gone North before; as Kroetsch has told us, the fiction – the story-telling – makes us real. This seeming obsession with naming, with genealogy, is one aspect of the discursive formation that ensures its longevity and flexibility, because each new play/text/statement repeats and then adds to the story, even when the clear intention of the play is to critique and problematize ideas of North.

As these plays make only too clear and as Herman Voaden knew in 1930, staging the North is a way of staging a national identity. Canada *is* North, these plays tell us, even on Clinton Street in downtown Toronto. Moreover, North is always opposed to South. Sometimes that South exists in the blind indifference of Ottawa bureaucrats and the Christian church; sometimes it is the urban world of boredom and civilization. Gould saw that South/North binary as fundamental to Canadian life, as did W.L. Morton, Lawren Harris, and D.C. Scott, who captured the opposition succinctly in his poem "The Height of Land":

Upon one hand
The lonely north enlaced with lakes and streams,
and the enormous targe of Hudson Bay,
Glimmering all night
In the cold arctic light;
On the other hand
The crowded southern land
With all the welter of the lives of men.   (Scott, 108)

R. Murray Schafer believes that Canadians will only be themselves when they face North again, and Rudy Wiebe would agree. "We are a northern nation," he insists, and "until we grasp imaginatively and realize imaginatively in word, song, image and consciousness that North is both the true nature of our world and also our graspable destiny we will always go whoring after the mocking palm trees and beaches of the Caribbean and Florida and Hawai" (*Playing Dead*, 111). Wiebe might have been talking with Butch, because they are saying the same thing – that the idea of Canada and an idea of North are one and the same.

When you sit down to watch Ann Claire Poirier's award-winning NFB documentary *Tu as crié Let Me Go* (1997), you may be surprised. The film is set in downtown Montreal and is about a personal tragedy: the murder of Poirier's daughter, a heroin addict and prostitute. This is *not* a film about the North. But Poirier is a Québécoise and a Canadian, and in this film she is reaching for a visual metaphor to contain her grief, love, and, possibly, acceptance (understanding is impossible for all the parents in the film); to do this, Poirier turns North. *Tu as crié Let Me Go* opens with a long, silent, slowly moving distance-to-close-up shot of a massive iceberg. The camera is unseen, but we know it must be fixed on a slow-moving boat that is circling the berg. Suddenly, the berg calves – that is, a massive piece breaks loose from the mother berg and plunges into the sea. Without explanation, the scene shifts abruptly to an urban street and Poirier's voice-over begins.

Why an iceberg? And where? The answers come in the closing sequence, when we return to the iceberg and the sea, but this time we catch a glimpse of Poirier at ship-side watching the berg, and we hear her speaking of her daughter, who wanted to be free, and of herself, who must let her daughter go, like the many-thousand-year-old mother berg returning parts of itself to the sea. The child, a beloved daughter, is this woman's, this *Canadian* woman's beloved "northern light."[38] It would be absurd, of course, to argue that this film is a northern film, but it is not absurd to say that it conveys something about the profound importance, to the southern imagination, of the North. As we have seen from several of the plays, North is that symbolic place of freedom, of letting go, of spiritual sustenance, and, yes, of death. But in Poirier's visual language that death is represented as a return to the sea, to the inescapable cycle of death and life, to a North that eventually melts southwards. The iceberg unites mother/child, birth/death, North/South in a northern discourse beyond words, a discourse that informs so many Canadian paintings, non-verbal texts, and films.

Two of the earliest films to represent the North are Nell Shipman's *Back to God's Country* (1919) and Flaherty's *Nanook of the North* (1922), and since this period of black and white silent film there has never been a time when the North has not been represented on screen.[39] While an exhaustive study of film representations of North is beyond my present scope, it seems to me that Shipman and Flaherty signal two distinct traditions for Canadian filmmaking about the North that are still strong at the turn of the twentieth-first century: highly romanticized narrative constructions of place, characters, and story, typically found in feature films and novel adaptations; and authenticated, documentary representations of actual people, places, historical events, and of natural phenomena and of other films – self-quotation and intertextuality being as common in film practice as in other modes of artistic production.

The documentary tradition in Canada can be traced back to early Canadian Pacific Railway advertising shorts and to Robert Flaherty, but it is most centrally associated with the National Film Board of Canada, which was created in 1939

with a mandate that includes informing Canadians about themselves and reproducing and reinforcing the discourse of nation (see Morris). My research in NFB
archives has turned up a daunting number of documentaries about the North that
I have not seen (and could not manage to view); they are ethnographic, historical,
scientific, artistic, or broadly cultural, and they range from *The Baffin Island Oil Spill
Project* (1982) to the very moving *Coppermine* (1992), about tuberculosis among the
Copper Inuit, and from *The Land That Devours Ships* (1984), yet another look at
nineteenth-century Arctic disasters, to a series of films for children called *The
Stories of Tuktu* (1994), which emphatically recall Flaherty's *Nanook of the North*, and
Sedna, the Making of a Myth (1992), about three Inuit carvers from Baffin Island creating the massive sculpture that now resides in the lobby of a Toronto bank. The
romantic feature-film tradition comes forward in time from *Back To God's Country*
and its Hollywood remakes (see Armatage, 27, and Berton) to late twentieth-century co-productions like *Map of the Human Heart* (1993) or *Kabloonak* (1994) and to a
film adaptation like *Shadow of the Wolf* (1992). The documentary tradition remains
strong, not only in NFB productions and on television but also with independent
films such as *Project Grizzly* (1996), *The Herd* (1998), *Amarok's Song* (1998), and Peter
Mettler's experimental and highly parodic documentary *Picture of Light* (1994).

But first, let me set the scene by going back to God's country with Shipman and
Flaherty. *Back to God's Country*, based on a story by James Oliver Curwood and
filmed in part in northern Alberta, is about the heroine's (Dolores, played by Nell
Shipman) attempts to escape a wicked would-be seducer/rapist who follows her
to the Arctic, where it seems that he has her where he wants her at last. But no,
Dolores has an affinity for nature and all animals, wild or domestic, and in her
hour of need she befriends Wapi the killer-dog, who is instantly tamed (after constant abuse from white men) by her woman's touch and successfully defends her
against her assailant. The (melo)drama of the basic plot is heightened by the titles,
close-ups of Dolores with bears, racoons, and, of course, Wapi, and most of all by
protracted long, distant, panning shots of the dog-sled race that is the film's climax. But because this sequence is possibly the first film creation of what is now a
cliché of northern film representation, it warrants some close scrutiny.

Picture this: Dolores is fleeing across the tundra, with her seriously wounded
husband on her sled and the villain in hot pursuit; she has her husband's handgun, but – being a woman, after all – she drops it in the snow: cut to the gun
sticking out of the snow as her dogs speed on; pan to the two sleds, with the
villain's closing the gap on Dolores; cut to Wapi, who leaps to her defence by
attacking the villain's dogs. The film ends with domestic bliss restored, as we see
Dolores, her Canadian engineer husband, their new baby, and Wapi gathered before the fire in a modest northern cabin. The husband has learned to shun southern cities and material goods (prior to their Arctic adventure, he had taken an
unhappy Dolores to his mansionlike home in the city), and Dolores, the eternal
feminine, has found paradise living close to the pristine natural world of which
she is so much a part: God's country, which, according to the visual logic of the

film's images, is northern Canada.[40] I think there is a sense in which Flaherty also creates an image of God's country in *Nanook of the North*. Because there is very little plot upon which to hang the film (Flaherty rejected story), both the camerawork and the representation of the "Eskimos" and their simple lives suggest a pre-lapsarian realm of survival in a harsh but beautiful and bountiful land. Nanook is a great hunter, as is amply demonstrated in shot after shot of his spearing fish, hunting walrus, harpooning seals, trapping fox, and so forth. Moreover, he does all this work with the greatest good cheer, surrounded by his ever-smiling family. The film ends with a close-up of his sleeping, contented face. Nanook's North is removed from place and history; no one starves or dies in this pristine, timeless world; no cultural conflict or southern interference intrudes upon his simple, primitive, yet heroic life.

The differences and similarities between these two films are instructive, and they suggest the blurring that so often occurs in practice between the documentary and romantic narrative styles in film. Both were filmed on location and can therefore claim a certain authenticity. Both rely heavily on dramatic cinematography such as the iris-in close-ups contrasted with the long-distance panning shots of the Arctic and sub-Arctic landscape, which are used particularly for scenes of dog-sleds moving slowly across a low horizon. And both celebrate this pristine natural world of snow, ice, and whiteness, constructing it as a realm of beauty and spiritual interconnection, where death and evil have no place. There, however, the similarities end, for where *Nanook* removes the Inuit from history (thereby romanticizing and idealizing them), *God's Country* shows the negative impact on the North of evil whites, who kill a Chinese miner at the beginning, abuse animals, distribute alcohol freely, and exploit the Inuit women (not to mention the villain's violent designs upon the heroine). Although I cannot pause to compare more fully the construction of race and gender in these two early films, it is safe to say that Flaherty side-steps these issues *in the film*, while Shipman thematizes and, to a degree, critiques them. Whereas *Nanook of the North* is important for having represented a lifestyle and an environment (in which just making a film was a challenge), *Back to God's Country*, for all its melodramatic trappings, is significant because it places a woman at the centre of an already masculinist northern discourse long before Canadian novels or plays would do so, but, in doing this, it equates woman with nature – and with North.

Never Cry Wolf (1983), despite the decades that separate it in time and technology from the 1920s, recuperates many of the semiotic signs and themes developed in these two early films.[41] More importantly, it has been an immensely popular family film (rivalling the popularity of both *God's Country* and *Nanook* in their heyday) that has reached a very wide audience, both on screen and on home video, and thus become a significant statement in the discursive formation of North. Its significance as a statement is further enhanced by the fact that it quotes from earlier films, like *God's Country* and *Nanook*, combines aspects of both the documentary and the romance-narrative film styles, and uses, as well as parodies, several familiar northern tropes.

The hero of the story, Tyler, goes North for the Canadian government to study and prepare a report on wolves. Current science argues that wolves, as voracious predators, are decimating caribou herds, but as Tyler quickly learns, this so-called scientific logic is a myth. Dumped on a frozen sub-Arctic lake by Rosie, the wild, cunning bush pilot, and surrounded (shades of Sir John Franklin) by stacks of utterly useless *things* – tinned asparagus, boxes of toilet paper, sheafs of requisition forms, a typewriter, and a radio that won't work – Tyler does not have long to wait before the North finds him. In the dying light and over the sounds of wind, crunching snow, and the meaningless static from the radio, Tyler hears howling. The camera tracks his anxious gaze off to the distant dark shapes moving across the snow. With visions drawn from European legends and fairy-tales, not to say scientific lore, racing through his mind, Tyler dives for the only cover around – his canoe overturned on the ice. There he awaits his fate and the first blow to his southern illusions about the North. The wolves turn out to be huskies pulling a sled, driven by an Inuk elder, who will, as these stories always go, save Tyler from himself and teach him how to live in and with the North.

As the months pass, Tyler will establish a number of strategic relationships with his new northern world, and each of these relationships will free him *from* a southern-constructed misconception *into* a profound identity with the North. First, he sets up a base camp from which to observe and study a white wolf family. Within no time he has named them, Angeline and George, and discovered that they live and raise their pups on lemmings (or mice). He has also realized that the wolves are studying him – looking back at him and accepting him into their world. Then he gains a greater familiarity with the Inuk, Ootek, and his family, from whom he learns much about the spirit and habits of the great wolf. Bit by bit, he sheds his southern ignorance and his civilized shibboleths. He is going Indian, as it were, and rediscovering – or so the film suggests – a truer, better, more essential self that is in tune with the wolves, the Inuit, and the North. This essentializing, and essentially romantic, construction of identity is visually reinforced in several scenes, but the most memorable and symbolic ones all focus on the body: in one, Tyler mimics the male wolf by peeing a boundary around his territory, and he drinks quantities of tea to accomplish this masculine feat; in another, he proves that a large carnivore can in fact thrive on a diet of mice by emulating the wolves once more (although Tyler cooks his); in another scene he runs naked, except for his boots, with a stampeding herd of cariboo that is being culled by a pack of wolves. This last scene is the most symbolically powerful because in it Tyler becomes physically (that is, in the film, *visually*) natural, an animal with other animals. Not until he finds the wolf-kill does the human being resurface, when, still naked, he approaches the feeding wolves, checks the dead caribou, and discovers, deep in the bone marrow, what the Inuit told him he would find: disease. The wolves kill the weak, aged, and diseased animals, thereby preserving a healthy herd.

Up to this point *Never Cry Wolf* constructs an image of the North that draws upon the visual language and the themes made so familiar by films going back to

God's Country and *Nanook*. It recapitulates the concept of North as God's country, a friendly Arctic place of purity and natural interconnection that might even have pleased Stefansson, where food is plentiful and life secure; and it asserts the possibility – indeed, the existence – of an essential humanity (albeit, here, a man's) capable of coexisting fully and happily within a northern paradise. However, it was the South that sent Tyler north, and the South is not so easily dismissed. Southern science, capitalism, and technology, in the person of Rosie the bush pilot, are penetrating Tyler's world, shattering its peace, and forcing it to enter history. Rosie is a white man on the make, eager to exploit the tourist potential of the North, and when Tyler refuses to leave with him at the scheduled pick-up time, Rosie decides that either Tyler is on to something financial or has simply gone mad, become bushed. To make matters worse, Rosie, this corruptive serpent in paradise, has helped Mike, a young Inuk with experience of whites and the South, to obtain the white man's goods he desires: a rifle and a new set of false teeth. And Rosie's help has come through trade in furs, white wolf furs; he has taken the pelts of Tyler's wolves in exchange for the cash that Mike needs to buy the goods.

In its penultimate scene *Never Cry Wolf* shows how vulnerable the North is to invasion from the south. To look, the film says, is to kill. Yet this is a film. It must be looked at, and the gaze it turns upon the North is one trained in a documentary tradition using a technology that inscribes an ideology based on the premise that to know is to understand and to understand is to be empowered, possibly to do good. The footage of the wolves hunting, playing, caring for their pups, is unimaginable without the language of wildlife documentary. When he realizes that the pups are orphaned, Tyler even crawls into the wolf den, taking the camera with him, thereby penetrating and revealing the innermost secrets of a feminized landscape. In a visual gesture that collapses documentary into romance, thereby returning us to an earlier visualization of harmony within the story, the film ends with a lengthy sequence showing Tyler and Ootek sitting on the tundra, juggling stones, and laughing together. Tyler has turned his gaze away from the wolves, to be sure, but not very far away. We leave him in the North, in childlike communion with an Inuk elder, as if in fulfillment of his adventure and his desired escape from the hegemonic forces of science, technology, big business, and southern governments. This homosocial bond recapitulates Flaherty's with "Nanook" and points forward to a similar configuration in *Kabloonak*. *Never Cry Wolf*, with its white man-of-nature hero, its corrupting bush pilot, its wise, smiling Inuit, its majestic scenery, and its beautiful wolves, uses documentary legitimation to romance the North and to reinforce, through quotation, allusion, and repetition, the idea of North as a place of escape, primitive spirituality, and wildlife adventure.[42]

The 1990s have witnessed the release of a number of films that contribute to and participate in the discursive formation of North, but, like *Never Cry Wolf*, they do so less by reformulating or "writing back" to the dominant discourse than by reproducing familiar statements, repeating documentary or romance narrative codes, and recycling northern themes. *Shadow of the Wolf* (1992) and *Map of the Human Heart* (1993) both present dramatic stories of love, hate, murder, revenge, and suicide set in a gothicized Arctic that bears little resemblance to any actual northern setting or situation. *Shadow of the Wolf*, based on Yves Thériault's novel *Aggaguk*, is simply a bad film, with non-Inuit playing Inuit parts and large dollops of sex and violence. *Map of the Human Heart* is a more complex and successful portrayal of Inuit experience between the wars and after the Second World War, despite its emphasis upon interracial sexual obsession; it represents an Inuk as part of a rapidly changing world to which he cannot successfully adapt. In the former film the North is already corrupt, a place of primitive violence, superstition, and animality. In the latter the North is a place of idealism, community, and happiness, at least until whites intrude, bringing mixed-race offspring, disease, and southern hospitalization, which shatters Inuit families, and war. These constructions of North are familiar: either it is beyond the pale, an exotic place inhabited by primitives, or it is a paradise corrupted by southern interference and white influence.

Although NFB documentaries, such as *Between Two Worlds: The Story of Joseph Idlout* (1990), and films produced by the Inuit, Dene, or northern Cree, such as *Power* (1996), a documentary about the Great Whale hydroelectric project in Nunavik, are certainly introducing representations of North that conform more closely to northern experience and serve northerners' priorities (see Balicki, Gale, Christopher Harris, and Roth), independent documentaries produced in the South by southerners seem caught within the old (and dominant) paradigm. Two recent films by Peter Lynch demonstrate what I mean. Both *Project Grizzly* (1996), which has already gained something of a cult following, and *The Herd* (1998) celebrate the confrontation between an individual white male and a hostile wilderness. In both cases the man is out to test his mastery of the situation and, on some level, to confirm his masculinity. It would be difficult to call Troy Hurtubise a hero, but this North Bay nut and Mackenzie brothers look-alike, who spends every cent he has building a robo-suit in which to study grizzlies up close, certainly has illusions of grandeur. Having survived one grizzly attack, he is sure he has the power to do it again and, in the process, come to *know* the grizzly – as long, that is, as he is grizzly-proofed. On some mythic level, or on some level of half-baked parody of myth, the film suggests that he has this power. While Troy stumbles about in the bush, looking like a cross between an astronaut and a deep-sea diver, Lynch's cameras capture his obsession and, by the very act of filming him, elevate the man and his story into a statement about one of the most archetypal encounters possible in the North: man meets grizzly. The journey from Tay John's epic fight with the grizzly to Tyler's bond with the wolves (that other animal symbol of the North) to Troy Hurtubise's quest for the ultimate face-to-face encounter with the North is not as great as it may at first appear. Troy came by his obsession naturally, so to speak, by saturation in the idea of North as a place of such mythic encounter.

If there are elements of irony and self-parody in *Project Grizzly*, the same cannot be said for *The Herd*. This film recreates the actual epic journey of Andrew Bahr, who was hired in 1929 by the Canadian government to herd three thousand rein-deer from Alaska to the Mackenzie delta in an ill-conceived effort to assist starving Inuit. A journey that was to take eighteen months took six years. While Lynch may have found the government's plan quixotic and the bureaucrats stupid, he makes an epic hero out of Bahr, whose Arctic experience and sheer masculine determination ultimately prevail over an unimaginably inhospitable northern landscape and the stubborn, unco-operative reindeer. Here, even more than in *Project Grizzly*, the vast, harsh landscape dominates the story to provide the visual power of the film. Bahr's ability to survive and succeed in such a desolate place only enhances his stature, making him a figure to rival Stefansson.

Not all recent documentary films that use the North as their setting, theme, or governing visual metaphor are constructed on quite the grand narrative scale of *The Herd. Thirty-two Short Films about Glenn Gould* (1993) uses North to frame and define Gould *as a Canadian* because the opening and closing shots depict Gould emerging from and disappearing back into a flat, snow-filled landscape (we can even hear the crunch of his boots on the snow) in a visual replication of Blair Bruce's *Phantom Hunter*, of the many uninhabited Group of Seven landscapes, possibly of Michael Snow, or of the stories about Franklin, Hornby, Tom Thomson, even pure fictions like Tay John or Solomon Gursky, each of whom disappeared into, was swallowed up by (to recall Frye's phrase from *The Bush Garden*), a northern landscape. The only film I know that pushes this northern documentary discourse of snow, cold, emptiness, and disappearance to its visual/logical extreme is, in fact, Michael Snow's *La Région Centrale* (1971; see Illus. 21). In this film, we can pass three hours watching as a camera moves continuously, in all directions, recording nothing but its own movement and empty northern space. Canada, says Snow, who set up his elaborate filming apparatus north of Montreal, *not* in the Arctic, *is* this *région centrale*, this uninhabited, inhospitable, northern space, stripped of all heroic possibility and all romantic adventure, "that just goes on without us" (60).

I cannot allow Snow the last word or image here, for in the realm of the documentary there are two films that reverse the shot, not only on Snow but on the entire tradition of southern documentary constructions of North: Ole Gjerstad's and Martin Kreelak's *Amarok's Song* and Mettler's *Picture of Light. Amarok's Song*, directed by Gjerstad and Kreelak, is a powerful and highly critical re-presentation of white/Inuit cultural contact in the Baker Lake area, first in the 1950s and then again in the 1990s. This film-video was made at the Banff Centre and is, therefore, free of some of the more constraining aspects of the NFB style. While focusing on the lives of the Netsilik, who were forced by starvation and the Canadian government to move into the community of Baker Lake and give up their traditional life on the land, *Amarok's Song* presents the Netsilik story in Inuit terms and from the Inuit perspective: the title alone captures the Inuit concept of life-story as song, and the use of the Kivioq legend to structure the narrative reminds viewers that this film is an Inuit story about *their* experiences of cultural encounter. But these

Illus. 21. Artist Michael Snow on the northern Quebec mountaintop "set" of the film *La Région centrale* with the film machine designed by Snow and Pierre Abbeloos. Photograph taken by Joyce Wieland in October 1969 and reproduced from *The Collected Writings of Michael Snow* with the permission of Michael Snow.

aspects of the film only mark the beginning of a sharp critique of white, southern representations of Inuit life, especially those created by the NFB. There is no dominant voice-over interpretation of events in the film (as is typical in NFB documentaries), and archival footage is deployed, through skilful editing and intertextual montage, to highlight the bitterly ironic juxtaposition of earlier images of "Eskimos" and the contemporary Inuit commentary on both those images and actual experience. For example, in one especially moving sequence, we see archival footage from the 1968 NFB documentary *North Country: Sister Pelagie* contextualized by a contemporary interview with the Inuuk whose life is celebrated in the film, but who left the church in the 1980s because of the injustices and abuses she witnessed. Although the former "Sister Pelagie" refuses to describe what happened, the film itself, relying on the interviewer (Martin Kreelak), names and specifies sexual abuse at Chesterfield Inlet as one of the chief crimes committed by the church against Inuit children. In a few frames and images *Amarok's Song* has exposed and rewritten the earlier, happy narrative of Christian conversion and assimilation into a story of suffering, betrayal, and abuse.[43]

Peter Mettler's *Picture of Light* is, for me, one of the most fascinating of non-heroic treatments of North, which, none the less, captures a particularly haunting aspect of the North: the Northern Lights. After much waiting around in a

Churchill, Manitoba, motel for just the right moment to arrive, Mettler and his all-male crew rush out into the snow, set up their cameras – and shoot. And there it is! In the warmth and comfort of an urban cinema in downtown Vancouver/Toronto/Montreal: the Aurora Borealis. Or is it? Is Mettler's picture of these Northern Lights not a construction after all, a celluloid simulacrum of the spirit of the North? Of course it is, and yet the Northern Lights are both real and the stuff of northern myth. As Mettler reminds us, in a voice-over comment on the sight: "We live in a time when things do not seem to exist if they are not captured as an image. But if you look into darkness you may see the light on your own retina – not unlike the Northern Lights – not unlike the movements of thought. Like a shapeless accumulation of everything we have ever seen. Before science explained, the Northern Lights were interpreted as visions, prophecies, spirits ... images provided by Nature framed by no less than the universe itself."[44] In *Picture of Light* Mettler has re-presented the Northern Lights as real, as myth, and always, in the movies, as pictures.

At the outset of my discussion of North on film I suggested that documentary and romance narrative styles have often overlapped in the practice of filming a northern subject, especially if the film involved working in a northern location. Where Mettler's documentary seems to problematize that overlap, Claude Massot's *Kabloonak* (1994) takes that threshold on which the two styles meet and makes that conjunction the subject of his film. *Kabloonak*, its title surely recalling Gontran de Poncins's autobiography, creates the story of (or *a* story *about*) Robert Flaherty's making of *Nanook of the North*, and thus it brings me and the film visualizations of North (almost) full circle. By returning to Flaherty and *Nanook*, and by filming in the Arctic, under circumstances that rivalled Flaherty's, Massot achieves several things. He pays homage to Flaherty while recognizing the awe-inspiring beauty and terror of the North, and he constructs "Flaherty" and his filmmaking as both heroic and very human. But he does not stop there, for *Kabloonak* is not simplistic hagiography or sequences of spectacular wilderness documentary, although it is both these too. Beyond "Flaherty," played by British actor Charles Dance, are all the Inuit we do not see in *Nanook of the North*, and while I agree with Noreen Golfman's reading of this representation as a romanticization of them, they are also represented both as complex human beings and as characters in a film about a film (Golfman, 24). In other words, *Kabloonak* allows us to see the documented North within the romantic one *and* the romantic construction within the documentary. In this film we can see how filming the North inescapably constructs it as an objectified document, and thereby writes it into the discursive formation that, in the realm of film at least, began in God's country.

(Alas, had I seen Zacharias Kunuk's magnificent *Atanarjuat* before going to press, I would have concluded my discussion of films by noting his manipulation of these elements, and I would have analysed his film in chapter 6 as a major example of re-writing North.)

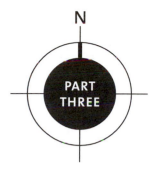

N

PART THREE

NARRATING A NORTHERN NATION

The things that are unobtrusive and differentiated by shadings only – grey in grey above all – like our northern woods, like our sparrows, our wolves – they held a more compelling attraction than orgies of colour and screams of sound. So I come home to the north.
Frederick Philip Grove, *Over Prairie Trails*

Maggie opened a map upon her knee ... The very strange beauty of this country through which she passed disturbed Maggie, and projected her vision where her feet could not follow, northwards – never southwards – but north.
Ethel Wilson, *Swamp Angel*

This air had come down from the empty far north of spruce and frozen lakes where there were no people, it had come down from the germless, sinless land.
Hugh MacLennan, *The Watch That Ends the Night*

Pourtant, ils sont beaux ces fleuves dont le voyage se fait à travers un si oppressant silence. J'identifie la Rivière George, la Falls, la Rivière-à-la-baleine, puis la fameuse Corok dont j'ai entendu chanter la beauté sauvage, là-haut, entre les montagnes, par un peintre.
Gabrielle Roy, *Voyage en Ungava*

FICTIONS OF NORTH

LOOKING FOR TAY JOHN

In a retrospective essay from *A Frozen Tongue* Aritha van Herk remarks that the "great Canadian north is not something that one can capture easily," and she goes on to say, somewhat surprisingly, that "Canadians have not written much about the north" (282–3). By "north" van Herk means "the magnificent barrenlands," and her point seems to be that this "infinite myth and place" defies or eludes our efforts to write about it (283). What van Herk is looking for but not finding is a writing beyond adventure story or regional, local wilderness colour, or writing that reaches out to acknowledge, embrace, and help to construct something far larger (her word is "universal," 283) that North evokes and can be seen or made to represent.

That something larger, beyond adventure story and wilderness description, is my subject in this chapter because, of all the media and genres and disciplines that I have considered thus far, the novel is the most powerful contributor to the network of statements constituting the discursive formation of North. Moreover, novels perform crucial "enunciative functions" (Foucault, 106) within the formation, and these functions are my chief concern in this book. Since its rise in the eighteenth century, the narrative impulse that takes shape in the novel has been implicated in the articulation of Western notions of individual identity, including the stories of origins and genealogy, and in the consolidation of and resistance to modern Western nation-states. Countries, like people, need their stories told and make their stories work in the socio-political domain; even the highly technologized, globalized forces operating at the beginning of the twenty-first century have diminished neither this desire for narrative nor the novel's capacity to elicit and satisfy this desire. And the jury deciding whether the concept of the nation-state is dying or experiencing a bloody resurgence is still out (see Benedict Anderson, Bhabha, and Ignatieff).

In what follows I argue that, over a period of approximately 170 years, from the 1830s to the 1990s, Canadian novels (or novels about "Canada"), both individually and together, have represented Canada-as-North and constructed Canadians as those quintessential northerners whom R.G. Haliburton, Vilhjalmur Stefansson,

Lawren Harris, and R. Murray Schafer (to mention a few) imagined themselves to be. To a significant degree I can speak of a discursive formation of North at all because of this large body of fiction. That said, however, I want to go back and start my story (my chapter) again, first to map the discursive terrain designated *novel* and then to problematize it. A novel can be many things: indeed, its very elasticity, hybridity, or generic promiscuity is what makes it so useful to any discursive formation, and certainly here to the idea of North. In his collection of autobiographical essays about writing, *A Likely Story*, Robert Kroetsch described the potential of narrative this way: "The North," he said, "makes possible a new story" (35).

So, let's begin again, with the *old* story, the one van Herk did not want to see, before contemplating what the new story or stories might be, or how it or they might contribute to this shifting, evolving discursive formation of North and hence to an "imagined community" called Canada.

To construct a detailed investigation of northern narratives about Canada would require another book, one I cannot write here. I would need to establish a narrative typology flexible enough to identify various kinds of novels and to distinguish them from their cognate fellows across several degrees of difference. Decisions would have to be made about where to draw a line between fiction and non-fiction, such as autobiography or essays, because many Canadian writers have used both modes in their writing about North, and capillary links inevitably exist within these single-authored systems. Further decisions would have to be made about narrative poetry, especially long narrative poems.[1] While it might be plausible to exclude individual poems from consideration, or even a volume of poems, such as Al Purdy's *North of Summer* (1967), the distinction becomes less clear in the face of Henry Beissel's *Cantos North* (1982), which I consider in my Epilogue, or Gwendolyn MacEwen's *Terror and Erebus* (1974, 1987), which is both narrative poem and verse drama.

But assuming that a satisfactory typology could be established, a set of narrative fictions loosely called novels agreed upon, the task of analysis would still be daunting. Jack Warwick performed this task for Quebec literature in *The Long Journey*, and the larger study I am imagining might begin by revisiting Warwick's theorizing and methodology and expand or modify his approach to suit the far more diverse and dispersed textual field of northern fiction written in English by Canadians. Allison Mitcham made a start in *The Northern Imagination*, and Atwood pushed the typologizing and thematic discussion further in *Strange Things*. Although some categories of analysis would be impossible (after all, an entire volume has been devoted to a narratological study of *La Montagne secrète*; see Malette), a typology similar to Warwick's could be generated by grouping texts according to nordicity indices (where the stories are set, in what northern region; see Illus. 6 and 9) and, more interesting perhaps, by identifying them with key topoi such as the NWMP (or RCMP), the Klondike and other major historical events, significant moments of cultural encounter, or the stories of heroic, mysterious, or tragic figures like John Hornby, Tom Thomson, Grey Owl,

Albert Johnson, and Franklin.[2] Certainly, there is no lack of relevant tropes, some of which recur so insistently as to constitute a cliché'd or formulaic script for *the* northern narrative – one where the writer takes large dollops of cold, snow, solitude, adds empty, vast spaces, wild animals (favorites are grizzlies, wolves, and caribou), and then tosses in the hero, typically a white man or boy who must struggle to survive (or die), face starvation (or cannibalism), and either go mad or find spiritual solace, even salvation, through endurance in this harsh yet potentially transforming landscape. Either this hero stays in the North (often disappearing into it or dying there; there is little to choose as far as plot is concerned), or, if he brings the North out with him, he is a changed man. Throw in some sex and violence, a murder or two, a trapline trespass, vary slightly by shifting seasons – winter is *de rigueur* and perfect for disappearing snowshoe tracks and dog-sled chases across snow and ice, but desolate taiga and tundra under relentless summer light (with millions of blood-thirsty insects) or claustrophobic spruce forests and dangerous rivers provide thrilling options – or make your hero a woman (a rare and risky choice), and ... Voilà! A northern novel.

It would be unwise, however, in this book-length study of the northern novel that I am proposing, to dismiss these tropes or the predictable, formulaic scripts they produce. Even van Herk is not immune to them, as we shall see, and embedded in these formulaic narratives, replicated and produced by them, are a host of ideological issues that invite scrutiny. Any comprehensive study of these northern novels would have to lay bare the assumptions informing representations of race, gender, class, and ethnicity. It would have to locate the politics of this representation and identify points of possible rupture, types of resistance, and traces of what Bhabha calls "supplementarity" ("DissemiNation," 305–6). In order to pursue this critical analysis of the politics of representation, my hypothetical study would have to examine in detail, at the microlevel, not one text but many, and this examination would of necessity return the discussion to questions of genre and narrativity because it is on this site of representation, where (as Bhabha tells us) generic hybridity makes its stand and where the destabilization of the formulaic northern potentially disrupts representation, that traces of the evolving discursive formation of North can be found. Finally, such a study of the northern novel would need to explore the continuities and discontinuities of such terms as "nation" and "national."

Of course, any discussion of the novel might choose to query ideas of nation; within the Canadian context several critics have already done so, but the corpus of *northern* novels written in English by Canadians highlights specific issues of regional versus national identity and of crises in the negotiation and construction of the rhetoric (if not the fact) of national unity.[3] Can one align Warwick's *The Long Journey* with Atwood's *Strange Things*, and if so, how? What role does northern narrative, in particular fictional narrative (however these are classified in the typology that must precede and direct discussion), play in the construction of Canada?[4] Is the Canada represented in and produced by these novels a Canada with Quebec or, given the symbolic importance of *le grand nord* and the *pays d'en haut* for Quebec identity and literature, are the norths sufficiently different and distinct to force a separation? And, in the last analysis, are these representations powerful enough to intervene in and contribute to a discursive formation of North that will effect and empower an imagined community of Canada-as-North?

Clearly, I cannot tackle this larger project here. None of the issues is simple; each opens out on to a host of attendant questions, problems, and challenges. Ultimately, of course, there are no easy answers, no templates or typologies or scripts that are fixed. Moreover, the very indeterminacy and fluidity of the enunciative field are both more interesting and more enabling than the clarity of closure. What I will tackle in this chapter is much more modest and tentative and much less detailed. While recognizing the risks of presuming to organize a vast array of primary materials, I will sketch a provisional typology of what van Herk and Kroetsch think of as *old* northern stories in order to examine a few specific examples of what are, arguably, *new* ones. My specific examples of new northerns are drawn from the works of six major contemporary artists, each of whom has written about the North several times and has visited, worked, or lived in one or more northern locales: Rudy Wiebe, Robert Kroetsch, Aritha van Herk, Elizabeth Hay, Mordecai Richler, and Gabrielle Roy.

In some senses, these six writers are obvious choices. Roy, Kroetsch, Wiebe, and Richler are among Canada's most celebrated novelists; Hay and van Herk, while more junior, with Hay the least known of the six, are making serious, often experimental contributions to story-making about the North. Despite their first-hand experiences of North, all six are southern Canadians who, with the exception of Roy, live and work in southern Canada, and despite their varied ethnic and linguistic backgrounds (which are of significance to each) they are all white Euro-Canadians. They consititute, in short, an ideal test group of literary, personal, and southern Canadian perspectives on the representation of North and on the evolving discursive formation of North. Finally, their northern novels are very different from each other and rich in narrative complexity, thematic scope, and metaphoric or symbolic texture; their works are fascinating individually and as a group, and they testify to the wide possibilities of writing serious northern fiction. None of their works constitutes a simple instance of taking snow, wolves, a hero, some tundra, and mixing. Moreover, there can be no doubt, I think, that North and Canada-as-North matter deeply to each of these writers. Each wrestles with questions of identity – individual and national – by turning northwards and trying to imagine and articulate North.

By choosing six, whom and what am I leaving out? Well, to focus on artistic creation for the moment (as distinct from more formulaic, popular examples), there are Margaret Atwood, Howard O'Hagan, Denis Chabot, Ann Tracy, Thomas Wharton, and Thomson Highway. Atwood has had much to say about North, not only in *Strange Things*, which I discuss in chapter 2, but also in such stories as "Death by Landscape" and "The Age of Lead" (see Grace, "Franklin Lives"). Even *Surfacing* could, I think, be approached as a northern novel. Chabot's *Eldorado dans les glaces* and Wharton's *Icefields* are surrealistic, postmodern evocations, not so much of Canada-as-North as of icy, northern dreamscapes populated by ghosts, phantoms, and miraculous, alluring presences (see Martineau, and Leroux). While each is beautiful in its own right, neither occupies a position either central enough to or critical enough of the representations of North in which I am primarily interested. Tracy's *Winter Hunger*, a feminist revenge fantasy and cannibalism parable, resonates in appealing ways with Highway's remarkable novel *Kiss of the Fur Queen*; however, stories of cannibals in general and Highway's novel in particular will have to wait. The *Fur Queen*, in fact, is waiting in the next chapter.

My decision not to examine O'Hagan's *Tay John* in detail (1960) was a much harder one to make because, for many reasons, I see it as the ur-northern novel, and it is always at the back of my mind. (Does it haunt me because it holds out the promise of origins to this study, which eschews origins?) But key aspects of the text's northern semiotics can be briefly summarized. Both in its narrative hybridity and in its construction of a mixed-race hero (drawn from life) *Tay John* encompasses most if not all of the key topoi of northern novels, and it moves beyond these topoi into absolutely central issues of representation, cultural encounter, nation-building, and the dream of escape from a corrupt Western civilization into a North of new stories, identities, and possibilities. The final image of Tay John – disappearing into the mountains, into the North, down into the snow, into death – pulling the dead Ardith behind him surely haunts every reader and every northern novel written since:

Blackie stared at the tracks in front of him, very faint now, a slight trough in the snow, no more. Always deeper and deeper into the snow. He turned back then. There was nothing more he could do. He had the feeling, he said, looking down at the tracks, that Tay John hadn't gone over the pass at all. He had just walked down, the toboggan behind him, under the snow and into the ground.   (263–4)

We know that O'Hagan was aware of and influenced by northern tall tales, his personal experiences, the historical record, Shuswap myth, and, perhaps surprisingly, Shanly's poem "The Walker of the Snow," all of which situates *Tay John* as a statement in a network of statements functioning within the discursive formation of North. However, it is interesting to speculate upon the extent to which the novel can be more directly linked with later novels. Jimmy, for example, in Roy's *La Rivière sans repos* (*Windflower*, 1970) is another of those hybrid figures resulting from a rape, which recalls Tay John's conception, and similar mixed-race figures who represent violent cultural encounters, who come to occupy key positions in many northern novels. My aim here is not to ferret out influence, let alone origins, but to suggest one of the traces, the Foucaultian continuities, marking the reproducibility of the discourse and its capacity to supplement and alter the story.

NARRATIVE ROUTES NORTH

By virtue of its sheer quantity, writing about the North and about Canada-as-North has had a major impact on shaping Canadian identity. Fictional narratives are important and complex constitutive elements in the narration of nation because they legitimize, authorize, and determine the boundaries within which a story or a history can be told. In a new country, developing from a process of external colonization, exploration, and settlement, narratives of origins and self-*identification* are urgently, nervously sought, and they are found typically in figures (of speech, symbols, characters) of appropriation and expropriation that enable the settler culture to claim, albeit retrospectively, their continuity with a past predating their arrival (a *pre-history*, as it has been called, without questioning the assumptions of such a term) *and* their break or difference from and superiority to such a past. This simultaneous assertion of continuity and discontinuity can take many forms, usually unconscious, seemingly innocuous and inadvertent; they become social practices that are, as Bourdieu reminds us, part of the habitus. They help to tell *us* who and what *we* are, and *we* take them for granted until someone or some event ruptures the story to bring into critical awareness an absence, aporia, loss, or exclusion, and allows/forces *us* to acknowledge the boundaries, the full presence of others and of other stories. Tay John leaving only his traces in the snow causes such a rupture. So too does the alteration to a handsome heritage sign that I recently saw on a British Columbia beach: the story, carved carefully in lacquered wood, tells of a white man's arrival on this beach in the 1830s, a spot important to the "pre-history" of local Indians, and of what the white man did after he arrived. However, someone with another story to tell has gouged out the "pre," leaving an obvious gap, and thereby changed, irrevocably, the story of origins, arrival, and colonization – at least on that historical plaque. The act of appropriation has been erased, though its mark remains visible, and the story is reappropriated.

The novels of Wiebe, Kroetsch, Roy, van Herk, Hay, and Richler are similar attempts to story and re-store-y the nation. On the one hand they recapitulate narratives of origins and settlement, often creating beautiful and powerful figures of appropriation and expropriation; on the other, they question the entire enterprise, recognize the violence of the story, and often reject outright its legitimating comforts. They invent other stories or oblige us to see the story of colonization in a new light. They erase the "pre," but its traces are still there, like Tay John's faint footsteps in the snow.

There is much less ambiguity or subtlety to most of the popular writing about the North that has shaped public opinion and the national imaginary since the middle of the nineteenth century. Beginning with Robert Ballantyne's hugely popular boys' adventure novels set in the Canadian Northwest, representation of Canada as an empty northern space in which white men seek adventure and prove themselves by challenging nature persists in a host of tales for children and adults. This corpus of work may be classified as boys' adventure, wilderness romance, travel/explorer narrative, wildlife story, or even northern detective and mystery fiction. My point is that it is popular; it sells, and thus is influential at some level of the popular imagination.

Before I consider this corpus more closely, however, it is helpful to pause long enough to acknowledge the cognate field of non-fiction and its steady output over more than one hundred years. As early as 1869 (the same year R.G. Haliburton published *The Men of the North and Their Place in History*), Alexandre-Antonin Taché had published *Esquisse sur le Nord-Ouest de l'Amérique*, followed some twenty years later by *Vingt Années de missions dans le Nord-Ouest de l'Amérique* (1888), and George Tuttle had published *Our North Land, Being a Full Account of the Canadian North-West and Hudson Bay Route*.[5] Though their terms and fundamental ideology of white colonization and development may be similar, Taché and Tuttle have different northwests in mind – one with little room for Protestant anglophones, the other oblivious of the presence of Catholic francophones – but my point is less their difference than their common purpose, which is to identify the nation, and its future, with the Northwest. These books were influential in their day because they formulated and focused current public debates. By the 1890s the popular imagination was captured by news of gold in what seemed the fulfilment of a northern promise and prophecy: the North was a land of such riches that it could pull a world economy out of depression and make untold fortunes for all – or so that story goes. All the North American newspapers were bursting with news of the Klondike, and the first book about it, Tappan Adney's *The Klondike Stampede*, appeared in 1900, before the rush was quite over and while going North was still the thing to do.

Closer to home, the home that is of Quebec, Arthur Buies insisted that the northern reaches of the province were the true home of the French Canadian nation – "Le boulevard inviolable et sûr de leur nationalité."[6] His *La Province de Québec*, published in 1900, at a strategic moment for French Canadian *rayonnement* owing to the negotiation of provincial borders, invoked the North in support of French Canadian identity, but Buies' North was as empty of prior claims or other peoples (at least, of other peoples whom he counted) as was Tuttle's.

Between 1901 and 1939 non-fiction books, usually based on first-hand accounts of adventure or exploration, continued to be published at a steady pace. The North, whether a provincial north, the territories and the Barrens, or the high Arctic and the North Pole, were constantly in the public eye. Where the early and mid-nineteenth century was the period of keenest search for the Northwest Passage, the early decades of the twentieth century witnessed a viciously competitive and nationalistic fight by Americans and the British to claim the Pole (see Lisa Bloom). *The Beaver* and *Canadian Geographic* (at first called the *Canadian Geographical Journal*), two important and popular Canadian magazines, began circulation at this time; both were devoted to representing Canada-as-North and to presenting the history and geography of the more remote provincial norths, the sub-Arctic, and the Arctic. The nationalist agenda of both publications was every bit as clear as that of the American *National Geographic*, although neither Canadian magazine had comparable resources to fund and promote polar exploration.

Of the many northern non-fiction books published during the first decades of the twentieth century, some are still familiar, and a few remain in print. In most cases, however, they are now known by association with historic events, their famous authors, or a literary tradition, such as writing about the North. Ernest Thompson Seton's *The Arctic Prairies* (1912), the account of his 2,000-mile canoe trip through the Barrens in 1907, north of Great Slave Lake, in search of caribou, is a narrative replete with derogatory remarks about the Indians on whom, like so many before him, he relied, and ecstatic descriptions of the northern landscape, the very sight of which, he exclaims, is "the culmination of years of dreaming" (244). *The Arctic Prairies* includes reproductions of many of the drawings and paintings Seton made during his trip, and in this respect, as also in his successful use of the canoe for such a long journey, Seton's story repeats aspects of nineteenth-century journeys (by George Back, for example) and reinscribes elements of what would become an archetypal story about the Canadian artist in the northern bush. Seton, as it were, prefigures René Richard, the real-life model for Gabrielle Roy's Pierre Cadorai, and he succeeds where Tom Thomson would fail.[7]

My favorite early twentieth-century northern narrative is by Mina Benson Hubbard, one of the very few women to make such a trip *and* to write about it. *A Woman's Way Through Unknown Labrador*, first published in 1908, has never been long out of print (see Grace, 1999). Like Arthur Stringer, in *Open Water* (1914), Hubbard captures the sense of northern adventure and joy in a wild landscape that Seton celebrates. But popular as all these narratives were in their day, the books written by Arctic explorers shaped more profoundly the growing sense of where North was and what it might mean for Canada. Robert Flaherty, Vilhjalmur Stefansson, and Diamond Jenness were all active in the Arctic during this period, and their best-known work appeared in the 1920s. In addition to his film *Nanook of the North* (1922) Flaherty published *Camera Studies of the Far North* (1922) and *My Eskimo Friends* (1924); Stefansson published his provocative *The Friendly Arctic* (1922), and Jenness his *People of the Twilight* (1928). Add Knud Rasmussen's *Across Arctic America* (1927) and Leacock's *Adventures of the Far North* (1922), and you have a powerful network of statements circulating in the twenties.

Taken together, these narratives construct the North (from Labrador to Herschel Island, and from northern Quebec and Manitoba to the Beaufort Sea) as a space for virile, white male adventure in a harsh but magnificent, unspoiled landscape waiting to be discovered, charted, painted, and photographed *as if for the first time*. It is a place of masculine romance, offering challenge and escape (which makes Mina Benson Hubbard's story all the more remarkable) to those special few who can go North, as C.R. Cooper commanded in *Go North, Young Man* (1926), and return safely to tell the tale.[8]

Before the end of the 1930s, however, a new type of northern narrative would emerge, one that combines elements of masculine adventure with conservation of the wilderness. The chief exponent of these views was Grey Owl, who championed the wilderness and its creatures in autobiographical works such as *Men of the Last Frontier* (1931), *Pilgrims of the Wild* (1935), and *Tales of an Empty Cabin* (1936). Grey Owl, that Englishman Archibald Belaney gone Indian, is a fascinating subject in his own right, as Robert Kroetsch, Gwendolyn MacEwen, and Armand Garnet Ruffo have realized through their literary reincarnations of the man. Passing as an Indian, whatever his own complex reasons may have been, provided him with an authority to speak for his beaver friends that he could not claim as a white, and to resist the practice and the adventure narrative of trapping, hunting, and dominating the North. Grey Owl and his conservation narratives introduce a new and significant story into the discursive formation of North, a story in which human beings learn to live with nature rather than against it. That such a script might be romantic, even nostalgic, and that its author might be a fraud who could deceive his audiences by manipulating their racial prejudices only serves to complicate the picture in interesting ways. Grey Owl was a cult hero in his lifetime and continues to have a certain cult status: his gravesite and cabin in northern Alberta are visited by tourists; his portrait, taken by Yousuf Karsh, is frequently reproduced; and a highly romanticized film has been made about the man, his Iroquois wife, Anahareo, and his conservation work (see Attenborough).

The next thirty years, 1940 to 1970, witness the publication of many more books about the North in new categories of non-fiction narrative. Richard Finnie's *Lure of the North* (1940) and *Canada Moves North* (1942) pick up the colonization and development themes of Taché, Tuttle, Adney, Stefansson, and Cooper. Charles Camsell's autobiography, *Son of the North* (1954), provides further corroboration of an idea as old as Haliburton – that the Canadian North produces the best men, and these men, in turn, acknowledge their northern origins. Camsell, the son of a Fort Liard Hudson's Bay factor and his part-Indian wife (a lineage Camsell does not identify in *Son of the North*), became a geologist with the Geological Survey and held the federal government post of deputy minister of mines and resources from 1920 to 1946. His is a success story, but it is a success story based on the ideology of British heritage and development of the North by the science and technology of white, Western civilization. Moreover, his story is deeply ironic, although he seems unaware of any irony in his construction of a genealogy, as a "son of the North," that denies part of his racial identity, or in his advocacy of development of a North that he celebrates for its pristine rivers, mystery, and power to lure and hold one.

One other book published in the 1940s has had a peculiar longevity and impact on non-fiction and fictional narratives alike. Gontran de Poncins's *Kabloona* (first published in 1941 and reprinted in 1965 and 1980) is the autobiographical account of this Frenchman's year, 1938–39, spent with the Inuit of the Kitikmeot region around Gjoa Haven and Pelly Bay, and it has been received and interpreted as model ethnography by a man perfectly suited to understand and report on a vanishing culture.[9] But *Kabloona* is not ethnography of the Inuit, certainly not as ethnography was practised by Stefansson, Jenness, and Rasmussen; as its title clearly indicates (Kabloona is Inuktitut for white person), this book is about de Poncins's deeply personal quest for the self (a civilized, Western subject) through a process of near total identification with an Other who is both loathed and desired. That de Poncins knew what he was doing and understood its implications seems clear from his commentary: the point at which he comes to acccept the difference between himself and his hosts is the point at which he can see not them but himself through their eyes, enough at least to recognize that he is an incompetent nuisance, "a barbarian" (83). *Kabloona* marks one of those vital points of rupture, or Foucaultian discontinuity, in the discursive formation of North. This story by an outsider (a non-Canadian, a non-Inuk) tells a story of cultural encounter in which the white man learns to "discard things – haste, worry, rebelliousness, selfishness" (291), and it is a story in which he leaves before disrupting the people he encounters. While it may not be a narrative of national identity, *Kabloona* exposes many of the myths about white masculine identity and Western cultural superiority that are embedded in the idea of North, from its earliest Canadian formulations in the nineteenth century to the present. Its circulation and citation within the discursive formation of North, its continuing popularity, if you will, may arise from its problematic and disruptive power.

Two major creators of northern narrative to emerge in the 1950s are Pierre Berton and Farley Mowat. The stories they tell differ, but these men share an abiding passion for the North, defined by both as the sub-Arctic territories and the Arctic. Mowat's first books, *People of the Deer* (1952) and *The Desperate People* (1959), are about the plight of the Inuit of the central Arctic and his recognition that southern Canadians know very little about the actual experience of these people. Like Berton in *The Mysterious North* (1956) and *Klondike* (1958), Mowat is intensely nationalist. For both men it is the North, its landscapes, peoples (of all races), stories, and history, that constitute a Canadian identity.[10] Both Mowat and Berton have rescripted nineteenth-century polar exploration as a Canadian story: Mowat in his *Top of the World Trilogy* (begun with *Ordeal by Ice* in 1960) and Berton in *The Mysterious North* and later *The Arctic Grail* (1988) and a series of children's stories, which appeared in the 1990s. Each has contributed greatly to the popular understanding of Canada-as-North, not only in these historical works but also in more personal narratives. Berton's autobiographical *Drifting Home* (1975), about a northern rafting trip, takes me into my next period, but it underscores the same sense of North as homeplace for Canadians that Berton constructs in his historical narratives and Mowat explores symbolically in his autobiographical tale *Never Cry Wolf* (1963).

Interestingly, the perspectives that Mowat develops on the Inuit in *People of the Deer* and *The Desperate People* echo de Poncins and share a common self-critical stance, based on the acceptance of difference, with Raymond de Coccola's *Ayorama* (1956), Roger Buliard's *Inuk* (1953), and Doug Wilkinson's *Land of the Long Day* (1955). Each of these narratives is a blend of autobiography, history, and ethnography, but in the last analysis they all represent the Inuit not so much as exotic others but as fellow human beings and citizens in a Canada that extends north to the Arctic archipelago. Where Finnie and Camsell contribute to a northern narrative of development in which native inhabitants scarcely figure, and Stefansson and Jenness write Arctic ethnography, these works by Mowat, de Coccola, Wilkinson, and Buliard represent, for the first time, an indigenous North existing in history and moving into the present, a North with its own identity as part of a large national whole.

This narrative development is crucial in several ways but most importantly for its representation of North as lived in, as occupied by people with stories and voices of their own. Because of this representation, these statements in the discursive formation of North prepare the way for the *writing back* that I examine in the next chapter. True, they prepare the way by presuming to speak for the other, by ventriloquizing (or by what might be called appropriating voice), but they prepare the way all the same; they open a space for a speaking and listening that had been denied, repressed, or simply ignored hitherto. By the end of the 1960s, and with R.A.J. Phillips's *Canada's North* (1967) and Jim Lotz's *Northern Realities* (1970), Canadian ideas of North had grown to include a wider vision of North and of Canadian identity than Haliburton, Taché, Tuttle, Finnie, and Camsell could have imagined or would, I suspect, have approved of. Non-fiction northern narrative in the 1970s, 1980s, and 1990s multiplies the questions, the possibilities, and the voices still further.

The period of 1971 to 2000 (my present moment of writing and arbitrary endpoint) has been so rich in non-fiction books about the North that it is impossible to do more than touch upon a few selected highlights and trends as I see them.[11] Possibly the single most important nordicity index of socio-political discourse about the North during this period is the formulation and creation of Nunavut, a process that has kept the North in the public eye in a way that is quite different from the Klondike or Diefenbaker's "Road to Riches" campaign in the 1950s. Then, the North was represented as there for others, especially southern, Euro-Canadians living in big cities; now, it represents itself *for* itself. News coverage of 1 April 1999, Nunavut Day, is a separate topic, which I will consider in due course, but I mention Nunavut here because I find it symptomatic of the changes being articulated at the end of the twentieth century; it is a benchmark that signals a dramatic shift in the discursive formation of North as well as in the map of Canada and the Canadian constitution, and it interpellates a new national ideology and identity.

Other discursive lines, already well established, remain powerfully present during these years. The past of Arctic exploration continues to mesmerize Canadians: Mowat completes his *Top of the World Trilogy* with *Tundra* (1973), an account of exploration by land from Samuel Hearne in 1769 to John Hornby and Thierry Mallet in the mid- to late-1920s; Frank Rasky publishes his *Explorers of the North* series, with the dramatically titled *The North Pole or Bust* appearing in 1977, and Berton publishes his *Arctic Grail. Frozen in Time*, Owen Beattie and John Geiger's galvanizing account of forensic anthropology on Beechey Island, appears, complete with graphic colour photographs, in 1987, and in one stroke elicits a new flurry of Franklin mania in documentary film, childrens' books, adult non-fiction, fiction, painting, and newspaper accounts around the world (see Grace, "Re-inventing Franklin" and "Franklin Lives"). Full-scale biography of Canada's explorers (notably William Hunt's *Stef* in 1986) and the 1991 publication of *Arctic Odyssey: The Diary of Diamond Jenness, Ethnologist with the Canadian Arctic Expedition in Northern Alaska and Canada, 1913–1916*, edited by his son, serve to spark renewed interest in the men, the North, and the representation of Canada-as-North.

Mowat's *Tundra*, however, incorporates another set of statements in addition to exploration; he uses the occasion of re-narrating exploration by land to reflect upon the land itself and its primary inhabitants. *Tundra* is a first-person narrative, not perhaps an autobiography by any narrow definition but an eye-witnessing, as it were, a personal meditation upon the past as a way of looking to the future; Mowat's claim to truth and his authority to speak derive from this witnessing. He concludes *Tundra* with a well-placed indictment of white, southern greed and exploitation that has, he insists, turned the fragile vitality of the Canadian North into a truly barren land. His plea for reclamation, while echoing Stefansson's "friendly arctic" rhetoric, picks up the conservationist position of Grey Owl and continues his own earlier message (especially in *Never Cry Wolf* and *The Desperate People*), and combines this discourse with an emphatic acknowledgment of the claims of indigenous northerners, like the Inuit, Dene, and northern Cree, which began to emerge in the narratives of de Coccola, Buliard, and Lotz. Moreover, Mowat connects his meditation on North with the nation and with an inclusive national identity that entails collective responsibility for the land. "In 1967 Canada entered her second century," he reminds us: "Her first was a hundred years of despoilment of a new and virgin world, and nowhere is this more bleakly demonstrated than in the North ... In Canada's second century we have the chance to undo some of the brutal, tragic errors of the past. If we turn northward again in imagination and in reality we can bring a dead world back to life, and we can share that life and be the richer for it" (*Tundra*, 396). While I might challenge certain phrases and assumptions here (is Canada "a new and virgin land," and who is this "we" who should "turn northward'?), and while I am challenged to wonder what Canada's third century will bring to the North, Mowat's/*Tundra*'s contribution to the discursive formation of North is none the less rich and complex, and it represents, in its resistance to former discursivity and its recapitulation *with difference* of earlier narratives (Hearne's, for example), a discursive turn that many other writers will endorse.

But if *Tundra* is less *autobiography* than a contribution to the meditative life-writing of a nation, a steady stream of northern autobiographies has developed over the past thirty years. If time and space allowed, I would argue that Gould's 1967 *The Idea of North* was his closest approximation to autobiography, and that it, like *Tundra*, is a national life-writing (or, in view of the medium, *telling*). There have been many other similarly hybrid non-fiction texts: Hugh Brody's *Maps and Dreams* (1981) and *Living Arctic* (1987), Barry Lopez's *Arctic Dreams* (1989), all of which are reiterated and re-cited in John Moss's *Enduring Dreams* (1994). Many more traditional autobiographical narratives have also appeared during these years: René Richard's *Ma vie passée* (1990), Toni Onley's *Onley's Arctic* (1989), Betty Lee's *Lutiapik* (1975), Sheila Burnford's *One Woman's Arctic* (1973), and Victoria Jason's *Kabloona in the Yellow Kayak* (1995) are but a few examples of life-stories constructed around living, working, or travelling in the North. For each man or woman the North constitutes a dream of freedom and self-reliance tested by reality and incorporated into a definition of personal and national identity.[12] In this context, James Houston's *Confessions of an Igloo Dweller* (1995) is both more individualistic and more self-aggrandizing; however, Houston is also intent upon tracing, if only as a subtext, the emergence of Inuit art as a form and a commodity that represents Canada to itself and the world.

Though not exclusively about the North, John Colombo's *Windigo: An Anthology of Fact and Fantastic Fiction* (1982) certainly drew popular attention to the convergence of cannibal myths and stories and realities of scarcity and starvation that are experienced, with terrifying seasonal regularity, in northern regions of Canada. Colombo also explored some of the more mysterious and violent possibilities of life in the North. Of the many popular narratives that cater to a public desire for factual accounts of mystery, death, and violence, I will mention three – Dick North's *Mad Trapper of Rat River* (1972, 1991), only one of several representations of Albert Johnson, North's *The Lost Patrol* (1978, 1995), about the 1911 RCMP tragedy in the Yukon near Fort McPherson, and Vernon Frolick's *Descent into Madness: The Diary of a Killer* (1993). Narratives of starvation, cannibalism, becoming lost in the Barrens (the phrase gives Mowat the title for a 1956 children's book), freezing to death, or going mad are among the most common and persistent statements in the discursive formation of North. In earlier chapters I traced this phenomenon in the nineteenth-century poetry and painting of Shanly and Bruce and in the twentieth-century drama of Voaden, Kavanagh, Adams, Jeffery, and MacEwen, but this is a discourse comprising a complex network of statements and tropes that stretches back to the narratives of the earliest explorers, reaches an apotheosis in the mid-nineteenth-century context of Franklin, and refuses to go away, as John Wilson's fiction-as-journal *North with Franklin* (1999) demonstrates (see Grace, "Arctic Journals").

There is at least one more set of statements in the formation that I must not neglect. Beginning with Seton's 1912 narrative of canoing in Canada's North, *The Arctic Prairies*, I could trace the non-fiction representations of wilderness adventure in magazines (from *Outing* in the United States and *The Beaver* in Canada to the North's own *Up Here*) and in books that combine sport and physical challenge with descriptions of pristine natural beauty and claims that the North is one of the few remaining places on earth where such beauty still exists. Bruce Hodgins and Gwyneth Hoyle's *Canoeing North into the Unknown* (1994) and David Pelly's magnificently illustrated *Thelon: A River Sanctuary* (1996), published by the Canadian Recreational Canoeing Association, are only two of the most recent and stunning examples of this non-fiction adventure genre. The ironies and problematics of claims made in such books for purity of wilderness on the one hand and for exciting adventure on the other, and of the eco-tourism industry now supporting these claims, are integral to the narrative and politics of representation negotiated in and through the discourse. Again, the rhetoric of pure wilderness is inseparable from North as physical place, idea, and as a discursive formation that can be traced back to Europeans' first arrival in what was, to them, a new world, a prehistoric space, and this rhetoric inscribes a central core of irreconcilable narrative positions about discovery, origins, identity, and progress that are still dominant, that the Inuit of Nunavut will face, and that are constitutive of any narrative of the Canadian nation. This core of irreconcilable positions is equally important in the domain of fiction, where through metaphor, symbol, and scene the artist can represent the fusion or transcendence of irreconcilable binaries and hierarchies. It is, finally, an aspect of the discursive formation of North that reminds me of Tay John disappearing "down ... under the snow and into the ground" (264).

FORMULAIC NORTH

My consideration of the narration of Canada as a northern nation and my contextualization of my six major writers are not complete, however, without a brief mapping of the discursive terrain occupied by popular fiction. As a preliminary step, I would divide the narrative field into three categories, with popular, formulaic texts occupying a middle ground between the non-fiction already touched upon and the serious fictions represented by the work of my six novelists.

The Northern Narrative Field

NON-FICTION

- exploration narrative
- history
- autobiography/biography
- hybrid text

POPULAR FICTION

- wilderness adventure
- historical romance
- children's fiction
- detective/mystery stories

SERIOUS/EXPERIMENTAL FICTION

- symbolic romance
- postmodern narrrative
- epic narrative
- realist narrative

These categories illustrate degrees of separation within a transdisciplinary discourse in which there is always intersection, overlapping, and duplication. Even within the single discipline of prose narrative (if one can speak of it as single or a discipline), this movement across and within boundaries is apparent and inevitable. As my earlier attempt to label *Tundra* an autobiography demonstrates, the narrative shifts, while I look at it, into historiography, documentary, ethnography, personal meditation, and national identity story; in this it shares much with Gould's *Idea of North* or Onley's *Onley's Arctic*. Moreover, Mowat also writes popular fiction.

Within the category of *popular* fiction I include children's literature, both the lavishly illustrated books for youngsters and the adventure novels for teens, primarily boys.[13] These adventure novels, however, blur into adult popular fiction inasmuch as they share a common interest in wilderness romance that relies upon a quest plot. One contemporary example of this wilderness-adventure-quest amalgam carries this advertisement on its cover:

Kidnapped along with his father's boat, thirteen-year-old Johnny Marton is forced to accompany "mad" Bill Somerville down the Yukon River to Dawson. But the adventure turns out far differently than either of them imagined.

The book is Lucy Berton Woodward's *Kidnapped in the Yukon* (1968, 1984), and all the ingredients familiar from Robert Ballantyne to Robert Service (who makes his own appearance right on cue in *Kidnapped*), James Oliver Curwood, Berton, and Mowat are here: wilderness, a boat, danger, the requisite madman crazed by the bush, ferocious animals (here, the inevitable grizzly), narrow escapes, a journey North, and finally safe haven in a world of women, home, and civilization. Usually that safe haven is in the South, but even when located in the territories, as here, it represents the sphere of southern/feminine order and values.

The message conveyed in *Kidnapped*, in Marie McPhedran's *Golden North* (1948), and most recently in Margaret Thompson's *Eyewitness* (2000) is much the same as for Ballantyne in the nineteenth century: boys go on these northern adventures to grow up; the journey itself is a sort of *rite de passage* into manhood, a discovery of masculinity, and a testing of courage, ingenuity, self-reliance, and endurance. The North is a testing-ground in which isolation, hunger, physical danger from racing rivers, savage beasts, and foul weather, together with overwhelming beauty, provide both the threat and the reward. It is rare for these stories to explore gender explicitly, and sex, as such, is invisible. However, these stories are insistently homosocial; to borrow from Richard Phillips' description of Ballantyne's fiction, I would say that they construct a "space [for] boyish men and manly boys."[14] But there is also a spiritual and ethical dimension to these narratives, which are, among other things, lessons about life. These boys learn not only how to survive in the bush but also how to behave as the civilized white men they must become; they learn about the responsibilities of meeting and surmounting challenges, about the stern duties of leadership, and they learn to recognize their own mastery of and superiority over nature, natives, weaker males, and all females. This ethos, embedded within the romance adventure formula, carries over directly into popular fiction for adults, where again, I would argue, the primary reading audience is assumed to be male.

These novels also use historical subjects, and in a few recent examples they reach out to include previously excluded groups – girls, and native girls and boys. Pierre Berton's Adventures in Canadian History series, devoted to "Exploring the Frozen North," have such titles as *Jane Franklin's Obsession* (1992) and *Trapped in the Arctic* (1993), and they follow the historical record while representing the Inuit more favourably than was the case in nineteenth-century British discourse. In *Trapped in the Arctic*, for example, the narrator comments that while the exploration of the Arctic was deemed a "great achievement by the white European community, [it] brought little but misery to the people whose lands were invaded" (46). Only since the 1950s has it been possible for the discursive formation of North to include the notion that Arctic exploration was an invasion. Each of Berton's volumes is prefaced with a brief introduction; each is dramatically illustrated and includes modern maps showing the explorers' routes; and each carries an index. Historiography, here mimicking the very apparatus of exploration narrative, merges with romance adventure in the far North to form an entertaining, educational discourse on Canadian identity.

Because he adheres to the received historical record, it is pretty well impossible for Berton to put girls or Inuk heroes into these adventure-histories, but other writers of juvenile northern adventure *fiction* have. Martin Godfrey's *Mystery in the Frozen Lands* (1988) retells McClintock's 1859 voyage in search of Franklin through the eyes (and journal entries) of fourteen–year-old Peter Griffin and his Inuk companion Anton. In *The Maestro* (1995) Tim Wynne-Jones creates a bit part for a female bush pilot,[15] and in *The Inuk Mountie Adventure*, from his Tom and Liz Austen Mystery series, Eric Wilson concocts a wonderful tale of snowmobile chases, igloo-building, and dope-dealing around Gjoa Haven. While uncovering a plot against Canadian identity, Tom Austen learns about life in the Arctic, about the crucial importance of the North to Canada, and about the futility of violence from his Inuk mentor, who, far from being a stereotypic noble savage or cheerful "Eskimo," is a highly articulate, technologically savvy RCMP officer. Along the way Tom learns about the Franklin disaster, Owen Beattie's research, the Inuk pop star Susan Aglukark, and Nunavut, and he discovers that the white guys are the bad guys. He learns his most important lesson from the Inuk Mountie, who tells him that "this land of ours is a good one, Tom. In Canada, people live in harmony ... We must work together, the young and the old, to cherish our land, and protect it" (106).

Trapped in Ice (1997) by Eric Walters pushes juvenile fiction about northern adventure in yet another new direction. In this historiographic novel about

Stefansson's 1913 Canadian Arctic expedition, Walters creates a thirteen-year-old white girl called Helen for his first-person narrator.[16] Once he gets her on Robert Bartlett's ship *Karluk*, it is a comparatively easy matter to present her story through her journal because all self-respecting Arctic explorers keep journals. The adventure unfolds much as these tales always do: Walters stays close to the facts, while making Bartlett (not Stef) his hero; introduces a long journey North, danger, ice and cold, a fight with a polar bear, near-death and -starvation, but victory at last. If there is one point worth stressing about *Trapped in Ice*, apart from its creation of an intrepid young female adventurer and its striking narrative sophistication, it is the final moral of the story, which the old Captain gets to pronounce. It is a moral that reaches across the discursive divide to what I am calling serious/experimental fiction. We get Helen's story because she heeds Bartlett's advice: "Ya got at least one more story in ya. Ya just lived an adventure ... An' this story is just a little part of a bigger story, the story of your life, the story you're living right now. Don't ever forget ya have *the power ta change the pages, to make the ending different*" (204, emphasis added).

In the narratives I want to examine next the story seldom changes and the ending is rarely different. *Trapped in Ice* is an exception that proves the rule. From a later nineteenth-century romance like Jules Verne's *The Fur Country, or Seventy Degrees North Latitude* (1873) and early twentieth-century works such as Ralph Connor's *The Prospector* (1904), Douglas Durkin's *The Lobstick Trail: A Romance of Northern Canada* (1921), or Robert Flaherty's *White Master: A Story of the North* (1939) and John Buchan's *Sick Heart River* (1941) to the novels of Yves Thériault, Harold Horwood, Tom York, M.T. Kelly, and James Houston, the ingredients are much the same. These novels represent North as an alien and alienating landscape, feminine in its alluring charm, and as deadly as a female in a misogynist's nightmare. To survive in such a place requires ruthless endurance, but as likely as not the North will drive you mad, starve you, and freeze you to death in the end. Female characters are useless sex objects in this North in so far as they play any role at all (though the occasional *right* wife does appear); native men and "half-breeds" (for whom the Caucasian half is usually French) are cunning primitives or dangerous savages; and wild animals (wolves or bears) are the most worthy animate opponents. So why do these writers send their white male heroes North in the first place? Because southern, feminized civilization is soft and corrupt. Because the North beckons with some promise – riches, renewed manhood, escape, freedom, a new beginning/rebirth, even the release of death. Because the desire to go North in search of one's self, to go where no (white) man has ever gone before, to penetrate the secrets of *terra incognita* (that feminine wild zone of the unknown) is, simply, irresistible.

Sometimes these novels construct fictionalized accounts of historical figures like Albert Johnson or John Hornby, who are represented as heroic men escaping the South. Sometimes there are moral lessons to learn and spiritual ordeals to undergo. Wayland Drew's apocalyptic novel about a modern couple fleeing North by canoe – "All the way" (255) – into the past, into an unrepresented union with the wilderness, tries to make the North a sanctuary, if a grim sort of one. And sometimes the male protagonist makes it back alive, although as happens with Conrad's Marlowe or James Dickey's Ed Gentry in *Deliverance*, the wilderness will haunt him forever. But the controlling images are those associated with an empty northern wilderness and the solitary hero, hunter or hunted, who dares to go there. Even Fred Bodsworth, in his two northern novels, *The Last of the Curlews* (1966) and *The Sparrow's Fall* (1967), provides the same basic story of death and survival in a harsh land. In Bodsworth's novels, however, the reader finds accurate wilderness lore and an element of moral complexity in what are otherwise sentimental narratives, whether his heroes are the doomed curlews or the Caribou Indian (Atihkanishini) couple in *The Sparrow's Fall*. In these respects Bodsworth gives us two early examples of a fictional discourse that problematizes the popular northern adventure narrative. More generally, however, his story is one of survival of the fittest, in which a man must kill a pregnant caribou in labour or starve himself. The land, here the boreal forest and sub-Arctic taiga of northern Ontario, just south of Hudson Bay, is the only true protagonist, and it is inhuman, "a big and lonely land of bog and forest ... a land of clashing contrasts ... a benign land sometimes, amiable, even indulgent, but at other times a cruel land of perverse hostility" (1).

I began this chapter by citing Aritha van Herk's observations that "the great Canadian north is not something that one can capture easily" and that "Canadians have not written much about the north" except to use it as "a good setting for action-packed adventure" (*A Frozen Tongue*, 282–3). She is in large part right, if not about the quantity then at least about the "action-packed adventure." It now remains to see what a serious writer, an artist, can do with this "great Canadian north" when, like the writer of children's fiction or the writer of adult fiction who follows a set script for northern adventure, she or he too decides to go North. The narratives will still involve a journey; the land will still be dominant, and familiar historical figures will make their ghostly appearances; protagonists will still go mad, die, disappear, and starve. But they will also, deliberately, reimagine the story, and they will try to expand it, fracture it, supplement it, and self-consciously re-produce it as a narrative of nation.

DISCOVERING NORTHERNS

Judging from the discursive evidence I have gathered thus far, it is possible to describe the dominant and popular narrative of North as predictable, comparatively stable, easily reproduced, and homogeneous. There are exceptions, of course, and some writers introduce changes, but the fundamental story of northern narrative has remained largely intact for roughly 150 years. This narrative, crossing and blurring boundaries between fiction and non-fiction, stories for children and for adults, represents, within the parameters of wilderness adventure and romance codes, a North empty, silent, mysterious, awe-inspiring, and yet an alienating and crucially "anachronistic space" that is static, "primitive," female, and outside the progressive laws of modernity.[17] Native inhabitants, especially in pre-1950s examples, rarely appear, and when they do they are represented as exotic others, as metonymies for a savage landscape. The journey North that must precede and/or precipitate the narrative is undertaken by a white man (or boy), usually alone, and this white, masculine identity is constructed as both normative and central to the narrative. The action of the story, its diegesis, is masculinist; the male figure may be explicitly escaping a southern, urban domain of women, but whether he is canoeing, hunting and trapping, prospecting, exploring, fleeing justice in the shape of the RCMP, or merely seeking solitude or physical or spiritual adventure, he must prove himself in a series of tests that, if passed, will confirm his superiority over the North (rivers, cold, emptinesss), its wild animals, and other human beings. If this figure leaves the North, he will be prepared to take up his position as a leader in southern society, a true son of the North or son of the true North; if he does not leave, it will be because he has died or deliberately disappeared there, whereupon his story becomes the stuff of heroic legend and myth. Certain historical figures, such as Franklin, Albert Johnson, Tom Thomson, René Richard, and Grey Owl, are continually reproduced by northern narrative because they fit the script. Indeed, their lives appear to authorize and thus legitimate the story. They are, diegetically, the right stuff. So important have these five figures become to the narrative that they persist, albeit it in a more ironic position, in the novels I am about to consider, where their representation becomes a key site for analysis.[18]

With rare exceptions this dominant narrative is generically simple, even simplistic (which accounts in large part for its reproducibility) and monologic. Possibilities for ambiguity, irony, and conflicting moral positions, perspectives, or points of view are focalized and contained by a forceful first-person voice (as with Mowat or Berton) or an omniscient third-person one (as with Bodsworth). The potential dialogics of any novel, or any narrative for that matter, is repressed. As a consequence, the discourse inscribes and validates a highly simplified and hierarchized ideology of white, masculinist agency prevailing over a feminized anachronistic space, and the more formidable that space, the more heroic the endeavour. In contemporary parlance, this narrative inscribes a zero-sum game but a win-win semiotic for the hero, who, even in apparent defeat, has gone where few men dare to go and has therefore earned our admiration. At times, and by late twentieth-century standards, this narrative has been violently racist, and it continues (with a few exceptions) to be sexist, but above all it is imperialist, even in some of its late twentieth-century examples (the novels of Kelly and Houston, for example), in part because of the narrative focus on the white hero, in part because of the unproblematized narrative structure and the monologic narrative voice, and in part because North itself is represented as anachronistic space. As Anne McClintock argues, such spaces are seen as "prehistoric, atavistic and irrational, inherently out of place in the historical time of modernity" (40). If such a space is to make sense, carry meaning, become part of the modern nation, it must be entered, dominated, explored, and exploited; it must, in short, be colonized by story.

This project of colonization through narration continues in the novels of Wiebe, Kroetsch, van Herk, Hay, Richler, and Roy, but in problematized, self-reflexive, often overtly parodic ways. The land itself, though still gendered feminine, is less romanticized. In the work of these novelists northern space is often represented as occupied, as full of histories, stories, myths, and voices. Female authors, narrators, and characters take up more visible/audible positions in these texts, and the story-teller him- or herself becomes one voice among many in a shared process of narration and representation. The narrative that begins to emerge with these texts is hybrid, heterogeneous, and unstable; the historical record, where it is evoked, is fragmented, questioned, rescripted. Perhaps most notably, these writers know they are narrating a nation that has colonized space and excluded a range of other voices and stories, and they knowingly wrestle with narrative itself to force it to tell different stories.

Rudy Wiebe features prominently in this book because, together with Robert Kroetsch, he identifies himself categorically with the North and with northern narratives of nation. "I desire true NORTH," he tells us, and true NORTH, as he shows us in *First and Vital Candle* (1966), *The Mad Trapper* (1980), and *A Discovery of Strangers* (1994), is *the* Canadian story. Between 1966 and 1994 Wiebe has tried three times to narrate a northern nation in novels, but *Playing Dead: A Contemplation Concerning the Arctic* (1989) represents, better than any other single text that I might choose, what true North means for Wiebe. Throughout this meditation Wiebe is haunted by narrative – I am tempted to say by Canada itself – and by secrets he will name and not name. True North is a place of secrets and, therefore, of stories waiting to be told. *Playing Dead* haunts me (I know I will have to return to it) because it holds so many northern stories and voices within its fragmented, undecidable, mutable form; they flicker on the margins, surface briefly, and slide from view in Wiebe's prose river, only to resurface in another's voice: Franklin, Back, Hood, Greenstockings (*Playing Dead* is about Greenstockings), Albert Johnson, Mackenzie, Hearne, Akaitcho, William Nerysoo, Edgar Millen, Johnny Moses, Lazarus Sittichinli, Peter Guy (a pure fiction?), Tony Aparkark Thrasher, Frobisher, Fanny Pannigabluk, Stefansson, Agnes Nanogak, Robert Flaherty, Kroetsch, van Herk, Yates, Rasmussen, de Poncins, Peter Pitseolak, Orpingalik (and many more) – story-tellers all! Story-tellers and keepers of secrets: "Secrets; secrets everywhere" (44). To play dead, to lie in wait for that grisly/grizzly northern story, is not the way to construct a genealogy or to assert national origins. It is, instead, a way of writing, a process, and a stunning image of the discursive formation of North.

But Rudy Wiebe had to learn how to play dead by discovering and listening to the Copper Inuit story about Upaum, who tricked the grizzly bear and created the Coppermine River (tricked that northern ogre into unquenchable story). *First and Vital Candle*, compared with the later works, is a faltering, if necessary, first attempt. In many respects this novel shares much with the formulaic romance narrative of North. The single white male hero, Abe Ross, flees southern cities, women, and so-called civilization to work as a factor with the Frobisher Company in a small Keewatin Ojibway community. Once there, he exposes and converts a corrupt white man, saves the dissolute Indians (while at the same time resisting the sexual advances of an Indian girl), and falls in love with the devout Christian white teacher. The North emerges, in descriptive passages and reiterated tropes, as violent, elemental, largely empty, deceptive, and dangerous – especially for whites. The isolated community, rotting from within as a consequence of white interference, alcohol, and sexual excess, is surrounded by an utterly amoral world of blizzards, starvation, ice, and raging rivers. Abe's white sweetheart will drown in such a river, but Abe will succeed in purging the native community of evil and preparing it for a new start.

Summarized this way, *First and Vital Candle* seems to be the familiar "novel of northern adventure" announced on its cover. However, the novel raises issues of form and meaning that it cannot answer. Abe's victory is pyrrhic, the teacher's death curiously unresolved and arbitrary, and the future of the Frozen Lake Ojibwa is vague at best. Certainly Abe, if not Wiebe, views the Indians as unable to retreat into a traditional lifestyle (old Kekekose can no longer lead; Ojibwa shamanism is ineffective against the whites, and the Indians are incapable of helping themselves), and the closing image of the Indian girl going south to train as a teacher suggests that only by relying on white values and systems can the Indians move forward. But given Abe's negative portrayal of urban white society, this hope seems slim indeed. Wiebe's narrative, although focalized through Abe, complicates his narrative by embedding Abe's memories of earlier experiences in the Arctic within the narrative of Frozen Lake. In this way the main story-line is disrupted, not so much by a subplot as by a mirror story of the far North as a place of death and starvation in which a generous and courageous people (the Inuit of Dubawnt) manage to survive. In his next northern novel, *The Mad Trapper*, Wiebe will abandon the overt moralizing and unresolved cultural encounter of *First and Vital Candle* for a psychological exploration of the North as experienced by whites, and not until *A Discovery of Strangers* will he fully address the narrative and cultural problematics contained in the Abe Ross story.

The story of Albert Johnson, the so-called mad trapper of Rat River, marks a significant turning-point for Wiebe. He has tackled the story at least four times: in an essay called "The Death and Life of Albert Johnson" (in which the very order of the terms indicates the persistence of this secretive man's narrative life after death); in a short story, "The Naming of Albert Johnson," in the novel *The Mad Trapper*, and in *Playing Dead*. Comparing these four accounts makes clear that Wiebe has studied the available records and documents and that, in so far as there are facts to be known, he knows them. The story begins when a strange white man appears, as if from nowhere, on the Peel River at Fort McPherson in the early fall of 1931. He buys a trapping outfit and sets up as a trapper on the Rat River, which leads to a fatal confrontation with the RCMP that leaves an officer dead and ends, after a protracted manhunt across the Richardson Mountains during the depths of a terrible winter, in the man's own death. Who is he? We do not know for certain because he takes the secret of his identity to his Aklavik grave. Was he mad, a criminal, or simply a loner who tried to turn his back on society? Again, we can never know.

The search for Johnson captured newspaper headlines for months to become one of the most famous RCMP chases of all time and to represent the quintessential northern adventure story. By retelling it (four times), Wiebe has achieved several things. He has, more than any other writer, mythologized Johnson and reproduced the North as a space *par excellence* of masculinist adventure, but he has also disrupted, destabilized, multiplied, and reinvented the story. What began for Wiebe as an initial fascination with the man's identity – his name – and an abiding terror of/desire for true North grew into a fascination with story itself. In the novel Wiebe reproduces key facts, which are anchored, as it were, by his inclusion of several familiar historical photographs of the key players, while he fabricates and weaves together several stories, including a story Johnson does not tell. Each RCMP officer involved in the manhunt is allowed a voice, a partial telling; so are Wop May (the famous bush pilot brought in to hunt the fugitive from the sky) and his reporter companion. But more importantly still, the First Nations tell their version of who Johnson is and how (not) to deal with him, and Constable Edgar Millen (in actuality murdered by Johnson on 30 January 1932, before the chase begins) becomes the driven, obsessed, and haunted hero – a Victor Frankenstein pursuing his largely self-created monster across the frozen wastes.

From among these many voices and stories I want to single out two: Spike Millen's and William Nerysoo's. According to the Gwich'in, Albert Johnson has become a Windigo, and you cannot, *must* not, hunt a Windigo. Well before Nerysoo names Johnson and warns Millen, Wiebe has prepared his readers for this revelation. A terrible winter has descended on the land by the time the native trappers report trouble with Johnson; the northern lights flame across the sky, and the cold is so intense that it gnaws at the Mounties' faces as they wait for some response from the man holed up in his cabin (60). When Johnson survives the dynamiting of his cabin, Nerysoo begins to suspect the truth (96). Once the chase begins, the RCMP and their native guides must locate Johnson from his tracks in the snow, tracks that double back, deceive his pursuers, and even walk "right through the middle of their base camp ... between the tethered dogs" (108). They are "tracking an indomitable ghost that moved as if weather did not exist and laid tracks in whatever deadly spot it pleased" (107). How else explain such a presence except as a manifestation of one of the oldest northern stories there is? And "nobody chases a wendigo," Nerysoo says. "It's here, it's there, it appears to those people it wants to [but ...] we leave a wendigo alone" (108–9). When Millen insists that the man-hunt continue, Nerysoo muses that he "never thought a white could become wendigo" (109), but now that one has, he warns Millen, "It could get you too" (109). And, of course, it does.

By delaying Millen's death until the final face-to-face shoot-out with Johnson on 17 February 1932 (the day the real man called Johnson died), Wiebe gives credence to the Gwich'in explanation. Manic, exhausted, frost-blackened, and injured, Millen pushes on, "forging ahead with awesome strength ... as if he were rushing towards a destiny" (182). After weeks of psychological and physical exertion, hunting Johnson by becoming him – almost – he is shot by the silent spectre before him without hearing the man (or Windigo) utter a word.

In *The Mad Trapper* Wiebe may be constructing another tale of white men going North, but he transforms that story, through the Gwich'in perspective, into one of the oldest, most widespread indigenous narratives of North. Millen becomes both hero and madman: hero because he dies in his pursuit of the North, and a madman because he is too white to believe the Indians while there is still time to turn back. Rather than reproducing the known facts or turning the renegade Johnson into a beleagured white hero who can survive alone in the frozen North, Wiebe radically changes the story by dialogizing it. Each person there, and some who were not, has his own version of the story, but the man called Albert Johnson (whom we learn on the last page is *not* Johnson) eludes all of them and disappears, Windigo to the end, until the next time a story-teller tries to fashion his "wordlessly silent scream" (189) into a northern narrative.

A Discovery of Strangers builds upon the lessons Wiebe learns about the North and northern narrrative from *First and Vital Candle* on. It builds upon and reinscribes what he has learned about Canadian history, historical figures, and the figures excised from the history. The roots of this novel (his masterpiece, rivalled only by *The Temptations of Big Bear*) surface from the interstices of *Playing Dead*. In turning back to the North, after the wests of the prairie novels (*The Blue Mountains of China*, *Temptations*, *The Scorched Wood People*), Wiebe affirms his search for true North and for the narrative large enough to be a foundation story of nation. The core sequence of events concerns John Franklin's first search, in 1820–21 by land, for a northern route across Canada and for the Northwest Passage. He and his British officers, George Back, Robert Hood, and Dr John Richardson, are assisted by Canadian voyageurs and by the Yellowknife Indians, whose lands, north of Great Slave Lake, they must traverse. In the end the Mohawk, most of the Métis (Indian–French Canadian), and Robert Hood are dead. One of the voyageurs, Michel Terohaute (whose very name – terre haute – invokes the *pays d'en haut*), will go down in history as a cannibal.[19] Franklin, Back, and the British sailor John Hepburn survive. A beautiful Yellowknife woman, whose only known image is a drawing by Robert Hood that prefaces *Playing Dead*, also survives, with the remnants of her people, to bear the half-white child she conceived, or so the record suggests, in a brief affair with Robert Hood. These are the facts, or most of them, but they are not Wiebe's story. His story is a discovery narrative in reverse, in which the self-designated discoverers are discovered by the Yellowknife people, by the land and its animals, by a woman who teaches self-discovery, and by the reader who follows the white men through the "labyrinth of their disaster, within their Great Lone Empire of the Arctic Snows" (220).

A *Discovery of Strangers* is a fragmented and strategically disrupted narrative. The reader must piece a linear story together from many different sources: italicized quotation from the public record (journals and letters), the fictional voices created for real people, and Dene oral stories of transformation (the caribou cow), of death (Birdseye's Snow Man story about "These English"), of creation (the story of the Snow-Shoes), and of war (the Stolen Woman). It is, as Greenstockings' father Keskarrah knows, a story "telling itself backwards" (152), because such a "telling" is the only way to understand what happened when these English were discovered, the only way to make the past speak in Canadian voices, and to enable this story of cultural encounter to rewrite a history told as the discovery of a new world by white European men. Wiebe has taken Todorov's question of the other and turned it, perhaps not into answers but at least into new stories. He has also changed the ending, first by refusing to go beyond the ending that Greenstockings knows, and second, by giving her the final spoken word: "Mine" (317). When she insists on the *mine*, she asserts her claim to the child she carries, refuses to relinquish it (with its one dark brown and one blue eye) to Back, or even to acknowledge that it had a father, and asserts her claim to the story and the future.

Wiebe makes it difficult to piece a linear story together because he is telling another story. In this novel of discovery that other story is the one he wants us to hear, even to believe. Although it circles around and contains the stories of many men, and may even at times be driven by their scripted ambitions (for sex, for fame, for conquest), I take Wiebe seriously when he tells us, in his acknowledgments, that this is Greenstockings' story. To be her story it must be non-linear; it must tell itself backwards until it finds the story-teller. But who is Greenstockings? Wiebe knows his cultural stereotypes; he knows the gendering of earth and of the North in the dominant discourse, and in *Playing Dead* (that other narrative haunted by Greenstockings) he insists, "you [I/we] cannot *not* have a story because you had a mother" (68). Greenstockings is that Mother, that mother country, that northern place into which she disappears "as the arctic light darkens around her in its impenetrable, life-giving cold" (317).[20]

While I am speculating that, for Wiebe, Greenstockings represents the Mother of Canadian northern narrative, I am certain that Robert Kroetsch's northern novels chart a search for the North-as-Mother. This search, allegorized in *But We Are Exiles* (1965) and carnivalized in *Gone Indian* (1973), is rescripted and consolidated in *The Man from the Creeks* (1998). That this search must always be a man's and must always be sexualized, however, is finally problematized, if not displaced entirely, in the last of these three novels. Why Kroetsch went North in the first place at the age of twenty in 1948, and what he learned when he got there, is another likely story that sheds oblique and ironic light on his fiction. Even his three northern poems – "Meditation on Tom Thomson," "F.P. Grove: The Finding," and "Poem of Albert Johnson" (all from *The Stone Hammer Poems*, 1975, 46–51) – provide indices to how he sees North and chooses to represent it.

In his first published comments about Canadian identity and the North, from the short 1971 essay "The Canadian Writer and the American Literary Tradition," Kroetsch summed up North as "silence ... a true wilderness, a continuing presence" (11), and he characterized Canadian writing as articulating the desire (as O'Hagan did in *Tay John*) to "vanish into blizzards, under snow ... to return to the condition preceding creation" (14). For Kroetsch, Tom Thomson is the "archetypal Canadian Artist," and it is worth quoting his explanation of what Thomson signifies (if not for us, then at least for Kroetsch) because of its bearing upon his novels and its relevance for Roy's *La Montagne secrète*: "Thomson is the paradigm. Of the man who took the risk, got free, perished. Strangely, the paintings of his which we most treasure are without people entirely. And now, with life imitating art, we learn of the delightful possibility that Thomson's coffin is empty. It is the 'if' of his life, confronting the primal wilderness, that intrigues us. The Tom Thomson mystery. The Canadian Mystery" (*Open Letter*, 14). He tried to capture *his* Tom Thomson in the poem "Meditation on Tom Thomson," but Thomson got away, "free, daddy, FREE FREE FREE" (*Stone Hammer*, 51). What Kroetsch caught instead was the "holy shit mother," "the muskeg snatch / of the old north the bait that caught / the fishing father" (*Stone Hammer*, 50); so Kroetsch kept on fishing and disappearing into his personal, imagined North in search of romance, death, escape, ghosts, and the new language he needed to tell his northern (Canadian) stories.

In "Why I Went Up North and What I Found When He Got There," written twenty years after "The Canadian Writer and the American Literary Tradition" and close to forty-five years after he first went North to Great Slave Lake, the Mackenzie River, Norman Wells, Aklavik, and Tuktoyatuk, Kroetsch finally explains (at least it makes a good story) that he went North because Robert Service tricked him, with the word *moil* (the men who "moil for gold"), into wanting to write in the first place and into wanting to begin in the North. Repeatedly in this central essay Kroetsch returns to the idea that the North both created him and taught him, through silence, waiting, and listening to the river and to native oral story-telling, how to escape the Western, European, above all *southern* stories he inherited in order to "tell stories of my own" (23). Even then, at this beginning, it seems that North was inextricably associated with sex and Woman, and that that conjunction freed him because the "North makes possible a new story ... not through encounter with the self (held dear by Western thought), but rather through the astonishing encounter with an Other that eradicates self into all its disparate potential" (35). In each of his three northern novels he will search out his story in such an encounter – in *Exiles* he will fail; in *Gone Indian* he will exceed the limits and disappear, and in *Man from the Creeks* he will return to Robert Service and mine the motherlode of northern narrative to tell "a new story."[21]

But We Are Exiles is the story of a young man's attempt to escape the past and a betrayed love by going North. When the story opens, Peter Guy, who is working as a river pilot on the *Nahanni Jane* running between Great Slave and Tuk, has already failed to escape. Michael Hornyak, the man who betrayed him, has followed him

North and drowned, or been killed, and Peter and the crew must drag the river for his body. But the Mackenzie River keeps its secrets and its corpses, and this one will not surface until after the boat completes its northward journey and is heading south again, and until after Peter fails to reach a reconciliation with Kettle (Caroline Fraser, *the woman born and bred in the North*), the woman he lost to Hornyak. The story ends with Peter stranded in a blizzard, by choice, on the barge in Great Slave Lake with the corpse. In a rage of remembering, Peter pushes the corpse overboard and takes its place in the makeshift canoe-coffin. Presumably, he still hopes for rebirth, but without the Other his flight north ("north and again north," 48) ends with Peter Guy haunted by the ghosts of stories he cannot escape, assuage, or retell. All we hear of Kettle is that she will be sent out, south, against her will by her old trapper father in Aklavik. Her story is no more than an adjunct to the men's; it will have to wait until Kroetsch is ready to see a woman as an agent in, as well as a symbol of, the North. Like Wiebe's *First and Vital Candle*, *But We Are Exiles* remains trapped by the limiting clichés of the dominant, masculinist narrative of North. Its salvation resides, ironically, in the fact that the story does not work. In *Gone Indian*, Kroetsch tried again.

When Jeremy Sadness, an American graduate student from SUNY with a "romantic interest in the northern forests" (2), arrives in Edmonton for a job interview, he is mistaken for an Indian trapper "down from the North" (15). And no wonder. When he leaves the Edmonton airport, he has transformed himself into his life-long hero, Grey Owl, complete with braids, moccasins, and buckskin jacket (11), and he heads not to the university but due North. He has "gone Indian." Jeremy's adventures begin when he arrives in Notikeewin during the February Winter Festival, and they end, as far as we know, when he disappears into a blizzard on a snow-mobile, with his ideal northern woman, heading further north. In between the transformative arrival and the apocalyptic end, a lot will happen, all of it framed and commented upon by Jeremy's sceptical, ironic, self-serving professor down South.

What *happens* in *Gone Indian*, at least as Jeremy tells it on his tapes and his SUNY professor retells it (*caveat lector*: Professor Madham is no more trustworthy a story-teller than his young protégé) in letters sent north, is a rollicking sequence of sexual, dog-sledding, snowshoeing, drinking, swearing, and fighting encounters that outdoes the wildest northern (or western, for that matter) ever written. Winter Festival is raging in Noteekewin; the Northern Lights flare "red and green across the open sky ... the sky consuming itself" (31), and North is a world upside-down, carnivalesque enough to delight Bakhtin. "The festival is in full swing," Jeremy chatters into his tape-recorder:

I want to tell you, everything has become a game in this mad place: wood-splitting, ice-cutting, flour-packing, log-sawing. Moose-callers are calling moose: I expect a great awkward animal to lumber out of a coulee and onto Elkhart Pond, quietly munching the hats off people's heads. Goose-callers call geese: whole honking flights of Canada geese should come down out of the sky and skid to a halt on the unexpected ice. (75)

And before he knows it, he is happily conscripted to replace Roger Dorck and choose the Notikeewin Winter Festival Queen. As Winter King, Jeremy is, quite simply, outside himself – othered. The wise professor, commenting from his safe, southerly distance, describes Jeremy as succumbing to "arctic hysteria": "the extreme cold, the long nights, the solitude of *unbounded* space: these are the enemies that induce that northern ecstasy" (123). However, Jeremy has not yet gone far enough North.

Everything in *Gone Indian* points North; every step taken (whether in a truck, on snowshoes, behind a dog-sled, or on a snowmobile) is northerly. If we follow the tracks in the text, we should be able to discover where Jeremy is headed at the end. At one point our hero, already "disguised" as himself (that is, as an Indian), gazes north across the empty space and snow obscuring the North Saskatchewan River and remembers that "somewhere north of that river, Grey Owl lay cold in his grave" (59). When the loudspeaker announces that the winner of the dog-sled competition is from Prince Albert, Jeremy thinks of his Grey Owl "dying in a Prince Albert hospital":

The wracked body of the truest Indian of them all, that strayed Englishman – that corpse, carried north again, the team of horses, the sleigh, moving in a solemn procession across the ice of the lake, into the bush. Into the wilderness. (80)

After surviving his carnivalesque ordeals, after crowning the Queen, and returning, "like a trapper ... Remembering a passage from Grey Owl" (144), to the house called "Worlds End," where Bea Sunderman, the mother and lover, waits, Jeremy is finally ready for the next, the last, step: locked in Bea's embrace, with her "smell of a northern forest ... the muskeg waters of the north ... redolent of all our beginnings" (147), Jeremy flees north towards his/Grey Owl's grave.

In one sense, of course, *Gone Indian* recapitulates the obsession with sex and death that drives *But We Are Exiles*. In another sense, however, it marks a clear advance over its predeccesor. First, while Jeremy may end up as frozen to death as Peter Guy, he has one hell of a lot more fun along the way. Second, he has learned an invaluable lesson – North is a woman, "cold, blank, oblivious, whimsical, murderous, amoral, stark. The stark, amoral virgin" (45), but she is also the "holy shit mother" of us all. Perhaps by listening to Rudy Wiebe, Jeremy Sadness has begun to see that he has a story because he has a mother, but he has also come to accept that (for him, as for Kroetsch) North demands "the diffusion of personality into a complex of possibility rather than a concluded self" (*Gone Indian*, 152). These are that outrageous SUNY professor's words, of course, but they are strikingly similar to Kroetsch's own discovery, through sexual initiation – retold in "Why I Went North and What I Learned When He Got There" – that North enables/invites a new story through an "encounter with an Other that eradicates self into all its disparate potential." To be sure, the self that consumes Kroetsch's interest is gendered, emphatically male, and the North/Mother/Woman topos does precious little for the feminine subject. Between Kettle and Jill Sunderman (Bea's beautiful, icy daughter) there is little to choose; both are rejected by their male heroes, each of whom instead chooses absorption in the Mother who, alone, can promise rebirth in a new story. In *The Man from the Creeks* Kroetsch allows his male artist/ story-teller to tell a woman's story about going North, and thereby invests the feminine with agency and takes his own search for northern narrative beyond the silence of the grave.

The Man from the Creeks is an elegaic romance in which a 114-year-old narrator retells Robert Service's familiar narrative in "The Shooting of Dan McGrew." Like all good elegaic romances, the novel triangulates the story, although in this case there are triangles within triangles (see Figure 5). If we can believe Kroetsch when he tells us (in "Why I Went North") that Robert Service is to blame, then here, in this novel, written late in his career, Kroetsch takes his revenge. Peek takes Service's version of the Klondike Gold Rush and explodes it into a "complex of possibility." Peek's hero is his Mother, the lady known as Lou; the main story is the saga of going North; and the truth is that Lou loved the man from the creeks and that she died with him in that famous shoot-out in the Malamute Saloon. What's more, Lou is buried with her gold in the permafrost beneath the very cabin from which her aged son now speaks as the poet and teller of *herstory*.

Figure 5
Robert Kroetsch and Robert Service

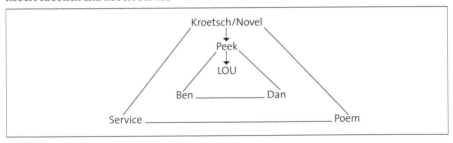

The Man from the Creeks is Kroetsch's most historiographic fiction. He has consulted the documents and the sources; he has reproduced facts, dates, and all the key historical players, from the infamous Soapy Smith to that famous enforcer of Canadian law and regulation Sam Steele of the NWMP; he has captured the narrative of waiting – in Skagway, in Sheep Camp, at Bennett Lake – and of climbing the Chilkoot Pass (one of the most famous photographs of the ordeal is reproduced on the dust-jacket and cited in the story, 114; see Illus. 22), and he reconstructs the drama of travelling down the treacherous, racing Yukon River, north to Dawson City. More than half the novel, in fact, is spent getting there, and as Tappan Adney, in one of the two prefacing quotations, reminds us, that *is* the story: "The newspapers were filled with advice, information, stories of hardship and good fortune; but not one [person] in ten, or a hundred, knew what the journey meant nor heeded the voice of warning" (quoted from *The Klondike Stampede*).

Certainly, Robert Service didn't. "The Shooting of Dan McGrew," the penultimate stanza of which provides the second prefacing quotation, Kroetsch's title,

Illus. 22. The chief route to the Klondike was to climb over the Chilkoot Pass in Alaska to reach the Yukon. Images like this one have become synonymous with the Klondike Gold Rush, but this distance shot is especially interesting because it shows the prospecting hopefuls waiting in Sheep Camp, their provisions scattered in the snow, for their turn to start the climb. If they could not afford to hire local people to transport their goods over the pass, they would make this climb several times with their provisions on their backs. Reproduced with permission of BC Archives (C-O4999).

and Peek's existence (he is "the kid that handled the music-box"), creates high romantic adventure out of the stuff of history.[22] Judging from Service's version of the Gold Rush in his immensely popular poem, the story of the Klondike and of Dangerous Dan McGrew was one of greed, sudden violence, betrayal, hard drinking, "fifty below" winters, and murder. It was a story about men and their battle with the land and competition with each other. The only role for a woman was that of whore-cum-entertainer, there to mine the miners. Although I cannot imagine that I need to reproduce Service's poem here, it is important to note that Kroetsch has selected his prefacing quotation from it with great care; he does *not* repeat Service's final interpretative stanza:

These are the simple facts of the case, and I guess
    I ought to know;
They say that the stranger was crazed with "hooch,"

and I'm not denying it's so.
I'm not so wise as the lawyer guys, but strictly
    between us two –
The woman that kissed him – and pinched his
    poke – was the lady that's known as Lou.   (*Songs of a Sourdough*, 56)

It is "the facts of the case," as Service's authoritative speaker/eye-witness puts it, that Peek must reinterpret outright, and most importantly must retell *not* as masculine adventure (or at least not only or primarily as that) but as a woman's determined, courageous, intrepid journey North with her young son (Peek), with the man who will help her, become her lover, and be "the man from the creeks," Ben Redd, and with her own search for gold.

Once Lou reaches Dawson City and has started to work at the Malamute, Peek is free to look around. His first foray is to visit Ben out on the creeks, where, in partnership with Dan McGrew, he is mining for gold. On his way, Peek tells us, he passed "the site of Discovery Claim" (232), and this fabled site elicits three different versions of that discovery: the official one, in which George Washington Carmack "noticed in the gravel bank a gold nugget the size of his thumb" (232) on 16 August 1896; the less official one, in which Skookum Jim finds the gold; and the third, unofficial but rumoured version:

Lou had her own version of the story, as you might expect. She believed with a kind of fervour that George's wife Kate made the discovery while she was doing the dishes in a mining pan. All three men, George and Jim and Tagish Charlie, were napping. She glanced down into the pan and saw a nugget staring at her like a golden eye.   (232)

And so, in a northern narrative that re-creates the North as a woman's place and story, Kroetsch/Peek/Lou reach back to problematize by dialogizing, not only a famous poem but also a famous historical moment, a foundational moment, a story of origins, discovery, and genealogy hitherto scripted as male (see my discussion of Kate Carmack in chapter 3).

The Man from the Creeks shares much with Kroetsch's other northern novels. Like both *Exiles* and *Gone Indian*, it begins and ends with a man; it is Peek, after all, who is the narrating, focalizing "I." As is true in both these earlier novels, in *Creeks* the journeying North is more important than the being there, and to be there is to die. But the *discontinuities* between *Creeks* and its predecessors are as significant as its continuities, if not more so, because here Kroetsch has made a personal search for North represent a larger, national, historic story (I would say even international, universal). Discovery of gold in the Klondike, whether by the American man George Carmack or by the native Canadian woman Shaaw Tláa, also known as Kate, brought Canadian law and policy into the North and led to the formal creation of the Yukon territory. Moreover, by keeping Peek in the North as the guardian of his mother's grave and story, Kroetsch has turned his own desire for/obsession with

North into a ghost story unlike the ghost stories of *Exiles* and *Gone Indian* because it is told by the ghostly poet/survivor himself.

The Man from the Creeks is in fact a ghost story with more ghosts than I can count. It is a narrative pieced together from ghostly voices out of the past, and it returns insistently to images of ghosts – dead and alive – glimpsed along the route North. Dawson City is a ghost town; the creeks are inhabited by "ghosts working wind-lasses ... more ghosts pushing wheelbarrows, moving out along planks or path-ways, emptying more muck and gravel onto more dumps ... ghosts that were darker than black" (269). In two of the most powerful scenes of the novel Kroetsch finally takes us where, thus far in his fiction, he has steadfastly refused to go: under the frozen ground, into the northern grave. In one of these scenes we descend with Lou and Peek into the tunnels Ben has scraped out of the bedrock and melted out of the permafrost in his search for "the old stream, the stream that wore the mother-lode itself into flakes and nuggets, and then hid them in gravel and sand" (270). That space under the earth is a hell, black, wet, full of smoke from fires melting permafrost, and unspeakably cold. Ben and his helpers are filthy, mole-like creatures (273), moiling for gold. The other ghostly grave scene, the scene of Kroetsch's ultimate ghost story, reveals not Peter Guy, Albert Johnson, Michael Hornyak, Grey Owl, Franklin, Hornby, Tom Thomson, or Jeremy Sadness, but Lou. As Peek, poet/story-teller to the end, tells us, he buried his beloved mother on a bed of spruce boughs and red crêpe roses, with the gold nugget given her by Ben filling her cupped hands, deep in the ground under his cabin. The coffins of McGrew and Redd have long since been swept into the Yukon River and disappeared, but not Lou's: "There in the permafrost she will endure long after I have played my last tune" (305).

In "Why I Went North" Kroetsch insists that "the North makes possible a new story" (35). *The Man from the Creeks* is Kroetsch's major contribution to that story. Here, finally, he has mined the North to discover that the gold of north-ern narrative is a multiple, complex, discontinuous story to be created from others' stories. Lou is that metaphorically embodied story – Mother, Mother-lode, Mother-country, and Muse – celebrated by a son of the North in true patriot love.[23]

Where Wiebe narrates a northern nation in *A Discovery of Strangers* as native myth and exploration, in *The Man from the Creeks* Kroetsch transforms a personal quest/adventure/ghost story into an allegory of self-as-other, self-as-North. What neither Wiebe nor Kroetsch can do is let a woman tell her own story of North. For that I must turn to Aritha van Herk and Elizabeth Hay.

It would be a mistake, however, to assume that because a woman writes a northern narrative, it will necessarily differ in fundamental ways from those writ-ten by men. As years of feminist scholarship have taught us, scripts are powerful, deeply engrained in a culture, and difficult to unlearn.[24] If Kroetsch found it difficult to free himself into story, especially into northern story, would it not be still more difficult for women, who have been denied an official role and agency in the North and whose presence has been reduced to a symbolic representation of the space to be desired, penetrated, conquered, and passed through, to find any voice at all, let alone a story? Children's fiction by women (Woodward and McPhedran are representative examples) usually follows the formulaic, masculinist pattern, and Canadian women have tended to write much less frequently in any mode about whatever northern experiences they may have had. Having first to create a subject position from which to speak, they have then had to fight for acceptance of the authority to speak and to write. However, women did go North prior to 1960, and they did write about it in autobiographical narratives that bear certain differences from men's (see Grace, "Gendering Northern Narrative").

Since 1960 serious women novelists, poets, and playwrights have also focused attention on the North; they have gone there, read about, and re-created northern heroes; they have written about their own experiences, and they have in many cases seen North as a source of Canadian identity. For Gwendolyn MacEwen, in *Terror and Erebus*, *Noman's Land*, and some poems (for example, "Grey Owl's Poem"), Canada *is* North and North is unquestionably dangerous, deadly, and female. It is, as MacEwen's Rasmussen warns, describing "the great virginal strait of Victoria" in *Terror and Erebus*, a formidable foe that might "hold you crushed forever in her stubborn / loins" (*Afterworlds*, 44).

Margaret Atwood is more ambivalent. While recognizing and ironizing the prevalence and authority of the masculine story, she nevertheless reproduces it in *Surfacing*, in "Death by Landscape," and in "The Age of Lead" (see Grace, "Franklin Lives"). In *Strange Things: The Malevolent North in Canadian Literature* she acknowledges that "the North [is] thought of as a frigid *femme fatale*, who entices and hypnotizes male protagonists and leads them to their doom" (3), but she does not so much critique or rewrite the story as describe and reproduce it. Most of Atwood's examples of North from *Strange Things*, at least in the "Linoleum Caves" chapter, which is dedicated to women's writing, take her no further north than the woods and summer cottage country just outside major Canadian cities, like Toronto or Vancouver. With one exception, Ann Tracy's Windigo fable *Winter Hunger*, she stays pretty far south, and in Tracy's North the worst Windigo is the hero's white wife. Women's literary norths, it seems, at least the ones Atwood enjoys, are female, icy-cold, and waiting out and up there ... to eat us.[25]

Van Herk and Hay try to do something different. Van Herk appropriates the masculinist story and displaces the male story-teller; Hay rewrites the story by supplementing it: she inserts herself and a sequence of forgotten women into the narrative metonymically, side by side with the men. The images of North that Hay and van Herk give us are intensely personal, lyrical, inner (even private); the identity they construct is their own. Both these writers seem suspicious of metaphoric grand narratives of a northern nation, and yet, I argue, they are trying to grasp such a story to write themselves into it, and possibly to rewrite it. Van Herk has two northern novels, *The Tent Peg* (1981) and *No Fixed Address* (1986), and one Arctic geograficione, *Places Far from Ellesmere* (1990). Hay has written a trilry: *Crossing the Snow Line* (1989), *The Only Snow in Havana* (1992), and *Captivity Tales: Canadians in New York*. For my purposes *The Tent Peg* is van Herk's key text and *Captivity Tales* is Hay's.

Places Far from Ellesmere, based on van Herk's camping trip to Ellesmere, is at one and the same time an autobiography-as-fiction and a fictional geography – a geografictione, as she calls it, of women. It is moreover a text self-consciously aware of its participation in a discursive formation of North (van Herk chooses a key passage from Foucault's *Archeology of Knowledge* as one of her three prefacing quotations). Although named for a man (the earl of Ellesmere, in 1852), the word Ellesmere signifies the feminine, maternal identity of the place; as such it haunts the narrative to become the goal of the narrator's retrospective account of this search for herself. Of the four topographical sections of the text (Edberg, Edmonton, Calgary, and Ellesmere), it is the largest (as long as the other three together), and it appears early on the textual horizon: "An island in the world: an arctic metaphor for escapation" (39). But once posited as escape and excavation, what is it that the narrator and I (for I am addressed insistently and directly: *you*) must search for, dig up, and why on Ellesmere? The answer lies in large part in what "Aritha" takes with her on her voyage: Tolstoy's *Anna Karenina*, which she calls "the North's invention" (113) and which she will unread and rewrite on Ellesmere in order to free Anna from the deadly family romance of its patriarchal, misogynist plot. However, in this fabrication of aphorisms – "Terror of women = terror of north" (123) – and of assertions – "Only the north can teach what reading means" (132) – I find it difficult to know what van Herk sees in Ellesmere, except herself, or what reading *her* means.[26] Her North seems to proffer the same old story of escape into the "white nights ... of a glacial narcolepsy" (143) and into the silent, frozen gravesite that she has been looking for all along. But this grave is already occupied by men (Franklin, Johnson, Grey Owl, Hornby) and already talked about (Robert Hood, Peter Guy, Jeremy Sadness) and written about (Wiebe, Kroetsch, et al.) by men. On Ellesmere, North is still a metaphor for a frozen woman (see Illus. 8), a grave, a mystery, a body written into history (not *her*story), an as yet "un/written northern novel" (*Places*, 113).

If "escapation" is both escape and excavation, perhaps going back to *No Fixed Address* will clarify the picture. Maybe here I can find van Herk's northern novel. *No Fixed Address: An Amorous Journey* is a road novel in which the road finally runs due north. The road queen, called Arachne Manteia, a picaresque heroine who peddles ladies' underwear and sleeps with whomever she pleases, has gone missing. The narrator of the frame narrative, titled "Notebook on a Missing Person," is telling her story as a parody of the male road novel that is destined to end in a flight north (instead of west). By turning north, however, Arachne has disappeared into conjecture and speculation:

If she turns north now, she will be going nowhere, into a lost and limitless world she might not emerge from.   (301)

She is steeling herself to enter the blank, the dislocated world of the North. Perhaps she will be able to find a place to settle in, colonize.   (302)

If she gets out of here, she will go north, north, north.   (303)

And she does get out – out of the narrative, out of the road plot, and out of sight, by driving a vintage Mercedes (a woman's name for a feminized conveyance) "away, slow, stately into the north" (303).

But why did she go north and what did she do when she got there? Since I cannot ask the question of *No Fixed Address*, I must go further back, dig deeper, practice escapation. Well, she went north in *The Tent Peg* to be a cook with an all-male (of course) geology survey crew working in the Yukon's Wernecke Mountains. Based on van Herk's own experiences as a northern bush-camp cook in 1977 and on her reading of explorers' narratives, *The Tent Peg* becomes an allegory of Canada-as-North and, I believe, van Herk's most interesting northern novel to date. She has described the book as a eulogy for the men who explore and map the country and of the Yukon mountain landscape, which is as "distinctively feminine, as changeable and arbitrary as any stereotyped woman" (*Frozen Tongue*, 280). To tell the story she creates a chorus of voices and an austere landscape, above the treeline of rock, mountains, flowers, and moss that hides its secret uranium and gold from all but those who learn to love and respect it. To speak for and embody this landscape, van Herk creates J.L. (Ja-el), the young cook, a woman who will signify more than the land or food. With one exception, the members of the crew have explorers' names: Mackenzie, Hudson, Hearne, Thompson, and Franklin.

The narrative motivation for the story is the desire to head north for the regular summer's exploration work; the complication to this simple plot is J.L., whom the men misread as a man – until it is too late. Women do not go north, and accepting her presence, even as a cook, proves as much of a challenge to the men as the land itself. By the novel's end, all but one of the men will have learned something they had not anticipated and be given J.L.'s gift of a sachet containing northern moss to take south. Jerome, the stereotypical misogynist, violent and stubborn, is the exception. He sees in women nothing but sex objects to use, in the land nothing but resources to pillage, and in both a field for his mastery and domination; however, he will be exposed and defeated by J.L. As the summer advances, her symbolic relationship with the land, as much as her physical presence in the camp and her defeat of Jerome, becomes the men's main subject of reflection. In their thoughts, as in their actions, they circle her in curiosity, in fear, in desire, and finally in acceptance and peace. By summer's end, they have found gold.

Although the narrative structure of *The Tent Peg* strains against my need for explanation (how do I come to overhear, gain access to, these many first-person voices? who or what is listening? can this round of solo voices be sustained or the speakers hear each other?), the core of the narrative is secure. This is J.L.'s story; she is its narrative and moral centre. Her relationship with the North is what holds this otherwise disrupted, fragmented, discontinuous story together. Two specific events image that relationship: one is her halting of a rockslide before it crushes the camp; the other is her communion with a female grizzly. In both cases, van Herk implies, it is because J.L. is a woman that the North stops short of murdering the men. It is J.L. who intercedes. When the "huge goddam grizzly bear" comes to the cook tent, J.L. goes out to meet her where she stands, "twenty feet away and reared up on her hind legs" (108). The men watch paralysed with fear as J.L. looks up at the bear "like they've met before ... sweeps off her hat and bows" (108), and the bear "drops to her feet," pauses, "as if in conversation," and "lumbers away" (108). No more is reported or said, but this is *not* the usual encounter with a grizzly found in northern adventure stories because this woman and this bear are represented as sisters sharing their space, agreeing to be different and to let live. J.L.'s relationship with the mountain is even more mysterious, and she describes this event in her own voice. Feeling the mountain move in the "perfect silence" (120) of the night, she wakes and goes out to wait, barefoot, at the base of the cirque. Through her feet she feels a "spasm," a shudder, as the "earth gathers herself" to give birth to the slide. As it thunders down towards her, she cries out and holds her palms against its descent. It stops ten feet before her:

I kneel then, press myself down and whisper, rock myself and whisper softly until the earth and I grow still, calm ourselves.

And they didn't hear it. When I finally slip back to my tent, they're still dreaming. Men with no ears, men with no connection to the earth.   (121)

Midwife, nurturer, conciliator, bringer of wisdom and peace, Ja-el, like her biblical namesake, none the less drives the tent peg of insight into each man's temple (each, that is, except Jerome's) before releasing them south with their moss sachets: *momenti borealis*. The northern story, as she re-creates it, transforms and heals. The men are absolved, freed from the conventionally scripted roles of conqueror and exploiter and denied the role of rapist. The Yukon, no longer a land, as Service puts it, waiting for men to rip and loot her, is left to itself with its power, mystery, and beauty intact.[27]

Unlike van Herk, or any of the others, Elizabeth Hay goes South to discover North and her own Canadian identity. Whether read individually or together, *Crossing the Snow Line*, *The Only Snow in Havana*, and *Captivity Tales* articulate Hay's identity as Canadian because she is northern, and she narrates that identity from her southern locations. In Mexico and New York the North haunts her; she is constantly finding the North in the South, locating images of snow and ice and fur in the sun and warmth and flowers of an alien geography. Through her travels from Yellowknife to southern Canada, Mexico, New York, and north again to Ottawa, she learns how to recognize the warmth, and she converts the longing for home into northern narrative. However, in so far as Hay can represent her story and identity as ours too – that is, as a national identity – then her story must include ours, and that is a lot to ask. The first-person voice in these three autobiographical narratives often seems self-absorbed, edgy, insecure: is that the Canadian voice? To balance this insecurity and narcissism, Hay incorporates an elaborately counterpointed set of others' voices and stories into her narratives, from David Thompson, Tookoolito, and Fanny Pannigabluk to Harold Innis, Glenn Gould, and Joyce Wieland. If this incorporation, alignment of stories, or supplementation of a familiar, dominant narrative does not always work to convince (though I think it often quite wonderfully does) the reader that he/she *is* included as part of Hay's northern nation, the language of desire certainly does, because that language captures the desire for what is missing in the South: cold, snow, silence, fur, and a paradoxical warmth.

Crossing the Snow Line, described as "stories," documents Hay's travels from Yellowknife, the world of the Thelon and Artillary Lake, where she can smell the tundra (17), to points further and further south. As she sheds a failed marriage, her cold climate, and the documentary about snow that she is preparing, she learns that small mammals such as "mice, voles, and shrews" live in the warm layers of snow next to the ground. She will take this knowledge with her to Mexico:

We split open the north and find the legend of a tropical valley: an orange grove in the middle of the arctic. Men stumbled upon it, the story goes, and could never relocate it. Maybe it was an ancient memory – before the last ice age the north was warm. (*Crossing*, 46)

In the next volume, *The Only Snow in Havana*, the components are not called stories; they read almost like journal entries. Hay has remarried, has a child, and has begun to move back north. Here her search for Canada intensifies in several ways: evocation of place and the naming of names, around which fragments of story can grow, are two key strategies for searching. Her mapping of personal identity with place emerges from a verbal, really a poetic, evocation of place through metonymies of cold, snow, and fur:

In the heat of a moment to remember something so cold. In the heat of Colombia to begin a book with ice. If we were to begin a northern story with a similar object of allure, what would it be?

Something warm. Glenn Gould's hands in gloves even in summer. (26–7)

To be writing about fur again – the connecting thread, the hair in my soupy geography. Draw a line from Yellowknife to Winnipeg, over to Toronto, down to Mexico City, back up to Salem, and over to New York and you'll see the hairline crack of my particular coming apart and staying together. (96)

An image occurs to me of three footprints in the snow. The first one fresh, made only yesterday; the second half-filled with snow, its contours rounded; and the third, older still, softened even more, the outline of a foot simply a hollow, and in that hollow, soft blue light. This suggests an advance that's a retreat, and a retreat that brings one home to oneself. (134)

It is in *Only Snow* that Hay seriously begins her naming of names, instead of the mere passing mention that characterizes *Crossing* (McLuhan, 29, Marilyn Bell, 48, Canuck, 88). From Harold Innis she moves back in time to Rasmussen, Thompson, and Hearne as she reconstructs her Canadian history by a naming process that is not a genealogy so much as a finding of herself through a remembering that becomes a ritual incantation: "Champlain, father of Canada, founder of the fur trade" (11) leads to Innis and his *Fur Trade* (13–14). Innis leads to David Thompson, and so it goes, criss-crossing a history, a geography, a country, in a verbal weaving of identity. The most important naming, however, is of a new name, one that is unfamiliar, not included in the histories of North even though it signifies "real snow": Hannah, Hannah Ebierbing, "an Eskimo interpreter for Charles Hall's Arctic Expedition" (57), born Tookoolito (see Illus. 23). Disliking the term "Eskimo," Hannah calls herself and her husband, Joe, Inuit; "she signs her name variously Hannah, Hannah-li-to, Too-koo-li-to" (61). Searching through archives and stumbling upon a few of her surviving letters, Hay learns that she was born in Igloolik, July 1866, but died, aged thirty-eight, in New England. The card index, however, tells Hay nothing: "Tookoolito – see Ebierbing. And under Ebierbing – only Joe" (65). In a narrative of understatement and allusion, woven from such fragments of stories, places, and names, Hay does not belabour the point. Hannah, however, becomes symbolic, a figure of erasure, of "real snow" and "hot furs" (58) taken south to melt and disappear, of memory, loneliness, and, above all, of desire – for North. She becomes for Hay a figure of the artist (interpreter/translator/writer) invoking Canada and a northern story, pushing Hay home.

Captivity Tales brings Hay back to Canada, literally to Toronto and Ottawa, but well before that return she has resurrected, named into her story, a lifeline of names so thick and dense that she virtually writes her way north. Living in New York, she raids the museums and libraries. In Toronto she searches out "books about the north [in ...] the quiet knowledge – the quiet joy – that this is the history I want to know" (145). These "warm" books are, she tells us, "at the source of all the stories we could ever want to know" (151). In their own right, and as reinscribed, reiterated, reproduced here in *Captivity Tales*, they are part of the discursive formation of North. Biding her time in American exile, Hay names them – people, places, titles – and quotes these fellow Canadian writers, explorers, thinkers, artists, and poets. Hannah reappears, bringing with her this time the story of Sedna (64–7), and so does Gould, this time with his *Idea of North* (53–5).[28] Joyce Wieland appears for the first time, tellingly, to remind Hay of *O Canada* (the national anthem and the quilt) and of "a new sort of mapmaking ... to reveal a snow underworld" (32). Hay identifies with Wieland, more so than with Tookoolito, for various reasons, but primarily because Wieland returned to Canada, worked with

Illus. 23. Tookoolito as she looked in the 1850s.
She was called Hannah Ebierbing by Charles
Francis Hall, but was known as Tackritow
by Margaret Penny. Reproduced with
permission of W. Gillies Ross from his book
on Penny called *This Distant and Unsurveyed
Country: A Woman's Winter at Baffin Island,
1857–58* (139).

the Inuit in Cape Dorset, and quilted I LOVE CANADA. Like Hay, Wieland began again in the North "at the source of all the stories we could ever want to know" (151), and so Wieland joins Tookoolito as a key symbol for Hay: where Tookoolito is the image of "real snow" in exile and of scattered, uncatalogued fragments, Wieland escapes captivity in New York and flees north to give Hay the *quilted* image of her country and her text.

Before I turn to my last two writers, Mordecai Richler and Gabrielle Roy, I want to reflect for a moment on where Wiebe, Kroetsch, van Herk, and Hay have brought the discursive formation of North. Wiebe and Hay seem largely concerned with national identity in history and with a history of excluded voices; Kroetsch and van Herk focus more closely on individual identity scripted by story and with the exclusions of narrative itself. But this difference is more a matter of emphasis and degree than of sharp distinction, and it is not the only difference among them. Questions of gendered differences also arise from the stories they give us, as does the still larger question of what each of them does to/with the representation of Canada-as-North. This last and large question I will defer until Richler and Roy are in place, but a few further comparisons can be offered now.

Both Wiebe and Kroetsch represent the journey north in terms of heterosexual male desiring, and both conflate North with Woman, whether as sexually alluring Indian (*First and Vital Candle, A Discovery of Strangers*) or as great white Mother (*Gone Indian, The Man from the Creeks*). That they also problematize, complicate, and enrich these representations testifies to their artistic and intellectual power and, surely, to the times in which they live. Both seem comfortable with the impulse to rewrite a national history and to insist that their rewriting reconfigure the nation. It is no accident, I think, that in their two most complex northern novels, *A Discovery of Strangers* and *The Man from the Creeks*, they take foundational events of historic and national significance, events already well and truly inscribed in the national psyche, and passionately, even aggressively, rewrite them. As writers authoring this rewriting, they distance themselves from their subjects and position themselves outside the narrative as new explorers, discoverers in their own right, with the power to find more than any man before them did (more than Franklin, Back, or Hood more than Grey Owl or Robert Service).

Van Herk and Hay write differently. In each set of three texts (they cannot simply be designated novels) they, of course, write as women, but they also write and rewrite Woman. Certainly, they too desire true North, but to find it they must first find themselves and acknowledge their prior inscription *by men* as synonymous with North. This identification means that it is almost inevitable that writing about the North will mean writing the self. For both of these writers, the desire for North is a desire for home, for that place where they can feel at home, secure, legitimized, and where their voices will be heard – where they can rest. Van Herk searches for this home/self/North geographically – from Ellesmere to Edberg, from Alberta to Vancouver Island, from Edmonton to Yellowknife to the Wernecke Mountains; Hay searches historiographically (albeit by removing herself in space), from Champlain to Thompson, Tookoolito to Wieland, Innis to Gould. What holds their radically disrupted, discontinuous narratives together is this personal quest and the emergence of what Sidonie Smith calls embodied subjectivity in relation to the earth, to other people, and to others' stories. Each takes the familiar equation of North with Female and gives it agency: J.L. praying to the mountain and halting the slide; "Aritha" freeing Anna and herself on Ellesmere; Elizabeth recognizing her longing in Gould's hands in gloves, in fur, in Tookoolito's "real snow," and finding herself in Wieland's quilts – a quilted self. Where Wiebe and Kroetsch construct an imagined community through metaphor (Woman *is* North and text *is* nation), Hay and van Herk construct crazy quilts of metonymies, assert themselves and their stories as part of this place they call Canada and North.

WRITING CANADA-AS-NORTH

Three-quarters of the way through Mordecai Richler's *The Incomparable Atuk* and well into the scene of a CBC television cultural showcase program, "Dinner with the Tastemakers," a gentle grey-haired Jewish "seeker after truth and beauty" (123) announces loudly, for all the dinner guests and the TV cameras to hear, that "the most boring, mediocre man in the world is the White Protestant goy, northern species, and in Canada he has found his true habitat" (130). Everything up to this point in the novel is wild comic satire; everything afterwards becomes serious. Both *The Incomparable Atuk* and *Solomon Gursky Was Here* are fundamentally satiric and parodic allegories of national identity and the creation of Canada's "imagined community." As such, they may seem to sit surprisingly, even preposterously, beside the northern novels of Gabrielle Roy. I find it hard to imagine, for example, two more different representations of the Inuit by white southern Canadians than Richler's *Incomparable Atuk* and Roy's *La Rivière sans repos* (*Windflower*), or two more different representations of artists creating their country's story than *La Montagne secrète* (*The Hidden Mountain*) and *Solomon Gursky Was Here*. But that difference is part of my point: the discursive formation of North exists because it reproduces and contains such discontinuity and difference. Moreover, underlying that difference, as I hope to show, is a continuity, for both writers are struggling with the same narrative challenge – the task of telling the Canadian story, which they both see (in these works) as a northern story.

The Incomparable Atuk, first published in 1963, is in many ways Richler's initial attempt at what would become the far greater national epic-as-parody of *Solomon Gursky*. It develops from a complex, farcical plot-line that brings the "chunky little primitive" (4), Atuk, to Toronto for a series of crazy encounters that will culminate in his ritual beheading. Atuk is found on the tundra by an RCMP officer who teaches him English. When Atuk insists on composing poetry, this good officer shows it around the trading post until Atuk is discovered by a visiting advertising executive from Toronto. One thing rapidly leads to another; the poems are published, first in advertisements, then in a volume; Atuk is a success and so is brought south as an example of the native Canadian poet and as a good marketing ploy for the corrupt and exploitative Twentyman Fur Company. Thus, the true North comes south to boost the credit ratings of the big business that lies at the origins of the Canadian state: fur. There is just one problem. Atuk has done something in his past, traditional life on the tundra that, when revealed, will necessitate his sacrifice by Mr Twentyman himself. The clue to Atuk's past is embedded in one of his poems:

O plump and delicious one
here in land of so short night
me
alone,

humble,
hungering   (57)

And Atuk's present opinion of the South, from business to government to cultural gurus, is quite clear in another of his pieces, this one written after his arrival in Toronto and therefore representative of Atuk's loss of "a certain arctic simplicity":

Twentyman Fur Company,
I have seen the best seal hunters of my
generation putrefy raving die from tuberculosis,
Massey, you square,
eskimos don't rub noses any more and the cats
around Baffin Bay dig split-level houses.
Listen to me, Pearson,
a house is not a home,
an igloo is not a pad.
And you, Diefenbaker, can kiss my ass
where holy most holy pea-soup hockey players have
rumbled.
Canada, wake up, you're all immigrants to me:
my people are living like niggers.   (47)

Disgusting, as Atuk's sponsor says? Perhaps. But this is what Richler intends as Atuk's real voice, and for those who don't read poetry, Atuk will put it in plain prose: "the land is ours and we'd like it back ... This is our country ... We're Canadians [... and] you're all white to me" (116). As Richler creates him, Atuk, despite the broad, cartoonlike strokes, is shrewd, angry, and contemptuous of the urban whites around him.

From this point on, however, the ad man who is marketing Atuk for the Twentyman Fur Company realizes he must censor the little primitive, a task that will prove challenging. As the plot unrolls, Atuk does rather well for himself: he seduces the beautiful blond swimmer, whom no other guy can get near, by appealing to her sense of *noblesse oblige*; he sets up "Esky Enterprises" by bringing his family down from Baffin Island to the city and locking them in a studio-warehouse, where they crank out cheap carvings for the tourist trade; and he becomes a national hero – "the Noblest Canadian of Them All" (155). His nemesis is a journalist who will help uncover what happened on the tundra, and this will lead to the rapid succession of events that follows the cbc's televised "Dinner with the Tastemakers." Atuk, it turns out, is responsible for the mysterious disappearance of an American intelligence officer operating in Canada's Arctic: "alone, humble, hungering" in the Arctic night, Atuk ate the American!

Now, cannibalism is a not unfamiliar spectre in northern narratives. From Windigo myths to actual cases resulting from starvation, the taboo and terror surrounding the eating of human flesh haunt the historical and fictional record. Although it is often a trope, a metaphor for states of mind or a symbol in religious and social practices, cannibalism is seldom treated as a joke. But that is what Richler makes of it. This act of cannibalism lies at the heart of Atuk's story, informing his doing and undoing, but before Richler is finished with his cannibal and Mr Twentyman has dispatched his marketing-ploy-turned-albatross, popular opinion and Canadian nationalism have transformed Atuk into a hero, then a martyr. While the Americans, "once Colonel Swiggert's bones were discovered and it was established, beyond a doubt, that Atuk had eaten him," demand "swift justice" (166), all the "Johnny Canucks" are united in defence of national identity, home and native land, and in their interpretation of Atuk's patriotic act: "Atuk's act was one of symbolic revenge. Culturally, economically, the Americans are eating our whole country alive" (168). "The fat," as Richler puts it (unavoidably) is "in the fire" (169). Voices rise in defence of the "noble Eskimo" and of "practices ... sacred to our brothers in the igloo" (169). The nationalist cry goes up: Yankees and Uncle Sam should go home and "above all, leave our Eskimos alone" (170). When Atuk is arrested, there are demonstrations, marches on Ottawa, parades, newspaper blitzes, and liberation contests. A communist newspaper headline announces that it is a wonder Atuk did not die, right there on the tundra, from "PTOMAINE POISONING" (170).

Good satire must have not only its target but also its clear message, and *The Incomparable Atuk* has both. The targets are everywhere; no individual, no activity, no race, gender, class, or ethnic group is exempt. Canadians, it seems, are a bad lot. The deeper, larger targets of Richler's satire, however, are not limited to his caricatures of individuals or even institutions, such as big business, education, government, and the media. Atuk represents Canada itself by embodying the country's northern identity. In his death at the hands of exploitative corporate ideology, represented by the Twentyman Fur Company in collusion with the media (he is beheaded, on national television, in Twentyman's quiz show "Stick Out Your Neck," when he cannot answer a question about Canada's first hockey star, Howie Morenz), Richler tells us that, whether Canadians like it or not, the national interest has already sold out to southern commodity and media markets. Still more fundamentally, Canada has so corrupted its own people, resources, and national image, so exploited and prostituted itself, that it deserves little sympathy. Canada has sold its northern soul to the devil, and that is always a bad bargain. At the end of the novel, the question of whether or not it is too late to change anything, to preserve a national identity, or even to save our own skins, is left open. Twentyman's henchman, Harry Snipes, has stepped up to a microphone before thousands of Atuk supporters, but his words are those of one of history's great betrayers: "Atuk is dead ... Friends, Canucks, countrymen ... use your noggins ..." (178). The only character who uses his head or his voice wisely is Atuk's father, the

"Old One," and he counsels against assimilation, refuses to renounce his "igloo mentality," and reminds Atuk that one day the Inuit will reclaim "the land that is rightly ours" (87).

Solomon Gursky is at once the most encyclopedic and parodic of texts within the discursive formation of North. In it Richler constructs a genealogy of Canada based on foundational myths of origins and discovery, and of indigenous and explorer/settler narratives. He includes as many representatives of race, class, and ethnicity as possible, together with their stories. To be Canadian, he tells us, is to write our story into national history by inscribing ourselves on a northern landscape. To do that, he brings the far North to the Eastern Townships in Quebec, Europe to the high Arctic, the prairies to the Laurentians, and the St Lawrence River to the Beaufort Sea. All travellers pass through Winnipeg and Yellowknife as they go north or south, and North, as Richler tells it, is the source. "Where ... North? Far" (4).

The novel comprises a history within a biography that contains fragments of many biographical and autobiographical stories. On both main narrative levels – biography and history – it is a mystery novel, a vast whodunit, proliferating with accurate facts, false clues, murders, disguises, disappearances, and ghosts. All the clues and the ghosts lead the narrator-cum-biographer-cum-historian, Moses Berger, who has decided to write the biography and family history of Solomon Gursky, into the northern wilderness in pursuit of a survivor from Sir John Franklin's fatal 1845 expedition in search of the Northwest Passage. Once Moses has done the necessary historical research and visited the North himself (Yellowknife to King William Island), he learns why Canada is a tale told by a trickster in which walking into and out of the Arctic alive is the measure of a man's identity.

Berger's subject and hero, the man whom he adopts as his preferred father, Solomon Gursky, typifies these qualities of survival, exile, and cunning. As Moses will eventually realize, Solomon is the direct descendant of Ephraim Gursky, the only Franklin survivor, who lived with the Inuit, became one with them, and scattered the Gursky seed and name across the Arctic. Ephraim survived because he and his Jewish companion smuggled kosher food on board the *Erebus* and therefore did not succumb to scurvy or lead poisoning. Once his only legitimate heirs arrive in Canada, immigrants to the prairies, Ephraim teaches his favourite grandson, Solomon, everything he knows about survival in Canada (thus, in the North). When the time comes Solomon will disappear into the North in his raven-black Gypsy Moth (a disappearance he effects three times as the story progresses) and into the story Moses Berger will tell. That story will also be about Solomon's only son, Henry, who lives in the Arctic, marries an Inuuk, and fathers *his* only son, the white-Inuk Isaac.

By tracing this one genealogical thread through Richler's long and hugely complex narrative interweaving of people, places, texts, and stories, I am neglecting a lot to emphasize what I take to be the main point: Solomon Gursky is both Moses Berger's biographical subject and his creation, and *Solomon Gursky Was Here* is a

Canadian history that centres on Solomon's northern origins and identity. That this novel is so much else besides only demonstrates Richler's capacity to include and connect the multiplicities, contradictions, and discontinuities of Canadian history as he sees it into this hybrid textual representation of country.[29] What holds the text together is the North, and I will examine just a few of the ways in which Richler creates his unity-in-diversity: his use of familiar tropes and images of North; his reproduction and inscription of key nineteenth- and twentieth-century Arctic narratives; his strategic use of native myth; and his development of one (among many) key visual *mises en abyme*. Along the way, and despite Berger's suffering-artist-as-drunkard persona, Richler shows us that Canadian history is anything but boring or uneventful. To the contrary. As he tells it, our "imagined community," built on furs, booze, and exploitation, rests on one incredible, ruthless, ambitious, rollicking plot after another, most of them masterminded by the fabulous Gurskys.

Among the most important tropes and images of North in the novel are the frequently repeated phrase that anchors the frame narrative of Berger's search in the present of 1983 to the 1851 history – "Where ... North? Far" (4, 148, 316, 484, 556) – and Isaac's survival in the Arctic by cannibalizing his father, Henry (526–7). Others include references to bush planes and pilots, a mysterious harpoon that appears when and where least expected, the gimel ("G," the third letter in the Hebrew alphabet) that occurs in the most inappropriate places, and the transformations and translations of the word *raven* (Tulugaq, Corbeau, Corvus, Cuervo, and Otto Raven) that follow the Gurskys wherever they go. The simple question "Where ... North?" serves several purposes: it connects the narrative in time by linking the embedded narratives; it connects the story at all levels with the process of going north; it reminds us that all good southern things come from and return to the North; and it functions as a verbal mnemonic for the reader, who is trying to stay on track, to locate his or her position on the map of Richler's text. Partly because Moses Berger is a very disorganized historian, with more than the usual historian's trouble getting his dates in order, and partly because the story we read is the story he is writing between bottles of Macallan consumed in his Lake Memphramagog cabin, repetitions like this are essential.

Cannibalism is, of course, the quintessential northern trope. It figured strategically in *The Incomparable Atuk*, and it plays a similarly symbolic role here. While family, friends, the Jewish faithful, and the newspapers find euphemisms for what Isaac does on the tundra, and while Isaac tries to excuse himself by pointing out that it was either eat his dead father or die himself because he could not, after all, eat the third member of the group, a decidedly unkosher Netsilik, the entire novel could be said to embody cannibalism. The fathers in the novel, like the founding fathers of a nation (according to Richler), try to devour their sons, so it should not be surprising if some of the sons turn the tables. Indeed, the so-called brotherhood of man is imaged, by Richler, as cannibalistic, from the Franklin disaster through the Second World War, as allied countries like Canada fed Jews to the enemy by refusing them asylum, to Isaac's survival strategem. The Gursky financial empire, founded on booze, maintains its control of business and profits by pitting ravenous siblings against each other, and Solomon, in his Sir Hyman Kaplansky incarnation, reminds his gentile dinner guests of their complicity in various cannibalisms by forcing them to participate in a bloody Passover Seder (506–11).

The textual rescriptings in *Solomon Gursky Was Here* are far too numerous to catalogue, let alone discuss. The crucial ones are citations of versions of the 1845 Franklin disaster and the nineteenth-century searches for Franklin that are part of the official record, but Owen Beattie's contemporary *Frozen in Time* gets a mention, as does Franklin's first expedition, by land in 1820–21, which is Wiebe's subject in *A Discovery of Strangers*. The Klondike, Robert Service (represented by Richler's inspired parody of "The Cremation of Sam McGee," 527), and the formation of the RCMP from the NWMP all appear, as does *The Beaver*, *Captain Al Cohol Comics*, the history of Yellowknife, Grey Owl, the Mad Trapper, and more.[30] But the search for the Northwest Passage and the texts that plot it form the key intertextual set in the novel. To make matters more interesting, Richler quotes from real source texts, modifies some of them, and fabricates others, and he scatters fragments of text, dates, names, places, and occurrences across his 557–page canvas. At one point we learn that Ephraim has settled down with an Indian woman called Lena Green Stockings in her cabin on the prairies (47), while at another we get a ribald account of Robert Hood's liaison with the real Greenstockings (415–17); at another we get a terse reference to Sir John Franklin's *Narrative of a Journey to the Shores of the Polar Sea* (204), while at still another we read the entire verbatim (I have checked) quotation of an advertisement in the Toronto *Globe*, 4 April 1850, announcing huge awards for anyone "who shall render efficient assistance to the crews" of the *Terror* and *Erebus*, or provide accurate information about their fate (413–14).

Two more examples of how Richler reproduces Franklin narratives, repeating, participating in, and adding to that most frequently cited set of statements, will serve to confirm the centrality of Franklin to the novel. Studying the documents of the Arctic Society, of which he has become a member, and an interview published in *The Yellowknifer*, Moses is able to recount what is known about the 1845 expedition (44–52). However, interspersed with the known facts – the complement of officers and men aboard the ships, details of their supplies and their route, and the ships, routes, and men who conducted searches for the missing Franklin, John Rae's discovery of evidence of cannibalism (also reported in the *Globe*), and Charles Dickens' heated denials – are a host of fabrications: not only did two strangers creep aboard the *Erebus* before it sailed from Stromness Harbour, but they smuggled their kosher food on board, including "uncounted jars of chicken fat" (46). These two characters will turn out to be Ephraim and his older friend Izzy Garber, and the Netsilik people of King William Island will save them and name them Tulugaq and Doktuk. Now there is some evidence that Crozier, captain of the *Terror*, was known to the Inuit as Aglooka and that he was accompanied by other white men called Toolooa (for raven) and Doktook (see Woodman, 195–9), but no one like Ephraim or Izzy was actually on either ship. Richler creates an apocryphal account of a search expedition, *Life with the Eskimos* by Waldo Logan, and quotes from it to confirm that Ephraim was called Tulugaq (meaning black for raven) because of his black eyes and beard. Then Richler goes further to claim that the grave of Isaac Grant (aka Izzy Garber) has been located on King William Island and that, when the body is exhumed in 1969, it is found to be wrapped in "a *talith*, the traditional prayer shawl common to the Ashkenazi Jews of Northern Europe" (51). That leaves Tulugaq (aka Ephraim) the sole survivor of the 1845 disaster, but this fictional survival only establishes, as it were, his presence in the Arctic; it does not explain how he survived or his subsequent adventures, the revelation of which will have to wait some four hundred pages before Moses finds the journals Solomon leaves for him on King William Island.

Solomon's journals, containing the tales within the history within the biography of the text, are pure fabrication drawn from the sources Richler consulted:

Trying to reconstruct Ephraim's interminable winters in the high Arctic, the sun sinking below the horizon for four months, Moses had to rely on conjecture and the accounts of other nineteenth-century explorers. Then there were the fragments from Solomon's journals, those tales told by Ephraim on the shores of a glacial lake, man and boy warming themselves by their camp-fire under the shifting arch of the aurora.   (432)

This description should warn any seasoned reader of northern novels about the authenticity of what follows. Ephraim's tales, told to and recorded (apparently) by Solomon in his own Arctic journals, provide an account of the crew's decline from saucy, homosocial theatricals to scurvy, delirium, death, and cannibalism (433–4). Only Ephraim and Izzy escape, which takes the reader back to the earlier account (44–52), as if to validate, through completion, that earlier narrative fragment.

The key native myth used by Richler that I want to examine is the story of the trickster Raven, and the one visual *mise en abyme* I will consider is the nineteenth-century engraving of Ephraim that seems to hang in several Gursky offices and homes. The story of Raven is common to many First Nations and Inuit cultures (see *Solomon Gursky*, 42–3). The best-known representation of the myth is possibly Haida artist Bill Reid's massive carving *The Raven and the First Men* (1990), showing Raven perched on a half-open clam shell with naked human beings fearfully emerging or crawling back inside.[31] Sir Hyman Kaplansky owns a picture illustrating this myth, and as he explains the story to Moses (he begins on page 493, but he had already warned Moses about the Raven: 191), it becomes quite clear that Kaplansky is Solomon and that Solomon is the Raven trickster, creator and destroyer, artist and con-artist, who has time and again terrified and seduced his hapless biographer-historian with his "smooth trickster's tongue" (500). By using this myth in this way, Richler has both incorporated native Canadian history into the fabric of his story and indentified his Gurskys with one of the major creation stories of Canada. He has, moreover, through the multilingual changes he rings on the word *raven*, multiplied the raven's identity and added to its transforming power. He has, in a sense, appropriated the myth to enhance his own trickster/artist fable and, to reverse the connection, rooted his version of Canadian history deep within the "imagined community" of Nation.

The engraving works in a similar way.[32] It provides clues to the story Moses Berger is researching; it pops up to remind us of important connections; and it inscribes, literally, Ephraim within an Arctic iconography of Canada. One of the best descriptions of the image comes shortly after a dead raven, skewered by a harpoon, is found at the grave of Bernard Gursky, the corrupt business tycoon who tried to destroy his brother Solomon and failed. The engraving we are told about is a copy (the original hangs in the Gurskys' Montreal boardroom) that hangs in the New York office of Bernard's son:

> Ephraim was drawn alongside a blow-hole, with both feet planted in the pack ice, his expression defiant, his head hooded, his body covered with layers of sealskin ... He held a harpoon in his fist, the shaft made of caribou antler. There was a seal lying at his feet, the three masts of the doomed *Erebus* and jagged icebergs rising in the background, the black Arctic sky lit by paraselenae, the mock-moons of the north.   (266)

And this is as clear a visual image as we will ever get of the original Canadian Gursky, the man whom Solomon so clearly resembles that he might be Solomon himself.

For all its satire of Canadians and big business, culture, founding families, and the writing of history and biography, *Solomon Gursky Was Here* is serious parody on an epic scale. It is, in the final analysis, a northern ghost story – history as northern ghost story – in which Richler has added one more ghost to the genealogy. Canadian history, he tells us, must include these ghosts even if (especially when) they do not fit the stereotypic model (white, male, Christian, and of British descent). By repeating and adding to a vast archive of Arctic lore, this novel, more than any of the other northern novels written to date, insists that, to be truly Canadian, a man must know how to disappear into and reappear from the Barrens. Like Wiebe, Richler wants true North, not passage to somewhere else. Like Solomon, the trickiest ghost of them all, he must go North. Where ...? Far.

The shift from Richler to Roy is, at first glance, considerable – from satire and epic to realism and allegory – except that, despite the scope of *Solomon Gursky*, Richler has not said all that can be said about ideas of North or made the ultimate contribution to the discourse. Roy's novels are written in another, complementary register. Where Richler delights in representing the artist as trickster, Roy returns us to the human being and, in this way, to one of the most basic of northern stories: the representation of the North itself. For this reason (and because the novel holds a special place in my heart), I will conclude my discussion of her work and the narration of nation in this chapter with *The Hidden Mountain*, that parable *par excellence* of what it means to be a Canadian/northern artist. But *The Hidden Mountain* is not Roy's only northern narrative, and she, as did each of my other writers, went north to see something of the place for herself.

In July of 1961 Gabrielle Roy visited Fort Chimo on Ungava Bay, a tiny village on the shores of the Koksoak River. Judging from her account, *Voyage en Ungava*, the experience moved her deeply.[33] She was struck, first and last, by the land itself – its tragic beauty, its silence (unimaginable in the South), its space and isolation, and yet, at the same time, "its delicate harmony of colours ... from a hand that had painted the wide canvas of the North" (Roy from *Voyage*, quoted in Gagné, my translation). She was equally impressed with the Inuit she met on this trip, among whom she found the inspiration for her characters in *Windflower* and in the three "Eskimo Stories" included with the French edition of *La Rivière sans repos* (Gagné, 373, 376). Her conclusions about the impact of white culture upon the native community are negative, the most prophetic being her comment that one drop of white blood in a Inuk's veins makes that person less content with life. Without doubt, this trip inspired her to write *Windflower*, her third northern novel, which she considered calling *Fleur boréale* (Ricard, 1972, 307), but ideas of North had been with Roy from the beginning of her writing career, and they always circled around what she saw as a fundamental, irreconcilable opposition between North and South. Long before she became so keenly interested in Ungava and the cultural encounter taking place there, she admits to a fascination with the very words "Frobisher" and "Baffin Island" (Roy, quoted in Gagné, 370, 383), and the North, or the going north away from crowded cities, is central to *Where Nests the Water Hen*, *The Cashier* (*Alexandre Chenevert*), and the story of Pierre Cadorai in *The Hidden Mountain*.[34]

Where Nests the Water Hen and *Windflower* are deeply tragic stories on a theme of perennial and personal significance for Roy – the departure of children from the home and the consequent abandonment of a mother. In the first novel that story unfolds in an isolated community in northern Manitoba, a land "just at the edge of the everlasting tundra" (31). This is a provincial North of hunting and trapping, dependent on the fur trade, and part of the southern government's northern colonization program. As the Tousignant family grows (finally to thirteen children), the mother wants a school built, and ironically, as a result of her efforts, a teacher arrives from the South with the knowledge that will lure each child away to southern cities. The bleakness of this inevitability is balanced, though never resolved, by the qualities associated with the northern landscape, qualities at once harsh yet pure, where life is simple but free. The lessons of the North are expressed by the priest, who gets a better price for his parishioners' furs in Toronto by pointing to the quality of the pelts: the farther north and the colder the climate, the darker, richer, and thicker the fur. The final, moral message of the story is that, while the South, signifying the advance of civilization, cannot be stopped, and that, as with the furs, it will absorb all the good things the North produces (including its children), the North still offers something precious and unique.

Again, it is the priest who explains that "the farther he had gone into the North, the more free he had been to love" (160).

By comparison, *Windflower* is almost devastating in its seemingly unqualified and unmediated portrayal of loss. When the South enters the tiny Inuit community on the Koksoak River, the life of at least one woman is changed forever. Elsa Kumachuk, who is raped by an American soldier stationed at the military base outside the town, bears a child who becomes the absolute centre of her world. This blond Inuk baby precipitates a cultural struggle for Elsa that drives her to emulate a white lifestyle, which she can only support through domestic work. Unhappy with this artificial life, she returns to her traditional way of life until the day when her Jimmy must attend school. When the local RCMP officer comes to take Jimmy, Elsa flees with him on to the land, only to be driven back to the community by a blizzard and the child's illness. Elsa is trapped. Unable to return to her former Inuit life, and unable to satisfy the increasing demands of the boy, she loses both. Jimmy abandons her to search for his American father, and our last glimpse of Elsa is as a prematurely old woman, dreaming of this son as she wanders the shores of the Koksoak. Even Elsa's grandfather Thaddeus, an Inuk artist and philosopher, cannot assuage her grief or carve the features of this alien child. Neither the love of Thaddeus nor the utter devotion of Elsa can hold the boy in the North.[35]

Together these two novels represent a North inhabited by realistic characters facing actual hardships and challenges within a modern, changing society that they cannot understand or control. Of the six writers I have examined in detail, Roy is the only one to explore the social impact of contemporary southern technology and so-called *civilized* values on a simpler, remote northern world. (*First and Vital Candle* does not focus on these issues.) Although muted by the lyricism of her language and by her refusal to preach, Roy's representation of North in these novels has more in common with Jim Lotz's *Northern Realities* and Tester and Kulchyski's *Tammarniit* than with stories about Franklin, the Mad Trapper, or dreams of romantic escape. Her mothers must carry out their existence in close relation with family and community, and in daily dependence upon the land. The ethnic or geographic differences between the Franco-Manitoban Luzina Tousignant and the Inuut Elsa Kumachuk are far less important than their shared fate. Both women serve to represent Roy's vision of a nurturing, sustaining North that can only lose in any contest with the South. And yet, despite this bleak vision, the artistic care Roy lavishes on her evocations of the North remains in the imagination long after the novels end. It is that fundamental sustaining freedom and beauty that she captures so well in *The Hidden Mountain*.

The Hidden Mountain celebrates both the Canadian North, from the Mackenzie to Ungava, and the Canadian artist's need, even duty, to represent it. Although it is emphatically a novel, constructed through a narrative focus on fictional characters who are located in time and space, embody an ideology, and enact a sequence of events over time, the novel has much in common tonally with the contemplative meditation of Wiebe's *Playing Dead*. When the novel opens, we are situated on the shores of a river from which a lone stranger will appear. The river itself, the watcher(s), the man who will appear – all these are deeply familiar and resonant elements within the discursive formation of North. Kroetsch's *But We Are Exiles* opens on the Mackenzie, and that river carries and haunts the plot. Wiebe's *The Mad Trapper* opens on a river, the mighty Peel, and the reader watches a man enter the story by water. Consider these beginnings:

And bent over he could feel the stillness strike the back of his bare head, half knocking life into him, half knocking it out. His breath came in lumps. He glanced up at the breath-tripping hush; at the broad river, mirror-smooth in the afternoon sun; at the old riverboat where she lay tied up beside her two steel barges. No one had seen the canoe stop. The lifting bow bobbed gently. He looked down again at the water and this time saw his own face watching him; the prematurely balding blond head, the full lips and squinting deep-set eyes suggesting a moodiness that didn't belong with his tall and hard body. He studied the reflection as if not sure whom he might see.   (*But We Are Exiles*, 2)

The autumn sun was almost gone behind the Richardson Mountains. Its last light flamed against an underbelly of cloud, polished the water of the Peel River into uneasy boils of glistening black and vivid, almost bloody, red. Distant sounds drifted by: geese flying south, water lapping against rocks, but over all lay the immense Arctic silence of the coming winter.

A spot of blackness appeared on the edge of a red gleam that cut across the river. Slowly the spot grew larger, lengthened into the light so slowly that it seemed to be standing still in the shining water without a ripple or a wave to reveal its movement. Gradually the shape emerged: in the middle of the huge empty river was a man.   (*The Mad Trapper*, 11)

More and more often, though, the old man would punctuate his labours with an intense contemplation of the river as it flowed along its course ...

The river had little depth, but was wide, of lovely aspect, and with a swift current. Its steep and difficult banks could only be scaled, a little farther on, just where the cabin was perched above, and where, below, a small landing dock rested on piles. All else was wilderness, silence, sky beyond measure. And this somewhere in the Northwest Territories, that vast top of Canada, almost half a continent, and still almost wholly the possession of a few scattered handfuls of men.   (*The Hidden Mountain*, 3–4)

Rivers. Rivers flowing north, rivers moving us into story. Rivers that bear the very rhythm of these northern narratives. Northern rivers are, inevitably, major characters in northern novels because they are, inescapably, major players in Canadian history, economics, geography, and myth. *Playing Dead* takes the creation of a river (the Coppermine) as its central metaphor; *First and Vital Candle* features a beautiful but deadly river. *Gone Indian*, *The Man from the Creeks*, *Windflower*, and *Where*

Nests the Water Hen: they are all obsessed with rivers, the Mackenzie, the Yukon, the Coppermine, the Peel, the Koksoak, the North Saskatchewan, the Water Hen ... and so many more.

The man about to enter *The Hidden Mountain* by river is Pierre Cadorai, a Canadian painter. This is his story, and a story of the rivers that carry him across the North, west to east, until he finds his grail – a sacred mountain. Although Roy bases her story upon the actual northern journeying of painter René Richard (1895–1982), she creates a character, in Pierre, and a story of allegorical significance that exceeds and supplements any actual biography.[36] The text has three parts, each one charting Pierre's course across the North in parallel with his artistic awakening and development. In part 1, where he enters the narrative by water, he is young, full of curiosity, fulfilling himself by sketching the scenery around him in pencil. He meets the old trapper, who is watching by the shore as the novel opens, the trapper's daughter, who has left for Arctic Red River, and then Steve Sigurdsen, with whom he will spend two long Yukon winters trapping. Through Steve's intervention he begins to sketch in colour, with crayons, and through Steve he learns the responsibility of his calling: to represent the Canadian North, its wildlife, its people, and its seasons *for others*, so that they can see the North country too, and rejoice.

In part 2, Pierre leaves the relative security of his friendship with Steve to continue his search for the soul of his country, because he has come to understand what he must do with his life:

Yes, here was what really deserved to be recorded on paper: the return of the sun, the trees coming back to life, the end of damnable winter!

Thus it was that Pierre discovered what men expected of persons like himself – that they should, thanks to them, rejoice and be sustained by hope.   (44)

He arrives in Ungava by river and discovers what he realizes is his goal and ultimate challenge: a uniquely beautiful mountain. However, his desire to paint the mountain in all its moods and guises nearly destroys him (as a river, too, has almost done), and he only narrowly escapes the onslaught of winter by making his way to an Inuit community. Once there, he is nursed back to health, but a fatal contact has been made, not with the North or the Inuit but with white, southern, European values and expectations. Pierre's sketches are admired; he is encouraged by a priest to study abroad to become a real artist.

Part 3 depicts Pierre's life in Paris and his downward path of despair, exile, and death. A stranger in an alien place, he walks the shores of the Seine, dreaming that this river is one of his northern rivers. He is befriended by a young man who comes down the Seine and into his life, and he struggles to draw and paint according to classical precepts. He fails, of course, and withdraws further and further into the northern landscape of his memory and imagination. In a stark and stunning reversal of his physical journey east to the site of high culture, and of the assumptions North Americans often hold about Europe, especially in matters of the arts, Pierre rejects the formal, well-lighted studio routine of his fellow painters and establishes himself in a tiny, cold garret, heated by a wood stove. He chooses this place because its spatial confinement is conceptually and imaginatively *right*: "he had shaped himself to this law of the North: vast spaces outdoors; indoors kept small" (161). He will die of a heart attack in this room while struggling to paint his "montagne secrète."

Roy's novel has been criticized for lacking dramatic action and interesting characters (and character relations), but these criticisms miss the point (see Ricard, 1999, 408–9). That the narrative should be seen as lacking action, or plot, is especially interesting because it suggests the close association in a reader's mind of North with adventure, and of the novel as a genre with a prescriptive set of realist conventions. But as should be clear by now, *The Hidden Mountain* is a northern novel with a difference. The descriptions of the landscape are realist to a point, but Roy's realism shifts imperceptibly into symbolism, and I want to examine two key points at which this shift occurs. The same shift occurs with characterization, as is clear from Pierre's lack of contextualizing familial or psychological background and from the increasingly symbolic weight of his human relationships. In fact, there is a marked degree to which all human relationships in this novel are primarily with (or are represented in terms of) the land.

Although other symbols might be isolated as keys to reading this novel (the mountain itself or the image of a tree), I see the river, or rivers, as the symbolic heart of the text. In this, as in much else, I share Antoine Sirois's reading of the symbolic and mythic qualities of Roy's writing and intention. Rivers unite the narrative, from the Mackenzie to the North Saskatchewan to the Churchill to the Seine, and back, in image and imagination, to those northern rivers from which Pierre is separated in Paris. Rivers carry the story and its artist-hero, from West to East, from North to South, as he traverses the country attempting to find his vocation and the soul of the land he must paint. Both temporally and spatially, the river provides a cumulative metaphoric network (created from repeated metonymic images that posit rivers as essential parts of life and of North) that connects the three parts of Pierre's story and resonates, as I suggested through my comparative quotations, with other northern statements in the discursive formation of North. In another kind of analysis than the one I am concerned with here, I would also develop the broader philosophical, mythological, and religious associations of rivers as metaphors for time itself, for life and death, and for purification and rebirth – all of which Roy evokes. If I stress the power of the river imagery to convey the movement and process of Pierre's search for and discovery of the land he must identify with and represent in art, it is because this imagery facilitates my reading of the text as a narrative river of statements, which is coherent within itself and part of the large shifting discourse that is my primary concern. Moreover, in her use of rivers Roy constructs the artist-parable and national-allegory aspects of her novel, and these are the qualities that made *The Hidden Mountain* difficult or frustrating for her early critics.

A close examination of one river scene, in which Pierre almost dies, will suggest what I mean by parable and allegory. At the end of part 1 Pierre decides that he must leave Steve and their Yukon traplines to continue his search for the country he will paint. After a brief farewell and Sigurdsen's warning about the dangers of northern rivers, Pierre sets out in his canoe to follow the rivers across the Northwest Territories. He has felt tortured by his failure to capture in line and colour the qualities of water, but now, completely alone on the river, he realizes that "his soul seemed to find rest here, as though close to this world's wild heart" (64). Towards the end of August he reaches the "northern limits of Manitoba" and the Churchill, "another great river whose name had been for him so full of enticement" (65). But the Churchill proves impossible to navigate, and Pierre falls in love with the country by exploring and sketching smaller waterways until he discovers "a river of enchantment" (66) that appears on none of his maps: "It simply appeared: an utter stranger. It was lovely. It flowed narrow, rapid, and certainly deep, between steep embankments of rock moistened by spume" (66).[37] Completely mesmerized, Pierre forgets the river itself in his effort to capture its colours, vegetation, and reflections. Suddenly, he is caught up in a violent current sweeping him towards rapids. Unable to pull to shore, he has a few seconds to decide what to save before grasping a tree branch ("salvation") and hauling himself to safety; he takes his rifle with him and leaves his precious sketches and paints in the runaway canoe.

The scene Roy describes, in the third person but focalized through Pierre, has the force of parable and the resonance of myth: at the microlevel of the text she creates an image of man's ineluctable fate before the greater forces of nature; at the mesolevel, where this scene connects across the narrative, she is building an allegory of the northern artist. At the macrolevel, where the novel connects with other statements in the discursive formation, this scene evokes a familiar northern trope of death by drowning. Here, in part, is the scene: As Pierre hangs, swinging from the branch, he watches his canoe shatter against the rocks, spilling paints and drawings into the river:

Then this strange river, covering itself with spots of colour, offered the strangest of sights. Scattered in every direction, his sketches with their fresh colours hurtled over each other, twirled, moved apart, then drew together as though to fashion on the surface of the water a series of broken images, without relation or meaning, though of amazingly brilliant loveliness. All one saw was carmine, acid greens, sunny yellows, spinning about ... Meanwhile the last born of the little sketches seemed to want to return to Pierre. Eddies jostled it back and forth between each other. With its painted surface facing the sky it circled around a narrow area, for a moment almost found refuge in calmer water along the bank. Pierre reached out, was about to try to recover it ... and then it slid quickly, was in its turn snatched by the whirlpools, and sucked into the river's mighty funnel.   (67)

Pierre survives, having lost his entire summer's work, and typically Roy provides only the most laconic observation – possibly "those summonses to his soul" (68) have really been his "foes, eager to jeer at all he did" (68). Whether friends or foes is not, I think, Roy's point. This extraordinary scene, captured in words, while representing the visual world of the painter and his hubris, symbolizes both the near impossibility and the obsesssive desire to see, know, and celebrate the North. Unlike Tom Thomson (an inspiration to Richard and clearly an avatar for Pierre), Roy's hero lives to paint again. It will not be a northern river that kills him. But he has been warned about the stakes for which he is playing and reminded, surely, in those brilliant broken images of colour swirling briefly on the water's surface before being sucked into its dark depths, that he has given his heart's blood to this North: that it, in fact, possesses him.[38] This is a lesson he will ignore or forget until he finds himself in a Paris garret.

Before Paris becomes even a distant possibility, let alone a depressing reality, Pierre continues east into Ungava, where he finds the secret or hidden mountain. Drawing upon Richard's stories and her own imagination (she made the trip to Ungava in July 1961, after writing this novel), Roy describes Ungava, in the extreme north of Quebec, as "a land fashioned ... in the realm of hallucination" (71). Pierre is sighted entering this land, by canoe on "the River of a Thousand Thunders," by a young Inuk who realizes that this white man is the "Man-of-the-Magic-Pencil" (74) whose reputation has preceded him across the North. It is *there*, somewhere in Ungava, that Pierre discovers "a high and solitary mountain that glowed in the red sunlight and burned brilliantly like a great pillar of fire" (81). This discovery is almost apocalyptic, in several senses. It seems to Pierre as if this mountain has "chosen ... to reveal itself" (82), that it is pleased with his gaze and talks to him (83), that he and this mountain are one. Revelation, holy grail, ultimate object of his quest and the inspiration of his art, Pierre prays for the capacity to paint it, to capture it. Caught up in his obsession to represent this "resplendent" being (as he thinks of it), he paints frantically, oblivious of approaching winter, which catches him low on supplies and far from an Inuit settlement. Painting this mountain very nearly kills him and leads to another of Roy's profoundly symbolic moments of northern awareness.

Just as Pierre realizes how blind he has been to the "pitiless implacablity" (94) of the North, he sees an aged caribou bull, which he must kill to survive. A protracted and appalling hunt ensues, with Pierre wounding the animal and tracking it by its blood. Sighting the creature, he fires again, but the animal refuses to die, and now, out of ammunition, he is forced to kill it by hand. He catches up with the staggering bull several times, and strikes it with his hatchet. He runs beside it, begging it to die, and striking it again and again.[39] By the time the beast finally succumbs, night has fallen; Pierre is exhausted and far from his camp by the mountain:

Pierced with cold, Pierre let himself slip down next to the dead caribou, which gradually began to give him its warmth. In the endless stretches of the tundra they formed a tiny, motionless, almost fraternal patch of shadow ... the caribou was to become for him flesh, blood, and his very thought.   (98)

Once more Roy has constructed a scene of archetypal signficance; man and animal, hunter and hunted, become one in a brutal, yet necessary communion. But this scene is more than an example of mere survival of the fittest. On the one hand, Roy has drawn upon a familiar northern trope of human survival by hunting, while on the other she invests this violent hunt with the spiritual qualities of sacred ritual, sacrifice, and a recognition of the interdependence of all living things in the North. On a practical and realist narrative level, Pierre must live to continue his life's work, but on a symbolic level – one that is not spelled out by Roy or recognized, *yet*, by Pierre – this fusion of man and beast identifies Pierre Cadorai as a northerner, as a man who will not survive apart from this place.

When he finally makes it back to camp, a bear has destroyed his work and remaining provisions; the mountain has withdrawn its face in wintry rebuke, and he longs for release in death. Only the greater desire to create future art forces him to struggle to the coast, where the Inuit save him. There he meets the priest who will recognize the quality of his few surviving paintings and set the wheels in motion for his journey to Montreal, and then to France. Pierre flies out of the North filled with terror and apprehension and into a South of cities, noise, crowding, and a far greater loneliness than he ever knew in the North. Before his first day in Paris ends, he finds himself dreaming, with "a primitive surge of the soul," of "the great North" (131). From this day to the day he dies some months later, Pierre searches Paris for echoes and reminders of who he really is. He is unable to paint well again until he paints what he wants – not the city streets but the rivers, trees, people, and animals of the North – and he is unable to do that well until he finds his garret, where the light reminds him of daylight on "the Upper Mackenzie, during the month of October" (162). Roy's Canadian trapper-turned-painter, this quintessential northerner, finds solace for his deracination and alienation in his room with a woodstove that resembles a northern cabin. And there he begins to paint: "Under his brushes the woods of the North surged into life" (165).

As the North returns in his mind's eye and to his canvases, he becomes increasingly obsessed with representing and capturing it. Finally, he turns to a self-portrait, as if in mute recognition that by re-creating his North he is, in fact, creating himself, and the portrait he paints is haunting indeed. We see it through the eyes of a fellow painter, Pierre's friend Stanislas: the face is "disproportionately long," the eyes looking down, with pupils dilated, and on the top of the head Stanislas detects "a hint of curious protuberances, a suggestion of antlers" (177). In this extraordinary image Pierre has represented himself as acknowledging the "close alliance of the soul to all that is primitive" (178) and, because his head emerges from a tracery of northern trees, as virtually inseparable from the land. In the language of paint (captured in Roy's words), Pierre images himself as figure *and* ground, human and beast, creator of and created by the North. Although I do not for a minute wish to overemphasize the relation of Richard to the fictional creation of Pierre, it is worth noting that one of René Richard's self-portraits (and Roy knew his work well) bears an uncanny resemblance to the painting Roy attributes to her character (see Illus. 24). Clearly Richard has done with shadow and line in this expressionist portrait what Roy suggests through her cryptic description, couched in suggestive words and her qualifications ("perhaps," "yet," "somewhat"), and then completes with questions and a deliberately inconclusive statement: "Its appeal lay in that kind of fascination with which it pointed – counter to all clarity – toward the harrowing enigmas of existence" (178).

However, Roy, for her own complex reasons, does not end her narrative at this symbolic point of recognition and reconciliation. Nor does she permit Pierre to return to his beloved North (as *she* had done, as René Richard had done). Instead, she has Pierre die in his garret, still longing to "return there," where he would like "to die" (183), and still struggling to paint his resplendent mountain. He collapses before his easel as "the lofty mountain faded away" (186), and Roy ends with a simple question: "Who, in the mists, would ever find it again?" (186)

This question, taut with ambiguity, promise, and uncertainty, resonates on every level of the narrative. The simplest answer, or so it seems to me, is also the obvious one: the reader. The reader of *The Hidden Mountain* will "find it again" if he or she looks in the right place: in the great North constructed in the words and narrative of Roy's text, and in so many other texts. Paradoxically (given the relative brevity and seeming simplicity of the story), Roy has found a great deal in the North to express and represent on her verbal canvas. In the foreground are the rivers and trees of the Yukon and the NWT; in the middle distance are the many northerners (man and beast) who inhabit the vast spaces, and in the distance looms a mountain, beautiful, austere, rounded with age, mysterious and beckoning. The entire work is suffused with a luminosity, that light of the Mackenzie in October, reminiscent of a Richard or a Lawren Harris (see, for example, Plates 6 and 8). Moving forward towards me through the picture plane (perhaps like Blair Bruce's ghostly trapper with whom I began this study; see Plate 2) is some barely discernible shape, part human, part animal, the unrepresentable, uncapturable face of the North.

I have already suggested that, as a realist novel, Roy's text gives us a recognizable picture of various aspects of the Yukon, the southern stretches of the NWT, and the barrens of Ungava, and of the human beings who actually inhabit the North – trappers, Indians of various northern First Nations, and the Ungava Inuit – by living a hard life on the land. She does not romanticize or sentimentalize this existence, and she captures something of its variation from region to region. The two supporting characters who emerge most distinctly from among those people Pierre meets on his journey are Steve Sigurdsen, the white trapper, and Orok, the Inuk, himself a hunter and an artist, who will work beside Pierre and help him survive. These two are very different men, but they share a love for and a shrewd

Illus. 24. René Richard, *Autoportrait* (1934), pencil on paper, 20.7 × 19.4 cm. 2001 ©, all rights reserved, Fondation René Richard. Reproduced with the permission of the Fondation René Richard. In this image Richard bears an uncanny likeness to Roy's description of Pierre Cadorai's self-portrait. Here, as in the novel, the elongated face and exaggerated ears of the man suggest the resemblance to a deer or caribou.

understanding of the North. They also share the capacity to understand the role and value of the artist, and *The Hidden Mountain* is above all a portrait of the artist as Canadian and (to paraphrase A.M. Klein) as *northern* landscape. Both in his life and in his premature death, Pierre Cadorai represents Roy's idea of the artist who lives in and for his art, mostly in isolation, and inextricably involved with his spiritual home. For Pierre that home is the North, the source of his inspiration and the core of his identity. He believes it is his sacred duty to paint that world in the best work he can create, and this task, or duty, will destroy him if he allows his attention to wander.

Standing in opposition to this North is a South composed of cities, noise, hordes of people, material demands and ambitions, and all the pressures and standards inimical to the true, the northern artist – or so Roy conceives of this artistic mission. South is made to include the temptations of Europe, specifically of a Paris arrogantly claiming itself to be the arbiter of true art. Roy's extension of the idea of South to include not just a southern Canadian city but also a European art centre is what leads me to suggest that, in addition to and resting upon the realist depiction of northern lives and landscapes that informs this narrative of an artist's life, *The Hidden Mountain* is an allegory of the Canadian nation united by its great northern rivers, which can carry a man from the Mackenzie to Ungava Bay, and by its longing for the freedom, beauty, purity, and elemental simplicity of North.

Here, in this allegorical North, is where I locate Roy's own self-portrait, which the novel is commonly taken to be, and her ultimately romantic vision of a possibility for the country that, she believed, only the totally committed artist could see. She has acknowledged the fascination the North holds for her, and she has taken several of her characters north in search of spiritual renewal, but as a Franco-Manitoban with Quebec roots, living through the troubled post-war years and the rise of Quebec nationalism, Roy remained a Canadian; she was fully aware that, for all French Canadians of her generation, "le grand Nord" symbolized identity, history, and freedom.[40] Her North, then, is doubly hers and northern: it evokes the past of the voyageurs, early exploration, and provincial *rayonnement* associated with the *pays d'en haut*, and it promises a future, stretching from east to west and back again, from the Yukon to Labrador, with the potential to enrich and hold us all.

Like so much that is radically ambivalent in Roy's vision, however, this symbolic North, with all it represents, eludes our grasp. If we leave it to go, as Wiebe puts it in *Playing Dead*, "whoring" after the South, we will die in exile, longing but failing to return. If we stay, will we find the home and identity we seek? Why does Roy kill Pierre in Paris? What does this narrative decision mean? Perhaps it only means that Roy, like Hay, had to go away to understand the value of home and the nature of *her* task. Perhaps it means that, as far as Roy is concerned, the Canadian/northern artist is doomed to create little more than artistic fragments, that the North is too big, too overwhelming to capture in art. Perhaps she wants to suggest (as have other Canadian artist parables, from Klein to Ross, Buckler, Richler, Atwood, MacEwen, and Kroetsch) that the true Canadian artist must lose him or herself entirely in and to the North; perhaps she sees in Tom Thomson the inevitable Canadian artist story, what Atwood calls "Death by Landscape."[41]

But haunting this novel, hidden by Roy within it, is another perhaps – the possibility, at once more exciting and potentially tragic, that Canada will either recognize its northern identity by continually forming new ideas of North *or* it will die, with its story in brilliant fragments, in a foreign, *southern* place. By holding out this question and opening out the possibility of continued searching and finding, Roy enables *The Hidden Mountain* to be read as an allegory of Canada-as-North and as a vital contribution to the discursive formation of North. If it is true, as I am convinced it is, that in some deeply personal, displaced, and symbolic manner Roy often (always?) wrote about the Mother (her own mother, her need for and fear of mothering), then the deepest, most profound "secrète" in this great novel is the representation of the Mother country, of the immense challenges it presents, of its deadly hold on us (perhaps especially if we are Franco-Canadian?), of the obeisance it demands, of its inexpressible beauty, and of our need for "mon pays," "the true North."[42]

Although Canadian landscape painters rarely include signs of human life, let alone of themselves, in their work (Richard is something of an exception), the same cannot be said of the novelists. In fact, the writers I have discussed in this chapter all privilege the figure of the artist, who emerges as a centre of discursive and symbolic importance. For Wiebe, he/she is a story-teller and mythographer very close to Wiebe himself. For Kroetsch he is a poet and a liar, a clown and an old fart; he is definitely a he and has much in common with Richler's artist as drunkard, biographer, and finally as trickster. The artists in the women's narratives are equally varied: from bush cook to freedom fighter (van Herk), and from biographer to autobiographer (Hay and Roy). What all these fictional artists and their actual creators have in common is some degree of personal, first-hand understanding of the norths that lie far north of the wintry landscapes on the southern boundaries of the country. All these artists go north, often far north and west, and all make that journeying the motivation for the story. None of them wastes any time representing Canadian winter, wandering around Algonquin Park, or getting lost in the scrubland north of Belleville. There is, in short, an artistic purposefulness to these novels and to the northern setting, which has expanded to include the territories and the high Arctic and to explore the possibilities of the discourse far beyond the parameters of earlier and more formulaic work.

As a group these writers have problematized, complicated, and multiplied our ideas of North. One of the most fundamental ways in which they do this is by placing the artist figure at the centre, where he/she can see what is there and be seen there (Orok watching Pierre, Peek watching Lou, Solomon spying on Moses, and so on). Tropes of arrival in the North, of eating or being eaten (even if only swallowed by a river, as in *The Hidden Mountain*), of documentation in written, pictorial, or oral records – all these strategies both represent North and validate a human presence there. The discursive formation of North produced by these novels lays imaginative claim to that space without pretending to fill or define it. And, as most of these novels imply, there are stories out and up there that cannot be told by the southern-based Euro-Canadian writer, no matter how travelled or informed he or she may be. This acknowledgment of continuing desire to go North, to listen, see, and understand, is finally what is most significant about these texts. Wiebe is the most insistent in reminding us about those original northerners, who have yet to be heard, but Hay and Roy also point to them, name them, and make room for their stories. It is time for me to do the same.

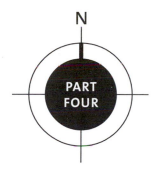

THE NORTH WRITES BACK

I say for the last time. We have been silent too long.
Anthony Apakark Thrasher, *Thrasher*

Let us write passages that will sway the centuries-old impressions that others have about our true colours. Let us put, without a moment's hesitation, a voice in the mouth of our silent mind.
Alootook Ipellie, *Echoing Silence*

Dene legends don't all have a nice beginning, middle, and end like on television. But these are the stories of my people. I am very happy to share them.
George Blondin, *Yamoria*

PELAJIA: So what! And the old stories, the old language. Almost all gone ... was a time Nanabush and Windigo and everyone here could rattle away in Indian fast as Betty Bingo could lay her bingo chips down on a hot night.
Thomson Highway, *The Rez Sisters*

We will continue to protest. We will walk again on our land together with our children, our husbands and our elders, always singing and praying in our own language, and always in the hope that our prayers will be answered. Together with your help, we can build a better future for our children and the world.
Anne Marie Andrew, *It's Like the Legend: Innu Women's Voices*

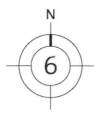

WRITING, RE-WRITING, AND WRITING BACK

A THEORY OF NORTHERN DISCOURSE

When the Inuit want to explain where the Qallunaat came from, they tell the story of a girl who was hard to please and did not want to marry. This Inuuk eventually mated with a dog and gave birth to half-human and fully human offspring: the half-human pups were sent away, one to father whites, the other to father Indians. Only the fully human offspring became people: Inuit. There are, of course, variants to this story and links between it and the stories about Sedna (another Inuuk with marital problems!), but the key points are consistent: first, this is a creation story that accounts for different races, most importantly the Inuit, and that helps to explain white and Indian behaviour – from an Inuit perspective. According to the Inuit, the Qallunaat are descended from the greedy white pup; therefore no one/Inuk should be surprised by their irrational, greedy, capricious natures, and they must be treated with caution.[1]

Northern First Nations have similar stories that help to explain racial, ethnic, and cultural difference and to account for the Other. One of the more succinct of these is the Anishinabek (Sandy Lake Cree) story about Wee-sa-kay-jac (the trickster), who was trying to create people from clay after the great flood. His first two attempts were disappointing: on the first try he produced a man who was too dark, and on the second he produced a man who "was pale and unhealthy looking" (Ray and Stevens, 24). Needless to say, these two sorry specimens were discarded, and Wee-sa-kay-jac tried once more. On the third try he produced an attractive olive-coloured man, who looked just right! This, then, was the perfect man – an Indian – and he was kept.

The beauty of these stories is that they allow *us* (by whom I mean, in this instance, southern Euro-Canadians) to see ourselves as an other sees us. The picture is not flattering, and it is by no means all that the Inuit or Cree have to say about whites, but these stories serve as valuable markers of discourse that preceded the present period of colonization and development by English- or French-speaking strangers in the traditional lands of Denendah, Nunavik, and Nunavut, lands now designated part of northern Canada. Moreover, these two stories make up but a very small part of a large, rich, and powerful body of myth, legend, and story in which Canada's original peoples account for creation, construct their histories, and develop their spiritual, social, and political codes. While it is certainly not my intention (nor am I able) to discuss this complex "orature" (Ashcroft *et al.*, 181), I believe that a minimal awareness of this material is important, both to the project of *writing back* and to the appreciation of how North is *written* by northerners and, increasingly, by southerners.

For example, it is important for any reader (or listener) to realize that the Dene can tell us how the Deh Cho was created, long before someone called Mackenzie paddled down river, that the legendary Yamoria brought law and order to Denendeh ages before the RCMP arrived in the Northwest Territories, that the pan-Arctic myth of Sedna informed the core activities and theology of the Inuit, and that the concept of the Windigo articulates terrors, taboos, and moral imperatives central to the Cree, Ojibwa, and many other northern peoples.[2] It is important to know something about this rich orature, not only because it focuses recognition and validation of oral history but also because this orature produces/is produced by culture, because it informs a literature now produced in, or translated into, English, and it has begun to influence the writing (and thus the law, politics, and habitus) of the dominant discourse. Indeed, I would go further and say that this orature, which *as oral* ideology interpellated native subjectivity for centuries, has now begun to interpellate hybrid subjectivities. But before I get too far ahead of my material and my argument – for the question of subjectivities interpellated by an inevitably ideological and changing discursive formation of North must wait for the conclusion to this chapter – I want to return to issues of terminology and theory.

After much deliberation I have called this chapter "The North Writes Back," and this is why. By the North, I actually mean several particular geographical and political areas: the provincial norths, particularly those of Manitoba, Ontario, Quebec, and Labrador, and the sub-Arctic and Arctic territories of the Yukon, the Northwest Territories, and Nunavut. In other words, I have shifted my focus away from southern ideas of North to ideas of North arising from the norths found north of sixty, or north of the treeline, or well north of populated areas easily reached by car, train, or boat. This move northwards entails a shifting not only of sites but also of sights. This North is, first of all, multiple and multifaceted, marked by topographical and meterological diversity. Secondly, it is *home* to the people who live there, most of whom are Inuit, Indian, or Métis. Thirdly, this northern home is occupied by many different peoples, speaking many different languages, developing different cultures, and experiencing different pre-contact and contemporary histories. The significance of this difference is conveyed in the stories with which I began: for the Inuit, it is whites and Indians who must be accounted for; for the northern Cree (as for the Dene) it is the "Eskimos" and whites.[3] Because I cannot hope to account fully for this diversity or begin to discuss the wealth of self-representation produced by the North, I have had to be highly selective in my choice of materials for close attention and highly general in my summary of what I understand of the larger picture.

Over the years, and especially through several trips north, I have glimpsed this diversity first-hand. The Canadian Inuit are in fact a multiplicity of distinct groups with a complex history scattered across the Arctic and sub-Arctic in small, isolated communities in Nunavut, Nunavik, the NWT, and the Yukon (see McGhee). Despite local differences, most of them are united by language, Inuktitut, and a shared orature and culture, but one need only reflect upon the marked differences in sculpture (a medium familiar to most southern Canadians and non-Inuit) coming from Kingnait (Cape Dorset on Baffin Island), Arviat (formerly Eskimo Point on the west coast of Hudson Bay), and the Kitikmeot region of the central Arctic (Iqaluktuutiak/Cambridge Bay, Uqsuqtuuq/Gjoa Haven, and Kurvigjuak or Arviligjuaq/Pelly Bay) to appreciate the differences in material culture and artistic expression.[4] Similar diversity of peoples is represented by the terms Yukon First Nations and Dene, which includes the Carrier, Chipewyan, Dogrib, Gwich'in, Hare, and other groups in the Northwest Territories, and the Cree are also diverse (see Blondin, and Beardy and Coutts). But my purpose here is not ethnographic; I am not interested in describing, interpreting, or analysing peoples, cultures, and artifacts. Contemporary scholars such as Julie Cruikshank, Dorothy Harley Eber, Robin McGrath, and Penny Petrone, building upon their own research and using changing ethnographic methodologies, are doing this work. My purpose is both more specific and more speculative: by considering a few examples of works published in English and by situating them within a broader discursive context, I want to explore what this discourse tells us about itself as northern and what impact it might be having on the discursive formation of North. Above all, I am constructing a northern discourse of North (of Nunavut, Nunavik, Denendeh), shaping, delimiting, and *using* it within my larger project: the examination of Canada and the idea of North.

This northern North I am constructing is, of course, a re-presenting of what is already constructed in the publicly funded heritage centres, historic sites, arts co-ops, museums, and private galleries scattered across the North in major centres like Inuvik, Whitehorse, Yellowknife, and Iqaluit, and in small local places like Teslin, Igloolik, or Pangnirtung. The very existence of such institutional centres speaks to northerners' desire to collect, store, preserve, select, and display – in short, to construct – their time and place, to celebrate and interpret the events and objects of their lives, to make sense of their North by representing and narrating it themselves, and to share that cultural knowledge with others. The architecture of the northern Quebec Cree village of Oujé-Bougoumou, designed by Douglas Cardinal and completed in 1999, is yet another example of how northern peoples can reclaim cultural identity in material form (see Stevens and Acland); this village of concentric circles and teepee-like structures is an aboriginal text, what Ruskin might have called a sermon in *wood*. The proliferation of journals, magazines, books, news coverage, marketing strategies, and the products of popular culture that represent the North (to itself and to others) also indicates the degree to which North remains a construction, and an idea. Of course, it is not a pure, original, or *true* North, any more than southern representations are. This

North is a function of a complex interaction between the colonizing imposition of southern and western norms, assumptions, technologies, and institutions *and* the increasing capacity of northerners to appropriate these mechanisms and regimes of power in order to "write back."

But what does it mean to "write back"? I have borrowed the term, and my modified application of the theory it inscribes, from *The Empire Writes Back: Theory and Practice in Post-Colonial Literatures* by Bill Ashcroft, Gareth Griffiths, and Helen Tiffin, who borrowed it, in their turn, from Salman Rushdie. The very concept of *writing*, let alone of writing *back*, however, raises some immediate concerns. The discursive evidence I am exploring is not always written, if by written one understands only language as written down. Just as I considered the widest possible range of activities as grist for my discursive mill in preceding chapters, so I insist upon being similarly eclectic here. Thus, I use the terms writing, writes, and written very loosely indeed to include many forms of address and activity, many semiotic codes and modes of representation, from music and wall-hangings to radio, television, comic strips, festivals, conferences, and speeches. My *texts* are oral/aural and visual/graphic; they exist in print, to be sure, but also in prints, in CDs and CD-ROMs, in Web sites, maps, photography, sculpture, and plays. The public (filmed, photographed, televised, documented) signing of treaties and agreements is textual, a form of writing, a formal, shared discourse – even, I would suggest, a story. And it is for me this notion of story-ing, of narration, that provides the connective tissue of this heterogeneous discourse, that allows me to think of such diverse statements as contributing to and participating in the discursive formation of North.

Inevitably, there are other reasons for insisting upon writes and writing, and here I take my cue directly from *The Empire Writes Back*. Like it or not, the North must write in order to write back because, to repeat (rewrite) the eloquent statement with which Anthony Apakark Thrasher concludes his autobiography: "I say for the last time. We have been silent too long" (104). Or, as Ashcroft, Griffiths, and Tiffin explain: "the appropriation which has had the most profound significance in post-colonial discourse is that of writing itself. It is through an appropriation of the power invested in writing that this discourse can take hold of the marginality imposed on it and make hybridity and syncreticity the source of a literary and cultural redefinition" (78). Or, again, as an Inuuk once said (giving Robin Gedalof her title): "paper stays put" (4). Once colonization has occurred, the colonized do learn to use the tools of the colonizer, not only to assimilate but also to survive, to fight back, to resist, to bring about change. And the key sign of what I take, in my present context, to be *post*-coloniality is the appropriation and deployment of writing, whether the colonization being negotiated is external, between an imperial centre and a settler society, or internal, between the dominant settler culture and the aboriginal cultures being dominated (see Ashcroft *et al.*, 32–3).

In addition to insisting upon writes and writing because of their pivotal role in post-colonial power politics, I also use the terms because a majority of northern statements that are readily accessible in southern Canada are written and published in English; because the words and stories of Inuit, Yukon First Nations, Dene, and Cree have been translated into English for at least one hundred years, and those peoples have themselves been writing (since at least 1970) in English; because there is, in short, a tradition of orature and literature on which I can base my own writing about their writing, and because my focus on writing (albeit in the inclusive, eclectic sense I have outlined) allows me to address the problematics of language and the strategies of writing back.

Not all the work I will consider can be described as a deliberate writing back, and some important distinctions must be made between a more transparent or universalized writing *about* or writing *to*, and those texts (Billy Diamond's speech, Kananginak Putugak's print [see Illus. 25], and Thomson Highway's novel) that are overt, even aggressive examples of writing back. To complicate matters further, I want to reserve a theoretical space for work that *re*-writes, as distinct from writing about or to, or writing back. Although I preserve the term writing back for those few texts that deliberately accost the dominant discourse in order to disrupt, supplement, supplant, and even disregard it, I nevertheless believe that the cumulative weight of writing about or to, as of rewriting, has contributed to the phenomenon of writing back. The first two categories necessarily precede and prepare the way for the third; they also accompany, take place along side of, the third. While there are numerous sites for establishing my tripartite distinction, an absolutely fundamental one is the language in which something is spoken, narrated, performed, or written. As the authors of *The Empire Writes Back* demonstrate, for their purpose that language is English, the colonizing language of England (analogous cases can be made for Greek, Latin, French, American English, and so forth). However, they argue for a crucial separation between English and english, where English signals the language of the centre and english that of the margins (8–11). English is official, normative, authoritative, monologic; english is unofficial, obstreperous, disruptive, polyphonic, and, from the perspective of the centre (legislatures, courts, schools, publishing houses), ungrammatical, colloquial, unintelligible, wrong.

When texts – for example, the oral stories of the Inuit – are listened to, collected, translated into English, edited, tidied up, and polished for publication by a mainstream press for distribution and sale to southern, non-Inuit consumers (and the economics of publishing will dictate that this be done), we have books that primarily write to non-Inuit about Inuit, even when the Inuk's name appears on the dust-jacket and title-page. They are interesting, to be sure, and sometimes informative, but they are readily assimilated into or co-opted by the dominant discourse. However, when texts aim to rewrite events already inscribed by the dominant culture, they will cause some perturbation of the discourse, even if they are written in English, whether the language is mediated through an editor or translator or written by the Inuk/Dene/Cree author in English. So, when William Nerysoo tells Rudy Wiebe that Albert Johnson became a Windigo, and Wiebe

Illus. 25. *The First Tourist* (1992) by Kananginak Putugak, lithograph, 57 × 71 cm, edition of fifty, printer Pitseolak Niviaqsi, provides a wryly ironic commentary on non-Inuit southerners who go North to photograph what they imagine to be the *real* Inuit. Image reproduced with permission of the West Baffin Eskimo Co-operative, Cape Dorset, Nunavut and courtesy of the Department of Indian and Northern Affairs.

creates a character who tells Spike Millen this *fact*, the official story has been ever so slightly, yet strategically, rewritten in English and english. There are many more examples of this rewriting to which I will turn shortly, but for the moment I merely wish to identify my three degrees of writing (leaving writing *back* out) and to suggest that together and cumulatively they constitute a powerful counter-discourse in which the North can be, as it were, heard, in which it breaks an imposed silence, and through which it eventually writes back.

TRADITIONAL NORTHERN DISCOURSE

There are many forms and ways in which northerners have caught southern, Euro-Canadian, and non-Canadian attention. The twentieth century has witnessed a concentrated attention on North and on northern indigenes, from the ethnographic gaze scripted for non-Inuit consumption by early twentieth-century explorer/ethnographers like Stefansson, Flaherty, and Rasmussen, to the equally carefully constructed gaze of the late-twentieth-century media (notably on television) coverage of the inaugural ceremonies for Nunavut on 1 April 1999. Like the books, photographs, translated poems, stories, songs, and the film *Nanook of the North* from the 1920s, televised coverage of Nunavut Day contributes to a writing about the Inuit and the North that is addressed to the nation at large – indeed, to the world. There are differences between the writing *about* and the writing *to* of the 1920s and the 1990s, the most obvious being the CBC's voice-over translation of Inuktitut into English (not english) and French, but my point is that Nunavut Day had been prepared for acceptance by the Canadian public less by governments and constitutional experts than by decades of writing about and to.[5]

Contributions to this writing include special stamp issues featuring North and the Inuit; festivals like the Great Northern Arts Festival in Inuvik (covered by the media and at which non-northerners are welcome), or the June 1998 Northern Festival of the Arts, held in Toronto; and conferences held in Canada and abroad, such as the annual Circumpolar Universities Cooperation Conferences, the triennial Nordic Association of Canadian Studies Conferences, or the 1996 "Imagining the Arctic" Conference (to name only a few) – all of which have produced books in recent years. Newspapers, popular southern magazines (*Maclean's*), and journals (*Canadian Geographic* and *The Beaver*) have set the stage for public acceptance by familiarizing Canadians in general with the history leading up to Nunavut, the challenges facing Nunavut, and the stastistics used (in the South) to define Nunavut: 1,994,000 square kilometres; 27,219 people (85 per cent Inuit, 15 per cent non-aboriginal); a nineteen-member legislative assembly; and an estimated government budget of $587 million.[6] Relentless marketing and tourist advertising for everything from genuine art to all-terrain vehicles, beer, and kitsch ("ookpik" dolls and polar bear licence plates or key chains) have played an enormous part in writing North into the southern imagination, especially when this writing is produced by northerners (as in *Up Here*, the *Nunavut Handbook*, and Yukon or NWT Web sites).

The most lasting contribution to this phenomenon of writing about and to, however, is not to be found in advertising or media coverage but in material objects, such as sculpture, painting, prints, and wall-hangings acquired and displayed in museums and galleries across the country, in compact disks that reproduce and commodify performers like Northern Tutchone singer/composer Jerry Alfred or Inuut singer Susan Aglukark, and in edited books that deliver northern writing in English and, more recently, in english to southern readers.[7]

The number and range of these volumes is considerable. Beginning with Rasmussen's *Across Arctic America* (1927), "Eskimo" poems and songs continued to be collected and reproduced up to the 1980s (see Colombo, Lewis, Lowenstein, and Petrone); through these collections, as well as through frequent quotation in other texts and by being set to music (see Adaskin, Applebaum, Freedman, and McIntosh – notably her composition *Kivioq, an Inuit Legend*, 1985), this orature in translation remains in circulation outside of its source culture, removed from its originating cultural context. "Eskimo" (later Inuit) myths, legends, and stories have received similar attention, beginning with Edmund Carpenter's edition of

The Story of Comock the Eskimo, as told to Robert Flaherty (1968) – a text that has under-gone at least three translations, from Comock to Flaherty, presumably through a translation in english by Flaherty, who retold it, in English, on the BBC, to Carpen-ter, who edits, introduces, and situates the transcribed story in its finalized, published form, and continuing with Maurice Metayer's translation and editing of *Tales from the Igloo* (1972), Agnes Nanogak's *More Tales from the Igloo* (1986), both illustrated by Nanogak, and with *Stories from Pangnirtung* (1976), illustrated by Germaine Arnaktauyok.

Each of these volumes of stories is beautifully illustrated with narrative draw-ings or full-colour prints, and these illustrations help both to keep the books in print (or, in the case of Carpenter, to make it a collector's item) and to bridge the gap between the native source and its intended non-native audience. Moreover, each volume is carefully introduced by the non-Inuit translator and/or editor, and it is this introductory positioning that operates strategically to mediate, to make the stories palatable, interesting, and acceptable, even important. As Stuart Hodg-son insists, in his foreword to *Stories from Pangnirtung*: "By recognizing and record-ing the thoughts of our [sic] northern elders, these stories from Pangnirtung will strengthen an awareness and respect of Inuit heritage and culture by younger and future generations" (7). He concludes by congratulating and thanking the people of Pang and by instructing the non-Inuit reader to "listen carefully to the true experts of the North" (8). However, in order to help the reader listen, the Inuit material has been carefully selected and transformed, through translation and ed-itorial polishing, into English. The only editor to describe this process in detail is Robin McGrath, an expert in Inuit orature and literature, who reminds *us* in her foreword to Agnes Nanogak's *More Tales from the Igloo* that "each step away from the original Inuktitut distances us" (xi). Elsewhere, in several scholarly articles, McGrath analyses the whitewashing of Inuit myth, legend, and story, and de-scribes the misreadings and misunderstandings that can arise from this process.[8]

Among the many books that educate *us* about Inuit sculpture, I will mention only three that strike me as representing some of the more interesting and pro-vocative ways in which this art has been presented and mediated for a non-Inuit audience: *Eskimo* (1959), by Carpenter, with Frederick Varley and Robert Flaherty; *Inuit Stories/Légendes inuit* (1988), edited by Zebedee Nungak and Eugene Arima; and Dorothy Harley Eber's *Images of Justice* (1997).[9] Between the late 1950s and the late 1980s, of course, an art market developed for Inuit sculpture, prints, and wall-hangings, but Carpenter's book represents an early attempt to present the exotic through ethnographic explanation, social context, and familiarization strategies. Thus, in his text Carpenter focuses on the sculpture of the Aiviluk from Igloolik, and he makes no comment on why Varley's images are included, or on why or how Flaherty obtained the sculptures photographed for the book.[10] Instead, he describes the "comfortless and desolate" Arctic home of the Aiviluk and explains the sculpture by describing what he understands of their "acoustic space," their lack of focus or fixed perspective, the mechanical ability they reveal, and the absence of artistic intention. In other words, he familiarizes the sculpture by comparing it with Western norms and aesthetics and by emphasizing its difference from *our* culture, instead of its relevance to Aiviluk culture. The inclusion of Varley's stunning images, produced during his 1938 trip to the eastern Arctic aboard the patrol ship *Nascopie*, both visually overwhelms the photographs of the small, subtle carvings and provides a complex, non-Inuit, visual semiotic framework within which to place, and thereby re-contextualize, the Aiviluk and their "art."

As might be expected, a book co-edited by an Inuk who has become a political activist and leader in Nunavik presents a different picture and tells a different story. All the carvings photographed for *Inuit Stories/Légendes inuit* are from the Povungnituk area, and each carver is identified with a portrait photograph and by name. More importantly, each carving is explained by an accompanying story *in english*. The reader can see the carvings and read them through the story, in which she can hear the voice of the Inuk artist. Here, for example, is Saali Arngnaituq telling us about "the one who turned into a wolf," which is also the story narrated in five accompanying sculptures: "Then again, there is the story about Qisaruatsiaq. The one who became a wolf is called by this name. It is also a story of a time long ago when there were no white men here in this country" (61). The shift from Carpenter's *Eskimo* to *Inuit Stories/Légendes inuit* is enormous, and certainly prepared for by the intervening thirty years of art marketing, social and cultural awareness, and land-claims negotiations in Nunavik (which I will address shortly), but among the many points that might be made, let me stress just two: first, the art is contextualized in its own terms and by reference to the cultural knowledge and practices of the people who produced it, and, second, the stories retain their often ungrammatical, oral qualities, which allow the Inuk story-teller to be heard through the english prose.

In *Images of Justice: A Legal History of the Northwest Territories as Traced through the Yellowknife Courthouse Collection of Inuit Sculpture* Eber pushes the lessons learned from a book like *Inuit Stories/Légendes inuit* several steps further. Drawing upon her extensive knowledge of the Canadian North, Eber constructs the legal history of the NWT through its first fifteen years, 1955 to 1970, when John Howard Sissons and William George Morrow were its first two resident chief justices. The story is one of repeated attempts to make the punishment fit the crime by forcing Canadian laws to recognize and accommodate the exigencies and practices of a culture and a lifestyle they were never designed to address. Certainly, Sissons emerges as a sort of hero – I am tempted to liken him (in some ways) to Kivioq – but his story and the legal history he and Morrow carved out of their first-hand on-site experiences of isolated Inuit communities and traditional methods for handling problems is told, in part, by the sculptures created by the Inuit to tell their own version of events, in part by Eber's mediation, and in part by extensive quotation of the Inuit. What emerges from this hybrid narrative is a history that demonstrates the function of a dynamic appropriation-in-process, which produces a degree of legal hybridity and narrative supplementarity (especially in the stone narratives). Let me be clear: I am not assessing the law here, or praising (or condemning) the justices or their judgments. It is Eber's text that fascinates me because it tells legal history in a thoroughly unorthodox way and argues that even the law, which, as with the church and educational system, has been most violently imposed on a colonized people, can, in practice, be modified to fit, perhaps not the crime *per se* but the cultural context within which that crime must be understood. In *Images of Justice* Inuit images, values, and modes of narrative expression (sculpture, like prints and wall-hangings, is often used to tell stories) supplement the non-Inuit story; they appropriate the story, retell it, and make it their own. In the narrative process (as also in the actual case-by-case legal process) a dominant discourse is changed by the presence of each sculptural statement. This book could not have been written one hundred years ago, or even during the fifteen years covered in its pages, because Eber must rely upon the institutionalized collection for primary material and upon her non-Inuit readers' intimate familiarity with Inuit sculpture as a form and with a discursive formation of North that, steadily over the twentieth century, expanded to include Inuit voices and statements.

It is not, however, only Inuit voices that can be heard in edited collections and other narrative forms, although, for reasons I will consider later, the installation and legitimation of Inuit discourse within the dominant discourse appears to be more advanced than does that of the Yukon First Nations, Dene, Cree, or Innu. In an important early text, *Sacred Legends of the Sandy Lake Cree* (1971), Cree artist Carl Ray and co-author James Stevens retell traditional Anishinabek myths, legends, and stories with accompanying line drawings. Before presenting this pre-contact material, however, Ray and Stevens situate the Cree of Sandy Lake in the present by describing their post-contact history (dating from about 1894) and their current problems on reserve. This introductory material serves several purposes; it is generally informative about where and who these people are and how contact occurred, but more importantly it places a contemporary people in a complex, evolving history of relationship with the past, the land, and the invading culture. The myths and legends reproduced tell us about how the world was made, explain the Cree twelve-moon cycle, and introduce us to the adventures of Wee-sa-kay-jac, "the sex maniac of the north" (11), Guy-an-way, a god who destroyed cannibalistic creatures, and the Windigo. This is a writing by and about the Cree addressed primarily to a non-Cree, southern audience, produced by a major mainstream publisher (McClelland and Stewart), and presented without apology for the libidinous and violent characteristics of the stories.

Four collections published in the 1990s also reproduce myth, legend, and story, but through the more immediate and less mediated practice of oral history. In *Life Lived Like a Story*, written by Julie Cruikshank in collaboration with three Yukon elders – Angela Sidney, Kitty Smith, and Annie Ned – Cruikshank allows these women's stories to appear *in english* and with the characteristics of their orality (asymmetry, repetition, mythic structuring and parallels, etc.). In her introduction she explains her role and methodology in what is a sophisticated working model for any non-native trying to approach, collect, and edit oral narratives. George Blondin, a Dogrib from the NWT, has followed his 1990 book, *When the World Was New*, with *Yamoria, the Lawmaker: Stories of the Dene* (1997), in which he expands his narrative and geographical reach to include many Dene voices and stories from a wide range of places. As with Cruikshank and my other examples (Beardy and Wachowich), Blondin's *Yamoria* is addressed to non-Dene southern readers, but it refuses to cater to that audience by regularizing, sanitizing, or editing the material; his one concession is to provide (in parentheses) the European names for Dene places: thus, S'omabak'e (Yellowknife), Deninu (Fort Resolution), Teetl'it Gwinjik (Peel River), but the Deh Cho is always the Deh Cho, which we are already expected to know.

My last two examples provide a helpful bridge to the autobiographies at which I also wish to look. Flora Beardy, a Cree/Métis interpreter with Parks Canada, and Robert Coutts, a historian with Parks Canada, have collected, transcribed, translated, and edited what they describe as "narrated life histories" on "autobiographical themes of daily life" (xiv), granted to Beardy in interviews with elders from the western lowlands of Hudson Bay, around York Factory, who call themselves the Maskêkowininiwak. Beardy and Coutts seem to me to have combined the approaches of Ray and Stevens and Cruikshank in that they introduce and historicize the people and their stories but allow the "voices from Hudson Bay" to speak, *in english*, for themselves. Unlike the Sandy Lake Cree of northern Ontario, the so-called Swampy Cree have a long post-contact history dating back to 1670 and characterized by smallpox epidemics, treaty signing, and major disruption to their traditional way of life; therefore, the editors can include many historical photographs and documented facts. The stories, most of them short and practical, with a few showing the incorporation of myth through allusions, themes, and structure, serve to balance the white record represented in the photographs and the well-documented arrival of church and school. Taken as a whole, *Voices from Hudson Bay* is a complex, hybrid, and dialogic narrative that shares much with the rewriting of North, and begins to resemble what I call writing back.

Nancy Wachowich's *Saqiyuq: Stories from the Lives of Three Inuit Women* (1999) is one of the most recent examples of a rapidly emerging tradition of autobiography among the Inuit, Innu, Yukon First Nations, Dene, and Cree.[11] Wachowich has reproduced (with minimal editing) the life-stories of three generations of women from one Baffin Island family – a grandmother, Apphia Angalati Awa, her daughter, Rhoda Kaujak Katsak, and Rhoda's daughter, Sandra Pikujak Katsak. For me, the most interesting of these autobiographical narratives is Apphia's, because her voice, like her experience, is so different from those of her modern daughter and young granddaughter. There is a sense in which Apphia invites me to listen to a story (as my own mother might) and to learn about a world I do not know and could not have survived in. I experience a sense of being privileged in listening to her story, which mixes elements of the traditional story with frank accounts of her personal experiences. Rhoda's story, like her English, is much more familiar and terse; she is a modern Canadian – if also an Inuuk – and her problems, like her anger, are all too common. It is her attempt to recover a traditional past, erased by Christianity and a southern school curriculum, that most moves me. Sandra's voice is something of a shock because she sounds like a member of the younger generation almost anywhere in North America – a generation I don't really understand or always like. But perhaps that is the (or a) major point and lesson: contemporary voices in English, influenced by the globalized world of the Internet, television, email, T-shirts, Coca Cola, American movies and popular culture, do sound much the same. Juxtaposing Sandra with Rhoda and Apphia allows the reader to glimpse (to overhear, as it were) the change and, for me at least, the loss. Sandra, I realize, does not sound northern. Whether she should or not is another matter.

If *Saqiyuq* is not formally called autobiography, this is less because it has been mediated by a non-Inuit than because of its fragmented, multiple stories. Of the many autobiographies written by Inuit or First Nations people, the majority have undergone a complex process of transcription, translation, and editing, all of which, as McGrath reminds us, puts the non-native reader at a considerable distance from the autobiographer and the story. However, as she also notes (see "Oral Influences"), autobiography is a favoured form among the Inuit, as it would also seem to be for other northern natives. A very few examples will serve to illustrate this point and enable me to make some observations about the ways in which this life-writing writes about and to, as well as rewrites, or even writes back to, the dominant discourse.

Tom Boulanger's *An Indian Remembers* (1971), with illustrations by Edward Howorth, is a first-person account, apparently unedited by anyone else but the author, written in english. Born in 1901 and raised by a Protestant minister, Boulanger describes his life, devout faith, trapping, illnesses, dreams, and so forth in considerable detail. Despite his praise for the whites he knew, his great care never to complain, and his genuine affection for the man who raised him, Boulanger gently insists throughout on the value of a traditional northern Cree life and the importance of the land. It is with regret, if also with realism, that he remarks how "everything had nearly passed away nowadays that was used in the old times in the north countries, and new generation is starting" (50). John Tetso's *Trapping Is my Life* (1970), illustrated by Lorne H. Bouchard, strikes a jarring note beside Boulanger's narrative. Tetso, a Slavey from the upper Mackenzie area near Fort Simpson, agreed to write about his life because "I am always willing to help bridge the gap between our two worlds. Integration, that is" (1), but the introductory preface presents "John [as] unlike any other Indian" because he is "quiet, thoughtful, sincere," and hard-working (viii). However well-meaning such comments by Claire Molson may be, they do not help to situate Tetso or his work in any useful context. How the narrative was compiled, by whom, and with what changes, if any, are matters not addressed. Molson only tells us that "John's stories may seem simple and short," but they "are all true" and took place in a harsh part of Canada, where mistakes often cause death (ix).[12] The truth of Tetso's life is indeed compelling, for the stories it comprises are about a trapping life, lived on the land, following the seasons, and rich in the detail and joy of his work; his memories of residential school are less happy, but he does not dwell on the negative and shifts quickly to hockey, skating, and the making of snowshoes. He repeatedly asserts his belief that traditional Dene life in the bush is better than any other, and he articulates an unmistakable pride in this life and in Dene heritage, while recognizing that things are changing.

Of the four Inuit autobiographies – *I, Nuligak* (1966), *People from Our Side: Life Story with Photographs and Oral Biography* (1975), *Thrasher ... Skid Row Eskimo* (1976), and *Life among the Qallunaat* (1978) – only Peter Pitseolak's *People from Our Side*, co-authored with Dorothy Harley Eber, remains in print, and only Minnie Aodla Freeman's *Life among the Qallunaat* approaches the kind of decisive writing back that characterizes texts by Alootook Ipellie and Thomson Highway. *I, Nuligak*, translated and edited by Maurice Metayer, who also prepared *Tales from the Igloo*, is subtitled *The Autobiography of a Canadian Eskimo*, and it may well be the first full-scale publication of its kind (see McGrath, "Circumventing the Taboos," 218). Through the translating and editing process Metayer has transformed Nuligak's first-person memoir into standard English, and he has provided the text with an explanatory introduction, notes, and appendices. Nuligak's story is none the less a moving and remarkable one about an Inuk orphan's growing up in the coastal area of the Beaufort Sea, east and west of the Mackenzie delta. As Metayer notes, Nuligak structures his story in the form of Inuit legend, in his case the story of Lumaq, the orphan boy (10–11; see also McGrath in *Canadian Inuit Literature*, 91). *People from Our Side* differs from any other Inuit narrative I have discussed because of Pitseolak's strong personality and commitment to photography. Eber most decidedly plays second fiddle or editorial midwife to Pitseolak's emphatic first-person voice, which dominates every page on which it occurs, and Pitseolak's (and his wife's) photographs of himself (see Illus. 26), of family and community members, and of traditional activities on the land occupy the true foreground of the text.[13] As Pitseolak informs us, "I am telling a story about how Seekooseelak grew" (63), and thus about a former way of life, now vanishing. He took seriously his role of documentary cultural historian, and he understood that his own life exemplified the rapid changes experienced by the Inuit.[14]

Life among the Qallunaat, as its title suggests, tells quite a different story. Minnie Aodla Freeman, who was born in 1937 and grew up in the James Bay area of Moosenee and Moose Factory, spent several lonely years in a residential school before coming south to Ottawa in 1957 to work for the Welfare Division of the Department of Indian and Northern Affairs. The first half of her autobiography, and her play *Survival in the South*, describe her initial culture shock and present her observations on southern urban whites. This young Inuuk, fresh from her northern home, turns what amounts to an ethnographic gaze on these strange people,

Illus. 26. This famous photograph of Inuk photographer Peter Pitseolak was taken, c 1947, by his wife Aggeok. It is reproduced here with the permission of Louis Campeau, courtesy of the Canadian Museum of Civilization (#2000–180).

analysing the oddity of their habits, criticizing their ignorant assumptions and stereotyped views about Inuit, and metaphorically shaking her head over their absurd expectation that she like the South or be pleased to don a parka in July to advertise cool, refreshing ginger ale – just because she is an Inuuk. But Freeman's gaze is often bitterly reflective as well as ironically bemused. She is appalled by white unwillingness to help her, when she knows how much Inuit have helped whites in the North; she is sharply critical of racist remarks, weary of stereotypes, and quick to compare white and Inuit men and describe whites as domineering and exploitative. Freeman knows precisely what she is doing when she calls her play *Survival in the South* and her autobiography *Life among the Qallunaat*: she is echoing the sorts of titles and phrases so commonly used to describe southerners' experiences of the Arctic and the bizarre people they study when they go there. This echoing is a way of "returning the gaze" and of deliberately creating an unflattering, two-dimensional representation of southern life as she, a northerner, sees it (see Bannerji). In this sense, then, her work is a very early Canadian example of writing back by a member of a dominated group within Canada; it represents a marginalized voice addressing the centre in an effort to be heard, but also in the hope of modifying the dominant discourse. To return to useful terms employed by Ashcroft, Griffiths, and Tiffin in *The Empire Writes Back*, I would say that Freeman first *abrogates* the norms of the dominant discourse and then neatly *appropriates* and reverses them to articulate her own cultural experience (38–9).

I will return to Freeman in the context of rewriting, but before I move on it is important to pause long enough to reflect upon where the northern statements I have examined thus far have taken the discursive formation of North. In the first place, there has been a persistent interest in the Inuit that has shifted from representations of them by non-Inuit, who speak for them, to carefully mediated texts (Eber, McGrath, Petrone, Wachowich) in which they speak for themselves. The language in which northerners write, when it is not Inuktitut, Gwich'in, or Cree, has shifted from normative English to english, and this has both produced and participated in an increased acceptance of and appreciation for orature and oral history as legitimate forms. There have also been significant changes on the legal and political fronts; the fact of Nunavut is the most dramatic example of this change. But the picture is by no means rosy; the dominant remains dominant and, for the most part, stable in these statements. Moreover, if my brief summary of northern texts has not misled me, I detect a marked disproportion in the number of Innu, Dene, or Cree examples compared with the Inuit, and consequently a lesser degree of impact on the dominant discourse. The possible reasons for this difference are many: the Inuit may occupy a more positive position in the southern, Euro-Canadian view of North because they were constructed, early on, as childlike and smiling (by Flaherty most notably) and because they are geographically distant, remote, well removed from competitive proximity with the South. The Innu, Cree, or Dene may have been more reluctant to talk about, re-present, publish, or otherwise reproduce aspects of their culture, either because it is wrong to represent the sacred, because they have lost the languages and stories as a result of enforced acculturation, or because they fear further damage to their culture if it is made widely accessible.[15] However, this too is changing, as the books by Beardy and Coutts, Blondin, Cruikshank, Wadden, Byrne and Fouillard, and Ray and Stevens demonstrate. In so far as these works participate in a wider sphere of North American First Nations literature, it is possible to speak of a tradition, if not a canon, to which these voices belong. By writing about and to, these texts provide a rich discursive ground for the production of new texts that rewrite aspects of the dominant discourse or that write back to assert another reality.

The 1970s saw the beginning of several attempts by northerners to write their own stories, with Markoosie's *Harpoon of the Hunter* being the most famous example, and to rewrite the stories of events, people, and so-called facts that had become part of an accepted southern discourse about the North. By first examining a few examples of the latter, I will be able to clear the way for consideration of the former. When I describe this process of correcting or modifying the dominant discourse, I do not wish to imply that the knowledge acquired by the North was recent but that the rewriting, which entails reaching the dominant discourse to correct or alter the record, did not become really apparent until the 1970s. The Dene always knew what the Deh Cho was and how it came to be; this knowledge is new only to others. The Inuit always knew how Indians and Whites came to be, but it took time for this news to reach southern, non-Inuit ears. There are many examples of such rewriting, and there are others that more directly address recent events that are documented, according to Western priorities and in the service of Euro-Canadian regimes of power, as official history. The creation of Nunavut, based as it is on a settlement of land claims and requiring a full-scale modification of cartography (a change of internal borders) and naming (Frobisher Bay, a prime sign of external colonization imposed through internal and unconscious colonization in the 1940s, has gone, leaving Iqaluit – meaning "a school of fish" – overlooking Koojesse Inlet) is a stunning example of what I mean by rewriting.[16] Naming, of course, is a powerful means of control, and as Valerie Alia has shown, it has caused considerable trauma among the Inuit.

Other examples of rewriting might include the development in the 1980s of the IBC (Inuit Broadcasting Corporation), which broadcasts in Inuktitut, the incorporation of TVNC (Television Northern Canada) in 1990, the creation of Igloolik Isuma Productions (started in 1988 and Inuit owned), or the reconstruction of events at Bloody Falls, or recent attempts to replace Kate Carmack within the accepted story of the Klondike, or the story of Weetaltuk, or validation of Inuit accounts of the Franklin disaster. Peggy Gale has provided a valuable overview of Igloolik's Isuma Productions, with its early 2001 release of a first dramatic feature film, *Atanarjuat*, and, in *Un/Covering the North*, Valeria Alia surveys the entire field of northern communcations.[17] One of Alia's most interesting observations is that, today, *southern* media and programs are "alternative" in the North (63). I have argued for a rewriting of the Carmack stories in chapter 3, but rewritings of Bloody Falls, Weetaltuk, and Franklin also illustrate how this process works.

The story of what happened at Bloody Falls is well-known and obsessively reproduced in the version recorded by Samuel Hearne, who witnessed the 1791 massacre (as he saw it) of Inuit by Dene in the central Arctic place on the lower Coppermine River that bears this name. Hearne published his emotional and graphic account in *A Journey From Prince of Wales Fort to the Northern Ocean* (1795), and, while few Canadians have read the entire volume, thousands have read the widely anthologized excerpt about Bloody Falls (see Brown, Bennett, and Cooke;

Daymond and Monkman; and Morrison, 64–6). In his preface to *Tales from the Igloo* Metayer summarizes Hearne's account by way of explaining "Copper Eskimo" and Indian relations: both groups, he tells us, visited the boundary area between traditional Inuit lands to the north and Dene lands to the south in search of raw copper, and during one of these encounters "Hearne's Indian guides massacred an entire settlement of sleeping Inuit people" (10). However, quite another interpretation of events is possible if one turns to Inuit orature, especially the Navanana story, where conflict involving a stolen woman complicates a long history of trade and strife between the Copper Inuit and the Chipewyan. In her examination of Hearne's version, Robin McGrath argues that the white man subscribed to racist, sexist constructions of the violent male Indians, on the one hand, and of the gentle, sensuous Inuit women on the other (see McGrath, "Samuel Hearne") – he saw, in other words, what he was conditioned to see, without having the language, history, or cultural context to interpret the event.

Weetaltuk, Minnie Aodla Freeman's grandfather, was the patriarch of Cape Hope Island in his day. According to Freeman, he met and assisted Robert Flaherty in 1913, when Flaherty was exploring islands in Hudson Bay for minerals, but he was then written out of the official record when the islands he had named for himself were renamed – the Belcher Islands – and Flaherty credited with discovering them. Weetaltuk died in 1957, but Freeman recalls him, and his example and legacy, vividly. In *Life among the Qallunaat* she describes the disintegration of Weetaltuk's extended family group after his death, their forced relocation by the government, and the ways in which they "were taken advantage of" by the intruders (68–71). If one compares Freeman's description of her ancestors, especially Weetaltuk during his prime and at the time he knew Flaherty, with Flaherty's description, the difference is striking. In *My Eskimo Friends* Flaherty devotes a section to "Winter on Weetaltuk's Island" but describes the people as "shaggy beings" emerging from their igloos "on hands and knees" (16); they are, from his point of view, "as primitive looking a lot as I have ever seen" (55).

Illuminating as this comparison of writings is, the Franklin story is even more impressive in its rewriting scope. Briefly, Inuit accounts of what happened to Franklin, his ships, and his men were not only discounted by the British, but the people themselves were denigrated by no less a person than Charles Dickens (see Brannan, Grace, "Re-inventing Franklin," and Woodman). Although Rasmussen recorded Qaqortingneq's version of what the Inuit had observed, and that version has been reproduced since, it was not until David Woodman published *Unravelling the Franklin Mystery: Inuit Testimony* (1991) that Inuit oral testimony appeared side by side with written accounts drawn from the official records.[18] By treating Inuit accounts in this way, Woodman has created a fully dialogized narrative of the Franklin disaster in which a new, inclusive discourse emerges, one that is not so intent upon establishing Truth (what happened remains a tantalizing mystery) as orchestrating truths, as allowing the Other to speak within (instead of from the margins of) the dominant discourse. To do this is to rewrite the story of Franklin and of non-Inuit acceptance of Inuit truth, and in the rewriting to change both stories.

The Arctic Sky: Inuit Astronomy, Star Lore, and Legend (1998) resembles Woodman's work in some ways, but it also moves closer to the writing of stories I considered earlier. Authored by John MacDonald, who lives in Igloolik, and published jointly by the Royal Ontario Museum and the Nunavut Research Institute, this fascinating volume gathers the centuries-old astronomical wisdom of the Inuit, mainly from the Igloolik area, from myth, legend, earlier published sources (such as Jenness or Rasmussen), contemporary interviews with twenty-eight elders who contributed to the Igloolik Oral History project, numerous maps, photographs, drawings, and the reproduction of prints, in order to tell the story of the stars as the Inuit know them. The collaborative, multi-media, interdisciplinary narrative that emerges reminds non-Inuit, southern Canadians of many things – for example, of how profoundly Inuit art narrates Inuit life and knowledge; how different from Toronto, say, the night sky appears when you look at it from Igloolik, where Polaris, the Pole Star, is almost directly overhead and is called Nuntuittuq, meaning "never moves" (59); and how richly interrelated the legends and myths are with the practical lives of the people, who, like travellers everywhere, once relied on the stars to guide them. *The Arctic Sky* provides a reading of Ulluriat (the stars and constellations), telling their stories of shamanistic power, mythological roles, and horological use that is also an indigenous story of North.[19]

Of the Inuit, Dene, and Cree stories available in English/english, including those about Yamoria, the Windigo, Wee-sa-kay-jac, and Kivioq, or Michael Arvaarluk Kusugak's stories for children, I want to mention only two for which I have a personal affection: *Harpoon of the Hunter*, the first work of Inuit literature I read, shortly after its publication in 1970, made a lasting impression upon me; and Mary Carpenter's story of "Skeleton Woman," to which I listened spellbound one spring afternoon in 1995, reawakened my initial fascination with the literature and dramatically increased my appreciation for Inuit story-telling. Markoosie's novella (or long short story) is now considered a classic of Inuit writing in English and an accepted part of the larger Canadian canon. Set in the area of Cornwallis Island, it combines oral traditions with a romantic love interest not found in traditional Inuit orature (see McGrath, "Editing Inuit Literature," 167). The story of "Skeleton Woman," as Carpenter explains, comes from the western Arctic, where she, an Inuvialuit, heard it in the whaling camps at Kittigazuit (Mary Carpenter, 226). Unlike Markoosie's story, it could scarcely be described as having a love interest, but also unlike Markoosie's, it has a happy – if unusual – ending.

Harpoon of the Hunter was first written in Inuktitut and then translated into English by the author.[20] It is the story of Kamik, a boy on the verge of manhood, who must learn to be a hunter to avenge the death of his father (killed by a polar bear) and to survive alone when all the other hunters and their dogs are dead. Thus far, the story is familiar from Inuit legend (as indeed it is also from plays like Henry Beissel's *Inuk and the Sun*). Further complications arise, however, when neighbouring Inuit, who live on the far side of a dangerous channel, arrive to search for the lost hunters. They find Kamik, who is returning to camp alone and on foot, just in time to save him from another bear, and Markoosie's story seems to be moving towards a qualified happy ending in which Kamik has survived to comfort his widowed mother and to marry the daughter of the man who found and rescued him. However, life in the Arctic is cruel; while the little group is trying to re-cross the channel, Kamik's mother drowns; his sweetheart disappears under the ice trying to reach her father, and Kamik gives up all desire for life. Stranded on drifting ice, he refuses to jump to safety; he is carried out to sea and commits suicide by driving the harpoon into his throat: "And, for the last time, the harpoon of the hunter made its kill" (81). Thirty years after its first appearance in English, this tale, told simply, without embellishment or histrionics, is still impressive. Although there are some jarring notes (for example, regarding the musk oxen – see McGrath, "Editing Inuit Literature," 4), the modest incorporation of Kamik's love interest does not seem inconsistent with modern Inuit experiences (it is still the girl's father who decides on his daughter's husband) or myth (like Sedna, she has refused other men), and the governing impulse of the narrative is the struggle for survival ending in death. Markoosie seems to have considered the romantic possibilities of his story but rejected them in favour of both lived experience and mythic imperative.

"Skeleton Woman" moves in the opposite direction – from death under the sea to rebirth and plenitude on land. One day, Carpenter tells us, a young Inuk out fishing snags something heavy and difficult to land. When he finally gets the thing to the surface, he is terrified by what he sees: a skeleton woman, all teeth, skull, and bones, tangled in his net. He races for shore and dives into his snow-house thinking he is safe, but "Safe?" Carpenter asks – "Ha. Imagine ..." – and from there the tale unfolds. Skeleton Woman, who was thrown into the sea long ago by her angry father, has been dragged back to land, and she lies there now, a jumble of bones tangled in the net, on the floor of the man's snow house. Horrible as she is, he takes pity on her; he gently untangles and reorganizes her, then he covers her bones with furs to keep her warm. Exhausted at last, he sleeps. Carpenter pauses and surveys her audience, but we know that more trouble is brewing and that the young man should not have fallen asleep. (Wake up! Wake up! I want to say, but being an adult kabloona I remain quiet.) Sure enough, Skeleton Woman spies a tear at the corner of his eye and, being thirsty, crawls over, puts her skeletal mouth to the tear, and drinks. Feeling stronger, she reaches into the sleeping man for his heart – things are going from bad to worse! – but somehow the man continues to sleep while Skeleton Woman beats upon the drum that is his heart, summonsing flesh, eyes, hair, hands, "the divide between her legs and breasts long enough to wrap for warmth" (228), all the good things, in fact, that a woman must have. Her task complete, she returns his heart and lies down with the young man, who is in for a pleasant surprise when he awakes. Although Carpenter does not put it this way, she tells us that the couple live happily ever after;

they go away and are always well fed by the sea creatures with whom Skeleton Woman once lived. The story ends, but for the southerners gathered in an Ottawa classroom on a May day in 1995, the North has just spoken. Later, reading the story as written, I recapture its life, recalling something of its spoken power, realizing that the telling was a gift I can keep because "paper stays put."

THE NORTH WRITES BACK

Writing back comes in stages, gradually, and it can take many forms. *Life among the Qallunaat* has elements of writing back; so too does Carpenter's story, embedded as it is in her awareness of cultural oppression, the hegemonic power of discursive domination, and in her ability to arouse and then defeat a host of Qallunaat expectations that her story is about death, vampires, and Poe-like demons. Writing back can also be light-hearted, whimsical, satiric ... in a gentle way. Kananginak Putugak's "The First Tourist" (see Illus. 25) is such a writing back, and so is Judas Ullulaq's "Art Dealer on Phone" (see Illus. 27). Like the Putugak print, Ullulaq's sculpture cuts both ways in that it comments as much on southern codes and power as on northern ways of negotiating, manipulating, and playing along with southern expectations and demands: You want a traditional Inuk or a new sculpture – a Shaman? a dancing musk ox? No problem, these pieces seem to say; it's a deal. Alootook Ipellie uses just this kind of satiric humour in his *Ice Box* cartoon strip, which I want to consider at greater length.

Ipellie began publishing *Ice Box* in the January 1974 issue of *Inuit Monthly*, an Inuktitut/English magazine published in Ottawa by the Inuit Tapirisat of Canada, after he had spent some years in Ottawa and had been working as a translator and columnist for the magazine.[21] As he explains in his interview with Michael Kennedy, trips home to Iqaluit reminded him forcibly of the old "culture that was dying," and he began trying, in his poetry, to "write about the old ways" (Ipellie, quoted in Kennedy, 158). He describes "the idea" for *Ice Box* as a "mixture of the two cultures" (southern, Euro-Canadian and northern, Inuit) in which "you'll see the setting is the Arctic, but the storyline itself is very often from the South" (159).

This concept of mixing cultures, or of supplementarity (Bhabha 306), is fundamental to much of what is understood as contemporary Inuit literature and art, but it carries the particular edge of writing back in most of Ipellie's work. In "The Development of Inuit Literature in English" Robin McGrath notes that contemporary work contains "elements borrowed or adapted from" Euro-Canadians, while maintaining "strong ties to the oral material" (195). According to McGrath, the combination of verbal and visual material can be traced back to the Inuit precontact cultural tradition of *illustrating* stories with "music, facemaking, string games, dance, puppets and other dramatic forms" (200). Post-contact Inuit culture commonly links narrrative with many visual forms, from sculpture and photography to drawing, and these media are "an important part of Inuit literature" (201). Indeed, McGrath goes further to note that "texts are often produced in conjunction with specific illustrations in the manner of Japanese art, and the comic strip form can be found in literature for adults as well as children" (201).

Illus. 27. *Art Dealer on the Phone* (c 1995) by the late Inuk master sculptor Judas Ullulaq, 11 × 10 × 7 in., is a fine example of Kitikmeot art. It is also a gently satiric comment on North-South relations and the deals to be made in the Inuit art market. Photograph by Kenji Nagai. Reproduced with the permission of Derek Norton and the Spirit Wrestler Gallery.

Ice Box is just such a comic strip. The line-drawn characters, Nanook, Papa Nook, Bones, and Mama Nook, will appeal to all age groups in the North and the South, and many of the episodes in the lives of these cheerful Inuit (school, games, Santa Claus) are directed at children. But the strip cannot be separated from its context on the page, where it often contributes to and comments on a particular social or political event (land claims *non*-settlement, environmental policies, communications systems, International Women's Year, etc) that is discussed, in Inuktitut and English, in the columns above it. Whatever the particular focus of the strip in a given episode, however, the comic is emphatically family- and community-based; the Nook family is always interacting with the land and the weather (often in extremely amusing ways), with each other, or with the community of Ice Box. That community, of course, is itself a parody of how southern Canadians *construct* the North, with its smiling "Eskimos," and, like all good parodies, it cuts two ways – against the source of the parody and against those who misread the source text. For the non-Inuit southern reader the comic is full of surprises, not the least of which is that the North has families who are a lot like ours.

Although there is a strong Inuit tradition of superhuman mythic heroes (Kivioq is perhaps the best known), there is nothing heroic about the Nooks. Ipellie's focus is deliberately and strategically on the social and political dynamics of every-day life, an everyday life that is changing as a result of southern, governmental, non-Inuit technological pressures while remaining rich in traditional practices, assumptions, values, and problems. And both sides of this cultural equation are parodied, satirized, and pilloried. As McGrath has noted, Ipellie "has no hesitation about fusing traditional and modern elements to come up with works that attack Inuit and non-Inuit alike" ("Development," 198). Consequently, an Inuk can look pretty silly rolling his kayak, harpooning rock instead of seals, or waiting for spring to arrive, and a Kabloona can be smelly, useless, and downright destructive, as, for example, when he knocks on an igloo, waits to be asked to enter, but then throws explosives at it when no one tells him to come in. The irony of Ipellie's image of women's rights coming to the Arctic is a fine example of his skilful mix-ture of northern and southern social semiotics (an Inuuk carries a heavy load on her back that turns out to be the round badge and slogan of the women's move-ment); what the narrative adds to the visual message (or vice versa) is precisely the incongruity and incompatibility of old and new values, especially when the new values are perceived as imposed from without. Ipellie's handling of alcohol abuse is much less complex or subtle but no less effective: the Arctic and its people must be saved, not from the "Ether people" or mad scientists with German names (found in a southern comic set in the North, like *Nelvana of the Northern Lights*) but from the dangers at hand. In the familiar pow-wham-bang of the last frame depicting target practice with a liquor bottle, Papa Nook shoots the bottle. Here Ipellie uses the visual semiotics of adventure comics to destroy the immediate, tangible enemy within the community.

As an example of writing back, whether to southern comics like *Nelvana* or to complex contemporary social problems and politics, *Ice Box* depicts a family working and playing together despite a harsh climate, government interference, and cultural instability. The Nooks' North is home, and its landscape is full, not barren or empty. Ipellie's representation of space, while simple, usually depicts a world full of snow, igloos, animals, and human activity. The existence of words within this space accounts for another striking difference between this comic and one like *Nelvana*, where we have only English in a fairly formal, expository mode. In *Ice Box* we have english and Inuktitut, predominantly as dialogue. As with the visual space, the verbal semiotics constructs an economy of plentitude and social presence. What is more, in *Ice Box* Ipellie identifies the imperialist forces as the agents of southern Canadian government and industry – the

Illus. 28. This strip by Inuk artist Alootook Ipellie from his *Ice Box* cartoon first appeared in *Inuit Today* 8.1 (1979): 4–5. Compared with the Ullulaq or the Putugak, it makes a more sarcastic comment on southern attempts at colonization of the North. Reproduced with permission of the artist. © Alootook Ipellie.

census-takers, environmentalists, educators, and entrepreneurs who treat Arctic communities as marginal colonies without distinct identity or value. One of the subtlest and most amusing of the *Ice Box* critiques of southern administrations is a sequence depicting Papa Nook discovering a fresh source of soapstone for carving: "pretty ocean green ... perfect hardness ... great chip-a-bility!" (see Illus. 28) On closer inspection, however, the devout Papa discovers "some kind of ancient writing" on a corner of the stone that protrudes from the snow. His son, Bones, translates it as an inscription on a monument "ERECTED IN MEMORY OF ONE OF OTTAWA'S GREATEST GOVERNMENTS," and in the fourth frame we see, on the stone beneath the snow, the word YELLOWKNIFE carved in English and Inuktitut. Many possible interpretations come to mind, but given that this strip appeared in July 1979, I would suggest that Ipellie has moved beyond the irony of hyperbole to the voice of prophecy: before long, Yellowknife will be ancient history, buried in

Arctic snow, its monuments ready for recycling and, in this case, for Papa Nook's sculptured writing back.

In *Ice Box* Ipellie appropriates aspects of white, southern culture, albeit from his cultural and ethnic position on the margins of Canadian society (one could scarcely call his physical place in Ottawa the margin!), and this appropriation – of comic genre, cultural reference, and iconography – is a key strategy in a writing back (Ashcroft *et al.*, 38–9, 114–15) that resists reappropriation or co-optation by the dominant group and asserts its own construction of identity and reality. He has seized the means and modes of communication (writing/image) and used them to assert "mixture," hybridity, a both/and of cultural discourse that re-places by supplementing the dominant discourse.[22]

However, writing back can be angry, expressing both the rage and the outrage that build up under silence and marginalization. This edge appears in Ipellie's cartoon despite the laughter, but if I was delighted listening to Carpenter, I was moved to anger and jolted into awareness by the story of another great story-teller on another public occasion. That story-teller was Billy Diamond, chief of the Waskaganish Band of James Bay Cree and former grand chief of the Grand Council of the Cree of Quebec. The occasion was the Third Triennial International Conference of the Nordic Association of Canadian Studies; the place was Oslo, the date August 1990. Back home, the Kahnesetake/Oka crisis was mounting, and against this backdrop Chief Diamond spoke about the James Bay Hydroelectric Project, proposed for northern Quebec, now Nunavik, in 1970 by then Quebec premier Robert Bourassa, and about Quebec's current proposal to push ahead with the Great Whale River phase of the project. The Cree had not been consulted in the 1970s, despite the fact that a royal proclamation of 1763 called for the securing of native title to land prior to settlement in the provincial north and despite the terms set forth in two Quebec Boundaries Extension Acts (in 1898 and 1912). To drive home the enormity of just one phase of the James Bay Project plan, the Le Grand River Project, Diamond equated the area of Cree lands to be flooded with "submerging the whole of Northern Ireland" (88). So the northern Cree organized and, through strenuous negotiation, forged the James Bay and Northern Quebec Agreement, which they signed on 11 November 1975.

Since that day, Diamond tells us, the Cree have had to fight to force the governments to honour their commitments under the agreement. His voice intense with emotion, Diamond exclaims: "*No one can buy a way of life and culture with dollars*" (90), but the italics of the published text fall far short of his voice. Now, in the 1990s, he tells us, his people are threatened with the Great Whale Project and the Nottaway/Broadback/Rupert Rivers Project: Bourassa insists that James Bay II will go ahead. But the Cree say no. If he had known what he knows now, Chief Diamond tells us, he would never have signed the 1975 Agreement (92). This time, however, he will fight against Canada's "institutional racism and apartheid" (99). Although his dealings with governments are not widely known, in this speech he had the floor, and in the publication of the text, his story is repro-

Illus. 29. This picture shows the Cree and Inuit protesting Quebec's proposed Great Whale hydroelectric project by paddling their "Odeyaks" in the New York City harbour in 1990. The photograph was first published in *Never without Consent* and is reproduced here with permission of the photographer Chase Roe. © Chase Roe.

ducible; his are fighting words, and this fighting is a writing back. But the fight over James Bay II was only beginning with Billy Diamond's words. During the summer of 1990 and the following months, the Cree took their battle to the courts, to the international press, and to national television; they demonstrated before the Americans by paddling a traditional boat down the Hudson River past New York City (see Illus. 29).[23]

THE FUR QUEEN'S LESSON IN WRITING BACK

In *Sacred Legends of the Sandy Lake Cree* we are told that the "dreaded windigo is the most horrible creature in the lands of the Cree and Ojibwa Indians. Nothing strikes more terror in the hearts of the Anishinabek than the thoughts of windigo" (122). Windigos are cannibals who strike from the North during the winter months (though they can attack in summer), and they show no mercy, even to their own families, when they are seized with the lust for human flesh. Although a Windigo was formerly human, once it has been possessed by the spirit of cannibalism it turns to ice; hair grows over its face and body, and it craves *only* human flesh (see Illus. 30). According to all northern Cree, the Windigo can be male or female, and a particular Windigo can, with skill and courage, be overcome; however, the Windigo spirit is never absolutely annihilated. There are many stories

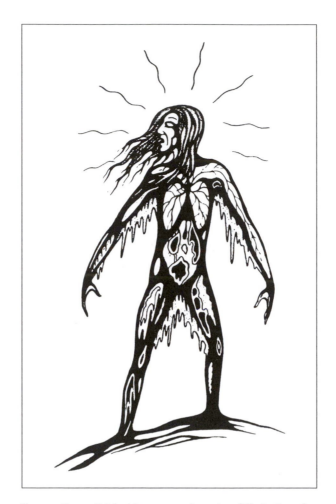

Illus. 30. Cree artist Carl Ray prepared a series of illustrations for *Sacred Legends of the Sandy Lake Cree* (1971), edited by James R. Stevens. This drawing depicts Windigo, the dread cannibal spirit, and it introduces the chapter called "Stories of the Windigo." It is reproduced from the book with the permission of Penumbra Press.

about ordeals involving Windigos that stretch back over countless generations, but unfortunately the Windigo is not a thing of the past. The Windigo spirit is still alive amongst us, and if William Nerysoo was surprised (in Rudy Wiebe's telling of it) that a white man could go Windigo, Thomson Highway is not. In *Kiss of the Fur Queen* he tells us about the most appalling, the most destructive Windigos ever to ravish the Canadian North.

Highway's autobiographical/biographical novel is about two Cree brothers from the northern Manitoba sub-Arctic who try to go white in the south – Winnipeg, Toronto, and the wider Western world – and discover a full share of tragedy, despair, and disillusionment.[24] Gabriel Okimasis dies young in a Toronto hospital; Jeremiah, his older brother, lives to tell the story of his people and his family, and it is a story of colonization and cannibalism of the North by the South, or, to put it more precisely, of the Cree of northern Manitoba, of a community (here the fictional reserve of Eemanapiteepitat), and of a family by the cultural, linguistic, and religious Windigos of the white, southern, Euro-Canadian system, as represented first and foremost by the Catholic Church and the Oblate fathers who penetrate, occupy, and control through terror this remote northern community. In truth, the Okimasis boys did not need to come as far south as Winnipeg to be touched by the cannibal breath of the South. The Oblate residential school at Birch Lake, to which they are flown out of Eemanapiteepitat at six years of age, is where this personal battle with the Windigo begins.

It is strategically important, I think, that Thomson Highway has chosen to tell this story as a novel, because the novel form reaches a much wider audience than a play and is, unlike a play, much more amenable to the focalized authority of a narrator (here a third-person, omniscient trickster). In addition, the novel is capable of deploying the complex interweaving of myth, vision, dreams, and daily reality that also characterizes Highway's plays.[25] In this novel Highway constructs a powerfully dialogized, hybrid narrative that enables him to write back, not only to expose and condemn the evil that so traumatized an entire generation of native people, and not only to attack and condemn the profoundly misogynistic racism at the root, as he sees it, of colonialist thinking, but also to create a text – a work of art – that mixes cultures, languages, and modes of story-telling into a new heterogeneous discourse. *Kiss of the Fur Queen* is one of the finest examples I know of writing back, and because it is, at every turn, a story about the North, it is writing back to the dominant discourse of North and wrenching it into new possibilities.

The story opens with the word "Mush," as appropriate a northern word as one can find. Abraham Okimasis, champion Cree dog-sled driver from Eemanapiteepitat, husband of Mariesis Okimasis, and father-to-be of the brothers whose life-stories are this novel, is racing towards the finish line of the three-day dog-sled race in the annual "Trappers' Festival of Oopaskooyak, Manitoba, February 23–25, 1951":

Three days. One hundred and fifty miles of low-treed tundra, ice-covered lakes, all blanketed with at least two feet of snow – fifty miles per day – a hundred and fifty miles of freezing temperatures and freezing winds. And the finish line mere yards ahead. (4)

Abraham will win this race, and his reward will be a silver bowl and a kiss from the winner of the festival's beauty contest: the Fur Queen.

There are many other competitions in this winter festival, all of them reminding me of the festival Jeremy Sadness (aka Grey Owl) stumbles upon in Kroetsch's *Gone Indian* – muskrat-skinning, trap-setting, bannock-baking, snow sculpture, even a "dreaded Weetigo look-alike contest" (7) – but the dog-sled race and the crowning of the Fur Queen are the highlights. This conjunction of winners and events is memorialized in a photograph of the 1951 Fur Queen kissing the 1951 champion musher, and this framed document will accompany father and sons through the rest of the story. However, photography does not capture Abraham's truest experience of winning and being kissed by the Fur Queen. What Abraham, "Cree gentleman from Eemanapiteepitat, Manitoba, caribou hunter without equal, grand champion of the world" (9) sees, as the Fur Queen approaches, is a vision in white fur, "chiselled out of arctic frost, her teeth pearls of ice" (10): she is "the Goddess," carrying a sacred vessel, "her person sending off ripples of warm air redolent of pine needles and fertile muskeg and wild fireweed" (11). And what Thomson Highway has done, within the few opening pages of his story, is to move us into another world, a world in which the realities of myth and daily life intersect – the world of the northern Cree. For this is no ordinary Fur Queen, no pretty chit from Wolverine River; this is the Fur Queen of the North, wearing a white fur cape that becomes the Aurora Borealis and carrying in the stars of her tiara the ghostly baby who will be born to Abraham and Mariesis nine months later: Jeremiah Okimasis.

In one magical stroke Highway has indigenized the Christian Holy Family, and inscribed the Cree version of how babies arrive on earth into the discursive formation of North. Already, ideas of North are expanding. Moreover, he has established the spirit presence of the trickster, who will reappear in various guises and preside over the unfolding story. This trickster, of course, is Wee-sa-kay-jac (the Fur Queen, the Arctic Fox [see 231–4], other women "in white fur" [96] or polyester [106], and Thomson Highway himself), without whom native culture would be lost to the "Weetigo" forever.[26] Later in the novel, as Jeremiah and Gabriel search a Winnipeg mall for new clothes for Gabriel, who has just joined Jeremiah in the South, Jeremiah will have a vision. This startling occurrence is precipitated by the disturbingly surreal world of the mall, where the "t" in Eaton's looks like a crucifix and where a mannequin in white fox fur can talk: "*ooteesi*," she whispers, "this way" (117), and the brothers find themselves at the men's underwear counter in Liberty's. Fingering the "spirit-white Stanfield's," Jeremiah recalls the legend of how "Weesageechak" transformed himself into a white weasel to attack a Windigo. He killed the monster by crawling into his "bumhole" and chewing up his entrails, but when he crawled out he was covered in shit. Horrified, "Weesageechak" cried until the Great Spirit washed him off in a river; however, because God held the trickster by the tip of his weasel tail, that tip has remained black to this day (118–21). Thoughtfully, Jeremiah remarks, "You could never get away with a story like that in English" (118), but, of course, he, and Highway, just have. By telling this story in English (not a single Cree word appears during the telling) and by situating it within the Winnipeg mall, Highway not only inserts Cree legend into the great Western form of the novel; he also forces us to see the powerful analogy between the mall and the Windigo (both equally soulless figures of ravenous consumption) on the one hand and the risk of confronting or entering such *places* on the other. Without yet facing the fact, both Okimasis brothers, but especially Gabriel, have been indelibly marked by their encounter with the Windigo. By extension (by reading and listening), so have we. And in a deft play on white and black, and a north-izing of their symbolic functions, Highway has Gabriel buy "three pairs of black jockeys by Alberto Bergazzi" (119).[27]

But the mall, horrible as it is, is by no means the most dangerous, devouring, deadly Windigo in *Kiss of the Fur Queen*. The worst of these Windigos is one Father Lafleur, head of the residential school to which the Okimasis boys are sent. This priest visits the boys' beds at night, his heavy silver crucifix slapping their mouths as he leans over them to masturbate while pulling at their young bodies. Many years late, after abandoning his career as a concert pianist and losing his brother to a successful career as a ballet dancer and to a series of white male lovers, Jeremiah remembers his worst encounter with this Windigo: "Now he remembers the holy man inside him, the lining of his rectum being torn, the pumping and pumping and pumping, cigar breath billowing somewhere above his cold shaved head" (287). This is what happened to him, what happened to Gabriel and to other boys held in the clutches of the school. The only explanation the child could find for this pain was that he was being punished for speaking Cree. Now, as an adult, he is still trying to explain it through the play he is writing, in which Gabriel will dance, a play that retells the history of his people: "Scene Four: 1860. The first missionary arrives on Mistik Lake" (291).

This play is called "Chachagathoo, the Shaman" (302), and Gabriel will die as its run comes to an end. However, Gabriel's death, and the play's closing night, coincide with the end of Highway's novel, which, through a series of repetitions, returns us to the novel's opening scene, to the Fur Queen, who comes to Gabriel's hospital bed in Toronto to kiss him: a kiss of life (for the father) now a kiss of death and rebirth as Gabriel leaves his body to float away with the Fur Queen, while "the little white fox on the collar of [her] cape" winks at Jeremiah. In order to accomplish this ritual, Jeremiah has had to stage-manage this dying by barring the hospital room door against a Catholic priest come to administer the last rites. He does this over the desperate protests of his devout mother and the screaming hospital fire alarm, set off by the burning of sweetgrass for Gabriel. His determination to defy and overcome the Church is born in part from his recognition of the alien Windigos of his personal past, in part from his anger at the destruction they have wrought more generally, and in part from his father's dying words. Re-presented in a scene that occurred years before Gabriel's death, Abraham's final words to his sons are shocking because they suggest his death-bed belief, not in Catholicism and the hovering Father Bouchard (the parish priest in Eemanapiteepitat) but in Cree spirit power, and because they confirm the presence of the Windigo among them. With his dying breath he tells them the story of the Cree hero Son of Ayash, who comes to earth to destroy evil and remake the world, which "has become too evil ... Evil after evil ... the most fearsome among them the man who ate human flesh" (227).

In Thomson Highway's telling, this is a stunning scene, in many ways the key turning-point of the narrative for Jeremiah, his *Adagio espressivo* (217).[28] The Oki-masis family has gathered in the house; the whole community seems crowded into its small space. But the brothers draw close to their father, hoping in these final moments to tell him what happened to them at the residential school. Then suddenly the priest enters, "his crucifix wedged like a handgun in the sash of his cassock" (226). And the battle for truth and Abraham's spirit begins. As Father Bouchard intones the last rites, the Cree hunter speaks *in Cree* of the Cree hero who must "make a new world" by destroying the Windigo, "the Cree descant whirring, light as foam, over the English dirge" (227). And yet, when the priest holds the communion wafer to the dying man's lips, the hunter's "tongue darted out, grabbed the body, flicked back in" (228). It would seem that the Windigo of Roman Catholicism, that cannibal spirit, has taken over the soul of Abraham Okimasis. Watching, understanding, outraged, Jeremiah will not let it happen again. When the time comes, he will call upon the help of Wee-sa-kay-jac, the Fur Queen, and Chachagathoo, the last of the great Cree shamans, the woman who was condemned and outlawed by the priest, to help him remake the world.[29]

To remake the world, Highway (aka Jeremiah in this autobiographical story) begins by remaking the story and the language in which it is told. In *Kiss of the Fur Queen* rewriting *is* writing back, repositioning the former colonizer beside the formerly colonized, reinstating by reinscribing an outlawed power. Highway practises this writing back power in many ways. He uses irony, satire, and scatalogical humour with Rabelaisian vigour for a subject that is anything but comic; this humour is a means of disrupting normative Anglo-Saxon, non-Cree codes of decorum; it is what Bakhtin calls the carnivalesque. He writes the Cree language with, and without, parallel English explanations slipped into the text, *into* his narrative, thereby making its unfamiliarity to non-Cree speakers gradually familiar while always reminding *us* (his non-Cree readers) that this strange language belongs here and is in control of the story. To put this in the form of one of the governing metaphors of the text, Highway buggers English and the great English form of the novel. But he does more: he creates a cast of characters (as he does in his plays) who are human and non-human, and he treats them with the most even-handed, vernacular realism. Who could have imagined, for example, that a powerful demi-god sort of person like Wee-sa-kay-jac would turn up with "missile-like tits, ice-blond meringue hair," and "kewpie-doll lips" (231)? And who could have dreamed that he – ah, she – would show up talking like a cheap nightclub floosie, a "Cree chanteuse" in drag, to argue with a guy about the meaning of life? Poor Jeremiah. He is slow to get it. But when he collapses in the snow calling on God for help, it is this "torch-singing fox with fur so white it hurt the eyes" (231) who appears, and if we have read this far, we know we have met this lady before. What "Miss Maggie

Sees" wants to do is "slice" the "goddamn balls" off that "frustrated old fart" of a Christian God, and she leaves Jeremiah with this decisive idea and with "the sound of the north wind, slow, persistent, moaning, the most beautiful sound he had ever heard" (234).

At the microlevel of the text, then, Highway deploys a range of techniques for writing back: hybrid language, imagery, allusions, legends, mythic characters – all drawn from and reformed by northern Cree culture – which invade the English, Christian, classical (Chopin and ballet), consumer world of southern Canada and the narrative space of the novel to stomp all over Euro-Canadian sensibilities and expectations and to explode stereotypes as rapidly as Wee-sa-kay-jac's bumhole can fart. Even the structure of the novel bends to the power of Cree story-telling as its linear progression, which begins emphatically with Abraham's race and his sons' birth and growing up, slows, then circles back to its beginning, then repeats earlier scenes with disrupting variations and speed, until the narrative soars free of Western, Christian teleology to float off into mythic space and cyclic time with the Fur Queen. Our sense of any boundary between the real, material world and an even more real, spiritual one blurs as voices and visions appear, disappear, and reappear as if by magic, orchestrated by an absent, third-person, all-knowing narrator whose only traces can be found in the dedication, the two prefacing quotations – one an injunction against dancing by D.C. Scott, the other a warning from Chief Seattle of the Squamish that the Indian dead are not powerless – and in the enigmatic subtitles to the six parts of the narrative, which tell us how to *perform* the story: from *Allegro ma non troppo* to *Presto con fuoco*: fast, but not too fast, to very fast with passion.[30]

Through his maccaronics, his dream vision, his characters, the stories within stories, and the non-linear narrative form Thomson Highway has created a novel in which the stereotypes of North are turned inside out. His North is not a place for white male adventure and escape; it is a home invaded by monsters from the South. From the northern Cree perspective, the evil Windigos of white religion, sexual abuse, colonization, racism, sexism, and the enforcement of prohibitions – against language, indigenous spiritual power, dancing – all come from the South, and all these evils inflicted upon the Cree are contained within/figured by the governing, all-consuming trope of cannibalism. In other words, *Kiss of the Fur Queen* makes sense of this cannibalistic invasion of the North by imaging the invading forces of evil in the stories that it knows best: those of the Windigo. The question that remains, haunting the story as we finish it, is this: Can the northern Cree, can we, can anything, survive?

Cree wisdom tells us that, while Windigos are deadly, they can be overcome; the story of how weasel got the black tip on his tail is only one, comparatively light-hearted version of how to kill a Windigo.[31] However, the Windigo that Highway confronts seems unstoppable. Like all artists and story-tellers, the most he can do is to give us some weapons with which to fight back and a renewed energy for the fight. On this score he has achieved a lot. Drawing upon the tragedies of his own and his brother's lives, he has fashioned a story in which the North writes back to the South, naming it for what it is and describing the evils it has perpetrated upon the body of the North. By doing this, he has changed irrevocably, if not as cartographically as Nunavut, the discursive formation of North. Once one has been kissed by the Fur Queen, one can never go North again with southern assumptions about empty spaces ripe for adventure, freedom, escape, and exploitation intact. One can no longer go North in the self-righteous belief that North is an absence of civilization and history, a place just waiting for, intended for, development by the superior culture and technology of Europe or the South. By writing back to the South and its construction of a dominant national discourse of Canada-as-North, Highway makes it impossible to look at the North and at Canada in the same way. What is more, in a move that recalls the map "Inuit View to the South" (see Illus. 13) in Rudy Wiebe's *Playing Dead*, he makes it impossible to see South and all it represents in the same way. By bringing North to the South, by reading South in terms of northern values and assumptions, and by calling southern penetration of northern spaces and bodies a violation, Highway simply changes the picture.

Eemanapiteepitat, complete with Wee-sa-kay-jac, Chachagathoo, the Northern Lights, the Fur Queen, Windigo, and the winking Arctic Fox (and many others) is home. It is home and native land, a true north of trapping, fur, huskies, caribou, fish, the love and safety of family, the simplicity of survival with independence, stories, and a history that gives meaning to existence. But to formulate North this way, in the images of humanity and plenitude, is to return to my question, now rephrased: Can *this* North survive? Is it not already gone? Certainly, Highway does not flinch from describing the degree to which South has penetrated North and is devouring his people – with the loss of story and language, with alcohol, television ("the Weetigo finally arrived," 187), airstrips, airplanes bringing more and more southern goods, violence, poverty, and despair. Neither Gabriel nor Jeremiah can return North and go back to the life their father knew. And yet, or so it seems to me, the Fur Queen holds out a different promise. Just possibly we can change the discourse, modify the ideology it inscribes, and transform the subjectivity interpellated by that hierarchical binary system of dominator/dominated, White/Other, South/North, into a multiplicity of shared, equal subjectivities. By definition, a discursive formation changes and is changed by the statements that constitute it. In so far as *Kiss of the Fur Queen* is a statement in the discursive formation of North, it has introduced change. From *The Men of the North and Their Place in History* to the Okimasis brothers is a long and fruitful journey.

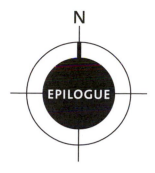

MAGNETIC NORTH

I could even have pardoned anyone among us who had been so romantic or absurd as to expect that the magnetic pole ... was a mountain of iron, or a magnet as large as Mont Blanc. But nature has here erected no monument to denote the spot which she had chosen as the centre of one of her great and dark powers.
James Clark Ross, quoted in *Polar Pioneers*

"All the energy of the world radiates from the Magnetic North Pole."
CANADIAN PROVERB (ought to be)
R. Murray Schafer, *Music in the cold*

On the first of June in 1831, on the Boothia Peninsula, James Clark Ross found the Magnetic North Pole – or, at least, he came as near to finding it with precision as he could. Using a dip circle and suspended horizontal needles (primitive instruments by today's standards), he measured the dip at 89° 59′ N; it took him an hour to get his measurement, and he realized "that the magnetic pole was moving even as he tried to locate it" (Ross, 153–4). But Ross was more a scientist than an explorer. He was after accuracy and discoveries of a factual, physical sort rather than heroic achievement and glory. As the nineteenth century passed into the early twentieth, it would not be the Magnetic North Pole that captured public attention.

Franklin, McClintock, Back, Hall, Cook, and Peary were the names in the news, and these men are inextricably associated with the Northwest Passage and the race to discover and claim the North Pole. And it is not hard to understand why. How can you find something that refuses to stay put? How can you plant a flag on the spot, or leave a message recording your victory, or have your picture taken to prove you got there? Magnetic North, for all its mystery and "dark powers" (as Ross described its strange lure), cannot be a fixed goal.

But that is why, perhaps, I find Magnetic North infinitely more fascinating than a Northwest Passage (there is, in fact, more than one passage). For me the North Pole is a bore. I am fascinated by the fact that Magnetic North cannot be located with absolute precision except in the measuring of its movement, and I am intrigued by its power, its magnetic force. Gwen Boyle recorded the music of the Magnetic North Pole in *Tuning* (Plate 7), and R. Murray Schafer claims its energy as the perfect image for Canada. I cannot associate music or energy with the North Pole. But I confess that I find many other attractions in the existence of a Magnetic North Pole, and these attractions are why I want to end *Canada and the Idea of North* with this Pole. As an image of constant movement and energy, Magnetic North represents perfectly what I understand as the discursive formation of North. Most importantly, Magnetic North suggests a politics of locations – mine, yours, voices from the past, from north of sixty, from newly arrived Canadians – because it is only one of several northern poles: North Pole, Geographic North

Pole, North Magnetic Pole, North Geomagnetic Pole, and (of course) the Pole of Inaccessibility (see Lopez, 18–19).

As must already be clear, I am drawn to Magnetic North as metaphor and metonomy; the very word *magnetic* pulls me into its sphere of influence. From the Greek, *Magnes lithos* (the stone of Magnesia, or lodestone), and folklore to computers, from the earliest navigation to molecular physics, magnetism is everywhere and Magnetic North is a part of/a synecdoche for Canada: from metaphor to metonomy! I repeat the word aloud – magnetic, mag/net/ic, magne/tic (a great nervous tic?). I look it up and find proliferating possibilities: magnetic circuit, magnetic flux, magnetic induction, magnetic moment (my alliterative, metaphoric favourite), magnetic pick-up, magnetic roasting, magnetic storm, magnetic variation; and there are more – magnetomotive or magnetooptics (with two Os)! But what about the *North* in the Magnetic North? What I am really after here is not magnetism but North, ideas of North; going North, being North, captured me, pulled me inexorably into a magnetic field of representation, formation, construction, and seemingly endless discursive permutation. Don Proch's exquisitely crafted mask *Magnetic North* (see plate 1) speaks to me so powerfully because it is both metaphor and metonymy for this entire field of representation.

To speak of the politics of location in the context of North is to speak personally. At many points in my long, unfinished journey of northern exploration I have asked myself when I started and why, and I have often been asked these questions by others (students, colleagues, friends, family): how did *you* become interested in the North, they want to know, as if to say, how did a white, middle-aged English professor like *you* end up doing *this*? I begin, or so I tell it now when I tell my story, with a serious illness at the age of two. Get your baby out of the city, the doctors told my parents, and thus began, for me, the journeying North into memories of the smell of pines in the heat of summer sun, of needles and cones on the forest floor, of shafts of golden light filtering through the bush, of wild berries, cold lakes, and the call of the loon. Of course, I was then, and have always been, a southerner living and working in a city (Montreal, Toronto, Vancouver), and I cannot imagine living in the bush, off the land, without cinemas and art galleries to hand. Nevertheless, I date a pattern of going North from those earliest experiences and sensuous memories. In some vague but persistent way, North for me has always meant health, spiritual and physical, happiness, peace, and going North has always been a process, an idea, evoking anticipation, relief, joy, and yes, adventure. How romantic, I can say now; how blind, even ignorant I was of the complex realities of living in northern Canada. The pattern, however, is very familiar, and it was first articulated by W.L. Morton: Canadians huddle in their southern cities for most of the year, but flee to the northern lakes and forests for their ritual summer *fix* of outdoors beauty, fresh air, fishing, canoeing, hiking, and swimming that will get them through another year, another long urban winter until the next escape in July or August.

I had not heard of Morton in the 1950s or even the early 1960s; Canadian history written by Canadian historians was rarely taught in the schools, and growing up in eastern Canada, I was brought up unconsciously on the "Laurentian thesis" without knowing anything specific about it or about Donald Creighton. But the pattern, established so early, of making summer pilgrimages to the North continued. Now, in hindsight, I can see that I would have to shed Creighton to appreciate what Morton could tell me about being Canadian. It also took three years in England and Europe, in the late 1960s, to show me that, like Roy's Pierre Cadorai, I belonged in Canada and that Canada for me would always be inextricably associated with northern spaces, trees, lakes, snow, wild animals, and the sounds and smells of childhood, despite the working reality of life in a city. Returning from England to Montreal in 1968, I entered a psychological spatial disappointment, despite the city's urban joys and amenities, that drove me to travel west and always northwards in the effort to recapture those childhood memories: to the Laurentians, to Algonquin Park, to the north shore of Lake Superior, but still not far north, at least not far enough.

Leaving home does have its good points, of course. If nothing else it forced me to see my country anew and much more consciously. Not until 1970 was I ready, or equipped, to *see* where I was or why I wanted to be there. Without knowing it yet, I was asking myself one of Frye's questions – where is here? – and I was starting to formulate an answer. For me the 1970s were years of calculated immersion in Canada marked by many revelations: the shock of recognition in a Group of Seven painting; the eerie attraction of Blair Bruce's *Phantom Hunter*; the tantalizing promise hidden in Gould's *The Idea of North*; the discovery of Gabrielle Roy, who spoke to me as George Eliot, Thomas Hardy, and James Joyce could never do. Somewhere along the way I read Morton for the first time, and more pieces of understanding fell into place. Malcolm Lowry's description of his Consul as some poor soul fleeing north stuck in my imagination, even if North for Lowry would only be Dollarton, on the north shore of Burrard Inlet opposite Vancouver. Everything is relative, and North/South is a tension of shifting opposites, as Elizabeth Hay would explain to me in due course. Leaving *home* again, this time Montreal for Vancouver at the end of the 1970s, was another new start and another impetus to travel because Vancouver, for all its amenities and natural beauty, became another urban centre to leave behind. But where do I go on the west coast of Canada if the Gulf Islands hold none of the necessary magnetism, if even Emily Carr's forests cannot hold me?

As Margaret Atwood puts it, "the journey north has the quality of dream" ("True North," 143), and I found myself in Lotus Land dreaming about "the journey north." Why? Because *it* was there, up there, somewhere I had not yet gone, more northerly than the Laurentians or Lake Superior, much more. Going from east to west in Canada helped me to understand how large the country is; the travelling forced me to consult maps, and the maps showed routes, even the most northerly of them, tracing thin lines across the southern quarter of the country. Beyond these roads stretched a vast expanse of Canada I did not know. Moving from east to west also reminded me of Morton (that champion of the west), and it taught me to watch for differences, to question my middle-class, white, eastern, central Canadian assumptions – my own version of the Laurentian thesis. I ventured cautiously out of Vancouver, looking for something, always turning north at Hope, discovering, step by step, the Cariboo, where those childhood memories could be recaptured, Prince George, the Peace River country, Cassiar, Atlin. By the early 1980s I was poised and ready for the flood of northern ideas that would push me into the 1990s – the music of Harry Somers, Inuit sculpture, the history of the Klondike, *Nanook of the North*, Susan Aglukark, Whitehorse, Yellowknife, learning the saga of the Mackenzie pipeline debate (which rivalled James Bay in its scope and significance). Rumours of a place called Nunavut reached me in my southwest corner of British Columbia, and it was either those rumours or the story of Franklin – as sung by Stan Rogers in "Northwest Passage" – that sent me reaching for my Beaufort Sea.

Four Arctic journeys later, all four made in the 1990s, what have I learned? Flying over Great Slave Lake, I learned what a forest fire can be; crossing from Pangnirtung to the Kekertons in an open boat, when the Coleman stove caught fire, I had a few seconds to imagine burning to death or dying in the glacial water; crossing the Peel River, I learned that a Dene teenager, Walkman tuned to the latest hip-hop tune, found Whitehorse alienating and returned *north* to Arctic Red River. Hiking the tundra around Bathurst Inlet I saw not empty space but human traces in the wolf-traps, meat caches, and caribou fences used by the ancestors of my Inuuk guide.

Above all I learned that there is no *true North* unless I can accept the true multiplicity and diversity of weather, geology, history, languages, and people, and that ideas of North, like what we insist on calling northern places, change. I have learned to be haunted by Gwendolyn MacEwen's question –

> You ask yourself are you
>   the fixed centre of this scene
> and will you stand forever witnessing
> the movement of stars, politics of the northern sky,
> kinesis of snow?

– and my answer is no ("Polaris," *Afterworlds*, 20). It is no because there are no fixed human centres and because the "politics of the northern sky," like Magnetic North, is kinetic, not static.

In the world of Canadian literature, where I have lived and taught for the past twenty-five years, I have gradually come to believe that if Canada has a great epic poem, it is not Pratt's *Toward the Last Spike*. As the telling of a foundational myth, *Toward the Last Spike* strikes many resonant chords, and yet, although Pratt's narrative follows the railway west, *Toward the Last Spike* is a Laurentian poem. Pratt's west is a hinterland to be opened by and for eastern centres of culture and trade, and his North is only there as a hostile force of Canadian Shield and muskeg to be dominated. No, if Canada has an epic poem, it is Henry Beissel's *Cantos North* (1982). In this twelve-part celebration of the country, Beissel does not focus so much on building or founding a nation as on what and who were always already here and on all those aspects of here that have built us: "the north," he insists, "discovered us / fell upon our vanity / with tomahawks of ice" ("Third Canto: Map of Discoveries," 17).

For Beissel, the human discoveries, like the mapping, are multiple, and the history-ing includes first peoples, who themselves encounter a land written into existence "a thousand generations / before a dream of pioneers became a nightmare" (16). In the fifth canto the epic poet tells us "How to Build an Igloo / Into History" (27) and reminds us that to do so, and to survive, is to *live* an epic story "beyond any Homer" (29). By contrast, the exploits of explorers seem modest, unheroic; modern efforts to map, control, settle, and tame the country amount to little more than "*folie des bois*," "*folie de la neige*" (39), and the idea of building a nation with railway tracks is reduced to "hammerblows" "to crucify a tribal culture" (56). But Beissel's songs of the North are by no means merely a condemnation of European and Euro-Canadian imperialism. By far the greatest cumulative weight of the twelve cantos is in the voice they create for the land itself, which in turn contains a multitude of indigenous voices. Beissel's "I" is always shifting, at times prophetic and apocalyptic but at others gentle and personal; it is never the epic "I" telling a master narrative but often the lyric "I" tracing a geometry of love for a history and a place that resists fixed versions of identity and becoming and defeats all pretensions of a "master race" (2). Beyond the desecration of colonial history, Beissel tells us, the North persists, "a threshold / in the mind," that direction "where all parallels / converge" (43). *Cantos North* is, in fact, not an epic but a love poem that can be sung by anyone who has been kissed by the Fur Queen: look north, the song tells us, "look north for the future" (1).

The idea that Canada's future is somehow linked to the North is, as the discursive formation I have traced shows, hardly new. Depending upon where North is located and how it is determined, it has symbolized future hopes for purity, freedom, adventure, wealth, fame, and regional and national identity – for Quebec *rayonnement* and for national unity – as long as there has been a Canada. Just as there is always a personal politics of location, there is as well a national politics of location, and at the beginning of a new century that politics of northern location seems to hold challenges and promises beyond anything Haliburton or Stefansson or Diefenbaker could have imagined. Nunavut is one of those promising challenges, as is the writing back of the northern Cree or the land-claims agreements of the Inuvialuit and Nishga peoples.

Thomas Berger might as well have been speaking about the survival of the country when he said:

It is in the North that the survival of the native subsistence economy is essential; it is there that the place of native peoples will be determined; it is there that our commitment to environmental goals and international co-operation will be tested. In the North lies the future of Canada. (*The Arctic*, 43)

To say that Canada's future lies in the North, however, is to raise a number of questions, such as: whose North and why North? As Canada enters the twenty-first century, it could well be argued that we are beyond the ideology of nation-states and that the Free Trade Agreement, even more than NAFTA, merges Canada with its ancient nemesis – the United States. There will soon be a common currency, the "Amero," and anyway, Hollywood North is just that: Hollywood. At the beginning of the twenty-first century the magnetic attraction pulling Canada due south seems stronger than ever before.

However, if we want to preserve a national identity (and I do), North still seems to me to hold the greatest attraction as a force and as an idea. But the idea must keep changing. We must abandon any lingering allegiance to the Laurentian thesis and endorse another story and ideology: let me suggest the Magnetic North thesis. To endorse the Magnetic North thesis is to understand ourselves as a people drawn by ideas of North, who accept the practical, exigent realities measured by Hamelin's nordicity indices. Indeed, to reject these indices would be nonsensical, as the 1998 Ice Storm surely reminds us and as Lawren Harris told us in *Winter Comes from the Arctic to the Temperate Zone* (see Plate 3 and Illus. 5). To endorse Magnetic North is to recognize the landscaped face in Proch's mask as our own. Moreover, the magnetism of North can attract (is even irresistible to) everyone who lives, or comes to live, in Canada. Jin-Me Yoon confirms this in her photographic writing-back called *A Group of Sixty-Seven* (1996), depicting Korean Canadians superimposed on an image of a Harris painting (see Plate 9), and Dionne Brand states this categorically in her essay "Driving North, Driving Home": born and bred in the Caribbean, Brand now defines home as North, two hundred kilometres north of Toronto, a landscape of snow and cold that you must enter like a bear (32).

To accept the Magnetic North thesis of our national identity is to listen to Beissel's love song, to *see* what contemporary artists like Yoon and Brand show us, or to write a book like *Canada and the Idea of North*, which is my statement in the discursive formation of North. It is to accept North as multiple and always changing and to respect the diversity and heterogeneity of our home and native land. It is to search for new ways of creating an inclusive nationality that inscribes an empowering ideology of dialogic hybridity. To go North now is to seek not Wiebe's "true north" but the Magnetic North. To go North now is to be kissed by the Fur Queen.

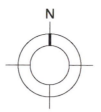

NOTES

PROLOGUE

1 Joan Murray provides a detailed discussion of *The Phantom Hunter* in *Letters Home: 1859–1906, The Letters of William Blair Bruce* (22 and 29), where she notes that Bruce intended the painting to be exhibited in Europe as a representation of Canada. In a 1 October 1884 letter from France to his mother, Bruce insists that it is Canada's "northern blood that will tell" (100) – that will make the country noble, benevolent and good. According to Murray, the man in the painting is Bruce and the painting a self-portrait (21).

2 "The Walker of the Snow," first published by Shanly in the *Atlantic Monthly* (May 1859), was frequently quoted and anthologized (see Chalykoff). Bruce discovered it in *Locusts and Wild Honey* (1879), *edited* by the American naturalist John Burroughs, and *he* pestered his father to send it to him in France (Murray, 21). See my discussion of reprintings in chapter 3.

3 *Nanook of the North* has achieved prestige as the first documentary film and as an authentic portrayal of Inuit life. See my analysis of the film's authenticity, marketing, and ideology in "Exploration as Construction: Robert Flaherty and Nanook of the North." The film was being used in introductory university anthropology courses as recently as the late 1980s, and it is frequently used in film courses.

4 In his introduction to *Six Canadian Plays*, Voaden articulated what amounts to a manifesto on Canadian drama for his day. He announced that the volume was "dedicated to the north" because, as he explained (quoting Lawren Harris), the north "has a 'spiritual clarity' which flows into our lives and makes them clearer and richer, giving distinction and national character to our idealism"(xix–xx). Voaden's passion for the North must be understood in the context of his day, which included a sharp rise in national sentiment following the Great War, pride in the work of the Group of Seven, and opposition to negativity about a national arts scene by contemporaries like Merrill Denison, who derided what he called the "unheroic North." I have discussed this context and Voaden's vision in detail in chapter 5 of *Regression and Apocalypse*.

5 *The Standardization of Error* (1928) is an ironic, witty castigation of cultural misrepresentations that serve the interests of established, civilized, political regimes and reinforce mainstream ideology. The occasion for this attack is Flaherty's film, and Stefansson devotes several pages (86–94) to a detailed exposure of the errors and deliberate misrepresentations in *Nanook of the North*. Moreover, he claims to have observed many screenings of the film in schools, where children are indoctrinated with false ideas about the North and the Inuit, and he goes so far as to call the practice a deliberate deception. *The Standardization of Error* is remarkable for several reasons, not least the accuracy of Stefansson's charges, charges that few Flaherty scholars take seriously, but the most striking aspect of the book, and one it shares with *The Friendly Arctic*, is Stefansson's astute and articulate critique of representation itself and of its cultural manipulation.

6 Peary's self-pronounced claim to the North Pole is critiqued and seriously questioned by Lisa Bloom in *Gender on Ice*; see, in particular, 15–56.

7 Pearson's article is fascinating for many reasons, not least his careful deployment of sovereignty-claims rhetoric; for example, he lists the official activities of Canada in "her Arctic"(639) and insists that Canada "accepts responsibility for its own sector," when the Arctic sector concept was and still is disputed by the United States. Moreover, Pearson quietly qualifies Canada's co-operation with the United States by declaring that "each northern nation should cooperate with every other in all Arctic problems"(643) and that, for the sake of peaceful development in the Arctic, all nations must "work together within the United Nations"(647).

8 Pearson's language here bears striking resemblance to Robert Service's poem "The Call of the Yukon"(1907) – "This is the Law of the Yukon, that only the strong shall thrive; / That surely the weak shall perish, and only the Fit survive" – and to R.G. Haliburton's rhetoric in *The Men of the North and Their Place in History*; see chapter 2.

9 This version of Diefenbaker's remarks is quoted from Peter Newman's *Renegade in Power* (218). Typescripts of the speech, held with the Diefenbaker Papers (vol. 19, file 650) at the University of Saskatchewan, give slightly different wording, and the transcript of the broadcast of his speech on CKY Winnipeg radio suggests that, at this point in his remarks, Diefenbaker did not speak of fulfilling Macdonald's dream but did say that "Macdonald gave his life to this party" (broadcast transcript, 8). Newman's own slant on Diefenbaker's "Northern Vision" is quite derisory (see 217–23), apparently because he is personally sceptical. Judging by his final comment, Newman had not been persuaded by Stefansson: "The trouble was, rather, in the character of the North itself. Political rhetoric, no matter how inspired, could work little magic in that inhospitable barren land" (223).

10 Harris visited the Arctic with A.Y. Jackson in the late summer of 1930 aboard the government supply ship *Beothic*. This was Jackson's second trip; the first took place in 1927, when he went on the *Beothic* with Dr Frederick Banting. Jackson made a total of twelve trips to the far North or the Arctic between 1927 and 1965. Frank Johnston, who had changed his name from Franz and had painted with members of the Group in Algoma in 1919 and 1920, spent five months of 1939 – years after he had left the Group – at Eldorado on Great Bear Lake and at Coronation Gulf in the Northwest Territories.

11 The term "mystic north" was first used by J.E.H. MacDonald after he and Harris saw the 1913 exhibition of Scandinavian art in Buffalo (see Nasgaard, 3). In "Revelation of Art in Canada" (1926) Harris *insisted* that Canadians live "on the fringe of the great North and its living whiteness … its cleansing rhythms. It seems that the top of the continent is a source of spiritual flow that will ever shed clarity into the growing race of America, and we Canadians being closest to this source seem destined to produce an art somewhat different from our Southern fellows – an art more spacious, of a greater living quiet, perhaps of a more certain conviction of eternal values. We were not placed between the Southern teeming of men and the ample replenishing North for nothing" (86). This particular statement, with its geographical determinism, has been quoted at length or alluded to in many studies of Harris; see, for example, Grace (1985: 436), Christopher Jackson (73), Larisey (4), and Hjartarson (71). The deliberate linking of the North with Canadian nationalism has been made, most recently and exhaustively, by Charles Hill in his monumental study/exhibition catalogue *The Group of Seven: Art for a Nation* (1995).

12 He is also, of course, echoing several of his own earlier canvases. See, for example, *Lake and Mountains*, 1928 (Plate 6) and *Albert Harbour, North Baffin Island*, 1930, both of which are reproduced in Christopher Jackson's *Lawren Harris* (48 and 52).

13 Studies by Pierre Berton, Frank Norris, and, to a lesser degree, Ann Fienup-Riordan confirm the flagrant stereotyping and enormous popularity of these northern constructions of Canada. Berton overstates the case against Hollywood, however, when he insists that it was Hollywood that single-handedly promulgated the idea of the North

as physically and morally rejuvenating (54–5) and as a site of white, masculinist, racist rhetoric about the North (78). These ideas were deeply embedded in Canadian rhetoric from at least the 1860s on. The all-Canadian radio series *Men in Scarlet*, sponsored by Lowney's Chocolates and introduced by Harry "Red" Forster was very popular during the Second World War. It was based on actual RCMP records and aimed at celebrating the real exploits of the Mounties and boosting patriotic pride. The television series *Sergeant Preston of the Yukon* was created by Blake W. Owensmith, an Englishman working in Hollywood who knew little about Canada or the RCMP, and produced by Charles E. Skinner in Hollywood, and a few episodes are now available on video. The series was based on the popular radio drama created by George W. Trendle.

14 In 1992 the National Archives of Canada mounted a major exhibition on the history of Canadian comic books. The catalogue *Guardians of the North/Protecteurs du Nord*, prepared by curator John Bell, provides fascinating information about Nelvana and other northern heroes such as Northguard, who made his appearance in the 1980s. A series of trading cards for children was published along with the catalogue. In October 1995 Canada Post released a stamp series celebrating Canada's superheroes of the forties, including Superman (the creation of Canadian-born Joe Shuster), Nelvana (see Plate 4), Johnny Canuck, Fleur de Lys, and Captain Canuck. Dixon of the Mounted was not in this series.

15 Gould makes these connections in his introduction to *The Idea of North*; see the unpaginated liner notes to his *Solitude Trilogy*, and *The Glenn Gould Reader*, 391.

16 These differences are particularly clear in Gould's introductions. For example, in the CBC Northern Services introduction, which I consulted in the Gould Collection (MUS 109-5.32.1) of the National Library, Gould provides more detail about the possible train routes into the North (across the Alaska/Yukon border, the "Muskeg Express" from Winnipeg to Churchill, Manitoba, and the Polar Bear Express across northern Ontario from Cochrane to

Moosonee). Most importantly, however, Gould addresses his own southern bias, something barely touched upon in the published introduction (*Glenn Gould Reader*, 392), by frankly stating that the program "is inevitably limited by being a southerner's nostalgic look at the north ... and ... by that envy with which we in the South ... regard those of you who reside in Northern Canada" (4).

17 As André Loiselle notes in his review of the film, Girard was "conscious of the self-reflexive import of 'The Idea of North' [and] made it one of the central ingredients in his production" (10). The film opens and closes with the black-clad figure of Gould approaching and retreating from the camera across a flat, barren expanse of ice and snow. At the end the solitary figure in effect disappears into the whiteness from which it had emerged in the opening sequence.

18 The quotations from *The Idea of North* in the following discussion have been taken directly from the 1992 CBC compact disk *Glenn Gould's Solitude Trilogy*. I have consulted the manuscripts and drafts for the composition, however, and it is clear that Gould had the most difficulty with Marianne Schroeder's voice. Although she began with as much material as each of the men, her contributions are the last to be finalized, and her voice is pared down more extensively than any of the others. The final effect is to marginalize the female voice, and this marginalization conforms to the dominant gendering of northern discourse and myth. In Gould's defence I should add that he, at least, included a woman's perspective.

CHAPTER ONE:
REPRESENTING NORTH

1 In addition to these authors, all of whom are listed in my Bibliography, I would also like to acknowledge the lessons I learned in a parallel research group at UBC on "Race, Gender, and the Construction of Canada" between 1993 and 1996. Some of the practical results of those fruitful years of debate are published in *Painting the Maple: Essays on Race, Gender, and the Construction of Canada*, co-edited and co-authored with Veronica Strong-Boag, Avigail Eisenberg,

Joan Anderson, Gabriele Helms, Matt James, and Paddy Rodney.

2 Because I use the social semiotics of Hodge and Kress to analyse specific examples of the North in the discursive formation of North, I will not take time here to summarize their eloquent arguments and model (see chapter 3.) It should be noted, however, that in their social semiotics, Hodge and Kress draw in part, on the work of Voloshinov/Bakhtin in *Marxism and the Philosophy of Language* to establish a semiotics that contradicts and resists an arbitrary Saussurean system of language and signs. As a result, their social semiotics provides an analytical tool that is congruent with Foucault, Bakhtin, and Bourdieu, each of whom has contributed to their theorizing of signs, and is consistent with my theorizing of North and my methodology. In addition to stressing the importance of dialogic process, plus the interdependent domains of time *and* space (what Bakhtin calls the "chronotope"), their conception of discourse includes language and other sign systems and their model of social semiotics can be applied precisely across disciplines to connect, link, and locate bridges. Because they stress the relevance of social context, use, social action, and ideology (resulting from dialogic relations among signs), their theory is dynamic. Like Bakhtin (and to a lesser degree Foucault) they allow for transformation and contestation at the level of social interaction, and this interaction accounts for the forces of power and solidarity and the ways in which both are negotiated in an on-going manner within what Bourdieu calls the habitus. Lastly, and of particular importance for my work, Hodge and Kress see all social semiotics as gender inflected.

3 In her useful study "Realism Reconsidered: Bakhtin's Dialogism and the 'Will to Reference,' " Ann Jefferson plots a number of congruencies between Foucault and Bakhtin. She argues for an explicit analogy between Foucault's explanation of power as the "will to truth" functioning within discourse and Bakhtin's "consistent and fairly unconcealed assumption … that discourse … is representational in intent" (177). She calls this intent the "will to reference" (77) and argues that "it is this very impulse toward the referen-

tial object that engenders dialogism" (77). My thanks to Gabriele Helms for bringing this useful study to my attention.

4 Both François Lyotard in *The Postmodern Condition* (1984) and Jean Baudrillard in "The Ecstasy of Communication" and "The Precession of Simulacra" analyse the dangers (and possibilities) of the virtual world of postmodernity and the obscene power of simulacra and simulation.

5 I will return to Diana Fuss's article "Interior Colonies: Frantz Fanon and the Politics of Identification" in subsequent chapters, but the point to stress here is her description of identity (of self and of nation) as an imperialist process of interior and exterior colonization that comes very close to cannibalization. Thus, she argues that identification is "a form of violent appropriation in which the Other is deposed and assimilated into the lordly domain of Self" (23). See chapter 6 for my discussion of the trope and politics of cannibalism in Thomson Highway's *Kiss of the Fur Queen*.

6 In "Notes towards a Politics of Location" from *Blood, Bread, and Poetry*, Rich reminds me, in the strongest terms, to remember who I am and the privileged position from which I speak. I/we ("Who is *we*?" [231]) must begin by "recognizing our location, having to name the ground we're coming from, the conditions we have taken for granted" – "because our lived experience is thoughtlessly white" (219).

7 The texts of primary importance to me are Bakhtin's *Speech Genres and Other Late Essays* and *Problems of Dostoevsky's Poetics*, although *The Dialogic Imagination* and the Voloshinov/Bakhtin *Marxism and the Philosophy of Language* have also influenced my thinking.

8 To the best of my knowledge, very few theorists or literary or cultural critics have made a detailed comparison of Foucault and Bakhtin, although many make passing references to both and allude to common ground; see, for example, Amigoni, Hitchcock, Jefferson, Pile and Thrift, and Shields. Doug West links Said and Foucault, in his analysis of northern discourse, to argue that southern Canada orientalizes the North.

9 In "Questions on Geography" Foucault finally agrees that "Geography must indeed lie at the heart of my concerns" (77) because

it is at the heart of power relations "exercised over bodies, multiplicities, movements, desires, forces" (74). Bakhtin develops a spatio-temporal concept that he calls the "chronotope": speaking of Goethe, he explains that "time, in all its essential aspects, is localized in concrete space ... Everything in this world is a *space-time*, a true *chronotope*" (*Speech Genres*, 42). For Bakhtin's detailed explication of the chronotope "as a formally constitutive category of literature" (84), see his essay "Forms of Time and the Chronotope in the Novel."

10 Foucault's archeology and genealogy are methods that can be applied to any "discourse-object" (*Archeology*, 140), and Bakhtin's dialogics describes that dynamic of all utterances that necessarily partake in heteroglossia. According to Bakhtin, "dialogic relationships ... are extralinguistic" (*Problems*, 183); they are "possible ... among images belonging to different art forms" (185), but "discourse," says Bakhtin, "is by its very nature dialogic" (183).

11 It is worth pointing out, however, that even with Foucault some*one* must *use* the archeological method. Although the method does not address the subject, either in its attention to statements or to discursive formations, there is nevertheless a Foucaultian "speaking subject, who reveals or who conceals himself in what he says, who, in speaking, exercises his sovereign freedom" (*Archeology*, 122).

12 Two discussions of Bourdieu's habitus that I have found instructive are those of Pile and Thrift in "Mapping the Subject" (27–32) and Craig Calhoun in "Habitus, Field, and Capital: The Question of Historical Specificity" in Calhoun, LiPuma, and Postone (61–88). Charles Taylor also finds the concept of the habitus important and "potentially fruitful," and, although he does not cite Bakhtin as such, his discussion of "embodied understanding" and the "dialogical" versus "monological" recalls Bakhtin at every turn; see "To Follow a Rule."

13 Foucault's comments on the rules of discursive practice suggest to me a more general application to non-verbal sign systems. He insists that we *not* treat "discourses as groups of signs ... but as practices that systematically form the objects of which they

speak" and "do more than use these signs to designate things" (*Archeology*, 49). Both Bakhtin and Hodge and Kress, who also see discourse as signs, extend the applicability of discourse *through their signifying systems* to the non-verbal.

14 As Lois McNay points out, "a more central problem with Foucault's notion of an aesthetics of existence [and, thus, with subjectivity] is that it privileges an undialectical and disengaged theory of the self" (157). Foucault's subject, or "techniques of self," is, therefore, non-dialogic, and lacking in the full capacity of participation and resistance that comes with agency.

15 The lowest temperatures recorded in Canada are discussed by David W. Phillips in "Canada's Coldest Day." Mayo in the Yukon formerly won the prize for this record, with temperatures sinking to −81°F on 3 February 1947, but colder temperatures have been recorded using more sophisticated alcohol thermometers with markings to −94°F.

16 The decisive linking of Harris and the Group with the North and with a northern nationalism began with Frederick B. Housser's *A Canadian Art Movement: The Story of the Group of Seven* [1926], continued with Herman Voaden's *Six Canadian Plays*, studies by Christopher Jackson, Hjartarson, Eli Mandel, Michelle Lacombe, Douglas Cole, and Ann Davis, to mention only a few, and culminated in Charles Hill's comprehensive *The Group of Seven: Art for a Nation* almost seventy years later in 1995. *Music in the cold* was first published by Coach House Press in 1977, but for ease of reference all my quotations are from *On Canadian Music*, which is paginated. However, in his important article, "The Myth – and Truth – of the True North," about nineteenth-century artists and early twentieth-century illustrators such as C.W. Jefferys, Robert Stacey argues that the Group did not invent the idea of northern wilderness so much as capitalize upon an already well-established discourse and iconography.

17 It is well beyond the space at my disposal or my capacity to examine every contributor to this descriptive/critical/theoretical aspect of the discursive formation of North, and it is entirely possible, indeed likely, that I will have missed some contributions. But in addition to the individuals named or the

studies examined here, I must add all the critical essays in my own *Representing North* and in John Moss's *Echoing Silence*. Both volumes contain some excellent work by young scholars on everything from epistemic narrations of the North to *métissage* in memoir and analyses of gender. The 1997 Klondike conference at the University of Edinburgh, with proceedings forthcoming, is one further contribution to the discourse.

18 Allison Mitcham's *The Northern Imagination: A Study of Northern Literature* (1983) is particularly interesting for its inclusion of novels by Anglo-Canadian and Quebecois novelists and its illustrations by Carl Schaefer. These illustrations are black and white ink drawings of skeletal trees, rocks, and water; there are no people in his landscapes. Although Mitcham's first chapter is titled "Northern Utopia," the norths presented in the fictions she describes are threatening and potentially annihilating.

19 While I would not quarrel with McGregor's formulation of Canada "as the archetypal incarnation of the northern nation" (61) or disagree with her claim that "Canadian consciousness is ... derived explicitly from the peculiar relation between the northerner and his environment" (77), many of the sweeping generalizations that she builds on these basic premises are deeply flawed. The most misleading of these generalizations, to my mind, are her insistence that as a consequence of northern nature perceived exclusively as negative, our artists and writers are obsessed with isolation and death (109, 114), and her claim that the hostile northern landscape is masculine, as distinct from the feminine garrison (134–5). For a different approach to the construction of Canada-as-North, see James Doyle's *North of America*.

20 Davis's argument is more complex and nuanced than this brief quotation suggests, and her comparison of Harris and Kent, and of specific canvases, provides a richer context for interpreting and theorizing the North than does, say, McGregor. See "Northern Explorers: Lawren Harris and Rockwell Kent" in *A Distant Harmony* (103–37) for her specific comparisons (with plates) of Harris's *Algoma Country* (1920–21) with Kent's *The Trapper* (1921) and of Harris's *Icebergs and*

Mountains (c1930) with Kent's *Iceberg, Greenland* (1932–33).

21 Warwick draws a map of Quebec on which he places the "Pseudo-North" around Montreal, the "Near Pays d'en Haut" reaching west to Lake Abitibi and east to Lake St John, the "Pays d'en Haut" stretching north to James Bay, with beyond that the "Far North." On his map of Canada he extends these categories, as they are represented by the literature he examines, across the Northwest. His description of novels and poems, against the history and culture of Quebec, provides a much more complex and convincing discussion of the imagined North than that found in other studies. In his study of Duncan Campbell Scott, Stan Dragland goes a step further than Warwick by identifying both Scott and himself with an imagined northern Ontario. For a different reading of *le grand nord*, see Morissonneau's *La Terre promise*; Morissonneau describes the occupation of northern Quebec as "la Mission par excellence des Canadiens français" (100).

22 Leacock's *Adventures of the Far North* is especially interesting in this regard because it marks, to the best of my knowledge, the earliest *Canadian* recuperation of British Arctic exploration in that Leacock quotes the published narratives of Franklin, Hearne, and Mackenzie within his own re-narrativization of their adventures. In doing so he notes Mackenzie's discovery of strategic natural resources, and he quotes Hearne's description of the massacre at Bloody Falls, a scene that has been anthologized and repeated and written about by scholars and poets (such as John Newlove and Don Gutteridge) until it has become a familiar and haunting statement in the discursive formation of North; see the rewriting of this in chapter 6. According to Ian MacLaren, George Back's poem "Recollections of our unfortunate Voyage ..." (1819–22) is the "earliest poetic re-casting of the massacre" (MacLaren, "Commentary" in *Arctic Artist*, 282).

23 I have coined this rather cumbersome term for *Kabloona* because, like that earlier travel memoir with pseudo-ethnographic trappings by Pierre Loti, *Japan; Madame Chrysanthèmum* (1893), or later works like Barry Lopez's *Arctic Dreams* (1986), *Kabloona*

is *not*, finally, about the North, a part of the Arctic, or about the Netsilik people, even though its ostensible purpose is to report on these things; it is about the experiencing, reporting, representing I – de Poncins, the white man.

24 At several points in his discussion of "True North" Shields classifies *it* as masculine (163, 183, 188), thereby conflating the environment, landscape (or land), with the human agents who map, name, strive to penetrate, and sometimes die there. Despite his lengthy critique of McGregor (184–5), he appears to have adopted uncritically her gender classification, even though he goes on to quote a passage from the *Catholic World* (1865) that emphatically genders Nature and North as feminine (194). Indeed, as should be clear, the space of North, whether we call it a liminal zone, a myth, or a textual Other, is constructed as a female space for the exploration, conquest, adventure, etc., of the white, usually southern male. See my discussion in chapter 4, and R.S. Phillips.

25 It is regrettable that in a serious study of North such as this one, the social scientist's (here geographer's) "suspicious glance" (167), as he calls it, blinds him to three-quarters of the cultural evidence before him. In his one extensive quotation and discussion of a creative writer – Margaret Atwood (167) – he chastizes "this novelist" for daring to speak for the "average" Canadian, and he thereby seeks to dismiss her comments as "prescriptive" (167). Prescriptive of what? and why? If a country's artists do not, to some degree, echo public perception (as well as shape it, as they are shaped by it), then it is hard to imagine who does, and not wise to imagine that geographers and other social scientists (or scholars) do.

26 John Sutherland, who was largely responsible for the merger of *Preview* and *First Statement* in the mid-forties, first thought of calling the new journal "Portage" (Vanneste, 74); see chapter 2, n 10.

CHAPTER TWO:
CONSTRUCTING A
NORTHERN NATION

1 Jack Shadbolt's mural was commissioned for the Edmonton International Airport, and a full-colour reproduction of his 1962 acrylic and ink study has been reproduced for the cover of *Open Letter* 5–6 (1996), where it accompanies my discussion of Robert Kroetsch's *Gone Indian*. Paterson Ewen's massive painting on gouged plywood was featured in a special room for the Art Gallery of Ontario's 1996 retrospective of Ewen's work. In the accompanying audio commentary Ewen (and others, including filmmaker Peter Mettler, who made *Picture of Light*, 1994), discusses the Mercator distortion of his imagined Canada, which dominates the globe and depicts a Canadian Arctic that fills most of the visual space.

2 In his table for "Nordicity compared by criteria (in VAPO)," Hamelin compares five northern places to demonstrate that the interior of Keewatin has the highest total nordicity. What Hamelin does not sufficiently allow for in these VAPO criteria is the psychological and poetic constructions of North, what Amanda Graham examines as "subjective" factors; and yet the elegance and the utility of indexing, especially as developed by Hamelin, continue to be highly valued (Graham, 33).

3 It is remarkable how little appears to be known by scientists and social scientists about the variety of artistic representations of North (and the reverse is no less true and regrettable). The exceptions to this apparent rule are Carl Berger in "The true north strong and free" and Shelagh Grant in "Myths of the North in the Canadian Ethos," where each examines a range of poetry, fiction, and non-fiction narrative. By and large, however, the same few literary examples are cited and re-cited, most notably Robert Service's poems, which reinforce romantic clichés about the "spell," "love," "peace," "silence," and "wonder" of "nameless" mountains and "valleys unpeopled," or construct a female Yukon who will destroy the weak and reward "the men who will win" her, men "Desperate, strong and resistless" who will, in a word, ravish her; see "The Spell of the Yukon" and "The Law of the Yukon."

4 On 1 June 1831 James Clark Ross tried to locate the North Magnetic Pole, in his words "the spot which [nature] had chosen as the centre of one of her great and dark powers," (quoted in M.J. Ross, 153), using a dip circle

and horizontally suspended needles. As M.J. Ross describes the scene, "the dip was 89° 59', and Ross was satisfied that he was as nearly on the exact spot of the magnetic pole as he could possibly be" (153); he hoisted the British flag on the spot and erected a cairn. However, Ross knew that the pole was moving *while he was taking his measurements*, and he was careful to acknowledge this fact. Contemporary scientists have praised Ross, who was using slow, primitive equipment by our standards, and they assert that James Clark Ross "spent a day closer to the magnetic pole than any observer since" (quoted in M.J. Ross, 154).

5 As a Social Darwinian with extreme racist views about *white* northern racial superiority, Tuttle makes for uncomfortable reading today, and I shall return to *Our North Land* in my discussion of race and gender. It should be added here, however, that Tuttle was one of the earliest and loudest proponents of northern development: everything he saw, from polar bears (which he delighted in slaughtering) to birds, whales, and mineral resources, were meant for exploitation by southern Canadian businesses. For a fine contemporary consideration of the hapless James Knight, see Geiger and Beattie, *Dead Silence.*

6 The North-West Mounted Police force was officially established by Sir John A. Macdonald on 30 August 1873. In 1904 they were granted the title Royal North-West Mounted Police, and in 1920 they received their current name, Royal Canadian Mounted Police (RCMP). The history of the North from the 1890s to the present is closely bound up with the history of the Mounties. In 1895 they were sent into the Yukon to manage the increasing American influx and to control the Gold Rush, which hit its peak in 1898. Their most northerly post in 1895 was at Fortymile on the Yukon River, but by 1903 there were police posts on Herschel Island in the Western Arctic and Cape Fullerton in the east. By 1920 there were posts across the NWT, and some difficult patrols had taken place. The Lost Patrol of 1911, the hunt for the mad trapper in 1932, and the navigation of the Northwest Passage by the St Roch in 1940–42 are among the most famous of their northern exploits.

7 In "Re-searching the North in Canada," West offers what strikes me as a fine reading of the semiotics of the Prince of Wales Northern Heritage Centre in Yellowknife. He measures nordicity not in VAPO but in architecture, museology, and artifacts. Thus the centre, he argues, "re-presents the history of the Canadian North from two very different perspectives": that of official, Western, and southern-trained specialists, who, as it were, universalize North, and that of aboriginial northerners, who emphasize the local, the regional, and the land, languages, and lifestyles (112). I am not certain that I can agree with his optimistic conclusion that the "cultural blending" of accounts of North in the centre indicates a sharing of North, but his semiotic reading makes a good beginning to what could be a fascinating comparative study of such centres across Canada.

8 I am thinking here not only of Morton's stress on satire and epic (thus Leacock and Pratt) but of his notion of northern art as puritanical, of the northern frontier as perpetual, and of a psychology of Canada-as-North that is informed by "endurance and survival" (112), all of which echo through the work of major writers like Atwood, Wiebe, Kroetsch, Roy, and Richler, not to mention a host of other novelists, poets, playwrights, and visual artists. This is not the place to trace in detail Morton's impact upon Canadian culture in the widest sense, but such a study should be undertaken.

9 In "The Limits of Northern Identity: An Assessment of W.L. Morton's Northern Vision" West bristles at Morton's description of a "too terrible" North and chastizes Morton for refusing to grant a status to the North equal to that of the west. He accuses Morton of wrapping "himself in a Northern flag ... a characteristic gesture of Conservative intellectuals and politicians of the 1960s" (106). What West fails to understand fully is the consequence of Morton's radical call for a historiography of the North that inscribes northern difference while retaining the North for a larger, more diverse, evolving, and complex Canadian whole.

10 For a detailed history of the merger and creation of *Northern Review*, see Vanneste, who notes in passing (74) that the name "Portage" had been suggested but does not

explain how "Northern Review" was chosen. In my 10 March 1997 conversation with her, Sandra Djwa suggested that the name likely came from the *Preview* group, which included F.R. Scott, who had written poems about Canada's northernness and the Laurentian Shield by 1946.

11 At the beginning *The Northern Review* was published by the Northern Review Society, "a non-profit organization devoted to the development of scholarship in the North" (see title page, vol. 2, 1988), based at Yukon College, Whitehorse.

12 Davey's argument is not a new one; it can be traced back to the theories of Marshall McLuhan and related to the growth of regionalist studies in the 1970s and 1980s (see Westfall). Davey's study is new in so far as he applies the regional/global nexus that erases nation-states and nationalism (which are viewed, *tout court*, as obvious evils) to literature. I have presented my argument for Canadian nationalism, with specific reference to Davey, in "Canada Post."

13 I am thinking here of *Writing North* (1992), but, as my bibliography suggests, the growth and variety of studies of the Yukon blossomed in the 1980s. Without question the opening of Yukon College in Whitehorse in 1983 (something called for by Lotz in *Northern Realities*) and the excellent research and art gallery facilities of the Yukon Archives and Cultural Centre played a key role in facilitating this growth. However, to reverse the equation, it would be as accurate to say that the college and the centre would not have been created without the prior knowledge and pride of Yukoners.

14 The Great Northern Arts Festival began in 1989 and is held annually for ten days in July. The festival draws artists from across the North and encourages all fields of art from sculpture and painting to music, storytelling, and crafts. Although visitors are welcome, the festival is designed for the artists, with workshops, seminars, masterclasses, and demonstrations. Works are on exhibition and are for sale.

15 In its early years the *Canadian Forum*, begun in 1920, relied heavily on illustrations by members of the Group. *The Beaver*, the official magazine of the Hudson's Bay Company, also begun in 1920, has always focused on the North, as has the *Canadian Geographic*, which began in 1930 under the name *Canadian Geographical Journal.*

16 Despite his disparaging remarks about Diefenbaker's northern vision and his insistence that no amount of political rhetoric or practical effort could transform the North into anything but an "inhospitable barren land" (223), Peter Newman does admit that Diefenbaker's Conservatives accomplished a lot during their term.

17 In his contribution to the *Canadian Forum* Richard Rohmer describes the Mid-Canada Development Corridor project, one goal of which was to move 10 per cent of Canadians into the boreal or "green north," and he sets forth the ideology of the project in language reminiscent of Diefenbaker's: the project will give Canadians "a common goal," "behind which all of us can gather as a nation" (191).

18 To compare accounts of the Gold Rush, especially with reference to the original find on Rabbit Creek in August 1896 that sparked the great rush, is to be confronted with an array of contradictory stories. Many agree that George Carmack made the discovery, which he certainly claimed for himself, while others say that Bob Henderson deserves credit, and still others say, as does Ken Coates, that Skookum Jim "made the first discovery of the gold-lined creek beds" (*Canada's Colonies*, 76; see also Whyte). Some say that Kate, Carmack's Tagish wife, discovered the gold; see my discussion of Kate Carmack in chapter 3.

19 I have discussed the Molson's advertisement, which was the first of these ads using images of Canada-as-North to market our products and resources, elsewhere (see Grace, "Canada Post," 131–2). Within a year of the Molson ad, Toronto-Dominion (the name itself speaking ironically to the use of the North in its ads) and Fidelity Investments Mutual Funds were appealing to Canadian national pride and loyalty by exploiting images of northern wilderness, Inukshuks, pristine lakes and snow, mountains, and so on. The TD Evergreen image uses colours and exposition that effectively evoke Lawren Harris's paintings of Lake Superior, and all three endorse and assume a national North (as opposed to a regional

one) at the disposal of a metropolitan, southern Canadian centre.

20 In addition to the major figures already mentioned I would add the following scholars, artists, and creative writers who are tackling these issues as they pertain to the North: Valerie Alia, Goehring and Stager, Lisa Young, Cameron and White, Marlene Creates, Elizabeth Hay, David Woodman, Mary Shiell, and Geoff Kavanagh. I have begun to analyse and disentangle some of these threads in specific case studies of the reinventions of Franklin, of Robert Flaherty's *Nanook of the North*, and in a joint-authored paper on Wendy Lill's play *The Occupation of Heather Rose* (see Anderson *et al.*).

21 I am thinking very generally here of such problems as the spread of tuberculosis and other white-man's diseases that decimated native populations across the country (for example, at Coppermine on the Beaufort Sea), the relocations of families in the eastern Arctic, drug and alcohol abuse, violence, and suicide. The list is long and growing, as reports about Innu children sniffing gasoline during the winter of 2000–01 demonstrate. For discussion of some of these problems see Alia, Hill, Tester and Kulchyski, Speck, Raine, Mowat (1952), videos such as *Coppermine: Consequences of Contact with the Outside*, and the CD-ROM *Spirit of Davis Inlet*.

CHAPTER THREE:
VISUALIZING NORTH

1 I do not wish to enter the debate about whether or not Harley understands or applies Foucault correctly or whether he has pushed a postmodern theorizing of maps far enough. For responses to Harley, see Belyea, Rundstrom, and Sparke. To this non-specialist, Harley's analysis is both familiar (from literary theory) and refreshing, inasmuch as his approach serves to open up for investigation received ideas about the scientific objectivity, truth value, and representational utility of maps.

2 This is not the place to summarize Woodman's arguments in favour of taking both the stories and the maps of the Inuit seriously in our attempts to revisit and rediscover what happened to Franklin or the possible survivors of his expedition. Suffice it to say here that Woodman presents the

case convincingly in both *Strangers among Us* and *Unravelling the Franklin Mystery*. When Robert Rundstrom turns to Inuit maps, he focuses on contemporary maps of Nunavik (the Inuit area of northern Quebec), on which Inuit names appear with Qallunaat names in French and English (Rundstrom, 10–11). For another interesting discussion of indigenous mapping, see Sparke, who insists that the Beothuk had a geographic imagination; by placing Shawnadithit's maps beside those of the colonizers, he achieves the kind of cartographic dialogue (dialogization) that Rundstrom advocates. See also Robin McGrath's "Maps as Metaphors."

3 I cannot begin to analyse in depth the ideological and aesthetic complexity and challenging quality of these assemblages. To enter the gallery space of the exhibition is to share the private domains of the subjects and, in a sense, to enter into dialogue with them. As Jacqueline Fry puts it in her catalogue essay: "Marlene Creates succeeds in sharing with us the play of memories of long ago, rooted in pre-urban places. These memories are falsely thought to belong to a world other than our own, yet they are so close!" (54)

4 Scots historian James Mackay has published a definitive biography of Service called *Vagabond of Verse*, in which he claims that Service is the most widely read poet of the twentieth century, and Margaret Atwood, with her uncanny instinct for the precise insight that characterizes all her work, has called her witty, ironic examination of Canadians' obsession with the North *Strange Things: The Malevolent North in Canadian Literature*, after Service's famous poem.

5 In paper after paper given to the 1997 Conference on the Klondike held at the Canadian Studies Centre of the University of Edinburgh, these popular notions of the Klondike, now taken as representative of Yukon life more generally, were disproved, but at the same time scholars from Whitehorse like Carolyn Moore, Amanda Graham, and Brent Slobodin demonstrate that attempts to alter the dominant discourse are vehemently resisted. Thus the icon on Yukon licence plates and government letterhead is still a gold miner with his pan. Perhaps more important for my purposes, and

for an understanding of the discursive formation of the Klondike, is Jim Burant's evidence that, of the thousands of photographs taken of the Gold Rush, the vast majority are of working men (and women) and of daily life, and yet it is the same few showing men climbing the Chilkoot Pass, scantily clad entertainers, or the red-light district of Dawson City that are recycled and have come to be seen as synonymous with and decisively constitutive of Yukon life. In her study of the Klondike, Charlene Porsild analyses the class hierarchy and conditions for non-native women, including prostitutes, and claims that by 1898 Dawson City had a population that was 12 per cent women (292).

6 Languirand's play, with music by Gabriel Charpentier, comprises a two-part series of twelve scenes that creates a carnivalesque music-hall routine out of the mad scramble for gold in 1896–97. Despite its strong parodic style, with moments of sharp satire, burlesque, and slapstick comedy, Languirand's larger purpose is serious. In his essay "Le Québec et L'Americanité," which follows the play, he develops a theory of national identity in which the United States is characterized as masculine and Quebec (by extension all of Canada) is feminine. According to Languirand, the Klondike Gold Rush represented one of the last great bursts of male dionysian energy on this continent, an energy once embodied in Quebec by the *coureurs des bois*. As one of the least lucky figures in the play chants, perhaps echoing Robert Service: "C'est le pays du soleil de minuit / C'est le grand Nord qui fascine et qui tue" (32).

7 One of the most extraordinary and destabilizing additions to the discursive formation of the Klondike is the story of Katherine Ryan (1869–1932), a farm girl from Johnville, New Brunswick, who set out for the Klondike in 1898 by the all-Canadian route through northern British Columbia via Glenora and Telegraph Creek to Atlin, and from there to Whitehorse. While wintering over in Glenora, she opened a restaurant in a tent, and her appreciative customers called it "Klondike Kate's" (142). According to Brennan, however, the title "Klondike Kate" was appropriated by the notorious American actress Kitty Rockwell, and Ryan

suffered much embarrassment over the resulting confusion in their identities. Until Brennan's book appeared in 1990 to set the record straight, a distinguished woman (Ryan became a nurse, a businesswoman, a special constable with the RCMP, and a politician) was forgotten to Canadian history. The colourful American actress took Katherine's title and gave it the distinctly unsavoury ring that it still carries. Perhaps the best known of the Yukon's (and the Klondike's) respectable women is Martha Black, who, as a member of Parliament for the Yukon, told her own story, but there are others, like Eva MacLean, who travelled to Hazelton in northern British Columbia in 1911 as a minister's wife and whose truly enlightened views about Indians, prostitutes, and white racism, sexism, and hypocrisy are striking for her time and place; see *The Far Land*.

8 James Albert Johnson states that Marguerite Carmack cut out all references to both Kate and Graphie Grace when she went through her husband's papers after his death (156) and prior to preparing his autobiography, *My Experience in the Yukon*, for publication in 1933. Angela Wheelock has found some alleged quotations by Kate in newspapers, and she also believes that material exists that is not available to researchers. Native elders have maintained the stories passed on to them by Kate, Skookum Jim, Dawson Charlie, and Patsy Henderson, but those who actually knew Kate are now all dead. Moreover, the privileging of an individual's voice as *individual*, with the concomitant desire to preserve it, does not appear to be of first importance in these oral narratives; see Cruikshank, *Reading Voices*, 142–4.

9 The following summary of events has been drawn from a wide range of studies of the Klondike and the Yukon more generally; see the Bibliography. I am, however, especially grateful to Julie Cruikshank, Mary Shiell, and Angela Wheelock for their generous help with materials and for their advice.

10 As Cruikshank explains (133), in a matrilineal culture, where a child belongs to the mother's clan, this loss of Graphie was an ultimate blow. While one can speculate at length about Carmack's motives in taking Graphie, no explanation of them absolves him of profound racism and sexism: to say

that he wanted the best for his daughter is to say, in short, that white society is better than Indian and that a father's claim to know what is best and his authority to impose it supersedes a mother's. He had the money and the social position, and thus the power to act, and act he did. Graphie was married at seventeen, within months of her arrival in Seattle, to her father's brother-in-law Jacob Saftig, a man of thirty-two (Johnson, 141). Clearly, her chances of returning to the Yukon, or even of developing her own perspectives and priorities as an adult, would have been severely limited. George's letters to his sister in July and November of 1900 reveal that it had always been his intention to separate Kate from her daughter: in July, when Kate was trying to sue for divorce, he wrote to Rose that Kate "must not take Graphie away. If she does, I will take her by law," and in November he wrote again that "the less I seem to care for the child the less will be the fight for her" (Johnson, 117, 121).

11 The parallels between the Butterfly story and the actual events in Kate and George Carmack's lives are striking, but I do not want to aestheticize Kate's real life by stressing these parallels too much. The most important point to make by comparing the tragic opera with the Carmacks' lives is that the opera offers a catharsis and prettification of an ugly practice that was common enough in colonialist encounters in Canada (and elsewhere). Moreoever, the opera gives the abandoned woman a voice – indeed, a diva's dominant voice – which was not the case for Kate. In the versions of the Butterfly story by Long and Bellasco (see also Loti) that influenced Puccini, American culture is seen as superior to Asian, and Butterfly becomes so infatuated with Pinkerton and the *idea* of America that she tries to become, through mimicry, an American wife. This archetypal story of European/American orientalism and imperialism was enormously popular during the 1890s and early 1900s in one or more of its forms (memoir, novel, play, or opera). The popularity and general adaptability of the story attest to its profound significance for Western culture at a critical juncture in its history. My thanks to my colleagues in the UBC research group on the Butterfly narratives; our discussions have taught me a lot about *Madama Butterfly* and its related texts.

12 The common description of the women who went to the Klondike is that they were mostly "camp followers," a euphemism for prostitutes, or entertainers, like "the lady that's known as Lou" (Service, 52), whose purpose it was to part miners from their gold. How these women were treated by employers and customers, what their health and living conditions were like, and why they would have gone to the Gold Rush are rarely touched upon, and the assumption that women of dubious or ill repute *naturally* flock to such places to prey on men is not examined; for some consideration of this situation, see Frances Backhouse, 85–111, and Porsild, 170–95. For an analysis of prostitution under patriarchy and in isolated, male-dominated communities, see Goldman and, more generally, Fingard, Walkowitz, and White. Berton states that Carmack's second wife, "a pretty, dark woman named Marguerite Laimee … was obviously a camp-follower" (427) and probably involved in prostitution. As recently as 1991 Ken Coates describes Klondike prostitutes as there to "mine the miners," with no attention to their wider socio-economic context or actual conditions; see *Best Left as Indians*, 45–6.

13 Miners' maps of the Klondike area show names associated with the Queen of Sheba's treasure and King Solomon's mines, such as Ophir Creek and King Solomon Dome; for an illustration and brief description of these maps by Stephen Fox, see *Canadian Geographic* (Nov./Dec. 1996): 48. In light of the immense popularity of Haggard's novel, which was available in cheap paperback in North America and Europe by the time of the Gold Rush and has remained continuously in print and been widely translated since its publication, it is not difficult to imagine that some of the miners, at least, were consciously echoing the novel. Certainly Robert Service knew Haggard's famous text.

14 The analyses of the fur trade developed by Van Kirk and Brown are much more complex than can be summarized here, but they concur that after about 1830 and with the

advance of Victorian mores and prejudices, circumstances worsened for all women, and the combination of Victorian racism and sexism made native women particularly vulnerable. See Brown (150) and Van Kirk (146–60). The history of women in the fur trade needs to be used to inform the history of women in the Klondike, and this has begun with Porsild's dissertation. According to Porsild, "racism was a mainstay of Yukon life" (292).

15 McClintock makes some striking points about the conjunction of imperialism, racism, sexism, and the fetishization and commodification of cleanliness through soap: "soap took shape as a technology of social purification, inextricably entwined with the semiotics of imperial power and class denigration" (212). When George went south with his fortune, he wanted to become a gentleman, and he could assert this status by owning property, dressing elegantly, living fashionably, and, necessarily, observing the highest standards of middle-class hygiene for himself and those who belonged to him.

16 Johnson's descriptions of Kate are invariably sexist and pejorative; Carmack is his hero. Thus, Kate is described as a shrew who drinks, kicks, screams, and generally carries on (48–51). Moreover, Johnson asserts that she "was the envy of other Tagish women, who considered it a great honour to be sleeping with a white man" (56). According to Johnson, the two never marry but just start living together (50), and when Kate is in Seattle her behaviour is "outrageous" (110), "unpredictable," and "troublesome" (111).

17 The 26 July 1899 *Seattle Post-Intelligencer* article is quoted at length by Johnson (105–8); in it George is called a "wealthy squaw man" who has angered "Mrs Carmack" by paying attention "to women fairer than his dusky spouse." Kate is described in ironic, condescending terms that make a mockery of her identity as an Indian, a wife, and a woman, and the reporter states that she was drunk, swearing, and fighting "with the strength of a wild animal." How he could *know* such things and purport to give an eye-witness account are never clarified.

18 I claim no expertise in women's fashions, but judging from discussions of the subject (see Buck, Careless, and Cunningham), Kate is wearing a fairly formal day or walking dress that is quite fashionable, if not up to Paris standards. Blouses with different skirts were very popular as informal day attire during the 1890s. It was typical of formal dresses in the 1890s to make the bodice the feature of chief importance and the skirt simple (Buck, 74). The colour of Kate's dress is almost certainly black, which, together with the high lustre of the material, provides an ideal background for the display of the gold necklace and accessories. My special thanks to Lisa Chalykoff for her help on these points.

19 Mary Ann Doane has examined the psychoanalytical concept of masquerade as a theory of the feminine stemming from Freud, and she concludes, among other things, that "while the male is locked into sexual identity, the female can at least pretend she is other" (25). Men, therefore, can transvest because their masculine identity is given, but women cannot transvest because feminine identity "is constructed as mask" (25): feminine identity *is* masquerade. I am using the term masquerade differently, however, and in accordance with Bhabha, Fuss, and McClintock, as a mode of *social practice* related to mimicry; thus, for my purposes here masquerade is associated with the behaviour of the man and mimicry with the woman, although either classification could apply to both genders depending upon the socio-historical context.

20 In this remark from act I, "And to the day when in a real wedding ceremony I shall marry a real American wife" (85), Pinkerton is joking with Sharpless, the American consul in Nagasaki.

21 "Fanny" Pannigabluk was Stefansson's seamstress and companion during his 1908–12 and 1913–18 expeditions, and the mother of his child; Alice Nuvalinga, who played the role of Nyla in *Nanook of the North*, bore a son who carried the name Flaherty, and Robert Hood's affair with the Yellowknife woman he called Greenstockings is mentioned in narratives of the 1819–21 Franklin expedition and fictionalized in Wiebe's *A Discovery of Strangers*; see also Wiebe's *Playing Dead* and Grace's "Exploration as Construction."

22 When William Connolly took his Cree wife and children to eastern Canada in 1831, he found them unsuitable and repudiated them to marry his cousin; he sent Susanne to a convent in Red River (Van Kirk, 188).

23 Ghosts and their close relatives – demons, spirits, hallucinatory presences, doubles, revenants, tricksters, even Windigos (who are in a class by themselves) – are some of the most prevalent images of the North. They appear throughout our literature, from the popular poetry of Robert Service to the plays of Herman Voaden, from the myths of the Indians and Inuit to the contemporary fiction of Atwood, MacEwen, Richler, Kroetsch, Drew, Houston, and Tracy, to mention only a few examples. Farley Mowat gives us a memorable version of death as a snow walker in the title story of his collection of stories about the Inuit and the Arctic called *The Snow Walker*.

24 Mitchell describes the exhibition of "orientals" at events like the 1889 Exposition Universelle in Paris (290–2), but similar exhibitions of "Eskimos" took place at events like the Chicago Exposition of 1892–94. The most infamous of these exhibitions is the one staged by Robert Peary in 1897; see Kenn Harper's *Give Me My Father's Body.*

25 This summary of the complex system developed by Hodge and Kress is my own, and I have stressed those aspects of greatest use to my argument. They do not provide such a reductive abstraction of their system. For their discussion of this preliminary material, see chapters 1 and 3 of *Social Semiotics.*

26 Murray explains that Bruce's breakdown occurred in France and was "caused by the double burden of overwork and poverty," and she suggests that the painting "shows his reaction to his poverty. He believed that God, or a spiritual power, had pulled him through" (Murray, 1985, 30). The entry on Bruce in the *Dictionary of Canadian Artists* claims that he lost 200 paintings when the ship carrying them back to Canada for an exhibition sank, and that this was the cause of his breakdown (97).

27 At several points in his letters Bruce describes this painting, in which he placed high hopes at this stage in his career, asks his family to send him snowshoes and other things needed for the scene, asks for copies of the poem, and stresses the value and importance of the North: "*It is the northern blood that will tell,*" he wrote to his mother in 1884 (*Letters Home*, 100). Although Bruce never returned to Canada to live, he did travel to the Arctic and he lived on Visby, a Swedish island, until his sudden death in 1906.

28 After long admiring the painting from reproductions, I was delighted to have a chance to examine it closely in May 1996. My thanks to Art Gallery of Hamilton curators and archivists.

29 The second of Bruce's paintings to be recognized as a major work, both in his lifetime and since, is *The Smiths* (1894), now in the National Gallery of Canada.

30 I have not found any precise references to or quotations from Shanly in *Tay John*, but the final scene of the novel, related to us through Denham by the trapper Blackie (a story told within the story), of Tay John appearing out of a blizzard as Blackie snowshoes through a valley in northern British Columbia, is one of the most disturbing and memorable in Canadian fiction; see my discussion in chapter 5. I suspect that O'Hagan is not the only writer to have been impressed by Shanly. Grey Owl (Archibald Belaney) describes similar disturbing presences in his *Men of the Last Frontier* (1931), and this work in turn influenced Robert Kroetsch's *Gone Indian*; see Grace, "Robert Kroetsch and the Semiotics of North."

31 For more information on this fascinating subject, see Colombo and Johnston. Colombo reprints Shanly's poem (27–9), which he describes as "no more than a distant cousin of the Windigo" that nevertheless strikes "terror in the hearts of lonely travelers in the northern woods" (27). There are many versions of the story, both Indian and white, but they stem from traditional Ojibwa and Cree myth, which Johnston locates in northern Manitoba, Ontario, and Quebec, and the main difference, according to Colombo, is that the Indians stress cannibalism in their versions while the whites stress madness, and both usually end in death (119). I return to the fictional accounts of the Windigo in chapters 5 and 6.

32 This quotation is attributed to Rae in an interview he gave to a reporter for the *Globe*, 23 Oct. 1854, 2. Similar stories appeared in

other Canadian papers and made sensational headlines in England, where the news was received with outraged disbelief and Rae was vilified for making such allegations; see McGoogan. Charles Dickens took up the fight to protect the honour of the British Navy and the reputation of Sir John Franklin in articles and in the play he co-authored with Wilkie Collins, *The Frozen Deep*; see Brannan; Grace, "Re-inventing Franklin"; and Woodman, *Unravelling the Franklin Mystery.*

CHAPTER FOUR:
PERFORMING NORTH

1 Richard Gwyn called his biography of Trudeau *The Northern Magus: Pierre Trudeau and Canadians (1968–1980)*, and the Mission Hill winery in British Columbia has recently bottled a new Canadian wine with this label.

2 Northern Encounters was arranged through the Arctic Council, a circumpolar arts organization founded in September 1996, to bring the eight circumpolar countries (Canada, Sweden, Denmark and Greenland, Finland, Russia, Norway, Iceland, and the United States [Alaska]) together. Canada held the first chair for a two-year term. The description of the festival quoted here is from the festival Web page and other advertising.

3 This version of the song is quoted from Richard Finnie's *Canada Moves North* (204); Finnie attributes it to "four chaps" from the Yukon and notes that Slim Behn brought it to Norman Wells, NWT, and that Gerry Murphy confirmed the lyrics. See also Edith Fowke's comments in the *Encyclopedia of Canadian Music* II:1399. "When the Ice Worms Nest Again" was recorded in 1964 by the Loewen Orchestra for Smithsonian-Folkways Recordings. The liner notes to the 1994 Polygram CD release state that the ballad was written by Norma Booth, with co-authors from Le Pas, Manitoba, and published in 1949; they add that it "dates back to an old folk song from the Yukon Gold Rush." Ice worms, of course, are mysterious creatures (ice-worm cocktails have been known to have bits of spaghetti in them), but the echo in the song of the faithless Pinkerton's promise in *Madama Butterfly* to return "when the robins nest again" is less mysterious. Certainly it is too strong to pass over without comment.

The lover in the ballad is as racist, deceptive, and exploitative as Pinkerton (or as George Carmack), although the light-hearted song gives us little idea of what the self-centred singer's Inuuk girfriend might be thinking.

4 Aglukark, who won a Juno Award in 1995 and shortly thereafter signed a contract with EMI, enjoys growing popularity across the North and in southern Canada for her compact disks *This Child* and *Arctic Rose*, and her music videos. She adds an important female voice to the otherwise dominant male profile of northern music, sings in a combination of English and Inuktitut, and combines elements of popular and country music with gospel to create a striking hybrid sound for her strong personal and ethical lyrics. See Schmaltz.

5 Admittedly, both Clément and McClary are examining opera – that is, music with verbal text and narrative – but McClary also looks at other, non-text-based, non-programmatic works. For example, she comments that "the paradigms of tonality and sonata have proved effective and resilient" because they "are taken for granted as aspects of autonomous music practice" instead of being interpreted as "the most powerful aspects of musical discourse" (16), and she applies her method to the "Master Narrative of 'Absolute Music' " (55) in an analysis of the first and second themes of the first movement of Tchaikovsky's Fourth Symphony (1877); see *Feminine Endings*, 69–79. Her comments on the "feminine endings" of secondary themes in other compositions by Mozart and Schubert are equally provocative and illuminating.

6 The discussion that follows is by no means exhaustive. For a more musicological description of compositions inspired by the Canadian landscape in general, see Parsons.

7 See Kallmann (34), the *Tableau* CD liner notes (which use Harris's *Fog and Ice, Kane Basin* [1930]), and Parsons, 15–16.

8 Most musicologists and music critics resort to metaphor and representational imagery, as I do here, in the attempt to describe or capture the qualities of musical language and its effect upon a listener.

9 See Longtin's remarks, and his praise for the most famous northern composer, Sibelius, in Tannenbaum, "Secrets of the North Wind."

10 See Parsons, 60–3; Garant's *Anerca* (1961–63); and Louis Applebaum's *Innuit* (1977). Although he does not use voice or lyrics, Murray Adaskin has created two exquisite pieces based on Inuit song and story in his *Qualala and Nilaula of the North* (1969). Written for woodwinds, strings, and percussion, Freedman's *Anerca* (1966) captures a sense of Inuit rhythm, story-telling, and life far better than setting English translations of songs or poems to music could do. Adaskin's pieces were composed after he had visited Rankin Inlet in the 1960s with the sculptor Eli Borenstein. While there he listened to the stories of Qualala and Nilaula, the throat-singing of the women, and Inuit drumming, and he has drawn on these experiences, plus his sensitive observation of life at Rankin, to create these two pieces.

11 The poem has a fascinating history. It was published in three distinct versions, with only the third receiving the final imprimatur of the poet. The first two versions, which appeared in the *McGill Fortnightly Review*, 9 Jan. 1926, and *Canadian Forum*, July 1927, respectively, are highly conventional in form and content and rather preachy, but the third version marks an exciting breakthrough for Smith. The poem was originally inspired by an early exhibition of the Group of Seven.

12 This consideration of Archer's music has benefited greatly from my 17 Dec. 1996 conversation with Bryan Gooch, who played the music and analysed the score in detail for me. In his recent anthology of nineteenth-century Canadian poetry, *The Emergence of the Muse*, Gooch remarks on the fruitfulness of looking at "poetry within the cultural context of ... music and painting" (xii).

13 Parsons considers a number of these composers and their works. In addition to the ones he treats, I would add Alexina Louie's *Winter Music* (1989), Malcolm Forsyth's *Atayoskiwin* and *Auyuittuq* (a setting of Inge Israel's poem of the same name), the young Inuit composer Jason Akearok, who won the 1995 Murray Adaskin composition prize at the University of Victoria for "Iikkii," and François Houle's *Au coeur du litige*.

14 There are, for example, striking differences between the 1948 CBC performance, which lasts twelve minutes fifty seconds, and the 1991 recording with the Edmonton Symphony Orchestra, which lasts fourteen minutes forty-four seconds. Such differences affect the mood of the piece and, thus, an interpretation of it.

15 Parsons analysis depends upon the negative interpretation of the Canadian landscape first promulgated by Northrop Frye in *The Bush Garden* and continued by Margaret Atwood in *Survival* and Gaile McGregor in *The Wacousta Syndrome*. The notion that the Canadian landscapes created in literature, painting, and music are exclusively, or even primarily, threatening and destructive, is far too restrictive and simplistic; the reality is much more nuanced and complex than this "survival" paradigm allows. For alternative discussions of the Canadian landscape, see Harris, McLaren, Hay, Moss, New, Wiebe, and van Herk, and my analysis of critical mappings of North in chapter 1.

16 Woodwinds, notably the clarinet, are often used in the sound track for feature films, documentaries, and television programs about the North. Two such examples are Robert Flaherty's classic documentary *Nanook of the North* (1922) and *Never Cry Wolf* (1983), the feature film based on Farley Mowat's novel of the same name. In *Au coeur du litige*, the most recent composition I consider, Houle builds his music on and around the clarinet.

17 See, for example, the poems in *Anerca* (an Inuktitut word for breath) and *Playing Dead* (116–18), where Rudy Wiebe quotes a song by Orpingalik of the Netsilik called "My Breath," which instils a hope for renewed creativity – be it mercy or the grace of God – in the Christian writer. According to Richard Lewis, words for "breath" or "to breathe" also mean "to make poetry or song" (6).

18 The word *iikkii* appealed to Morel in part because it is a palindrome. The quotation from Beaulieu appears at the top of the score; it is taken from the first section of "tout mon sang s'anordit" of the unpaginated poems.

19 In his interview with Harry Elton of CBC's *Mostly Music*, just before the November 1984 world première of *Atayoskiwin*, Forsyth described the composition as inspired by a recent winter trip to northern Alberta. He was deeply moved by the "barren and forbid-

ding" land and by its "majesty" and "quiet," which are like the northern Cree people. "Atayoskiwin" means "sacred legends." The composition has three parts: part 1, "The Spirits," opens with what Forsyth describes as "the taste of silence," but that silence is quickly animated by woodwinds, harp, and strings; part 2, "The Dream," draws more on the brass, with contrasts supplied by the strings, and Forsyth borrows a theme from Sibelius's *Fifth Symphony*; part 3, "The Dance," has a lively, almost Copeland-like quality with a dramatic use of drums. All quotations are from the CMC tape #1907 of the 3 Dec. 1984 *Mostly Music* CBC broadcast of the Edmonton Symphony Orchestra's première of the piece conducted by Uri Myer.

20 My discussion of Schafer is strictly limited to some of his essays in *On Canadian Music, Music in the cold*, "The Canadian Soundscape" from *Voices of Tyranny, Temples of Silence*, and the composition *North/White*. I am not attempting a thorough analysis of Schafer's work or his personal mythology (which is beside the point in a Foucaultian analysis). Schafer is one of the most complex and articulate of twentieth-century composers, and his oeuvre and thought have yet to be analysed as a whole; for a detailed discussion of *Patria* and a good bibliography, see Haag.

21 In addition to recommending that the CBC use "the call of the loon as a spacer between programs," Schafer used it "as the model for the unaccompanied Princess's aria in *The Princess of the Stars*," which he calls his "most 'Canadian' work" ("The Canadian Soundscape," 83). The CBC may not have taken Schafer's advice, but other institutions have: loons are now used to market everything from T-shirts to decorator night-lights; they commonly appear as logos or are sold as handicraft tourist carvings, and they glorify the Canadian one-dollar coin.

22 *Music in the cold* (1977) was published by Coach House Press in a specially designed paperback edition measuring 12.5 cm × 22 cm. The cover is dark blue, and the text is printed in the same blue on cream paper in what closely resembles verse paragraphs. This edition, which I use throughout, is unpaginated.

23 *Music in the cold* ends with the image of a middle-aged man surrounded by young men sitting around the campfire, at which point Schafer shifts to the first person and announces: "I will build a new culture." Schafer's Canada is not only North – "I am a Northerner," he insists – it is also deeply sexist and fractured by an unexamined set of binaries that inscribe North as pure and South (by which he means the United States) as corrupt, North as masculine and South as feminine and effeminate. "The art of the North is the art of restraint," he tells us, whereas "The art of the South is the art of excess"; it is the "soft art of dancing girls and of the slobber." In *Princess of the Sun*, which draws on Indian myth, Schafer's allegory is more inclusive, and in "Canadian Culture: Colonial Culture" (*On Canadian Music*, 90) he calls for a return to "native culture," not as a rehabilitation of that culture merely but as our empowering common heritage.

24 Gwen Pharis Ringwood's *The Road Runs North* (1967), with music by Art Rosoman, Gordon McCall's *Running on Frozen Air* (1996), and Jacques Languirand's *Klondyke* (1971), with music by Gabriel Charpentier, are just three examples. Jim Bett's *Colours in the Storm* celebrates Tom Thomson; I discuss this play, with other works about Thomson, in *Inventing Tom Thomson*.

25 In his 1928 essay "Nationalism and Drama" Denison describes a "Canadian theatre" as a "mirage" (66); his "unheroic North" was aimed at debunking the northern myth of Canadian identity and superiority that he, like Voaden and the Group, had inherited from the nineteenth century and from thinkers like R.G. Haliburton; see my discussion of Haliburton in chapter 1 and my analysis of Voaden's *Six Canadian Plays* manifesto in "Re-introducing Canada's 'Art of the Theatre.'" Paradoxically, even Denison was not immune to the heroics of romantic adventure in a deadly alluring North; in his radio plays *Henry Hudson and Other Plays* (1931) he dramatized the explorers Hudson and Alexander Mackenzie.

26 It is surprising that Garebian, who is writing in 1988, does not comment on the racist assumptions that underlie this southern construction of "Eskimo" life, note the mistake about penguins, which are not found in the Arctic, or provide any social context for

what Gardner (and seemingly Herbert Whittaker, who designed the "arctic tea gowns" for Lear's daughters) confidently believed to be an authentic representation of Inuit culture. The production, however, was not well received, and in the United States critics thought it was set in Alaska – a fine touch of poetic justice.

27 The title of the play, in its first publication, was *Inook and the Sun*, but Beissel has since changed it to *Inuk*, the "name" of his main character, and I use this revised title; Inuk is the preferred English spelling of the masculine singular for person in Inuktitut; see *Staging the North*, 56. Many myths inform the play, from Inuit myths of Sedna and the Northern Lights to Parsifal, Oedipus, and Persephone, but the final effect, especially when puppets, instead of actors, are used, is of an abstract, symbolic, universal story that moves from darkness to light, from death, winter, and cold to rebirth, spring, and warmth, and that blurs the separation between physical and spiritual realms.

28 For a further discussion of this play, see *Staging the North*, 116–20. In "Gendering Northern Narrative" I have argued that the masculine subjects and phallic images of key paintings in the discursive formation of North (such as Blair Bruce's *The Phantom Hunter* and several works by the Group) work to subdue and contain a threatening feminine natural world, while the subjects and images of paintings by Judith Currelly and other women artists celebrate and humanize a feminine nature. North may be a woman in Currelly's paintings, or in a painting like Mary Pratt's *Venus from a Northern Pond* (1987), but she is not the Medusa or Vagina Dentata of male imagining.

29 Usually Hornby is depicted as the central figure, if not the hero, of this story because we know most about Hornby and because he was the eldest and the leader of the trio. Hornby had had extensive experience in the bush and some very narrow escapes from death, and yet he was determined to conquer the Barrens. His fatal mistake was to rely on the great Barrenland herds of caribou for food, but the caribou did not pass by the cabin that year; the spring came late, and one by one the men died. Hornby went first, followed by Harald, and finally young Edgar. For a very different dramatic treatment of the story, see Bruce Valpy's *Hornby*.

30 For the details of Michael Oros's life, crimes, and death, when he was finally shot by the RCMP in 1985, see Vernon Frolick's *Descent into Madness*. Adams had met Oros and reported on him for the *Whitehorse Star*; he also had access to the diaries and creates a somewhat different, and more sympathetic Oros, in his character Mick, than the Oros created by Frolick.

31 By the term documentary mode I mean an aesthetic form of representation that works from a base in physical or historical facts and in documentary or archival material (see Nichols). To be documentary does not mean something is necessarily authentic, real, or true, but that it is created in accord with certain conventions, as an analysis of a film like *Nanook of the North* makes clear (see Grace, "Exploration as Construction"). There is no contradiction to finding documentary elements in an expressionist play like *Free's Point* or in a minimalist play like *Who Look In Stove*. I have not examined Geoff Kavanagh's play "Canoe Lake," but like everything inspired by Tom Thomson, from Kroetsch's poem to Joyce Wieland's film *The Far Shore* (1976) and Andrew Hunter's 1997 novella-cum-exhibition cataglogue *Up North* (the exhibition opened at the McMaster Museum of Art on 11 Jan. 1998), the play celebrates the painter, mythologizes him, and strives to preserve his mysterious disappearance into and almost totemic union with the water and forest of the North; see *Inventing Tom Thomson*.

32 I have discussed Voaden's work at length in *Regression and Apocalypse* (117–37), so will not do so again here; for Voaden's own commentary on his plays and a number of excellent production photographs, see his *A Vision of Canada*.

33 In Bunraku the puppeteers are fully visible, and Beissel sees them as integral to the imaginative world of his play (see Illus. 20). This style of puppetry is also appropriate to Beissel's Inuit subject, and to the nature of myth, because the human beings in the play are subject to the whims of greater forces (nowhere more emphatically than in the Arctic), and the puppeteers embody those

forces and provide a visible, symbolic link between the Moon, Sun, Sedna, and the other gods and Inuk.

34 For this quotation, see Walker. Thompson's romantic quasi-religious reaction no doubt stems in part from her Roman Catholic upbringing; however, this mystical sense of communion with nature mixed with feelings of dread, while it exists not only in Canada or only in the northern wilderness, is a staple element at all levels, from macro to micro, of the discursive formation of North. For a more detailed discussion of North in the play, see Grace, "Going North on Judith Thompson's *Sled*."

35 Among the many studies of the impact and consequences of white, southern values, laws, and institutions on northern peoples, some of the best are Tester and Kulchyski, *Tammarniit*; Dorothy Harley Eber, *Images of Justice*; Betty Lee, *Lutiapik*; and Inuit autobiographies like *I, Nuligak* or Freeman's *Life among the Quallunaat*. See also the CD-ROM *Spirits of Davis Inlet*.

36 For a more detailed discussion of this play, see Anderson *et al.* and *Staging the North* (295–7), and for other perspectives on the lives of northern nurses, see Speck's *An Error in Judgement* and Lee's *Lutiapik*. Lill had not read *Lutiapik* when she wrote her play, which grew out of her own experiences in a remote northern community, but the resemblances between the experiences of Dorothy Knight (the northern nurse called Lutiapik) in Lake Harbour and Heather's are striking. Nurse Marianne Schroeder, in Glenn Gould's *The Idea of North*, also provides glimpses into the kind of colonialist attitudes and southern impositions that characterize government and institutional Canadian behaviour in the North.

37 Judith Thompson and Henry Beissel make the most overt use of the Aurora and its First Nations or Inuit associations. Thompson provides a prefacing quotation to *Sled* from Candace Savage's *Aurora*, and in *Inuk and the Sun* Inuk talks to the Lights, seeking their help and support. The Lights also play a crucial role in *Sixty Below*, a play written by Yukoners Patti Flather and Leonard Linklater, and in Thomson Highway's *Kiss of the Fur Queen* (see chapter 6). I have discussed various uses of the Northern Lights

in "Representing the Northern Lights," an essay for the *catalogue raisonnée* on Richard Prince's 1999 sound sculpture installation called "The Aurora on All Three Channels."

38 This striking Arctic frame for an otherwise southern Canadian, deeply urban story is explained, emotionally, in terms of metaphor, by Poirier's closing description of her daughter as "my northern light." Perhaps Poirier also alludes to Inuit and First Nations myths associating the Northern Lights with the spirits of the dead; if so, the allusion reminds me of Judith Thompson's *Sled*.

39 Much has already been written about cinematic presentations of the Canadian North and about the film's construction of Canada-as-North by Americans; see my comments on the creation of Sergeant Preston and the American image of Canada as a northern wilderness in my Prologue. The most exhaustive historical treatment of Hollywood's creation of a stereotypic North is Pierre Berton's *Hollywood's Canada*; less analysis has been given to Canadian-made films or to joint productions from the 1970s, 1980s, and 1990s, but see Balicki, Norris, and Roth, and Ann Fienup-Riordan's *Alaska Eskimos in the Movies*. Because I have already discussed Flaherty's film in detail (see "Exploration as Construction"), here I will focus on its comparisons with Shipman's film. For a general treatment of Canadian film, see Peter Morris's *Embattled Shadows*.

40 Much of the Shipman film was shot in California, but the Arctic scenes were shot outdoors in northern Alberta (with disastrous consequences for the first leading man, who died of pneumonia), and the film discourse (its action, images, editing, etc) constructs "god's country" as an extension of the far North.

41 *Never Cry Wolf*, a Walt Disney production directed by Carroll Ballard, is based upon Farley Mowat's 1963 autobiographical novel of the same name. This fact is important for the construction of the film's hero, Tyler (played by Charles Martin Smith), who looks like a younger Farley Mowat and also, through the film, instals "Mowat" as a northern hero in the discursive formation of North. However, the film adds elements and characters to the story that are not part of Mowat's text, the most significant addition

being Rosie, the bush pilot, who represents the corrupt whites, with exploitative southern attitudes and a lust for technology, who defile the North.

42 The phrase "romance the North" is borrowed from Lorna Roth. In "(De) Romancing the North" she offers a thoughtful critique of film representations of Inuit and other northern peoples. She comments on *Nanook of the North* and on several NFB documentaries, but she does not look at *Never Cry Wolf*. It should be noted that the documentary representation of Inuit and Dene are not all anachronistic; films like *Nuhoniyeh: Our Story*, aired on CBC television in May 1996, present a sensitive, three-dimensional portrayal of northerners; see Christopher Harris.

43 I would like to thank Peter Harcourt for bringing this film to my attention by screening it at a conference in August 1999 and for discussing its differences from standard NFB work. As Harcourt also noted, the contrasts between *Amarok's Song* and *Between Two Worlds*, which does attempt to explore the damage caused the Inuit by the encounter with southern, white culture, are also striking and worth separate study.

44 I have based this quotation on my transcription of the voice-over in the film; however, certain phrases also appear in Urquhart (47) and Oxtoby (39).

CHAPTER FIVE:
FICTIONS OF NORTH

1 For many reasons and after much deliberation, I have decided not to devote a chapter or section exclusively to poetry. This does not mean that Canadian poets have not written about North or contributed to its discursive formation and representation – to the contrary! Specific examples of lyric poems, narrative poems, series of poems, and long poems are easy to find, from powerful nineteenth-century pieces like Charles Shanly's "The Walker of the Snow" and rather vague, generalized *winter* poems like Kipling's "Our Lady of the Snows" (1897) or Machar's *Lays of the 'True North'* (1899) to well-crafted poems like Archibald Lampman's "Temagami" (1896) and influential and popular turn-of-the-century poems such as Robert Service's volume *Songs of a Sourdough*

(1907), which has never been out of print. A tradition of twentieth-century poetry that either draws on northern imagery or explores northern subjects is very strong and includes work by major modernist poets like D.C. Scott, A.J.M. Smith, F.R. Scott, Dorothy Livesay, and Earle Birney, and contemporary poets like Beissel, Lane, Purdy, MacEwen, Atwood, Gutteridge, Kroetsch, Newlove, Yates, Drummond, Farmiloe, Flood, Gom, Hume, Pickthall, Precosky, Ruffo, and Margaret Thompson. To this list must be added the many collections of Inuit songs, which are often called poems; see Rasmussen, Petrone, and Lowenstein. For critical discussions of poetry about the North, see Dickinson, Djwa, Grace, and MacLaren (1992 and 1996).

2 I have made efforts in this direction with articles about Franklin, and on Atwood and Kroetsch; see also *Inventing Tom Thomson*. John Moss has collected several essays on Arctic narrative in *Echoing Silence*.

3 Among studies of the Canadian novel in English that explore questions of national identity, those by Dickinson, Davey, Moss, McGregor, and New (1997) are particularly interesting.

4 For an interdisciplinary discussion of the "construction of Canada," see *Painting the Maple*, ed. Strong-Boag *et al.*; the essays by Chalykoff and Verduyn address the novel as a site of such construction.

5 For a detailed discussion of Taché and of other French-Canadian proselytizers of French Catholic identity and *rayonnement* into *le grand Nord*, see Warwick and Morissonneau.

6 Quoted by Guy Lecomte in "L'Appel de la forêt et l'appel du Nord: Mythes et réalités" (94), where Lecomte discusses the impact of ideas of North for French Canadians as they were promulgated by writers like Buies, Father Labelle (as early as 1880), Félix-Antoine Savard, and Georges Bugnet. For all these men true French Canadian, Catholic identity could flourish, protected, in *le grand Nord*, where francophones would be free of southern, English Canadian, and American influence.

7 On his return south up the Athabaska River, Seton's canoe capsizes and he panics at the thought that his precious journals and

drawings will be lost; see pages 292–3. The genuine horror and despair he evokes are recaptured by Roy in a similar scene in *La Montagne secrète*; my discussion of Roy's novel and this scene follows.

8 Cooper was American and had his own economic agenda in this book. During the twenties, 1926–27 to be precise, John Hornby was starving to death on the Barrens with his two companions, Edgar Christian and Harold Adlard, and several men would die on Stefansson's Canadian expedition.

9 The unnamed editors of the 1965 edition, in a preface reprinted in the 1980 edition, insist that the book is *about* "Eskimos" and that Malinowski praised it as a book about primitive people, written as these things should be written. Poncins himself never makes this mistake; in comment after comment he explains that he is learning about himself. *Kabloona* has had a remarkable "trickle-down" effect, showing up as an influence on Leonard Peterson's play *The Great Hunger*, where the plot-line is taken from de Poncins, and appearing in the references of most post-1941 studies of the North.

10 The limitations of Berton's appreciation of cultural plurality in the North have been critiqued by Lorna Roth, who notes that Berton's nine images of "northerners" identify them by profession, with one exception: the ninth face is identified as "Eskimo" (see Roth, 39–41). Mowat, too, has been criticized for pronouncing on matters he does not fully understand; his nickname, fondly pronounced by those who know him, is "hardly-know-it," and yet, in contrast with Berton, Mowat has frequently criticized Canada for doing less for the Inuit than does Greenland, and he has written extensively and critically about their treatment by Ottawa.

11 Over the past several years I have reviewed, on average, six non-fiction books annually for various journals; many other publications have been reviewed by other readers. The range of these publications is itself quite impressive – from exhaustively researched academic and scientific works to popular studies, memoirs, letters, biographies, collections of essays, photography, travel, a wide range of art books, and documentaries on CD-ROM. Many of these titles are provided

in the Bibliography, but a few comments are called for here. Two massive historical collections have appeared, *Tales of the Canadian North* (1984) and *The Great North* (1990), which include essays and short fiction culled from magazines, roughly between the 1880s and the 1940s (dates and sources are not always given), and demonstrate the marketing and representation of Canada by both Americans and Canadians as synonymous with a vaguely defined northern wilderness. The period 1970 to 1999 marks the beginning of publication, in English, of work by the Dene, the northern Cree, the Innu, and the Inuit; often these are in the form of collections, and they are usually edited by non-natives, but these peoples are speaking in their own voices (see chap. 6 for my discussion of this material). This period has also seen the massive popularization of the Group of Seven as *the* Canadian art force in everything from major exhibitions to coffee mugs, jewelry, place mats, calendars, videos, CD-ROMs and Web sites, and the publication of art books that focus on the North. A few examples of this phenomenon are Callaghan and de Visser's *Winter* (1974), William Kurelek's *The Last of the Arctic* (1976) and *A Northern Nativity* (1976), Jackson's *A.Y. Jackson: The Arctic 1927* (1982), Toni Onley's *Onley's Arctic* (1989), René Richard's *Ma vie passée* (1990), Peter Pitseolak's *People from Our Side* (1993), and Dorothy Eber's *Images of Justice* (1997).

12 Although I have listed them together here, there are interesting differences as well as commonalities among men's and women's representations of self and North in their autobiographies. I have examined some of these, as well as other autobiographies not mentioned here, in "A Woman's Way."

13 There are many illustrated books for young children that use northern imagery, storylines, and settings; see, for example, work by Cleaver, Kurelek, Kusugak, Munsch, Owens, Tessier, and Wynne-Jones and Beddoes.

14 See Phillips' article by this title. I have explored aspects of gender in "Gendering Northern Narrative," but I think the masculine/feminine binary is especially clear in *Zoom Away* by Wynne-Jones and Beddoes.

15 This novel has an unusual plot: its teenaged hero runs away from home and meets a

bizarre, reclusive pianist/composer who is staying in an isolated cabin on a northern lake in order to work. When this strange man returns to Toronto, where he lives (and dies), the boy thinks he may be the man's natural son. However, the cabin is destroyed, along with the great work of the "maestro," and the boy eventually accepts the truth and returns to his family. It is hard not to see some elements of Glenn Gould in the creation of the maestro figure.

16 The only Helen on the actual expedition was an Inuuk child, the daughter of Kiruk; see Hunt, 76. And for a different interpretation, as well as a confirmation, of events aboard the *Karluk*, see Hunt, 71–88.

17 In *Imperial Leather* Anne McClintock examines this concept of "anachronistic space" and its function within colonizing and commodifying regimes of power; see 40–2. In so far as North has been represented as an "anachronistic space," it has come to signify a place of colonization and commodification *within* the nation-state.

18 During the research on Tom Thomson, I quickly discovered that he has attracted so much attention from biographers, novelists, poets, playwrights, and visual artists that I would have to treat him separately; see *Inventing Tom Thomson*.

19 The subject of cannibalism, as it relates to North and as a trope, is treated briefly in chap. 6. To a degree Wiebe is recuperating, by contextualizing, Michel Terohaute's posthumous reputation; he shows that the extremity to which the men were driven leaves them little choice for survival but to eat human flesh, and he has one of his white characters, John Hepburn, comment quite brutally upon the practice among British seamen of resorting to the eating of "long-pig" (*Discovery*, 286–93).

20 Wiebe has faced a major challenge in this portrayal and representation of Greenstockings. First of all, we know almost nothing about her except what survives in passing references (usually sexist and racist) in British explorer narratives and in the one visual image made by Hood. Second, Wiebe's sexualization of her in both *Discovery* and *Playing Dead* runs the real risk of replicating negative stereotypes of women generally and of native women in particular. Third, his

conflation of her, through symbolism and imagery, with the land itself (mother earth and mother country) once again invites the kind of reductive and controlling association of the feminine with physical matter that lies at the heart of Western concepts of the subject, which are fundamentally binary and hierarchical and privilege mind over body, spirit over matter, and male over female. While I recognize these problems in his representation of Greenstockings (as I am certain he does himself), I would argue that his desire to tell and honour a narrative of Canada that not only includes but is founded upon a female native figure is both a powerful renegotiation of typical colonialist explorer narratives and a sincere attempt to celebrate what he believes to be the uncelebrated and forgotten foundations of our so-called new world.

21 Kroetsch's conflation of Woman with North is a familiar trope, but what he does with the concept is very interesting. For example, in the poem "F.P. Grove: The Finding" the woman (Grove's wife) is there waiting in/as the North, the place for which he is heading and the haven that he reaches. However, in "Poem of Albert Johnson," where there is no woman to represent and mitigate North, Kroetsch (and Johnson, as Kroetsch sees him) refuses the encounter with this Other and, thus, with story. In "Why I Went North" Kroetsch is explicit: he does not want to write Johnson's story because "he was the death of the author" (31). And Kroetsch turns away from Johnson immediately to describe his first sexual encounter, with a Métis woman of the North (32–5), and this encounter leads him to "a new story" (35).

22 This description of the kid who would become Kroetsch's Peek is from the first verse of the poem: "A bunch of the boys were whooping it up in the Malamute saloon; / The boy that handles the music-box was hitting a jag-time tune" (*Songs of a Sourdough*, 52).

23 To a feminist critique that described Kroetsch's Lou as another sexist identification of woman with earth and with story, both of which must be mined (penetrated, forced, raped) by the creative will of the male miner/writer/story-teller, I can only say: yes, I agree. And yet, relatively speaking,

Kroetsch has represented his Woman, like his North, as active, powerful, proud, and precious, which is a long way from the Lou of Service's poem or from the still-popular idea that the women who went to the Klondike were worthless creatures, there to mine the miners – whores with (or without) hearts of gold.

24 For a feminist discussion of these issues, see Benstock, de Lauretis, McClintock, and Sidonie Smith.

25 In fairness, I should note that Atwood ends *Strange Things* on the serious note of conservation. She concludes by warning us about the ozone layer, pollution, exploitation, and the fragility of the North. Imagery and symbolism, she notes, are based on reality, and the destruction of that reality – here, the North – will leave humanity bereft of one of the great sources of story: "The things that are killing the North will kill, if left unchecked, everything else" (116).

26 In the title essay to her collection *In Visible Ink* van Herk speaks of her experience on Ellesmere as being "invisibled" (8). She goes on to describe her sense of self as "glass," "fragile," "a tracement of arctic essence" (8); she has been found by the North and occupied, disrupted (9), and "freed from words" to take a "different" story south (11).

27 My reference is to Service's poem "The Law of the Yukon," where the Yukon is represented as a vengeful female who speaks in the first person and warns that she will destroy weaklings but welcome "the men of my mettle," who can conquer, develop, and civilize her by "scaling my ramparts of snow," "Ripping the guts of my mountains, looting the beds of my creeks" (*Songs of a Sourdough*, 16).

28 The human threads in the story include Hearne, Hornby, Boas, Minik (and the other Inuit with him and with Peary), Michael Snow, Thompson, Wieland, Gould, Marie Prevost, Cook, Harris, Carr, Hudson, McLuhan, Seton, G.D. Roberts, Flaherty and "Nanook," P.K. Page, McClintock, Hall, Hannah, Thierry Mallet, Innis, Pitseolak, Pegi Nicol Macleod, David Milne, John Drainie, Teresa Stratas, and more, most of them Canadians, many of them sojourners in New York.

29 Among some of the more important aspects of this novel that I cannot address here are its parody of Canada's leading liquor barons, the Bronfmans, his portrait of Jewish Canadian culture, his savage satire of Canadian literature (notably of A.M. Klein) and Canadian art, and his precise evocation of the Eastern Townships, Montreal, and Winnipeg during Prohibition.

30 Richler finds room to mention Back and Greenstockings, the Hudson's Bay Company, voyageurs, and many other bits of northern lore; the only name I could not find was Hornby's. For Richler's description of Yellowknife, see "North of Sixty."

31 Reid's carving, housed in the Museum of Anthropology at the University of British Columbia, depicts the Haida creation story in which Raven, the trickster, finds a huge clam shell on the beach and, noticing tiny creatures inside, coaxes them to come out and play. However, he finds only timid, male creatures in the shell and grows tired of playing with them. His next attempt at meddling produces little male and female creatures, who are much more interesting, even though they do not have glossy black feathers and cannot fly. These creatures are the progenitors of the Haida Nation, and Raven continues today to enjoy the game of life he started with them so long ago. The Yukon First Nations, Dene, and the Inuit also have stories about Raven the trickster; see *Solomon Gursky*, 42–3.

32 There are several important paintings with interesting intertextual roles to play in this novel. One is the portrait of Diana McClure, which Solomon will steal and Kaplansky will hoard in his cellar, where it waits for Moses to discover it. Diana, it should be noted, is not only the great love in Solomon's life but also a woman with one brown and one blue eye – just like the baby girl Greenstockings holds in *A Discovery of Strangers*. Another intertextual painting is Dov HaGibor's *Gloriana* (489), a complex Richler spoof on postmodern art and on some of the minor characters and themes of his own story.

33 For a discussion of this trip and the unedited *Voyage en Ungava*, see Gagné, in particular part 3 of his long article (published in *Revue de l'Université d'Ottawa* 46.3 [1976]: 364–90). Gagné provides substantial quotation from

Roy's text and comments on the influence of this trip upon *La Rivière sans repos*. The full text, with editorial notes, has been published in *Gabrielle Roy: Le Pays de "Bonheur d'occasion" et autres écrits autobiographiques épars et inédits*; see Ricard and Marcotte. It is clear that Roy had long been fascinated by the Arctic and that she had read de Poncins.

34 I will not consider *The Cashier* here, but Alexandre's one break for freedom and peace is the trip he takes to a Laurentian lake north of Montreal. Roy herself often fled the city to Rawdon, one of her special havens just north of Montreal, in order to find the space she needed to write. The name Cadorai is of Breton origin, and Roy may have chosen it for its association with a Saskatchewan family called Cadorais (see Ricard, 358). She may also have chosen the name for its link with a Quebec boat-building company called Cadorette. Whatever the spelling (Cadorai, Cadorais, Cadoret – the name of a settler, Georges Cadoret, who came from Bretagne in 1657), the name is pronounced Cadoré, with the obvious echo of golden. I am grateful to Antoine Sirois for this information. The name also incorporates Roy's childhood nickname, "Cad"; see Shek, 38.

35 The original French publication of the novel included three short stories about the Inuit, "The Telephone," "The Satellite," and "The Wheelchair." Each of these moving stories depicts the Inuit struggle to deal with white technology and its impact on their lives. Of all Roy's fiction, *Windflower* received the coolest reception, and Roy's American publisher rejected it (Ricard, 1999, 413, 428). In my view this novel – simple and direct, even bare in its basic plot – was ahead of its time in its frank portrayal of cultural encounter and loss. Although the American soldier is barely described and is not presented as a violent predator, he represents the South and its incursions into a fragile world order, and that South (whether Canadian or American) brings little of any real value to the Inuit in this novel.

36 The initial critical reception of this novel was qualified, even negative (see Ricard, 1999, 408–9). The key exception and earliest appreciation of the novel's strengths was Antoine Sirois's first study. Gradually, however, and with time for critical reflection, the novel has attracted as much serious attention as any of Roy's texts; see, for example, Amprimoz, Bessette, Brochu, Lacombe, Malette, Morency, Morissonneau, Ricard, and Sirois. The novel bears the dedication, in its original French and in the English translation: "à R.R., peintre, trappeur, fervent du Grand Nord, dont les beaux récits me firent connaître le Mackenzie et l'Ungava." It is now generally accepted that *The Hidden Mountain* closely follows many of the events in the life of Canadian painter René Richard and that it also dramatizes many aspects of Roy's own personal and aesthetic concerns. That said, it would be a mistake to insist upon a tight equation of Pierre with either Richard or Roy; indeed, the factual differences, which highlight the fictional choices made by Roy, are as interesting as the similarities, and perhaps more revealing of her purposes.

37 Without wishing to stress the obvious, I should note that the feminine gender of the French *la rivière* ascribes an erotic/sexualized quality to this description that will only intensify as the scene unfolds: Pierre will be saved from death in the yawning jaws of this female natural force by the phallic tree.

38 Although this is his most dramatic and terrifying near-disaster on a river, Pierre loses his work to rivers on other occasions as well; see 78–80.

39 Judging from Roy's representation of this hunt, she was horrified by the entire process, whereas René Richard, on whose story this hunt is based, enjoyed hunting; see Lacombe. See also Roy's story "La Légende du cerf ancien," where the wanton killing of an animal provokes a transformation in a hunter. My thanks to Antoine Sirois for bringing this story to my attention. Roy's decision to stress this hunt and to link it with the mountain may owe something to her knowledge of the Innu and Labrador Inuit myth of a mountain in Ungava sacred to the caribou; see Speck, 82–7.

40 As François Ricard makes unequivocally clear (410–11), Roy avoided overt politics as much as possible, but she always remained a staunch Canadian nationalist and deplored the polarization and hostility she saw surfacing during the Quiet Revolution. Her

position may even have contributed to the very qualified and lukewarm reception her work received from Québécois critics in the 1960s; see Ricard, 408–9.

41 In this short story from *Wilderness Tips* Atwood combines a remembered tragedy and mystery from her character's childhood with an evocation of the landscapes of Algonquin Park, both as the young campers discover it and as the Group of Seven painted it; in effect, the reader is pulled into an unsolved mystery, the answer to which lies hidden in the paintings on the wall of a downtown Toronto apartment.

42 Scholars of Roy's work and life agree about the crucial importance of Mélina Roy to Gabrielle's writing (see Ricard, *inter alia*). To my knowledge, no one has gone so far as to claim that the land, or country of Canada, as celebrated in *The Hidden Mountain*, symbolizes the Mother as Mother country; however, I believe that this reading is well supported by the text itself, by Roy's family history, by the recurring significance of mothers in her work, *especially* in the northern novels, and by Roy's well-known federalist views. She was never a political writer, but she endorsed the idea of a multi-ethnic Canada, stretching from sea to sea to sea (Ricard, 214–16, 410). Moreover, there is enough evidence in the fiction and the biography to suggest that a feminist, Freudian (or modified Lacanian) approach to Roy would confirm the significance of the symbolic Mother.

CHAPTER SIX:
WRITING, RE-WRITING, AND WRITING BACK

1 For more information about this story, its variations, connections with the core Inuit myth of Sedna, and its multiple interpretations, see McGrath's "The European in Inuit Literature," and for particular focus on how Indians came into existence and why they became traditional enemies of the Inuit, see Igjugarjuk's account in Rasmussen (89–90) and Qaqortingneq's in Petrone (29–31).

2 For contemporary discussions, see Blondin, Colombo, Cruikshank, Gedalof, King, Petrone, and Ray and Stevens. Just as creation stories are central to the cosmologies of all native cultures (not just the

northern Canadian groups under discussion here), so stories of cannibals and cannibalism are widespread; in the Canadian context, see McDowell, and in the broader context, see Barker *et al.*

3 Throughout this chapter I use the term Inuit. However, this term is the designation of choice for the people of Nunavut; the Inuvialuit of the Western Arctic still use the term Eskimo. It is generally accepted that this term, commonly used by Europeans and Euro-Canadians and -Americans, derives from the Cree *escee* (meaning sickening) and *mau* (meaning human or person), and alludes to the Inuit as eaters of raw meat (Freeman, *Life among the Qallunaat*, 88). As such, it carries pejorative connotations; see the *Nunavut Handbook*, 365.

4 All words in indigenous languages appear without italics; they are not foreign. In the context of this chapter, English is the foreign language. Because of orthographic variations commonly found in the spellings of indigenous names and words, I have relied on the spelling given in the *Nunavut Handbook* or in the source texts cited. My spellings of Windigo and Wee-sa-kay-jac are from Ray and Stevens, but spellings vary widely.

5 Analysis of cbc's coverage is beyond my scope, but a few impressions can be noted in passing. Although the main language in use was Inuktitut, it was barely audible under the interpreter's voice-over and only surfaced in gaps in the translation. I found the bifurcation simultaneously fascinating (when has Inuktitut been heard before on southern cbc?) and dissonant; an odd disjunction emerged in the story of the changing Canadian constitution. Although the new legislature is Inuit, the forms, symbols, and rituals of power (the mace, seating plan, use of flags, etc) and constitution are borrowed and adapted from Canadian (and thus British) parliamentary protocols and policies. The resulting Nunavut narrative represented on television is thereby rendered safe and familiar, even boring.

6 I have taken these statistics from "Nunavut: Up and Running" by Dane Lanken and Mary Vincent, in the special Nunavut issue of *Canadian Geographic* 119.1 (1999); other sources quote different statistics, but I have

found this article to be generally sound and balanced. *Up Here* devoted its April 1999 issue to Nunavut, and a stream of articles has appeared in the *Globe and Mail*. Many of the latter are critical and/or condescending and focus on suicide rates, substance abuse, crime, and poverty. The impression left by these pieces is negative and one-sided: the citizens of Nunavut have created dreadful social problems and a population explosion; the new territory contributes nothing to Canada but will be a huge drain on the public (that is, southern, non-Inuit) purse; and Nunavut is a mistake that will fail. See Anderssen, Lagji, and Simpson.

7 A 1995 CD like *Nunavik Concert*, produced by Sunshine Records in Winnipeg, brings the Inuit musicians who performed in Inukjuak, Nunavik, on 5 Aug. 1993 into quasi-permanent circulation for listeners, very few of whom could have attended the live concert. In so far as these singers use some English, as do Alfred and Aglukark, they make their work accessible to a non-native audience. Edited books are an increasingly important source of northern material, and I discuss some of these below; see, for example, Gedalof, Petrone, *Staging the North*, ed. Grace *et al.*, which contains *Sixty Below* and two Tunooniq plays, and *Writing North*, ed. Friis-Baastad and Robertson.

8 Three of McGrath's articles to date are particularly helpful in explaining what is lost, not only in translation but also in the Englishing of the prose and in the sanitizing of material, either by altering or by excluding it. In "Monster Figures and Unhappy Endings," she describes the role of monsters, cannibals, trolls, murder, and suicide in Inuit literature. In "Editing Inuit Literature" she discusses Markoosie's *Harpoon of the Hunter* as an example of some of the pitfalls faced by contemporary Inuit writers working in English and relying on non-Inuit editors. Finally, in her chapter for *The Native in Literature* she stresses the importance of oral traditions to contemporary Inuit writing and the hybridity of such non-fictional forms as autobiography.

9 I am not including a wider range of journals and books, which are often produced as *catalogues raisonnés*, by art historians because,

while they no doubt contribute to the discursive formation of North, they focus on the sculpture or prints as art within or in relation to a Western tradition. Debates about the issues raised by the creation of an Inuit art history and art market are complex, but I cannot digress to consider them here.

10 Flaherty collected these pieces during his early geological surveying in the Hudson Bay area, and they were given to the Royal Ontario Museum in 1914 by Sir William Mackenzie, Flaherty's employer. The Varley drawings and paintings (four in full colour) represent the landscape and the people; his sketches of Inuit faces and clothing are the only images of the people in the book. Carpenter, an anthropologist and colleague of Marshall McLuhan's at the University of Toronto in the 1950s, had lived with and studied the Aiviluk. See also Flaherty's *The Captain's Chair* for his publication of "The Story of Comock," which he presents within quotations as if Comock were speaking (139–50).

11 I would like to thank Aurèle Parisien of McGill-Queen's Press for allowing me to read *Saqiyuq* in page proof so that I might consider it briefly here. For a theoretical discussion of Yukon First Nations autobiography, see Cruikshank's *Life Lived Like A Story*, and for a discussion of Inuit autobiography, see McGrath's "Circumventing the Taboos." *It's Like the Legend: Innu Women's Voices* (2000) is the most recent example of such antiobiography of which I am aware.

12 Partial explanation is provided on the dust-jacket and in letters to Mrs Molson, included at the end, in which Tetso mentions his stories being "collected in a book" (111) that appeared in 1964 and overlaps with *Trapping Is My Life*.

13 Eber is scrupulous, however, about describing her role and the collaborative creation of the text, both in the introduction to the first edition in 1975 and in the preface to the 1993 reprint.

14 Comparable appreciations of change are apparent in texts I am not examining, such as Armand Tagoona's *Shadows*, narratives by Margaret Baikie and Elizabeth Goudie (see Blake), and the Labradorian lives represented by installation artist Marlene Creates.

15 While I hesitate to speculate further on this question on the basis of impressions, I do not think it is an error to say that Indians generally have been demonized by the dominant settler culture, from the period of first contact, when many resisted the invaders, to the present, when they fight for land claims by insisting upon an oral history or, as with Oka, when they take up arms. When they have not been demonized (in history, movies, paintings), they have been romanticized as noble savages, or as innocents about to disappear for good; Indian princess images of Pauline Johnson, the Grey Owl phenomenon, and a character like Rita Joe in George Ryga's play are possible because of this stereotyping. For a contemporary play about Yukon First Nations, which mixes myth and social realism in a hybrid structure, see Flather and Linklater, *Sixty Below*.

16 Iqaluit is the capital of Nunavut, but prior to the 1940s the site was used by generations of Inuit, and before them by Thule and Dorset, as a prime seasonal hunting-place. The Canadian government officially named the place Frobisher Bay, after allowing the United States Air Force to build an airstrip there in 1942. The name they chose honours Martin Frobisher, a British explorer/pirate, who landed there in 1576. It would scarcely be an exaggeration to call Frobisher a violent, greedy fool and the choice of name an odd one. He fought with local Inuit, captured four of them to display in England (they died there), and scooped up tons of what turned out to be fool's gold.

17 Gale describes *Atanarjuat: The Fast Runner*, directed by Zacharius Kunuk, as an overt celebration of the ideology informing Nunavut (62), and this film, as well as other projects for television or video, are examples of re-writing or writing back. I did not see this film until October 2001; thus I have not been able to discuss it; see Purvis. Alia's research indicates that despite the electronic sophistication of northern communications such as TVNC (the "world's largest aboriginal television network," 103) and the recent development of Web sites (see Alia's Appendix E), the Norths (provincial and territorial) still see radio as their primary medium of communication (89).

18 I have discussed Woodman and the Franklin stories in "Re-inventing Franklin" and in my review of Woodman's book, "Multiple Discoveries." Qaqortingneq's description of the Franklin disaster was first published by Rasmussen in *Across Arctic America* (239–40), then reprinted by Petrone (31–2), and quoted by Gwendolyn MacEwen in *Terror and Erebus*, where it continues to live another kind of re-scripted life.

19 In a brief summary I cannot do justice to the scope of this volume or its visual beauty, let alone assess the impact it might have on ideas of North among southern Canadians, who do not see the same sky. MacDonald's text is scrupulously documented with respect to sources, orthography, and cultural context, and he stresses, among other things, the importance of Inuit place-names and the rapid erosion of astronomical knowledge in recent decades.

20 In his foreword James McNeill introduces Markoosie, a pilot living in Resolute, and explains the genesis of the story. However, he does not describe the degree to which he edited Markoosie's translation in order "to commit these stories to writing in such a way that they could become part of the world's popular literature" (6).

21 *Inuit Monthly* changed its name to *Inuit Today* in 1975, and Ipellie's cartoon strip continued until 1982. He has also created the current comic strip called *Nuna & Vut* for the Iqaluit daily *Nunatsiaq News*. Ipellie, who was born on Baffin Island to a semi-nomadic hunting family, was educated in Iqaluit, Yellowknife, and Ottawa, where he now lives and works as a writer, columnist, and artist.

22 In "DissemiNation" Homi K. Bhabha describes the intervention of minority discourse in the culture of a nation as supplementarity: "The supplementary strategy interrupts the successive seriality of the narrative plurals and pluralism by radically changing their mode of articulation" (305). The power of supplementarity that facilitates the emergence of minority discourse within the dominant discourse is not so much a negation of received history but "the renegotiation of those times, terms, and traditions through which we turn our uncertain, passing contemporaneity into

the signs of history" (306). Ipellie is performing precisely this type of "renegotiation."

23 *Never without Consent*, prepared by the Grand Council of the Crees, is itself an act of writing back in forceful political rhetoric. In this book the Cree analyse the James Bay Hydroelectric Project in the context of Quebec's move for separation, and they make their own independent stand. Among the photographs, which they include as overt propaganda, is one showing the Cree and Inuit of Nunavik demonstrating on the Hudson River with New York City in the background. The native perspective on the James Bay projects and process has also been documented in the 1994 NFB documentary *Amisk* and in the 1996 film *Power*. For an earlier but very interesting and dialogic treatment of the James Bay development struggle, see Boyce Richardson's *Strangers Devour the Land*. See also Clerici and Illus. 29.

24 Although I cannot pursue the autobiographical and biographical aspects of this novel in any detail, Highway has been clear about the fact that his narrative is closely based on his life and on that of his younger brother, René, who died of AIDS-related complications in the early 1990s. The character of Jeremiah represents Thomson (his birth, his training as a concert pianist, his social work with native people, and his turn to writing), and Gabriel represents René in his successful career as a ballet dancer, his sexual abuse and promiscuity, and his early death. The sexual abuse by Oblate priests suffered by both characters, Highway declares, happened in life, and it damaged his and his brother's lives. This story, he says, should not only be told but should be headlines until Canadians understand what happened to a generation of native children (see Posner). *Kiss of the Fur Queen* is dedicated to his brother.

25 In inteviews Highway has said that he needed the money that a successful novel (unlike a play) would bring, and he has described the gruelling effort required to produce his own plays by establishing the Native Earth Performing Arts Company in Toronto. However, it would be a mistake to leave his choice of medium at that. Since the successful productions and publications of his plays, *The Rez Sisters* (1986) and *Dry Lips Oughta Move to Kapuskasing* (1989), Highway

has experienced personal tragedy, and the novel form is the most flexible and accessible mode for managing and directing his rage and grief. Highway has been interviewed on CBC television; see also Posner and Mandel.

26 The trickster, whom Highway calls "Weesageechak" (Cree) or "Nanabush" (Ojibwa), has a central role in his plays as well as in this novel, and Highway always includes an explanatory note on this important figure. In the *Fur Queen* he tells us that "Weesageechak" has no gender or "is both simultaneously," and he asserts his belief that "she/he is still here among us" because, without this figure, "the core of Indian culture would be gone forever."

27 As with so much in this complex text, I cannot linger over the evolving associations of white and black created through imagery and symbol, but it is through moments like this, and through the verbal echoes he sets up, that Highway links the priests (black robes) and their rape of the boys with black, and the spirit world of the Cree with white – white fur, white Stanfield's, white snow, and so on. This troping on white/black reverses the southern construction of white as good because it is racially and culturally superior, and dark (or black) as evil because it is Other. Here the notion of the great white North is Cree.

28 In a classical composition the tempo *adagio* indicates slow but also thoughtful, contemplative, possibly serene. *Adagio espressivo* suggests a performance (for the reader, as for Jeremiah) that is especially slow and thoughtful; see n 30.

29 The story of Chachagathoo is delivered in fragments over the course of the narrative, as if to suggest that her power (erased by the strategic misogyny of Catholicism) can only be glimpsed and recovered very gradually; see *Kiss of the Fur Queen*, 90–1, 245–7. Highway has said that he believes change is possible because "the male god is totally dysfunctional. The goddess is coming back" (Posner, c5). For a version of the legend of Ayash, see "The Plight of Iyas" in Ray and Stevens, 112–20.

30 Each of the six parts is separate and carries an Italian tempo instruction for performing classical music, thus: "*Allegro ma non troppo*,"

"*Andante cantabile*," "*Allegretto grazioso*," "*Molto agitato*," "*Adagio espressivo*," and "*Presto con fuoco*." If I call these instructions enigmatic, it is because they are surprising in this otherwise Cree-English text and because I have not come fully to terms with what they are doing there. Trained as a classical pianist, Highway has chosen these terms with care, and they warrant further attention. Because Jeremiah, Highway's fictional counterpart, is also a trained pianist and then a writer, it is possible that *Fur Queen* can be read as his composition, a sonata, say, for orchestra, or a concerto, in which the classical four or five parts have been extended, through writing back, to six.

31 The story of weasel and the Windigo has variations (see Ray and Stevens, 31–2), and there are many stories among the northern Cree and Dene about how Windigos have attacked or been destroyed; see Colombo, Ray and Stevens (122–8), and Blondin (76–8).

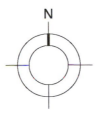

N

AN INTERDISCIPLINARY BIBLIOGRAPHY

This interdisciplinary bibliography includes both items cited in the book and works consulted. While I cannot claim to have created a definitive bibliography on the Canadian North, I have consulted a wide range of primary and secondary materials across several disciplines; by including all the items I have consulted, I hope to illustrate the vast range of materials available to scholars and to provide them with an interdisciplinary bibliography on the subject. No on-line or card-catalogue search will call up works across the disciplines; only persistent sleuthing will cut across library classification by discipline. Print materials are listed alphabetically by author (or title when an author is not given), without sub-divisions into genres or disciplines; music and film, video and CD-ROM have their own sections. Once again, it is a pleasure to thank Lisa Chalykoff for her patient and meticulous care in helping me to find materials and prepare this bibliography.

PRINT

Abel, Kerry. "Of Two Minds: Dene Response to the Mackenzie Missions, 1858–1902." In Coates and Morrison, eds., *Interpreting Canada's North*. 77–93.

Adams, Amy. "Arctic and Inuit Photography." *Inuit Art Quarterly* 15.2, 15.3, 15.4 (2000): 4–16, 4–19, 4–11.

Adams, Philip. "Why Theatre, Lawrd?" *Theatre Memoirs*. Toronto: Playwrights Union of Canada 1998. 43–7.

– *Free's Point*. In Grace, D'Aeth, and Chalykoff, eds., *Staging the North*. 237–78.

Adams, Stephen. *R. Murray Schafer*. Toronto: University of Toronto Press, 1983.

Adney, E. Tappan. *The Klondike Stampede*. 1900. Introduced by Ken Coates. Vancouver: University of British Columbia Press 1994.

"A Frightful Place To Die." *Prime Time News*. CBC Toronto, 14 Sept. 1994.

Alia, Valerie. "Another Look at Nanook." *Up Here: Life in Canada's North* (Aug.–Sept. 1987): 63–4.

– *Names, Numbers, and Northern Policy: Inuit, Project Surname, and the Politics of Identity*. Halifax: Fernwood 1994.

– *Un/Covering the North: News, Media, and Aboriginal People*. Vancouver: University of British Columbia Press, 1999.

Ames, Michael M. *Cannibal Tours and Glass Boxes: The Anthropology of Museums*. 2nd rev. ed. Vancouver: University of British Columbia Press 1992.

Amigoni, David. *Victorian Biography: Intellectuals and the Ordering of Discourse*. New York: Harvester Wheatsheaf 1993.

Amprimoz, Alexandre L. "L'Homme-arbre de *La Montagne secrète*." *Canadian Literature* 88 (Spring 1981): 166–71.

Anderson, Benedict. *Imagined Communities: Reflections on the Origin and Spread of Nationalism*. Rev. ed. London: Verso 1991.

Anderson, Frank W. *The Death of Albert Johnson, Mad Trapper of Rat River*. Surrey, BC: Heritage 1986.

Anderson, Joan, Sherrill Grace, Gabriele Helms, Patricia Rodney, and Matt James. "Women Speaking: *Heather Rose* and the Culture of Health Care." In *Northern Parallels: 4th Circumpolar Universities Cooperation Conference Proceedings*, ed. Shauna McLarnon and Douglas Nord. Prince George: University of Northern British Columbia Press 1997. 84–101.

Anderson, Patrick. "Poem on Canada." *The White Centre*. Toronto: Ryerson 1946. 29–45.

Anderssen, Erin. "Nunavut to be a Welfare Case." *Globe and Mail*, 5 June 1998, A1ff.

Andrew, Anne Marie [Anami Antane]. "The Government of Mischief." In Byrne and Fouillard, eds., *It's Like the Legend*. 242–4.

Angus, Ian. *A Border Within: National Identity, Cultural Plurality, and Wilderness*. Montreal: McGill-Queen's University Press 1997.

Aquin, Benoit. "Lethal Beauty." *Canadian Geographic* 118.2 (Mar./Apr. 1998): 30–5.

Arctic Images/Images de l'Arctique: The Dawn of Arctic Cartography, Fourth Century to 1822/Débuts de la cartographie de l'Arctique (du IVe siècle à 1822). Ottawa: Public Archives/Archives publiques 1977.

Arctic Images/Images de l'Arctique: The Frontier Photographed, 1860–1911/Photographie de sa frontière (1860–1911). Ottawa: Public Archives/Archives publiques 1977.

Arctic Images/Images de l'Arctique: Pictorial Witnesses, 1819–1854/Témoignages iconographiques (1819–1854). Ottawa: Public Archives/Archives publiques 1977.

Armatage, Kay. "Nell Shipman: A Case of Heroic Femininity." In *Gendering the Nation: Canadian Women's Cinema*, ed. Kay Armitage *et al.* Toronto: University of Toronto Press 1999. 17–38.

Armstrong, John. "A Rec Room Requiem." *C Magazine* (Nov. 97–Jan. 98): 18–22.

Ashcroft, Bill, Gareth Griffiths, and Helen Tiffin. *The Empire Writes Back: Theory and Practice in Post-Colonial Literatures*. London: Routledge 1989.

Ashley, Kathleen, Leigh Gilmore, and Gerald Peters, eds. *Autobiography and Postmodernism*. Amherst: University of Massachusetts Press, 1994.

Atwood, Margaret. *Surfacing*. Toronto: McClelland and Stewart 1972.

– *Survival: A Thematic Guide to Canadian Literature*. Toronto: Anansi 1972,

– "True North." *Saturday Night* (Jan. 1987): 141–8.

– "The Age of Lead" and "Death by Landscape." *Wilderness Tips*. Toronto: McClelland and Stewart 1991. 157–75, 107–29.

– "Concerning Franklin and His Gallant Crew." *Books in Canada* (May 1991): 20–6.

– *Strange Things: The Malevolent North in Canadian Literature*. Oxford: Clarendon 1995.

– "The Labrador Fiasco." In *Turn of the Story: Canadian Short Fiction on the Eve of the Millenium*, ed. Joan Thomas and Heidi Harms. Toronto: Anansi 1999. 1–13.

Babby, Ellen Reisman. *The Play of Language and Spectacle: A Structural Reading of Selected Texts by Gabrielle Roy*. Toronto: ECW, 1985.

Back, George. *Arctic Artist: The Journal and Paintings of George Back, Midshipman with Franklin, 1819–1822*. Ed. C. Stuart Houston. Montreal: McGill-Queen's University Press 1994.

Backhouse, Constance. *Colour-Coded: A Legal History of Racism in Canada, 1900–1950*. Toronto: University of Toronto Press 1999.

Backhouse, Frances. "Women of the Klondike." *The Beaver* 68.6 (Dec. 1988–Jan. 1989): 30–6.

– *Women of the Klondike*. Vancouver: Whitecap 1995.

Bakhtin, M.M. *The Dialogic Imagination: Four Essays*. Ed. Michael Holquist, trans. Michael Holquist and Caryl Emerson. Austin: University of Texas Press 1981.

– "Forms of Time and the Chronotype in the Novel." In Bakhtin, *The Dialogic Imagination*. 84–258.

– *Problems of Dostoevsky's Poetics*. Ed. and trans. Caryl Emerson. Minneapolis: University of Minnesota Press 1984.

– "The Problem of Speech Genres." In Bakhtin, *Speech Genres*. 60–102.

– *Speech Genres and Other Late Essays*. Ed. Caryl Emerson and Michael Holquist, trans. Vern W. McGee. Austin: University of Texas Press 1986.

Balikci, Asen. "Anthropology, Film and the Arctic Peoples: The First Forman Lecture." *Anthropology Today* 5.2 (Apr. 1989): 4–10.

Ballstadt, Carl, ed. *The Search for English-Canadian Literature: An Anthology of Critical Articles from the Nineteenth and Early Twentieth Centuries*. Toronto: University of Toronto Press 1975.

Bannerji, Himani. "Re: Turning the Gaze." In *Beyond Political Correctness: Toward the Inclusive University*, ed. Stephen Richer and Lorna Weir. Toronto: University of Toronto Press 1995. 220–36.

– , ed. *Returning the Gaze: Essays on Racism, Feminism and Politics*. Toronto: Sister Vision 1993.

Banting, F.G. "With the Arctic Patrol." *Canadian Geographical Journal* 1.1 (May 1930): 19–30.

Barbeau, Marius. "Indian Songs of the Northwest." *Canadian Music Journal* 2.1 (Autumn 1957): 16–25.

Barbour, David. *The Landscape: Eight Canadian Photographs/Le Paysage: huit photographes canadiens.* Kleinburg, Ont.: McMichael Canadian Art Collection 1990.

Barker, Francis Duncan, Peter Hulme, and Margaret Duncan Iversen, eds. *Cannibalism and the Colonial World.* Cambridge: Cambridge University Press 1998.

Barnouw, Erik. *Documentary: A History of the Non-Fiction Film.* New York: Oxford University Press 1974.

Barrett, Andrea. *The Voyage of the Narwhal.* New York: Norton 1998.

Barsam, Richard Meran. *The Vision of Robert Flaherty: The Artist as Myth and Filmmaker.* Bloomington: Indiana University Press 1988.

Barthes, Roland. *S/Z.* Trans. Richard Miller. New York: Hill and Wang 1974.

Bastedo, Jamie. *Reaching North: A Celebration of the Subarctic.* Red Deer, Alta.: Red Deer College Press 1997.

Baudrillard, Jean. "The Ecstacy of Communication." *The Anti-Aesthetic: Essays on Postmodern Culture.* Ed. Hal Foster, trans. John Johnson. Port Townsend, Wash.: Bay 1983. 126–34.

– *Simulations.* Trans. Paul Ross, Paul Patton, and Philip Butchman. New York: Semiotext(e) 1983.

– "The Precision of Simulacra." *Simulacra and Simulation.* Trans. Sheila Faria Glaser. Ann Arbor: University of Michigan Press 1995. 1–42.

Bauer, Dale M., and S. Jaret McKinstry, eds. *Feminism, Bakhtin, and the Dialogic.* New York: State University of New York Press 1991.

Beardy, Flora and Robert Coutts, eds. *Voices from Hudson Bay: Cree Stories from York Factory.* Montreal: McGill-Queen's University Press 1996.

Beattie, Owen, and John Geiger. *Frozen in Time: Unlocking the Secrets of the Doomed 1845 Arctic Expedition.* New York: Plume 1987.

– "Frozen in Time." *The Beaver* 68.5 (Oct.-Nov. 1988): 19–27.

– *Buried in Ice.* Mississauga: Random House of Canada 1992.

Beaudry, Nicole. "The Language of Dreams: Songs of the Dene Indians (Canada). *The World of Music* 34.2 (1992): 72–90.

Beaulieu, Maurice. *Il fait clair de glaise.* Montréal: Les Éditions d'Orphée 1958.

The Beaver: Exploring Canada's History 74: 6 (Dec. 1994–Jan. 1995). Special Seventy-fifth Anniversary issue (1920–95).

Beckwith, John. "A Portrait." *Musicanada* 6 (Nov. 1967): 8–9.

Beeby, Dean. *In a Crystal Land: Canadian Explorers in Antarctica.* Toronto: University of Toronto Press 1994.

Behiels, Michael, ed. *Aboriginal Peoples in Canada: Futures and Identities.* Montreal: Association of Canadian Studies 1999.

Beissel, Henry. *Cantos North.* Moonbeam, Ont.: Penumbra, 1982.

– *Inuk and the Sun.* In Grace, D'Aeth, and Chalykoff, eds., *Staging the North.* 49–100.

Belasco, David. "Madame Butterfly: A Tragedy of Japan." *Representative American Plays: From 1767 to the Present Day.* Ed. Arthur Hobson Quinn. 7th ed. New York: Appleton-Century-Crofts 1957. 621–36.

Bell, John. *Guardians of the North: The National Superhero in Canadian Comic-Book Art.* Ottawa: National Archives of Canada and the Minister of Supply and Services Canada 1991.

Bellam, David. *Peter Pitseolak (1902–1973): Inuit Historian of Seekooseelak.* Montreal: Musée McCord, McGill University 1980.

Belyea, Barbara. "Images of Power: Derrida/Foucault/Harley." *Cartographica* 29.2 (1992): 1–9.

Bennett, Donna. "Weathercock: The Directions of Report." *Open Letter* 5.8/9 (Summer/Fall 984): 116–45.

Benson, Eugene, and L.W. Conolly. *English-Canadian Theatre.* Toronto: Oxford University Press 1987.

Benstock, Shari, ed. *The Private Self: Theory and Practice of Women's Autobiographical Writings.* Chapel Hill: University of North Carolina Press 1988.

Bentley, D.M.R. *The Gay] Grey Moose: Essays on the Ecologies and Mythologies of Canadian Poetry, 1690–1990.* Ottawa: University of Ottawa Press 1992.

Berger, Carl. "The True North Strong and Free." In *Nationalism in Canada*, ed. Peter Russell. Toronto: McGraw-Hill 1986. 3–26.

Berger, Thomas R. *et al. The Arctic: Choices for Peace and Security: Proceedings of a Public Inquiry.* West Vancouver: Gordon Soules 1989.

Berton, Laura Beatrice. *I Married the Klondike.* 1954. Toronto: McClelland and Stewart 1961.

Berton, Pierre. *The Mysterious North.* Toronto: McClelland and Stewart 1956.

– *Klondike: The Life and Death of the Last Great Gold Rush.* Toronto: McClelland and Stewart 1958.

– *Hollywood's Canada: The Americanization of Our National Image.* Toronto: McClelland and Stewart 1975.

– *The Arctic Grail: The Quest for the North West Passage and the North Pole, 1818–1911.* Toronto: McClelland and Stewart 1988.

– *Jane Franklin's Obsession.* Ill. Paul McCusker. Toronto: McClelland and Stewart 1992.

– *Dr. Kane of the Arctic Seas.* Ill. Paul McCusker. Toronto: McClelland and Stewart 1993.

– *Trapped in the Arctic.* Ill. Paul McCusker. Toronto: McClelland and Stewart 1993.

Bertram, John, and Jim Betts. *The Shooting of Dan McGrew.* Music and lyrics by Jim Betts. Toronto: Playwrights Union of Canada 1985.

Bessette, Gérard. "La Route d'Altamont, clef de *La Montagne secrète.*" *Trois romanciers Québécois.* Montréal: Éditions du Jour 1973. 185–99.

Betts, Jim. *Colours in the Storm.* Toronto: Playwrights Canada Press 2000.

Bhabha, Homi K. "DissemiNation: Time, Narrative, and the Margins of the Modern Nation." In Bhabha, ed., *Nation and Narration.* 291–322.

– "Of Mimicry and Man: The Ambivalence of Colonial Discourse." *The Location of Culture.* London: Routledge 1994. 85–92.

–, ed. *Nation and Narration.* London: Routledge 1990.

Bilby, Julian W. *Nanook of the North.* London: Arrowsmith 1925.

Birney, Earle. *The Straits of Anian: Selected Poems of Earle Birney.* Toronto: Ryerson 1948.

– *The Collected Poems of Earle Birney.* Toronto: McClelland and Stewart 1975.

– "Can. Lit." *Ghost in the Wheels: Selected Poems.* Toronto: McClelland and Stewart 1977. 49.

– *The Mammoth Corridors.* Okemos, Mich.: Stone 1980.

bissett, bill. "i dreem uv northern skies." *northern birds in color.* Vancouver: Talonbooks 1981.

Black, Martha Louise. *Martha Black: Her Story from the Dawson Gold Fields to the Halls of Parliament.* Ed. Flo Whyard. Anchorage: Alaska Northwest Books 1976.

Blais, Marie-Claire. *Wintersleep.* Trans. Nigel Spencer. Vancouver: Ronsdale Press 1998.

Blake, Dale. "Re-inventing Labrador: Elliott Merrick's Persuasive Northern Mythology." *The Northern Review* 14 (Summer 1995): 116–29.

– "Women of Labrador: Realigning North from the Site(s) of *Métissage.*" In Grace, ed., *Representing North.* 164–81.

Blodgett, Jean, and Lee-Ann Martin, eds. *The McMichael Canadian Art Collection: Twenty-fifth Anniversary Edition, 1965–1990.* Kleinberg: McMichael Canadian Art Collection 1989.

Blondin, George. *When the World Was New: Stories of the Sahtu Dene.* Yellowknife, NWT: Outcrop 1990.

– *Yamoria the Lawmaker: Stories of the Dene.* Edmonton: NeWest 1997.

Bloom, Harold. *Anxiety of Influence: A Theory of Poetry.* New York: Oxford University Press 1973.

Bloom, Lisa. *Gender on Ice: American Ideologies of Polar Expeditions.* Minneapolis: University of Minnesota Press 1993.

Boden, Jurgen R., and Elke Boden, eds. *Canada North of Sixty.* Toronto: McClelland and Stewart 1991.

Bodsworth, Fred. *The Last of the Curlews.* 1955. Ill. T.M. Shortt. London: Longmans 1966.

– *The Sparrow's Fall.* Garden City, NY: Doubleday 1967.

Bondar, Alanna F. " 'Life Doesn't Seem Natural': Ecofeminism and the Reclaiming of the Feminine Spirit in Cindy Cowan's *A Woman from the Sea.*" *Theatre Research in Canada* 18.1 (Spring 1997): 18–26.

Booth, David, comp. *Images of Nature: Canadian Poets and the Group of Seven.* Toronto: Kids Can 1995.

Booth, Michael R. "Gold Rush Theatres of the Klondike." *The Beaver* 42.1 (Spring 1962): 32–7.

Boris, Eileen. "Dialogue: Gender, Race, and Rights: Listening to Critical Race Theory." *Journal of Women's History* 6.1 (Summer 1994): 111–24.

Boulanger, Tom. *An Indian Remembers: My Life as a Trapper in Northern Manitoba.* Ill. Edward Howorth. Winnipeg: Peguis 1971.

Bowering, George. "Windigo." In Colombo, ed., *Windigo.* 187–91.

– "Selections from *Errata.*" *Prairie Fire* 8.4 (1987–88): 6–11.

– *Urban Snow.* Vancouver: Talonbooks 1992.

Bowlby, Rachel. "Breakfast in America – *Uncle Tom's* Cultural Histories." In Bhabha, ed., *Nation and Narration.* 197–212.

Boyle, Gwen. "Artist's Statement." *Tuning.* Exhibition. Richmond, BC: Richmond Art Gallery 1993.

Bradley, Ian L. *Twentieth Century Canadian Composers.* 2 vols. Agincourt, Ont.: GLC 1977.

– "Altitude ... Claude Champagne." 1:24.

- "'To the Lands over Yonder' ... John Weinzweig." 1:90–7.
- "Images ... Harry Freedman." 1:144–5.

Brand, Dionne. "Driving North, Driving Home." *Canadian Forum* (Oct. 1998): 30–2.

Brannan, Robert Louis, ed. *Under the Management of Mr. Charles Dickens: His Production of "The Frozen Deep."* Ithaca: Cornell University Press 1966.

Brask, Per, and William Morgan, eds. *Aboriginal Voices: Amerindian, Inuit, and Sami Theatre.* Baltimore: Johns Hopkins University Press 1992.

Brekke, Asgeir, and Alv Egeland. *The Northern Light: From Mythology to Space Research.* New York: Springer-Verlag 1983.

Brennan, Ann. *The Real Klondike Kate.* Fredericton, NB: Goose Lane 1990.

Brennan, Timothy. "The National Longing for Form." In Bhabha, ed., *Nation and Narration.* 44–70.

Brochu, André. "*La Montagne secrète*: le schème organisateur." *La Visée critique: essais autobiographiques et littéraires.* Montreal: Éditions du Boréal 1988. 186–203.

Brody, Hugh. *The Living Arctic: Hunters and Trappers of the Canadian North.* Vancouver: Douglas & McIntyre 1987.
- *Maps and Dreams: Indians and the British Columbia Frontier.* 1981. Vancouver: Douglas & McIntyre 1988.
- *The Other Side of Eden: Hunters, Farmers, and the Shaping of the World.* Vancouver: Douglas & McIntyre 2000.

Brown, Emily Ivanoff, "Ticasuk." *Tales of Ticasuk: Eskimo Legends and Stories.* Ill. Eugene C. and Mary Lou Totten. Fairbanks: University of Alaska Press 1987.

Brown, Jennifer S.H. *Strangers in Blood: Fur Trade Company Families in Indian Country.* Vancouver: University of British Columbia Press 1980.
- and Robert Brightman. *"The Orders of the Dreamed": George Nelson on Cree and Northern Ojibwa Religion and Myth, 1823.* Winnipeg: University of Manitoba Press 1988.

Brown, Russell, Donna Bennett, and Nathalie Cooke, eds. *An Anthology of Canadian Literature in English.* Rev. abr. ed. Toronto: Oxford University Press 1990.

"Bruce, William Blair." *A Dictionary of Canadian Artists*, comp. Colin S. MacDonald. Ottawa: Canadian Paperbacks 1967. 97–8.

Bruce, William Blair. *Letters Home, 1859–1906: The Letters of William Blair Bruce.* Ed. Joan Murray. Moonbeam, Ont.: Penumbra 1982.

Bruffee, Kenneth A. *Elegiac Romance: Cultural Change and Loss of the Hero in Modern Fiction.* Ithaca: Cornell University Press 1983.

Bryne, Nympha, and Camille Fouillard, eds. *It's Like the Legend: Innu Women's Voices.* Charlottetown, PEI: gynergy 2000.

Buchan, John [Lord Tweedsmuir]. *Sick Heart River.* London: Hodder and Stoughton 1941. Ed. David Danielle. Oxford: Oxford University Press 1994.

Buck, Anne. *Victorian Costume and Costume Accessories.* London: Herbert Jenkins 1961.

Buitenhuis, Peter. "Born out of Fantasy and Cauled in Myth: The Writer and the Canadian North." In Carlsen and Streijffert, eds., *The Canadian North.* 1–13.

Buliard, Roger P. *Inuk.* London: Macmillan 1953.
- *Nanouk.* Paris: Éditions Fleurus 1956.

Burant, Jim. "Getting Gold from Silver: Photography of the Klondike Gold Rush from the 1890s to 1905." *The Northern Review* 19 (Winter 1998): 204–17.

Burnford, Sheila. *One Woman's Arctic.* Toronto: McClelland and Stewart 1973.

Burns, Mary. "Yukon Quintette." In *Take Five: The Morningside Dramas*, ed. David Carley. Winnipeg: Blizzard 1991. 1–36.

Burns, Nick. *Super Shamou.* Created by Barney Pattunguyak and Peter Tapatai. Ottawa: Inuit Broadcasting Corp., n.d.

Burt, Page. *Barrenland Beauties: Showy Plants of the Arctic Coast.* Yellowknife: Outcrop 1991.

Burwash, L.T. "The Franklin Search." *Canadian Geographic* 1.7 (Nov. 1930): 587–603.

Butler, Judith. *Gender Trouble: Feminism and the Subversion of Identity.* New York: Routledge 1990.
- *Bodies That Matter: On the Discursive Limits of "Sex."* New York: Routledge 1993.
- *The Psychic Life of Power: Theories in Subjection.* Stanford: Stanford University Press 1997.

Byrne, Nympha, and Camille Fouillard, eds. *It's Like the Legend: Innu Women's Voices.* Charlottetown, PEI: gynergy books 2000.

Calder-Marshall, Arthur. *The Innocent Eye: The Life of Robert J. Flaherty.* New York: Harcourt 1963.

Calhoun, Craig, Edward LiPuma, and Moishe Postone, eds. *Bourdieu: Critical Perspectives.* Cambridge: Polity 1993.

Callaghan, Morley, and John de Visser. *Winter.* Toronto: McClelland and Stewart 1974.

Cameron, Agnes Deans. *The New North: An Account of a Woman's 1908 Journey through*

Canada to the Arctic. Ed. David R. Richeson. Saskatoon: Western Producer Prairie 1986.

Cameron, Kirk and Graham White. *Northern Governments in Transition: Political and Constitutional Development in the Yukon, Nunavut and the Western Northwest Territories*. Montreal: Institute for Research on Public Policy 1995.

Campbell, David. *Writing Security: United States Foreign Policy and the Politics of Identity*. Minneapolis: University of Minnesota Press 1992.

Camsell, Charles. "The New North." *Canadian Geographical Journal* 33.6 (Dec. 1946): 264–77.

– *Son of the North*. Toronto: Ryerson 1954.

Canada. Department of the Naval Service. "Eskimo Songs." *Report of the Canadian Arctic Expedition 1913–18*. Vol. 14. Ottawa: King's Printer 1925.

– Environment Canada Parks Service. *Chilkoot Trail: National Historic Park, Canadian Parks Service*. Anchorage: Alaska National History Association, n.d.

– House of Commons. Standing Committee on Foreign Affairs and International Trade. *Canada and the Circumpolar World: Meeting the Challenges of Cooperation into the Twenty-First Century: Report of the House of Commons Standing Committee on European Affairs and International Trade*. Ottawa: Canada Communication Group 1997.

– Indian and Northern Affairs. *Canada's North: The Reference Manual*. Rev. ed. Ottawa 1990.

– Indian and Northern Affairs. *Canadian Inuit Sculpture*. Ottawa 1992.

– Office of the Official Languages Commissioner. *The Languages of Our Land: The Northwest Territories Official Languages Act*. Ottawa 1994.

Canada First: A Memorial of the Late William A. Foster, Q.C. Intro. Goldwin Smith. Toronto: Hunter Rose 1890.

Careless, Virginia A.S. *Responding to Fashion: The Clothing of the O'Reilly Family*. Victoria: Royal British Columbia Museum 1993.

Carlick, Alice. "The Girl and the Grizzly: Bringing Traditional Narratives into Yukon Classrooms." *The Northern Review* 14 (Summer 1995): 34–47.

Carlsen, Jørn, ed. *Literary Responses to Arctic Canada*. Nordic Association for Canadian Studies Text Series 7. Lund, Sweden: Nordic Association for Canadian Studies 1993.

– and Bengt Streijffert, eds. *The Canadian North: Essays in Culture and Literature*. Nordic Associa-

tion for Canadian Studies Text Series 5. Lund, Sweden: Nordic Association for Canadian Studies 1989.

Carmack, George W. *My Experiences in the Yukon*. Marguerite Carmack 1933.

Carmack, Kate. Obituary. *The Pathfinder*, 1920, 22.

Carpenter, Edmund. "Witch-Fear among the Aivilik Eskimos." in Valentine and Vallee, eds., *Eskimo*. 55–66.

– *Oh, What a Blow that Phantom Wind Gave Me!* New York: Holt, Rinehart and Winston 1973.

– ed. *Anerca*. Toronto: J.W. Dent 1959.

– and Marshall McLuhan, eds. *Explorations in Communication: An Anthology*. Boston: Beacon 1960.

– with Frederick Varley and Robert Flaherty. *Eskimo*. Toronto: University of Toronto Press 1959.

Carpenter, Mary. "Stories: 'Skeleton Woman,' 'Woman of the Sea.' " In Moss, ed., *Echoing Silence*. 225–30.

Carruthers, Glen, and Gordana Lazarevich, eds. *A Celebration of Canada's Arts, 1930–1970*. Toronto: Canadian Scholars' 1996.

Case, Sue-Ellen *et al.*, eds. *Cruising the Performative: Interventions into the Representation of Ethnicity, Nationality, and Sexuality*. Bloomington: Indiana University Press 1995.

Cavanagh, Beverley. "Imagery and Structure in Eskimo Song Texts." *Canadian Folk Music Journal* 1 (1973): 3–16.

Chabot, Denys. *L'Eldorado dans les glaces: roman*. Montreal: Éditions Hurtubise 1981.

Chalykoff, Lisa. "Tracing C.D. Shanly's 'The Walker of the Snow.' " *Canadian Literature* 160 (Spring 1999): 187–9.

Chaput, Simone. "Un Solitaire: The Life and Art of René Richard." *The Beaver* 79.6 (1999/2000): 41–5.

Charles, John. "Janacek's Time Has Come." *Financial Post*, 29–31 Jan. 1994, S7.

"Charting New Territories." Narr. Lister Sinclair. *Ideas*. 3 episodes. CBC, Toronto, 4, 11, 18 March 1998.

Cherney, Brian. *Harry Somers*. Toronto: University of Toronto Press 1975.

Churchyard, Charles. *Arctic Critiques*. Devil's Thumb Press 1992.

Cleaver, Elizabeth. *The Enchanted Caribou*. Toronto: Oxford University Press 1985.

Clément, Catherine. *Opera, or, The Undoing of Woman*. Trans. Betsy Wing. Minneapolis: University of Minnesota Press 1988.

Clemente, Linda M., and William A. Clemente. *Gabrielle Roy: Creation and Memory.* Toronto: ECW, 1997.

Clerici, Naila. "The Cree of James Bay and the Construction of Their Identity for the Media." In Behiels, ed., *Aboriginal Peoples.* 143–65.

Clifford, James, and George E. Marcus, eds. *Writing Culture: The Poetics and Politics of Ethnography: A School of American Research Advanced Seminar.* Berkeley: University of California Press 1986.

Coates, Colin and Ken, eds. *The Northern Review,* special issue on the Klondike Gold Rush, 19 (Winter 1998).

Coates, Kenneth S. *Canada's Colonies: A History of the Yukon and Northwest Territories.* Toronto: Lorimer 1985.

– *Best Left as Indians: Native-White Relations in the Yukon Territory, 1840–1973.* Montreal: McGill-Queen's University Press 1991.

– "The Rediscovery of the North: Towards a Conceptual Framework for the Study of Northern/Remote Regions." *The Northern Review* 12/13 (Summer/Winter 1994): 15–43.

– and William R. Morrison. *The Forgotten North: A History of Canada's Provincial Norths.* Toronto: Lorimer 1992.

– eds. *For Purposes of Dominion: Essays in Honour of Morris Zaslow.* North York, Ont.: Captus 1989.

– eds. *Interpreting Canada's North: Selected Readings.* Toronto: Copp Clark Pitman 1989.

Cole, Douglas. "Artists, Patrons and Public: An Enquiry into the Success of the Group of Seven." *Journal of Canadian Studies* 13.2 (1978): 69–78.

Coleridge, Samuel Taylor. "The Rime of the Ancient Mariner." 1797–98. *English Romantic Writers.* Ed. David Perkins. San Diego: Harcourt 1967. 404–13.

Colgate, William. *Canadian Art: Its Origin and Development.* 1943. Toronto: Ryerson 1967.

Collier, Eric. *Three against the Wilderness.* 1959. Don Mills, Ont.: General Paperbacks 1991.

Colombo, John Robert. *Poems of the Inuit.* Ottawa: Oberon 1981.

– ed. *Windigo: An Anthology of Fact and Fantastic Fiction.* Saskatoon: Western Producer Prairie 1982.

Comock. *The Story of Comock the Eskimo, as told to Robert Flaherty.* Ed. Edmund Carpenter. New York: Simon & Schuster 1968.

Conrad, Joseph. *Heart of Darkness.* New York: Norton 1963.

Cook, Ramsay. "Imagining a North American Garden: Some Parallels and Differences in Canadian and American Culture." *Canadian Literature* 103 (Winter 1984): 10–23.

Cooke, Alan. "A Woman's Way." *The Beaver* 291 (Summer 1960): 40–5.

Cooper, Courtney Ryley. *Go North, Young Man!* Boston: Little, Brown, and Co. 1929.

Copeland, Donalda M., and Eugenie Louise Myles. *Nurse among the Eskimos.* London: Souvenir Press 1964.

Cornwell, Regina. *Snow Seen: The Films and Photographs of Michael Snow.* Toronto: Peter Martin 1979.

Cowan, Cindy. "Beast of the Land" and "The Trap of Cultural Specificity: Seeking Intercultural Solidarity." In Cowan and Rewa, eds., *Beast of the Land.* 3, 24–8.

Cowan, Cindy, and Natalie Rewa, eds. *Beast of the Land: Arctic Theatre Makers. Canadian Theatre Review* 73 (Winter 1992).

Craniford, Ada. *Fiction and Fact in Mordecai Richler's Novels.* Lewiston, NY: E. Mellen Press 1993.

Creates, Marlene. *Marlene Creates: The Distance between Two Points is Measured in Memories, Labrador, 1988.* North Vancouver: Presentation House Gallery 1990.

Creighton, Donald. *Dominion of the North: A History of Canada.* 1944. Toronto: Macmillan 1957.

– *Canada's First Century, 1867–1967.* Toronto: Macmillan 1970.

Crompton, Liz. "Michael Kusugak, Storyteller." *Up Here: Life in Canada's North* (Sept.–Oct. 1994): 40–1.

Cruikshank, Julie. *Reading Voices: Oral and Written Interpretations of the Yukon's Past.* Vancouver: Douglas & McIntyre 1991.

– "Images of Society in Klondike Gold Rush Narratives: Skookum Jim and the Discovery of Gold." *Ethnohistory* 39.1 (1992): 20–41.

– with Angela Sidney, Kitty Smith, and Annie Ned. *Life Lived Like a Story: Life Stories of Three Yukon Native Elders.* Vancouver: University of British Columbia Press 1990.

Culhane Speck, Dara. *An Error in Judgement: The Politics of Medical Care in an Indian/White Community.* Vancouver: Talonbooks 1987.

Cunningham, Cecil Willett. *English Women's Clothing in the Nineteenth Century.* London: Faber and Faber 1937.

Currelly, Judith. "Artist's Statement." 1990. Unpublished ts.

Curwen, Eliot. *Labrador Odyssey: The Journal and Photographs of Eliot Curwen on the Second Voyage of Wilfred Grenfell, 1893.* Ed. Ronald Rompkey. Montreal: McGill-Queen's University Press 1996.

Curwood, James Oliver. *Steele of the Royal Mounted.* 1911. Montreal: Pocket Books of Canada 1946.

Custen, George F. "The (Re)Framing of Robert Flaherty." *Quarterly Review of Film Studies* 7.1 (1982): 87–94.

Dacks, Gurston. "The Politics of 'Partnership' in the Northwest Territories." In Coates and Morrison, eds., *For Purposes of Dominion.* 225–43.

Dafoe, Christopher. "Early Days at the Beaver." *The Beaver* 74.6 (Dec. 1994–Jan. 1995): 2–3.

Dahlie, Hallvard. "North by West: The Northern Vision and the Structures of Ambiguity in Western Canadian Fiction." In Carlsen, ed., *Literary Responses.* 33–40.

Dalpé, Jean-Marc. *Le Chien: pièce en un acte.* Sudbury, Ont.: Éditions Prise de Parole 1987.

Dalton, Annie Charlotte. *The Neighing North.* Toronto: Ryerson 1931.

Danky, James P., ed., and Maureen E. Hady, comp. *Native American Periodicals and Newspapers, 1828–1982: Bibliography, Publishing Record, and Holdings.* Westport, Conn: Greenwood 1984.

Darroch-Lozowski, Vivian. *Antarctica Body.* Waterloo, Ont.: Penumbra 1990.

Davey, Frank. *Post-National Arguments: The Politics of the Anglophone-Canadian Novel since 1967.* Toronto: University of Toronto Press 1993.

Davidson, James West, and John Rugge. *Great Heart: The History of a Labrador Adventure.* 1988. Montreal: McGill-Queen's University Press 1997.

Davies, Robertson. *Question Time: A Play.* Toronto: Macmillan 1975.

Davis, Ann. "An Apprehended Vision: The Philosophy of the Group of Seven." MA, York University 1973.

– *A Distant Harmony: Comparisons in the Painting of Canada and the United States of America.* Winnipeg: The Gallery 1982.

Davis, Richard C. "Thrice-Told Tales: The Exploration Writing of John Franklin." In Carlsen and Streijffert, eds., *The Canadian North.* 15–26.

– "The Canadian North and the Novelist's Art." In Carlsen, ed., *Literary Responses.* 41–50.

– "Cultural Ventriloquism: Speaking Truth with a Forked Tongue." In Peepre-Bordessa, ed., *Transcultural Travels.* 9–17.

– *Lobsticks and Stone Cairns: Human Landmarks in the Arctic.* Calgary: University of Calgary Press 1996.

Daymond, Douglas and Leslie Monkman, eds. *Literature in Canada.* Vol. I. Toronto: Gage 1978.

Dean, William G. "Atlas Structures and Their Influence on Editorial Decisions: Two Recent Case Histories." In Winearls, ed., *Editing.* 137–62.

De Bray, Emile Frédéric. *A Frenchman in Search of Franklin: De Bray's Arctic Journal, 1852–1854.* Ed. and trans. William Barr. Toronto: University of Toronto Press 1992.

De Certeau, Michel. "Montaigne's 'Of Cannibals': The Savage 'I.'" *Heterologies: Discourse of the Other.* Trans. Brian Massumi. Minneapolis, Minn.: University of Minnesota Press 1986. 67–79.

De Coccola, Raymond, and Paul King. *Ayorama.* Toronto: Oxford University Press 1955.

DeGraf, Anna. *Pioneering on the Yukon, 1892–1917.* Ed. Roger S. Brown. Hamdon, Conn.: Archon 1992.

de Jouvancourt, Hugues. *René Richard.* Montreal: Éditions La Frégate 1974.

de Laguna, Frederica, ed. *Tales from the Dena: Indian Stories from the Tanana, Koyukuk, and Yukon Rivers.* Ill. Dale DeArmond. Seattle: University of Washington Press 1995.

De Lauretis, Teresa. *Technologies of Gender: Essays on Theory, Film, and Fiction.* Bloomington: Indiana University Press 1987.

Delisle, Jeanne-Mance. *Un reel ben beau, ben triste.* Montreal: Les éditions de la pleine lune 1980.

– *A Live Bird in Its Jaws.* Trans. Yves Saint-Pierre. Montreal: NuAge 1992.

Dene Traditional Life Series, Northwest Territories. Photographs. Yellowknife: Department of Information, Government of the Northwest Territories in co-operation with the Hudson's Bay Company, 1981.

Denison, George T. *Struggle for Imperial Unity.* London: Macmillan 1909.

Denison, Merrill. *The Unheroic North.* Toronto: McClelland and Stewart 1923.

– *Henry Hudson and Other Plays.* Toronto: Ryerson 1931.

Den Ouden, Pamela. "'My Uttermost Valleys': Patriarchal Fear of the Feminine in Robert

Service's Poetry and Prose." *The Northern Review* 19 (Winter 1998): 113–21.

De Poncins, Gontran. *Kabloona.* 1941. Chicago: Time-Life 1980.

Derrida, Jacques. "Of an Apocalyptic Tone Recently Adopted in Philosophy." Trans. John P. Leavey. *Semeia* 23 (1982): 63–97.

DeShaw, Rose. "The Ragtime Kid Checks Out." In Skene-Melvin, ed., *Secret Tales.* 47–61.

DeVere Brody, Jennifer. "Hyphen-Nations." In Case *et al.*, eds., *Cruising the Performative.* 149–62.

Diamond, Beverley. "Narratives in Canadian Music History." In Diamond and Witmer, eds., *Canadian Music.* 139–71.

– and Robert Witmer, eds. *Canadian Music: Issues of Hegemony and Identity.* Toronto: Canadian Scholars 1994.

Diamond, Billy. "The Development of the North: Confrontation and Conflict." In Seyersted, ed., *The Arctic.* 87–99.

Dickason, Olive Patricia. "Three Worlds, One Focus: Europeans Meet Inuit and Amerindians in the Far North." In *Rupert's Land: A Cultural Tapestry,* ed. Richard C. Davis. Waterloo: Wilfrid Laurier University Press 1988. 51–78.

Dickerson, Mark O. *Whose North? Political Change, Political Development, and Self Government in the Northwest Territories.* Vancouver: University of British Columbia Press 1992.

Dickey, James. *Deliverance.* New York: Dell 1970.

Dickie, Bonnie. "Marie Bouchard and the Baker Lake Renaissance." *Up Here: Life in Canada's North* (Sept.–Oct. 1994): 28ff.

Dickinson, Christine Frances, and Diane Solie Smith. *Atlin: The Story of British Columbia's Last Gold Rush.* Atlin, BC: Atlin Historical Society 1995.

Dickinson, Peter. "Documenting 'North' in Canadian Poetry and Music." In Grace, ed., *Representing North.* 105–22.

– *Here is Queer: Nationalisms, Sexualities, and the Literatures of Canada.* Toronto: University of Toronto Press 1999.

Dickson, Lovat. *Half-Breed: The Story of Grey Owl (Wa-She-Quon-Asin).* London: Peter Davies 1939.

Diefenbaker, John. "Opening Campaign Speech." 12 February 1958. John Diefenbaker Papers, University of Saskatchewan Archives, Saskatoon.

Dingle, Adrian. *Nelvana of the Northern Lights.* Toronto: Triumph Adventure Comics 1941–47.

Djwa, Sandra. " 'A New Soil and a Sharp Sun': The Landscape of a Modern Canadian Poetry." *Modernist Studies* 2.2 (1977): 3–17.

Doane, Mary Ann. *Femmes Fatales: Feminism, Film Theory, Psychoanalysis.* New York: Routledge 1991.

Dobi, Steve. "Restoring Robert Flaherty's *Nanook of the North.*" *Film Library Quarterly* 10.1–2 (1977): 6–18.

Dobrowolsky, Helen. *Law of the Yukon: A Pictorial History of the Mounted Police in the Yukon.* Whitehorse: Lost Moose 1995.

Dorland, Keith. "True North." Unpublished play.

Doyle, James. *North of America: Images of Canada in the Literature of the United States, 1775–1900.* Toronto: ECW 1983.

Dragland, Stan. *Floating Voice: Duncan Campbell Scott and the Literature of Treaty 9.* Concord, Ont.: Anansi 1994.

Drew, Wayland. *The Wabeno Feast.* Toronto: Anansi 1973.

Drummond, Robbie Newton. *Arctic Circle Songs: Fifty "Delta Hushpuppies."* Waterloo, Ont.: Penumbra 1991.

Drummond, Susan G. *Incorporating the Familiar: An Investigation into Legal Sensibilities in Nunavik.* Montreal: McGill-Queen's University Press 1997.

Dubé, Marcel. *Au retour des oies blanches.* Montreal: Leméac 1966.

Duchesne, Scott, and Jennifer Fletcher. "*Sled*: A Workshop Diary." *Canadian Theatre Review* 89 (Winter 1996): 33–38.

Duffy, R. Quinn. *The Road to Nunavut: The Progress of the Eastern Arctic Inuit since the Second World War.* Montreal: McGill-Queen's University Press 1988.

Dufresne, Guy. *Les Traitants.* Ottawa: Leméac 1969.

– *The Call of the Whippoorwill.* Trans. Philip London and Laurence Bérard. Toronto: New 1972.

Dunning, John. *Tune in Yesterday: The Ultimate Encyclopedia of Old-Time Radio, 1925–1976.* Englewood Cliffs, NJ: Prentice-Hall 1976.

Easingwood, Peter, Konrad Gross, and Wolfgang Klooss, eds. *Probing Canadian Culture.* Augsburg: AV-Verlag 1991.

Eather, Robert H. *Majestic Lights: The Aurora in Science, History, and the Arts.* Washington, DC: American Geophysical Union 1980.

Eber, Dorothy Harley. *When the Whalers Were Up North: Inuit Memories from the Eastern Arctic.* Kingston: McGill-Queen's University Press 1989.

– *Images of Justice: A Legal History of the Northwest Territories as Traced through the Yellowknife Courthouse Collection of Inuit Sculpture.* Montreal: McGill-Queen's University Press 1997.

Ede, Charles. "Zero or Harlequin Lights." *Canadian Drama/L'Art dramatique canadien* 16.1 (1990): 49–61.

Egoff, Sheila, and Judith Saltman. *The New Republic of Childhood: A Critical Guide to Canadian Children's Literature in English.* Toronto: Oxford University Press 1990.

Elder, Kathryn, ed. *The Films of Joyce Wieland.* Toronto: Toronto International Film Festival Group and Wilfrid Laurier University Press 1999.

Elder, R. Bruce. *Image and Identity: Reflections on Canadian Film and Culture.* Waterloo, Ont.: Wilfrid Laurier University Press 1989.

Eldridge, Judith A. *James Oliver Curwood: God's Country and the Man.* Bowling Green, Ohio: Bowling Green State University Popular Press 1993.

Eliot, T.S. "Burnt Norton." 1935. *Collected Poems, 1909–1962.* London: Faber and Faber 1963. 189–95.

Ellmann, Maud. *The Hunger Artists: Starving, Writing, and Imprisonment.* Cambridge, Mass.: Harvard University Press 1993.

Engle, Lars. "Discourse, Agency, and Therapy in *Hamlet.*" *Exemplaria* 4.2 (Fall 1992): 441–53.

"Eskimo Nell." *The Faber Book of Blue Verse.* Ed. John Whiworth. London: Faber and Faber 1990. 3–10.

Études Inuits Studies. Laval, PQ: Inuksiutiit Katimajiit 1977–.

Evans, Chad. *Frontier Theatre: A History of Nineteenth Century Theatrical Entertainment in the Canadian Far West and Alaska.* Victoria: Sono Nis 1983.

Falck-Ytter, Harald. *The Aurora: The Northern Lights in Mythology, History and Science.* Photographs by Torbjörn Lövgren, trans. Robin Alexander. Edinburgh: Floris 1985.

Farmiloe, Dorothy. *Elk Lake Diary: Poems.* Cobalt, Ont.: Highway Book Shop 1976.

Fawcett, Brian. *The Secret Journal of Alexander Mackenzie.* Vancouver: Talonbooks 1985.

Fee, Margery, ed. *Silence Made Visible: Howard O'Hagan and Tay John.* Toronto: ECW 1992.

Feher, Michel, W. Ramona Naddaff, and Nadia Tazi, eds. *Fragments for a History of the Human Body.* Vol. 3, *Zone 5.* New York: Urzone 1989.

Ferron, Jacques. *Grands Soleils.* Montreal: Éditions D' Orphée 1958.

Fiedler, Leslie A. *Return of the Vanishing American.* New York: Stein and Day 1968.

Fienup-Riordan, Ann. *Freeze Frame: Alaska Eskimos in the Movies.* Seattle: University of Washington Press 1995.

Filewod, Alan. "National Theatre/National Obsession." *Canadian Theatre Review* 62 (Spring 1990): 5–10.

Fingard, Judith. *The Dark Side of Life in Victorian Halifax.* Porters Lake, NS: Pottersfield 1989.

Finnie, Richard. *Lure of the North.* Philadelphia: David McKay 1940.

– *Canada Moves North.* 1942. Toronto: MacMillan 1948.

– "When the Ice Worms Nest Again." *Canada Moves North.* 1942. Rev. ed. Toronto: Macmillan 1948. 204.

Flaherty, Frances Hubbard. *The Odyssey of a Filmmaker: Robert Flaherty's Story.* Urbana, Ill.: Beta Phi Mu 1960.

Flaherty, Martha, and John Bennett, eds. *Inuktitut 70* (1989). Ottawa: Indian and Northern Affairs 1989.

Flaherty, Robert. *Camera Studies of the Far North.* London: Putnam 1922.

– "Life among the Eskimos." *The World's Book* (October 1922): 632–40.

– *My Eskimo Friends: "Nanook of the North."* Garden City, NY: Doubleday, Page & Co. 1924.

– *The Captain's Chair: A Story of the North.* New York: Scribner's 1938.

– *White Master: A Story of the North.* London: Routledge 1939.

– "Robert Flaherty Talking." In *The Cinema 1950,* ed. Roger Manvell. Harmondsworth, Middlesex: Penguin 1950. 11–29.

Flather, Patti. "Apprehending the Canadian Landscape: A Profile of Playwright Leslie Hamson," "Nakai Theatre Ensemble," and "The Yukon Writers' Festival: Building a Northern Literary Voice." In Cowan and Rewa, eds., *Beast of the Land.* 33–5, 42–4, 51–3.

– and Leonard Linklater. *Sixty Below.* In Grace, D'Aeth, and Chalykoff, eds., *Staging the North.* 435–501.

Flood, John. *Land They Occupied.* Erin, Ont.: Porcupine's Quill 1976.

– *No Longer North.* Windsor, Ont.: Black Moss 1987.

– ed. *Mooskek Reader.* Coatsworth, Ont.: Black Moss 1978.

– and Jacques Albert, eds.. *Boreal: Journal of Northern Ontario Arts.* Hearst, Ont.: University College of Hearst.

Flucke, A.F. "Whither the Eskimo?" *Social Problems: A Canadian Profile.* Ed. Richard Laskin. Toronto: McGraw-Hill 1964. 124–8.

Fogel-Chance, Nancy. "Living in Both Worlds: 'Modernity' and 'Tradition' among North Slope Inupiaq Women in Anchorage." *Arctic Anthropology* 30.1 (1993): 94–108.

Foster, W.A. *Canada First.* Toronto: Adam, Stevenson 1871.

Foucault, Michel. *The Archaeology of Knowledge.* Trans. A.M. Sheridan Smith. London: Routledge 1972.

– "Questions on Geography." *Power/Knowledge: Selected Interviews and Other Writings, 1972–1977.* Ed. Colin Gordon, trans. Colin Gordon, Leo Marshall, John Mepham, and Kate Soper. Brighton, Sussex: Harvester 1980. 63–77.

Frances, Daniel. *National Dreams: Myth, Memory and Canadian History.* Vancouver: Arsenal Pulp 1997.

Franklin, Colleen. " 'Steering Against the Tyde of Satan's Malice': *The Strange and Dangerous Voyage of Captaine Thomas James." The Northern Review* 17 (Winter 1996): 85–96.

Franklin, Sir John. *Narrative of a Journey to the Shores of the Polar Sea, in the Years 1819, 1820, 1821, and 1822.* 1823. Edmonton: Hurtig 1969.

Freedman, Harry. Interview. By Michael Schulman. *Canadian Composer* 96 (Dec. 1974): 4–10.

Freeman, Minnie Aodla. *Life among the Qallunaat.* Edmonton: Hurtig 1978.

– "Survival in the South." In Gedalof, ed., *Paper Stays Put.* 101–12.

Freeman, Randy. "Believe it or not!" *Up Here* 16.2 (2000): 41–3.

Friedrich, Otto. *Glenn Gould: A Life and Variations.* Toronto: Lester and Orpen Dennys 1989.

Friis-Baastad, Erling, and Patricia Robertson, eds. *Writing North: An Anthology of Contemporary Yukon Writers.* Whitehorse, Yukon: Beluga 1992.

Frolick, Vernon. *Descent into Madness: The Diary of a Killer.* Surrey, BC: Hancock House 1993.

Fry, Jacqueline. Catalogue Essay. Trans. Elizabeth Ritchie. In Creates, *Marlene Creates: The Distance.* 53–8.

Frye, Northrop. *The Bush Garden: Essays on the Canadian Imagination.* Toronto: Anansi 1971.

Fuss, Diana. "Freud's Fallen Women: Identification, Desire, and 'A Case of Homosexuality in a Woman.' " *Yale Journal of Criticism* 6.1 (1993): 1–23.

– "Interior Colonies: Frantz Fanon and the Politics of Identification." *Diacritics* 24.2–3 (Summer/Fall 1994): 20–42.

Gaffin, Jane. *Edward Hadgkiss: Missing in Life.* Whitehorse, Yukon: Word Pro 1989.

Gagné, Marc. "*La Rivière sans repos* de Gabrielle Roy: Étude mythocritique incluant *Voyage en Ungava* (extraits) par Gabrielle Roy." *Revue de l'Université d'Ottawa* 46.1 (1976): 83–107; 46.2 (1976): 180–99; 46.3 (1976): 364–90.

Gale, Peggy. "A White Light." *Canadian Art* 15.4 (1998): 58–65.

Garneau, Michel. *Les Neiges suivi de Le Bonhomme Sept-Heures: théâtre.* Montreal: VLB 1984.

Garreet-Petts, W.F., and Donald Lawrence. "Thawing the Frozen Image/Word: Vernacular Postmodern Aesthetics." *Mosaic* 31.1 (Mar. 1998): 143–78.

Gates, Michael. *Gold at Fortymile Creek: Early Days in the Yukon.* Vancouver: University of British Columbia Press 1994.

Gedalof, Robin, ed. *Paper Stays Put: A Collection of Inuit Writing.* Ill. Alootook Ipellie. Edmonton: Hurtig 1980.

Geddes, Gary, ed. *Skookum Wawa: Writings of the Canadian Northwest.* Toronto: Oxford University Press 1975.

Geiger, John, and Owen Beattie. *Dead Silence: The Greatest Mystery in Arctic Discovery.* Toronto: Viking 1993.

Genest, Miche. "The Fasting Girl." Shrinking Violet Theatre, Vancouver, BC, 1 Mar. 1998.

George, Peter G. "Native Peoples and Economic Development: Prospects for the Cree and Ojibway Indians of Northern Ontario." In Carlsen and Streijffert, eds., *The Canadian North.* 27–47.

Georgia. *Georgia: An Arctic Diary.* Edmonton: Hurtig 1982.

Geyshick, Ron. "Cannibal Woman," "A Windigo." In Moses and Goldie, eds., *Canadian Native Literature.* 200.

Gibbons, Jacqueline A. "The North and Native Symbols: Landscape as Universe." In Simpson-Housley and Norcliffe, eds., *The Arctic.* 99–108.

Gilmore, Leigh. *Autobiographics: A Feminist Theory of Women's Self-Representation*. Ithaca: Cornell University Press 1994.

Glasmeier, Michael. "Cold Genius – The Arctic Seen from Afar." Trans. H. Whyte. In Seppala, ed., *Strangers i the Arctic*. 82–5.

Goddard, John. "A Real Whopper." *Saturday Night* (May 1996): 46ff.

Godfrey, Martyn. *Mystery in the Frozen Lands*. Toronto: Lorimer 1988.

Goehring, Brian, and John K. Stager. "The Intrusion of Industrial Time and Space into the Inuit Lifeworld: Changing Perceptions and Behaviour." *Environment and Behaviour* 23.6 (Nov. 1991): 666–79.

Goldberg, David Theo. *Racist Culture: Philosophy and the Politics of Meaning*. Cambridge: Blackwell 1993.

Goldie, Terry. "A Northern People?" In Carlsen and Streijffert, eds., *The Canadian North*. 49–60.

Goldman, Marion S. *Gold Diggers and Silver Miners: Prostitution and Social Life on the Comstock Lode*. Ann Arbor: University of Michigan Press 1981.

Goldman, Marlene. "Earth-Quaking the Kingdom of the Male Virgin: A Deleuzian Analysis of Aritha van Herk's *No Fixed Address* and *Places Far from Ellesmere*." *Canadian Literature* 137 (Summer 1993): 21–38.

Golfman, Noreen. "*Kabloonak*: Robert Flaherty and the Making of *Nanook of the North*." *Canadian Forum* (Oct. 1994): 23–4.

Gom, Leona. *Northbound: Poems Selected and New*. Saskatoon: Thistledown 1984.

Gooch, Bryan N.S., and Maureen Niwa, eds. *The Emergence of the Muse: Major Canadian Poets from Crawford to Pratt*. Toronto: Oxford University Press 1993.

Gordon, Charles William. *Prospector: A Tale of the Crow's Nest Pass*. Toronto: Westminister 1904.

Gould, Allan. *The Great Wiped Out North*. Illustrated by Graham Pilsworth. Toronto: Stoddart 1988.

Gould, Glenn. " 'The Idea of North': An Introduction." *The Glenn Gould Reader*. Ed. Tim Page. New York: Knopf 1984. 391–4.

Grace, Sherrill E. "A Northern Modernism, 1920–1932: Canadian Painting and Literature." *Bibloteca Della Ricera, Cultura Straniera 12. Canada Ieri e Oggi*. Rome: Schena Editore 1985. 425–40.

– " 'Mapping Inner Space': Canada's Northern Expressionism." In Carlsen and Streijffert, eds., *The Canadian North*. 61–70.

– *Regression and Apocalypse: Studies in North American Literary Expressionism*. Toronto: University of Toronto Press 1989.

– "Comparing Mythologies: Ideas of West and North." In *Borderlands: Essays in Canadian-American Relations*, ed. Robert Lecker. Toronto: ECW 1991. 243–62.

– "Re-introducing Canadian 'Art of the Theatre': Herman Voaden's 1930 Manifesto." *Canadian Literature* 135 (Winter 1992): 51–63.

– "Articulating North." In Carlsen, ed., *Literary Responses*. 65–75.

– "Canada Post: – Modern? – Colonial? – National?" *Transactions of the Royal Society of Canada*, Sixth Series, 6 (1995): 127–37.

– " 'Franklin Lives': Atwood's Northern Ghosts." In *Various Atwoods: Essays on the Later Poems, Short Fiction, and Novels*, ed. Lorraine M. York. Concord, Ont.: Anansi 1995. 146–66.

– "Re-inventing Franklin." *Canadian Review of Comparative Literature*. 22. 3–4 (Sept.–Dec. 1995): 707–725.

– "Multiple Discoveries." *Canadian Literature* 149 (1996): 136–7.

– "Exploration as Construction: Robert Flaherty and *Nanook of the North*." In Grace, ed., *Representing North*. 123–46.

– "Robert Kroetsch and the Semiotics of North." *Open Letter* 5/6 (Spring/Summer 1996): 13–24.

– "Gendering Northern Narrative." In Moss, ed., *Echoing Silence*. 163–81.

– " 'A Woman's Way': Canadian Narratives of Northern Discovery." In *New Worlds: Discovering and Constructing the Unknown in Anglophone Literature*, ed. R. Beck, I. Gutiérrez, and M. Kuester. Munich: Verlag Vögel 1999. 177–202.

– "From Nelvana to Ice Box: Popular Constructions of 'the Arctic.' " *The Northern Review* 21 (Summer 2000): 22–37.

– "Representing the Northern Lights." In *The Aurora on ALL Three Chanels, catalogue raisonnée* of the sound-sculpture installation by Richard Prince. Barrie, Ont: MacLaren Art Centre 2000. 10–11.

– "Staging the 'North' in BC: Two Cariboo Gold Rush Plays." *Canadian Theatre Review* 101 (Winter 2000): 19–24.

– "Representations of the Inuit: From Other to Self." *Theatre Research in Canada* 21.1 (2000): 38–48.

– "Arctic Journals." *Canadian Literature* 170/171 (2001): 247–9.

– " 'Hidden Country': Mina Benson Hubbard's Story." *Biography* 24.1 (Winter 2001): 273–87.

– *Inventing Tom Thomson.* Unpublished ms.

– ed. *Representing North. Essays on Canadian Writing* 59 (Fall 1996).

– Eve D'Aeth, and Lisa Chalykoff, eds. *Staging the North: Twelve Canadian Plays.* Toronto: Playwrights Canada 1999.

– and Stefan Haag. "From Landscape to Soundscape: The Northern Arts of Canada." *Mosaic* 31.2 (June 1998): 101–22.

Graham, Amanda. "Indexing the Canadian North: Broadening the Definition." *The Northern Review* 6 (Winter 1990): 21–37.

Grand Council of the Crees (Eeyou Astchee). *Never without Consent: James Bay Crees' Stand against Forcible Inclusion into an Independent Quebec.* Toronto: ECW 1998.

Grant, George. *Technology and Empire; Perspectives on North America.* Toronto: Anansi 1969.

Grant, Shelagh D. *Sovereignty or Security? Government Policy in the Canadian North, 1936–1950.* Vancouver: University of British Columbia Press 1988.

– "Myths of the North in the Canadian Ethos." *The Northern Review* 3/4 (Summer/Winter 1989): 15–41.

The Great North: A Collection from Harper's Magazine. New York: Gallery 1990.

Green, Jim. *North Book.* 1975. Ill. Nauya. Winlaw, BC: Polestar 1986.

Greenwood, Michael. "Myth and Landscape: An Introduction." *Artscanada* 25.222–3 (Oct./Nov. 1978): 1–8.

Grey Owl [Archie Belaney]. *The Men of the Last Frontier.* London: Country Life 1934.

– *Pilgrims of the Wild.* London: Lovat Dickson & Thompson 1935.

– *Tales of an Empty Cabin.* London: Lovat Dickson 1936.

Griffin, John. "Film about the Inuit and Pioneer Film-Maker is a Triumph." *Montreal Gazette,* 16 Sept. 1994. C1–2.

Griffith, Richard. *The World of Robert Flaherty.* New York: Duell, Sloan and Pearce 1953.

Griffiths, Franklyn, ed. *Politics of the Northwest Passage.* Montreal: McGill-Queen's Press 1987.

Gross, Konrad. "North of Canada – Northern Canada: The North in 19th-Century Juvenile Fiction." *Zeitschrift für Kanada-Studien* 15.2 (1995): 19–32.

Grosz, Elizabeth A, ed. *Feminism and the Body. Hypatia: A Journal of Feminist Philosophy* 6.3 (Fall 1991).

– *Volatile Bodies: Toward a Corporeal Feminism.* St Leonards, NSW Australia: Allen & Unwin 1994.

Grove, F.P. *Over Prairie Trails.* Toronto: McClelland and Stewart 1970.

Gunnars, Kristjana. "The Idea of North and the Disclosure of Agency." In *Canada and the Nordic Countries in Times of Reorientation: Literature and Criticism,* ed. Jørn Carlsen. Aarhus, Denmark: Nordic Association for Canadian Studies 1998. 7–19.

Gutteridge, Don. *The Quest for North: Coppermine.* Ottawa: Oberon 1973.

Gwyn, Richard. *The Northern Magus: Pierre Trudeau and Canadians (1968–1980).* Ed. Sandra Gwyn. Toronto: McClelland and Stewart 1980.

Gzowski, Peter. "The Morningside Years: An Interview with Peter Gzowski." By Glenn Sumi. *The Book Review* 2.1 (1997): 6.

Haggard, H. Rider. *King Solomon's Mines.* London: Cassell 1933.

Haley, Susan. *The Complaints Department: A Northern Novel.* Wolfville, NS: Gaspereau Press 2000.

Haliburton, R.G. *The Men of the North and Their Place in History: A Lecture Delivered before the Montreal Literary Club, March 31*[st]*, 1869.* Montreal: John Lovell 1869.

– *A Review of British Diplomacy and its Fruits: "The Dream of the United Empire Loyalists of 1776."* London: Sampson Low, Marston, Low, and Searle 1872.

Halliday, D.S. *Tales, Trials and Tragedies of the Arctic.* Dawson Creek: D.S. Halliday 1990.

Hamelin, Louis-Edmond. *Canadian Nordicity: It's Your North Too.* Trans. William Barr. Montreal: Harvest 1979.

– *The Canadian North and Its Conceptual Referents.* Ottawa: Canadian Studies Directorate 1988.

– "Development of Nordology." *The Canadian North and its Conceptual Referents.* Ottawa: Canadian Studies Directorate 1988. 11–17.

– "Images of the North." In Coates and Morrison, *Interpreting Canada's North.* 7–17.

Hamilton, John David. *Arctic Revolution: Social Change in the Northwest Territories, 1835–1994.* Toronto: Dundurn 1994.

Hamilton, Walter R. *The Yukon Story: A Sourdough's Record of Goldrush Days and Yukon Progress from the Earliest Times to the Present Day.* Vancouver: Mitchell 1964.

Hamson, Leslie. *Last Rites. Canadian Theatre Review* 75 (Summer 1993): 55–71.

– "Land(e)scapes." Unpublished play, 1997.

Hancock, Geoffrey, ed. *Arctic of Words. Canadian Fiction Magazine* 83 (1993).

Hancock, Lyn. *Winging It in the North.* Lantzville, BC: Oolichen 1996.

Haraway, Donna. *Primate Visions: Gender, Race, and Nature in the World of Modern Science.* New York: Routledge 1989.

Hardin, Herschel. *Esker Mike & His Wife, Agiluk.* In Grace, D'Aeth, and Chalykoff, eds., *Staging the North.* 1–48.

Harley, J.B. "Maps, Knowledge, and Power." In *The Iconography of Landscape: Essays on the Symbolic Representation, Design and Use of Past Environments,* ed. Denis Cosgrove and Stephen Daniels. Cambridge: Cambridge University Press 1988. 277–312.

Harper, Kenn. *Give Me My Father's Body: The Life of Minik, the New York Eskimo.* Frobisher Bay, NWT: Blacklead 1986.

Harré, Romano. *Physical Being: A Theory for a Corporeal Psychology.* Cambridge, Mass.: Blackwell 1991.

Harris, Christopher. "Haunting Story of Hard Times." *Globe and Mail,* 4 May 1996, C1.

Harris, Eric. "Struck Powerless." *Canadian Geographic* 118.2 (Mar./Apr. 1998): 38–41.

Harris, Lawren. "Revelation of Art in Canada." *Canadian Theosophist* 7.5 (July 1926): 85–8.

– *Lawren Harris.* Ed. Bess Harris and R.G.P. Colgrove. Toronto: Macmillan 1969.

– *North by West: The Arctic and Rocky Mountain Paintings of Lawren Harris, 1924–31.* Calgary: Glenbow Museum 1991.

Harris, R. Cole. "Maps as a Morality Play: Volume I of the *Historical Atlas of Canada.*" In Winearls, ed., *Editing Atlases.* 163–79.

– *The Resettlement of British Columbia: Essays on Colonialism and Geographical Change.* Vancouver: University of British Columbia Press 1997.

Harrison, Keith. "Samuel Hearne, Matonabbee, and the 'Esquimaux Girl': Cultural Subjects, Cultural Objects." *Canadian Review of Comparative Literature* 22.3–4(1995): 647–57.

Hartsock, Nancy. "Foucault on Power: A Theory for Women?" In *Feminism/Postmodernism,* ed. Linda J. Nicholson. New York: Routledge 1990. 157–175.

Hay, Elizabeth. *Crossing the Snow Line.* Windsor, Ont.: Black Moss 1989.

– *The Only Snow in Havana.* Dunvegan, Ont.: Cormorant 1992.

– *Captivity Tales: Canadians in New York.* Vancouver: New Star 1993.

Heffel Gallery. *W.P. Weston, A.R.C.A.* Vancouver 1991.

Heming, Arthur. "The Snow Wetigo." 1907. In Colombo, ed., *Windigo.* 51–8.

Hemsworth, Wade. *The Songs of Wade Hemsworth.* Ed. Hugh Verrier, ill. Thoreau MacDonald. Waterloo, Ont.: Penumbra 1990.

Henighan, Tom. *Ideas of North: A Guide to Canadian Arts and Culture.* Vancouver: Raincoast 1997.

Hesse, Marta Gudrun. *Gabrielle Roy.* Boston: Twayne 1984.

– " 'The Invasion of Progress': Yves Thériault's Portrait of the Inuit in *Agaguk, Tayaout,* and *Agoak.*" In Carlsen and Streijffert, eds., *The Canadian North.* 73–85.

Highway, Thomson. *The Rez Sisters.* Saskatoon: Fifth House 1988.

– *Dry Lips Oughta Move to Kapuksasing.* Saskatoon: Fifth House 1989.

– *Kiss of the Fur Queen.* Toronto: Doubleday 1998.

Hill, Charles C. *Canadian Painting in the Thirties.* Ottawa: National Gallery of Canada 1975.

– *The Group of Seven; Art for a Nation.* Ottawa: National Gallery of Canada 1995.

Hinton, A. Cherry, and Philip H. Godsell. *The Yukon.* Toronto: Ryerson 1954.

Hirsch, Marianne. *Family Frames: Photography, Narrative, and Postmemory.* Cambridge, Mass.: Harvard University Press 1997.

Hirschkop, Ken, and David Shepherd, eds. *Bakhtin and Cultural Theory.* New York: St. Martin's 1989.

Hirsh, Michael, Patrick Laubert, Clive Smith, and Alan Walker. *Great Canadian Comic Books.* Toronto: Peter Martin 1971.

Hitchcock, Peter. *Dialogics of the Oppressed.* Minneapolis: University of Minnesota Press 1993.

Hjartarson, Paul. "Of Inward Journeys and Interior Landscapes: Glenn Gould, Lawren Harris, and 'The Idea of North.' " In Grace, ed., *Representing North.* 65–86.

Hodge, Robert, and Gunther Kress. *Social Semiotics.* Ithaca, New York: Cornell University Press 1988.

Hodgins, Bruce W. "The Canadian North: Conflicting Images, Conflicting Historiography." In *Voyageur: Collected Papers and Proceedings*

of the Work-in-Progress Colloquium, ed.
A.G. Martel and F.A. Hagar. Vol. 2 (1979–80).
[Peterborough, Ont.]: Department of History,
Trent University, n.d. n.p.

– and Gwyneth Hoyle. *Canoeing North into the
Unknown: A Record of River Travel, 1874 to 1974.*
Toronto.: Natural Heritage/National History
1994.

– et al., eds. *The Canadian North: Source of Wealth
or Vanishing Heritage?* Scarborough, Ont.:
Prentice-Hall 1977.

Hoeg, Peter. *Smilla's Sense of Snow.* Trans. Tiina Nun-
nally. New York: Farrar, Straus and Giroux 1993.

Holling, Holling Clancy. *Paddle-to-the-Sea.* Boston: Houghton 1941.

Homer-Dixon, Thomas. "Dealing with a major-
league ice hole." *Globe and Mail*, 8 Sept. 2000
A17.

Honderich, John. *Arctic Imperative: Is Canada
Losing the North?* Toronto: University of
Toronto Press 1987.

Hong, Ahnes. "Judith Thompson: A Bibliography." *Canadian Theatre Review* 89 (Winter
1996): 42–4.

Hood, Hugh. *Dead Men's Watches.* Don Mills,
Ont.: Anansi 1995.

Hood, Robert. *To the Arctic by Canoe, 1819–1821: The
Journal and Paintings of Robert Hood, Midshipman
with Franklin.* Ed. C. Stuart Houston. Montreal:
McGill-Queen's University Press 1974.

Horwood, Harold. *White Eskimo: A Novel of Labrador.* Don Mills, Ont.: Paperjacks 1972.

Hossack, Phil. "Return of the Kayak." *Canadian
Geographic* 119.1 (Jan./Feb. 1999): 58–64.

Houle, Alain. "Les Voyageries de Gabrielle
Roy at de René Richard." *North/Nord* 24.6
(Nov./Dec. 1977): 36–43.

Housser, Frederick B. *A Canadian Art Movement:
The Story of the Group of Seven.* 1926. Toronto:
Macmillan 1974.

Houston, James. *Whiteout.* 1988. Toronto:
General Paperbacks 1991.

– *Confessions of an Igloo Dweller.* Toronto:
McClelland and Stewart 1995

– "Art of the Arctic." *Vancouver Sun*, 20 Jan. 1996,
D1ff.

– *The Ice Master: A Novel of the Arctic.* Toronto:
McClelland and Stewart 1997.

Houston, John. *Spirit Wrestler.* Toronto:
McClelland and Stewart 1980.

Howell, Mike. "B.C. crew led to graves from
Franklin expedition." *Vancouver Sun*, 26 Aug.
2000, A1–2, B6–8.

How Summer Came to Canada. Retold by William
Toye, ill. Elizabeth Cleaver. Toronto: Oxford
University Press 1969.

Hoyle, Gwyneth. "Women of Determination:
Northern Journeys by Women before 1940."
In *Nastawgan: The Canadian North by Canoe and
Snowshoe: A Collection of Historical Essays*, ed.
Bruce W. Hodgins and Margaret Hobbs.
Toronto: Betelgeuse 1985. 117–40.

Hubbard, Mina Benson. *A Woman's Way through
Unknown Labrador.* Toronto: William Briggs
1908.

Hulan, Renée. "Representing the Canadian
North: Stories of Gender, Race, and Nation
(Identity)." PhD,. McGill University 1996.

Hume, Christopher. "Doris McCarthy." *Weekend
Sun* (Toronto), 9 Jan. 1982, "Today," 13.

Hume, Stephen. *Signs against an Empty Sky.* Dunvegan, Ont.: Quadrant 1980.

Hunt, William R. *Stef: A Biography of Vilhjalmur
Stefansson.* Vancouver: University of British
Columbia Press 1986.

Hunter, Andrew. *Up North: A Northern Ontario
Tragedy.* Owen Sound, Ont.: Thomson 1997.

Hutcheon, Linda. *Narcissistic Narrative: The
Metafictional Paradox.* Waterloo: Wilfrid
Laurier University Press 1980.

Ignatieff, Michael. *Blood & Belonging: Journeys
into the New Nationalism.* Toronto: Viking 1993.

Ingstad, Helge Marcus. *The Land of Feast and
Famine.* 1933. Montreal: McGill-Queen's University Press 1992.

Innis, Harold. *The Fur Trade in Canada: An Introduction to Canadian Economic History.* Rev. ed.
Toronto: University of Toronto Press 1970.

Inuit Traditional Life Series, Northwest Territories.
Photographs. [NWT]: Department of the
Northwest Territories 1981.

Ipellie, Alootook. "Ice Box." Cartoon. *Inuit
Monthly*, Jan. 1974 to Feb. 1975. Continued in
Inuit Today, Feb. 1975 to Spring 1982.

– *Arctic Dreams and Nightmares.* Penticton, BC:
Theytus 1993.

– "Alootook Ipellie: The Voice of an Inuk
Artist." Interview with Michael P.J. Kennedy.
Studies in Canadian Literature 21.2 (1996): 155–64.

– "Thirsty for Life: A Nomad Learns To Write
and Draw." In Moss, ed., *Echoing Silence.* 93–101.

Israel, Inge. *Unmarked Doors: Poems.* Vancouver:
Cacanadadada 1992.

Jackson, A.Y. *A Painter's Country: The Autobiography of A.Y. Jackson.* 1958. Toronto: Clarke, Irwin
& Co. 1976.

- A.Y. Jackson, The Arctic 1927. Intro. Naomi Jackson Groves. Moonbeam, Ont.: Penumbra 1982.

Jacobus, Mary, Evelyn Fox Keller, and Sally Shuttleworth, eds. Body/Politics: Women and the Discourses of Science. New York: Routledge 1990.

James, William Closson. A Fur Trader's Photographs: A.A. Chesterfield in the District of Ungava, 1901–4. Kingston: McGill-Queen's University Press 1985.

- Locations of the Sacred: Essays on Religion, Literature, and Canadian Culture. Waterloo, Ont.: Wilfrid Laurier University Press 1998.

Jason, Victoria. Kabloona in the Yellow Kayak: One Woman's Journey through the Northwest Passage. Winnipeg: Turnstone 1995.

Jay, Paul. "Posing: Autobiography and the Subject of Photography." In Ashley, Gilmore, and Peters, eds., Autobiography and Postmodernism. 191–211.

Jeannotte, Ken. "A Pale Caress." Photographic Series. Yukon Arts Centre, Whitehorse. 27 June to 4 Aug. 1996.

Jefferson, Ann. "Realism Reconsidered: Bakhtin's Dialogism and the 'Will To Reference.'" Australian Journal of French Studies 23.2 (May–Aug. 1986): 169–84.

Jeffery, Lawrence. Who Look In Stove. In Grace, D'Aeth, and Chalykoff, eds., Staging the North. 187–235.

Jenness, Diamond. Arctic Odyssey: The Diary of Diamond Jenness, Ethnologist with the Canadian Arctic Expedition in Northern Alaska and Canada, 1913–1916. Ed. Stuart E. Jenness. Hull, PQ: Canadian Museum of Civilization 1991.

- The People of the Twilight. 1928. Chicago: University of Chicago Press 1959.

- "A Human Being Transformed." 1935. In Colombo, ed., Windigo. 125–6.

- Dawn in Arctic Alaska. Minneapolis: University of Minnesota Press 1957.

Jenness, Stuart E. "Conflicts and Adversities: The Southern Party of the Canadian Arctic Expedition, 1913–1916." The Beaver 76.4 (Aug.–Sept. 1996): 34–41.

Jiles, Paulette. North Spirit: Travels Among the Cree and Ojibway Nations and Their Star Maps. Toronto: Doubleday 1995.

Johnson, James Albert. Carmack of the Klondike. Ganges, BC: Horsdal & Schubart 1990.

Johnson, Phyllis J., and Peter Suedfeld. "Coping with Stress through the Microcosms of Home and Family among Arctic Whalers and Explorers." History of the Family 1.1 (1996): 41–62.

Johnston, Basil. Ojibway Heritage. Toronto: McClelland and Stewart 1976.

Kallmann, Helmut, Gilles Potvin, Kenneth Winters, eds. Encyclopedia of Music in Canada. Toronto: University of Toronto Press 1981.

Kalluak, Mark, ed. How Kabloonat Became and Other Inuit Legends. Yellowknife: Program Development, Dept. of Education, Government of NWT, 1974.

Kasemets, Udo. "John Weinzweig." Canadian Music Journal 4.4 (Summer 1960): 4–18.

"Kate Carmacks [sic]." Alaska Sportsman 34 (Oct. 1968): 3.

Kavanagh, Geoff. "Canoe Lake." Unpublished play.

- Ditch. In Grace, D'Aeth, and Chalykoff, eds., Staging the North. 135–85.

Keenainak, Simeonie. "The Native Photograph." In King and Lidchi, eds., Imaging the Arctic. 221–5.

Keenleyside, Anne, Margaret Bertulli, and Henry C. Fricke. "The Final Days of the Franklin Expedition: New Skeletal Evidence." Arctic 50.1 (Mar. 1997): 36–46.

Kelcey, Barbara Eileen. "Lost in the Rush: the Forgotten Women of the Klondike Stampede." MA, University of Victoria 1987.

Kelly, M.T. The Ruined Season. Windsor, Ont.: Black Moss 1982.

- A Dream Like Mine: A Novel. Toronto: Stoddart 1987.

- Breath Dances between Them: Stories. Toronto: Stoddart 1991.

- Out of the Whirlwind: A Novel. Toronto: Stoddart 1995.

Kennedy, Michael P.J. "The Sea Goddess Sedna: An Enduring Pan-Arctic Legend from Traditional Orature to the New Narratives of the Late Twentieth Century." In Moss, ed., Echoing Silence. 211–24.

Kenney, Gerard I. Arctic Smoke & Mirrors. Prescott, Ont.: Voyageur 1994.

Kenyon, Walter. Arctic Argonauts. Waterloo: Penumbra 1990.

Kerr, D.G.G., ed. A Historical Atlas of Canada. Cartography by C.C.J. Bond. Toronto: Thomas Nelson 1960.

King, J.C.H. and Henrietta Lidchi, eds. Imaging the Arctic. Vancouver and Seattle: University of British Columbia and University of Washington Press 1998.

Kipling, Rudyard. "Quiquern." *The Second Jungle Book*. Ill. J. Lockwood Kipling. London: Macmillan 1895. 143–71.

– "Our Lady of the Snows." 1897. *The Complete Verse*. London: Kyle Cathie 1990. 148–9.

– "Recessional, 1897." *The Collected Verse of Rudyard Kipling*. Toronto: Copp Clark 1910. 219.

Kirchhofer, Anton. "The Foucault Complex: A Review of Foucauldian Approaches in Literary Studies." *ZAA: A Quarterly of Language, Literature and Culture* 45.4 (1997): 277–99.

Kitigawa, Muriel. *This Is My Own: Letters to Wes and Other Writings on Japanese Canadians, 1941–1948*. Ed. Roy Miki. Vancouver: Talonbooks 1985.

Kiyooka, Roy. "letters purporting to be abt tom thomson." *Artscanada* 29 (Feb./Mar. 1972): 25–34.

– *Pacific Windows: Collected Poems of Roy K. Kiyooka*. Ed. Roy Miki. Vancouver: Talonbooks 1997.

Klengenberg, Lily. "Umialik's Daughters." *Up Here: Life in Canada's North* 15.3 (Apr. 1999): 59–61.

Klutschak, Heinrich W. *Overland to Starvation Cove: With the Inuit in Search of Franklin 1878–1880*. Trans. and ed. William Barr. Toronto: University of Toronto Press 1993.

Knott, Russell. "The Mounties in Print." *Book and Magazine Collector* 129 (Dec. 1994): 29–41.

Knowles, Richard Paul. "Representing Canada: Teaching Canadian Studies in the United States." *American Review of Canadian Studies* 25.1 (Spring 1995): 9–26.

– " 'Great Lines Are a Dime a Dozen': Judith Thompson's Greatest Cuts." *Canadian Theatre Review* 89 (Winter 1996): 8–18.

Konrad, Victor. "Recurrent Symbols of Nationalism in Canada." *Canadian Geographer* 30.2 (1986): 175–180.

Korte, Barbara. "In Quest of an Arctic Past: Mordecai Richler's *Solomon Gursky Was Here*." In *Historiographic Metafiction in Modern American and Canadian Literature*, ed. Bernd Engler and Kurt Müller. Paderborn: Ferdinand Schöningh 1994. 493–505.

Kraus, Robert, ed. *Nanook of the North [by] Robert Flaherty*. New York: Windmill 1971.

Kreimeier, Klaus. "Blaue Blume Wirklichkeit." *Die Zeit* 30.28 (July 1995): 15.

Kreisel, Henry. *The Betrayal*. Toronto: McClelland and Stewart 1971.

Kristeva, Julia. *Powers of Horror: An Essay on Abjection*. Trans. Leon S. Roudiez. New York: Columbia University Press 1982.

Kroetsch, Robert. *But We Are Exiles: A Novel*. Toronto: Macmillan 1965.

– "A Conversation with Margaret Laurence." In Kroetsch, ed., *Creation*. 53–63.

– *Gone Indian*. Toronto: New Press 1973.

– *The Stone Hammer Poems: 1960–1975*. Lantzville, BC: Oolichan 1975.

– *The Crow Journals*. Edmonton: NeWest 1980.

– "The Canadian Writer and the American Literary Tradition." *Open Letter* 5.4 (Spring 1983): 11–15.

– *The Lovely Treachery of Words: Essays Selected and New*. Toronto: Oxford University Press 1989.

– *A Likely Story: The Writing Life*. Red Deer, Alta.: Red Deer College Press 1995.

– "Playing Dead in Rudy Wiebe's *Playing Dead*: A Reader's Marginalia." *A Likely Story*. 87–109.

– "Why I Went Up North and What I Found When He Got There." *A Likely Story*. 13–40.

– *The Man from the Creeks: A Novel*. Toronto: Random 1998.

– ed. *Creation*. Toronto: New Press 1970.

Kroker, Arthur, and Marilouise Kroker, eds. *Body Invaders: Panic Sex in America*. Montreal: New World Perspectives 1987.

Kula, Sam. "Dreams Made in Canada: A History of the Feature Film, 1913 to 1995." *Archivist* 110 (1995): 16–25.

Kurelek, William. *The Last of the Arctic*. Toronto: McGraw-Hill Ryerson 1976.

– *A Northern Nativity: Christmas Dreams of a Prairie Boy*. Montreal: Tundra 1976.

Kuropatwa, Joy. "Durkin's *The Lobstick Trail*." In Carlsen, ed., *Literary Responses*. 97–103.

Kusugak, Michael Arvaarluk, and Vladyana Krykorka. *Baseball Bats for Christmas*. Ill. Vladyana Krykorka. Toronto: Annick 1990.

– *Hide and Sneak*. Ill. Vladyana Krykorka. Toronto: Annick 1992.

Laberge, Marie. *Ils étaient venus pour –*. Montreal: Boréal 1997.

Lacombe, Michele. "The Origin of *The Hidden Mountain*." *Canadian Literature* 88 (Spring 1981): 164–6.

– "Theosophy and the Canadian Idealist Tradition: A Preliminary Exploration." *Journal of Canadian Studies/Revue d'etudes canadiennes* 17.2 (1982): 100–18.

Laghi, Brian. "Inuit Find No Magic Solution on the Way." *Globe and Mail*, 4 June 1998, A1.

Laidlaw, G.E. "Six Traditional Tales." 1924. In Colombo, ed., *Windigo*. 119–23.

Lambert, Betty. "The Song of the Serpent." Unpublished play.

Lampman, Archibald. "Temagami." *Lampman's Sonnets, 1884–1899*. Ed. Margaret Coulby Whitridge. Ottawa: Borealis 1976. 158.

Lane, Harry. "Redefining the Comfort Zone: Nancy Palk, on Acting Judith Thompson." *Canadian Theatre Review* 89 (Winter 1996): 19–21.

Lane, Patrick. *Winter*. Regina, Sask.: Coteau 1990.

Languirand, Jacques. *Klondyke: Action dramatique*. Musique de Gabriel Charpentier. Montreal: Cercle du livre de France 1971.

Lanken, Dane. "The Vision of Grey Owl." *Canadian Geographic* 119.2 (Mar./Apr. 1999): 74–80.

– and Mary Vincent. "Nunavut, Up and Running." *Canadian Geographic* 119.1 (Jan./Feb. 1999): 38–46.

Larisey, Peter. "Nationalist Aspects of Lawren S. Harris's Aesthetics." *National Gallery of Canada Bulletin* 23 (1974): 3–9.

– *Light for a Cold Land: Lawren Harris's Work and Life – An Interpretation*. Toronto: Dundurn 1993.

Lazarevich, Gordana. *The Musical World of Frances James and Murray Adaskin*. Toronto: University of Toronto Press 1988.

Leacock, Stephen. *Adventures of the Far North, A Chronicle of the Arctic Seas*. Toronto: Glasgow, Brook & Co. 1922.

– "I'll Stay in Canada." *Funny Pieces*. New York: Dodd, Mead 1936. 284–92.

– Introduction to *Unsolved Mysteries of the Arctic* by Vilhjalmur Stefansson. New York: Macmillan 1945. v–viii.

– "Reflections on the North." In *A Northern Treasury: Selections from The Beaver*, ed. Clifford Wilson. New York: Thomas Nelson, n.d. 56–64.

Lecker, Robert, ed. *Borderlands: Essays in Canadian-American Relations*. Toronto: ECW Press 1991.

Lecomte, Guy. "L'Appel de la forêt et l'appel du Nord: Mythes et réalités." In Carlsen and Streijffert, eds., *The Canadian North*. 87–99.

Lee, Betty. *Lutiapik: The Story of a Young Woman's Year of Isolation and Service in the Arctic*. Toronto: McClelland and Stewart 1975.

Leer, Martin. "From Linear to Areal: Suggestions towards a Comparative Literary Geography of Canada and Australia." *Kunapipi* 12.3 (1990): 75–85.

Legault, E.T. *Dixon of the Mounted*. Toronto: Active Adventure Comics, 1942–.

Leroux, Jean-François. "Black Snow: The Arctic Infernos of Hubert Aquin and Denys Chabot." *The Northern Review* 17 (Winter 1996): 97–108.

Levasseur, Donat. *Les Oblats de Marie Immaculée dans l'Ouest et le Nord du Canada, 1845–1967: esquisse historique*. Edmonton: University of Alberta Press 1995.

Lewis, Richard, ed. *I Breathe a New Song: Poems of the Eskimo*. Ill. Oonark, intro. Edmund Carpenter. New York: Simon and Schuster 1971.

Lighthall, William Douw. *Songs of the Great Dominion: Voices from the Forests and Waters, the Settlements and Cities of Canada*. London: Walter Scott 1889.

Lightstone, Susan. "North Star Rising: Susan Aglukark Takes Off." *Arctic Circle* (Winter 1993): 14ff.

Lill, Wendy. *The Occupation of Heather Rose*. In Grace, D'Aeth, and Chalykoff, eds., *Staging the North*. 293–330.

Linsley, Robert. "Landscapes in Motion: Lawren Harris, Emily Carr and the Heterogenous Modern Nation." *Oxford Art Journal* 19.1 (1996): 80–95.

Little, James R. "Squaw Kate." *Alaska Life* (Mar. 1943): 17–18.

Littlejohn, Bruce, and Jon Pearce, eds. *Marked by the Wild: An Anthology of Literature Shaped by the Canadian Wilderness*. Toronto: McClelland and Stewart 1973.

Livesay, Dorothy. *The Two Seasons*. Toronto: McGraw-Hill Ryerson 1972.

Loiselle, Andre. "François Girard's Glenn Gould and The Idea of North." *Reverse Shot* 1.3 (1994): 8–13.

Long, John Luther. *Madame Butterfly*. New York: Century 1903.

Longfellow, Henry Wadsworth. *Evangeline*. 1847. Halifax, NS: T.C. Allen 1901.

Lopez, Barry. *Arctic Dreams: Imagination and Desire in a Northern Landscape*. Toronto: Bantam 1989.

Loranger, Françoise. *Encore cinq minutes et Un cri qui vient de loin*. Ottawa: Le Cercel du Livre de France 1967.

Loti, Pierre. *Japan; Madame Chrysanthèmum*. Trans. Laura Ensor. London: KPI 1985.

Lotz, Jim. *Northern Realities; The Future of Northern Development in Canada.* Toronto: New Press 1970.

Lyall, Ernie. *An Arctic Man: Sixty-Five Years in Canada's North.* Halifax: Goodread Biographies 1983.

Lynn, Marion, and Shelagh Wilkinson, eds. *Women of the North. Canadian Women's Studies* 14.4 (Fall 1994).

Lyotard, Jean-François. *The Postmodern Condition: A Report on Knowledge.* Trans. Geoff Bennington and Brian Massumi. Minneapolis: University of Minnesota Press 1984.

McCaffery, Steve. *North of Intention: Critical Writings, 1973–1986.* Toronto: Nightwood 1986.

McCall, Gordon. "Running on Frozen Air." Unpublished play, 1996.

McCarthy, Martha. *From the Great River to the Ends of the Earth: Oblate Missions to the Dene, 1847–1921.* Edmonton: University of Alberta Press 1995.

McClary, Susan. *Feminine Endings: Music, Gender, and Sexuality.* Minneapolis: University of Minnesota Press 1991.

McClintock, Anne. *Imperial Leather: Race, Gender, and Sexuality in the Colonial Conquest.* New York: Routledge 1995.

M'Clintock, Francis Leopold. *The Voyage of the 'Fox' in the Arctic Seas. A Narrative of the Discovery of the Fate of Sir John Franklin and His Companions.* Edmonton: Hurtig 1972.

McCourt, Edward. *The Yukon and Northwest Territories.* Toronto: Macmillan 1969.

MacDonald, Colin. S. "Francis Hans Johnston." *A Dictionary of Canadian Artists.* Vol. 3. Ottawa: Canadian Paperbacks 1967. 566–70.

MacDonald, Ian, and Betty O'Keefe. *The Klondike's "Dear Little Nugget."* Victoria, BC: Horsdal & Schubart 1996.

MacDonald, Janice. *True North: Canadian Essays for Composition.* Don Mills, Ont.: Addison-Wesley 1999.

MacDonald, J. Fred. *Don't Touch That Dial! Radio Programming in American Life, 1920–1960.* Chicago: Nelson-Hall 1979.

MacDonald, John. *The Arctic Sky: Inuit Astronomy, Star Lore, and Legend.* Toronto: Royal Ontario Museum/Nunavut Research Institute 1998.

MacDonald, Mike. *Seven Sisters.* Video Installation. Yukon Arts Centre, Whitehorse, NWT 27 June–4 Aug. 1996.

McDowell, Jim. *Hamatsa: The Enigma of Cannibalism on the Pacific Northwest Coast.* Vancouver: Ronsdale 1997.

MacEwen, Gwendolyn. *Terror and Erebus: A Verse Play for Radio. Tamarack Review* (Oct. 1974): 5–22. Repr. in *The Poetry of Gwendolyn MacEwen*, Vol. 1, *The Early Years.* 101–19.

– *Terror and Erebus.* In Grace, D'Aeth, and Chalykoff, eds., *Staging the North.* 115–33.

– *Noman's Land: Stories.* Toronto: Coach House, 1985.

– *Afterworlds.* Toronto: McClelland and Stewart 1987.

– *The Poetry of Gwendolyn MacEwen.* 2 vols. Ed. Margaret Atwood and Barry Callaghan. Toronto: Exile 1993, 1994.

McGee, Thomas D'Arcy. "Protection for Canadian Literature." *New Era* (24 April 1858): 2.

McGhee, Robert. *Ancient People of the Arctic.* Vancouver, BC: University of British Columbia Press 1996.

McGoogan, Ken. *Fatal Passage: The Untold Story of John Rae, the Arctic Adventurer Who Discovered the Fate of Franklin.* Toronto: HarperCollins 2001.

McGrath, Robin. "Editing Inuit Literature: Leaving the Teeth in the Gently Smiling Jaws." *Inuit Art Quarterly* 2.4 (Fall 1987): 3–6.

– "Oral Influences in Contemporary Inuit Literature." In *The Native in Literature*, ed. Thomas King, Cheryl Calver, and Helen Hoy. Toronto: ECW 1987. 159–73.

– "Maps as Metaphor: One Hundred Years of Inuit Cartography." *Inuit Art Quarterly* 3.2 (Spring 1988): 6–10.

– "Monster Figures and Unhappy Endings in Inuit Literature." *Canadian Journal of Native Education* 15.1 (1988): 51–8.

– "The European in Inuit Literature." In Carlsen and Streijffert, eds., *The Canadian North.* 109–18.

– "Circumventing the Taboos: Inuit Women's Autobiographies." In *Regard sur l'avenir/Looking to the Future: Papers from the 7th Inuit Studies Conference*, ed. Marie-Josée Dufour and François Thérien. Laval, PQ: University of Laval Press 1990. 215–25.

– "The Development of Inuit Literature in English." In *Minority Literatures in North America: Contemporary Perspectives*, ed. Wolfgang Karrer and Hartmut Lutz. Frankfurt am Main: Peter Lang 1990. 193–203.

– "Samuel Hearne and the Inuit Oral Tradition." *Studies in Canadian Literature* 18.2 (1993): 94–109.

– *Trouble and Desire.* St John's, Nfld.: Killick 1995.

McGregor, Gaile. *The Wacousta Syndrome: Explorations in the Canadian Langscape.* Toronto: University of Toronto Press 1985.

Machar, Agnes Maule. *Lays of the "True North," and Other Canadian Poems.* London: Elliot Stock and Copp, Clarke 1899.

McIntyre, Gordon. "Believe It!" *Up Here* 17.7 (2001): 31.

Mackay, James A. *Robert Service: A Biography: Vagabond of Verse.* Edinburgh: Mainstream 1995.

Mackay, J. Ross. "Arctic Landforms." In Wonders, ed., *Canada's Changing North.* 91–3.

McKillop, A.B., ed. *Contexts of Canada's Past: Selected Essays of W.L. Morton.* Toronto: Macmillan 1980.

MacLaren, Ian S. "Retaining Captaincy of the Soul: Response to Nature in the First Franklin Expedition." *Essays on Canadian Writing* 28 (1984): 57–92.

– "Samuel Hearne and the Landscapes of Discovery." *Canadian Literature* 103 (Winter 1984): 27–40.

– "The Aesthetic Map of the North, 1845–1859." *Arctic* 38.2 (June 1985): 89–103.

– "Samuel Hearne and the Inuit Girl." In Easingwood *et al.*, eds., *Probing Canadian Culture.* 87–106.

– "The Poetry of the 'New Georgia Gazette' or 'Winter Chronicle' 1819–1820." *Canadian Poetry* 30 (Spring/Summer 1992): 41–73.

– "Commentary: The Aesthetics of Back's Writing and Painting from the First Overland Expedition." In Back, *Arctic Artist.* 275–310.

– "Tracing One Discontinuous Line through the Poetry of the Northwest Passage." *Canadian Poetry* 39 (Fall/Winter 1996): 7–48.

MacLean, Eva. *The Far Land.* Prince George, BC: Caitlin 1993.

MacLennan, Hugh. *The Watch That Ends the Night.* New York: Signet 1959.

McLeod, Grace Dean. *Stories of the Land of Evangeline.* Boston: D. Lothrop 1891.

MacLeod, Margaret, and Richard Glover, eds. "Franklin's First Expedition as Seen by the Fur Traders." *Polar Record* 15.98 (1971): 669–82.

MacMillan, Rick. "Out of Technology, Back to Nature." *Music Scene* 293 (Jan.–Feb. 1977): 6–7.

– "Diana McIntosh Calls Winnipeg Home Base." *Music Scene* 300 (Sept.–Oct. 1978): 4ff.

McNay, Lois. *Foucault and Feminism: Power, Gender and the Self.* Boston: Northeastern University Press 1992.

McNeilly, Kevin. "Listening, Nordicity, Community: Glenn Gould's 'The Idea of North.'" In Grace, ed., *Representing North.* 87–104.

McPhedran, Marie. *Golden North.* Toronto: Macmillan 1948.

McPherson, Hugo. "Wieland: An Epiphany of North." In Elder, ed., *Films of Joyce Wieland.* 11–19.

MacPherson, M.A. *Outlaws of The Canadian West.* Edmonton: Lone Pine 1999.

Madsen, Ken. "Discovering the Music of the Wilderness." *Up Here: Life in Canada's North* (Mar.–Apr. 1998): 24ff.

Malette, Yvon. *L'Autoportrait mythique de Gabrielle Roy: analyse genettienne de La Montagne secrète de Gabrielle Roy.* Orléans, Ont.: Les Éditions David 1994.

Malinowski, Bronislaw. *The Argonauts of the Western Pacific: An Account of Native Enterprise and Adventure in the Archipelagoes of Melanesian New Guinea.* New York: Dutton 1922.

Mandel, Charles. "Kissed by a Fur Queen." *Calgary Straight,* 15–21 Oct. 1998, 12.

Mandel, Eli. "The Inward, Northward Journey of Lawren Harris." *artscanada* 222/223 (Oct./Nov. 1978): 17–24.

Mandy, E. Madge. *Our Trail Led Northwest: True Tale of Romance and Adventure in British Columbia.* Photographs by Joseph T. Mandy. Burnaby, BC: E.M. Mandy 1989.

Manera, Matthew. "The Act of Being Read: Fictional Process in *Places Far from Ellesmere.*" *Canadian Literature* 146 (Autumn 1995): 87–94.

Marchand, Philip. *Marshall McLuhan: The Medium and the Messenger.* Toronto: Random 1989.

Markoosie. *Harpoon of the Hunter.* Montreal: McGill-Queen's University Press 1970.

Marks, Laura. "Authorship and Audience in Inuit Video." Unpublished paper, 1998.

Marsh, Donald B. *Echoes from a Frozen Land.* Ed. Winifred Marsh. Edmonton: Hurtig 1987.

Martineau, Joel. "Landscapes and Inscape in Thomas Wharton's *Icefields.*" *Open Letter* 10.2 (1998): 41–50.

Mayer, Melanie J. *Klondike Women: True Tales of the 1897–98 Gold Rush.* Athens, Ohio: Swallow/ Ohio University Press 1989.

Mellen, Peter. *The Group of Seven.* Toronto: McClelland and Stewart 1970.

Memorial University of Newfoundland Art Gallery. *Marlene Creates: Landworks 1979–91.* Exhibition Catalogue. St John's, Nfld., 1993.

Merchant, Carolyn. *The Death of Nature: Women, Ecology, and the Scientific Revolution.* San Francisco: Harper 1980.

– *Ecological Revolutions: Nature, Gender, and Science in New England.* Chapel Hill: University of North Carolina Press 1989.

Merivale, Patricia. "The Biographical Compulsion: Elegiac Romances in Canadian Fiction." *Journal of Modern Literature* 8.1 (1980): 139–52.

Metayer, Maurice, ed. and trans. *Tales from the Igloo.* Ill. Agnes Nanogak, foreword by Al Purdy. Edmonton: Hurtig 1972.

Metcalfe, Robin. "Letters Out." *Books in Canada* (Mar. 1990), 21–4.

Mewburn, Charity. *N.E. Thing: Sixteen Hundred Miles North of Denver.* Vancouver: Morris and Helen Belkin Art Gallery 1999.

Michaels, Anne. *Fugitive Pieces.* Toronto: McClelland and Stewart 1996.

Mitcham, Allison. *The Northern Imagination: A Study of Northern Canadian Literature.* Moonbeam, Ont.: Penumbra 1983.

– *Atlin: The Last Utopia.* 1989. Hantsport, NS: Lancelot 1992.

Mitchell, Timothy. *Colonising Egypt.* Cambridge: Cambridge University Press 1988.

Montrose, Louis. "The Work of Gender in the Discourse of Discovery." *Representations* 33 (Winter 1991): 1–41.

Morency, Jean. *Un roman du regard: La Montagne secrète de Gabrielle Roy.* Quebec: Centre de recherche en littérature québécoise, Université Laval 1985.

Morissonneau, Christian. *La Terre promise: Le Mythe du Nord québécois.* Montréal: Hurtubise 1978.

– "Images d'Amérique et lieu du Nord." *Études françaises* 21.2 (1985): 53–9.

Morley, Patricia. "Canadian Art: Northern Land, Northern Vision." In *Ambivalence: Studies in Canadian Literature,* ed. Om P. Juneja and Chandra Mohan. New Delhi: Allied 1990. 22–38.

Morley, William F. *Ontario and the Canadian North.* Vol. 3 of *Canadian Local Histories to 1950: A Bibliography.* Toronto: University of Toronto Press 1978.

Morris, Alexander M. *The Hudson's Bay and Pacific Territories: A Lecture.* Montreal: John Lovell 1859.

Morris, Peter. *Embattled Shadows: A History of Canadian Cinema, 1895–1939.* Montreal: McGill-Queen's University Press 1978.

Morrison, David, and Georges-Hébert Germain. *Inuit, Glimpses of an Arctic Past.* Ill. Frédéric Back. Hull, PQ: Canadian Museum of Civilization 1995.

Morrison, William R. *Showing the Flag: The Mounted Police and Canadian Sovereignty in the North, 1894–1925.* Vancouver: University of British Columbia Press 1985.

– *True North: The Yukon and Northwest Territories.* Toronto: Oxford University Press 1998.

– and Kenneth A. Coates. *Working the North: Labor and the Northwest Defense Projects, 1942–1946.* Fairbanks: University of Alaska Press 1994.

Morton, W.L. "Clio in Canada: The Interpretation of Canadian History." 1946. In McKillop, ed., *Contexts.* 103–12.

– "Marginal." 1946. In McKillop, ed., *Contexts.* 41–7.

– *The Canadian Identity.* 1961. 2nd ed. Madison, Wisc.: University of Wisconsin Press 1972.

– "British North America and a Continent in Dissolution, 1861–71." 1962. In McKillop, ed., *Contexts.* 186–207.

– "The North in Canadian History." *Northern Affairs Bulletin* 7.1 (Jan./Feb. 1960): 26–9.

– "The 'North' in Canadian Historiography." 1970. In McKillop, ed., *Contexts.* 229–39.

Moses, Daniel David, and Terry Goldie, eds. *An Anthology of Canadian Native Literature in English.* 2nd ed. Toronto: Oxford University Press 1998.

Moss, John, ed. *The Canadian Novel.* 4 vols. Toronto: NC Press 1978, 1980, 1982, 1985.

– *Enduring Dreams: An Exploration of Arctic Landscape.* Don Mills, Ont.: Anansi 1994.

– ed. *Echoing Silence: Essays on Arctic Narrative.* Ottawa: University of Ottawa Press 1997.

Mowat, Farley. *Lost in the Barrens.* 1956. Ill. Charles Geer. Toronto: McClelland and Stewart 1993.

– *Never Cry Wolf.* Toronto: McClelland and Stewart 1963.

– *The Polar Passion: The Quest for the North Pole.* Toronto: McClelland and Stewart 1967.

– *Canada North.* Toronto: McClelland and Stewart, 1969.

– *Tundra: Selections from the Great Accounts of Arctic Land Voyages.* Vol. 3 of *The Top of the World Trilogy.* Toronto: McClelland and Stewart 1973.

– *The Snow Walker.* Toronto: McClelland and Stewart 1975.

- *Ordeal by Ice: The Search for the Northwest Passage.* Toronto: McClelland and Stewart 1989.
- "The Nature of the North." In *The Broadview Reader*, ed. H. Rosengarten and Jane Flick. Rev. ed. Peterborough, Ont.: Broadview 1992. 257–63.
- *Walking on the Land.* Toronto: Key Porter 2000.

Mulhallen, Karen. "Schaferscapes/Wolfbound: Twelve Notes Toward a New View of Camping." *Descant* 26.1 (Spring 1995): 133–76.
- "Schaferscapes." *Border Crossings* 15.1 (Winter 1996): 25–31.

Müller-Wille, Ludger, ed. *Franz Boas among the Inuit on Baffin Island, 1883–1884.* Trans. William Barr. Toronto: University of Toronto Press 1998.

Munro, John A., ed. *The Wit & Wisdom of John Diefenbaker.* Edmonton: Hurtig 1982.

Munsch, Robert, and Michael Martchenko. *50 Below Zero.* 1986. Toronto: Annick 1992.

Murphy, William T. *Robert Flaherty: A Guide to References and Sources.* Boston: G.K. Hall 1978.

Murray, Jeffrey S. "Selling Golden Dreams." *Canadian Geographic* 116.6 (Nov./Dec. 1996): 46–7.

Nanogak, Agnes. *More Tales from the Igloo.* Edmonton: Hurtig 1986.

Nasgaard, Roald. *The Mystic North: Symbolist Landscape Painting in Northern Europe and North America, 1890–1940.* Toronto: University of Toronto Press 1984.

Nattiez, Jean-Jacques. "Comparisons within a Culture: The Example of the *Katajjaq* of the Inuit." In *Cross-Cultural Perspectives on Music*, ed. Robert Falck and Timothy Rice. Toronto: University of Toronto Press 1982. 134–40.

Neff van Aertselaer, JoAnne. "Representations of the North: Space, Presence and Power in Anglo-Canadian Writing." In *Visions of Canada: Approaching the Millenium*, ed. Eulalia C. Piñero Gil and Pilar Somacarrera Iñigo. Madrid: Ediciones de la Universidad Autónoma de Madrid 1999. 47–59.

Nelles, H.V. *The Politics of Development; Forests, Mines & Hydro-Electric Power in Ontario, 1849–1941.* Toronto: Macmillan 1974.

Nerling, Thomas. "In the Teeth of the Shore." Unpublished play, 1992.

Neuman, Shirley. "Writing the Reader, Writing the Self in Aritha van Herk's *Places Far from Ellesmere.*" In Neuman, ed., *Reading.* 215–34.
- ed. *Reading Canadian Autobiography. Essays on Canadian Writing* 60 (Winter 1996).

New, William H. *Land Sliding: Imagining Space, Presence, and Power in Canadian Writing.* Toronto: University of Toronto Press 1997.
- *Borderlands: How We Talk about Canada.* Vancouver: University of British Columbia Press 1998.

Newell, Dianne. "Canada at World's Fairs, 1851–1876." *Canadian Collector* 11.4 (July–Aug. 1976): 11–15.

Newlove, John. "Samuel Hearne in Wintertime." 1968. In *The New Oxford Book of Canadian Verse in English*, ed. Margaret Atwood. Toronto: Oxford University Press 1982. 336–7.

Newman, Peter C. *Renegade in Power: The Diefenbaker Years.* Toronto: McClelland and Stewart 1963.

Nichols, Bill. *Representing Reality: Issues and Concepts in Documentary.* Bloomington: Indiana University Press 1991.

Nickle Arts Museum, Calgary. *Recollecting: J. Dewey Soper's Arctic Watercolours.* Calgary: University of Calgary Press 1995.

Nicol, C.W. *The White Shaman: A Novel.* Toronto: McClelland and Stewart 1979.

Nixon, H.H. "Inuit." *Northward Journal* 18/19 (1980): 126–9.

Nochlin, Linda. *The Body in Pieces: The Fragment as a Metaphor of Modernity.* London: Thames and Hudson 1994.

Nolan, Yvette, and Valerie Shantz. "New Theatre North Playwrights Festival." *Canadian Theatre Review* 89 (Winter 1996): 78–80.

Norcross, E. Blanche. *Pioneers Every One: Canadian Women of Achievement.* Toronto: Burns & MacEachern 1979.

Norris, Frank. "Popular Images of the North in Literature and Film." *The Northern Review* 8/9 (Summer 1992): 53–72.

North, Dick. *The Mad Trapper of Rat River.* 1972. Toronto: General Paperbacks 1991.
- *The Lost Patrol: The Mounties' Yukon Tragedy.* 1978. Vancouver: Raincoast 1995.
- *Arctic Exodus: The Last Great Trail Drive.* Toronto: Macmillan 1991.

Northern Review: A Multidisciplinary Journal of the Arts and Social Sciences of the North, The. Whitehorse, Yukon: Northern Review Society.

Northward Journal: A Quarterly Journal of Northern Arts. Moonbeam, Ont.: Penumbra Press.

Northey, Margot. *The Haunted Wilderness: The Gothic and Grotesque in Canadian Fiction.* Toronto: University of Toronto Press 1976.

Nuligak. *I, Nuligak.* Ed. and trans. Maurice Metayer, ill. Ekootak. Toronto: Peter Martin 1966.

Nunavut Implementation Commission. *Footprints in New Snow: A Comprehensive Report from the Nunavut Implementation Commission.* Ill. Alootook Ipellie. Iqaluit: Nunavut Implementation Commission 1995.

Nungak, Zebedee and Eugene Arima. *Inuit Stories: Povungnituk.* Hull, PQ: Canadian Museum of Civilization 1988.

– and Stephen Hendrie. "Contemporary Inuit Photography in Nunavik: Two Decades of Documentary, Photojournalism and Corporate Photography at Makivik Corporation." In King and Lidchi, eds., *Imaging the Arctic.* 69–75.

Nunn, Robert. "Strangers to Ourselves: Judith Thompson's *Sled.*" *Canadian Theatre Review* 89 (Winter 1996): 29–32.

O'Flaherty, Patrick. *The Rock Observed: Studies in the Literature of Newfoundland.* Toronto: University of Toronto Press 1979.

O'Hagan, Howard. *Tay John.* 1960. Toronto: McClelland and Stewart 1974.

– "An Interview with Howard O'Hagan." By Keith Maillard. In Fee, ed., *Silence.* 21–38.

Oleson, Robert V. "An Eskimo in New York." *The Beaver* 68.5 (Oct.–Nov. 1988): 51–3.

Olnick, Harvey. "Harry Somers." *Canadian Music Journal* 3.4 (Summer 1959): 3–23.

Oman, Lela Kiana. *The Epic of Qayaq: The Longest Story Ever Told by My People.* Ottawa: Carleton University Press 1995.

O'Neil, John D. "Democratizing Health Services in the Northwest Territories: Is Devolution Having an Impact?" *The Northern Review* 5 (Summer 1990): 60–81.

O'Neill, Patrick B. "*Zero* and the Arctic Dramatic Tradition." *Canadian Drama/L'Art dramatique canadien* 16.1 (1990): 42–8.

Onley, Toni. *Onley's Arctic: Diaries and Paintings of the High Arctic.* Vancouver: Douglas & McIntyre 1989.

Owens, Mary Beth. *A Caribou Alphabet.* Willowdale, Ont.: Firefly 1988.

Oxtoby, Susan. "Pictures of Light: An Extended Carte Blanche Spotlighting Toronto's Peter Mettler." *Cinematheque Ontario Film Programme Guide* (Fall 1996): 37ff.

Page, Tim, ed. *The Glenn Gould Reader.* Toronto: Lester & Orpen Dennys 1984.

Parker, Brian. "Is There a Canadian Drama?" In *The Canadian Imagination: Dimensions of a Literary Culture*, ed. David Staines. Cambridge, Mass.: Harvard University Press 1977. 152–87.

Parsons, David. "Landscape Imagery in Canadian Music: A Survey of Composition Influenced by the Natural Environment." MA, Carleton University 1987.

Patterson, David. *Literature and Spirit: Essays on Bakhtin and His Contemporaries.* Lexington: University Press of Kentucky 1988.

Pattison, Jeanne L. "The Group of Seven's Arctic." *Up Here: Life in Canada's North* (Sept.–Oct. 1996): 28–32.

Paul, Linda Joan. "Human Encroachments on a Domineering Physical Landscape." In Simpson-Housley and Norcliffe, eds., *A few Acres of Snow.* 86–98.

Pearson, Lester B. "Canada Looks 'Down North.'" *Foreign Affairs* 24.4 (July 1946): 638–47.

Pechey, Graham. "On the Borders of Bakhtin: Dialogisation, Decolonization." In Hirschkop and Shepherd, eds., *Bakhtin and Cultural Theory.* 39–67.

Peepre-Bordessa, Mari, ed. *Transcultural Travels: Essays in Canadian Literature and Society.* Nordic Association for Canadian Studies Text Series 11. Lund, Sweden: Nordic Association for Canadian Studies 1994.

Pegg, Barry. "Nature and Nation in Popular Scientific Narratives of Polar Exploration." In *The Literature of Science: Perspectives on Popular Scientific Writing.*, ed. Murdo William McRae. Athens: University of Georgia Press 1993. 213–29.

Pekarik, Christina. "Cloudberry." Unpublished play, 1997.

Pelly, David F. *Thelon: A River Sanctuary.* Merrickville, Ont.: Canadian Recreational Canoeing Association 1996.

Peterson, Leonard. *The Great Hunger.* Agincourt, Ont.: Book Society of Canada 1967.

Peterson, V. Spike. "Disciplining Practiced/ Practices: Gendered States and Politics." In *Knowledges: Historical and Critical Studies in Disciplinarity*, ed. Ellen Messer-Davidow, David R. Shumway, David J. Sylvan. Charlottesville: University Press of Virginia 1993. 243–67.

Petitjean, Leon et Henri Rollin. *Aurore, l'enfant martyre: Histoire et présentation de la pièce par Alonzo Le Blanc.* Montreal: VLB 1982.

Petrone, Penny, ed. *Northern Voices: Inuit Writing in English.* Toronto: University of Toronto Press 1988.

Phillips, David W. "Canada's Coldest Day." *The Beaver* 77.1 (Feb.–Mar. 1997): 30–7.

Phillips, R.A.J. *Canada's North*. Toronto: Macmillan 1967.

Phillips, R.S. "Space for Boyish Men and Manly Boys: The Canadian Northwest in Robert Ballantyne's Adventure Stories." In Grace, ed., *Representing North*. 46–64.

Pickthall, Marjorie. "Canada's Century." *The Complete Poems of Marjorie Pickthall*. 1927. Toronto: McClelland and Stewart 1936. 460.

Pile, Steve, and Nigel Thrift, eds. *Mapping the Subject: Geographies of Cultural Transformation*. New York: Routledge 1995.

Pitseolak, Peter, and Dorothy Harley Eber. *People from our Side: A Life Story with Photographs*. Trans. Ann Hanson. Montreal: McGill-Queen's University Press 1993.

Podedworny, Carol. "Tom ( ) Tom." *C Magazine* 38 (Summer 1993): 53–4.

Porsild, Charlene. "Culture, Class and Community: New Perspectives on the Klondike Gold Rush, 1896–1905 (Yukon Territory)." PhD, Carlton University 1994.

– *Gamblers and Dreamers: Women, Men, and Community in the Klondike*. Vancouver: University of British Columbia Press 1998.

Posner, Michael. "Highway Is Back with a Vengence." *Globe and Mail*, 17 Oct. 1998, c1ff.

Prairie Art Gallery, Grande Prairie. *Euphemia McNaught: A Regional Focus*. Exhibition Catalogue. Grande Prairie, Alta., 1994.

Pratt, Mary. *Venus from a Northern Pond*. Private Collection. In *The Art of Mary Pratt: The Substance of Light,* by Tom Smart. Fredericton, NB: Beaverbrook Art Gallery and Goose Lane 1995. 122.

Precosky, Don, ed. *Four Realities: Poets of Northern B.C.* Prince George, BC: Caitlin 1992.

Pretes, Michael. "Northern Frontiers: Political Development and Policy-Making in Alaska and the Yukon." In Lecker, ed., *Borderlands*. 309–28.

Prince, Richard. "The Northern Lights." In Seppala, ed., *Strangers*. 206–7.

Pringle, Heather. "Forgotten Claims." *Canadian Geographic* 116.6 (Nov./Dec. 1996): 36–46.

Proctor, George A. *Canadian Music of the Twentieth Century*. Toronto: University of Toronto Press 1980.

Pryde, Duncan. *Nunaga: My Land, My Country*. Edmonton: Hurtig 1971.

Pullman, Philip. *The Golden Compass*. New York: Alfred A. Knopf 1996.

Purdy, Alfred. *North of Summer*. Toronto: McClelland and Stewart 1967.

– *Reaching for the Beaufort Sea*. Madeira Park, BC: Harbour 1993.

Purvis, Mifi. "Igloolik's Fast Runner." *Up Here* 17.1 (Jan./Feb. 2001): 15.

Pylvainen, Tina. "Grasping the Power of Language: Name and Song in Inuit Culture." *The Northern Review* 17 (Winter 1996): 33–47.

Qamaniq, David. "On Independence and Survival: David Qamaniq in Conversation with Cindy Cowan." In Cowan and Rewa, eds., *Beast of the Land*. 18–21.

Quenneville, Jean-Guy R. *Voyage d'un solitaire: René Richard, 1930–1933*. Ill. René Richard. Montreal: Trécarré 1985.

Raine, David F. *Pitseolak: A Canadian Tragedy*. Edmonton: Hurtig 1980.

Ralph, Gordon, ed. *Boneman: An Anthology of Canadian Plays*. St John's, Nfld.: Jesperson 1995.

Ransmayr, Christoph. *Terrors of Ice and Darkness: A Novel*. Trans. John E. Woods. New York: Grove Weidenfeld 1991.

Rasky, Frank. *The North Pole or Bust*. Toronto: McGraw-Hill 1977.

Rasmussen, Knud. *Report of the Fifth Thule Expedition, 1921–24*. Copenhagen: Gyldendalske Boghandel, Nordisk Forlag 1924–42.

– *Across Arctic America: Narrative of the Fifth Thule Expedition*. London: G.P. Putnam's 1927.

– comp. *Eskimo Poems from Canada and Greenland*. Trans. Tom Lowenstein. Pittsburg, Pa: University of Pittsburg Press 1973.

Ray, Carl, and James R. Stevens. *Sacred Legends of the Sandy Lake Cree*. Ill. Carl Ray. Toronto: McClelland and Stewart 1971

Reeves, John. "Arctic Images." *Descant XXIV* 10.2 (1979): 57–88.

Remie, Cornelius H.W. "Nunavut? Perceptions and Realities at the Periphery." *Zeitschrift für Kanada-Studien* 16.1 (1996): 103–17.

René Richard. Montreal: Fondation René Richard 1986.

Renov, Michael, ed. *Theorizing Documentary*. New York: Routledge 1993.

Ricard, François. *Gabrielle Roy*. Montreal: Fides 1975.

– "Une Recontre de Solitaires." *René Richard, 1895–1982*. Catalogue Centre d'exposition de Baie-Saint-Paul 1994. 6–7.

– *Gabrielle Roy: A Life*. Trans. Patricia Claxton. Toronto: McClelland and Stewart 1998.

– Sophie Marcotte, and Jane Everett, eds. *Gabrielle Roy, Le Pays de "Bonheur d'occasion" et autres récits autobiographiques épars et inédits*. Montreal: Éditions du Boréal, 2000.

Rich, Adrienne. "Notes toward a Politics of Location." 1984. *Blood, Bread, and Poetry: Selected Prose, 1979–1985*. New York: Norton 1986. 210–31.

Richard, René. *Ma vie passée*. Montreal: Art Global 1990.

Richardson, Bill. "Filling in the Blanks between Bear Cubs and Bibles." *Georgia Straight*, 20–27 Feb. 1997, 24–5.

Richardson, Boyce. *Strangers Devour the Land*. Toronto: Macmillan 1975.

Richler, Mordecai. *The Incomparable Atuk*. Toronto: McClelland and Stewart 1963.

– "North of Sixty." *Home Sweet Home: My Canadian Album*. Toronto: McClelland and Stewart 1984. 210–23

– *Solomon Gursky Was Here*. Harmondsworth: Penguin 1990.

Ringwood, Gwen Pharis. *Still Stands the House: A Drama in One Act*. New York: Samuel French 1939.

– and Art Rosoman. "The Road Runs North." 1967. Unpublished play. Ringwood Papers. University Library, University of Calgary.

Ritchie, Sherri. "Digging Deeper." *NeWest Review* 20.5 (June/July 1995): 35.

Rivet, Rick. *Caribou Mask Series*. Yukon Arts Centre, Whitehorse, NWT, 27 June–4 Aug. 1996.

Robert Flaherty, Photographer/Filmmaker, The Innuit, 1910–1922. Exhibition catalogue. Vancouver, BC: Vancouver Art Gallery 1979.

Robertson, Gordon. "Nunavut and the International Arctic." *Northern Perspectives* 15.2 (May/June 1987): 9.

Robinson, Arthur, Randall Sale, and Joel Morrison. *Elements of Cartography*. 4th ed. New York: John Wiley & Sons 1978.

Robinson, Mansel. *Slag*. Saskatoon: Thistledown 1997.

– *Colonial Tongues*. In Grace, D'Aeth, and Chalykoff, eds., *Staging the North*. 356–428.

Rogers, Wendy. "Circumscribing Silence: Inuit Writing Orature." *The Northern Review* 17 (Winter 1996): 48–59.

Ross, James A. *Canada First, and Other Poems*. Toronto: McClelland and Stewart 1920.

Ross, M.J. *Polar Pioneers: John Ross and James Clark Ross*. Montreal: McGill-Queen's University Press 1994.

Ross, W. Gillies. *This Distant and Unsurveyed Country: A Woman's Winter at Baffin Island, 1857–58*. Montreal: McGill-Queen's University Press 1997.

Roth, Lorna. "(De)Romancing the North: The Canadian North in Books and Film." *Border/Lines* 36 (Apr. 1995): 36–43.

Rotha, Paul. *Robert J. Flaherty: A Biography*. Ed. Jay Ruby. Philadelphia: University of Philadelphia Press 1983.

Roux, Jean-Louis. *Bois-Brûlés*. Montreal: Éditions de Jour 1968.

Roy, Gabrielle. "Peuple du Canada." *Bulletin des agriculteurs*, Nov. 1942, May 1943. n.p.

– *La Montagne secrète, Roman*. Montréal: Beauchemin 1961.

– *The Hidden Mountain*. 1961. Trans. Harry L. Binsse. Toronto: McClelland and Stewart 1962.

– *Where Nests the Water Hen*. Trans. Harry L. Binsse, intro. Gordon Roper. Toronto: McClelland and Stewart 1965.

– *Windflower*. Trans. Joyce Marshall. Toronto: McClelland and Stewart 1970.

– *Voyage en Ungava*. In Gagné, 46.3 (1976): 364–90.

– *The Fragile Lights of Earth: Articles and Memories, 1942–1970*. Trans. Alan Brown. Toronto: McClelland and Stewart 1982.

– *Enchantment and Sorrow: The Autobiography of Gabrielle Roy*. Trans. Patricia Claxton. Toronto: Lester & Orpen Dennys 1987.

– *Letters to Bernadette*. Trans. Patricia Claxton. Toronto: Lester & Orpen Dennys 1990.

– "La Légende du cerf ancien." *Cahiers Franco-Canadiens de l'Ouest* 3.1 (Printemps 1991): 143–63.

Ruby, Jay. " 'The Aggie Will Come First': The Demystification of Robert Flaherty." In *Robert Flaherty, Photographer*. 66–73.

Ruffo, Armand Garnet. *Grey Owl: The Mystery of Archie Belaney*. Regina: Coteau 1997.

Rustige, Rona, comp. *Tyendinaga Tales*. Ill. Jeri Maracle Van Der Vlag. Montreal: McGill-Queen's University Press 1988.

Ryder, Mark and Myra, eds. *Life in the Yukon*. Whitehorse: Yukon Archives, n.d.

Said, Edward. *Orientalism*. New York: Vintage 1979.

– *The World, the Text, and the Critic*. Cambridge, Mass.: Harvard University Press 1983.

– *Culture and Imperialism*. New York: Vintage 1994.

St Maur, Gerald [G.S. Lock]. *Odyssey Northwest: A Trilogy of Poems on the Northwest Passage.* Edmonton: Boreal Institute for Northern Studies 1983.

Salutin, Rick. "The Great White North." *This Magazine* 15.5–6 (Dec./Jan. 1981/82): 28–9.

Sarsfield, Peter. *Running with the Caribou.* Winnipeg: Turnstone 1997.

Saul, John Raulston. "My Canada Includes the North." *Globe and Mail*, 9 Mar. 2001, A13.

Savage, Candace. *Aurora: The Mysterious Northern Lights.* San Francisco: Sierra Club 1995.

Savard, Félix-Antoine. *La Dalle-des-Morts: Drame en trois actes.* Montreal: Fides 1965.

Schafer. R. Murray. "The Limits of Nationalism in Canadian Music." *Tamarack Review* 18 (Winter 1961): 71–8.

– *Louis Riel: A Case Study.* Toronto: Institute for Music, Dance and Theatre 1971.

– *Music in the cold.* Toronto: Coach House 1977.

– *The Tuning of the World.* New York: Knopf 1977.

– *North/White.* Toronto: Universal 1980.

– *On Canadian Music.* Bancroft, Ont.: Arcana 1984.

– *Voices of Tyranny, Temples of Silence.* Indian River, Ont.: Arcana 1993.

Schmaltz, Ken. "Susan Rules!" *Up Here: Life in Canada's North* (Dec. 1993–Jan. 1994): 12–15.

Schulman, Audrey. *The Cage: A Novel.* New York: Avon 1994.

Scobie, Stephen. "Amelia, or: Who Do You Think You Are? Documentary and Identity in Canadian Literature." *Canadian Literature* 100 (Spring 1984): 264–85.

Scott, D.C. *The Poems of Duncan Campbell Scott.* Toronto: McClelland 1926.

Scott, F.R. "Laurentian Shield." *The Collected Poems of F.R. Scott.* Toronto: McClelland and Stewart 1981. 58.

Sedgwick, Eve Kosofsky. *Between Men: English Literature and Male Homosocial Desire.* New York: Columbia University Press 1985.

Selesky, Karen. " 'Singing of What They No Longer Are'? The Role of Traditional Inuit Myth and Legend in Contemporary Inuit Narrative and Visual Art." *The Northern Review* 17 (Winter 1996): 71–84.

Semeniuk, Robert S. "Inuit Mecca." *Equinox* 1.6 (Nov./Dec. 1982): 29–51.

– "On the Land." *Canadian Geographic* 119.1 (Jan./Feb. 1999): 48–57.

Sen, Amartya. "Nobody Need Starve." *Granta* 52 (Winter 1995): 213–20.

Senkpiel, Aaron. "From the Wild West to the Far North: Literary Representations of North America's Last Frontier." In *Desert, Garden, Margin, Range: Literature on the American Frontier*, ed. Eric Heyne. New York: Twayne 1992. 133–42.

Seppala, Marketta, ed. *Strangers in the Arctic: "Ultima Thule" and Modernity.* Helsinki: Finnish Fund for Art Exchange and Pori Art Museum 1996.

Service, Robert W. *Songs of A Sourdough.* 1907. Toronto: Ryerson 1940.

Seton, Ernest Thompson. *The Arctic Prairies; A Canoe-Journey of 2,000 Miles in Search of the Caribou; being an Account of a Voyage to the Region North of Aylmer Lake, by Ernest Thompson Seton.* London: Constable 1912.

Seyersted, Per, ed. *The Arctic: Canada and the Nordic Countries.* Nordic Association for Canadian Studies Text Series 6. Lund, Sweden: Nordic Association for Canadian Studies 1991.

Shadbolt, Jack. *Bush Pilot in the Northern Sky.* Edmonton Airport, Edmonton.

Shanly, Charles D. "The Walker of the Snow." *Atlantic Monthly* 3.19 (May 1859): 631–2.

Shek, Ben-Zion. "Yves Thériault: The Would-be Amerindian and his Imaginary Inuit." In Carlsen and Streijffert, eds., *The Canadian North.* 119–28.

– "The 'Arctic' and its Inhabitants in Yves Thériault's Shorter Fiction and Children's Writing." In Carlsen, ed., *Literary Responses.* 147–52.

– "The Inuit in Gabrielle Roy's *La Rivière sans repos.*" In Peepre-Bordessa, ed., *Transcultural Travels.* 37–45.

Shelley, Mary. *Frankenstein, or, The Modern Prometheus.* 1818. New York: Bantam 1991.

Shields, Rob. "The True North Strong and Free." *Places on the Margin: Alternative Geographies of Modernity.* London: Routledge 1991. 162–206.

Shiell, Mary. "Rediscovering Kate Carmack, True Queen of the Klondike." *Up Here: Life in Canada's North* (July–Aug. 1996): 60–2.

Shipman, Nell. *The Silent Screen and My Talking Heart: An Autobiography.* Hemingway Western Studies Series. Boise: Boise State University Press 1987.

Shorty, Sharon. *Trickster Visits the Old Folks Home.* In Grace, D'Aeth, and Chalykoff, eds., *Staging the North.* 331–53.

Shrive, Norman. *Charles Mair: Literary Nationalist.* Toronto: University of Toronto Press 1965.

Simonson, Gayle. "The Prayer Man: Ojibwa Henry Bird Steinhauer Brought Religion to the Cree." *The Beaver* 68.5 (Oct.–Nov. 1988): 28–33.

Simpson, Jeffrey. "Tough Times Lie Ahead for the New Territory of Nunavut." *Globe and Mail,* 5 June 1998, A20.

Simpson-Housley, Paul. *The Arctic: Enigmas and Myths.* Toronto: Dundurn 1996.

– and Glen Norcliffe, eds. *A Few Acres of Snow: Literary and Artistic Images of Canada.* Toronto: Dundurn 1992.

Sirois, Antoine. "Le Mythe du Nord." In *Gabrielle Roy,* ed. Roland M. Charland and Jean-Noël Samson. Ottawa: Fides 1967. 65–9.

– "Le Grand Nord chez Gabrielle Roy et Yves Thériault." In *Colloque international "Gabrielle Roy,"* ed. André Fauchon. Saint-Boniface: University of Saint-Boniface Press 1996. 605–16.

– *Lecture mythocritique du roman québécois.* Montreal: Triptyque 1999. 99–112.

Skene-Melvin, David, ed. *Secret Tales of the Arctic Trails: Stories of Crime and Adventure in Canada's Far North.* Toronto: Simon & Pierre 1997.

Smith, A.J.M. "The Lonely Land." *Poets between the Wars: E.J. Pratt, F.R. Scott, A.J.M. Smith, Dorothy Livesay, A.M. Klein.* Ed. Milton Wilson. Toronto: McClelland and Stewart 1967. 106.

Smith, Gordon. "Ernest Gagnon on Nationalism and Canadian Music: Folk and Native Sources." *Canadian Folk Music Journal* 17 (1989): 32–9.

Smith, I.N., ed. *The Unbelievable Land: 29 Experts Bring Us Closer to the Arctic.* Ottawa: Queen's Printer, for the Dept of Northern Affairs and National Resources and the Northern Service of the Canadian Broadcasting Corp. 1964.

Smith, Sidonie. *Subjectivity, Identity, and the Body: Women's Autobiographical Practices in the Twentieth Century.* Bloomington: Indiana University Press 1993.

– "Identity's Body." In Ashley, Gilmour, and Peters, eds., *Autobiography.* 266–92.

Smyth, Heather. " 'Lords of the World': Writing Gender and Imperialism on Northern Space in C.C. Vyvyan's *Arctic Adventure.*" *Studies in Canadian Literature* 23.1 (1998): 32–52.

Snow, Michael. *The Collected Writings of Michael Snow.* Waterloo, Ont.: Wilfrid Laurier University Press 1994.

Sontag, Susan. *Under the Sign of Saturn.* New York: Farrar, Straus & Giroux 1980.

Soublière, Marion. *The 1998 Nunavut Handbook: Travelling in Canada's Arctic.* Iqaluit: Nortext Multimedia 1997.

Sparke, Matthew. "Between Demythologizing and Deconstructing the Map: Shawnadithit's New-found-land and the Alienation of Canada." *Cartographica* 32.1 (Spring 1995): 1–21.

Speck, Frank G. *Naskapi: The Savage Hunters of the Labrador Peninsula.* 1935. Norman: University of Oklahoma Press. 1977.

Spufford, Francis. *I May Be Some Time: Ice and the English Imagination.* London: Faber and Faber 1996.

Stacey, Robert. "A Contact in Context: The Influence of Scandinavian Landscape Painting on Canadian Artists before and after 1913." *Northward Journal: A Quarterly of Northern Arts* 18/19 (1980): 36–56.

– "The Myth – and Truth – of the True North." In *The True North: Canadian Landscape Paintings, 1896–1939,* ed. Michael Tooby. London: Lund Humphries 1991. 36–63.

Stafford, Barbara Maria. *Body Criticism: Imagining the Unseen in Enlightenment Art and Medicine.* Cambridge, Mass.: MIT Press 1991.

Stager, J.K., and Harry Swain. *Canada North: Journey to the High Arctic.* New Brunswick, NJ: Rutgers University Press 1992.

Stearns, Sharon. *Hunter of Peace.* Victoria, BC: Scirocco Drama 1993.

Stefansson, Vilhjalmur. *The Friendly Arctic, The Story of Five Years in Polar Regions.* New York: MacMillan 1922.

– *The Northward Course of Empire.* London: Harrap 1922.

– *The Standardization of Error.* London: Kegan Paul, Trench, Trubner 1928.

Stevens, Caroline, and Joan Reid Acland. "Building Sovereignty: The Architectural Sources of Oujé-Bougoumou." In Behiels, ed., *Aboriginal Peoples.* 124–42.

Stevenson, Alex. "The Robert Janes Murder Trial at Pond Inlet." *The Beaver* 34.2 (Autumn 1973): 16–23.

Stewart, Bruce D. "In the Wake of Erebus & Terror." *The Beaver* 68.5 (Oct./Nov. 1988): 13–18.

Stone, Judy. "Nanook of the Nineties." *Globe and Mail,* 24 Aug. 1994, C1–2.

Stoneman-McNichol, Jane. *On Blue Ice: The Inuvik Adventure.* Yellowknife: Outcrop 1983.

Stories from Pangnirtung. Ill. Germaine Arnak-tauyok, foreword by Stuart Hodgson. Edmonton: Hurtig Publishers 1976.

Stringer, Arthur John Arbuthnott. *Open Water.* New York: John Lane 1914.

Strong-Boag, Veronica. " 'A Red Girl's Reasoning': E. Pauline Johnson Constructs the New Nation." In Strong-Boag *et al.*, eds., *Painting the Maple.* 130–54.

– , Sherrill Grace, Joan Anderson, and Avigail Eisenberg, eds. *Painting the Maple: Essays on Race, Gender, and the Construction of Canada.* Vancouver: University of British Columbia Press 1998.

Sutherland, Patricia D., and Robert McGhee. *Lost Visions, Forgotten Dreams: Life and Art of an Ancient Arctic People.* Ottawa: Canadian Museum of Civilization 1996.

Suvin, Darko. "The Subject as a Limit-Zone of Collective Bodies (Bakhtin, Hobbes, Freud, Foucault, and Counting: An Approach)." *Discourse social/Social Discourse* 2.1–2 (Spring/Summer 1989): 187–99.

Tagoona, Armand. *Shadows.* Ottawa: Oberon 1975.

Tannenbaum, Peter. "Secrets of the North Wind." *Music Scene* (Sept.–Oct. 1986): 18–19.

Taylor, Charles. "To Follow A Rule ..." In Calhoun, LiPuma, and Postone, eds., *Bourdieu.* 45–60.

– "Why Do Nations Have to Become States?" *Reconciling the Solitudes: Essays on Canadian Federalism and Nationalism.* Ed. Guy Laforest. Montreal: McGill-Queen's University Press 1993. 40–58.

Taylor, William Henry. *Canadian Seasons, Spring; Summer; Autumn; Winter; With a Medley of Reveries in Verse and Prose and Other Curios.* Toronto: Published by author, 1913.

Teitelbaum, Matthew, ed. *Paterson Ewen.* Vancouver: Douglas & McIntyre 1996.

Tempelman-Kluit, Anne, ed. *A Klondike Christmas: Celebrating the Season in a Northern Frontier.* Vancouver: Whitecap 1998.

Tennenhouse, Esther. "Chanukkah Menorah, in Yellowknife, sculpted of ice." Photograph. Cover image. *Canadian Jewish Studies* 1 (1993). Vancouver: Canadian Jewish Historical Society.

Tessier, Tess, and Janice Sheehan. *Iceberg Tea.* Penticton, BC: Rainbow Dogooders 1989.

Tester, Frank James, and Peter Kulchyski. *Tammarniit (Mistakes): Inuit Relocation in the Eastern Arctic, 1939–63.* Vancouver: University of British Columbia Press 1994.

Tetso, John. *Trapping Is My Life.* Ill. Lorne H. Bouchard. Toronto: Peter Martin 1970.

– "How the Mackenzie River Was Made: Translation of a Slavey Legend." In Wonders, ed., *Canada's Changing North.* 89–90.

Thériault, Yves. *Marcheur.* 1950. Ottawa: Leméac 1968.

– *Agaguk.* 1958. Trans. Miriam Chapin. 1963. Toronto: McGraw-Hill Ryerson 1967.

– *Agoak: The Legacy of Agaguk.* Trans. John David Allan. Toronto: McGraw-Hill Ryerson 1979.

Thom, Ian M. *W.P. Weston.* Victoria, BC: Art Gallery of Greater Victoria 1980.

Thomas, Colin. "Sex, Dreams, and a Bucket of Snake." *Georgia Straight,* 3–10 Apr. 1997, 47–8.

Thompson, Francis. "From Prestige Project to Simply Shell: The Short History of the Northern Arts and Cultural Centre." In Cowan and Rewa, eds., *Beast of the Land.* 45–50.

Thompson, Judith. *Sled: A Play.* Toronto: Playwrights Canada 1997.

Thompson, Margaret. *Squaring the Round: The Early Years of Fort St. James.* Fort St James: Fort St James Historic Society 1992.

– *Eyewitness.* Vancouver: Ronsdale Press 2000.

Thomson, James. *The Seasons and the Castle of Indolence.* 1726. Ed. James Sambrook. Oxford: Clarendon 1972.

Thrasher, Arthur Apakark, with Gerard Deagle and Alan Mettrick. *Thrasher ... Skid Row Eskimo.* Toronto: Griffin 1976.

Tippett, Maria, and Charles Gimpel. *Between Two Cultures: A Photographer among the Inuit.* Toronto: Viking 1994.

Todd, Richard. "Narrative Trickery and Performative Historiography: Fictional Representation of National Identity in Graham Swift, Peter Carey and Mordecai Richler." In *Magical Realism: Theory, History, Community,* ed. Louis Parkinson Zamora and Wendy B. Faris. Durham, NC: Duke University Press 1995. 305–28.

Todorov, Tzvetan. *The Conquest of America: The Question of the Other.* New York: Harper & Row 1984.

Tompkins, Joanne. *Teaching in a Cold and Windy Place: Change in an Inuit School.* Toronto: University of Toronto Press 1998.

Tom Thomson Memorial Art Gallery. *Allen Smutylo: Prints and Drawings, 1982–1989.* Owen Sound, Ont., 1990.

Tookoomie, Simon, with Sheldon Oberman. *The Shaman's Nephew: A Life in the Far North.* Toronto: Stoddart Kids 1999.

Torgovnick, Marianna. *Gone Primitive: Savage Intellects, Modern Lives.* Chicago: University of Chicago Press 1990.

Tracy, Ann. *Winter Hunger.* Fredericton, NB: Goose Lane 1990.

Tremblay, Michel. *La Maison suspendue.* Trans. John Van Burek. Vancouver: Talonbooks 1991.

Trinh, T. Minh-Ha. *When the Moon Waxes Red: Representation, Gender, and Cultural Politics.* New York: Routledge 1991.

Tunooniq Theatre. *Changes.* In Grace, D'Aeth, and Chalykoff, eds., *Staging the North.* 101–13.

– *In Search of a Friend.* In Grace, D'Aeth, and Chalykoff, eds., *Staging the North.* 279–92.

Turner, D.J. "Who Was Nell Shipman and Why Is Everyone Talking about Her?" *Archivist* 110 (1995): 31–4.

Turner, Frederick Jackson. "The Significance of the Frontier in American History." *A Nineteenth-Century American Reader.* Washington: United States Information Service 1987. 80–5.

Turner, Robert. "Barbara Pentland." *Canadian Music Journal* 2.4 (1958): 15–26.

Tuttle, Charles R. *Our North Land.* Toronto: C. Blackett Robinson 1885.

Urquhart, Peter. "Picture of Light." *Reverse Shot* (Fall 1994): 47.

Valentine, Victor F., and Frank G. Vallee, eds. *Eskimo of the Canadian Arctic.* Toronto: McClelland and Stewart 1968.

Valkenen, Markku. "Prologue: Without Ice, There Is No Life." In Seppala, ed., *Strangers.* 26–34.

Valpy, Bruce. *Hornby.* John Rafferty, ed. In Cowan and Rewa, eds., *Beast of the Land.* 60–76.

Vancouver Art Gallery. *Robert Flaherty, Photographer/Filmmaker: The Innuit, 1910–1922.* Exhibition Catalogue. Vancouver 1980.

van Dreumel, Maureen. "Kenojuak: Intentional Narratives as Interpretive Strategies." *The Northern Review* 17 (Winter 1996): 60–70.

Van Herk, Aritha. *The Tent Peg: A Novel.* Toronto: McClelland and Stewart 1981.

– *No Fixed Address: An Amorous Journey.* Toronto: McClelland and Stewart 1986.

– *Places Far from Ellesmere: A Geografictione: Explorations on Site.* Red Deer, Alta.: Red Deer College Press 1990.

– *In Visible Ink: Crypto-Frictions.* Edmonton: NeWest 1991.

– *A Frozen Tongue.* Sidney, NSW: Dangaroo 1993.

– "Shifting Form: An Interview with Aritha van Herk." Unpublished. 7 May 1996.

Van Kirk, Sylvia. *Many Tender Ties: Women in Fur-Trade Society, 1670–1870.* Winnipeg: Watson & Dwyer 1980.

Vanneste, Hilda M.C. *Northern Review, 1945–1956: A History and an Index.* Ottawa: Tecumseh 1982.

Venema, Kathleen. "Mapping Culture onto Geography: 'Distance from the Fort' in Samuel Hearne's Journal." *Studies in Canadian Literature* 23.1 (1998): 9–31.

Verne, Jules. *The Fur Country, or Seventy Degrees North Latitude.* 2 vols. New York: Richard Worthington 1873.

Voaden, Herman, ed. *Six Canadian Plays.* Ill. Lowrie Warrener. Toronto: Copp Clark 1930.

– *A Vision of Canada: Herman Voaden's Dramatic Works, 1928–1945.* Ed. Anton Wagner. Toronto: Simon & Pierre 1993.

Voloshinov, Valentin Nikolaievich. *Marxism and the Philosophy of Language.* New York: Seminar 1973.

Wachowich, Nancy. "Making a Living, Making a Life: Subsistence and the Reenactment of Iglulingmiut Cultural Practices." PhD, University of British Columbia 2001.

– in collaboration with Apphia Agalati Awa, Rhoda Kaukjak Katsak, and Sandra Pikujak Katsak. *Saqiyuq: Stories from the Lives of Three Inuit Women.* Montreal: McGill-Queen's University Press 1999.

Wadden, Marie. *Nistassinan: The Innu Struggle To Reclaim their Homeland.* Vancouver: Douglas & McIntyre 1996.

Waiser, William A. "Canada Ox, Ovibos, Woolox ... Anything but Musk-Ox." In Coates and Morrison, eds., *For Purposes of Dominion.* 189–99.

Waldron, Malcolm. *Snow Man: John Hornby in the Barren Lands.* 1931. Montreal: McGill-Queen's University Press 1997.

Walk, Ansgar. Trans. Timothy Spence. *Kenojuak: The Life Story of an Inuit Artist.* Manotick, Ont.: Penumbra Press 1999.

Walker, Susan. "A Woman of Letters." *Toronto Star,* 9 Jan. 1997, G3.

Walkowitz, Judith R. *Prostitution and Victorian Society: Women, Class, and the State.* Cambridge, Mass.: Harvard University Press 1980.

Wallace, Dillon. *The Long Labrador Trail.* New York: Outing 1907.

Walters, Eric. *Trapped in Ice.* Toronto: Viking 1997.

Walton, Paul H. "The Group of Seven and Northern Development." *RACAR* 17.2 (1990): 171–9.

Ward, William Peter. *White Canada Forever.* Kingston: Queen's University Press 1972.

Warkentin, Germaine, ed. *Canadian Exploration Literature.* Toronto: Oxford University Press 1993.

Warley, Linda. "The Mountie and the Nurse: Cross-Cultural Relations *North of Sixty.*" In Strong-Boag et al., eds., *Painting the Maple.* 173–86.

Warwick, Jack. *Long Journey: Literary Themes of French Canada.* Toronto: University of Toronto Press 1968.

– "L'Appropriation de l'identité autochtone dans la littérature québécoise." *Zeitschrift für Kanada-Studien* 16.1 (1996): 118–25.

Wasserman, Jerry. " 'It's the Do-gooders Burn My Ass': Modern Canadian Drama and the Crisis of Liberalism." *Modern Drama* 43.1 (Spring 2000): 32–47.

Watson, J. Wreford. "The Role of Illusion in North American Geography: A Note on the Geography of North American Settlement." *Canadian Geographer* 13.1 (Spring 1969): 10–27.

Watson, Scott. *Jack Shadbolt.* Vancouver: Douglas & McIntyre 1990.

Watson, Sheila. *The Double Hook.* 1959. Toronto: McClelland and Stewart 1985.

Watt, Frederick B. *Great Bear: A Journey Remembered.* Yellowknife, NWT: Outcrop 1980.

Watts, Allan. "Judith Thompson Casebook." *Canadian Theatre Review* 89 (Winter 1996): 3.

Weinberger, Eliot. "The Camera People." In *Visualizing Theory: Selected Essays from V.A.R., 1990–94,* ed. Lucien Taylor. New York: Routledge 1994. 3–26.

Weller, Geoffrey R. "The Devolution of Authority for Health Care Services to the Governments of the Yukon and the Northwest Territories." *The Northern Review* 5 (Summer 1990): 37–59.

West, Douglas A. "Re-searching the North in Canada: An Introduction to the Canadian Northern Discourse." *Journal of Canadian Studies* 26.2 (Summer 1991): 108–19.

– "The Limits of Northern Identity: An Assessment of W.L. Morton's Northern Vision." *The Northern Review* 14 (Summer 1995): 95–115.

Westfall, William. "On the Concept of Region in Canadian History and Literature." *Journal of Canadian Studies* 15.2 (Summer 1980): 3–15.

Wharton, Thomas. *Icefields.* Edmonton: NeWest 1995.

Wheelock, Angela. "Daughter of the Wolf." Unpublished typescript.

Whidden, Lynn. "Charlie Panigoniak: Eskimo Music in Transition." *Canadian Folk Music Journal* 9 (1981): 34–42.

Whitaker, Muriel, ed. *Stories from the Canadian North.* Ill. Vlastavan Kampen. Edmonton: Hurtig 1980.

White, Donny. "In Search of Geraldine Moodie: A Project in Progress." In King and Lidchi, eds., *Imaging the Arctic.* 88–97.

Whyte, Doug. "Robert Henderson and His Search for Recognition as Discoverer of Klondike Gold." *The Northern Review* 19 (Winter 1998): 181–203.

Whyte-Edgar, C.M., ed. *A Wreath of Canadian Song.* Toronto: William Briggs 1910.

Wiebe, Rudy. "Where Is the Voice Coming From?" 1971. *River of Stone: Fictions and Memories.* Toronto: Vintage 1995. 27–40.

– "The Death and Life of Albert Johnson: Collected Notes on a Possible Legend." In *Figures in a Ground: Canadian Essays on Modern Literature Collected in Honor of Sheila Watson,* ed. Diane Bessai and David Jackel. Saskatoon: Western Producer Prairie 1978. 219–46.

– *First and Vital Candle.* 1966. Toronto: McClelland and Stewart 1979.

– *The Angel of the Tar Sands and Other Stories.* Toronto: McClelland and Stewart 1982.

– "The Naming of Albert Johnson." *The Angel of the Tar Sands and Other Stories.* 88–99.

– "Oolulik." *The Angel of the Tar Sands and Other Stories.* 100–15.

– *The Mad Trapper.* 1980. School ed. Toronto: McClelland and Stewart 1987.

– *Playing Dead: A Contemplation Concerning the Arctic.* Edmonton: NeWest 1989.

– *A Discovery of Strangers.* Toronto: Knopf Canada 1994.

– "River of Stone." In Carlsen, ed., *Literary Responses.*

Wilkinson, Bryan. "Harry Freedman: An Exciting Composer." *Canadian Composer* 17 (Apr. 1967): 4ff.

Wilkinson, Doug. *Land of the Long Day.* Toronto: Clarke, Irwin 1955.

Wilson, Ann. "Canadian Grotesque: The Reception of Judith Thompson's Plays in London." *Canadian Theatre Review* 89 (Winter 1996): 25–8.

Wilson, Clifford, ed. *Northern Treasury: Selections from* the Beaver. Edinburgh, New York: Thomas Nelson & Sons, n.d.

Wilson, Eric. *The Inuk Mountie Adventure.* Toronto: Harper Collins 1995.

Wilson, Ethel. *Swamp Angel.* Toronto: McClelland and Stewart 1962.

Winearls, Joan, ed. *Editing Early and Historical Atlases.* Papers Given at the Twenty-ninth Annual Conference on Editorial Problems, University of Toronto, 5–6 Nov. 1993. Toronto: University of Toronto Press 1995.

Winston, Brian. "The White Man's Burden: The Example of Robert Flaherty." *Sight and Sound* 54.1 (Winter 1984–85): 58–60.

Wonders, William C. "Search for Franklin." *Canadian Geographical Journal* 76.4 (1968): 116–27.

– "The Canadian Northwest: Some Geographical Perspectives." *Canadian Geographical Journal* 80.5 (May 1970): 146–65.

– ed. *Canada's Changing North.* Toronto: McClelland and Stewart 1971.

Woodcock, George. *Northern Spring: The Flowering of Canadian Literature in English.* Vancouver: Douglas & McIntyre 1987.

Woodman, David C. *Unravelling the Franklin Mystery: Inuit Testimony.* Montreal: McGill-Queen's University Press 1991.

– *Strangers among Us.* Montreal: McGill-Queen's University Press 1995.

Woods, Grahame. *Bloody Harvest.* Toronto: McClelland and Stewart 1977.

Woods, Gurli Aagaard. "The Space in the Margins: Suzanne Brøgger's 'No-Man's Land', Kristjana Gunnars' *The Substance of Forgetting,* and Aritha van Herk's *Places Far from Ellesmere.*" In Peepre-Bordessa, ed., *Transcultural Travels.* 111–24.

Woodward, Lucy Berton. *Kidnapped in the Yukon.* Scarborough, Ont.: Nelson 1984.

Wynne-Jones, Tim. *The Maestro.* Vancouver: Groundwood 1995.

– and Eric Beddoes. *Zoom Away.* Toronto: Groundwood/Douglas & McIntyre 1985.

Yaeger, Patricia. "Afterword." In Bauer and McKinstry, eds., *Feminism.* 239–45.

Yardley, M. Jeanne. "Voyage into Oblivion, Voyage into Legend: The Albert Johnson Narratives." In *Voyages: Real and Imaginary, Personal and Collective*, Selected Proceedings of the Twentieth Annual Conference of the Association for Canadian Studies, ed. John

Lennox, Lucie Lequin, Michele Lacombe, and Allen Seager. 21–32.

Yates, J. Michael. "Ice Carnival." *Hunt in an Unmapped Interior and Other Poems.* Francestown, NH: Golden Quill 1967. 33–4.

– *The Great Bear Lake Meditations.* Ottawa: Oberon 1970.

– "Death the Second." *Nothing Speaks for the Blue Moraines.* Delta, BC: Sono Nis 1973.

– *Fazes in Elsewhen: New and Selected Fiction.* Vancouver: Intermedia 1977.

– "The Hunter Who Loses His Human Scent." In Yates, *Fazes in Elsewhen.* 39–44.

– "The Sinking of the Northwest Passage." In Yates, *Fazes in Elsewhen.* 91–9.

– *Insel: The Queen Charlotte Islands Meditations.* Moonbeam, Ont.: Penumbra 1983.

York, Geoffrey. *The Dispossessed: Life and Death in Native Canada.* London: Vintage 1990.

York, Thomas. *Snowman: A Novel.* Toronto: Doubleday 1976.

– *Trapper.* Toronto: Doubleday 1981.

Young, Lisa. "Gender Parity North of 60: Reflection on the Proposed Nunavut Electrical System." Unpublished essay, 1996.

Young, Robert. "Back to Bakhtin." *Cultural Critique* 1.2 (1985/86): 71–92.

Zapf, Kim. "Educating Social Work Practitioners for the North: A Challenge for Conventional Models and Structures." *The Northern Review* 7 (Summer 1991): 35–52.

Zaslow, Morris, *The Opening of the Canadian North, 1870–1914.* Toronto: McClelland and Stewart 1971.

– *Reading the Rocks: the Story of the Geological Survey of Canada, 1842–1972.* Toronto: Macmillan 1975.

– *The Northward Expansion of Canada 1914–1967.* Toronto: McClelland and Stewart 1988.

– ed. *A Century of Canada's Arctic Islands, 1880–1980.* Proceedings of the Twenty-third Symposium of the Royal Society of Canada, 11–13 Aug. 1980. Ottawa: Royal Society of Canada 1981.

MUSIC

Adaskin, Murray. *Qalala and Nilaula of the North.* (1969). CMC Tape #642.

– "In Praise of Canadian Painting in the Thirties." Dir. Victor Martin, perf. Canadian Players of Toronto String Orchestra and George Brough. Walter Hall, Toronto, 24 Jan. 1976.

Aglukark, Susan. *Arctic Rose*. EMI Music Canada 1992.

– *This Child*. EMI Music Canada 1995.

Applebaum, Louis. *Innuit*. 1977. CMC Tape #1171.

Archer, Violet. *Northern Landscape*. 1978. CMC Tape #323. 3 songs.

Bottenberg, Wolfgang. Score for opera based on Henry Beissel's *Inook and the Sun*. 1986.

Brandt, Paul. "Canadian Man." *Small Towns and Big Dreams*. BMG CD, 2001.

Elliot, Robin. *Tableau*. CBC 1989.

A Folksong Portrait of Canada / Un portrait folklorique. Polygram 1994.

Forsyth, Malcolm. *Atayoskiwin: Suite for Orchestra*. 1984. CMC Tape #1907, rec. #404.

– *Auyuittuq*. Première. Dir. Morna Edmundson and Diane Loomer, perf. Elektra Women's Choir. Blue Mountain Baptist Church, Coquitlam, BC, 10 May 1997.

Freedman, Harry. *Images*. LP. Toronto: BMI Canada 1960.

– *Tableau for String Orchestra*. 1960. On Elliot, *Tableau*.

– *Anerca*. Perf. Louis Marshall and Weldon Kilburn. CBC Radio broadcast, 2 Feb. 1967.

Garant, Serge. *Anerca*. 1961. RCI *Anthology of Canadian Music*. Vol. 2B. LP. RCI 1986.

Gould, Glenn. "The Idea of North." 1967. *Glenn Gould's Solitude Trilogy: Three Sound Documentaries*. CBC 1992.

The Gumboots. *Spirit of the North*. The Gumboots 1992.

Healey, Derek. "Arctic Images: A Suite for Orchestra." *Contemporary Canadian Compositions for Orchestra*. Ricordi 1977.

Hemsworth, Wade. "The Franklin Expedition." *Folk Songs of the Canadian North*. LP. Folkway Records 1955.

Houle, François. *Au coeur du litige*. Field 2 CD, with bilingual booklet. Uxbridge, Ont.: Spool 2000.

"Inuit Vocal Games (Caribou, Netsilik and Igloolik Inuit)." *Canada – Jeux Vocaux des Inuit (Inuit du Caribou, Netsilik et Igloolik)*. Ocora Radio France 1989. Liner notes, 17–28.

Jerry Alfred & the Medicine Beat. *Nendaä-Go Back*. Etsi Shon Productions 1996.

Lien, Matthew. *Bleeding Wolves*. Whispering Willows 1995.

Longtin, Michel. *Au Nord de Lac Superieur*. 1972. CMC Tape #946–B.

Louie, Alexina. *Winter Music*. 1989. On *Treeline*. CBC Records 1997.

McIntosh, Diana. "Paraphrase #1." 1978. Unpublished score. CMC.

– "Kiviuq, an Inuit Legend." 1985. Unpublished score. CMC.

Morel, François. *Nuvattuq*. 1967. CMC.RC I 409.

– *Iikkii (Froidure)*. 1972. CMC.RC I 367.

Night Sun. *Night Sun*. Night Sun 1991.

Norman, Chris. *The Beauty of the North: Traditional Favorites from Quebec and Maritime Canada*. Dorian 1994.

North Country: The Music of Canada. Toronto Symphony Orchestra. LP. Citadel 1976.

Nunavik Concert. Sunshine Records 1995.

Pentland, Barbara. "Arctica, For Young Pianists." 1971. Unpublished score.

– *Suite Borealis*. 1966. RCI Anthology of Canadian Music, vol. 4A. LP RCI, 1986.

Puccini, Giacomo. *Madama Butterfly*. Librettists Luigi Illica and Giuseppe Giacosa, trans. G. Ricordi & Co. Decca 1987.

Rabinovitch, Sid. *Oolik Seeks the Wind*. Première. Oratorio with narrator, Susan Aglukark, Manitoba Chamber Orchestra. Winnipeg, 24 May 2000.

Rogers, Stan. *Northwest Passage*. LP. Fogarty's Cove Music 1981.

Somers, Harry. *North Country: Four Movements for String Orchestra*. 1948. On *The Spring of Somers*. CBC 1996.

– *Magic Flute*. 1997. Broadcast of *Northern Encounters Festival of the Arts*. CBC Radio, Toronto, 22 June 1997.

Symonds, Norman. *Big Lonely*. National Youth Orchestra of Canada, cond. Harman Hoakman. RCI 431. CMC.

Weinzweig, John. "To Homelands over Yonder." 1953. Cond. Filmer Hubble. CMC Tape #138.

– *Edge of the World*. Winnipeg Symphony Orchestra, cond. Victor Feldbrill. Rec. 25 Feb. 1962. CMC Tape #144.

Winters, Ken. Introduction to *North Country* by Harry Somers. 1991. CMC, New DAT 2.

Zuchert, Leon, and Ellen Bobrow. *In the Gleam of Northern Lights*. 1974. CMC Tape #1888.

FILM, VIDEO, AND CD-ROM

Alaska's Great Race: The Sharon Butcher Story. Dir. Lazlo Pal. Pal Productions 1989.

Amarok's Song. Dir. Ole Gjerstad and Martin Kreelak. Words and Pictures Video 1998.

Atanarjuat (The Fast Runner). Dir. Zacharius Kunuk. Igloolik Isuma Productions/National Film Board of Canada, 2001.

Back to God's Country. 1919. Perf. Nell Shipman. Restored print. Idaho Film Collection, Hemingway Western Studies Center, Boise State University 1996.

Between Two Worlds: The Story of Joseph Idlout. Dir. Barry Greenwald. National Film Board of Canada 1990.

The Champagne Safari. Dir. George Ungar. National Film Board of Canada 1995.

Coppermine: Consequences of Contact with the Outside. Dir. Ray Harper. National Film Board of Canada 1992.

Drowning in Dreams. Dir. Tim Southam. National Film Board of Canada 1997.

The Far Country. Dir. Anthony Mann. Perf. James Stewart. Universal 1954.

The Far Shore. Dir. Joyce Wieland. 1975. Liberty 1978.

The 49th Parallel. Dir. Michael Powell. General Film 1941.

"Frozen in Time." By Owen Beattie and John Geiger. *The Nature of Things*. Intro. David Suzuki. CBC Television and Tensel Media Productions, 18 Nov. 1987.

The Frozen North. Dir. Buster Keaton and Eddie Cline. 1922.

Gold Rush Trail: Then and Now. Ed. John Booth. Logan Video 1995.

Grey Owl. Dir. Richard Attenborough. Perf. Pierce Bronsan and Annie Galipeau. 1999.

The Group of Seven: Art for a Nation. Dir. Katherine Jeans. Ottawa: Sound Venture Productions 1995.

Heart of Light. Dir. Jacob Grønlykke. Prod. ASA Film. Danish Film Institute 1998.

The Herd. Dir. Peter Lynch. Perf. Colm Feore, Don McKeller. Cinematography by Rudolph Blahacek. National Film Board of Canada 1998.

"Ice Man." By Denise Brun and Michel Brun. *Life and Times*. CBC, 16 Jan. 1998.

Kabloonak. Dir. Charles Massott. C/FP Distribution Inc. 1994.

Lypa. Dir. Sharon Van Raalte and Shelagh Mackenzie. Ottawa: National Film Board of Canada 1976.

Map of the Human Heart. Dir. Vincent Ward and Louis Nowra. Miramax Films 1993.

Nanook of the North. Dir. Robert Flaherty. Pathé 1922.

Never Cry Wolf. Dir. Carroll Ballard. Walt Disney Pictures 1983.

North: Landscape of the Imagination. Dir. Tim Joyce. Sound Venture Productions 1993.

Picture of Light. Dir. Peter Mettler. Domino Film 1994.

Power. Dir. Magnus Isacsson. Prod. Glen Salzman. Cineflix Productions and the National Film Board of Canada 1996.

Project Grizzly. Dir. Peter Lynch. Prod. Michael Allder. Perf. Troy James Hurtubise. National Film Board of Canada 1996.

La Région centrale. Dir. Michael Snow. 1971.

Rose-Marie. Dir. W.S. Van Dyke. Perf. Jeanette MacDonald and Nelson Eddie. MGM 1936.

The Savage Innocents. Dir. Nicholas Ray. Paramount 1960.

Sergeant Preston of the Yukon. Series. Rhino Video Distributors 1989.

Shadow of the Wolf. Dir. Jacques Dorfman. Perf. Lou Diamond Phillips, Toshiro Mifune, Jennifer Tilly, and Donald Sutherland. 1992.

Spirits of Davis Inlet. Interactive CD-ROM. Prod. Diana Nethercott and Sharon Oosthoek. Southam Interactive 1995.

The Spoilers. Dir. Ray Enright. Perf. Marlene Dietrich, John Wayne, and Randolph Scott. Universal 1942.

Thirty-two Short Films about Glenn Gould. By François Girard and Don McKellar. Dir. François Girard. Perf. Colm Feore. Prod. Niv Fichman. Rhombus Media 1993.

True North: The Myth. Ontario Educational Communications Authority.

Tu as crié Let Me Go. Dir. Anne Claire Poirier. National Film Board of Canada 1997.

Vision Man. Dir. William Long. Swedish Film Institute. Aby-Long Productions 1997.

Zero° Kelvin. Dir. Hans Petter Moland. Norway. 1995.

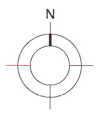

INDEX